Everygame

The NEW Official History of
KILMARNOCK FOOTBALL CLUB

Everygame

The NEW Official History of
KILMARNOCK FOOTBALL CLUB

BY DAVID ROSS

Published by:
KILMARNOCK FOOTBALL CLUB
RUGBY PARK
KILMARNOCK
KA1 2DP

Printed by:
FASPRINT SERVICES (IRVINE) LTD

ISBN 0-9541653-0-6

Published by:
KILMARNOCK FOOTBALL CLUB
RUGBY PARK
KILMARNOCK
KA1 2DP

© David Ross 2001

. . . .

British Library Cataloguing-in-Publishing Data.
A catalogue record for this book
is available from the British Library.

ISBN 0-9541653-0-6

Contents

Acknowledgments...9

About the Author...11

From the Chairman 13

Foreword - Bobby Williamson...15

Introduction 17

Everygame - A Kilmarnock A-Z..19-178

Statistics 179

The Legends...181

Killie Year-by-year..187-283

Advanced Subscribers 286-288

Acknowledgments

The following all provided invaluable assistance in the writing and production of this book and I would like to take this opportunity to thank them all. They are (in no particular order):

The staff of the **National Newspaper Library** in London, the **Mitchell Library** in Glasgow and the **Dick Institute** in Kilmarnock. **Andy Mitchell** of the Scottish Football Association and **David Thomson** at the Scottish Football League.

Alex Milligan, Allan Blane and the staff of the *Kilmarnock Standard.*

Kilmarnock FC club historian **John Livingston**, who has unearthed a mass of historical and statistical material for which I am grateful.

Allan Morrison and all at *Fasprint.* In particular **Tracey McGroarty** who dealt efficiently and kindly with last-minute alterations.

The directors, management and staff of Kilmarnock FC.

KFC's Commercial Manager **Jim McSherry**, who played the role of a true midfield general in providing material, organising publicity, and keeping things moving.

Richard Cairns for his assistance in sourcing photographs.

My wife **Josephine** for her support and encouragement.

Dedication

This book is dedicated to the memory of my mother, Elizabeth Ross 1925-1997.

About the Author

David Ross was born and raised in Dundonald in Ayrshire and has been a Kilmarnock supporter all his life.

Educated at Marr College in Troon, Kilmarnock Academy and the University of Teesside, he is a freelance journalist and writer. He is also a former parliamentary candidate for the Labour Party.

He has appeared on the television shows *'Mastermind'* and *'The People Versus'* taking football history as a specialist subject.

He and his wife Josephine now live in West Cornwall.

You can see more of David's work on his website **www.scottishleague.net**

The Board of Directors
Back row (l-r): Kevin Collins (Secretary), Robert Wyper (Director), David Heath (Chief Executive),
Jim Clark (Director), Jim Murdoch (Director).
Front row (l-r): Bill Costley (Joint Vice-Chairman), Sir John Orr OBE (Chairman),
Jamie Moffat (Joint Vice Chairman), Brian Sage (Director).

From the Chairman

As a Kilmarnock supporter since my boyhood it was a tremendous thrill as well as a great honour to be asked to serve as Chairman of the Board of Directors. To be following in the footsteps of so many distinguished predecessors is a task I was delighted to accept. And when I think of the effort and dedication so many have given to Kilmarnock Football Club over more than 130 years it is also an undertaking that I fulfil with all humility.

We have seen the transition from pre-war ground to 21st century all-seater stadium. There has been the establishment of the new fitness centre. And even as I write new developments are taking place at Rugby Park which will help secure a sound basis for the club's future and allow Kilmarnock to continue to make a "seriously strong" challenge for honours. It is thanks to the vision and efforts of my immediate predecessors that these developments have come about. Bill Costley, Jamie Moffat and all who have served on the Board of Directors over the past ten years have built on the foundations laid by Bobby Fleeting.

This past decade has seen Kilmarnock once again occupy a seat at the top table in Scottish football. For that much thanks must be given to the management and players. Bobby Williamson and his team have brought the Scottish Cup to Kilmarnock after nearly 70 years absence, taken the team to the Scottish League Cup Final for the first time in almost 40 years and delivered European football on a regular basis. These are achievements which are the envy of other provincial clubs in Scotland.

It would take up too many valuable pages in this book to thank everyone who works so hard to keep this club at the forefront of the Scottish game. But those involved know that their contributions are greatly valued by the Board and myself.

Of course football has its downs as well as its ups. And these too must be acknowledged. For it is only by recognising and learning from our failures that we can truly appreciate success. You will find both of Kipling's impostors - triumph and disaster - in these pages. And it is overcoming the disasters that make the triumphs all the sweeter.

But that is enough from me. It is time for you - the reader - to find your own personal favourite moments from over 4,000 games that Kilmarnock have played. Turn the page and start searching. Those memories are in these pages somewhere.

Sir John Orr OBE
Chairman, Kilmarnock Football Club

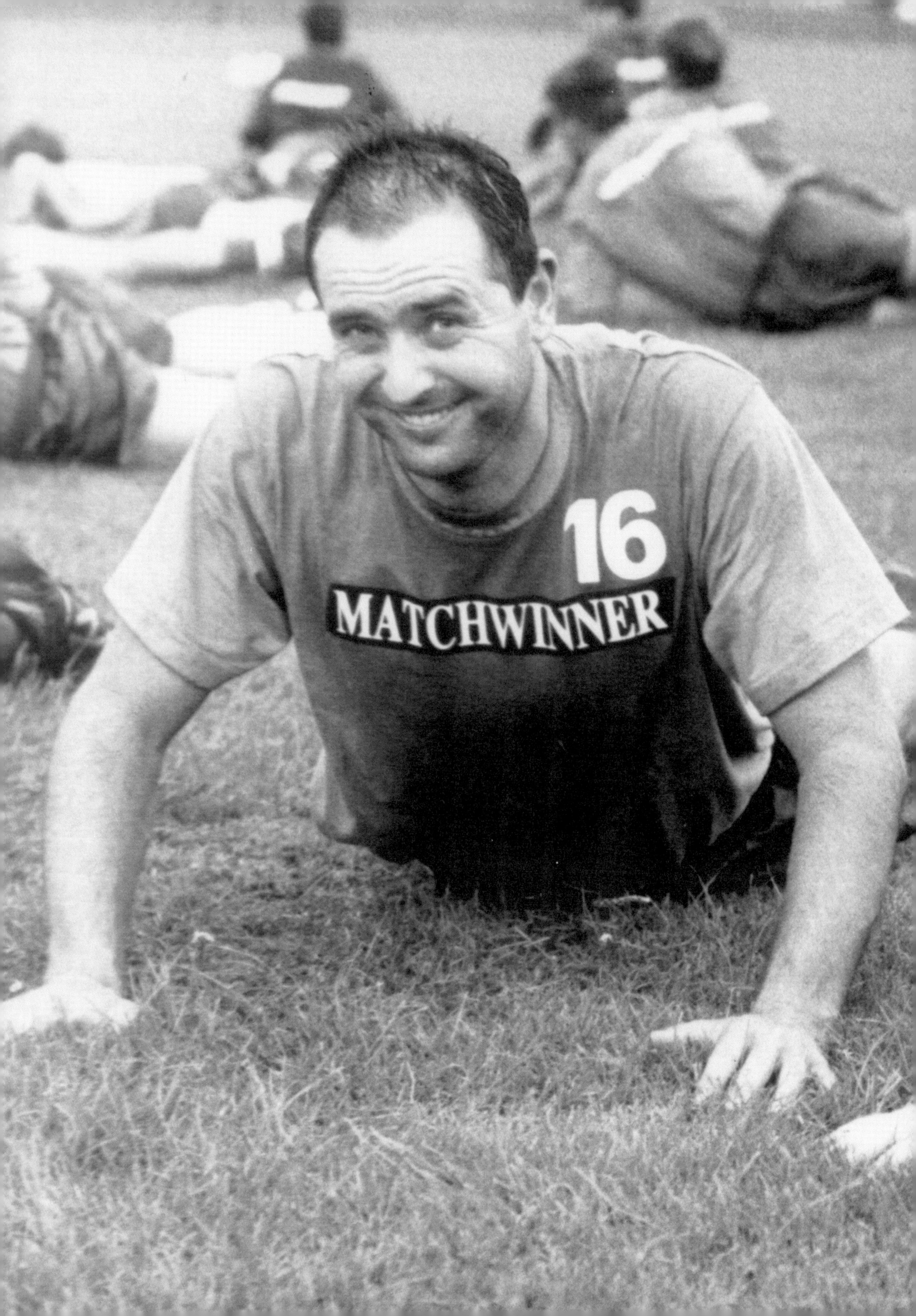
16
MATCHWINNER

Foreword

When I arrived at Rugby Park as a player over a decade ago I never thought for one moment that I would still be here and occupying the manager's seat now. The club had just been promoted from the Second Division but even then I could see that Kilmarnock were an ambitious club with a progressive outlook.

During my time here the club has returned to the Premier League and over the past few seasons has established itself as one of the leading lights in Scottish football by regularly finishing near the top of the table. That has brought European football back to Rugby Park on a regular basis. But of course the highlight of my career so far was when Kilmarnock won the Scottish Cup in 1997. To see over 25,000 Kilmarnock supporters cheering that triumph at Ibrox and to witness the celebrations of thousands more as the team made their progress through the town on an open-top bus is a memory I will cherish forever.

I have been fortunate to be able to work with a Board of Directors who have the enthusiasm and the drive needed to take the club forward. I have also had a strong team working with me. Jim Clark and Gerry McCabe have been magnificent as my assistants and Alan Robertson has done a first-class job in bringing through the youngsters who are the lifeblood of the game.

But it is the supporters who are the most important people at any football club. Without the fans there would be no club. The players, staff and myself all share in the joy of a victory and we all feel the pain of a defeat. Thankfully, in recent times there have been more highs than lows at Kilmarnock Football Club. It is my job to try and make sure that this continues and that the supporters have plenty to cheer about in the times ahead.

As for times past, there are details from over 4,000 matches in this book. There are countless opportunities in these pages for supporters to read about past glories while the team and myself attempt to provide more in the future.

Bobby Williamson
Manager, Kilmarnock Football Club

The way it was. **Rugby Park** before it became an all-seated stadium.

The way it is. The 18,000 all-seater is one of the most modern grounds in Scotland.

Introduction

I wrote the official history of Kilmarnock FC for the club's 125th anniversary in 1994 and thought then that there would be no need for a further volume for about 25 years. But so much has happened since then that I have no doubt that there is a need for this new history now.

The changes at the club both on and off the park since the publication of the '125' book have been both massive and beneficial. The Scottish Cup has been won for the first time in nearly 70 years. In 2001 Kilmarnock played in their first League Cup Final for almost 40 years. European football has been restored to Rugby Park on a regular basis. And the team - under manager Bobby Williamson - are firmly established as one of the best in Scotland. Indeed, no supporter under the age of 40 can ever remember a time when Kilmarnock have been as successful and as entertaining as they are now.

Off the field there has also been a total transformation. Kilmarnock now play in an all-seated stadium which is the fifth biggest in Scotland and the largest outside of Glasgow and Aberdeen. There has been the opening of the new Fitness and Health Centre and even at the time of writing new developments are taking place on-site at Rugby Park which will expand the club's commercial horizons.

All of this, coupled with the news that the '125' book was virtually unobtainable, prompted me to approach the club suggesting that a new book would be timely.

However I didn't want to just update the old book. In the big-business world of football today, fans are often asked to part with their hard-earned cash in return for what are often cosmetic changes to items they already possess - be that replica strips, souvenirs or even books! Adding on details from 1994 onwards with a few new photos and stats just didn't seem right. I'm glad to say that the club agreed with me.

So this is an entirely new publication. I have sought to interpret Killie's history in terms of the matches they have played from the first ever Scottish Cup tie in 1873 to the UEFA Cup campaign of 2001-02. I have approached this in what I think is an easily understandable manner by looking at matches against opponents in an A-Z format.

This has allowed me to give greater prominence to games against the clubs Kilmarnock have played more regularly than others while still affording adequate coverage of some of the more obscure opponents. It has also enabled me to provide some background details of the lesser-known sides.

This format has also given me greater scope in dealing with some of the more memorable matches such as Cup Finals, championship deciders and big European games.

The end result is, I hope, a volume that is easy to read either as a whole or to be dipped into as and when the reader fancies. To enable better integration between the text and the statistics I have compiled a series of 'mini-stats' for every club Killie have met more than twice in first class competition. This gives the reader an overview of matches against particular clubs, making it easier to know where to find greater match details in the statistical section.

I hope that I have been able to do justice to the story of one of Scotland's greatest football clubs. You - the reader - will be the arbiter of that. If you get half the pleasure from reading this book that I received from writing it then I'll know its been a job worth doing.

David Ross

Derrick McDicken in action against Hibernian

ABERCORN

Games	7	
League	6	1895-96, 97-99
Scottish Cup	1	1913
Top Scorer	'Bummer' Campbell 4	All SL
	Ritchie McAvoy 4	All SL
Top Home Crowd	8,000 Feb 8th 1913 SC	
Top Away Crowd	2,500 Oct 30th 1898 SL	

Abercorn were a Paisley side and had been one of the original members of the Scottish League but they had dropped into the Second Division by the time Killie first met them. The teams first crossed paths in Killie's debut League season in 1895-96 but Abercorn were too experienced for the League rookies, winning both matches.

Abercorn won the Division Two title that season and were elected to Division One where they lasted just one season. Killie were an entirely different proposition when the teams clashed again. In the first home match of the campaign, Killie raced into a 4-1 half-time lead and scored three more times in the second half to seal an easy win. This victory set the Ayrshire side up for a tremendous season which ended with the Second Division championship being won and Killie's first ever Scottish Cup Final appearance.

The following year 1898-99 saw Kilmarnock remain undefeated in the League all season and they won both matches with ease against an Abercorn side which finished bottom of the League.

The teams were destined to meet on only one further occasion. An Abercorn side which had won the Qualifying Cup and which was the only unbeaten team in Britain travelled to **Rugby Park** for a Scottish Cup Second Round tie in 1913. Despite the shock of losing the opening goal, Killie soon recovered with makeshift inside-forward **Dickie** the surprising inspiration. His hat-trick, alongside goals from **Andy Cunningham and 'Bud' Maxwell** ensured a comfortable home win. It was the end of the line for Abercorn. This was their last tie in the Scottish Cup proper and the club itself failed to re-start after the First World War.

*The late **Ian Fallis** drives a shot narrowly past the Aberdeen goal.*

ABERDEEN

Games	177	
League	153	1905-17, 19-47, 54-73, 74-75, 76-77, 79-81, 82-83, 93-2001
Scottish Cup	9	1921, 52, 59, 69, 70, 82, 84
League Cup	8	1959, 60, 77, 82
Other	7	1946,80
Top Scorer	Willie Culley 10	All SL
Top Home Crowd	18,128 Mar 5th 1969 SC	
Top Away Crowd	22,609 Mar 1st 1969 SC	
Highest Overall	25,812 Mar 14th 1970 SC	(Muirton Park, Perth)

Aberdeen's arrival in the First Division didn't exactly go down too well with Kilmarnock. Firstly, they had only got into the League at all at the expense of an Ayrshire side **Ayr Parkhouse**. Secondly, they had been elected to the top division after *just one season in Division Two* in which they had finished in *sixth* place. When Killie thought back to 1898, the year they had won the lower league and reached the Cup Final only to be rebuffed in their attempts to go up, a lot of gruff Ayrshire voices were heard to complain about favouritism.

And not without justification. The **Scottish League** were determined to bring top class football to Aberdeen. They recognised the potential that a club from the *Granite City* was capable of harnessing. But perhaps Killie's biggest complaint was the travelling involved. Although Killie were the southernmost side in the top division, most of their travel was to the central belt of Scotland. Only Dundee represented a sizeable journey. Until 1905. The addition of Aberdeen meant *a round trip of nearly 400 miles* to be undertaken in an era when road transport was a lot more primitive than today. Although it is only fair to say that the Edwardian rail network couldn't possibly have been any worse than the one we have to endure nowadays.

Certainly Killie never found **Pittodrie** to be the happiest of hunting grounds. They failed to even score a goal on their first four visits. The 1911-12 match was particularly problematic, as Killie's keeper was knocked unconscious by the ball in the pre-match warm-up. **Mattha Shortt** had to take over in goal and performed heroics as a rare away victory was achieved.

At home, results were much easier to obtain. The less parochially minded amongst the Rugby Park support realised that it was just as long a trek to Rugby Park for the Dons as it was to Pittodrie for Killie. And, although this was an era in which the term *'jet lag'* had yet to be coined, the effects of travelling long distances undoubtedly helped the home club's results.

During the First World War, Kilmarnock ran up some pretty spectacular scorelines. **5-2** in November 1914 then **5-0** in the opening game of the next season. Of particular significance in this game was the performance of **Willie Culley.** The centre-forward had struggled to win over the fans who had lionised **"Bummer' Campbell** and **Andy Cunningham**. Culley's strike rate before this season was less than one in three.

This season saw Culley go into overdrive. With Cunningham sold to **Rangers,** the responsibilities were greater than ever. And the hitman revelled in that. He smashed in his first hat-trick in this game against the Dons and ended the season with **23** League goals, his best-ever total.

Willie Culley remains Kilmarnock's all-time top goalscorer to this day. And it was his demolition of Aberdeen which really kick-started his career. He also holds the distinction of being top Killie scorer against Aberdeen with ten

League goals. Killie notched up a **7-0** thrashing of the Dons in 1916-17 in which *six different players scored*. Little wonder that Aberdeen withdrew from the Scottish League at the end of the season, citing war-time travel as too hazardous. Their journeys to Ayrshire were proving perilous enough.

Of course such results against a team like Aberdeen couldn't be maintained for long. In the inter-war period results were much closer at Rugby Park while Killie generally struggled on the road. In the five seasons immediately preceding the Second World War Killie failed to record a Rugby Park victory.

Mushroom clouds over **Hiroshima** and **Nagasaki** heralded the end of the **Second World War** and the advent of a new and terrifying era in which the very survival of humanity hung by the slenderest of threads. In the same month – **August 1945** – that brought one tyranny to a close and imposed another in the constant fear of human annihilation, it may seem wantonly self-indulgent to dwell on football, but dwell we must. For after six years of wartime restrictions, during which time the army had commandeered Rugby Park, people were desperate to return to normal life. And normal life meant football once again.

The Scottish League decreed that the 1945-46 season would be to all extents and purposes a normal one. Except that *there would be no promotion or relegation*. This was designed to help clubs such as Killie who had closed down for the duration of the conflict. **May 1940** had seen the last first eleven game at Rugby Park.

Killie had operated a reserve side in 1944-45 playing at **Blair Park** in Hurlford. With their ground handed back in April 1945 work desperately went on to prepare for the coming season with German prisoners of war busy building turnstiles almost up to kick-off.

Another blow to Killie was the loss of their

manager. **Jimmy McGrory** took over at **Celtic** and former Killie star **Tom Smith** succeeded him at Rugby Park. It was in these strange circumstances that Aberdeen came calling in the first home match for over five years.

Killie's time out of football took its toll. Only **Turnbull** and **Dornan** of the pre-war players were available. It was an almost unrecognisable eleven which took the field on August 18th 1945. Keeper **Wilson** made his Rugby Park debut. His next game there would be his last! For centre-half **Shufflebottom** his home debut was also his last appearance there. But compared to winger **Marshallsay** this pair were almost veterans. At least they had turned out for Killie away to **Queen's Park** in the League opener. The poor winger made just one appearance for Killie and this was it.

Aberdeen had played virtually throughout the conflict and it showed on the park. The Dons raced into a 3-0 interval lead, eventually winning 4-1. Even here there was no consolation for Kilmarnock. Their only goal came off an Aberdeen defender.

After Killie's seven years stay in the lower league from 1947-54 they returned to the top flight ready to give a chance to the men who had won promotion. Manager **Malcolm MacDonald's** loyalty was commendable if misplaced. The home fixture with Aberdeen on Dec 4th 1954 was destined to become a watershed.

After an embarrassing 4-0 defeat left Killie second bottom *with just four points from twelve matches,* MacDonald took drastic action. Four players were axed: the inspiring **Jimmy Middlemass**, 29 before he turned pro. **Bob Thyne**, rock solid centre-half and **Scotland** cap who would later join the Rugby Park board. **Jimmy Hood**, who like his father before him, was a legend in Killie's defence. And a raw youngster called **Frank Beattie**.

This quartet took the blame for Killie's plight. It was the end for them all bar Beattie. For Thyne and Hood it was particularly sad. They were the only survivors of the side relegated in 1947. For seven long years they plied their trade in the 'B' Division, spending their best playing days at football outposts like **Ochilview** and **Station Park, Forfar**. Now, after just a few short months back in the big time, their Killie careers were over. Some revenge was gained the following season when a **Davie Curlett** strike secured the points for Killie in front of 15,000 fans- a League record for Rugby Park in this fixture.

Frank Beattie came back of course to become perhaps the biggest legend of them all – the man who skippered Killie to the League title. To those who only saw Beattie in the 1960s or those too young to have seen him play at all, it is unthinkable that there was ever a time when this Kilmarnock icon ever enjoyed a status less than that of a demi-god. But this Aberdeen match demonstrates the bald truth. Big Frank was dropped and the fans applauded the decision. It wasn't until Beattie, who started out as an inside-forward, dropped back to the half-back line that his true ability shone through and the supporters who had jeered him began to lionise him.

After this, games between the clubs became a lot closer as Killie challenged at the top end of the table and they were more heated too. Killie striking legend **Eddie Morrison** lost his cool during a match, punching Dons keeper **Ernie McGarr** full on the chin right in front of the referee and was inevitably sent off. In 1971 over 19,000 turned up at Pittodrie, the most that ground has seen for this contest in the League. But with Killie's decline after the launch of the *Premier Division* in 1975 some of the results verged on the embarrassing. Crowd figures too were pathetic. The visit of the great Aberdeen side of the early 1980s – the team of **Strachan, Miller, McLeish** and **Leighton** which won the *Cup-Winners Cup* – attracted fewer than 2,500 spectators to Rugby Park.

How different it was in the 1990s as the crowds flocked back to the new-look ground. Over 9,000 saw Killie play the Dons in 1993-94. The season after that, **Alex Totten's** Killie created a record. *They defeated Aberdeen in all four League games*. Killie's 'whitewash' was something to be savoured. An achievement beyond the reach of any other club in Scotland, the Old Firm included, in 20 years of trying.

Gary Holt: *His first goal for the club ensured they avoided the play-offs in 1997.*

The most dramatic clash of recent times was the last League game of the 1996-97 season. Killie had reached the *Scottish Cup Final* but still faced the threat of relegation. There was a three-way battle going on with **Hibernian** and **Motherwell** to avoid a promotion/relegation play-off against **Airdrie**. Incredibly, *both play-off games were scheduled for the same week as the Cup Final*.

It's doubtful if any player needs an added incentive to avoid the drop but it was there for Killie – in spades. When Aberdeen took the lead at Rugby Park, the ground felt almost like a graveyard. Except that no mausoleum ever operated against a background noise of transistor radios and mobile phones as fans desperately tried to find out how events were shaping elsewhere.

It was then that in stepped **Gary Holt**. A trademark leap and lunge, a flick of the head and Killie were level. It was Holt's first goal for Killie. Like *Culley*, all those years ago, Holt had struggled to win over the fans. This, despite the fact that he was a Killie supporter through and through as his *tattoo* was to demonstrate.

1-1 was enough. And the first celebrations of 1997 took place that night. The perfect rehearsal for **Ibrox** two weeks later. For Gary Holt, this was a personal triumph. *Supporters who had previously called for his head now chanted for his selection by Scotland*

While there have been several **League Cup** tangles, games in the **Scottish Cup** have assumed greater significance. The first time they met was when Killie were the holders. A second round tie at Rugby Park in 1921 saw a mistake by Killie's **Hamilton** hand Aberdeen the lead. The defender redeemed himself by converting a penalty but Aberdeen's second half pressure finally paid off when their centre-forward **McDonald** eluded the offside trap to score the winner and end Killie's Cup reign.

There were two titanic Cup tussles in just over a year. The 1969 tournament saw Killie, in **Walter McCrae's** first season in charge, gain a creditable draw at Pittodrie in front of 22,609, an away record for this clash. The Rugby Park return was a nightmare. With a place in the last four at stake and in front of the biggest crowd to watch the fixture at home – 18,128 - Killie simply froze. 3-0 wasn't just a defeat, it was a capitulation.

It should all have been so different in the 1970 Semi-Final but Aberdeen struck the first blow

psychologically. They told the SFA they were sick of travelling to Glasgow for semi-finals and wanted a genuinely 'neutral' venue. **Muirton Park**, **St Johnstone's** ground was just less than 90 miles from both Kilmarnock and Aberdeen so the match went ahead there. Conditions for fans were appalling. Many couldn't see a thing; others scrambled on top of turnstiles or shimmied up floodlight pylons to get a view of the action. And, with no segregation either at the ground, or at the railway station, fighting broke out among sections of the supporters.

On the pitch a goal from the hitherto unheralded **Derek McKay** was enough to send Aberdeen into the Final, which they won. But the controversy over the choice of venue didn't die down. While it was generally admitted that Aberdeen's geographical position meant that they invariably drew the short straw, Killie supporters felt their team had been unfairly treated. If, as the SFA stated, their decision was fair to both clubs, then it left two questions unanswered:

When would Aberdeen complain about having to play Rangers or Celtic in Glasgow and offer to willingly forego their cut of a huge crowd against the Old Firm in order to play at a 'neutral' venue?

When would the SFA order Rangers or Celtic to meet Aberdeen at a 'neutral' venue outside of Glasgow?

More than 30 years later these questions are still unanswered. This writer suspects this will still be the case 30 years from today.

As for *Muirton Park,* it never hosted a big match again and this dilapidated wreck became a supermarket in the 1980s. Let us hope that shoppers have a better view of the fare on offer in the aisles than supporters had at this travesty of a cup-tie.

AIRDRIEONIANS

Games	182	
League	151	1895-99, 1903-36, 48-50, 55-65, 66-76, 77-79, 80-81,
		83-89, 90-91
Scottish Cup	7	1901, 32, 34, 57, 71, 73
League Cup	17	1956, 61, 63, 68, 69, 81, 82, 84, 99
Other	7	1940, 50, 64, 65
Top Scorer	Andy Kerr 14	SL 9 LC 5
Top Home Crowd	23,509 Mar 2nd 1957 SC	
Top Away Crowd	16,000 Feb 25th 1950 SL	
Highest Overall	28,138 Mar 26th 1932 SC	(Firhill)

Airdrieonians were one of Killie's earliest opponents, the clubs meeting for the first time in Kilmarnock's inaugural League season in 1895-96. And those first games produced some high-scoring affairs. That first season saw Killie lose **5-3** away before turning the tables with a **6-4** win at Rugby Park. The goal feast continued – Killie winning **5-4** away the following season then **5-2** at home in 1897-98 then **5-0** the next year. That season also witnessed an incredible **4-4** draw at **Broomfield**.

By the time Airdrie reached the top flight in 1903, defences had tightened up considerably and goals were much harder to come by. So too for Killie were victories, *there wasn't a single triumph in thirteen consecutive League matches from January 1905-January 1912.*

In the 1920s Airdrie occupied the same position in Scottish football that was to be Kilmarnock's in the 1960s – that of chief challengers to the Old Firm and the results between the two teams largely reflected the *Lanarkshire* side's superiority. But by the end of that decade Airdrie had faded badly and in 1929-30 Killie ran rampant in a **7-1** victory, being ahead 5-0 at half-time. **Bobby McGowan** notched up four goals. Four years later Killie repeated that amazing scoreline in another Rugby Park slaughter, with striker **'Bud' Maxwell** grabbing a hat-trick. Half-back **Jock McEwan** was the only Kilmarnock player to appear in both matches.

In the immediate post-war era, the most significant game between the clubs was in 1949-50. Killie were going strong in the 'B' Division but their promotion hopes were crushed in a 2-0 away defeat watched by 16,000 – a record gate at Broomfield for this fixture. Happier times returned, of course, towards the end of the fifties and **Vernon Wentzel** equalled *McGowan's* feat by scoring all four goals for Killie in 1959.

But that feat was soon to be eclipsed – by a man who was a goalscoring phenomenon at Rugby Park, the one and only **ANDY KERR**. *'Handy Andy'* scored **FIVE** in an **8-0** Rugby Park romp in 1962-63. Kerr had already stamped his authority on this fixture in 1959-60 when his solitary first half goal was enough to give Killie the points in front of nearly 14,000 – the best League crowd at Rugby Park against Airdrie. And it looked like the free-scoring days of the Victorian era had returned when Killie returned from Broomfield with a **5-4** success the following year.

Airdrie must have hated the sight of Andy Kerr. Not only did he score nine League goals against them, edging out *Willie Culley, Eddie Morrison* and *Brien McIlroy* to be Killie's top hitman against the *Diamonds*, he added another five in the League cup as well to bring his tally to 14. Kerr's goals came from just nine matches. In only two of these did he fail to hit the net. The only other Rugby Parker to reach double figures was the late Brien McIlroy with '11 (seven League, four Summer Cup).

The Championship-winning season of 1964-65 saw a New Year upset as leaders Killie slumped to defeat at Broomfield against an Airdrie side destined – even at the halfway point of the season – for relegation. Killie's 2-1 defeat was bad enough but another goal for the home team would have proved fatal to the Rugby Parkers title hopes.

For a few years in the 1970s the two clubs fates were closely entwined as both were relegated in 1973. Killie's double win over Airdrie wasn't quite enough to save them from the drop. But after a lacklustre start to life in the Second Division, it was an emphatic **4-0** drubbing of Airdrie that kick-started Killie's promotion campaign. Both clubs returned to the top after twelve months absence.

The next year was one of the most dramatic in Scottish football history. Only the top ten made the cut to form the new *Premier Division* and

Killie and Airdrie both just missed out, having played two entertaining, high-scoring draws against each other. The new set-up favoured Killie and they established their credentials early in the campaign at Broomfield, winning a marvellous game 4-3 after having led 2-0, then trailed 3-2 and seeing Killie scoring hero **Eddie Morrison** sent off.

The eighties saw crowds fall dramatically as football across Scotland lost its stranglehold on the nation's affections. *A paltry 727 watched one game at Broomfield.* On the plus side, there were some high scoring affairs reminiscent of the early encounters between the clubs. Unfortunately for Killie they were generally on the losing end of these.

The **Scottish Cup** has brought its fair share of dramatic matches too. None more so than in 1932 when Killie came out on top 3-2 in a closely fought semi-final at *Firhill.* The crowd of

Eddie Morrison and George Maxwell (dark shirts) challenge at a corner, watched by Ian Fleming.
No goals here but all three got on the scoresheet in this 4-0 win in 1973-74. Killie's other scorer that day was
Jim McSherry, now the club's commercial manager.

almost 30,000 was the biggest to watch any game between the clubs. In 1957 Killie met Airdrie in the last eight at Rugby Park. Two goals from **Gerry Mays** and another from **Willie 'Puskas' Harvey** easing the home side to a 3-1 triumph and another step along the path to their first post-war Final. The attendance that day was 23,509, easily the largest number ever assembled at Rugby Park for a game between the two sides. But an unbeaten record stretching back 70 years was lost in 1971 when an abject Killie side trailed in at the interval three goals down at Rugby Park. Not even a spirited second half fightback could save them. Worse was to come two years later when the two sides destined for relegation met once again at Rugby Park. In a scrappy affair Airdrie scored the only goal of the game. Killie have waited nearly 30 years for a chance of revenge but the teams have been kept apart in the draw ever since.

There have been several League Cup meetings too. The most recent seeing first division Airdrie knocking out Premier League Killie 1-0 after extra time in a quarter-final tie in 1998-99. But perhaps the most poignant fixture of them all took place in the wartime **Western League** on May 25th 1940. Not for the score – a rather embarrassing 5-1 home defeat for Killie – but for the occasion. Days later the military took control of Rugby Park as an arms dump – the only football ground in Scotland where this happened. **No one knew at the time but when the Killie players trooped dejectedly off the pitch after the loss to the Diamonds, it was the last match to be played at Rugby Park for five years.**

Gerry Mays scores with a spectacular header during Killie's 1957 Cup triumph over the *Diamonds*.

ALBION ROVERS

Games	45	
League	30	1919-23, 34-37, 38-39, 47-48, 49-54, 73-74
Scottish Cup	8	1893, 1904, 20, 29, 32, 34, 64
League Cup	2	1974
Other	5	1919, 40
Top Scorer	Walter Jackson 6	All SL
Top Home Crowd	12,000 Sep 3rd 1921	
Top Away Crowd	11,665 Feb 3rd 1934 SC	
Highest Overall	95,000 Apr 17th 1920 SC	(Hampden)

Games against **Albion Rovers** haven't exactly been commonplace down through the years but there have been several significant encounters. None more so than the **Scottish Cup Final** of 1920.

The first Final after World War One was a gala occasion for the clubs – even if the SFA didn't think so. The governing body estimated that, with no Old Firm presence, the crowd would be lucky to reach 50,000. In the event the fans of both clubs proved the authorities wrong. 95,000 – **a new record**, and easily the biggest crowd for a Killie v Rovers game- turned up and the prospect of a shock was on the cards early on as Rovers took the lead.

The Coatbridge side were bottom of the single-division Scottish League but Killie were wary of them, having already lost to the men from *Cliftonhill* in the War Cup of 1918-19. Gradually, though, Kilmarnock's superiority began to show and goals from **Willie Culley, Mattha Shortt** and **JR Smith** ensured victory for Killie, although Rovers never gave up. The final score was 3-2 to Kilmarnock and the Scottish Cup was on its way to Ayrshire for the first time.

The cup connection between the clubs continued when Killie overcame Rovers on their way to their second Cup win in 1929 and again in 1932 – when Killie reached the Final – Rovers were beaten along the way. But the Lanarkshire side gained revenge two years later when, as a

Second Division side, they humiliated Killie by winning 2-1 at Cliftonhill. There were 11,665 present that day, the most to have attended a Cliftonhill game between the clubs. Since then the clubs have only met once with Killie running out easy winners in 1964.

The only occasion the clubs have met in the League Cup was in 1973-74, in the Quarter-Finals. Killie returned from Coatbridge having received an embarrassing 2-0 defeat. They had their work cut out to turn things round at Rugby Park in the second leg but a 5-2 win was enough to squeeze through 5-4 on aggregate. **Five different Killie players were on target that day.**

With so few meetings between them it's a bit of a statistical oddity that Killie and Rovers have clashed in wartime cups during both global conflicts with the record standing at a victory apiece.

The first League meeting between the clubs was also in the cup-winning season of 1919-20 and although Rovers gave a good account of themselves at home, Killie generally had the better of things. Particularly so in 1922-23 when they won **7-0** at home with **Walter Jackson** grabbing four of the goals. With six in total, all in the League, Jackson is Killie's top scorer against Rovers. But there was to be a humiliating **6-1** away defeat, perhaps appropriately on April Fools Day, in 1939.

Killie's first loss at Rugby Park came in 1947-48; in their first season in the lower League for nearly half a century but one in which Rovers gained promotion to the top flight for the last time. In Killie's own promotion season of 1953-54 they had to endure another humiliating home loss.

The last League meetings took place in 1973-74 with Killie winning an incredible match at Cliftonhill **4-3,** having led **3-0** at half-time. That game took place three weeks after Killie's League Cup debacle at the same ground and was watched by just 295 spectators; far and away the lowest crowd to have watched this fixture and just a little over a tenth of the number who had attended the cup-tie. Crowds, other than for the Cup Final, have never been huge. 12,000 is the biggest crowd at Rugby Park and 9,000 is the best recorded at Cliftonhill in the League. On March 30th 1974 Killie claimed the points at Rugby Park. The two clubs have never met in a recognised competition since then.

The 1920 Scottish Cup winners.
The side which brought the Scottish Cup to Ayrshire for the first time.
The players in the photo are: Middle row: T. Hamilton, T. Blair, D. Gibson.
Front: J. McNaught, M. Smith, J.R. Smith, W. Culley, M. McPhail.
Sitting: A. Mackie, J. Bagan, M. Shortt, R. Neave.
Trainers P. Carrick and J. McWhinnie are the immediate either side of the middle row and
Secretary/Manager Hugh Spence is in the middle of the back row.

ALLOA ATHLETIC

Games	43	
League	27	1922-23, 47-54, 73-74, 77-78, 83-84, 85-86
Scottish Cup	4	1920, 72, 2000
League Cup	9	1949, 53, 79, 80, 85
Other	3	1949, 76
Top Scorer	George Maxwell 4	SL 2, SC 1 Oth 1
	Hugh McLaren 4	SL 2 Oth 2
	Sammy McGivern 4	SL 4
Top Home Crowd	10,683 Sep 6th 1952 SL	
Top Away Crowd	10,000 Feb 7th 1920 SC	

Alloa were the first side to gain automatic promotion from the Second Division, in 1922. And the next season is the only one in which Killie have played them in the top flight. Killie were trailing 5-2 at **Recreation Park** with just eight minutes left when the game was abandoned. **Incredibly, the Scottish League ordered the entire match to be replayed and Killie salvaged a precious point in a 3-3 draw.**

The clubs met regularly during Kilmarnock's seven-year sojourn in the 'B' Division and there were some pretty impressive Rugby Park victories, including **5-1** in 1948-49 and **6-0** the following season. In the promotion season of 1953-54 Killie won 2-0 at home with the scoresheet reading *"Jack, Russell."* Cue the jokes about having plenty of bite up front as Killie put in a dogged performance.

Twenty years elapsed before the sides met again and Alloa were left wishing it would be another twenty before they had to return to Rugby Park as Killie thrashed them **8-2. Iain McCulloch, Ian Fleming** and **Gordon Smith** all scored a brace with **Ronnie Sheed** and **George Maxwell** completing the rout.

The clubs met several times from then until the mid-80s. April 28th 1984 was a real low point for Killie. They beat Alloa 2-0 in their final game of the season but the attendance was a pitiful 460 – *the lowest recorded League crowd for any Rugby Park match.* Just 227 spectators paid at the gate.

There have been happier times in the knockout tournaments. 10,000 turned up at Recreation Park to see Killie begin the march to their first Scottish Cup triumph in 1920 and Alloa were also brushed aside in the League Cup as Killie strode to their first Final in 1952-53. But it was the *Wasps* who provided the sting the last time the teams met. After drawing at Rugby Park, Alloa knocked Kilmarnock out of the Scottish Cup in February 2000.

Oh happy day. Rampant Killie put eight goals past Alloa in this 1973-74 encounter.

ANNBANK

Scottish Cup	6	1885,86,90,91,96
Top Scorer	Andrew Kelvin 3	All SC
Top Home Crowd	4,000 Sep 7th 1889	

Killie faced **Annbank** five times in just over a decade in the Scottish Cup and won only once. The start of this dismal sequence was in the second round of the 1884-85 competition. Killie, newly-crowned Ayrshire Cup winners, were expected to see off their county rivals with ease but, playing away from home on a ground with a *"mysterious-looking incline"* and an area off the pitch *"resembling a jungle"* they were soundly beaten 4-1. For Annbank it was an opportunity to march to the last eight of the tournament where their cup dreams were dashed on the reality of a 5-0 loss to **Hibernian**.

The opportunity for revenge came swiftly. Drawn at home in the first round of the following year's competition, Kilmarnock exacted retribution with a stunning **7-1** success. There was no repeat four years later as Annbank won 3-2 at Rugby Park in another first round tie. Indeed, Annbank were proving to be a bogey team as far as Killie were concerned. Not content with removing the Rugby Parkers from the national competition this season, they proceeded to do the same in both the Ayrshire and Kilmarnock Charity Cups.

Twelve months on, the same depressing story occurred again. Killie had restored local pride by winning the Ayrshire Cup but when faced with the familiar sight of an Annbank eleven in a Scottish Cup tie they just couldn't overcome them. Killie led **3-2** at the interval before settling for a **4-4** draw. The replay was a humiliation; **4-1** down at the break, Kilmarnock eventually lost **6-2**. Annbank, buoyed by yet another claiming of the Killie scalp, continued to do well in the Cup. The following season they again reached the last eight, going down to **Rangers** 2-0.

But perhaps the worst result of all was the last one. By January 1896 Kilmarnock were a Scottish League side with international players like **Jocky Johnstone** and **'Bummer' Campbell** in their ranks. Yet they slumped to another Rugby Park dismissal in the Scottish Cup. Annbank triumphing 3-2 in another first round tie. Although Annbank went on to appear in the competition proper on two more occasions it was to be the last time they clashed with Killie. Something Kilmarnock at least would be thankful for.

ARBROATH

Games	48	
League	41	1935-39, 47-54, 60, 69, 73, 75-76, 78-79, 90
Scottish Cup	3	1903, 21, 91
League Cup	2	1953
Other	2	1940, 91
Top Scorer	Allan Collins 5	SL 4 Oth 1
Top Home Crowd	10,467 Jan 3rd 1949 SL	
Top Away Crowd	5,000 Jan 22nd 1921 SC	
	5,000 Aug 28th 1948 SL	

Killie first met **Arbroath** in a League game in 1935. A stunning **5-0** win with **Bobby Beattie** claiming a hat-trick set the pattern for a largely

successful sequence of victories at Rugby Park. To this day, Kilmarnock remain unbeaten at home in all competitions against the *'Red*

Lichties.' Although when faced with the journey to that outpost of the North Sea called **Gayfield** times have generally been tougher.

Even Kilmarnock's first ever triumph at Gayfield was hardly a cause for celebration. Killie travelled back to Ayrshire with both points on September 2nd 1939. Less than 24 hours later the country was at war. But it was in the drab immediacy of the aftermath of global conflict that saw Killie's best performance against Arbroath. In January 1949 Killie were labouring in the old 'B' Division yet their home New Year fixture warmed their supporters as effectively as any *'Ne'erday hauf.'*

Hugh McLaren was the outstanding player of the time at Rugby Park. Too good for this League, he was soon to move to **Derby County.** But on January 3rd 1949 he was outstanding. Scoring twice in the first 20 minutes, McLaren ran the game from his inside-left position as Killie took a 3-0 interval lead. Two quickfire goals after the restart from **Allan Sinclair** had Killie cruising. So much so that McLaren was even able to miss a penalty with scarcely a murmur from the crowd. Nine minutes remained and it was still 5-0 when Killie went into overdrive. First came centre-forward **Clive's** second goal and Killie's sixth. Sinclair obtained his hat-trick a minute later. Then, with five minutes still on the clock, McLaren notched his own third to complete the scoring in an 8-0 rout.

These years were desperate times for Kilmarnock and results such as this were rare. And make no mistake, 'B' Division or not, this was a truly remarkable scoreline. It had been more than *seventeen years* since a Kilmarnock side had run up eight goals in a League match

Appropriately, this match was watched by the biggest attendance ever to see this fixture.

The next season saw Killie's first 'official' win in a Gayfield league match – the 1939 game being struck from the records. But after Killie climbed out of the lower League in 1954, games between the two sides were confined to those

SATURDAY, OCTOBER 4, 1968
ARBROATH
versus
KILMARNOCK
FIRST DIVISION   PRICE — 6d.   KICK-OFF 3 p.m.

THE MANAGER SAYS . . .

Two goals from **Jim McLean** - his first strikes for the club - gave Killie a 2-1 victory in this 1968 League match.

rare occasions that Arbroath played in Division One. Reconstruction saw the two teams pitted against each other in the middle division in the new set-up but the last 20 years has seen combat between the clubs confined to Killie's season in the Second Division in 1989-90. The game at Gayfield in February 1990 was of immense significance as Killie toiled to escape the bottom flight. A 4-2 win with goals from **Callaghan, Tait, Sludden** and **Watters** was the catalyst for a five-match winning run which pushed Killie right back into the promotion race.

Killie have prevailed on each of the three occasions the teams have met in the **Scottish Cup.** 1920-21 being particularly sweet as Killie travelled to Gayfield as holders of the trophy. The teams have met just twice in the League Cup, sharing a victory apiece. Those games coming in 1952-53 when Killie reached the Final despite their lower league status.

ARBROATH ATHLETIC

Arbroath Athletic were a non-league side that crossed swords with Killie just once – in the 1924-25 Scottish Cup. The Angus team had been rejected for membership of the short-lived Third Division on the grounds that Arbroath was too small a town to support two League teams and they viewed the Cup as an opportunity to prove the powers-that-be wrong. But Killie easily saw off their challenge. Goals from **Bird, Rock** and the legendary **Mattha Smith** gave Kilmarnock a

3-0 win in front of 6,000 at Rugby Park.

Arbroath Athletic's only previous tilt at the Cup had also foundered in Ayrshire – **Ayr United** also winning 3-0. Their third – and final – attempt for Cup glory ended in a 7-0 defeat by **Dundee United**. After that, they faded into obscurity, quickly followed by oblivion. The Scottish League's assessment of their potential had been cruel but accurate.

ARMADALE

Armadale were the shock troops of the first Scottish Cup to take place after the First World War. No fewer than three First Division sides – **Clyde, Hibernian** and **Ayr United** – had fallen by the time Killie arrived to face them in a quarter-final tie and a large crowd of around 8,000 turned up for the match. But this was to be the end of the giant-killing line for the West

Lothian outfit. Killie made the game secure in the first half with goals from the deadly strike pair of **Willie Culley** and **JR Smith**.

Although Armadale pulled a goal back after the break, Killie were never in any serious danger. Their victory put them into the last four for the first time in a dozen years and took them one stage nearer that elusive first major triumph.

ARTHURLIE

Like many others in today's junior ranks, **Arthurlie** were once a senior team. But in over 50 years in the senior ranks Kilmarnock played the **Barrhead** team just once in a first class competitive fixture. That was in the Scottish Cup in 1881-82. Killie had undertaken an excellent run. For the first time they had progressed past the all-Ayrshire stages of the competition and had now reached the last sixteen.

A crowd of 2,000 (impressive for the time)

assembled at Barrhead and watched as Killie gave as good as they got for the first 45 minutes. At 0-0 at the break, Killie were in with a chance. But the second half witnessed a collapse as Arthurlie ran out easy 4-1 winners.

There was some sort of revenge in store however. In the last eight Arthurlie were drawn away to Killie's local rivals **Kilmarnock Athletic** and the red-shirted Athletic avenged their fellow townsmen by defeating the Renfewshire eleven 5-1.

ASTON VILLA

For the fifth time in less than a decade Kilmarnock were invited to the USA to take part in that country's showcase summer soccer tournament. But whereas in the early part of the

1960s these tournaments attracted the cream of European and South American talent, this was not the case in 1969 when Killie locked horns with **Aston Villa.**

The Birmingham side were in serious decline, struggling to stay afloat in the English Second Division (equivalent to the Nationwide First today) under their charismatic and volatile Scots manager **Tommy Docherty**. So when Killie lost 2-1 to Villa in Atlanta after leading through a **Jim McLean** goal it was regarded as a poor result.

In this particular tournament the British teams taking part adopted the personas of their host cities. Thus it was that when Killie claimed a revenge victory three weeks later thanks to goals from **Jim McLean** and **Gerry Queen** that the US press reported it (where they mentioned it at all) as '*St Louis 2 Atlanta 1.*'

This tourney had even odder rules concerning goals and points. Killie finished in last place in the competition yet had taken 26 points from the eight games played!

AUCHINLECK

In its early days the Scottish Cup drew entries from all over the country and the competition was played on a county basis in the early rounds. As a consequence Killie met many other Ayrshire teams in the national tournament. **Auchinleck** were one such foe and they travelled to Rugby Park in the second round of the 1881-82 Scottish Cup.

The first half was close with the teams changing ends at 1-1. But the home side's class began to tell after the break. Killie ran out **7-1** winners at full-time. Although the line-up is known details of some of the scorers have been lost as the 19th century was not as statistically-minded as the 21st.

One statistic that is available concerns the opposition. This was the last time that Auchinleck took part in the Scottish Cup. Glory for Auchinleck would come in the Junior equivalent some 100 years later.

AYR ACADEMICAL

This is not the occasion to enter into the esoteric and bewildering world of family trees of 19th century football clubs. Suffice to say that **Ayr Academical** were one of several teams plying their trade in the county town in the late 19th century and that they went on to merge with others – a process which did not reach fruition until the creation of **Ayr United** in 1910.

The second round of the 1877-78 Scottish Cup competition saw Killie drawn away to the Accies. The only goal of the game came in the second half and it was in the Ayr side's favour. The opportunity for revenge came just two seasons later when Killie were drawn to play the Accies at home in the first round.

And revenge it was, albeit of an odd kind. For the Accies had reached the end of the line in this incarnation. They didn't show up and Killie were awarded the tie.

AYR EGLINTON

The first round of the 1875-76 Scottish Cup was the only occasion Kilmarnock faced **Ayr Eglinton**. And a strange encounter it was. For a start, the Ayr side could only muster ten men, placing them at a distinct and immediate disadvantage. Perhaps they weren't too perturbed. After all, according to advertisements this was a '*friendly contest.*'

Yet according to Killie outside-left **Andrew Ferguson's** match list for the season it was definitely a cup tie. This is one of the oldest surviving artefacts of any Kilmarnock player and as a result we know that Andrew Ferguson scored in the game as he notes in his card that

he *"kicked one"* of the goals.

David Sturrock became the first Kilmarnock player ever to score a hat-trick, though the other scorers are unknown. It was 3-0 at half-time, ending up **8-0**.

AYR PARKHOUSE

Ayr Parkhouse enjoyed a long existence as an independent club before they merged with local rivals **Ayr** in 1910 to form **Ayr United** – including two spells in the Scottish League. But prior to that they embarked on a Scottish Cup run in 1897-98 which led to the first all-Ayrshire quarter-final tie when Killie were the visitors to their *Beresford Park* ground.

Parkhouse had already disposed of **Kilmarnock Athletic** and this tie was eagerly awaited throughout the county. 6,000 watched the amateur Parkhouse quickly grab a two goal lead

but this Kilmarnock side had plenty of fighting qualities and they not only battled back into the game, they overwhelmed their county rivals taking a 5-2 lead at half-time.

Killie scored twice more without reply in the second half to establish beyond all doubt just who were the premier team in Ayrshire. For the second successive season they had reached the semi-finals. And this team made history by going on to become the first Kilmarnock side to appear in the Scottish Cup Final.

AYR THISTLE

Ayr Thistle were yet another of the short-lived sides that proliferated in the county town in the 1880s. Killie met them for the first and last time in the opening round of the Scottish Cup in 1887-88 at Rugby Park.

As a contest the game was effectively over by the break as Killie amassed a five goal lead. The home side piled on the agony for their visitors in the second period, adding three more goals to complete an **8-0** rout.

With Bertie Black grounded, Willie Harvey (8) attempts to rise for the ball, watched by Frank Beattie. This 1957 cup tie at a packed Rugby Park saw Killie beat Ayr United 1-0 thanks to a goal from Beattie.

AYR UNITED
(Includes AYR FC to 1910)

Games	141	
League	113	1897-99, 1913-25, 28-36, 37-39, 47-54, 56-57, 59-61, 66-67,
		69-73, 74-75, 76-77, 78-79, 81-82, 83-86, 88-89, 90-93
Scottish Cup	9	1881, 1924, 38, 57, 81, 94, 98, 99
League Cup	14	1948, 51, 52, 66, 71, 77, 87, 97
Other	5	1940, 93
Top Scorer	'Bud' Maxwell 9	All SL
Top Home Crowd	27,442 Mar 19th 1938 SC	
Top Away Crowd	23,785 Mar 23rd 1938 SC	

Killie's position of pre-eminence in Ayrshire was challenged in the dying days of the 19th century by the election of **Ayr FC** to the Scottish League. But the *'mother club'* quickly saw off the upstarts from the county town by climbing into the top division and leaving their rivals floundering in the lower league alongside the amateurs of Ayr Parkhouse.

By 1910 it had become apparent that Ayr couldn't really support two league clubs and so they merged. In reality, as they played at Ayr FC's ground, the team comprised most of their players and the support also came from Ayr FC, the new **Ayr United** club was more of a takeover than a joining of equals.

The merger paid a quick dividend. Within three years the new club had been elected to the top flight. And the first few derby games were torrid occasions for Killie supporters. In the first seven games in Division One, United won six with the other drawn. *"A deep humiliation"* was how the *Kilmarnock Standard* described matters. The fans expressed similar sentiments, if in a more florid tongue.

Gradually Kilmarnock regained the upper hand, winning at **Somerset Park** for the first time in December 1916 and following that up the next season by doing the double. In 1925 the fixture was played for the first time on a New Year's Day. And a happy Rugby Park it was. Although the ground was lashed by wind and rain and the kick-off was at the unusual time of 1.55, nothing could dampen the spirits of the home support as Killie completed another double over United with an easy 4-1 victory. With both teams struggling those points were precious. At the end of the season United were relegated.

Ayr came back after three years and games between the pair were more evenly contested, although Rugby Park in particular was the scene for some spectacular results; **5-1** to Killie in 1931-32, **5-3** to United the next season, **4-2** to Killie the year after that then a **6-3** home triumph in 1934-35. But the biggest – and best – came in January 1936. Killie were on a roll – seven games without defeat – and Ayr were at the foot of the table. The relative merits of the sides appeared to be borne out in the opening 45 minutes as Killie raced into a 3-0 lead. But just five minutes into the second half, the game was turned on its head as Ayr came storming back, scoring twice.

But just as the game seemed to be running away from them, Kilmarnock rallied. **Jimmy Williamson** and **Bobby Beattie** restored the three-goal gap and Ayr collapsed as Killie scored twice more to run out **7-2** winners; striker **Jimmy Robertson** scoring four. It was a record win over the auld enemy. Once again, Ayr were relegated.

The teams clashed again in Killie's 'B' Division days in front of large crowds. Killie were first to escape the bottom rung but even as they did so – in 1954 – United did the double, including an embarrassingly easy 3-0 Rugby Park Ne'erday win. United fans celebrated that day – and with good reason; for it would be seventeen years before they took the points away from Rugby Park again and sixteen before they could do the same at Somerset.

The rest of the 1950s and the 1960s saw precious few derby encounters as Ayr rarely played in the top division. And when they did it wasn't for long. So poor were United that in 1965 as Kilmarnock were crowned Champions of Scotland, their rivals languished in ignominy – *second bottom of the entire League.*

Ally McLeod's arrival as Ayr boss changed things round. As Killie began to falter from their sixties glory days, United were a vastly improved side. So much so that when the Premier Division was formed in 1975 it was Ayr who joined the elite as Killie pressed their noses up against the big-time window.

Within a year though, Killie had won promotion and county hostilities resumed. October 30th 1976 saw an explosion of old-fashioned wing play from **Davie Provan** on the right and **Gordon Smith** on the left as Killie tore Ayr apart. With the tragic **Ian Fallis** rampaging through the middle, Kilmarnock thrashed United **6-1**, Fallis scoring three, to record their first victory in the Premier Division and equal the winning margin of 1936.

Sadly, the rest of the season was a tale of woe as Killie were relegated. And in the second Rugby Park encounter, Ayr came away with a 1-0 win. That day – March 12th 1977 – was this author's 21st birthday and even now he regrets that the 6-1 win could not have been served up on that occasion.

As part-timers, neither Killie nor Ayr could sustain a Premier place for long and there were plenty of First Division derbies in the 1980s. But

although as fiercely contested as before, some of the passion had gone out of the fixture. Perhaps it was over-familiarity, with the teams now meeting three times a season. Perhaps it was lack of atmosphere as crowds declined to record lows. Perhaps it was the recognition that here were two teams going nowhere – content to stay in the middle order of the Scottish game. Perhaps it was all of these combined.

Whatever it was, the spark was re-ignited in the early 1990s as a resurgent Kilmarnock, led by **Tommy Burns** – a man who knew a thing or two about heated derby matches- enjoyed regular victories watched by big crowds. A generation of fans had grown up unaccustomed to seeing Killie on top and they enjoyed their team's renewed success.

Promotion in 1993 brought an end to the Ayrshire derbies. Unless, or until, Ayr can build a ground capable of meeting Premier League requirements (and, incidentally, a team to match) the Cups will remain the only outlet for the two clubs to clash.

And the Cups have witnessed some epic clashes. The first pairing in the **Scottish Cup** was back in 1880-81 when Killie beat the old Ayr FC 6-3. The first tie against United was a defeat at Somerset in 1924. A loss all the more galling as Killie had already eliminated Celtic and were strongly fancied for the trophy. But the most thrilling of all the Ayrshire duels came in the space of a few short days in 1938.

Both teams were fighting against the drop in the League but were going strong in the Cup. Killie had claimed a famous **Parkhead** victory in the third round, followed that up in their next game with a League win over **Rangers** and then found themselves awaiting the arrival of **Ayr** in the quarter-finals of the Cup.

27,442 – *the largest crowd for any Killie-Ayr*

game watched as the Rugby Park side failed to protect **Benny Thomson's** first half goal. Ayr forced a 1-1 draw and were now favourites for the tie. Four days later, **23,785** – a Somerset Park record for an Ayrshire derby – assembled for the replay. Once again, Killie took a narrow first half lead, courtesy of Thomson. But those United fans expecting a reprise of their team's Rugby Park performance were to be severely disappointed. Killie came storming out in the second half. Thomson added to his earlier goal and **Collins, McAvoy** and **McGrogan** all weighed in as a rampant Kilmarnock won 5-0.

Killie continued to have the evil eye as far as Ayr and the Scottish Cup were concerned. In 1957 (another year they reached the Final), 1981 and 1994, Kilmarnock opened up their Cup campaigns with a home win over Ayr. It was not until 1998 that the *'Honest Men'* finally managed to conjure up a victory to repeat their feat of 1924. And for Killie it could not have been worse. For they lost, not only to their most bitter rivals, they also surrendered the trophy itself; having arrived at Somerset as holders.

Having acquired the habit, Ayr went on to repeat their triumph the following season. Jokes about

getting to keep Killie if they beat them a third time abounded in the taverns of the county town. Perhaps fortunately, the draw kept the teams apart the next year.

The clubs have clashed many times in the **League Cup**, mostly in sectional matches, which had little bearing on the outcome of the group, let alone the trophy. But in 1965-66, Killie –the Scottish champions – faced a quarter-final challenge from an Ayr team going strongly at the top of the Second Division. It was a hard-fought two-leg affair which saw Killie safely through to the semis. Since the League Cup adopted a knockout format the teams have met twice, both at Rugby Park, and both won by Ayr. The shock of losing the most recent of these – in 1996-97 - being more than offset by Killie's Scottish Cup victory at the end of that campaign.

Killie have also faced Ayr in the wartime Western League and War Cup as well as the B&Q Cup and are undefeated in these matches. **And while Ayr can take comfort from the occasional Cup upset and some famous League victories, there can be no doubt that Kilmarnock have by far the superior record in games between the clubs.**

Frank Beattie (next to ball) in action against Ayr.
Here, Big Frank is a stalwart in defence in this early 1960s League match.

BANGU

1959-60 had been a great season for Kilmarnock. Runners-up in both League and Cup (the former for the first time), they had been chosen to represent Scotland in the **New York** international tournament. At the time this was regarded as highly as qualification for Europe. And Killie did Scotland proud, winning their group against highly ranked opposition. The consequence of their success was that they were to face the winners of the other group in the Final.

That side was **Bangu**, of **Brazil**. Thanks to Brazil's amazing success in winning the World Cup in Sweden (they remain the only country to become World Champions outside their native continent) and the feats of the prodigious **Pele,** Brazilian football was the standard to which all others aspired.

Kilmarnock were no different. That was why they flew out to take on Bangu at the **New York Polo Grounds** almost two months after their last match in the tourney, some 50 weeks after the old season had started and just *seven days* before they were due to kick-off the 1960-61 season at Easter Road.

And the crowd appreciated it too. Over 25,000 (big by US standards) applauded both sides on to the pitch and although Killie fought tenaciously, conditions and the time of year were against them as Bangu won 2-0 The Killie players hoisted the victorious Brazilian captain on their shoulders and applauded his team-mates off the park. The organisers were begging the Scottish League to enter Killie for the next year's tournament before the Scots were even on the plane home.

Killie invited Bangu over for a friendly and beat them 1-0 in front of over 18,000 but when they returned to America in 1961 it was a different story. Playing seven games in 24 days and having to fly from Montreal to New York for their final fixtures took its toll and Killie were easily beaten 5-0 by the Brazilian maestros in their final match of the tournament.

The victorious Kilmarnock squad return to Prestwick Airport with the trophies won in the USA in 1960.

BAYERN MUNICH

Kilmarnock's introduction to competitive foreign opposition in the **1960 New York** tournament wasn't exactly gentle. **Bayern Munich** were formidable foes. And if they were not exactly the household name in 1960 that they are today, that didn't matter. For Killie – and all of Scotland – knew all about the strength of German football. Earlier that year **Eintracht Frankfurt** had humiliated Rangers 12-4 on aggregate in the European Cup and just seven days before Killie took on their Bavarian opponents, Eintracht took part in the marvellous European Cup Final of 1960 at Hampden Park against **Real Madrid**.

It was not surprising that Killie took some time to settle. This was their first match in the competition and they had to adapt to the style of **Tommy Bryceland**, a **St Mirren** player given dispensation to play on loan for the injured **Bertie Black**. In the circumstances a 1-0 half time deficit wasn't too bad.

But Killie came out buzzing after the interval. Bryceland scored, as did both **Andy Kerr** and **Jackie McInally** as Killie won 3-1 and left the Polo Grounds stadium with the cheers of over 10,000 supporters – many of them exiled Scots – in their ears. Their American adventure had started with a bang.

BEITH

For many years **Beith** flew the flag for North Ayrshire as a senior side in the Scottish game. They played in the ill-fated **Third Division** in the 1920s and took part in the Scottish Cup as late as 1937. Indeed, Beith had first competed in the national tournament as early as 1876 so it was something of a surprise that their name and Killie's did not emerge from the hat together until 1904-05.

Killie had been going through a rough time – they lost six in succession in late 1904 – but they should have taken care of their North Ayrshire rivals comfortably. But this was to be one of those ties Kilmarnock would regret ever having to play. They struggled at home, trailing 2-1 at the break and were lucky to force a replay. The second match was no better – drawing 1-1 at half-time, a slipshod Killie went down 3-1 in front of 4,000 (mostly) jubilant supporters. '*Big Brother*' had been taken down a peg or two. But

take nothing away from Beith. Over the piece they had thoroughly deserved their triumph. And they proved it was no fluke by demolishing **Cowdenbeath** 4-0 in the next round before losing to **Ranger**s at Ibrox in the last eight.

Tragically, the home tie with Beith was the last game ever seen by Killie full-back **Barney Battles**. He had come down with influenza playing at Ibrox in the League the week before the cup tie. After watching the game his condition worsened and he died shortly afterwards. 40,000 lined the route of his funeral in Glasgow in silent, yet eloquent, tribute to a popular player.

Battles – an internationalist while with Celtic – was probably unaware that his wife was pregnant. The child was named after his father and, a generation later, also played for Scotland.

BERWICK RANGERS

Games	10	
League	5	1973-74, 89-90
Scottish Cup	1	1939
League Cup	2	1983
Other	2	1976
Top Scorer	Willie Watters 3	All SL
Top Home Crowd	6,439 Jan 21st 1939 SC	
Top Away Crowd	992 Feb 24th 1990 SL	

Kilmarnock's first trip into England on League duty was not a happy one. Soundly beaten 4-1 by **Berwick Rangers**, worse was to come just under a month later. A humiliating home defeat marked the end of **Walter McCrae's** tenure as Manager. A reign, which had started with high hopes and two successive European qualifications, ended on a cold October night in 1973.

It meant that McCrae would not be around to see many of the youngsters he had signed – players like the two **McCullochs, Ian** and **Allan; Smith, Fleming, Stewart** and **McLean** blossom into stardom. McCrae, of course, would return to Rugby Park in an administrative capacity, but for now his seventeen-year association with the club was over.

The only other League season in which the teams met – 1989-90 - also saw Killie at a low ebb. But one they were swiftly recovering from. When Berwick could not be issued with a safety certificate for their crumbling stand roof, a League match scheduled for *Shielfield* had to be quickly shifted to *Tynecastle* and Killie slumped to defeat. They gained revenge later in the season. Playing at a roofless Shielfield, the Killie fans having to stand up between the waterlogged seats, the supporters discomfort was eased by a fine performance from the team. **Willie Watters** scoring a hat-trick in a 4-1 win which kept Killie on the promotion track. This remains the only

occasion Kilmarnock have won a League match on English soil.

The largest attendance for this fixture is 6,439. That was the crowd the first time the teams met. Killie won **6-1** in a Scottish Cup tie in 1939 against a Berwick team, which, at the time, was a non-League outfit.

A **Willie Watters** hat-trick kept Killie on course for promotion in this rare foray across the border on League duty.

BESIKTAS

Not a lot was known about Turkish football in the early 1960s. **Besiktas** had won the inaugural Turkish championship in 1960 and had been eliminated from the European Cup by **Rapid Vienna**, albeit winning their home leg. So when Killie faced them in their fifth match in the **1961 New York** tournament (and their last in their Montreal base) the Turks were something of an unknown quantity. Naturally, in those insular days, nobody bothered to ask if Besiktas knew much about their opponents from Scotland. As far as the locals were concerned, they didn't want to know either team. Just 2,000 fans (the lowest crowd of the 1961 trip) turned up to watch.

Killie found out soon enough that Besiktas were a decent side and headed for the dressing rooms a goal down. Left-winger **Billy Muir** brought the Scottish side back into it with a second-half equaliser, but, try as they might, Killie couldn't force a winner. A draw was a fair result but, in some media eyes, Killie had failed against a team of unknowns. That is more of an indictment on the media of the time than on the team. Today, a draw against the Champions of Turkey on neutral ground would be regarded as a decent result for any Scottish team.

BLACKPOOL

1980-81 was a dismal season for Killie, ending in relegation from the Premier Division. One of the rare highlights of the term was Killie's **Anglo-Scottish Cup** adventure. Playing away to **Blackpool** in early September was a fan's dream. Most of Killie's travelling support were as familiar with the holiday resort as they were with their own town and the trip south was a grand opportunity for a short holiday with a football match thrown in.

A closely contested first leg ended with Killie trailing 2-1. The game was put into the record books in the second half when **Eamonn Collins** came on as a substitute for the Seasiders. At 14 years and 323 days old, Collins became the youngest player to take part in a senior football match anywhere in the UK in peacetime. It was a 'double' for Killie as, in 1945, they had faced a **Queen's Park** side with **Ronnie Simpson** in goal at the age of 14 years and 310 days – the Scottish record. Simpson misses out on the UK peacetime record, as his appearance was three days before the end of the Second World War.

The second leg saw a rare triumph over English opposition as Killie raced into a 4-1 interval lead, eventually winning the game 4-2 and the tie 5-4 on aggregate. Although Blackpool were a Third Division side, it was still a fair achievement by Kilmarnock. They were the only one of the four Scottish teams to win their quarter-final tie. Worst result of all being **Rangers** defeat by **Chesterfield!**

BO'NESS

Games	5	
League	2	1927-28
Scottish Cup	3	1929, 31
Top Scorer	'Peerie' Cunningham 5	4 SL 1SC
Top Home Crowd	8,300 Mar 4th 1931 SC	
Top Away Crowd	6,258 Feb 28th 1931 SC	

Long-gone from the senior ranks, **Bo'ness** figured briefly in Killie's history in the late twenties and early thirties. They reached the First Division in 1927 and gave Killie two tough games in their solitary season in the top flight. A **'Peerie' Cunningham** hat-trick gave Killie the points at Rugby Park where the game had been all-square at half-time. Away from home Cunningham gave Killie the interval lead, but a Bo'ness fightback saw the West Lothian club capture both points by winning 2-1.

If Killie thought they had seen the last of

Bo'ness they were wrong. For they were drawn together in the following season's **Scottish Cup**. They provided stiff opposition in a second round tie at Rugby Park. But Killie prevailed to win 3-2 and take another step on their way to Hampden glory later that year.

Two years later Killie looked to be on the way out of the tournament in the last eight as Bo'ness led 1-0. A dramatic 87th minute equaliser from **John Aitken** brought the teams to Rugby Park for a replay four days later. A hat-trick from **Willie Connell** and a brace from **'Bud' Maxwell** gave Killie a comfortable 5-0 victory.

BRECHIN CITY

Games	23	
League	21	1973-74, 83-87, 89-91
Scottish Cup	2	1937, 62
League Cup	0	
Other	0	
Top Scorer	Sammy McGivern 5	All SL
Top Home Crowd	4,767 Mar 31st 1990 SL	
Top Away Crowd	1,834 Jan 27th 1962 SC	

Apart from two brief encounters in the 1970s League games with **Brechin City** are concentrated in a cluster between 1983-1991 in the First Division and in Killie's Second Division season in 1989-90. These games took place at a time of profound decline for Kilmarnock and, while wishing followers of the Angus team no disrespect, it is an indication of such decline that the teams were on a level footing for so long.

Indeed, things were so bad at the time that defeat at home by Brechin was not considered anything out of the ordinary, nor were gates of under four figures worthy of comment. Ironically, it was during the season which saw the start of the modern Kilmarnock revival – 1989-90 – that the rivalry between the clubs was at its height.

Brechin led the promotion chase for most of the season with Killie closing in on them towards

the end. Brechin held the upper hand in the League matches between the clubs winning two and drawing the other. But that drawn game was to prove vital come the season's end. Killie, trailing at half-time forced a 2-2 result to rescue a home point and with it, consolidated their promotion challenge. That crucial point was the difference between promotion and staying down. Had they *won* the game then Killie, not Brechin, would have lifted the Second Division flag.

The club chairman at the time, **Bobby Fleeting,** wasn't too upset about this. His attitude was that a club of Kilmarnock's stature should never have been in this division in the first place and he wanted no reminder of their fall, such as a flag, anywhere near Rugby Park.

The first time the clubs ever met was a celebration day for Brechin and a humiliation for Killie. Brechin, fifth bottom of Division Two, took the lead in a first round **Scottish Cup** tie at Rugby Park in January 1937. They had been camped around their own goalmouth for the first fifteen minutes of the match before scoring in a breakaway.

Less than five minutes later, as the Killie goalkeeper collected the ball from a Brechin free kick, City's No 10, **Bollan**, knocked the ball out of the goalie's hands and into the net. Today, that would be a bookable offence at least. Back then it counted as a goal.

For over an hour Killie pounded away but all their efforts could muster was a solitary goal. They were out of the Cup. It was one of the biggest Scottish Cup shocks ever and a contender for the unwanted title of 'worst game ever at Rugby Park.'

Almost 25 years to the day, Killie exacted

revenge. They travelled to **Glebe Park** in the Cup and, thanks to four goals from **Ernie Yard**, ran out **6-1** winners.

Defeat for Killie in their opening game sparked off massive changes. Only four of the starting eleven lined up for the promotion-clincher at the season's end.

BROXBURN

Broxburn were one of a clutch of West Lothian clubs who sustained an existence in the League for a brief period after the First World War. And while they had their moments they never really troubled the big guns when their opportunity came along.

They were drawn to face Killie at Rugby Park in the opening Scottish Cup tie of 1922-23 and after putting up a stuffy performance in the first half, conceding just the one goal, they collapsed

entirely after the break.

Walter Jackson was in superb form for Killie that day. The younger brother of the famous **Alex Jackson** (one of the Wembley Wizards), Walter was a superb player in his own right. A winger by inclination, he was shifted to the middle whenever Killie were lacking in strikers. That was the situation this day. Playing at centre-forward, Jackson scored four times, with **Mattha Smith** notching the other in an easy 5-0 victory.

BURNLEY

They may have been on the maximum wage of £20 per week as opposed to the £50,000-plus of the stars of today, but when it came to petted lips, the **Burnley** side of 1960 could outrank any superstars of the modern era. As far as tantrums were concerned, Burnley were in a

class of their own.

The Lancashire team were Champions of England, hard though it may be to believe now, and contained players of undoubted class in **Alex Elder, Jimmy Adamson, John Connelly** and

Jimmy McIlroy amongst others. Yet their behaviour in the **1960 New York** tournament where they met Killie was that of a group of spoiled brats. Their luxury hotel wasn't good enough for them. They couldn't get steak every day. It was too hot for them to play football properly. Unlike, we must presume, some of the others in their group like **Kilmarnock, Glenavon** and **Bayern Munich,** all of whom supposedly played their football in some sub-tropical paradise and were acclimatised to conditions in the USA.

Perhaps the real reason for the Burnley whinges can be traced to their game against Killie. The Ayrshire side outplayed their illustrious opponents. It was supposed to be the biggest test Kilmarnock would face in North America but the game was won easily. Goals from **Andy Kerr** and **Vernon Wentzel** gave the Scottish club a satisfying victory and stunned the English press.

In the minds of Burnley and their media followers, the Champions of England couldn't possibly have been beaten fair and square by a Scottish side. There had to be some other reason. Their pathetic attempts at finding one prompted Killie boss **Willie Waddell** to declare that *"The Shah of Persia wouldn't get the treatment Burnley were looking for."* Younger readers should substitute the name of their favourite rock act or supermodel for that of the Shah to understand fully what Waddell was saying.

Let nothing be taken away from Kilmarnock's performance. It was eleven against eleven. The Scottish runners-up against the English champions. And the Scots won hands down. Fair and square.

CELTIC

Games	198	
League	170	1899-1947, 54-73, 74-75, 76-77, 79-81, 82-83, 93-2001
Scottish Cup	16	1900, 01, 24, 26, 29, 31, 38, 55, 57, 65, 72, 78, 95
League Cup	8	1964, 65, 84, 2000, 01
Other	4	1940, 46
Top Scorer	Jackie McInally 9	7 SL 2 SC
Top Home Crowd	32,887 Feb 19th 1955 SC	
Top Away Crowd	59,791 Oct 30th 1999 SPL	
Highest Overall	109,145 Mar 23rd 1957 SC	

Games against **Celtic** are usually high-octane affairs and the very first meeting of the two clubs set the tone for things to come. **August 26th 1899** was an auspicious date in Kilmarnock's history. It was their first game in Division One. It was also the official opening of the new, revamped Rugby Park, complete with new grandstand. And the visitors were the reigning Scottish Cup holders – Celtic.

The Second Division flag was unfurled before the game kicked off in glorious sunshine in front of a raucous crowd of 11,000. The scene was set perfectly for a glorious entrance into the game's upper echelon. But Celtic were intent on spoiling the script. Surviving early Killie pressure, the Parkhead side settled down and scored twice before the break then started the second half by laying siege to the Killie goal. Inside-right **Howie** brought Killie back into the match with a fine goal from an awkward position then levelled proceedings. Howie hit the crossbar as Killie pursued a winning goal. Winger **Findlay** netted only for his effort to be disallowed. Come the final whistle Celtic were on the ropes. A draw was a fine result against such illustrious opponents but few would have denied Killie the victory their play had deserved.

To prove it was no fluke, Killie travelled to **Parkhead** later in the campaign and took the lead on three occasions only for Celtic to equalise each time. And against a Celtic side in **'Bummer' Campbell's** testimonial match Killie won **6-0**. If they didn't know before, then Celtic knew by the end of this season that Kilmarnock were in the big time to do more than just make up the numbers.

The following year Kilmarnock recorded their first League victory over Celtic at Rugby Park but after that they began to toil. Killie were on the receiving end of some pretty embarrassing scorelines, particularly at Celtic Park where they struggled to repeat their initial form. Sixteen straight defeats followed that drawn game

Then on April 21st 1917 came a footballing miracle. Celtic were top of the League with just their home game against **Killie** to play. They had gone a record **62 matches** undefeated. Indeed this Celtic team was so good that they once played two matches in the same day *and won both*! Standing between them and a triumphant end to the season was a Kilmarnock side burdened by the legacy of those sixteen straight defeats.

Yet, once Killie soaked up all the early pressure, they responded in surprising fashion. Scorer supreme **Willie Culley** gave them a shock lead. Before the interval, **Mattha Smith** added a second. Killie controlled the second half with ease and could have ran out winners by more but even 2-0 was a sensation. What a time for Killie to record their first Parkhead win. It was a result which adorns the record books to this day.

Revenge was in the air when Killie next visited Parkhead. Celtic, with a 100% League record looked to put the Ayrshire upstarts in their place. But in an exciting first half it was Killie's **Malcolm McPhail** who struck first. Celtic immediately equalised but **Mattha Smith** put Killie back in front four minutes from half-time.

At the start of the second half McPhail seized on slackness in the home defence to put Killie 3-1 up and although Celtic pulled one back the points were headed Ayrshire way.

Two wins in a row at Parkhead. The only team to have beaten Celtic in almost two full years. The icing on the cake came in the shape of the Sunday papers. Celtic had been knocked off the top of the League and a new name stood proudly at the apex of Scottish football. **For the first time that team was Kilmarnock**.

Killie didn't win the League of course but they kept giving Celtic a hard time of it when the teams clashed. There were some epic encounters, Killie winning a thriller 4-3 in 1921-22, with four different players scoring. The next season they won at Parkhead again then followed that up with another remarkable game at Rugby Park.

Killie had just been knocked out of the Cup by East Fife and the career of their greatest goalscorer **Willie Culley** was over, accused of not trying in the cup tie. When Celtic's **Jimmy McGrory** (then at the outset of his career as the most prolific scorer in British football) put the Celts ahead after ten minutes, all looked lost. But Killie's **Rattray**, on his debut, equalised two minutes later. **Walter Jackson** gave Killie the lead but Celtic came back to square things at half-time.

Killie took the lead again at the start of the second half, courtesy of a **McCulloch** goal, before their keeper **John Morton** mishit a clearance, turning the ball into his own net. 3-3. **Mattha Smith**, as so often before, came to the rescue, firing past **Charlie Shaw** in the Celtic goal to make it **4-3**. Killie held on to record their second successive 4-3 Rugby Park victory. More important than that, they had just done the double over the mighty Celtic for the first time. The significance of that can be gauged from the fact that, nearly 80 years later, no Kilmarnock side has ever repeated the feat.

For much of the rest of the inter-war period, Celtic had the upper hand; although Killie recorded another fine win at Parkhead in 1936-37, winning **4-2** after a goalless first half. When **Jimmy McGrory** was appointed Killie boss, there were those who thought his former Parkhead employers might give him an easy time. Far from it. McGrory's first game as Rugby Park boss was on Christmas Day 1937 and the only gifts handed out were by the Killie defence as they lost away to Celtic **8-0**. In the final season before the war, Killie lost **9-1** away – *after taking the lead!*

Killie's return from the 'B' Division in 1954 renewed their rivalry with Celts. They managed to score three times at Parkhead in their first season back. But to no avail, as Celtic powered six past Killie. In the following season a struggling Kilmarnock side travelled more in hope than expectation to face League leaders Celtic on 10th December 1955. Celtic were unbeaten at home but that was about to change as **Davie Curlett** fired Killie ahead after just four minutes. After weathering the expected storm, Killie strengthened their grip on the match seven minutes from the break when **Willie 'Puskas' Harvey** beat four Celtic defenders before setting up Curlett for a second goal.

Killie kept control of the game in the second half and their delighted, if astonished, supporters left Glasgow happy with the first victory there since 1936. Even the most pessimistic of Killie fans would not have thought that 46 years later, this remains Kilmarnock's last League success at Parkhead. The intervening years have seen many close run things, with Killie sharing the spoils on ten of their 42 subsequent League visits (including those played at Hampden), but it remains an incredible statistic that Killie have not won on this ground for nearly half a century.

Of course Killie have had many memorable wins since then but they have all been at home. During the glory years of the 1960s there was an unprecedented run of victories over Celtic at Rugby Park. It started in 1959-60 with Killie's

first home victory since the war, then continued with another win two years later with a draw sandwiched in between. But it was in 1962-63 that the fun really started.

For all their fine defence Kilmarnock were a free-scoring side this season as 92 League goals testifies. Coming up against Celtic in a midweek clash they were aiming for their eighth League win in succession. And they achieved it in style. 2-0 ahead at the break, Killie piled on the agony in the second half, running up a record **6-0** triumph, making it a debut to forget for Celtic's *Jimmy Johnstone*. **Bertie Black** and **Andy Kerr** scored a pair apiece with **Joe Mason** and **Davie Sneddon** joining in the fun. The next season, as the two teams slugged it out for second place, it was the turn of **Jackie McInally** and **Eric Murray** to each bag a brace as Killie won **4-0**.

At least in the Championship season of 1964-65 Celtic managed to score at Rugby Park. Twice in fact. But to little purpose as Killie ran *five* past them, **McInally** grabbing another pair, with a couple from **Jim McFadzean** and a lone strike from **Ronnie Hamilton** completing the scoring.

With the advent of **Jock Stein** at the helm this sequence couldn't continue and games at Rugby Park were much tighter. Though not in March 1968 when it was Celtic's turn to win 6-0. And although Killie couldn't win at Parkhead they were capable of giving Celts the occasional scare.

One such match was the last League game of the 1960s, December 20th 1969 to be precise when **Eddie Morrison** put Killie ahead in front of over 30,000. Celtic recovered to win 3-1 but the real significance of the match came in a bone-jarring moment fifteen minutes into the game as **Jimmy Johnstone** raced for a loose ball alongside Killie's legendary club servant **Frank Beattie**. The clash was accidental – Johnstone didn't have a malignant bone in his body – but the crack was heard all over the ground. Beattie, at 36 the club's longest-serving player, had broken his right leg. The fans feared the worst and that the skipper's career was over. They reckoned without Beattie's indomitable spirit. It would be a long, hard road to recovery but Frank would be back.

Killie's decline during the 1970s meant they were no longer a serious threat as far as Celtic were concerned. But in November 1979 came a rousing 2-0 victory, by virtue of goals from **Bobby Street** and **Ian Gibson**. It was Killie's first League win over Celtic since 1965. But the continuing decline into the 1980s meant that it wasn't until the reborn Kilmarnock reached the Premier Division in 1993 that they could stand tall against their Parkhead rivals again.

Since then Killie have performed with distinction and have achieved several excellent results. In particular there was a battling 0-0 draw at Parkhead in 1997 in strange circumstances. Here was a ground with over 40,000 Celtic supporters sitting in silence while a few thousand Killie fans sang and danced their way through the match. The reasons were not hard to find. The game kicked off fifteen minutes later than Rangers match at Tannadice the same evening and by the time the first whistle had blown the Celtic fans knew their deadly rivals were ahead and that their precious *'nine-in-a-row'* League titles was about to be equalled. As for Killie they knew that a draw sent them into their final game against Aberdeen with an excellent chance of avoiding the play-offs – and they had the Scottish Cup Final to look forward to. All the same it was an eerie experience to behold.

Then in May 2001 it was Celtic who were the visitors to Rugby Park on the last day of the season. **Alan Mahood's** late goal giving Killie a well-deserved victory and earning them fourth spot in the league and qualification for the UEFA Cup ahead of Hearts.

There were those who moaned down Gorgie way about Celtic fielding reserve players, saving their big names for the Cup Final the following Saturday. The same moaners conveniently forgot that a 'reserve' Celtic side had won 5-2 at Tynecastle in the League Cup. More to the point,

***Alan Mahood.** His goal put Killie back into Europe. Here, he shows his strength to fend off Celtic's Paul Lambert.*

Killie had only been out of the top four once since the end of August. Their Edinburgh rivals had spent just one week in the coveted Euro spot all season. **Let nothing be taken away from Kilmarnock. It was a fine performance and their European place was a deserved reward for the season's endeavours.**

The clubs have been drawn together in the **Scottish Cup** on thirteen occasions, three of which have gone to replays. And Killie have had their share of triumphs too. The first pairings, at the dawn of the 20th century saw easy Celtic victories. But in 1924, the tide began to turn as Killie took on Celts at Rugby Park and won a famous 2-0 victory. That was the start of a series of encounters in the inter-war years. Celtic gained revenge at Rugby Park two years later. Then came a visit to Ibrox for a semi-final in 1929. Killie were given no chance, especially as top scorer **'Peerie' Cunningham** was missing. But it was his replacement – **Jimmy Weir** – who scored the only goal of the game to send triumphant Killie into the Final. It was Weir's only Cup outing of the season.

Two years later the sides clashed again in the last four, this time at Hampden. But there was to be no joy for Killie as Celtic ran out 3-0 winners. The most memorable match of these years was a third round tie in 1938. Killie, under **Jimmy McGrory,** were drawn away to Celtic just two months after losing 8-0 there in the League. But this was an entirely different occasion as **Allan Collins** and **Felix McGrogan** scored the first-half goals which stunned the bulk of the near-40,000 crowd. Celtic pulled a goal back after the break but the game – and the glory- was Killie's. A side struggling against relegation had pulled off the biggest shock of the season. The magnitude of the victory can best be summed up by the decision of the *'Sunday Post'* to issue a special souvenir of the match a week later!

Post-war, the first meeting was in 1955. Over 30,000 crammed into Rugby Park to see a **Henaughan** equaliser save the day for Killie. A few days later, despite a fine performance, Killie lost 1-0. But revenge wasn't slow in arriving.

Two years later the clubs were drawn together in the last four. 109,145 turned up at Hampden to see a **Gerry Mays** goal take Killie to within minutes of the Final before a Celtic equaliser forced the teams to return to Mount Florida four days later. This time there was to be no mistake as a Mays double and a goal from **Bertie Black** powered Kilmarnock into their first post-war Cup Final.

Hopes of a League and Cup double in 1965 were shattered at the quarter-final stage as, with new boss **Jock Stein** in charge, Celtic edged a thrilling Parkhead match 3-2 – **Jackie McInally** scoring twice for Killie. The teams met again in the semi-finals in 1972 when players like **Bobby Murdoch** and **Jimmy Johnstone**, then at the peak of their powers savaged Killie's defence. Yet somehow the Ayrshire side held out until **'Dixie' Deans** struck just before half-time. But Killie weren't finished yet. A defence-splitting pass from **George Maxwell** found winger **Jimmy Cook**. Cook's shot from the edge of the box sailed home for the equaliser. Deans restored Celtic's lead, and when **Lou Macari** added a third, the game was over. It would be more than 20 years before a Kilmarnock side progressed as far in the Scottish Cup.

But Killie still had some of that old Cup fire in their bellies. In 1978 boss **Davie Sneddon's** part-time side took the lead at Parkhead in a fourth round tie thanks to **Donnie McDowell.** There were just six minutes left when Celtic equalised. Killie set about disproving the old adage about only getting one shot at the Old Firm in the replay. Killie dominated the first half but found Celtic's defence impregnable. After the restart it was Celtic's turn to be dominant. Until they lost their teenage captain **Roy Aitken**, sent off for a second bookable offence.

First Division Kilmarnock took the opportunity now presented to them, After **Colin Stein** had gone desperately close, extra time began to loom, a factor which would undoubtedly favour the full-time Celts. But with eight minutes to go, Killie won a corner. The ball was cleared, but only as far as **Derrick McDicken**. He lashed in an unstoppable drive from 25 yards to put Killie ahead, then found time to get back into defence to make a goal-line clearance. It was the first time in almost 30 years that Celtic had lost to lower League opponents in the Cup and the press acclaimed Killie's performance as their best since beating Eintracht. A touch hyperbolic, perhaps. But for one man, it was his finest hour among many in a Kilmarnock strip. The man of this particular match was undoubtedly **'Big D' - Derrick McDicken.**

The only meeting since then was a quarter-final tie in 1995. Played on a Friday night to accommodate satellite TV, and at Celtic's temporary Hampden home, the game was a passionless affair, which Killie lost 1-0.

League Cup clashes have been rarer. It wasn't until 1963-64 that the teams first met in sectional matches. They did so again the following season but there was little, if anything of significance in these encounters. They were thrown together in the convoluted sectional games in 1983-84 when the group took three months to complete. First Division Killie were Celtic's main threat, taking qualification down to the wire in a Rugby Park match which the Celts won 1-0.

There have been two more meetings in recent years, in the closing stages of the competition. The semi-finals in 2000 saw Celtic squeeze past Killie with the only goal of the game. Then came the Final of 2001 as Killie, in their first Final for 38 years, strove to win the only domestic competition to elude them.

They matched Celtic in the first half, man for man and ball for ball. **Ian Durrant** - playing his first match for over three months - had been the game's outstanding performer. Alas, the influential midfielder hadn't fully recovered from injury and was forced to leave the field shortly before the interval. As if this wasn't bad enough, Celtic had one advantage over Killie. Over every other club in Scotland for that matter. **Henrik Larsson.** The Parkhead goal machine put his club in front shortly after the break. But at 1-0 Killie still had a chance. More so when Celtic's **Chris Sutton** was deservedly sent off. But that man Larsson struck again, fortuitously perhaps, as his shot seemed to take a deflection. But they all count and 2-0 it was. There was nothing fluky about Larsson's third as he outran the Killie defence from the halfway line to grab his hat-trick and complete the scoring.

For Killie though, it had been a great achievement to get to their second major Final under **Bobby Williamson** in less than four years. **An achievement most clubs in the land would envy.**

Not this time Henrik. Killie's **Chris Innes** *fends off hat-trick hero Larsson in the 2001 League Cup Final.*

CLACHNACUDDIN

Killie have met Inverness side **Clachnacuddin** on just one occasion, in the Scottish Cup. Drawn at home in the first round in 1907, the match was called off on the Saturday morning. Both the match referee and a local official deemed the pitch unplayable. *Clach* had travelled the day before however, so permission was given for a friendly to be played! So the cup-tie couldn't go ahead but the two teams could play a full game. This was not unusual at the time, strange as it may seem now.

Killie won the friendly 1-0. The real thing took place seven days later and it was never a contest as Killie surged into a three-goal interval lead, finally winning 4-0. All of which suggested they may have extended some Ayrshire hospitality to their Highland guests in the friendly game but were less welcoming when it came to the cup-tie.

CLYDE

Games	144	
League	128	1899-1900, 1906-24, 26-47, 51-52, 54-56, 57-61, 62-63,
		64-72 74-76, 78-79, 83-89, 90-91
Scottish Cup	5	1906, 12, 60, 79, 97
League Cup	5	1947, 61, 2001
Other	6	1940, 46, 52, 93
Top Scorer	Mattha Smith 9	All SL
	Eddie Morrison 9	All SL
Top Home Crowd	20,000 Oct 26th 1946 LC	
Top Away Crowd	18,000 Sep 14th 1960 LC	
Highest Overall	43,900 Apr 2nd 1960 SC	(Ibrox)

Although the teams haven't met too often in recent seasons, Kilmarnock and **Clyde** have a long history. They first met in the League in Killie's first season in Division One in 1899-1900 with Killie winning both games. There were some high-scoring affairs in their early matches with Killie winning **6-3** in 1909-10 and **5-2** a year later against a Clyde side that led the League. There was also a **5-3** win in 1919. These goal extravaganzas came in an era when the three-man offside law applied, making them all the more remarkable.

Stuffy opponents though they were, Clyde usually played second fiddle to Kilmarnock. From March 1923 to December 1932 Killie were unbeaten in League games. There were fewer fixtures after the war as Killie played in the lower League. Then when they returned to the top it was Clyde's turn to go down. The *Shawfield* team, so successful in the Cup, was frequently relegated in the quarter of a century after the war.

Killie ran up some impressive scorelines during this period. In 1958-59 Killie won **4-2** away and **4-1** at home. In 1962-63 they came away from Shawfield with a **5-0** victory. It was a lot closer in 1964-1965, but no less significant, as Killie won both League games 2-1. The second of these, at Rugby Park, was the 31st match of the season and came at a stage when one slip would have cost Killie their title chances.

In 1988-89 it wasn't a game between the two teams which was of particular significance but what Clyde were doing after the season had officially finished that was important. As Killie celebrated their seeming escape from relegation with a last-day victory at Palmerston Park, Clyde scored a penalty in the *97th minute* of their game with St Johnstone to send Killie into the Second Division on goal difference.

The **Scottish Cup** hasn't seen all that many games against Clyde but they've usually been important matches. Killie prevailed in the first meeting of the sides in 1906 and were confident of doing so when the teams next clashed in 1912. There was a massive crowd (for the times) of **19,564** a then record for Rugby Park for the quarter-final meeting in February 1912 and they saw Killie have the better of the first half yet go in at the interval two goals down. When Killie pulled one back at the start of the second period, hopes were high, despite being reduced to ten men when full-back **Davie Kirkwood** had to leave the field. But poor defending allowed Clyde to re-establish their two-goal cushion. Killie collapsed after that, as Clyde scored three more times to win by 6-1. Thousands of supporters left well before the end, disappointed by the score. Clyde went on to the Final that year. For Kilmarnock the opportunity for revenge didn't arise for almost half a century.

It was the semi-finals of the 1960 competition before they met again in the Cup. The venue was **Ibrox** and, with nearly 45,000 watching, there was a record crowd for a game between the clubs. Clyde had a fantastic record in the competition having won it in both **1955** and **1958**. With Killie chasing a historic double, only

those supporters with the longest of memories would have regarded it as a chance to atone for 1912. But atone they did, **Andy Kerr** and **Billy Muir** scored the first-half goals which gave Killie a 2-0 win and took them into their second Cup Final in four seasons.

When the teams next met, in 1979, Killie were in the middle of a good run, which would end in promotion. But the horrific winter meant that they had played only once in a month before travelling to Shawfield for a third round tie. Killie took a narrow 1-0 half-time lead then ran riot in the next 45 minutes, running out **5-1** winners.

It was eighteen years before they met again, this time in a fourth round tie at Clyde's new *Broadwood* stadium. It was a close, tense affair, but **Paul Wright's** goal was like so many of his for Killie – absolutely vital. Killie had avoided slipping up in a tricky tie and took one more step towards the Final at Ibrox.

In the **League Cup** the teams met in the first official competition in 1946 with the 20,000 crowd at Rugby Park the largest to watch this fixture. When they met in the first leg of a quarter-final tie in 1960-61 it was Shawfield's

Alex Burke bursts through the Clyde defence on the road to the Scottish Cup in 1997.

turn to produce a record crowd for the fixture as 18,000 saw Killie grab a precious 2-1 lead. The second leg was won easily enough 3-1 as Killie marched on towards the Final.

The last meeting of the teams was also in the League Cup in 2000-2001. And it was almost an

embarrassment for Killie. First Division Clyde gave as good as they got and took the lead in extra time. Kilmarnock were seven minutes away from elimination when **Freddie Dindeleux** equalized. Sixty seconds later, sub **Ally McCoist** pitched in with the winner, keeping Killie on the road to Hampden.

CLYDEBANK (1914-31)

Games	14	
League	14	1917-22, 23-24, 25-26
Top Scorer	David Fulton 3	All SL
	Willie Culley 3	All SL
Top Home Crowd	7,000 Sep 25th 1920 SL	
Top Away Crowd	9,000 Mar 23rd 1918 SL	

This **Clydebank** team had a short-lived spell in the Scottish League and have no connections whatsoever, other than the name, with the club which has played in the Scottish League since 1966.

With the withdrawal of three east coast teams from the League during wartime, Clydebank were invited into the single-division Scottish league, purely to make up the numbers. Yet initially they did very well. 9,000 saw them beat Killie at *Clydeholm Park* that season – 1917-18 - after **Fulton's** hat-trick had assured Kilmarnock of the honours in a 4-2 home win.

They were one of the casualties of automatic

relegation with its introduction in 1922 but bounced straight back. It was in that next season, 1923-24, that Killie gained their only win at Clydeholm, winning 2-1. Relegated immediately, Clydebank won promotion again just as promptly before being relegated again. After five years in Division Two, the recession of the early 1930s forced them to give up the professional game and go out of the League.

Killie were glad to see the back of them because they proved to be awkward opponents. In the last-ever meeting of the two sides, the soon-to-be relegated Bankies beast Killie 5-1 at Clydeholm. Indeed, Kilmarnock won only three of the fourteen meetings between the sides.

CLYDEBANK

Games	36	
League	32	1973-74, 78-79, 81-82, 83-85, 87-89, 90-93
Scottish Cup	3	1981
League Cup	1	1991
Top Scorer	John Bourke 5	4 SL 1 SC
Top Home Crowd	4,777 Aug 21st 1990 LC	
Top Away Crowd	3,400 Feb 18th 1981 SC	

The present **Clydebank** side didn't join the League until 1966 and it was seven years after that before Killie played them, winning both games in the promotion-winning season of

1973-74.

In fact Clydebank's presence became something of a lucky omen for Kilmarnock. The next time the teams met was in the 1978-79 season, with both teams vying for a place in the Premier Division. The three League games could hardly have been closer. Both sides recorded a 2-1 victory at *Kilbowie* with a 0-0 draw at Rugby Park. By the season's end Killie just edged out the *Bankies* on goal difference, to secure their passage to the big time. In 1981-82 the teams met again and once more Killie claimed promotion.

But during Killie's decline in the 1980s there was to be no such joy. Indeed, they were on the wrong end of some embarrassing scorelines at Kilbowie. As the good times returned to Rugby Park, so did the results in this fixture. A certain **Bobby Williamson** recorded a hat-trick in 1990-91 and in the very last League meeting between the sides, Killie won in some style. Two up after just three minutes, they added another two just before the break. By time up the score stood at **6-0** as Killie demonstrated that they had outgrown the First Division.

The teams have met once in both major Cups. In the **Scottish Cup** in 1981 it was a fourth round tie which went to a second replay at neutral *Love Street* before the Bankies took the quarter-final spot. Ten years later in the first round of the **League Cup**, Killie came back from two goals down to snatch a 3-2 extra time triumph at Rugby Park.

"Big D's gonty get ye" The fearsome (for the opposition) sight of **Derek McDicken** in possession and running at the enemy.

Killie pile pressure on the 'Bankies goal in the promotion tussle in 1979.

CLYDESDALE

Clydesdale were one of the pioneers of Scottish football. They reached the very first Scottish Cup Final, losing to **Queen's Park**. In the second year of the competition they reached the semi-finals and it took a second replay before Queen's Park overcame them. Kilmarnock's only competitive meeting with them was in the same tournament twelve months later in a second round tie. Killie turned up with only ten players so were at a disadvantage from the start. And when they found themselves two goals down at the interval amid monsoon-like conditions, some of the players were minded to give up there and then.

But the *Corinthian* spirit of sportsmanship won the day and Kilmarnock decided to take the field for the second half. A brave decision and unrewarded by neither the elements nor the opposition. The rains continued to pour down as Killie slumped to a 6-0 defeat.

For Clydesdale there was to be no reward either. They ran into Queen's Park in the next round and were beaten for the third year running. They slowly faded away after that but thanks to their performances in that inaugural tournament their name lives on forever in the annals of soccer history.

COLERAINE

When Killie were drawn to face **Coleraine** from **Northern Ireland** in the **Fairs Cup** in 1970-71 it seemed a beneficial draw. A short hop over the water, and an easy passage into the next round. That was the almost universal assumption. Possibly only the players and management of Coleraine harboured any other thoughts and these must have been inspired more by blind optimism than by anything of substance.

A 1-1 draw in the province was not a bad result, setting things up for another European glory night at Rugby Park. And at half-time in the second leg, with goals from **Tommy McLean** and **Eddie Morrison** giving Killie a 2-0 lead, everything was proceeding as planned. Even a **John Gilmour** effort being disallowed seemed to have no impact on Killie's progress into the next round.

And then the roof fell in.

Coleraine's centre-forward, **Des Dickson**, went on a storming run through the middle two minutes into the second half and pulled a goal back for the part-timers. Five minutes later he grabbed the equaliser, putting Coleraine ahead on away goals. Dickson then took a knockdown from a corner on the hour mark and tucked the ball away to give his side the lead.

Thirteen minutes was all it had taken to turn the game entirely on its head. The last half-hour passed as if Killie were still too dazed by the change in events to do anything about it. Coleraine held out with ease to secure their greatest triumph and one of Northern Ireland's finest European results.

In retrospect this match was a watershed in Kilmarnock's history. In fifteen seasons prior to this they had never finished lower than eighth in the League. In 24 after it they would only reach such a lofty position once. They had qualified for Europe five times in seven seasons. It would be 27 years before another European tie was played at Rugby Park.

At the time though, it was an unbelievable result. To this day it is impossible to explain how a side so experienced in Europe could throw away such a strong lead against such weak opposition. Scottish sides have suffered many embarrassing European moments. That is true enough. Btu there has been nothing comparable in terms of throwing away a lead against a side expected to be cannon fodder. September 29th 1970 is a date never to be forgotten by those who were there.

COWDENBEATH

Games	49	
League	45	1924-34, 47-54, 70-71, 73-74, 89-90, 92-93
Scottish Cup	1	1965
League Cup	3	1983, 92
Top Scorer	'Peerie' Cunningham 7	All SL
	'Bud' Maxwell 7	All SL
Top Home Crowd	9,006 Nov 21st 1953 SL	
Top Away Crowd	7,000 Oct 25th 1924 SL	
	7,000 Nov 1st 1947 SL	

Difficult to believe nowadays, but **Cowdenbeath** were once a feared force in the land. In the 1920s and 30s they held their own in the First Division for a decade and **Central Park** was never a place Killie (or any other club) fancied visiting.

One particularly dreadful result came in April 1932 when Killie were beaten **7-1** after leaving the pitch at half-time level at 1-1. In fairness to Killie, they were resting several first team regulars ahead of the upcoming Scottish Cup Final with Rangers. But playing in goal was **Sam Clemie**, hero of the 1929 Cup Final. This proved to be Sam's last appearance for Killie – a sad way for a Rugby Park legend to bow out.

There were regular 'B' Division meetings in the immediate post-war era and while Killie usually came out on top at home, the away games still proved problematical. In January 1954 as Killie pushed for promotion they again suffered a second-half disaster at Central Park. Trailing by a goal at the interval, Killie ended up on the wrong side of a **6-0** beating.

But thanks to promotion that season there have been few meetings between the clubs ever since. Killie did the double in the old First Division in 1970-71 and repeated the feat three seasons later in Division Two in a pair of high-scoring affairs; 4-3 at Rugby Park and 4-2 away.

The next time the clubs met was in 1989-90 in the Second Division. Killie faced Cowdenbeath at home in the last match of the season needing a win to guarantee promotion. A **Tommy Burns**

free kick provided **Paul Flexney** with the opportunity to open the scoring with a header after just four minutes and settle Ayrshire nerves.

Although Killie appeared to be strolling to promotion, further goals proved elusive and when Cowdenbeath equalised with thirteen minutes remaining, everything was on a knife-edge. Flexney appeared to have settled matters with a second header nine minutes from the end, until a Fife defender's hand stopped the ball on the line.

The penalty was entrusted to skipper **Dave McKinnon**, who would later freely admit to not

Dave McKinnon blasts home from the spot to put Killie back in the First Division.

being exactly the world's most confident penalty taker. But this time he was on target, blasting the ball home in front of over 8,500 jubilant spectators. Those fans were still cheering when the final whistle blew and sparked a pitch invasion - something unseen at Rugby Park for many years.

The last clashes took place in 1992-93 with Killie winning 3-0 at Central Park on the second last day of the season to keep themselves in pole position in the promotion race.

There has only been one **Scottish Cup** meeting of the sides. In the championship season of 1964-65 Killie easily overcame the Fifers 5-0 at Rugby Park in a first round tie. In the **League Cup** they have met twice. Killie winning a nervy penalty shoot-out 4-3 at Central Park, to reach the last eight, after the two teams had tied after 210 minutes in 1982-83. And a first round game, also at Central Park in 1991-92 when a **Bobby Williamson** strike was all that separated the sides.

McKinnon bellows his achievement to the jubilant supporters

CUMNOCK

There are great tales told in **Cumnock** of their fierce rivalries with other sides in Ayrshire. Yet none will feature Killie. For although the teams were drawn together to play at Rugby Park in the first round of the Scottish Cup on September 11th 1886, the match never took place.

Cumnock scratched from the competition, allowing Killie a walk-over into the next round. There couldn't have been an easier introduction to the season's tournament for Kilmarnock as they marched to the last eight for the first time.

DUMBARTON

Games	82	
League	70	1896-97, 1913-22, 47-54, 72-73, 74-76, 77-79, 81-82,
		83-84, 85-88, 89-90, 92-93
Scottish Cup	5	1897, 1938, 49, 59, 76
League Cup	5	1951, 52, 96
Other	2	1940
Top Scorer	Willie Culley 9	All SL
Top Home Crowd	12,173 Sep 1st 1951 LC	
Top Away Crowd	10,090 Jan 22nd 1949 SC	

Although **Dumbarton** had been one of the giants of Scottish football in the 19th century, they had fallen a long way by the time Killie first played them. **5-1** at home and **6-0** away were two resounding victories in 1896-97, a year which saw the *Sons* drop out of the League altogether.

Dumbarton worked their way back into the League and by 1913 had reached the First Division but their next appearance at Rugby Park, in January 1914, was just as embarrassing as before as Killie ran out **6-0** winners with two players, **Andrew Neil** and **William Whittle**, both recording hat-tricks. Neil must have loved facing the *Sons* as he scored all Killie's goals in their 4-0 home victory the next season.

With Dumbarton's relegation in 1922 it was over a quarter of a century before they and Kilmarnock met again on League duty. And although most of the matches were close, Killie had developed superiority by the time they won promotion in 1954 as a **5-2** win at **Boghead** and a **7-2** success at Rugby Park that season amply demonstrates.

When the clubs next met, Division One survival was at stake as Dumbarton were back in the top flight after a gap of 50 years. With both teams near the foot of the table, Killie committed an act of hara-kiri in the transfer market. They sold striker **Ross Mathie** to Dumbarton for a measly £5,000. On March 17th 1973 Mathie cost the club at least a six-figure sum scoring twice as

Dumbarton came from behind to beat Killie 4-2 in a Boghead league match. Six games later when the season ended Killie were a solitary point behind the *Sons* and were relegated after nineteen years in the top division. Mathie's transfer had been an act of lunacy which ultimately sent Kilmarnock down.

But if Boghead was a nightmare venue that season it proved to be an unlikely 'theatre of dreams' six years later. It was the scene for Killie's final match of the season and although Killie topped the First Division table, promotion rivals **Dundee** and **Clydebank** had games in hand. Victory was imperative. **Joe Cairney's** 15th minute opener was good enough for the half-time lead but there were no signs of celebrations from the Killie support for Clydebank were also ahead in their match. Six minutes into the second half a **John Bourke** knockdown allowed **Ian Gibson** to notch a second and the fans found their voice at last.

Bourke added a third with twelve minutes remaining and even a late goal for Dumbarton couldn't dampen the celebrations as news filtered through that Clydebank had drawn at Arbroath. Barring a ten-goal win by the Bankies in their last match, Kilmarnock had been promoted. The fans knew their club was back in the Premier Division. They sang the praises of the players and of the manager, **Davie Sneddon**. The Rugby Park legend was a part-time manager of a part-time club and the achievement of promotion was something of a minor miracle.

The clubs have met a few times since then but with nothing of the drama of 1979 attached. The most recent meeting was an edgy 1-0 win at Rugby Park, thanks to a **George McCluskey** goal which kept Killie on track for promotion to the Premier in 1993.

The **Scottish Cup** has produced dramatic meetings too. None more so than the first occasion the clubs clashed. Killie were strong favourites to win the semi-final tie at **Boghead** in March 1897 against a Dumbarton team at the bottom of Division Two. But Killie were woeful. Not even a **'Bummer' Campbell** hat-trick could save them. They lost 4-3 but the match was never as close as the score suggests, Dumbarton having led 4-1 until late on. Killie protested to the SFA that the teams colours had clashed but the authorities were having none of it. Kilmarnock would have to wait another twelve months before playing in their first Final. As for Dumbarton they went on to face Rangers, heavily tipped to lose. They didn't let the bookies down, crashing 5-1 in the Final.

It was 1938 before they met again and Killie regained some belated revenge with a **6-0** home win on their road to the Final that season. The biggest crowd ever to watch this match at Boghead turned out in 1949 as the home team won through to the second round. But ten years later came a remarkable performance from Kilmarnock. It was a second round tie played on an appropriate date – 14th February – as Killie completed a *St Valentine's Day massacre* of their own. **Wentzel, Burns** and **Mays** (from the spot) put Killie three up before Dumbarton pulled one back. **Joe McBride** restored the three-goal advantage just before the break. In the second half it was McBride's turn to be on target with a penalty and Wentzel added a sixth before the *Sons* got their second. McBride's hat-trick was Killie's seventh and Vernon Wentzel added an eighth for a treble of his own. **8-2** away from home. A terrific result. Oddly enough, the only

A surprisingly hirsute **Gus MacPherson** In action against Dumbarton

forward not to score – **Bertie Black**- was universally acclaimed as *Man of the Match*.

There's been just one Cup meeting since then- a disappointing game in 1976 when heavy favourites Killie were beaten 2-1 at Boghead in a quarter-final tie.

There has been little **League Cup** history between the sides. They were drawn together in the sectional stages in the early 1950s and also a first round match in 1995-96 when Killie struggled to a 1-0 win in extra time at Rugby Park.

DUNBLANE

Killie have twice played this Perthshire club in the Scottish Cup. They met in the fourth round in the 1886-87 competition with Killie converting a comfortable 2-0 half-time lead into a **6-0** rout by the finish. It was a significant result because it put Kilmarnock into the quarter-finals for the very first time.

The second occasion was also at Rugby Park in the second round in 1908. Three first half goals were good enough to win the match and again put Killie into the last eight. By this time though, that was something they had been become accustomed to.

DUNDEE

Games	177	
League	151	1899-1917, 19-38, 54-73, 74-75, 77-80, 82-83, 90-92,
		93-94, 99-2001
Scottish Cup	7	1898, 1902, 27, 64, 91, 94
League Cup	16	1953, 56, 58, 69, 70, 71, 74, 81, 85, 96
Other	3	1980, 91
Top Scorer	Mattha Smith 10	All SL
Top Home Crowd	16,000 Aug 31st 1955 LC	
Top Away Crowd	16,000 Aug 17th 1955 LC	
	16,000 Oct 15th 1960 SL	
Highest Overall	51,830 Oct 25th 1952 LC	(Hampden)

Dundee were already well-established in Division One by the time Killie first played them and the pattern of their early games was familiar; Killie usually winning at home and losing away. Indeed, it took until their fifteenth visit to *Dens Park* before Kilmarnock returned with both points. And, occasionally, defeats there could be embarrassing. **5-0** in 1908-09 and 1921-22 and **7-0** in 1927-28. Although from time to time Killie could land equally emphatic victories at home.

Even when both clubs were at the top of the Scottish game, in the late 1950s and the 1960s, the pattern of home dominance continued It was rare for Killie to lose at Rugby Park, so it was more than a mild surprise when Dundee not only took the points in the Championship season of 1964-65, they demolished Killie 4-1. It was a defeat that nearly cost Killie the title. Dundee could claim to have helped Killie win the flag though, as they slaughtered Hearts **7-1** at Tynecastle the same season.

The second half of that decade saw some remarkable matches. In 1965-66 Killie won a thriller **5-3** at Rugby Park then drew **4-4** the following season. Then came a truly incredible game at Dens Park in January 1968. A goal down to a penalty in five minutes, **Eddie Morrison** replied for Killie by grabbing two goals with less than fifteen minutes played. Dundee levelled just before half-time then scored twice after the break before **Brien McIlroy** scored for Killie to make it 4-3. Dundee's **Billy Campbell** scored twice within three minutes to seemingly wrap the game up only for ex-Dens Parker **Kenny Cameron** to snatch a pair for Killie. **6-5** down and on the attack, looking for an equaliser, Killie ran out of time. They had been beaten but had played their role in one of Scottish football's most remarkable games.

Both teams faded from the big time in the 1970s but there was still a competitive edge to their meetings. Particularly so in 1978-79 as they fought for promotion with Dundee pipping Killie by a single point for the First Division title with both going up. In the Premier, Killie grabbed a rare Dens victory to ensure their own survival and send Dundee back down.

Even in recent years the pattern of a century has continued as both sides still find it difficult to win away from home.

The **Scottish Cup** has seen some titanic tussles. Their first meeting was in the semi-finals in 1898. In those days there were no neutral venues and the first team out of the hat played at home. So it was that **Rugby Park** found itself hosting the biggest event in its history to that time. A record crowd of 11,000 saw Killie come back from a 2-1 half-time deficit to win 3-2 and reach the club's first Scottish Cup Final. Dundee were again beaten in 1902 but knocked Killie out in 1927.

The next meeting, in 1964, was another semi-final. Played at *Ibrox* with Killie the favourites to go through. Unfortunately for Kilmarnock it turned out to be one of those days when nothing goes right. A goal down at the break, Killie surprisingly folded afterwards, losing 4-0.

Killie lost again to Dundee in 1991 but a **Tom Brown** goal at Rugby Park in 1994 was enough to send them into their first semi-final for 22 years and beat Dundee in the competition for the first time since 1902.

The clubs have met many times in the **League Cup**, but never with as much at stake as in their first meeting. Dundee were the League Cup holders, Kilmarnock the 'B' Division upstarts. The scene was **Hampden Park** and over 50,000 turned up for the **League Cup Final** in October 1952. Kilmarnock were the better side on the day, controlling the middle of the park and winning corners and free kicks with abandon. But that old Killie failing in front of goal let them down. With only eight minutes remaining a replay loomed, but Dundee's **Bobby Flavell** (who would later play for Killie) had other ideas and scored twice to keep the trophy on Tayside.

Killie's French international **Christophe Cocard** takes on the Dundee defence at Dens Park.

But there was little sign of the traditional celebrations from Dundee. Kilmarnock had been the better team on the day, their opponents knew it and they recognised they were lucky to still have the Cup in their hands.

The clubs met frequently after that in the sectional stages. Indeed, they were in the same section three seasons running at the end of the 1960s but the next important tie between the two was again at Hampden. It was a semi-final and Killie were again a lower division side but there the similarities with 1952-53 ended. For this was an eerie affair. 1973-74 was the winter of the three day week. Poor weather forced postponement twice before the game went ahead in front of just over 4,500 spectators. An **Eddie Morrison** strike was ruled offside before **Tommy Gemmell** scored the only goal of the game to put Dundee into the Final where they beat Celtic.

The third round meeting of the clubs in 1980-81 produced a statistical oddity. Both legs finished goalless and a further thirty minutes also failed to produce a goal so the tie was decided on penalties, 5-3 in Dundee's favour. **It meant that Killie had been knocked out of the competition while remaining unbeaten.** They had played six games, winning three, drawing three and conceding just one goal, but they were out.

Lightning can strike twice as Kilmarnock found out four seasons later, again being knocked out by Dundee on penalties and again departing the competition unbeaten. Although this time they had played only two matches (both drawn) before elimination. Dundee also won in 1995-96 and have also knocked Killie out of two other cup competitions; the Anglo-Scottish Cup in 1979-80 (on away goals after two drawn matches) and in the semi-finals of the Centenary Cup in 1990. Being drawn against the Dens Park side in knockout tournaments is not a happy omen for Kilmarnock.

Ally McCoist, in his last season as a player, shrugs off a challenge at a sparsely-attended Dens Park

DUNDEE UNITED

Games	111	
League	93	1925-27, 29-30, 31-32, 47-54, 60-73, 74-75, 76-77,
		79-81, 82-83, 93-95, 96-2001
Scottish Cup	6	1932, 86, 97
League Cup	8	1954, 72, 73, 76
Other	4	1940, 50, 69
Top Scorer	Andy Kerr 10	All SL
Top Home Crowd	13,538 Dec 20th 1998 SPL	
Top Away Crowd	12,969 Feb 13th 1932 SC	

Dundee United were only bit-part players in the Kilmarnock story until after the war. The most notable pre-war performance was in 1931-32 when **John Aitken** scored five goals from the wing in an 8-0 hammering of United at Rugby Park. Post-1945 both teams were struggling to get out of 'B' Division and if Killie supporters thought that seven years was a long time to spend in the lower League they should spare a thought for fans of the *Tannadice* club. After relegation in 1932 it was 1960 before they again appeared in Division One.

One man who was happy to see them return was Killie striker **Andy Kerr**. *'Handy Andy'* notched up a hat-trick at Tannadice in a **4-2** victory in November 1960, then went one better in February 1962, scoring four in Killie's **5-3** Rugby Park win. For good measure he scored another Tannadice hat-trick in a **3-3** draw in November 1962. Andy's ten goals make him Killie's leading scorer against United, ahead of **Eddie Morrison** and **Brien McIlroy**.

A plentiful supply of goals from these players was the chief reason why it took United thirteen years after their promotion to win at Rugby Park, finally taking the points by a solitary goal in 1972-73. Two seasons later, Killie featured in an incredible match at Tannadice four days before Christmas. Without an away win, Kilmarnock found themselves two up at the break. They added two more in the second half and were still leading 4-0 with thirteen minutes to go, when United hit back. All of a sudden Killie were on the ropes, clinging on for life. It was a relieved team which trooped off the park winners by just 4-3. United were the visitors to Rugby Park in the last game of the season. This was a match which Kilmarnock had to win if they were to have any chance of making the top ten, thus qualifying for the inaugural Premier Division. But after an early Killie flurry, their chances were destroyed by a United team enjoying their best League season to that point. **Andy Gray** and **Paul Sturrock** put Killie to the sword. Killie were three down before twenty minutes had elapsed.

Killie began to fight back. **Ian Fallis** and **Ian Fleming** restored hope by closing the gap to 3-2 at half-time. It was all-out Killie attack in the second period but it brought no more goals. Then, with six minutes remaining, Sturrock scored a fourth for United. Kilmarnock were condemned to start life in the revamped League in the middle division, courtesy of a team managed by Killie old boy **Jim McLean**.

Killie's attempts to live with the Premier outfits in the 70s and 80s sometimes descended into farce. Twice they lost **7-0** at Tannadice and once by 5-0 at Rugby Park. Since promotion in 1993 there has been a marked change in fortunes. Rugby Park has become a fortress when United visit and at Tannadice Killie have lost just once in thirteen Premier visits.

The clubs have been drawn together in the **Scottish Cup** on just three occasions and all have needed replays. In 1932 nearly 13,000 saw the sides draw at Tannadice before Killie won the replay 3-0 to march towards the Final. In 1986 it was Kilmarnock who were the underdogs against a Dundee United team that was a power at European level, let alone Scotland. Killic forced a creditable 1-1 draw away and gave everything in the replay before losing 1-0.

The next meeting was at **Easter Road** in the semi-finals in 1997. The first match was something of a bore. Killie were marginally the better side but were unable to score. The replay, although a better game, looked to be following the same path before **Jim McIntyre** popped up four minutes from the end to touch the ball home and put Killie into their first Scottish Cup Final for 37 years. There were fewer than 10,000 in attendance that night but the noise they made must have been heard back in Ayrshire. This was the game which marked the transformation in Kilmarnock's role in the Premier. **They were no longer just survivors. Now, they were contenders.**

The first **League Cup** meeting was in August 1953 when Killie won **4-1** at home and **3-0** away. They topped their section with ease, only to lose out to Partick Thistle in the knockout stages. They were drawn together three times in the 1970s in matches of little distinction.

Killie also played United in two other tournaments. There was the War Cup in 1940, a competition which saw Dundee United reach their first national Cup Final. They eliminated Killie in the last eight. And the 'B' Division Supplementary Cup ten years later, a tie which Killie won. But the strangest competition was the 1969 USA tournament. Officially it was **Dallas v St Louis**. In practice it was **Dundee United v Kilmarnock**. For the record it was a draw in Dallas and United won 1-0 in Killie's *'home'* city of St Louis.

Ian Fleming looks on as Dundee United keeper **Hamish McAlpine** takes the ball off **Derrick McDicken's** head. The central character in this photo offers three rarities. Firstly, there's the sight of **Andy Gray** in a Dundee United shirt. Secondly, he's in his own penalty area. But, strangest of all, he's sporting a full head of hair! Killie won this League Cup tie 1-0 in 1975.

DUNFERMLINE ATHLETIC

Games	115	
League	89	1926-28, 34-37, 47-54, 55-57, 58-72, 74-76, 81-82,
		86-87, 88-89, 92-93, 96-99, 2000-01
Scottish Cup	4	1932, 66, 67
League Cup	22	1950, 51, 53, 57, 59, 61, 63, 66, 68, 73, 81
Top Scorer	Brien McIlroy 8	6 SL 2 LC
	Jackie McInally 8	5 SL 2 SC 1 LC
Top Home Crowd	14,275 Sep 10th 1958 LC	
Top Away Crowd	19,363 Mar 5th 1966 SC	

Early games against **Dunfermline Athletic** turned conventional wisdom on its head. Of the five pre-war League games at Rugby Park, Kilmarnock won just one. But at *East End Park* they triumphed four times and drew the other match. And, although the teams met regularly during Killie's 'B' Division days it was only in the 1960s that this fixture became one to watch as both clubs were the main challengers to the Old Firm.

In 1960 Kilmarnock were making their first real push for the title. Two days after reaching the Cup Final they played Dunfermline away, knowing a win would out them one point behind leaders Hearts with three games to play. Killie were enjoying an amazing run. **Fifteen successive League victories** with five Scottish Cup wins and a draw thrown in for good measure. All told, they had gone 21 matches unbeaten in the space of four months. No one expected it to end at Dunfermline. But it did. Dunfermline's **Ron Mailer** launched a shot from all of forty yards, which whizzed past **Jimmy Brown** in the Killie goal. There was no more scoring. The incredible run was over, and with it went Killie's hopes of the flag.

Most of the games at this time were tense affairs, many settled by a single goal, often the only goal. That was the case in 1964-65 as both teams battled for the Championship, each winning 1-0 at home. Dunfermline's title bid only failed on the second last Saturday of the season.

Like Killie, the *Pars* were also regular European contender throughout the sixties. Also, like Killie their star began to fade in the 1970s and

they spent several seasons in the new Second Division. Incredibly, from 1971-72 to 1992-93 these teams could hardly spend more than a season in the same division without one or the other being promoted or relegated. The sequence started in 1972 with Dunfermline going down from the old Division One. It continued in 1975 with both clubs failing to qualify for the inaugural Premier Division. The next season saw Killie achieve that goal while the Fifers went down to the Second.

They next met in 1981-82 with Killie again going up. In 1987 it was the Pars turn to win promotion. And in 1989 came a reversal of the fortunes of thirteen years previously with Dunfermline going up to the Premier and Killie

Fans favourite **Freddie Dindeleux** in action against Dunfermline in 2001

heading for the basement. For the *seventh* occasion in a row there was movement when the teams next met, in 1992-93. This time it was Killie who went up, but Dunfermline chased them all the way. In truth, the Fife side had much the better of the exchanges between the pair, winning three of the four League games (including twice at Rugby Park) and drawing the other. But it was Killie who ground out the results against the lesser lights. There were no shock defeats against the likes of Cowdenbeath for the Ayrshire side.

The first Premier pairings were in 1996-97, sparking off memories of the golden era of the 1960s with close matches where the home side usually triumphed. Indeed, Dunfermline have never won at Rugby Park in a Premier match and Killie found it hard to win at East End Park. Until, that is, 1998-99. With the two home games sending in 0-0 draws, Killie carved out some excitement away from home by beating Dunfermline 3-0, then by an unbelievable **6-0**. In a truly amazing performance, Killie led by a solitary **John Henry** goal with 54 minutes on the clock. Then, **Ian Durrant** and **Ally Mitchell** both struck within sixty seconds to wrap up the game **Jerome Vareille** added a fourth in 68 minutes with Henry grabbing his second six minutes later. **Ally McCoist** rounded off the scoring with two minutes to go. This defeat totally shattered Dunfermline. It sunk them to

the foot of the table. They managed just one more point from their remaining games and were relegated.

The clubs have met just three times in the **Scottish Cup**. Killie won easily at East End Park in a quarter –final tie on their way to Hampden in 1932. Then they met two seasons running in the sixties. Nearly 20,000 turned up to see the previous season's losing Finalists (Dunfermline) take on the reigning League champions (Kilmarnock) in a quarter-final tie at East End Park. Despite taking a half-time lead, thanks to **Jackie McInally**, Killie couldn't contain the Pars and ended up losing 2-1. Their chance for revenge was swift. They were drawn at home to Dunfermline in the first round the next year. But poor defending saw Killie slump to a 2-0 deficit at the break. McInally and **Andy King** rescued the home side and forced a replay. But, in another tense match, Killie lost 1-0.

Although the clubs haven't meet in the **League Cup** for more than twenty years, Dunfermline remain the team Killie have played most times in this competition. 22 in total, dating back to the 'B' Division days of 1949-50 when Dunfermline won the group and reached the Final where they lost to rivals East Fife. In 1952-53 four welcome points from the fixtures helped Killie on their way to winning the section as the first stage of their journey to the Final. A convincing 4-1 Rugby Park victory in September 1958, followed

The first of two own goals from Dunfermline sets Killie on their way to a 4-0 victory
in the promotion-winning season of 1975-76.

by a 3-3 draw away put Killie into the last four that year and in 1960-61 Dunfermline were the only team to lower Killie's colours in the sectional matches, but it wasn't enough to prevent the Ayrshire team from going on to reach the Final again. With the Pars once again in their group as Killie marched to the Final in 1962-63 they were something of a talisman for Kilmarnock.

There was another run to the semis in 1965-66 with Dunfermline one of the teams eliminated en route in the sectional matches and Killie also topped the mini-league in 1967-68 to reach the last eight. Of the eight times they had been grouped together, Killie had won the section six times and the Pars twice. A fine record but one, which was tarnished the next time they met. With two teams qualifying from the group in 1972-73, neither Killie nor Dunfermline were able to dislodge little **Stenhousemuir** from a qualifying spot. Killie triumphed the last time they met, winning 2-1 at Dunfermline in the second round in 1980-81 after drawing 0-0 at home in the first leg.

DYKEBAR

Killie drew 2-2 away to **Dykebar** in a third round Scottish Cup tie in 1887-88 after trailing 2-1 at half-time. The replay was hailed as one of the best games ever seen at Rugby Park. If it was it certainly wasn't on account of it being a close encounter as Kilmarnock led 6-0 at the interval and ended up winning **9-1**. Two of the goalscorers have been lost to posterity but we do know that in addition to doubles from **McGuiness** and **Taylor**, there was a hat-trick from **Sandy Higgins**. Higgins was possibly Killie's first 'superstar.' He was a miner and the fact that he even played in this tie was something of a miracle, given that he had been badly burned in a pit fire just two months previously.

For years Killie had resisted all attempts to lure Higgins south of the border and Sandy himself had been immune to several instances of *'tapping.'* But, possibly as a consequence of his accident, this was his last year at Rugby Park. He signed professional forms for **Derby County** but returned for one final season at Rugby Park seven years later.

As for Dykebar, this was their first season in the Cup and it was their best. Along with many others of their ilk, they vanished after the big clubs started getting byes in the competition once the Scottish League was formed in 1890.

DYKEHEAD

Dykehead were actually a Scottish League side when they visited Rugby Park for a third round Scottish Cup tie in February 1925. They were members of the original Third Division which ran from 1923-26 and included Ayrshire sides **Beith** and **Galston** among their number.

They gave a solid account of themselves in the first 45 minutes and the teams left the pitch with the score 0-0. But Killie's superior class told in the second period as **Lindsay** (twice), **Bird, Rock** and **Weir** all scored to give the home side a convincing **5-0** victory at the close.

Dykehead weren't finished though. They protested to the SFA, claiming that Killie wing-half **Joe Willis** had been guilty of some close-season infringement and should not have played. At one time the SFA overturned Cup results right, left and centre after appeals and replays were not uncommon. But those days had passed. With or without Willis, Killie would have won easily and the appeal was thrown out.

The cynic may have noted that a home tie with **Rangers** was the reward for reaching the quarter-finals and might have wondered if the *Shotts* side would have been so insistent if all they had to look forward to was an away match to a Highland League side!

DYNAMO BACAU

Dynamo Bac-Who? was the reaction of much of the supporters and the media when Killie were drawn against this **Romanian** team in the third round of the **Fairs Cup** in 1969-70. Hardly surprising when, in the same season, **Rangers** had asked the same question when drawn to face Romania's most famous side **Steaua Bucharest** in the Cup-Winners Cup. It's unthinkable nowadays when we know that Steaua have won the European Cup one more time than Rangers have and have appeared in two more European Cup Finals than the Ibrox side, but that was how insular Scottish football was, just over 30 years ago. No one bothered to think that if **Romania** had qualified for the **Mexico World Cup** and **Scotland** hadn't, that maybe, just maybe, they could play a bit. Wha's like us, indeed.

Kilmarnock's supporters were just as superior. When they found out that **Bacau** had got to this stage by beating **Maltese** and **Norwegian** opposition in contrast to Killie's two fine results against **Swiss** and **Bulgarian** clubs, most thought this would be an easy tie. They could never have suspected that it was going to be nearly 28 years before they'd see a European victory at Rugby Park.

Killie struggled in the home leg, just before Christmas and had **Ross Mathie** to thank for getting them a 1-1 draw. It was almost a month before the second leg was played and in the meantime Killie were going through a bad patch. In addition to losing **Frank Beattie** with a broken leg at Celtic Park, they went into the return on the back of a spell of seven games without a win. **Hugh Strachan** replaced Beattie and the experienced **Jim McLean** was restored to the side. But Killie were short on numbers this season as the presence of **George Maxwell** on the bench proved. Maxwell would become a Killie all-time great but at this stage of his career, his first-team experience was limited to a substitute appearance at Love Street on New Year's Day. Now, he was Killie's only alternative if things went wrong on the pitch.

And go wrong they did. On a poor surface, covered in ice and mud and with 20,000 fans roaring on their opponents, Killie were quickly a goal behind. Maxwell came on for Gilmour but to no avail. At 1-0 there was still a chance, but when Bacau scored again, in the second half, that was the game over. Killie's European ventures this season had actually cost them money so defeat was even more galling when the club realised that a victory would have meant a money-spinning quarter-final tie with **Arsenal**. As it was, the *Gunners* easily overcame Bacau and went on to win their first European trophy.

DYNAMO BUCHAREST

The first Romanian opponents Kilmarnock played were **Dynamo Bucharest** in the **New York Tournament** in 1961. Previously known as CCA Bucharest they had been taken over by the army and were the top team in their country.

They had already played in three European Cups by the time they faced Killie in June 1961. Only 3,000 watched what wasn't exactly the most exciting game Kilmarnock have ever taken part in. To be fair it was the second last match of a season nearly ten months old and a 0-0 draw against a team of Dynamo's calibre wasn't a bad result. But the most significant event of the game was the debut of a young defender called **Andy King**. King, of course would go on to give Killie a decade of service and would earn a League Championship winner's medal.

EAST FIFE

Games	57	
League	38	1930-31, 47-48, 54-58, 71-73, 75-76, 77-78, 84-88, 89-90
Scottish Cup	12	1923, 32, 38, 48, 55, 57, 65, 95
League Cup	4	1948, 95, 98
Other	3	1946, 91
Top Scorer	Ian Bryson 5	All SL
Top Home Crowd	18,656 Feb 20th 1957 SC	
Top Away Crowd	12,000 Jan 24th 1948 SC	
Highest Overall	92,716 Apr 27th 1938 SC	(Hampden)

East Fife only played once at Rugby Park in a League game prior to World War Two. They were demolished **5-1** in 1930-31, with four of the goals coming from **Abraham Wales**. Wales was only a reserve player, standing in for **'Bud' Maxwell**, but he took his opportunity with aplomb.

Killie missed out on playing East Fife in their great days as the **Methil** side's golden age co-incided with Killie's time in 'B' Division. By the time the teams met in the top flight the **Bayview** team were on the slide towards relegation in 1958. When they came back up in the early 70s, they gave Killie a torrid time. And they continued to do so in the 80s. In 1988 with both teams fighting against the drop, the Fifers won 3-1 at Rugby Park on the second last day of the season, a game in which Killie needed just a point to ensure safety and relegate their opponents. Killie did avoid the drop and East Fife did go down, but it certainly wasn't for lack of effort on the Fifers part.

The last time the teams met on League duty was in 1989-90. This season marked the debut of **Tommy Burns** as a Kilmarnock player and he first pulled on the jersey in farcical conditions at Bayview. The team bus broke down, the players changed in taxis, the match was played in the teeth of a howling gale, and there were players at risk of contracting hypothermia. The match was abandoned with fifteen minutes to go, much to the relief of Kilmarnock and the chagrin of East Fife, who were leading. It didn't make any difference – the Fifers won the replayed game 4-2.

But if that was controversial then it was nothing compared to the clubs first meeting – a **Scottish Cup** tie in 1923. Killie could only draw at home against their lower league foes thanks to a **Willie Culley** goal in a 1-1 tie. In the replay the Second Division side won 1-0. Three Killie players were accused of not trying, the worst crime a footballer can commit. Sensationally, one of the three was Willie Culley.

Culley was Killie's top striker. No one has ever scored more goals for the club than Willie Culley and he had been a servant of Kilmarnock's for twelve years. It seemed unthinkable that he wouldn't give of this best. Yet Culley was the only one of the trio to be found guilty and he was suspended sine die. Fortunately for Culley, Clyde came in to rescue him but for Kilmarnock it had been a traumatic time. The club's most favoured son had been 'convicted' of cheating on them.

Killie got their revenge nine years later, winning **4-1** at home in a first round tie on their way to the 1932 Final. But it was the next time they appeared in the Final which stands out – even more than 60 years later – as an epic occasion. And their opponents were East Fife.........

It was one of the most unlikely Finals in the history of the Scottish Cup. On the one hand, Kilmarnock, with a pedigree second to none outside the Old Firm, but deep in relegation trouble. And, on the other, East Fife, a Second Division side many supposed had got lucky. Lucky, because they had beaten only one top-flight side – **Aberdeen** – on the road to **Hampden.**

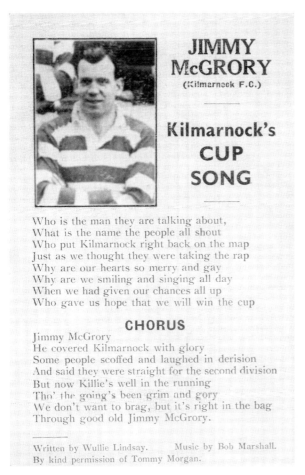

JIMMY McGRORY
(Kilmarnock F.C.)

Kilmarnock's CUP SONG

Who is the man they are talking about,
What is the name the people all shout
Who put Kilmarnock right back on the map
Just as we thought they were taking the rap
Why are our hearts so merry and gay
Why are we smiling and singing all day
When we had given our chances all up
Who gave us hope that we will win the cup

CHORUS

Jimmy McGrory
He covered Kilmarnock with glory
Some people scoffed and laughed in derision
And said they were straight for the second division
But now Killie's well in the running
Tho' the going's been grim and gory
We don't want to brag, but it's right in the bag
Through good old Jimmy McGrory.

Written by Wullie Lindsay.   Music by Bob Marshall.
By kind permission of Tommy Morgan.

Optimism before the Final, as expressed in *'Kilmarnock's Cup Song'*

The first game had little in it to enthuse the 80,000 present. East Fife took the lead before **McAvoy** equalised for Killie. In terms of excitement, that was it. But the replay, watched by an incredible crowd of **92,716** saw history made. Unfortunately for Kilmarnock they were not the history-makers. The pattern followed the first game with the Fifers taking the lead then Killie, this time with a **Benny Thomson** penalty, equalising. But then Killie went ahead for the first time thanks to an exhilarating run and goal from **Felix McGrogan** after 25 minutes.

An injury-ridden Kilmarnock tried desperately to defend that lead but it was no great surprise when East Fife levelled and the game went to extra time. The extra half-hour was too much for a team on its last legs and the Fifers scored twice to lift the trophy. **It was the only time a Second Division team ever won the Cup**. It was the first time since Queen's Park, as a non-league side, in 1893 that a side from outwith the top division had won the Cup. And, to date, also the last.

There have been more meetings since then. East Fife won again in 1948, Killie in 1955. After a replay, Killie emerged triumphant in 1957 on the way to their first Final since 1938, and also won after a replay in 1965. Most recently, there was another Killie victory in 1995. Indeed, Kilmarnock have met only Rangers, Celtic, Hearts and Partick Thistle more often in the Scottish Cup. But, even if they were to play East Fife 100 times, it's unlikely there will ever be a game as historic as that of 1938.

League Cup pairings have been fewer. Killie came off best in the section matches in 1947-48 and also knocked the Methil men out of the competition twice in the 1990s. They've emerged successful too in both the Victory Cup in 1946 and in the Centenary Cup. **But for all their success in these competitions it's established firmly in the record books that they lost the one that mattered the most.**

So near and yet so far. The team that played in the memorable 1938 Scottish Cup Final

Back: J A Herries, N D Robinson (directors), Fyfe, Hunter, Milloy, J Henderson (President), T Wylie (director)
Sitting: J McGrory (Manager), Thomson, Reid, Collins, McAvoy, McGrogan, J McWhinnie (Trainer)
Front: G Robertson, Stewart, Ross.

EAST STIRLINGSHIRE

Games	29	
League	14	1932-33, 48-49, 63-64, 73-74, 81-82, 89-90
Scottish Cup	9	1892, 95, 99, 1900, 36, 51, 97
League Cup	4	1949, 74
Other	2	1981
Top Scorer	'Bummer' Campbell 3	All SC
	Ian Fleming 3	All SL
	Sandy Higgins 3	All SC
	George Maxwell 3	1 SL, 2 LC
	Eddie Morrison3	1 SL, 2 LC
	Bobby Muir 3	All SC
	Jimmy Robertson 3	All SC
Top Home Crowd	12,211 Aug 14th 1948 SL	
Top Away Crowd	6,500 Feb 11th 1899 SC	

Killie have a 100% home record in League matches against **East Stirlingshire**, though admittedly, games have been few and far between. The clubs first meeting was in the old First Division in 1932-33 and *'Shire* were relegated after just one season in the top flight. In fact all Kilmarnock's games against them have been in seasons which have featured either promotion for Killie or relegation for East Stirling. The next meeting was in 1948-49 which ended with East Stirling plummeting into the 'C' Division.

They made a remarkable comeback by reaching the top league in 1963-64, but were promptly relegated. The clubs have also met in 1973-74, 81-82 and 89-90, all years in which Kilmarnock gained promotion. Killie's record at **Firs Park** is

Tom Brown's diving header against East Stirling makes it 2-0 in the 1997 cup-tie. Killie's first triumph on the road to glory

not quite as good as at home but they have still won the majority of matches.

The clubs have met fairly often in the Scottish Cup. There was a flurry of games at the end of the19th century with the teams drawn together four times in eight years. Killie won all of these, though the tie in 1899 had to go to a second replay at *Cathkin*. Killie also won in 1936 but suffered one of their worst-ever defeats in 1951 when the 'C' Division side won 2-1 at Firs Park.

Their most recent Cup meeting was a happier affair as Killie embarked on their glory run of 1997 with a home win over East Stirling in the third round.

The clubs have also met twice in the League Cup sectional stages with all four games played won by the home side. Oddly enough, East Stirling also played Killie in the Anglo-Scottish Cup. They were the Rugby Parkers first victims in the run to the semi-finals in 1981.

EASTERN

Eastern were a Glasgow side who had taken part in the inaugural Scottish Cup, losing narrowly to **Queen's Park** in the last eight. In the competition's second season they were drawn to play Kilmarnock in the second round. Although Kilmarnock were an improving team (having won a tie for the first time in the previous round) they were still not up to the standards of the Glasgow sides. Despite giving it their all, Killie were beaten 3-0.

Eastern went on to the last eight where they again lost narrowly, 1-0 to **Renton**. Within a few seasons they had vanished from the scene altogether.

In the era of **Bobby Charlton, Denis Law, Jim Baxter** and **Jimmy Greaves,** it says a lot about **FRANK BEATTIE's** ability that he featured on the cover of the prestigious 'Football Monthly'.

EINTRACHT FRANKFURT

"Here was a game that will be remembered as long as football is played in Ayrshire."

That was the press verdict on September 23rd 1964, the day after Killie's historic triumph over **Eintracht.** Almost 40 years later that verdict has endured. More dramatic than the title-clinching match at Tynecastle at the end of the season. More celebrated than any of the cup victories. A greater achievement than winning 3-0 at Ibrox. **This was the game which made the name of Kilmarnock Football Club resound throughout the footballing world.**

Consider the circumstances: In one corner, the Champions of the *Bundesliga,* the team that thrilled the continent in their Hampden Park European Cup Final against **Real Madrid.** A side, which in their last game against Scottish opposition, had humbled **Rangers** *12-4* on aggregate. A team known and feared the world over.

And in the other? A provincial team from South-West Scotland which had never played in a European tie. A side which had been in the bottom division ten years before this match and had been part-time only five years previously.

Add to that mixture a 3-0 home win for the Germans in the first leg and a quickfire addition to that in the second and you have a recipe for slaughter. Instead you get the footballing comeback of all comebacks. **You get Kilmarnock, the Lazarus of Scottish football.**

Killie's debut in Europe had been long overdue. Shunted off to America while lower placed sides took up a European slot by virtue of their city status had been Killie's lot over the five preceding seasons. Belatedly, the SFA finally consented to put forward Scotland's runners-up into the **Fairs Cup** (later the UEFA Cup). And their introduction to continental football had been torrid. Despite weathering the Eintracht

storm for the first half of the away leg, Killie's inexperience eventually showed and they left the *Waldstadion* beaten 3-0 and seemingly on their way out.

Rugby Park prepared for its first European tie in inauspicious circumstances. A combination of the first leg score and a battering by the elements conspired to produce a crowd of just under 15,000 for the return. And any confidence the super-optimists among the support may have had took a severe knock before kick-off when the teams were announced. Injuries forced manager **Willie Waddell** to field the versatile **Jim McFadzean** at left back and to promote a boy of 17 to the starting eleven.

That boy was **Tommy McLean,** whose previous outings had been restricted to a couple of Summer Cup appearances. Within 90 seconds of kick-off McLean and his team-mates saw what was already an uphill task become one the size of Mount Everest when German inside-left **Huberts** cracked home a shot from around 30 yards to make the score 4-0 on aggregate.

Then the most incredible fightback in the history of Scottish football began…

As the thirteenth minute approached, a **Davie Sneddon** pass found **Ronnie Hamilton** who knocked the ball past **Loy** in the Eintracht goal. 1-4. Three minutes later, the Germans clumsily failed to repel a McLean cross and **Brien McIlroy** pounced to put Killie ahead on the night. 2-4.

Now the fans got behind the team. A wall of sound enveloped Rugby Park and urged on the Ayrshire side. But the Germans held out till the interval without further loss. The second half started with only **Jackie McGrory** beside keeper **Campbell Forsyth** in defence as Killie surged forward in search of goals. Seven minutes into the second period and a McGrory free kick was met by a glancing header from McFadzean. 3-4. And well over half an hour to play. But now it was Eintracht's turn to attack. But their brief assault on Forsyth's goal yielded nothing and Killie assumed control again.

McIlroy netted only to be given offside and as the game entered its final ten minutes it looked like that most traditional of Scottish football results – the 'glorious' failure – was the most likely outcome. Then came a cross from McIlroy, and there was **Jackie McInally** soaring high above the German defence and heading past the keeper to square the tie. 4-4.

The terraces erupted as ecstatic supporters invaded the pitch. But the game wasn't over yet and McLean continued to weave his magic on the right flank until felled on the edge of the penalty area with two minutes remaining. Sneddon nudged a short free kick to Hamilton whose shot took a deflection off a defender on its way into the net. 5-4. And bedlam as thousands ran onto the pitch. After order had been restored the remaining two minutes were played out before the Northern Irish referee called time on the most amazing game Rugby Park has ever seen.

Now there was another pitch invasion and the fans refused to leave until their heroes had taken a bow. Mostly barefooted, the players returned to take the plaudits of the fans and the sight of the youngster McLean hoisted high on the shoulders of Sneddon, McInally and McIlroy inspired delirium among the crowd.

The evening was summed up perfectly by Willie Waddell who said: *" I have never been so proud of any team. The crowd gave us tremendous support and I have never witnessed scenes like this in my life."*

The next day Scotland awoke to find Killie's deeds plastered all over the front pages. Britain was in the middle of a general election campaign, as was the USA. China was on the brink of exploding an atomic bomb and a coup was in the offing in the Kremlin. But none of that was allowed to intrude on the story of the day – Kilmarnock's magnificent fightback. Perhaps even more significant in the world of Scottish football than knocking **Harold Wilson** and **Lyndon Johnson** off the front pages, Killie even managed to knock the Old Firm off the back ones!

Killie's European adventures began in Frankfurt in September 1964.

ELGIN CITY

When Kilmarnock were drawn to play **Elgin City** away in the fourth round of the Scottish Cup in 1972 it looked like a tricky tie. The then **Highland League** side had a proud record at their **Borough Briggs** ground. *It had been twelve years since they had last tasted defeat at home in the Cup* and in that time they had established themselves as Scotland's premier *giant-killers*. Indeed, Elgin had reached the quarter-finals in 1968.

So it was with some apprehension that Killie travelled north. But Elgin failed to live up to their billing and Killie soon established control, leading 2-0 at the interval. They continued to dominate and eventually ran out 4-1 winners in front of a crowd of over 10,000 which included a large contingent from Ayrshire. It was a long, but happy, journey home for their weary supporters.

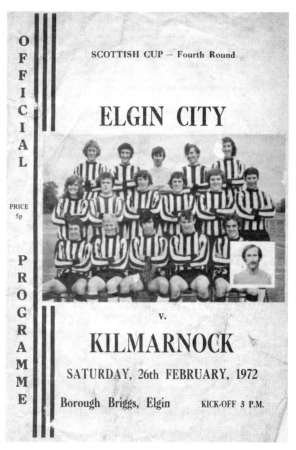

Elgin may have been Scotland's *'giant-killers'* but Killie were in no mood to play Goliath to the Highland David in this cup-tie.

Jim Fleeting unveils new signing **Bobby Williamson** in 1990.

EVERTON

Games	3	
UEFA	2	
Other	1	
Top Scorer	Andy Kerr 1	Other
	Brien McIlroy 1	UEFA
Top Home Crowd	23,561 Nov 11th 1964 UEFA	
Top Away Crowd	30,730 Nov 23rd 1964 UEFA	

Killie's first experience of **Everton** came in the **1961 New York** Tournament. Losing 2-0 at half-time, Killie pulled a goal back thanks to Andy Kerr but their first match in the competition ended in a narrow defeat.

After defeating Eintracht, the Merseyside giants were Killie's next European opponents. **Everton** were a terrific team in the 1960s. Champions in 1963, Cup Winners in 1966. Their team contained players with both skill and brawn. The artistry was provided by their Scottish playmakers **Jimmy Gabriel** and **Alex Young** – *'The Golden Vision'* as he was known on Merseyside. The strength came in the shape of iron man defender **Brian Labone**. There was also the promising young **Colin Harvey**. And with forwards like **Derek Temple, Fred Pickering** and **Johnny Morrissey,** there was no shortage of firepower either.

The first leg at Rugby Park, watched by a crowd in excess of 23,000 proved to be a disappointing affair for Killie. It was goalless at the interval but goals from Temple and Morrissey saw Killie lose at home for the first time this season. A quick goal from McIlroy at **Goodison** briefly restored hope but there was to be no Eintracht-style comeback for Kilmarnock. The English side ran out 4-1 winners on the night, 6-1 on aggregate.

EYEMOUTH UNITED

Eyemouth United, from the little Berwickshire fishing village, were the shock troops of the Scottish Cup of 1960. They disposed of **Albion Rovers** and **Cowdenbeath** to battle their way into the last eight. With the crowd restricted to just under 3,000 Kilmarnock travelled there on a hiding to nothing. Win easily, and that was what was expected. Lose, and it would be the biggest Cup shock ever.

But Killie played like the professionals they were. Goals from **Bertie Black** and **Jackie McInally** allowed them some leeway, although Eyemouth pulled one back before half-time. Killie were always in control of the game but with just a goal in it couldn't afford to be complacent. While under little pressure from the non-leaguers, it was a nervous second half for a Kilmarnock team relieved to hear the final whistle with score still 2-1 in their favour.

FALKIRK

Games	147	
League	130	1905-35, 36-47, 51-52, 54-59, 61-69, 71-73, 75-76,
		81-82, 83-86, 88-89, 90-91, 94-96
Scottish Cup	10	1897, 1936, 47, 56, 57, 64, 76, 97
League Cup	2	1959
Other	5	1946, 52, 76
Top Scorer	Brien McIlroy 16	14 SL 2SC
Top Home Crowd	15,132 Mar 12th 1955 SL	
Top Away Crowd	20,000 Feb 8th 1936 SC	
Highest Overall	81,375 Apr 24th 1957 SC(Hampden)	

Although they have played **Falkirk** almost 150 times in over 100 years, one game and one game alone springs to the mind of Kilmarnock supporters immediately. That, of course, is the match played on **May 24th 1997** at **Ibrox** - the **Scottish Cup Final**.

What an occasion as 25,000 blue-and-white bedecked Kilmarnock supporters travelled the short journey up the A77 for their team's first appearance in the Final for 37 years. It was the longest period between Finals in Killie's history. An entire generation had grown up knowing nothing but struggle. No one under the age of 40 among the throng that approached Ibrox could remember a time when Killie paraded a national trophy at Rugby Park. As for the Cup . . . well it had been 68 long years since a Kilmarnock side had won the trophy Killie first contested back in 1873.

The day was made for drama. Opponents Falkirk had beaten Killie in the Final 40 years previously and this was their first Final since then. The *Bairns* were led by **Alex Totten,** himself the occupant of the Rugby Park hot seat

Paul Wright swivels and turns to fire home the goal which brought the Cup back to Ayrshire after a gap of 68 years.

just five months beforehand. All of the Killie players had played for Totten and most had been signed by him.

Killie, in turn, were managed by **Bobby Williamson**. Totten's successor had little time to get his feet under the table before having to lead the club in a fight against relegation. That battle won, attention focused on the Cup.

The atmosphere at Ibrox (hosting its first Final since 1924) was electric. Nearly 50,000 fans filled the ground, singing the praises of their heroes. A far cry from the sectarian chanting of the Old Firm. It had been dubbed '*The Friendly Final*' and the match lived up to that billing. It could not, however, be said to be a classic game. Final nerves took care of that. Most of the players present were only too aware that this could be their only opportunity to take part in the Scottish season's showpiece match. None more so than Killie skipper **Ray Montgomerie.**

Monty hadn't joined the club he supported as a boy until his late twenties and he had seen the bad times. He had played in the Second Division at **Montrose** and **Stenhousemuir.** Now, at the age of 36, he led Killie out at Ibrox.

It was a game Killie controlled and when an unmarked **Paul Wright** slid the ball home, following an **Alex Burke** corner, in the 20th minute it was no more than they deserved. Falkirk had only one club in their bag. The long throw from the prodigious **Andy Gray** aimed at the 6ft 7ins **Kevin James.** But at times in the second half it had Killie under pressure. The Ayrshire side could have secured the game midway through that period but **Jim McIntyre**, celebrating his 25th birthday, failed to hit the target. With five minutes remaining, Falkirk's **Neil Oliver** had the ball in the net but was ruled offside. Despite protests, the TV replays showed that referee **Hugh Dallas** had made the correct decision.

That was the last scare. After three minutes of injury time, the whistle blew to spark off a frenzy of celebration both on the pitch and in the stands. Back in Ayrshire thousands more cheered

The scoreboard has yet to register it, but Wright's goal sparks off celebrations in the crowd and on the pitch as **Dylan Kerr** and **Gary Holt** rush to congratulate the goalscorer, watched by **Jim McIntyre** (10).

their heroes. All over Scotland and around the globe, wherever they could find a satellite TV, Kilmarnock supporters roared their appreciation of the men who brought the Cup to Ayrshire for the third time.

Back in Kilmarnock over 35,000 lined the streets to cheer the side home. From old men who could remember the 1929 victory to young girls the same age now as the ancients had been then, all united in their praise for Williamson and his team. It was a victory procession that had been a long time coming. A celebration the likes of which had not been seen for a generation. And a sign that, once again, Kilmarnock FC were a force to be reckoned with in Scottish football.

This was the culmination of a century long series of Cup duels with Falkirk. And controversy has never been far away. Their first encounter had taken place at Rugby Park in a second round tie back in January 1897. Killie won the game 3-1 but Falkirk successfully appealed, claiming the pitch markings were inadequate. Forced to replay the tie, Killie wasted no time in despatching their opponents a second time, winning easily 7-3 after leading 6-2 at half-time.

In 1936 Falkirk, then in Division Two, knocked out Killie at Rugby Park after a drawn game at Brockville in front of 20,000. Hard to believe now, how that dilapidated old ruin of a ground ever held so may people. Killie's first post-war Scottish Cup tie was also a Brockville defeat in 1947 but they gained revenge with a 3-0 win on the same ground in 1956. Twelve months after that came the first Scottish Cup Final between the sides.

Killie, third in the League, were strong favourites against a Bairns team near the bottom. But on the day they just didn't perform anywhere near as well as they could. In fact they were poor. Trailing to a **John Prentice** penalty, a **Davie Curlett** goal gave Killie a somewhat lucky second chance. The replay was even worse. Killie were punchless in attack and when they went behind in the 24th minute all seemed lost.

But it was now, when defeat was staring them in the face, that Kilmarnock sprung into action with attempts from **Bertie Black, Rab Stewart** and **Gerry Mays** before **Davie Curlett** again equalised. A defensive mistake in extra time allowed Falkirk to score again to take the Cup. The 40-year wait for revenge had begun. Victories for Kilmarnock in 1964 and 1976 proving to be merely the prelude to Ibrox 1997.

In the League Falkirk proved surprisingly successful at Rugby Park. Until, that is, December 1925. Kilmarnock lost that day but it would be an incredible *60 years* before a Falkirk team ever claimed full points at Rugby Park again. There were some close games, true, and a glut of draws. But, generally speaking, Killie supporters could look forward to a visit from Falkirk confident about the destination of the points. And there were plenty of those supporters

The scoreboard says it all. Kilmarnock have won the Scottish Cup.

too. Over 15,000 turned up at Rugby Park in 1954-55 to see Killie, in their first season back in the big time, win easily 2-0.

But if that game was an easy win, it wasn't a patch on what happened in February 1964. Within sixty seconds of the kick-off **Brien McIlroy** had rattled in the first goal. The same player saw an effort just three minutes later beaten away by the keeper only for **Frank Beattie** to pounce to grab the second. A clever passing move saw **Jackie McInally** score the third and the same player scored again before running through the Bairns defence, rounding the keeper and popping in number five – claiming his hat-trick in the process. Just before half-time, McIlroy attempted a shot from the bye-line which evaded a despairing **Willie Whigham** in the Falkirk goal to make it 6-0 at the break.

Whigham was at fault early in the second half, dropping a **Sneddon** cross which fell to **Hugh Brown** to make it seven. McIlroy notched up his hat-trick three minutes later and with just 54 minutes on the clock, fired in number nine. Double figures beckoned when Killie were awarded a penalty on the hour mark but a weak McIlroy effort was easily saved. Killie took the foot off the pedal after that and Falkirk managed to score a couple of late goals. **9-2** it finished. An amazing day, and one which restored Killie to the top of the League.

That match was the fourth in a sequence of *eleven* straight home wins over Falkirk. So when the *Bairns* were the visitors on the last day of the 1972-73 season with Killie needing a win to stay up, there was little to suggest that victory number twelve would not be forthcoming.

After all, Falkirk themselves were a poor team, only just above the relegation area. When **Eddie Morrison** netted after thirteen minutes and **Ronnie Sheed** did likewise fifteen minutes later, all was well. At half-time Killie were still two goals to the good and looking a safe bet for a 20th consecutive season in the top flight.

But it was an edgy, nervy, indeed panicky Killie team which took the field for the second half. Even this lacklustre Falkirk side eventually got

the message that their opponents were just hanging on to their lead. **Doug Somner** scored after an hour. Then, with three minutes remaining, **David Cattenach** equalised. Killie's winning run against Falkirk was over. More important than that, as news filtered through that relegation rivals **Dumbarton** had won, Kilmarnock had been relegated after nineteen years in Division One.

Unlike the Cup, revenge came swiftly in the League. It was three seasons later, the first year of the three division set-up, and Killie entertained Falkirk at Rugby Park for the first time since that fateful day, needing a draw to win promotion to the Premier Division. **Ian Fallis** put them ahead after just six minutes. But just like 1973, nerves took hold. Killie couldn't add to their score but Falkirk had little to offer in the way of attack. 1-0 it remained and the Ayrshire team were back with the big boys.

All runs have to come to an end sometime. And in April 1985 Killie finally lost to Falkirk at home. 0-0 at half-time, the *Bairns* scored three times in the second half to end that 60-year wait. They've managed just one more win at Rugby Park since. Two defeats in over three quarters of a century, coupled with that 100% record against **East Stirling**, it doesn't take much detective work to discover which Scottish town provides the most popular visiting sides to Rugby Park.

The clubs have met in just two seasons in the Premier. The first of these, 1994-95, produced an amazing midweek game at Brockville as Killie, courtesy of **Mark Skilling, Tom Black** and **John Henry** took a 3-0 interval lead. The game turned on its head in the second half and in the end Killie were happy to escape with a point from a 3-3 draw.

Surprisingly, the two sectional games in 1958-59 remain the only times the teams have met in the **League Cup**. For Kilmarnock supporters the last time the teams met in any competition is still the best. Ibrox on May 24th 1997 remains the pinnacle of achievement for the modern Kilmarnock FC. **The benchmark by which all else will be judged by the support.**

To the victor belongs the spoils. Cup-winning hero **Paul Wright** shows off the Scottish Cup to
25,000 jubilant Kilmarnock supporters as his team-mates await their opportunity to lift the precious trophy –
the oldest football trophy in the world.

FERENCVAROS

Many Eastern European teams were unknown quantities in the 1960s. Not so **Ferencvaros**. Their meeting with Kilmarnock was a clash of the respective champions of **Hungary** and **Scotland** in Killie's first match in the 1965 **New York** tournament.

While Killie had been making a name for themselves with that epic victory over **Eintracht,** the Hungarian side were blazing their own trail through continental football in the same competition. They eliminated top quality opposition in **Roma** and **Bilbao** before defeating the **Manchester United** of **Law, Best** and **Charlton** to reach the **Fairs Cup Final**. The Final was a one-off match, staged on the ground of their opponents **Juventus**. Amazingly, Ferencvaros pulled off a shock 1-0 victory to become the first Eastern European team to win a European trophy.

With acclaimed players like **Fenyvesi, Varga** and **Rakosi** in their side they were a match for anyone. But the jewel in the Hungarian crown was **Florian Albert**, later to emerge as one of the stars of the 1966 World Cup. Surprisingly Killie took a 1-0 lead by virtue of an own goal. But the sheer class of the Hungarians told as the game progressed and Killie's 2-1 defeat was no disgrace.

When the teams met again in Kilmarnock's last match of the tournament the strain of the championship season was beginning to tell on Killie. A **McIlroy** goal kept them in the game with the score 1-1 at half-time. But the second half was a different story as Killie felt the effects of a 60-match season. Ferencvaros ended up easy victors 4-1

FORFAR ATHLETIC

Games	42	
League	36	1949-54, 73-74, 84-89, 90-92
Scottish Cup	1	1928
League Cup	5	1952, 80, 89
Top Scorer	Willie Harvey 8	All SL
Top Home Crowd	11,983 Aug 29th 1951 LC	
Top Away Crowd	3,600 Jan 21st 1950 SL	

Forfar Athletic are comparative latecomers to the Kilmarnock story. Apart from their solitary **Scottish Cup** pairing in 1928 when Killie won 2-1 away in a second round tie, it was 1949-50 before they clashed. Forfar had won promotion from the 'C' Division and they proved to be awkward opponents on their inappropriately named **Station Park** turf. Inappropriate because the ground is actually fourteen miles from the nearest railway station!

Killie's first League visit in January 1950 ended in defeat but the attendance that day – 3,600 – is the largest to have watched this fixture in Forfar. Killie won all but one of their home games in their 'B' Division meetings (the other was drawn) but had to endure a **6-0** thrashing away in 1952-53. It wasn't until the promotion season of 1953-54 that they actually managed to record an away win.

Apart from one season in the 1970s it wasn't until 1984 that the teams began to meet regularly again. It is no disrespect to Forfar to say that it was a measure of how far Killie had fallen in the game that they were now considered the equals of the Angus club. Not just in status but in crowds too as the gate for one Rugby Park game in 1984-85 fell below the 1,000 mark. Killie couldn't win at Station Park and even lost a

League game to Forfar at home. That 2-0 defeat in 1988 remains the *Loons* only Rugby Park success.

Kilmarnock returned from their season in the Second Division reinvigorated. In their remaining League fixtures with Forfar they remained undefeated over two seasons. In October 1991 an **Ally Mitchell** goal gave them what was only their third League victory in eighteen visits to Station Park. Forfar's relegation in 1992 ended their time as Rugby Park regulars.

There have been three **League Cup** pairings. The sectional stages in 1951-52 with the clubs each winning their home games *(the Rugby Park one producing the fixture's record gate of nearly 12,000)*, a two-legged tie in 1979-80 which Killie won on aggregate with a home win and away draw and a 1-0 second round success for Killie in a Rugby Park match in 1988-89.

Calum Campbell positions himself to score in Killie's 2-0 home win over Forfar in 1992.

GALA FAIRYDEAN

Gala Fairydean, those seemingly perennially unsuccessful contenders for Scottish League membership, have met Kilmarnock on just one occasion. It was a first round Scottish Cup tie in January 1964 which brought the Borders side to Rugby Park. They arrived to face a Kilmarnock team in awesome form. Six straight victories had propelled Killie to the top of the League and almost 9,000 fans turned up for the cup-tie, most expecting to see a barrowload of goals.

It didn't work out that way. Gala fought manfully and that, combined with a Killie 'off-day' kept the interval score down to a single goal deficit, thanks to a **Jackie McInally** strike. The second half was just as frustrating for the fans. **Eric Murray** (who played most of this season as a striker) added a second but the fighting non-leaguers managed to score themselves. Gala kept battling to the end and it was a relieved Kilmarnock eleven that trooped off at the final whistle with just a narrow 2-1 win to show for their efforts.

GALSTON

An Ayrshire derby with a difference was the prospect facing Killie in the first round of the Scottish Cup in January 1935. **Galston** had been members of the Third Division in the 1920s and had kept up their membership of the SFA after that division had collapsed. Thus, they were annual entrants in the Scottish Cup. Indeed, the *Irvine Valley* club had been taking part in the national tournament since 1894 and although they never got past the second round, they had some pretty good results to their credit, including a win over **Motherwell** and a draw with **Hibs**.

So, it was a wary Kilmarnock side who stripped in their own dressing rooms, then put on overcoats to make the short journey to **Portland Park**. It wouldn't be that unfamiliar an experience for some of the players as Killie's reserves were regular visitors to the ground in the *Scottish Alliance*. Galston had a fair few ex-Rugby Parkers in their ranks and they kept the game tight. There were fewer than twenty minutes remaining when outside-right **James Black** gave Killie the lead. Despite a frenzied finish from the home side, Killie held on and were able to go back to Rugby Park for a bath with their heads held high.

So too, could Galston. It was a superb performance from them and worthy of the record crowd of 4,211. Galston could easily have switched the tie to Rugby Park. But they deserved full credit for sticking to their guns and keeping the game at home. Sadly, it wasn't long before they disappeared from the Cup. Despite the best efforts of Kilmarnock and Ayr United, the other clubs in the Alliance voted to axe Galston and Beith from the set-up just three years later.

GLASGOW UNIVERSITY

Forty years separates the two visits of **Glasgow University** to Rugby Park. Their first appearance was in a first round tie in 1929. Just 3,500 bothered to turn up to watch. Those who did saw a clinical Killie performance. Any thoughts the students might have had about creating an upset were blown away in the opening 45 minutes as Killie raced to a 4-0 lead.

They doubled that score in the second half although the students managed one in reply. There were *five* different scorers in the 8-1 win, with pride of place going to **Jimmy Ramsay** with a hat-trick. It was a gentle introduction to that season's competition. Killie would have to face two more Glasgow sides before going on to win the trophy. Both, it can be safely said, offered a slightly tougher proposition than the students.

The Glasgow students didn't often qualify for the national competition and interest could hardly be described as being at fever pitch in 1969. Just *eighty-three* spectators bothered to watch them knock out St Cuthbert's Wanderers to earn the right to face Killie.

But by the time of their first round appearance at Rugby Park it was a different story and there was a fair amount of support for the University among the nearly 8,000 strong crowd. The students appeared to have learned something of the modern game and managed to keep the score down to 2-0 at the break.

But superior fitness told in the second period and Killie eventually ran out winners by 6-0 with **Gerry Queen** grabbing a hat-trick. **Brien McIlroy** scored twice with an own goal completing the scoresheet.

For one Uni player though, playing against Killie was more than just a break from studies. The University captain **Jimmy Graham** put in a sterling performance which didn't go unnoticed by Kilmarnock. They signed him from **Queen's Park** a year later. Unfortunately a promising career was dogged by injury from the start.

GLENAVON

Games	3	
UEFA	2	2002
Other	1	1960
Top Scorer	Innes, Mitchell 1	Both UEFA
	Muir, Watson 1	Both Oth
Top Home Crowd	7,462 Aug 23rd 2001	
Top Away Crowd	3,000 Aug 9th 2001	

Glenavon were *'weel kent'* faces when Killie faced them in the 1960 **New York Tournament**. The teams had flown together from Prestwick and were based in the same Brooklyn hotel. This was Killie's second match of the tour and they followed up their opening win over Bayern with another comfortable victory. **Matt Watson** scored the opener with a fierce drive from the edge of the penalty area and **Billy Muir** added a second. Killie also hit the crossbar three times. Though to be fair to the Northern Irish champions it should be noted that they hit the woodwork twice themselves.

It was over 40 years before the teams met competitively again (though Killie won a friendly away to the Lurgan side 7-2 in 1968). Drawn together in the qualifying round of the **2001-02 UEFA Cup**, Killie, as the seeded side, were expected to progress. Though even a cursory look at Glenavon's European record would have told them to expect a stiff test. Since 1990 they had lost just once in seven home games, and that was to German giants **Werder Bremen**. Teams from **France, Belgium, Iceland, Poland** and **Croatia** had all been held and **Finnish** opposition beaten. However, in twelve previous European campaigns, they had won over two legs just once.

The first leg went more or less as scripted. Killie did most of the pressing but the part-timers compensated for lack of fitness with sound organisation. They got men behind the ball and tried to close things down in midfield. A goalless draw seemed on the cards until an injury-time corner from Killie saw **Chris Innes** soar above everyone to nod home the winner. *It was Killie's first away win in Europe in thirteen matches spanning 35 years.*

The home leg saw more of the same. Glenavon were content to absorb pressure, hoping to strike from a breakaway. The longer it stayed 0-0 the more restless the home fans grew. But a superb **Ally Mitchell** header edged Killie ahead. At last both fans and team could relax and Killie dominated the rest of the proceedings though they were unable to add to their tally. The job had been done efficiently enough. It was Killie's name that went into the first round draw and Glenavon returned over the water with their pride intact.

A hard-fought tie brought Killie's first away win in Europe for 35 years.

HAMILTON ACADEMICAL

Games	141	
League	123	1897-99, 1906-53, 65-66, 73-74, 75-76, 77-79, 81-82,
		83-86, 87-88, 90-93
Scottish Cup	8	1908, 12, 14, 30, 53, 59, 64
League Cup	5	1961, 74, 83
Other	5	1940, 46, 52
Top Scorer	Andy Cunningham 11	10 SL 1 SC
Top Home Crowd	14,000 Aug 21st 1946 SL	
Top Away Crowd	19,210 Feb 7th 1953 SC	

Hamilton Academical joined the Scottish League in strange circumstances in 1897. The season was already four games old when **Renton** resigned. Hamilton were not only invited to take their place, they also picked up from where the Dunbartonshire side left off, taking over not only Renton's fixtures but their record as well.

No matter the circumstances of their joining, there can be little doubt that Kilmarnock were pleased to see them, winning **5-0** at Rugby Park that season and **3-2** away. The following year the Accies were an even more welcome sight as Killie won both matches **7-1**. That was their last meeting until Accies joined the First Division in 1906. After that the two clubs met every season for almost half a century.

Killie maintained their excellent home form in the fixture and had a more than reasonable record away too, replicating their 7-1 win in 1909-10. From time to time they took the occasional beating at **Douglas Park** but generally it was one of the happier venues to visit. Most of the games accounted for little though. In the 20-strong First Division of the 1920s and 30s Killie and Accies were usually mid-table sides. Consequently there was often little at stake when the teams met.

That changed after the war. Both teams were relegated in the first post-war season – though the **14,000** who watched a Rugby Park draw was the largest for the fixture - and the fight back to the top was a long, hard slog. Hamilton made it before Killie, winning promotion in 1953. But Killie served notice of their own intent during

that campaign with a **6-1** home win over Accies. The following year it was Kilmarnock's turn to go up as Accies were relegated again.

Davie Provan scores against Hamilton in the first game in the new First Division in August 1975.

The two sides, so accustomed to their annual meetings, became virtual strangers over the next twenty years. They met just once, in 1965-66 when reigning champions Killie easily won both League games. The rivalry was renewed with a new intensity in 1973-74. Both teams chased a promotion spot with Killie just edging out their Lanarkshire rivals. And it was Accies who were the first visitors to Rugby Park when the new three-division structure got under way in 1975-76.

There were frequent clashes in the new First Division with first Killie, then Hamilton gaining the upper hand. But the decline of the Ayrshire side was exposed in 1984-85 when Accies won a Rugby Park league match for the first time since

1926-27. For the next few seasons Hamilton flirted with the Premier Division but never lasted more than a season.

By the early 90s both sides were established as among the best in their division and regarded as promotion prospects. And the most significant League meeting of all was also the last League meeting between the sides.

May 15th 1993 was the date. Rugby Park the venue. Hamilton the visitors. At stake? A place in the Premier Division. It had been ten long years since Kilmarnock had played in the top flight. A draw against Hamilton would end that decade in exile.

The pre-match build-up was intense. **Malky McCormick's** cartoons, exhorting Killie supporters to aid manager **Tommy Burns's** side by joining *"Uncle Tam's blue and white army"* were plastered all over Ayrshire. The turnstiles were closed almost an hour before kick-off, such was the clamour to see the game. Only police restrictions on the crowd limit prevented a record gate for this fixture. But it was an occasion to test the nerves of both fans and players alike.

With nothing but pride at stake, Hamilton were able to play a fast, free-flowing game which knocked Killie back on their feet in the early stages. Twice, keeper **Bobby Geddes** had to rescue his team mates and when a Hamilton shot smacked off the underside bar, the supporters feared the worst. Fortunately the ball rebounded safely enough and referee **Hugh Williamson** ignored the pleas of the Hamilton players for a goal.

Gradually, Killie began to come more into the match and their two main playmakers – **Shaun McSkimming** and **George McCluskey** – exerted more influence and initiated some clever moves of their own. News arrived on the terracing that promotion rivals **Dunfermline** were losing. A result that guaranteed promotion regardless of the Rugby Park outcome.

The players got the message. McSkimming almost broke the deadlock with an effort that hit the bar. That was as close as it got. Full-time blew on the only goalless draw of the season. But no one cared. Kilmarnock were back in the big time. There was a pitch invasion, reminiscent of the sixties glory days, fans and players joined each other in celebration. **Tommy Burns** emerged from the dressing room to tell the assembled media that this was *"the greatest moment of my career."*

And, irrespective of what was to transpire at the end of his tenure, it was a Burns-made achievement. His signing had been the catalyst in the club's transformation from a sixties relic to a modern, progressive club. And without his name, the club could never have attracted the kind of players needed to win promotion. The day Tommy Burns moved to Kilmarnock was the day the club stated its intent to be part of the elite again. And this was the day that made it all worthwhile. As 0-0 draws go, there can hardly have been any more glorious than this one.

Scottish Cup meetings have seen mixed fortunes for Kilmarnock. The clubs meetings have always been in the early stages of the competition and things started brightly enough for Killie. They won their first three encounters with the Accies but, as trophy holders, lost their title at Douglas Park in 1930. Having done the hard bit in 1953 by snatching a draw in front of almost 20,000 away – the highest Douglas Park attendance for the game – Killie then threw it away, losing 2-0 at home. That lapse was avenged with an easy 5-0 away win in 1959 and Killie also won at Douglas Park in 1964, the last time the teams met.

Killie have a superb **League Cup** record against Hamilton. Unbeaten in five games, they have conceded only one goal. On both occasions Hamilton have been drawn in their qualifying section, Killie have won the group. But the most significant League Cup meeting was their first. 1960-61 saw Killie romp through their group, disposing of **Hibs, Airdrie** and **Dunfermline**, only losing a game after the section had already been won. **Clyde** were beaten home and away in the last eight and only **Hamilton** stood between them and the Final. And the Accies were easily brushed aside. Although only 1-0 up at the break, Killie turned the screw after the interval and ran out easy winners 5-1. **Bertie Black** and **Andy Kerr** had a brace apiece with **Jackie McInally** the other scorer. The only disappointment was the crowd. Just 15,000 turned up to watch the clash at **Ibrox**.

Party On! The players celebrate the return to the Premier Division in 1993.

HEART OF MIDLOTHIAN

Games	204	
League	168	1899-1947, 54-73, 74-75, 76-78, 80-82, 93-2001
Scottish Cup	16	1907, 09, 13, 25, 31, 35, 60, 61, 70, 75, 87, 96
League Cup	18	1947, 58, 59, 60, 62, 63, 65, 69, 82, 88, 2000
Other	2	1946
Top Scorer	Gerry Mays 8	6 SL 2 LC
	Brien McIlroy 8	7 SL 1 LC
Top Home Crowd	26,584 Feb 19th 1960 SL	
Top Away Crowd	36,863 Feb 9th 1935 SC	
Highest Overall	51,280 Oct 27th 1962 LC	(Hampden)

In the pantheon of great Kilmarnock matches one game against **Hearts** stands out above all others. Just like **Eintracht** in 1964 and **Falkirk** in 1997, the game played at **Tynecastle** on **April 24th 1965** has seared itself into the memory of all who were there. Like the sagas told around ancient campfires, the tale of this match has passed down through the generations. It was a performance of epic proportions. And none of its glory fades by yet another re-telling...

It wasn't the first time the Scottish League championship ended with two teams level on points. It wouldn't be the last. It wasn't the only time the top two met on the last day to decide the destination of the flag. But it was, without fear of contradiction, the most dramatic, the most exciting, the most heroic end a season has ever seen.

Kilmarnock and Hearts had been locked together at the top of the table from day one of the 1964-65 season. But, as the teams entered the New Year, Killie's challenge had tailed off. **Dunfermline**, **Hibernian** and **Rangers** all had chances to seize the flag. One by one they fell away. Kilmarnock, meanwhile, had steeled themselves for one last effort. An unbeaten run in March and April brought them to Tynecastle on the final day of the campaign. And an appointment with destiny.

Goal average (which separated teams with the same points) may have been difficult to calculate but as the sun rose on the morning of April 24th the situation facing Killie was clear enough. They were playing away to leaders Hearts. They were two points behind. They needed not only to win, but also to win by two clear goals if they were to win the championship. That much, at least, was simple.

No one would have blamed the Kilmarnock players if they felt any nerves on this day. They had finished in second spot in four of the five preceding seasons. Manager **Willie Waddell** had already stated that he would be leaving at the end of the season. Many of the players had been at Rugby Park for a long time. They knew, deep down, that not only would they never have a better chance, there would never be *another* chance.

Hearts, by contrast, should have been confident. This would be their third title in seven years. They were an experienced side. They knew an early goal could extinguish what little chance Kilmarnock had. And they nearly got it. Their Norwegian winger **Roald Jensen** ran clear of the Ayrshire defence, drew keeper **Bobby Ferguson** out of his goal and then, inexplicably, blasted the ball wide. Perhaps that was an omen.

CHAMPIONS OF SCOTLAND
Celebrating on the Tynecastle turf are: L-R **Davie Sneddon, Eric Murray, Bobby Ferguson, Andy King, Jackie McInally, Frank Beattie.** Behind them is **Jackie McGrory**.

At any rate, this let-off gave the Kilmarnock defence the chance to muster themselves properly. Steadily, they repelled the Hearts onslaught and patiently waited for their own opportunities to come along. And after the Hearts whirlwind blew itself out midway through the first half, come along they did.

The forward line began to gel. Clever interplay between **McIlroy, McInally** and **McLean** allowed the young winger to send over a cross which was met by a downward header from **Davie Sneddon** to put Killie ahead. With Hearts still reeling from the shock, Killie struck again just three minutes later. **Bertie Black** was the instigator sending a pass through to **Brien McIlroy** whose unerring shot found the left hand corner of the net. 2-0. The dream was alive.

There was still an hour to play and although Killie controlled the rest of the first half, shell-shocked Hearts regained their composure at the start of the second period. Wave after wave of attack was broken down by the Killie rearguard. The game was already three minutes into injury time when Hearts' **Alan Gordon** broke through. His shot looked goalbound all the way, but the young Ferguson, making only his eighth league appearance, flung himself at the ball, tipping it round the post for a corner.

As the corner was cleared, the whistle sounded and Kilmarnock, the nearly-men, the perennial runners-up, had achieved the impossible. **At last they were Champions of Scotland.** By the closest margin in Scottish football history, four-hundredths of a goal.

It was only the third time that a team from outwith Scotland's four big cities had won the title. It was also the last. It was an achievement which, in all likelihood, no provincial club will ever attain again. **April 24th 1965. For Kilmarnock supporters all over the globe, a day that will never be forgotten.**

Yet there have been other great battles with Hearts over the years. Their League jousts have thrown up many memorable encounters. Back in

January 1905 a Kilmarnock team visited Tynecastle - a ground where they had never won – without a win in twenty away games and returned with a 3-1 victory. All Killie's goals came from centre-forward **Sandy Graham** who had been playing junior football just a month beforehand.

In December 1927, at Rugby Park, a Hearts side in the running for the title were soundly beaten 5-0 with five different players netting for Killie. In 1958 Hearts visited Rugby Park *eighteen* points clear at the top of the table. A fighting performance earned Killie a 1-1 draw, thus forcing Hearts to postpone their championship celebrations for a week. It was only the sixth point Hearts had dropped all season and it was also the last.

Then in March 1960 Killie beat a Hearts team that would again end up champions 2-1 at Rugby Park in front of a crowd of 26,584 – easily the biggest the fixture ever attracted at home. Nor did the pattern come to an end with the championship victory. After the funereal atmosphere of 1981 with fewer than 1,500 in the ground to watch two sides doomed to relegation, there was the raucous atmosphere of a near-10,000 crowd a year later as a tense 0-0 draw kept both sides on track in their personal promotion duel – a contest Killie ended up winning.

There was **Mark Skilling's** 30-yard drive at Tynecastle in 1993. A stunning goal to win any game and proof, if any were needed, that Killie were back as one of Scotland's top sides. Four seasons later, the same venue was the scene for an incredible game. Killie took the lead through **Pat Nevin** but Hearts went in at the interval 2-1 ahead. **Gary Holt** levelled for Killie only for Hearts to score twice more. **Mark Roberts** pulled one back but the *Jambos* replied again to finish up 5-3 winners.

August 1998 brought another chapter in the **Ally McCoist** story as the veteran striker bagged a hat-trick against Hearts at Rugby Park and earned a recall to the Scotland team in the process. And in September 2000 **Paul Wright** and **Freddie Dindeleux** scored to give Killie their first League win at Tynecastle since Skilling's screamer.

But stirring contests have not been confined to the League. All told, Killie and Hearts have faced each other 34 times in the two knockout tournaments. Only **Rangers**, with 35, have played Killie on more occasions. Killie lost the first few meetings in the **Scottish Cup**. Indeed, in six pre-war pairings they were successful only once. The 2-0 defeat at Tynecastle in 1935 saw the biggest attendance for the fixture – 36,863.

It was a different story post-war. With both teams in the hunt for a League and Cup double in 1960 there was a terrific second round clash at Tynecastle. Trailing 1-0 at half-time, **Billy Muir** equalised to bring Hearts to Rugby Park. A crowd of nearly 25,000 saw Muir give Killie the lead. Hearts equalised but an 86th minute strike from **Rab Stewart** put Killie into the next round.

The two clubs were drawn together again at the same stage of the competition twelve months later but this time Hearts left Rugby Park with a 2-1 win under their belts. 1970 brought a superb performance from Killie as goals in each half from **Jimmy Cook** and **Ross Mathie** gave them victory. There was no such joy in 1975 as Hearts won 2-0 at Tynecastle.

By 1987 Kilmarnock were languishing in mid-table in the First Division and Hearts were challenging for honours so when Killie were drawn out of the hat to play at Tynecastle in the third round, few held out much hope for their prospects. But Killie took over 2,000 supporters to the match – more than they were averaging at home - and they put up a fantastic fight to emerge with a goalless draw.

In the Rugby Park replay things were going Killie's way when Hearts had a player sent off and **Ian Bryson** put Killie ahead from the penalty spot. But a 66th minute equaliser sent the game into extra time. Despite Killie's best efforts, the ten-man *Jambos* clung on to force a second replay.

Killie won the toss for venue so the game went ahead at Rugby Park. For the second time more than 14,000 turned up, Proof that the support was there if the side ever became successful. A **Gary Mackay** goal in the 25th minute gave Hearts the interval lead. Just sixty seconds had elapsed after the break when Killie found themselves two down. Still, they refused to give up and a **Paul Martin** header in 73 minutes brought them back into the tie. Killie put on a storming finish and saw shots blocked and the woodwork scraped. But with just a minute to go a Hearts breakaway ended in a third goal. Despite the result the supporters knew just how well their team had performed against one of the best sides in Scotland and they left the pitch to that rarest of sights – *a defeated team receiving a standing ovation.*

The most recent meeting was in 1996 and a Killie side which had defeated Hibs at **Easter Road** in the previous round looked forward to an 'Edinburgh double.' Sadly, it wasn't to be. A close encounter ended with Hearts 2-1 winners.

In the **League Cup** the teams met in the very first competition, each winning their home match. They didn't meet again until the late 1950s when it began to be an annual occurrence. The 1957-58 sectional matches saw Killie take three of the four points on offer on their way to winning the section. Those three dropped points represented exactly half the total Hearts were to drop in the entire League campaign that season. The next year the teams clashed in the semi-finals. Laughably, **Easter Road** was selected as a supposedly 'neutral' venue and it was no surprise that Killie lost 3-0. Though Killie had no cause for complaint the following season when they lost both sectional games – the Rugby Park contest by 4-0

They also lost both games in 1961-62 but it was the meeting the next season that was the most memorable of them all and the occasion of an injustice that still rankles today.

It was the **League Cup Final** on **October 27th 1962**.There were over 50,000 in attendance at

Hampden Park and Killie got off to a bright start but lacked penetration in the opposing penalty area. Halfway through the first half **Willie Hamilton,** the best player on the pitch, sent over a lovely cross for **Norrie Davidson** to convert and give Hearts the lead. Killie fought back with **Frank Beattie** bringing a tremendous save out of keeper **Gordon Marshall** *(whose son is the present Kilmarnock custodian).*

Killie forced the pace in the second half but as the minutes ticked away it looked like they were getting nowhere. With only seconds remaining **Jim Richmond** hoisted a free kick high into the penalty area. **Frank Beattie** leapt above everyone to head home the 'equaliser.' Then, to everyone's (including the Hearts players) astonishment, referee **Tom 'Tiny' Wharton** awarded a free kick to Hearts.

Pandemonium! Killie were furious. They pleaded with Wharton, cajoled him, begged him to consult his linesman. That official's flag had stayed studiously down. Eventually Wharton spoke to the linesman, only to return and insist on the free kick being taken. Was it handball? Beattie denied it. Manager **Willie Waddell** stood by his player. Wharton had been nowhere near the penalty area when he gave his decision. No flag was raised. No reason ever given.

Whatever the reason, Killie had lost. The Rugby Park faithful never forgot Wharton's decision. Every time he officiated at Rugby Park, a storm of boos echoed around the ground. To this day, the Scottish League Cup remains the one major trophy never to have found a resting place in the Rugby Park trophy room. For that there are many who still blame 'Tiny' Wharton.

Later meetings between the clubs had little at stake until the quarter-final meeting at Rugby Park in February 2000 when a goal from **Michael Jeffrey** was good enough to send Kilmarnock into the semi-finals for the first time in 26 years.

Craig Dargo evades a tackle in this game against **Hearts** in 2000.

HIBERNIAN

Games	189	
League	158	1899-1931, 33-47, 54-73, 74-75, 76-77, 79-80, 82-83,
		93-98, 99-2001
Scottish Cup	5	1908, 39, 74, 96, 2001
League Cup	19	1959, 61, 67, 72, 75, 80, 84, 89, 92, 93, 2000, 01
Other	7	1946, 64, 75
Top Scorer	Willie Culley 14	All SL
Top Home Crowd	19,059 Feb 12th 1955 SL	
Top Away Crowd	32,394 Feb 4th 1939 SC	

Hibernian were difficult opponents right from the start. It wasn't until their sixth League visit to Rugby Park that Killie managed to record a victory. And it took until their twelfth trip to **Easter Road** for full points to be collected. But once Killie got those initial wins under their belts, results against the Edinburgh side improved and by 1917-18 Killie were able to claim their first League *'double.'* They repeated that feat the next season with the Rugby Park victory a spectacular affair.

Killie demolished Hibs **7-1** and even allowed themselves the luxury of missing a penalty. Record scorer **Willie Culley** bagged four of the goals. Also scoring two goals that day in September 1918 was **Sandy Goldie**. Tragically, just two months later, Goldie was dead. He was a victim of the Spanish influenza epidemic which killed more people in Europe than the First World War. Culley himself was fortunate to survive the epidemic, but not without cost. His wife was one of the victims.

Not all results against Hibs were obtained so easily and sometimes Killie found themselves on the receiving end. August 22nd 1925 at Easter Road was a case in point. Somewhat unlucky to be two goals down at the break, a freak gust of wind blew a seemingly innocuous shot under the bar instead of over it to leave Killie three down. It was 5-0 before Killie attempted a shot on goal. Three further strikes left a stunned Killie suffering an 8-0 defeat – one of their worst ever scorelines. It was part of a dreadful sequence of results for Killie at Easter Road. Between January 1919 and September 1938 they were unable to record a League victory on that ground.

Killie were to mete out vengeance for that depressing run. For almost two decades they were invincible against Hibs at Rugby Park. Hibs won 4-1 in December 1957 and next recorded a League triumph in February 1977, *eighteen* games in all, including ten successive Killie wins from 1960-69. **In all competitions the record stretched to 24 matches unbeaten at Rugby Park.**

And there were some impressive as well as vital wins during this period. Most important of all was the championship season. Killie faced Hibs at Rugby Park when their title bid was in crisis. They had lost three on the trot. Four out of the last five. But a **4-3** win over Hibs ended the slump and put Killie back on the title track. Goalscorers that night were **Eric Murray, Andy King**, and, most significant of all, two from **Bertie Black** who was playing his first League game of the season. Earlier that season Killie had won 2-1 at Easter Road thanks to a pair from **Ronnie Hamilton**. They had been forced to give a debut to a rookie goalkeeper thanks to regular **Campbell Forsyth** being away on Scotland duty. The newcomer was **Bobby Ferguson**, whose display that day was immense.

The February 1967 match at Easter Road saw manager **Malcolm McDonald** forced to give debuts to two youngsters to get over an injury crisis. For **Brian Rodman** and **Eddie Morrison** it was the first of many appearances in a Kilmarnock shirt. Morrison marked his debut with a goal in just four minutes. Unfortunately Killie lost 3-1.

In January 1980 the League match at Rugby Park produced an outstanding performance and a hat-trick from **Bobby Street** in a 3-1 win. A showing which totally overshadowed the undoubted skills of **George Best** who was playing for Hibs. But two seasons later came a repeat of 1925 as Hibs crushed Killie 8-1 at Easter Road. Incredibly the score had been just 2-1 at half-time.

Ally Mitchell gets the better of **Murdo McLeod** as Killie knock holder Hibs out of the League Cup.

More recently Easter Road was the setting for one of Killie's most crucial games in modern times. Over 6,000 fans trekked from Ayrshire to Edinburgh on May 14th 1994 for the last game in Kilmarnock's first Premier season in a decade. They knew their team needed to win to ensure survival. But they also knew that unless **St Johnstone** beat **Motherwell 4-0** at **Fir Park** the same day that a draw would be good enough. Defeat though was unthinkable.

The legions of Ayrshire fans erupted after just

five minutes as **Tom Brown** bundled the ball into the net. A raised flag indicating offside quickly silenced the support. Chances were made but not taken by Kilmarnock who were always in control of the match. But when word filtered through that St Johnstone had gone in front, doubts began to creep in. Should Killie lose a goal now then it was all over. Their hard-won Premier status gone after just a year.

The news spread from the terraces to the bench to the pitch. But the players held their nerve. They continued to seek the goal which would guarantee safety. It never came but the final whistle which heralded a goalless draw, also signalled Kilmarnock's survival. They had been tested and they hadn't been found wanting. Killie were not only back, they were back for good.

There were joyous scenes all around the ground and one in particular has gone down in infamy. Manager **Tommy Burns** and assistant **Billy Stark** bowed in homage to the fans and kissed the jerseys. One month later they departed Rugby Park for Parkhead in acrimonious circumstances. Their leaving of Rugby Park caused bad feeling enough amongst the support. Memories of the badge-kissing just made matters worse.

But a more celebratory atmosphere enveloped Rugby Park on a Friday evening in 1996-97 when both Kilmarnock and Hibernian put on a show for the cameras. In a match televised live on Sky, both sides paraded a feast of football before the watching public's eyes. **John Henry** gave Killie a 15th minute lead only for **Kevin Harper** to equalise four minutes later. **Jim McIntyre** quickly restored the lead three minutes after that but with only half an hour played **Andy Dow** made it 2-2. Second half goals from **Paul Wright** and an own goal from **Pat McGinlay** gave Killie a magnificent **4-2** triumph. It was a game which showed all that was good about Scottish football and it demonstrated to many that there was more to Scottish football life than the Old Firm.

Surprisingly for two sides with such a long pedigree, there have only been five **Scottish Cup** meetings. Killie have met **Annbank** and **Hurlford** more often than they've faced Hibs. The first meeting, in 1908, saw a shot from distance by Killie's **John McAllister** win them the game 1-0. That put Killie into the last four for the first time in the 20th century and it was also their first ever victory at Easter Road in any competition.

The next meeting was in 1939. A record crowd for the fixture of 32,394 saw Hibs beat Killie 3-1 in a second round tie despite **Sammy Ross** giving Killie the half-time lead. The 1974 third round meeting was even more painful. **Eddie Morrison** scored twice for Killie at Easter Road but Hibs struck back to take a 3-2 interval lead and ended up winning 5-2.

Killie claimed their first cup win since the Edwardian era thanks to two goals from **Paul Wright** in a third round tie in 1996. The most recent meeting was in a quarter-final game in 2001. Amazingly, it was the first time Hibs had ever appeared at Rugby Park in a Scottish Cup tie. With both teams going strongly in the League it was expected to be a closely-contested affair. And so it was. Killie also had the League Cup Final to look forward to, a week after this cup tie. But hopes of a Cup *'double'* evaporated a minute from the end. Just when it looked like a replay was on the cards, up popped **Tom McManus** to edge Hibs into the last four with the game's only goal.

League Cup meetings have been much more frequent. Only **Dunfermline** have played Killie more times than Hibs in that competition. Good results in 1958-59 and 1960-61 helped Killie win their section in both those seasons but they were less successful in 1966-67 and 1971-72, although the latter season provided a moment for Killie fans to cherish. In only his third match since recovering from his horrific broken leg, **Frank Beattie** struck a magnificent goal from 25 yards at Easter Road in Killie's 3-1 defeat. It was also *Big Frank's* last for Kilmarnock. The 1974-75 meeting saw the teams meet in the

quarter-finals. A 3-3 draw in an exciting game at Rugby Park was never going to be good enough for Killie and despite making a fight of it at Easter Road a late collapse allowed Hibs the luxury of a 4-1 scoreline in their favour.

A *'double'* over Hibs helped Killie win the section in 1979-80 but the 1983-84 competition which saw the end of the sectional format was a disappointment for both teams as crowds totalling less than 5,000 for the two fixtures combined indicates.

Since the tournament switched to a straight knockout format there have been mixed fortunes for Killie. A narrow 1-0 defeat at Easter Road in 1988-89 was followed by a spirited 3-2 defeat at Rugby Park in a third round tie in 1991-92. Killie's goals – from **Calum Campbell** and **Shaun McSkimming** – were the only ones conceded in the entire tournament by Hibs as they went on to lift the trophy.

Revenge came swiftly. At the same venue, in the same round, the next season, holders Hibs were put to the sword by a rampant Killie in extra time. **McSkimming** again, aided by **George McCluskey** and **Ross Jack** gave Killie a 3-1 victory. 1999-2000 saw yet another third round Rugby Park tie and again Killie won a close game, this time by 3-2 with **Ally McCoist (2)** and **Jerome Vareille** the scorers.

Twelve months on and it was a quarter-final tie, again at Rugby Park. **Russell Latapy** gave Hibs the lead after just two minutes. It took Killie until three minutes into the second half to restore parity through **Andy McLaren**. A **Craig Dargo** goal seventeen minutes from time sent Killie into their second successive semi-final.

The vagaries of the draw are quite amazing. Kilmarnock have played Hibs in the League Cup as many times in the past dozen years as they have in the Scottish Cup in over 120 years.

Hibs were also one of Killie's opponents in the Southern League Cup (the fore-runner of the present competition) in 1945-46 and the clubs have clashed in two other competitions as well. There was the **Summer Cup** in 1964. This competition lasted only two years. Failure to support it by the Old Firm led to its demise but it was not as unpopular as some have suggested. Hibs only finished second in their group but went through to the semi-finals because group winners **Hearts** were playing in **America**. After a play-off with **Dunfermline**, Hibs emerged as Killie's opponents.

Killie had an easy run to the last four, disposing of **Airdrie, Motherwell** and **Queen of the South** for the loss of a solitary point. In an amazing first half at Rugby Park the teams left the field locked together at 3-3. Killie scored again in the second period to take a narrow lead to Easter Road. It wasn't enough; Hibs won 3-0 and went on to win the competition.

What was significant for Kilmarnock about it though was that these two games marked the first appearances of one of the most naturally talented players ever to grace a Kilmarnock strip. The teenage **Tommy McLean** made his debut at Rugby Park and kept his place for the second leg.

As for this being an unpopular competition. Nearly 9,000 watched the Rugby Park match in

midweek and over 17,000 attended the Easter Road tie. Hardly poor figures. The other cup tie was a **Drybrough Cup** match at Easter Road in July 1974. **Ian Fallis** netted for Killie in a 2-1 defeat but again the notable thing here is the crowd figure. Despite being played 'out of season' over 13,000 watched this match. A sign that the public would watch whatever the season? Or a by-product of **Scotland's** magnificent **World Cup** performance in **West Germany**? Probably a bit of both.

Derek Anderson fends off the attentions of Hibs' **Darren Jackson.**

HURLFORD

Games	7	
Scottish Cup	7	1878, 83, 84, 85, 86
Top Scorer	Smith 2	Both SC
Top Home Crowd	2,000 Oct 17th 1885 SC	
Top Away Crowd	2,000 Nov 7th 1885 SC	

Hurlford were frequent opponents in the early days of football. They were beaten **5-1** in a first round Scottish Cup tie in September 1877 but on their next appearance showed how determined they were to be a thorn in Killie's flesh.

1882-83 was the start of four successive meetings of the clubs in the Scottish Cup and they were to be contentious occasions too.

Drawing 1-1 at half-time in their second round tie, Killie lost 6-2 at home in a game condemned by the press for its savagery. It was said to have been *"the wildest and most rough game ever played in Ayrshire."* And that was saying something!

Killie gained revenge the following season with a 3-0 home victory. But it was in 1884-85 that the bitterness between the clubs exploded. In the interim Killie had won the **Ayrshire Cup** for the first time by beating Hurlford in the Final but were forced to wait until protests from Hurlford had been heard before the players received their medals. Coupled with existing local rivalry it made for an unpleasant atmosphere when the teams clashed in the first round of the 1884-85 Scottish Cup.

Killie had seemingly cruised through to the next stage of the competition by beating Hurlford 6-1 at Rugby Park. But Hurlford protested to the SFA. Protests were common, often made on the flimsiest of evidence concerning registration, more seriously on grounds of fielding professionals or players from other clubs. On this occasion Hurlford's protest on breach of registration rules was successful and a replay was ordered to be played at Hurlford. Kilmarnock took part in the match and lost 3-1. But they had submitted a protest of their own prior to the kick-off, accusing Hurlford of the same breaches they had themselves been found guilty of!

Amazingly, although the result wasn't rescinded, Hurlford were disqualified and Killie reinstated to the competition. Not that it did them much good, going down at **Annbank** in the next round.

But the teams had saved the worst till last. They were again drawn together in the second round of the 1885-86 tournament. On October 3rd Killie were beaten 4-3 at home. That was the signal for a protest. The appeal was successful and on the 17th October the teams fought out a 1-1 draw, Killie's goal coming from the legendary **Sandy Higgins**. Then the fun started. Kilmarnock failed to turn up for the replay on the 24th. Instead of throwing Killie out of the Cup, the SFA ordered both sides to play in **Ayr** on the 31st. This they did, only for the match to be abandoned with ten minutes to go and the teams level at 1-1. So it was off to Hurlford on November 7th and a 2-2 draw after extra time. The marathon was finally ended on November 14th at Rugby Park with Hurlford winning 5-1. To little avail for Hurlford were soundly beaten by **Arthurlie** in the next round. Although they did reach the quarter-finals in 1887. Fortunately for Killie and Hurlford they were never drawn together again.

Hurlford kept entering the Scottish Cup though and last appeared in the competition proper in 1923 when they reached the second round before losing to **Celtic**. The enmities faded over time and in 1944 it was Hurlford, now a junior side, who came to Killie's rescue in their hour of need.

Without a home since 1940 when the army requisitioned Rugby Park, Killie wanted to operate a 'reserve' side in the 1944-45 season to prepare for the restart of football after the war. And it was old enemies Hurlford who provided the solution to Kilmarnock's problem, allowing them to play at **Blair Park** until Rugby Park was fit for football once more.

INVERNESS CALEDONIAN THISTLE

A fourth round away Scottish Cup draw to **Inverness Caledonian Thistle** in 2001 was always going to be a tricky tie. Killie had found difficulty enough in the past in visits to the Highlands but this was an entirely different matter. Their opponents were now a professional outfit, a good First Division side. And it proved to be a difficult game. Just as the supporters began making their way to the exits and a replay looked inevitable, the Highlanders pounced on a defensive error and struck in the last minute of the game.

Another embarrassing Cup exit stared Killie in the face but they immediately carried the ball up the park and **Garry Hay** atoned for his defensive lapse by scoring the equaliser. At Rugby Park, events descended into near-farce.

Given the go-ahead in the morning, Killie informed the Inverness club that it was ok to travel – the match was in no danger. But after just 27 minutes the game was abandoned because the pitch was frozen.

It went ahead a week later and the Inverness team stung Killie by taking the lead six minutes into the second half. But this Kilmarnock team was a resilient one and **Kevin McGowne** squared things on the hour mark. Eight minutes later a penalty from **Paul Wright** proved to be Killie's passport to the last eight.

INVERNESS CALEDONIAN

Killie's first visit to the Highlands on Scottish Cup duty was a first round tie in 1922 away to Inverness Caledonian. For almost half an hour the Highland League side kept the First Division team at bay. **David Gray** broke the deadlock in Killie's favour and then the Ayrshire side missed a penalty. **John Scott** scored his only goal for the club to give Killie a two goal lead at the break.

Any hopes of a Caley fightback ended when **Willie Watson** scored a third just after the restart. Then **Willie Culley** got in on the act to make it 4-0. Caley pulled a goal back but Culley netted again to make it 5-1 and cap a professional performance from Killie in what was a potentially tricky tie. Indeed, had it not been for some excellent goalkeeping the score could easily have reached double figures.

INVERNESS THISTLE

February 9th 1985 is a dark day in the history of Kilmarnock Football Club. Along with defeat at **East Stirling** and at home to **Brechin City**, both also in cup matches, it must rank right up there as a contender for that most unwanted of prizes; the one reserved for worst performance ever.

Of course any trip to the Highlands must be regarded with caution but even this poor Kilmarnock team should have won this third round tie. **Inverness Thistle** were hardly out of the giant-killing mould. They were second bottom of the Highland League. For over half an hour Killie dominated but without scoring. Nine minutes from half-time criminal defending left Thistle's **Milroy** unmarked at a corner and he put the home team ahead.

Apart from hitting the woodwork once, Killie made little headway in the second half and with time running out as they pushed forward in search of the equaliser they left gaps at the back. There were only nine minutes left when Thistle scored again to effectively kill off the game.

But more humiliation was to come as the Highland side added another in the 87th minute to make the final scoreline 3-0. Manager **Eddie Morrison** was later to describe it as the worst game of this time at Rugby Park. Angry fans surrounded the team bus which was given a police escort out of town. In all their years in the game there can be few, if any, worse results endured by Kilmarnock FC.

INVERNESS CITADEL

Kilmarnock's trip north to face **Inverness Citadel** in the first round of the Scottish Cup in 1931 was the least fraught of any of their Highland outings. Their opponents had never

progressed beyond the second round of the tournament. And their only two victories had come at the expense of **Clackmannan** and **Armadale**. Both League sides admittedly when they had played Citadel, but hardly of the calibre to warrant the Inverness side being accorded the status of giant-killers, nor to strike fear into Kilmarnock.

So it proved. Killie took a 2-0 interval lead and wrapped the game up easily in the second half, treating the 3,000 spectators to some exhibition football as they completed a highland clearance of their own, winning **7-0.** Those heroes from 1929 **John Aitken** and **Willie Connell** were both on the scoresheet and there were two goals from **Jimmy Muir** who had only made his first team debut at Tynecastle the week previously.

But the hero of the day was the new darling of the Rugby Park terraces. **'Bud' Maxwell** had made his debut earlier in the season and he had been scoring with abandon. This game was tailor-made for him and he celebrated by scoring the first hat-trick of his career.

KAISERSLAUTERN

Kaiserslautern were a plum draw for Killie in the **1999-2000 UEFA Cup.** Four times German champions; this was a team at the peak of their game. Two of their titles had come in the 1990s, most recently in 1998. And they had won the German Cup twice in the same decade as well. They were a team packed with international experience from all over the world. **Michael Schjonberg**, a defender with over 30 caps for Denmark. **Hans Ramzy,** a Scottish sounding surname but with nearly 100 appearances for Egypt. In midfield: **Marian Hristov** a Bulgarian internationalist, **Martin Wagner**, capped six times for Germany. Their squad had international class running throughout it. **Jorgen Pettersson** (Sweden), **Olaf Marschall** (Germany), **Marco Reich** (Germany), **Slobadan Komljenovic** (Yugoslavia), **Janos Hrutka** (Hungary), **Igli Tare** (Albania), and **Jeff Strasser** (Luxembourg) a one-time target for Killie.

But the jewel in their crown was undoubtedly the attacking midfielder **Youri Djorkaeff,** not only a regular for France but also a man who had played in the 1998 World Cup Final. A player capable of turning a game in an instant with a visionary pass, or a superb shot.

So it was a daunting task which faced Killie as they made their bow in the **Fritz Walter Stadion,** an impressive 38,000 capacity ground named after Kaiserslautern's most famous son –

the man who had captained the West German side to its first World Cup victory in 1954.

Killie started well, defending in depth and breaking when they got the opportunity. **Jerome Vareille, David Bagan** and **Ian Durrant** all had attempts on goal. But with the half hour mark reached and the game still scoreless, Killie's hopes crumbled in less than ten minutes. A **Koch** header put the Germans ahead. Seven minutes later Killie were dealt a devastating blow when **Djorkaeff** smashed home a free kick. Two minutes after that another header, this time from **Marschall** made it 3-0.

All Killie could do in the second half was attempt to stop the scoreline from becoming a rout. They managed to prevent any further goals and the super optimists among the support remembered the last time Killie had been beaten 3-0 in Germany – Eintracht – and consoled themselves with thoughts of a repeat of that fabulous night.

The supporters themselves had been terrific ambassadors for their club. They sang, they danced, they drank, but always with a smile on their faces. And yet another continental venue wondered what it was about the Scots, that they could be so cheerful and friendly in defeat.

The home leg's kick-off was altered to 5pm in order for the game to be shown live on German

TV. Undoubtedly that had an effect on the crowd with just over 8,000 turning up. The early goal Killie were looking for to give them renewed hope failed to materialise but at least the first twenty minutes passed by without further loss.

Then, just like the first leg, the game was decided in a matter of minutes. Again, **Djorkaeff** was the destroyer, opening the scoring in 22 minutes. Seven minutes later **Ramzy** added a second and suddenly even an Eintracht-style win wouldn't be good enough. The Germans relaxed after that and the game meandered towards its inevitable conclusion – a 5-0 aggregate defeat. Killie had been outclassed. The gulf between the *Bundesliga* and the *SPL* was all too obvious. It was their worst European result in terms of the scoreline, since losing to Everton all those years ago.

"I realised the way your eyes deceived me…"
Killie fans make their presence felt in Germany
before the game in Kaiserslautern

KARLSRUHE

Karlsruhe were Killie's second opponents in the 1961 **New York** competition. Having lost to **Everton** in the opener, Killie were forced to travel from Montreal for this fixture five days later. It was a game they had to win if they were to repeat their feat of the previous year and reach the Final.

A **Bobby Kennedy** goal in 24 minutes gave them the perfect platform. But although dominating the rest of the half, Killie failed to add to their lead. They were stung by an equaliser two minutes after the resumption but had regained the lead within a minute thanks to **Billy Muir**.

Another breakaway goal by the Germans just after the hour mark levelled the match. And a third on the counter-attack fifteen minutes from time left Killie with a 3-2 defeat in a match which should have been comfortably out of their opponents reach. Those first half misses cost Killie the tie and their hopes of winning the group.

KILBIRNIE

Games	4	
Scottish Cup	4	1879, 82, 84, 89
Top Scorer	Brodie, Hay, Wallace 1	All SC
Top Home Crowd	5,000 Sep 22nd 1888 SC	

Kilbirnie were another in the long list of local rivals that proliferated in the early days of organised football. Kilmarnock had been going through a difficult period when they first met them in a home Scottish Cup first round tie in 1878-79. Splits with the local rugby and cricket clubs had enticed players away. And many of those who remained had seen better days so the 2-0 defeat wasn't a total surprise.

The opportunity to avenge that loss came along three years later in the third round. Goals from **Wallace** and **Hay** gave them a 2-0 win and a place in the 'national' stage of the competition for the first time. Two years later clubs like Kilbirnie were finding it difficult to survive and their failure to assemble a team for the first round tie gave Killie a walkover to the next stage.

But Kilbirnie were still good enough for one last hurrah in 1888-89. A 5,000-strong crowd assembled at Rugby Park to see the away team take a 2-1 half-time lead in a second round match. And Kilbirnie scored again in the second half to claim a famous victory. They had a grip on Killie that season, also eliminating the Rugby Park side from both the Kilmarnock and Ayr Charity Cups.

The next season Kilbirnie were good enough to reach the last eight of the Scottish Cup before losing to **Third Lanark.** But within a few seasons they had vanished from the game.

LA GANTOISE

Having demolished another Belgian side, *Royal Antwerp,* in the previous round, Kilmarnock supporters could be forgiven for thinking that this 1966-67 third round Fairs Cup tie against **La Gantoise** would be a walkover. It turned out to be anything but. **Eric Murray's** first half goal was all Killie had to protect when they travelled to **Belgium** for the second leg.

In those days European football virtually shut down in the winter and the sides had to play the second leg, just seven days after the first, and four days before Christmas in the full knowledge that it would be four months before the competition resumed!

Killie were well experienced in Europe by now and they were going along comfortably, protecting their narrow lead with ease. They were just thirteen minutes away from full time when a bizarre incident occurred. **Frank Beattie**

(and how many times was Beattie at the heart of controversy?) placed the ball for a free kick, only to stagger back in bewilderment. The referee ruled that Beattie had handled the ball and awarded the Belgians a free kick of their own. In the ensuing confusion, they took the kick and scored from it. With no further activity of note Killie now had to face 30 minutes of extra time.

The game grew ugly. **Jim McFadzean** fouled an opponent and was then sent reeling to the ground by the Belgian. McFadzean was sent off but La Gantoise saw *two* of their players receive their marching orders in the extra period. But it was Killie who remained the calmer of the sides as **Jackie McInally** grabbed the goal which effectively ended the tie. **Tommy McLean** added another to give Killie a 2-1 win. It was their last away triumph in Europe for 35 years.

LANEMARK

Lanemark made their only Scottish Cup visit to Rugby Park in the first round of the 1886-87 competition. By this time Killie had outgrown the local opposition and, the odd shock result notwithstanding, usually took care of the minnows with ease.

That was certainly the case here as they effectively killed off the game well before the interval. They reached the dressing rooms **6-1** up and meted out more punishment in the second half, eventually winning **10-2.**

Lanemark were a resilient side though. They came back from this defeat to twice reach the fourth round (the 'all-in' stage) of the Cup where they met accomplished teams like Renton and St Mirren. What did for them, as for so many of the little teams, was the major change in the Scottish Cup after 1891 when the big teams were given byes until the last 32.

They also earned themselves a place as an unwanted footnote in Killie's history when they were beaten **15-0** in an Ayrshire Cup tie in November 1890 – Kilmarnock's record victory in any competition.

LARGS ATHLETIC

Largs Athletic came visiting in the first round of the Scottish Cup in 1881-82 and must have wished they hadn't bothered. Kilmarnock brushed them aside with ease, winning **6-0**. It was an excellent start to a fine season for Killie in which they reached the last 16 of the Cup. For Largs it was their first ever Scottish Cup-tie. Undaunted by this introduction to the national tourney they entered again the next year only to be beaten **7-0** by **Annbank**. After that they didn't bother to enter again.

LEEDS UNITED

Leeds United were undoubtedly one of the best sides in Europe in the 1960s. **Billy Bremner, Peter Lorimer** and **Eddie Gray** were the Scots trio at the heart of many of their successes. **Paul Reaney, Terry Cooper, Norman Hunter** and **Jack Charlton** added English steel to the side. And in manger **Don Revie** they possessed one of the shrewdest and most progressive thinkers in the game.

So when they were drawn to play Kilmarnock in the **Fairs Cup** semi-finals in 1967 Ayrshire was alive with anticipation. For Killie there was the added incentive that victory would give the Finals of all three European tournaments a Scottish presence –**Celtic** and **Rangers** having already claimed their places in the other two tournaments. Throw in the possibility of

Eintracht winning the other semi-final and there was a scenario that would have been laughed right out of Hollywood, so implausible did it seem.

But it was real enough and on a Friday night in Yorkshire Killie faced the might of England. There were over 40,000 at **Elland Road** that evening and they must have been totally bemused during the first 45 minutes. Leeds had the meanest defence in England. Killie's was reputedly the best in Scotland. Yet an astonishing first half saw the keepers beaten six times with the English side claiming a **4-2** lead.

The second half was more in keeping with spectators expectations. Both defences got back on top of their games and no more goals were scored. Killie were left facing an uphill battle at Rugby Park.

But the team didn't think the tie was beyond them. **Brien McIlroy's** two away goals might yet prove crucial for this was the first year that away goals counted as double in event of a tie. 2-0 or 3-1 would be good enough.

The teams faced each other just five days later in a Rugby Park cauldron. 24,831 supporters – *Killie's largest ever for a European tie* – turned out, many of them with Yorkshire accents, and they created a magnificent atmosphere around the ground.

Leeds, however, had made their reputation on defence away from home. In this season and the previous one they had won in **Leipzig**, in **Amsterdam** and *twice* in **Valencia**. They had drawn in **Turin** and in **Hungary**. Their only defeats had been narrow ones, in **Zaragoza** and **Bologna**. In short, if there had been 100,000 inside Rugby Park, Leeds would not have been intimidated.

They came prepared to spend 90 minutes in their own penalty area if necessary. And for much of the game that's exactly where they were camped as Killie tried to break them down. But after 45 minutes only a **Brien McIlroy** shot had troubled keeper **Gary Sprake**. The Welsh international was notably unreliable but not on this night. Here, he dealt with everything Killie could throw at him while, at the other end, **Gray** and **Lorimer** reminded Killie just how dangerous Leeds could be on the break.

The second half saw Killie hopes briefly raised when **Cooper** blatantly felled **Tommy McLean** in the box, but Killie's penalty claims were ignored. Leeds got the 0-0 draw they played for. The 180 minutes of football had produced six goals in the first thirty-eight and none at all in the remaining 142. Eintracht too missed out on the Final. For Killie keeper **Bobby Ferguson** it was farewell to Rugby Park. After the match he signed for **West Ham United** who paid Kilmarnock £65,000 – *a world record for a goalkeeper.*

For Killie there was nothing but memories of a glorious European run. Their best ever in continental competition.

So far.

In the Rugby Park match, **Gary Sprake** gathers under pressure from **Carl Bertelsen** with **Billy Bremner** looking on. The other Killie forwards in the picture are **Gerry Queen** and **Brien McIlroy**.

LEITH ATHLETIC

Games	17	
League	14	1895-99, 1930-32, 47-48
Scottish Cup	3	1898, 1912, 28
Top Scorer	William Reid 6	4 SL 2 SC
Top Home Crowd	5,000 Feb 7th 1931 SL	
Top Away Crowd	7,000 Jan 21st 1928 SC*	*Played at Easter Road
	7,000 Oct 4th 1930 SL	

August 17th 1895 is an auspicious date in the history of Kilmarnock Football Club. That was the day when they travelled to face **Leith Athletic** in their very first Scottish League match. The Division Two clash ended 3-1 in the home side's favour – hardly surprising considering that Leith had spent the previous four years in Division One. **Ritchie McAvoy** claimed the honour of scoring Killie's first goal in league football.

Although Killie's record against Leith at home was exemplary, they found it difficult to take anything from their travels. In April 1899 Killie were unbeaten throughout their entire League programme. But with two games to go they still hadn't secured the Second Division title. They faced closest rivals Leith needing a point to secure the flag.

But horrendous defending with just five minutes played left them a goal down. **'Bummer' Campbell** equalised but a headed own goal put Leith ahead again. The 'Bummer' equalised again. 2-2 at half-time. Killie needed only to hold the line and the title was theirs.

But disaster struck in the second period as Leith took the lead for the third time. Killie winger **Bob Findlay** let fly with a shot shouting at the Leith players to let it through. Incredibly, they did just that. Killie were level again at 3-3 and the title was theirs for the second season running.

That was the last League meeting between the sides for over 30 years. Leith were briefly in the top flight in the early 1930s, during which period Killie picked up full points away for the first time. On March 12th 1932 there was a simply amazing game which saw Killie fall 3-0 behind at home. Despite only having pulled one back by the break, they went on to win **6-3. John Aitken, Willie Connell** and **'Bud' Maxwell** all scored two each. *Killie even missed two penalties!*

The last time the teams ever met on League duty was in January 1948 with Killie winning **6-2** at Rugby Park.

There were three **Scottish Cup** clashes and Killie won them all, including two away from home. Despite going behind at Rugby Park in 1898, Killie won a second round tie **9-2!** Two goals from **Andy Cunningham** gave them a 2-0 win away at the same stage in 1912. And a hard-fought tie played at **Easter Road** saw Killie emerge victorious 3-2 in a first round game in 1928.

LINTHOUSE

Games	8	
League	8	1895-99
Top Scorer	Davie Maitland 6	All SL
Top Home Crowd	2,000 Feb 1st 1896 SL	
Top Away Crowd	2,000 Mar 19th 1898 SL	

Linthouse were a Govan-based team who walked hand-in-hand with Kilmarnock into Scottish League membership. They not only joined at the same time as Killie, they received the same number of votes. But that was where the similarities ended. For there was already a well-established club in Govan, by name of Glasgow Rangers. There was little support for another team and Linthouse struggled to survive.

Killie completed a 'double' over Linthouse in their first season, but managed just one point the following year. They did the 'double' again in 1897-98 and once more in 1898-99, winning **8-0** at Rugby Park, a match in which **Jim Howie** scored four goals.

The 3-0 away victory that season was to be the last time the teams met. The next year saw Kilmarnock in the top flight. It was also the last of Linthouse's five seasons in the League. The two teams may have come in together, but for Killie it was upward and onward while for the Govan side it was obscurity followed by extinction.

LIVINGSTON (MEADOWBANK THISTLE)

Games	27	
League	24	1983-85, 87-89, 90-93
Scottish Cup	2	1992
League Cup	1	1999
Top Scorer	Colin Harkness 5	All SL
	Bobby Williamson 5	All SL
Top Home Crowd	6,565 Aug 18th 1998 LC	
Top Away Crowd	2,301 Jan 25th 1992 SC	

It was hardly a day to put the flags out when Kilmarnock entertained **Meadowbank Thistle**, as **Livingston** were then known, for the first time on September 14th 1983. Only 1,028 spectators bothered to watch as Killie won the First Division match 3-1. But even that pitiful attendance was almost double the number who watched the Rugby Park fixture later in the season. 539 saw a 1-1 draw.

It was a measure of how far Killie had fallen in the game that they were playing Meadowbank at all. For *Livvy's* previous incarnation was nothing like the go-ahead progressive outfit of today. Meadowbank had been a non-league works team by name of **Ferranti Thistle** who had been invited to join the League to make up the numbers and to act as cannon fodder for others.

That they had managed to gain promotion within eight years was quite an achievement considering that they played in an athletics stadium in front of crowds often as low as 200. They even proved good enough to come back after relegation and actually finished second in 1987-88. As only one club went up that season they were denied promotion. But it showed what could be done with limited resources. Meanwhile, Killie were struggling badly and defeats both at home and away to Meadowbank were no rarity.

It was only when the Kilmarnock phoenix emerged from the ashes of the Second Division that they began to record regular victories over Meadowbank. One in particular has gone down in the record books.

It was a midweek end-of-season match on April 10th 1991 watched by just over 1,000 fans. A tight game was the general forecast. But when two goals from **Calum Campbell** wrapped around one from **Billy Stark** put Killie 3-0 up with less than fifteen minutes played, that prognosis was dead and buried.

Bobby Williamson notched up Killie's fourth and fifth before **Trevor Smith** made it 6-0 at the break. **Tommy Burns** added a seventh then a huge cheer went around the ground as Meadowbank pulled one back. Burns grabbed another to make the final score **8-1**, Killie's best away win in modern times.

But Meadowbank could still be awkward opponents as they proved earlier in the same season, coming back from 2-0 down after 45 minutes to win 3-2 at Rugby Park. Not the most memorable of starts for the new Killie striker making his debut that day – one **Bobby Williamson.**

The clubs solitary **Scottish Cup** meeting the next season was a different matter. Lucky to leave Edinburgh with a 1-1 draw, by virtue of an **Ally Mitchell** strike, Killie found themselves a goal down at the break in the third round replay at home. **Hugh Burns** saved some face by scoring the goal which took the tie into extra time. With no further scoring, the game was decided on penalties. Killie lost out 4-3; their

penalty misses coming from opposite ends of the age spectrum – teenage substitute (and debutant) **Mark Roberts** and veteran **Tommy Burns**.

The only game against Livingston, as opposed to Meadowbank, that took place prior to the 2001-02 season was a third round **League Cup** game in 1998-99. A **Paul Wright** goal gave Killie the first half lead but Livvy levelled just after the break. It took an extra time goal from substitute **Ally McCoist** to put Killie back in front before Wright added a third near the end to give the scoreline a more comfortable look.

Not this time. **Ally Mitchell's** face is a picture of despair after a missed opportunity against **Meadowbank.**

LOCHGELLY

Lochgelly had been a League team for a short period either side of the First World War. They had lost League status several seasons before they arrived at Rugby Park for a first round Scottish Cup tie in 1933 and this was their only opportunity to play against top calibre opposition.

Killie, losing Finalists the previous year, didn't treat their Fife opponents lightly. It was a full-strength side which took the field in front of just over 3,500 spectators. And, once on the pitch, they went about their job clinically. Two goals from **'Bud' Maxwell** and one from **Campbell Gilmour** meant the tie was all but over by half-time. Killie eased up in the second half and Lochgelly managed to pull a goal back to make it 3-1 at the finish.

For Killie a job done well. For Lochgelly the satisfaction of avoiding a massacre like they had suffered the previous year when they lost **13-3** away to Hearts. But for Lochgelly, it was also to be a sad occasion. They never played in the Scottish Cup proper again.

LOKOMOTIV LEIPZIG

Lokomotiv Leipzig were strongly fancied to dispose of Kilmarnock in the Quarter-Finals of the **Fairs Cup** in 1967. After all, the **East German** outfit had already beaten strong opposition from **Sweden** and **Belgium** in the competition then surpassed all expectations by eliminating the star-studded **Benfica** side in the third round. If they could get past *Eusebio, Simoes, Torres, Coluna* and co, then surely Kilmarnock wouldn't be much of a threat?

After just three minutes it seemed the 'experts' were right as Leipzig snatched the lead in their **Zentralstadion** home. Killie had a real job on their hands just to keep the score down. Superb defending and some excellent goalkeeping by **Bobby Ferguson** enabled the Ayrshire team to reach the interval without further loss.

Four minutes into the second half, Killie's prospects suffered a savage blow when influential inside-forward **Gerry Queen** was sent off for retaliation. Forced to play for 40 minutes with ten men, Killie relied on Ferguson to be at his best. Fortunately, he was, demonstrating the kind of form which had earned him the *'Player of the Year'* award from the fans. At 1-0, Killie had a great chance to progress.

The second leg was almost a mirror image of the first. It was Killie who scored early in the game, **Eric Murray** netting in eight minutes. And it was the German goalie **Weigang** who had to be on top of his game to prevent further loss. Save for the sending-off the two games were identical until the 63rd minute. That was when **Jim McFadzean** ran more than half the length of the park, shrugging aside challenge after challenge en route only to see the keeper parry his shot away.

But it fell right into the path of goal-snatcher supreme **Brien McIlroy** who prodded home to put Killie 2-0 up on the night, 2-1 on aggregate. That was enough. Killie were into the last four and Rugby Park was the scene for another crowd invasion as well over 15,000 fans acclaimed their team.

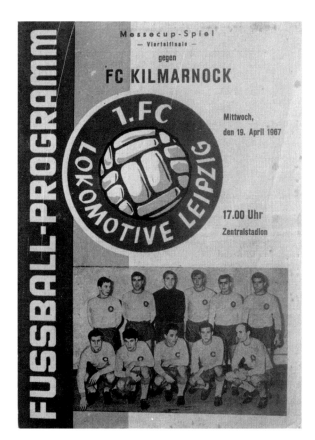

A 5pm kick-off after four months idle was Killie's re-introduction to Fairs Cup business in East Germany.

LUGAR BOSWELL

Killie faced **Lugar Boswell** twice in the Scottish Cup in the 1880s. Lugar didn't have a bad record in the national competition. They had forced the mighty **Vale of Leven** to a replay in a last sixteen tie a few years beforehand and claimed their place in the third round in the 1886-87 competition with a 6-1 thrashing of **Dalry**.

And at first they gave Killie a hard time at Rugby Park. The home team led by just 2-1 at the break. But the second half saw a reinvigorated Kilmarnock They ran riot, winning easily **7-2**.

Two years later Killie travelled to Lugar for a

first round tie. There was a similar pattern to the previous game. In a close first half Killie managed just a 1-0 lead. But after the break it was no contest, Killie winning **5-0**. Among the goalscorers that day was one **James Campbell**. The legendary *'Bummer'* scored his first Scottish Cup goal playing in an unfamiliar position on the left wing.

For Lugar, like so many others, their time in the national tourney was nearing its end. They had just one more season to play in the Cup before vanishing from the senior ranks.

MANTOVA

Kilmarnock were going well in their section in the **1963 New York** tournament when they played Italian team **Mantova**. In an entertaining first half **Bertie Black** and **Jim McFadzean** gave Killie a healthy-looking 2-0 lead. But it wasn't to last. The effects of a long season began to take their toll. It was Killie's *51st* competitive game and their fifth in less than three weeks in the States. So it wasn't a great surprise when the Italians fought back to level the match at 2-2.

What did come as a shock though was Mantova's attitude afterwards. They accused Killie of cheating, alleging that **Jim McFadzean** was an impostor. Of course the assertion was preposterous and the Italians were forced to back down. But it gave manager **Willie Waddell** an opportunity to demonstrate his scathing wit when he asked: *"Who did they think he was? Pele?"*

MAUCHLINE

Games	5	
Scottish Cup	5	1877, 80, 81, 83
Top Scorer	Hay, McSkimming, Thomson	
	all 1	

Nowadays Mauchline is renowned as a hotbed of Kilmarnock support. Strange to think that over 100 years ago **Mauchline FC** were one of Killie's greatest rivals. The teams clashed many times in friendlies and in local competitions but they were also drawn together four times in the Scottish Cup.

The first occasion was a second round tie in

1876-77 which Killie lost 2-1 at home. Kilmarnock's objection to Mauchline's winning goal was upheld by the match referee but overturned by the SFA who awarded the tie to Mauchline and declared that the result should stand.

But if there had been any doubts about that result there could be no objections the next time the teams met. Killie were soundly beaten **6-2** away in another second round tie in 1879-80. In a third round clash the next season Mauchline 'won' 2-1 before what was thought to be a disappointing crowd of around 3,000. Killie immediately found cause to issue another protest, claiming that the game hadn't lasted a full 90 minutes.

This time the SFA backed Kilmarnock and ordered the match to be replayed. Killie came back with a 3-3 draw to take the tie to Rugby Park. But hopes that home advantage might

prove decisive were dashed as Mauchline won easily, 3-0

Two years later, in a first round tie, Kilmarnock beat their bogey team at last. A goal in each half from **McSkimming** and **Hay** gave Killie a 2-0 home success. *It was the first time that the proud men of Mauchline had been eliminated from the trophy at the first time of asking.*

The side, which had once reached the last eight, struggled on for a few more years, but fell victim to the post-1891 structure of the competition, never appearing after that date.

MONTREAL CONCORDIA

Killie came up against the exotically named **Montreal Concordia** in the 1961 **New York** tournament. Despite the name of the competition Killie actually played four of their seven matches in Montreal. Unsurprisingly, in view of the opposition, this was one such.

The first half didn't exactly see the Scottish representatives hit top form and they reached the break level with their hosts at 1-1. Killie upped the stakes in the second half, winning

comfortably in the end 4-2. The goals came from **Bertie Black, Jackie McInally** and two from **Andy Kerr**.

Kerr had equalled **'Peerie' Cunningham's** League record for Killie of 34 goals. His two goals in this match were his last of the season and brought his tally in all competitions to 45, establishing a record which stands to this day. Given the way the modern game is played it is possible it may last forever.

MONTROSE

Games	30	
League	24	1973-74, 75-76, 77-79, 85-87, 89-90, 91-92
Scottish Cup	4	1931, 69, 82
League Cup	2	1975
Top Scorer	Iain McCulloch 4	All SL
	George Maxwell 4	3 SL 1 LC
Top Home Crowd	7,385 Feb 12th 1969 SC	
Top Away Crowd	3,000 Feb 14th 1931 SC	

Games against **Montrose** have been few and far between. Killie won both matches when they first clashed in the old Division Two in 1973-74 but took just one point when the teams next met two seasons later. This was the first season of the new set-up and Montrose enjoyed the best season in their history. They reached the last four of the League Cup, last eight of the Scottish Cup

and finished third in the table, one place behind Killie. Despite their success this season they were never really contenders for promotion. Killie and Partick Thistle got away from the pack early in the season and stayed well in front.

Although they have proved to be troublesome opponents occasionally on their own **Links**

Park turf, Montrose have never really bothered Killie at Rugby Park. Their last League visit resulted in a **5-1** Kilmarnock victory in 1991-92. Indeed, Kilmarnock are unbeaten at home against them in all competitions and have also won the majority of matches away.

The clubs met twice in the **Scottish Cup** before they faced each other in the League. Killie won 3-0 away to then non-league Montrose in a third round game in 1931 but found them to be stiffer opponents in 1969. Trailing at the break, it took a goal from **Eddie Morrison** to force a replay. The Rugby Park match was an altogether easier affair. Morrison netted again and **Tommy McLean** scored a hat-trick as Killie won 4-1.

John Bourke scored the only goal the last time the teams met in the Cup in a third round Rugby Park tie in 1982. Killie also took three of the four points on offer in 1974-75 - the only time they ever met in the **League Cup**.

A crucial victory here set up the last-day crunch match with Cowdenbeath.

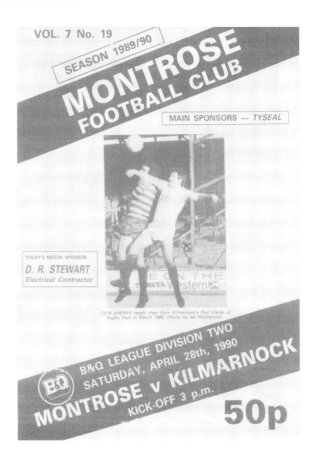

MORTON

Games	164	
League	139	1895-99, 1900-27, 29-33, 37-38, 46-47, 49-50, 52-54, 64-66,
		67-73, 74-76, 77-78, 79-81, 82-84, 85-87, 88-89, 90-93
Scottish Cup	8	1920, 66, 71, 94, 95, 97
League Cup	10	1954, 68, 79, 80, 93, 94
Other	7	1918, 40, 46, 92, 93
Top Scorer	Willie Culley 10	All SL
Top Home Crowd	19,245 Jan 7th 1950 SL	
Top Away Crowd	10,306 Dec 12th 1964 SL	
Highest Overall	50,000 Mar 27th 1920 SC	(Hampden)

Rivalry with **Morton** stretches right back to Kilmarnock's first season in the League in 1895-96. They were the second side to visit Rugby Park in the League and **Cappielow** was the scene of Killie's first away win in League football.

Even when Killie reached the top division, Morton weren't far behind them, being elevated to that sphere twelve months afterwards. And there were some cracking games played too. Killie's first home game in 1902-03 was against the Greenock men. Killie started poorly and were soon two goals down. In the second half a frantic fifteen minutes saw them go 3-2 up. Morton then missed a penalty before Killie rounded off an amazing fightback by scoring again to win 4-2.

Killie had a fine record at home against Morton

and although Cappielow was always a difficult venue they picked up a few wins there too. But the start of the 1920-21 season brought disaster there. Killie had a nightmare of a match, 6-1 down at the break they ended up losing **9-2.**

Morton's heyday was during the First World War and its immediate aftermath. For the rest of the inter-war period they found it difficult to survive in the top flight and relegation was a constant threat and sometimes reality. This gave Killie opportunities to exact some sort of revenge for the 9-2 hammering. And in February 1930 they seized their chance winning **7-2** at home. **Bobby McGowan**, on loan from **Rangers,** hit *five* of the goals that day. He was the first Killie player to do so in the League. This was part of a great run at home. Between 1924-1978 Killie lost just one League match to Morton at Rugby Park.

Those who complain about fixture congestion today should consider the problems Killie faced in 1938 when they had to play four matches in seven days.

It didn't help that the first two of these happened to be the Cup Final and a replay that went to extra time. But after Killie lost to **East Fife** on the Wednesday they were faced with a trip to **Tynecastle** on the Saturday. *Before that they had to play Morton at Rugby Park on the Friday!*

If nothing hinged on those games then things wouldn't have been too bad. But Kilmarnock were fighting for their lives. After nearly 40 years in the top flight, relegation stared them in the face.

To make matters worse, injuries had decimated the team. Killie were forced to make five changes and two players – goalkeeper **John McIntyre** and left winger **Martin Borthwick** – were making their debuts.

This pair performed sterling service but it was the three other replacements who were the heroes of the hour. **Robert Gallacher** was playing at inside-right for the first time, **Hamilton Henry** in his first game since

November and **John Gillespie** in his first outing since Christmas Day scored the goals which beat Morton 3-0 and kept Kilmarnock in Division One.

The biggest crowd at Rugby Park for this game came on January 7th 1950 when Killie took on a Morton side who boasted the proud title of *only undefeated side in Britain*. A claim that was buried in Ayrshire thanks to a 2-0 home victory. Morton went up that season but they were back in the 'B' Division two years later.

1953-54 was to see Kilmarnock gain promotion but the league campaign got off to a dreadful start. Three straight defeats left Killie at the bottom of the table. No points and no goals. Hardly the right preparation for a visit to Cappielow. But Killie began to turn their season round in Greenock. Ahead 4-1 at the break, they eventually won **6-4.** Killie's participants in this goal feast were **Willie Harvey (2), Gerry Mays (2), Davie Curlett** and **Tommy Henaughan**.

There were no further League meetings until Morton rejoined the top flight in 1964-65. And Cappielow was again the scene for an amazing match, but this time it was one that Killie would want to forget.

By December 1964 Killie had played fifteen League matches and were unbeaten with eleven wins and four draws. They led the League on goal average from **Hearts**, one of only two teams they had yet to play. The other was Morton. And on December 12th Killie took their unbeaten record to Cappielow and left it trampled underfoot in the Greenock mud. Two down at the break, things got worse in the second half as Killie were taken apart. **5-1** was the final score. A sore defeat to take for a side that had conceded just nine league goals up to that point. It was also the largest attendance at Cappielow for this fixture.

In a season of consistency it was an inexplicable aberration. Not even the absence of **Jackie McGrory** through injury could explain away the defeat. For Killie had won 2-0 against Falkirk the week beforehand with McGrory also absent. Sometimes matches come along which provide results with neither rhyme nor reason. This was one such game.

Ronnie Hamilton, Killie's lone scorer that day, also scored at Cappielow the next season while **Brien McIlroy** added a hat-trick in Killie's 4-1 win there. Revenge hadn't taken long.

There was an entertaining game in the 1971-72 season which saw Killie win 4-2 thanks to goals from **Jimmy Cook (2), John Gilmour** and **Ross Mathie**. It was also the last time League football was played at Rugby Park on Christmas Day.

The arrival of the *Premier Division* in 1975 meant that clubs like Killie and Morton were often either vying for a place in the top flight or battling to stay there. But in the 1982-83 season it was apparent from early on that these were the two clubs going down. Killie won only *three* League games all season. But two of them were against Morton! There was a 3-1 home win in November 1982 with **Jim Clark, Brian Gallacher** and **John Bourke** scoring the goals. And the following March came Killie's best performance of the term as they won, again at home, **4-0**. Gallacher netted twice with **Sammy McGivern** and **Paul Clarke** completing the scoring.

Several First Division meetings followed but the clubs haven't met in the League since Killie's promotion to the Premier in 1993. In recent seasons Morton have concentrated more on simple survival than on rejoining the game's elite.

Morton first played in the **Scottish Cup** in 1877. In the 116 years thereafter they and Kilmarnock were drawn together just *three* times. *In the four years after that they were drawn together another three times!*

But if the pre-1990s meetings were few, they were always dramatic. Their first clash was a Semi-Final at **Hampden** in 1920. Killie were affected by the occasion more than Morton,

John Bourke is thwarted by the keeper in this Rugby Park clash with Morton.

though neither side was used to playing in front of 50,000 spectators. But the Greenock team were more composed and it was little surprise that they went 2-0 up. Even though Killie pulled a goal back before half-time, they didn't look like winning the game. But what a difference a break makes. The roles were reversed in the second half as Killie took control, brought themselves back into the game with an equaliser and eventually won 3-2 to put themselves back into the Final after a 22-year absence. **JR Smith** with two goals and **Malcolm McPhail** with the other were the heroes of the hour.

If Morton were downcast it didn't last too long. Two years later they won the Cup for the only time in their history.

The first round meeting in 1966 was a tense affair. Kilmarnock were reigning League champions. Morton fighting (unsuccessfully in the end) against the drop. But the old saw about the Cup being a leveller proved to be correct when Morton took the lead at Cappielow. But **Gerry Queen**, recently signed from St Mirren, so already a demon in Greenock eyes, was in terrific form and he scored the goal that took the tie to Rugby Park where the result was never in doubt. Queen struck again and so did **Frank Beattie** and **Bertie Black** as Killie won 3-0.

The fourth round tie in 1971 at Cappielow was a close affair which Killie edged 2-1 to keep their Cup record against Morton intact. It was 1994 before the teams met again but once more it was a tense fourth round tie in Greenock which was determined in Killie's favour by a first half goal from **Bobby Williamson**.

When Killie could only manage a goalless draw at home in the third round the next season, it looked like they had blown their chance. But **Stevie Maskrey** came off the substitutes bench to score twice as Killie won 2-1 at Cappielow after extra time.

The last time they met was at the Quarter-Final stage in 1997 and Morton fancied their chances of finally beating Killie as the teams met at Cappielow once again. Killie looked to have the game wrapped up by half-time as **John Henry** put them ahead in thirteen minutes, **Paul Wright** added a second after half an hour and Henry made it 3-0 five minutes from the interval.

Bu Morton came out with all guns blazing in the second half and **Alan Mahood** pulled a goal back after ten minutes play. Seven minutes later Mahood grabbed another. He may be a hero to the Killie support now but Alan Mahood was hardly the object of their affections then.

Just as things looked like turning Morton's way, **Jim McIntyre** stepped in four minutes later to make it 4-2 and steady Killie nerves. With two minutes remaining Henry secured his hat-trick to make the final score 5-2 and take Kilmarnock one step closer to glory at Ibrox.

Killie took four points and conceded no goals on their way to winning the section when the teams first met in the **League Cup** in 1953-54. In their next meeting, in the last eight in 1967-68, Killie lost the first leg 3-2 away but were fancied to

overturn the deficit at Rugby Park. Despite support from a crowd in excess of 14,000 it was a disappointing night as they lost 2-1 on the evening, 5-3 on aggregate.

Killie hoped to make up for that defeat in a third round tie in 1978-79. Goals from **Joe Cairney** and **George Maxwell** gave them a 2-0 lead to defend at Cappielow. It wasn't enough. Killie lost 5-2 after extra time to go out 5-4 on aggregate. Twelve months later the teams met in the last eight and this tie proved to be a classic.

Both sides were going strong in the Premier Division at the time. In fact, Morton topped the table. The first leg at Cappielow ended 3-2 in the Greenock team's favour but those goals from **Stuart McLean** and **Bobby Street** gave Killie hope that they could turn things around at Rugby Park.

Killie pressed for most of the match but Morton looked comfortable in defence. There were just under twenty minutes remaining when **Paul Clarke** cracked in a fierce shot from twelve yards to take the game into extra time.

Within two minutes **Joe Cairney** scored to put Killie ahead on aggregate. Three minutes later it was all square again as Morton scored. So it stayed until the second period of extra time got under way. Shortly into the final fifteen minutes Morton's **Jim Tolmie** scored a classic solo goal after beating five men. Now Killie were behind again.

Bu they weren't finished yet. **Ian Gibson** made it 3-2 to Killie and 5-5 on aggregate. Now it was down to penalty kicks.

Morton went first and scored. Killie replied. After six penalties it was 3-3. Tolmie took the seventh and duly scored. Now it was **Bobby Street's** turn. Street's effort was hit with venom but it cracked off the crossbar. Morton scored with their fifth to win the tie.

There were those who reckoned it had been the finest match seen at Rugby Park since Eintracht.

That may have been exaggeration but it was a tremendous exhibition of football, laced with tension throughout, even if the players didn't quite merit the knighthoods one Sunday paper thought they deserved. Killie were left to rue the fact that had 'European' rules applied, Killie would have won in regulation time on account of their away goals.

Kilmarnock finally managed a League Cup win at Cappielow in 1992-93. It was another terrific match which saw Killie fall behind. Again it went to extra time before a winner could be found. But two magnificent goals from **Tommy Burns** and another from **Ross Jack** gave the Ayrshire team a 3-2 victory. But while Killie held the upper hand in the Scottish Cup, it seemed Morton did likewise in the League Cup and when the teams clashed again in the second round at Rugby Park it was Morton who emerged as winners by 2-1 in 1993-94.

It seemed these teams just couldn't avoid meeting one another in the 1990s. They were even drawn together twice in succession in the

B&Q Cup for non-Premier teams, with Morton winning twice. All told they were paired off seven times in five years with both having varying degrees of success. But that last Scottish Cup meeting was undoubtedly the most important of them all. It reinforced the belief that 1997 was going to be Kilmarnock's year.

Extra time joy for Killie in this League Cup encounter at Cappielow thanks to a spectacular goal from **Tommy Burns**.

MOTHERWELL

Games	196	
League	167	1895-99, 1903-47, 53-68, 69-73, 74-75, 76-77, 81-83,
		84-85, 93-2001
Scottish Cup	10	1897, 1933, 60, 66, 70, 77, 88
League Cup	7	1954, 55, 72, 90
Other	12	1940, 46, 64, 65, 77
Top Scorer	'Bummer' Campbell 12	10 SL 2 SC
Top Home Crowd	29,412 Feb 27th 1960 SC	
Top Away Crowd	23,000 Mar 8th 1933 SC	

Motherwell were the first side to ever visit Rugby Park in the Scottish League. There were worries that crowds may not turn out to watch League football as admission prices had doubled from 3d to 6d (*1.25p to 2.5p*). But in the event there were around 2,000 in attendance at the match on **August 24th 1895** come the 4.00 kick-off. That doesn't sound like many but attendances have to be put into perspective. The

first Old Firm League match attracted a crowd of just 8,000 and that was regarded as a big turnout.

Motherwell put a bit of a damper on proceedings by taking the lead but outside-right **David Watson** equalised, thus claiming the honour of scoring the first home goal in the League. Killie took the lead and after the break they simply destroyed Motherwell, running in goal after goal to end Rugby Park's introduction to the Scottish League with the resounding scoreline: **KILMARNOCK 7 MOTHERWELL 1. Richard Cox,** the Killie left-winger scored the first hat-trick.

The following year over 500 supporters made the trek to Glasgow on a rainy day in December to see Killie beat Motherwell 4-1 in the **Scottish Qualifying Cup Final** at **Hampden**. *It was the first trophy won by Killie at national level.*

Four years after Kilmarnock were elected to Division One Motherwell joined them in that exalted company. At first Killie had the upper hand, especially at Rugby Park. But after World War One, the 'Well developed into a potent force and Killie suffered some heavy beatings. Particularly in 1922-23 when they lost **6-0** at home.

For over a decade Motherwell were the most serious challengers to the **Old Firm** and in 1931-32 they captured the championship – the only non-Old Firm title winners between 1904-48. They lost just twice all season and one of those games was at Rugby Park. 12,000 watched as **'Bud' Maxwell** gave Killie a victory over the champions-to-be. It was Killie's only home League victory over Motherwell from 1929-47.

At **Fir Park** Killie found it even tougher, going from 1929-54 without picking up full points. 1953-54 was Kilmarnock's seventh successive season in the lower division and they were struggling to establish their promotion-challenging credentials until they visited leaders Motherwell. The game was heading for a 0-0 draw until Killie's **Willie *'Puskas'* Harvey** struck, scoring twice within a minute to record the first Fir Park success for a quarter of a century,

'Well had already booked their place in Division One by the time they visited Rugby Park with four games to play. But for Kilmarnock victory was absolutely essential as they strove to join the Lanarkshire side in the top flight and a fine 4-2 success kept them on course to end their seven-year exile.

It was time now for Killie to take control of this fixture From 1962-83 they remained unbeaten at Rugby Park. And there were some spectacular triumphs during this period. In December 1960 Killie won a thrilling game **5-3,** having led **3-2** at half-time. **Andy Kerr** scored four of the goals with **Jackie McInally** getting the other.

In October 1962 there was another quite incredible game. Leading just 2-1 at the break, Killie really turned on the style in the second half, to win **7-1.** Amazingly the goals came from *seven* different players! And in November 1965 the reigning Scottish champions thrashed Motherwell **5-0** with four of the goals coming in the second half.

Although things were more difficult at Fir Park, Killie still enjoyed some success there. Sometimes even in defeat there would be a match to remember. Such was the case in the Premier Division in November 1976. In a wonderful exhibition of football from both teams, Killie led 2-0 at the interval only to lose out **5-4.** That was the sixth defeat in a run of twelve in succession away to Motherwell. Indeed Killie went from 1968-96 without a win at Fir Park.

Once that losing streak came to an end, Killie found Fir Park to be a friendlier place with four more victories since then. Including a wonderful 4-0 win in February 2000 when all the goals came from Killie's *French 'Foreign Legion.'* Both **Jerome Vareille** and **Christophe Cocard** scored twice.

The **Scottish Cup** has seen plenty of crucial matches between the clubs. Killie had to play Motherwell in the Scottish Cup proper for the first time in a first round tie just over a month after their Qualifying Cup win. After forcing a 3-3 draw away, they reprised their Hampden triumph with a **5-2** replay win at home.

Kilmarnock also fancied their chances the next time the teams clashed, in a quarter-final tie in

Paul Wright scores from the spot against Motherwell. Wright's goal in January 1996 gave Killie their first League win at Fir Park since 1968.

1933. After all Killie had reached the Final the previous year, losing to **Rangers** after a replay. And they had just eliminated the Ibrox side from the competition. The match with Motherwell drew a crowd of 20,658 to Rugby Park who watched Killie come back from behind to force a 3-3 draw.

23,000 – *the biggest attendance at Fir Park for the fixture* – saw the replay. Killie fell three goals behind to the then Scottish champions at the interval and in a goalscoring extravaganza after the break, ended up losing **8-3**.

When the teams next met, in a third round clash in 1960, it was Killie's turn for a record gate. **29,412** were in attendance – **the largest Rugby Park crowd for *any* game apart from the Old Firm.** And they were rewarded with two **Jackie McInally** goals in the second half which gave Killie victory and kept them on the road to Hampden.

Having already won the Rugby Park League

match 5-0 a second round visit from the Lanarkshire team in the Scottish Cup in 1966 hardly had Killie quaking in their boots. What few could have envisaged through was that Killie would win by the same score again. Over 13,000 saw another **5-0** triumph with goals from five different players – including an own goal!

In a quarter-final tie at Fir Park in 1970, Killie were under the cosh for long periods in the first half. But, having survived the storm, they took control after the break and a **Ross Mathie** header halfway through the second half was good enough to send them into the last four. Sadly, their next trip to Motherwell on Cup business was less successful, losing 3-0 in a third round tie in 1977. The tie was effectively over by half-time, all the goals being scored by then.

By 1988 Killie were struggling to retain First Division status while 'Well were an established Premier side. But the indomitable Ayrshire spirit was shown by more than 2,000 fans – more than usually watched home games – who travelled to Motherwell and saw a superb goalkeeping performance from **Allan McCulloch** help Killie to a 0-0 draw. But the pattern around this time was always the same. Draw with a Premier team away, take them to Rugby Park, and put up a good fight. And lose. This tie was no different as Killie, having kept it goalless at the break, went down 3-1 in the replay.

In the **League Cup** the teams were drawn in the same section two years running. Firstly, in 1953-54 they exchanged home victories. Fir Park was Killie's only sectional loss as they went through to the last eight. The next season saw Motherwell win both matches as they marched all the way to the Final where they lost to Hearts.

By 1971-72 and their next League Cup meeting, much had changed in football. Particularly crowds. Whereas over 21,000 had seen the last League Cup game with Motherwell at Rugby Park, now there were only a little more than 5,000 in attendance. And at Fir Park the crowd had slumped from 17,000 to less than 3,500. Both teams won their home games but neither progressed beyond the sectional stage.

There has only been one meeting since the League Cup became a straight knockout tournament. Killie lost 4-1 at home in 1989-90. Hardly a surprising result as they were then in the Second Division.

Kilmarnock have met Motherwell far more times in other recognised first class fixtures than any other club – *twelve* in total. There were two meetings in the aborted 1939-40 League season

and two in the wartime Western League in the unofficial 1945-46 term. The clubs also met in both Summer Cup campaigns in the mid-1960s. The latter of these saw Killie surprisingly lose out to Motherwell in the group stage. The Fir Parkers went on to win the trophy.

Finally, there was the Anglo-Scottish Cup in 1976-77 when after gaining a 1-1 draw away Killie won the second leg easily 4-0.

Fir Park held no fear for Killie in the 1990s, though they lost this closely-contested game 1-0.

NENTORI 17 TIRANA

Albania was uncharted territory as far as Kilmarnock were concerned when they travelled there to play in the **European Cup** in 1965. The team were forced to fly to **London**, then on to **Rome** before their chartered *Alitalia* flight took them to **Tirana**. It was touch and go. The Albanian authorities insisted the flight had to arrive before dusk or it wouldn't be allowed to land. In his centenary history of Killie, '*Go Fame...*', the late **Hugh Taylor** tells of the fear experienced by all on board as they were hit by a lightning storm. And of how, when landing, armed police wouldn't even say where the game would be played or at what time.

Taylor also goes on to relate just how friendly the Albanians were the following day when nothing was too much trouble for them.

At this time Albania was almost cut off from the rest of Europe. Under its eccentric leader **Enver Hoxha** it followed a *Maoist* path, deliberately isolating itself from outside influence. If a foreigner arrived with long hair, it was cut before they could enter the country. Fortunately the Kilmarnock team were a clean-cut crew. Beatles-style moptops were nowhere in sight.

Killie's opponents **17 Nentori Tirana** took their name from the date (November 17th 1944) when Hoxha's partisans and their Soviet and Yugoslav allies liberated the Albanian capital from Axis rule. It was not only their first ever game in Europe, it was the first by any Albanian team.

The term '*unknown quantity*' could have been invented for them. Everything had been done to make the game as comfortable for the home team as was possible. Kick-off was 3.30pm in blazing heat and with the factories being given a day off, there were 30,000 in the **Qemal Stafa** stadium to watch the game.

Killie skipper **Frank Beattie** laughed off the heat, saying the club had played in hotter conditions in New York. But the opposition couldn't be shrugged off so easily. The Albanians turned out to be a skilful lot, particularly, as Taylor notes, their midfield. As he put it, they attacked Killie "*with everything but their Chinese allies.*"

Killie defended in depth for much of the match and the 0-0 draw they emerged with was a fine result achieved in difficult circumstances.

The return leg at Rugby Park saw Killie well on top but it was late in the day – less than fifteen minutes remaining – before **Bertie Black** scored the only goal of the game to put Killie into the last sixteen and send close on 16,000 supporters home happy.

NEW YORK AMERICANS

The **New York Americans** were ostensibly the host team in the **1960 New York** tournament, although they encompassed players from different nationalities. They were the last team Killie faced in their section. And with Burnley still capable of catching them if they slipped up, it was a game Killie needed to win if they were to clinch the group and meet Bangu in the Final.

The game itself was played in the **Roosevelt Stadium** in **Jersey City.** The effects of a long season were definitely in evidence as Killie were more lethargic in this match than in others. But they were still too good for their hosts. **Jackie McInally, Billy Muir** and an own goal helped them to a 3-1 win over their hosts in front of 11,704 spectators.

Killie met the same opposition in the same competition the next year. But as it was earlier in their itinerary (their third match), a fresher Kilmarnock team won easily 4-0, with **Bertie Black, Hugh Brown, Andy Kerr** and **Matt Watson** all scoring.

The crowd on this occasion was only 7,000. An indication that despite the best efforts of Kilmarnock and the other sides taking part that the American public really weren't taking to the game in any great numbers.

NICE

Games	3	
UEFA	2	
Other	1	
Top Scorer	Jackie McInally 1	Oth
	Mark Reilly 1	UEFA
	Paul Wright 1	UEFA
Top Home Crowd	8,402 Oct 2nd 1997 UEFA	
Top Away Crowd	10,812 Sep 18th 1997 UEFA	

Nice were not the unknowns some opponents were in the **1960 New York** tourney. For having beaten **Rangers** in the **European Cup** a few seasons beforehand, Killie knew that the French side had to be respected. They had won the French title four times in the previous nine years and had reached the quarter-finals of the European Cup this same season. And although beaten by mighty Real Madrid, they had defeated the Spanish legends in their home leg.

It may have added further insult to **Burnley's** pride, but as far as Kilmarnock were concerned, Nice were their most dangerous opponents in America.

And it showed too. The French played well and for much of the match were the better team. But **Jackie McInally's** goal ensured Killie a 1-1 draw. It may have been a point dropped but it was the only one in the section and it kept Killie at the top of the group, ready for their showdown with the New York Americans.

It was 37 years before the teams paths crossed again. In 1997 Nice, like Kilmarnock, had been busy on two fronts domestically. Unlike Killie they couldn't avoid relegation, finishing bottom of the table, twelve points adrift of the nearest side. But, just like Killie, they won their national Cup Final. Again, like Killie it was their third success. For Nice it was also their first trophy since their golden age in the 1950s.

So it was that the teams met in the **1997-98 European Cup-Winners Cup.** The Kilmarnock support was happy with the draw. After being exiled from Europe since 1970 the draw had

taken them firstly to the **Republic of Ireland,** now to the **French Riviera.** All things considered, there are worse places to spend a few days.

The first leg started badly for Killie as they went behind after only thirteen minutes. After that it was a major effort to reach the dressing rooms still just one goal behind. But all that first half effort was undone three minutes after the restart

A visit to the French Riviera was just what the supporters wanted even if the result wasn't to their liking.

when the French side doubled their lead. But Killie were undaunted. They began to force their way into the match and make some attacks of their own. They received their reward with a penalty twelve minutes from time, coolly converted by **Paul Wright**. But while the fans were still celebrating, Nice scored again to leave Killie facing a 3-1 deficit in the home leg.

Needing to win 2-0 at home the task was difficult but not impossible as the teams prepared to do battle at Rugby Park. An injury to **Kohn,** who had scored twice in France, forced him to leave the field before ten minutes were played. Nice's misfortune was Killie's opportunity but the early goal many considered to be crucial was unforthcoming. But, just as in the first leg, Killie kept plugging away and a

Mark Reilly strike just after the half-hour mark, sparked renewed hope both on the pitch and in the stands.

One more goal needed and an hour to get it. But the French defence was impregnable. As time dragged by Kilmarnock began to commit more men forward in search of the winner, thus leaving themselves vulnerable to a counter-attack. And, with fourteen minutes remaining Nice equalised. It was a dagger blow to the Kilmarnock heart. Now, with time running out, they needed to score twice just to take the game to extra time. Despite an almost immediate double substitution, with **Nevin** and **Roberts** replacing **Mitchell** and **Vareille**, there was to be no last minute goal rush from Kilmarnock. Their first venture into Europe for over a quarter of a century was over.

NITHSDALE WANDERERS

Games	4	
Scottish Cup	4	1904, 13
Top Scorer	James Blair 2	Both SC
Top Home Crowd	6,000 Jan 25th 1913 SC	
Top Away Crowd	900 Jan 23rd 1904 SC	

Sanquhar side **Nithsdale Wanderers** were Kilmarnock's first round **Scottish Cup** opponents in 1904. It was Killie's worst season since joining the top flight. They were bottom of the table and destined to go begging for re-election at the end of the season. So the fact that they found the game at Nithsdale's **Crawick Holm** ground a struggle was not too surprising. They were lucky to come back from Sanquhar with a 2-2 draw.

But if that result was bad, the replay at Rugby Park was even worse. First Division Kilmarnock struggled to a 1-1 draw with their non-League opponents. The tie went to a third game – also at

Rugby Park – and again it finished 1-1. Fortunately for Kilmarnock there were thirty minutes of extra time to be played and this period allowed the superior fitness of the League side to tell as Killie scraped a lucky 2-1 win.

Nithsdale visited Rugby Park again in the same round nine years later. But Killie were a more formidable outfit by then. They were only a goal up at half-time, sparking off fears of another embarrassing encounter with the Wanderers. But Killie tightened their grip on the game in the second half and ran out comfortable 3-0 winners at the end.

NOTTINGHAM FOREST

Nottingham Forest were Killie's opponents in the quarter-finals of the **Anglo-Scottish Cup** in 1976-77. Forest were a fast-emerging side managed by the inimitable **Brian Clough**, on track for promotion to the English First Division. So for Killie to return from the **City Ground** with just a 2-1 deficit, thanks to a **Gordon Smith** goal was quite an achievement.

Ian Fallis struck for Killie in the home leg but Forest equalised after half-time. Fallis scored again to make it 2-1 to Killie after 90 minutes. With the teams locked together at 3-3 on aggregate, the game went into extra time. It was then that the superior fitness of the full-time team told and Forest managed to tie the game on the night and take the tie 4-3 overall.

With basically the same squad of players Clough and Forest would go on to become **English champions** a year later and win the **European Cup** the year after that. *When put into that perspective, it can be seen that Kilmarnock put up a truly valiant fight against a highly talented team.*

NOTTS COUNTY

Four years after meeting their city neighbours, Kilmarnock came up against **Notts County** in the **Anglo-Scottish Cup**. Although not possessing the glamour names of their neighbours, County still had a fine team. One that was good enough to earn them promotion to the top flight in England for the first time in nearly 60 years.

Players like Scottish internationalists **Don Masson** and **Eddie Kelly** weren't exactly unknown to the Rugby Park faithful. But the most familiar of them all was **Iain McCulloch**, sold by Killie to County for £80,000 in 1978.

For a **semi-final** there was a poor turnout of fewer than 3,000 at Rugby Park for the first leg.

They saw an entertaining first half which left Killie trailing 2-1. **Jimmy McBride** getting the goal for Killie. The second half saw no further scoring.

Killie's hopes of retrieving the situation in Nottingham were soon dashed as County took a 2-0 lead at half-time to kill off the tie. With nothing at stake both teams put on a show in the second half. **Bobby Street** and **McBride** again managed to score for Killie as they lost 5-2 on the night and 7-3 on aggregate.

Killie were left with a couple of consolation prizes. They had gone further than any other Scottish side in the competition that year. And at least they had prevented McCulloch from scoring against his former team-mates.

Gordon Smith strikes from the spot in 1975.

ORION

Orion were a team from **Aberdeen** who were regular competitors in the **Scottish Cup.** Their first meeting with Killie was a first round tie in 1899. Travelling to Aberdeen for a cup-tie in January in the 19th century wasn't exactly a pleasure trip. And with a hostile crowd of 5,000 on their backs Killie braced themselves for a testing time. That it didn't materialise was thanks in no small measure to **Bob Findlay.** A ball-playing winger effective on either flank, Findlay took up his favoured position on the left for this match and scored twice in the first half to give Killie a comfortable cushion. The second half was an anti-climax as the home side failed to fight back, allowing Killie a comfortable passage into the next round.

The next season the same two names came out of the hat in the second round. But this time it was Orion who were forced to make the long journey to Ayrshire. They never really stood a chance. The difference between local Leagues and the Scottish First Division was apparent throughout the match. Killie raced to a 4-0 lead at the interval and cruised through the second half, scoring apparently at will. It ended up **10-0** one those rare occasions a Kilmarnock side has notched up double figures. Pride of place on this occasion going to **Davie Maitland** who netted five times.

Orion learnt from this tie. It was clear to them (and others) that the city of Aberdeen had too many teams and not enough quality opposition. Three years later Orion were one of the sides that joined together to form a new team. One that is still going strong today under the name **Aberdeen Football Club.**

ORO

The organisers of the **New York** tournament invited Kilmarnock back for a third time in 1963; such was the popularity of the Rugby Park side. And in their third match in the competition they came across opposition from **Mexico** for the first time.

Oro represented a different style of football for Killie and it took them some time to come to terms with it. They trailed by 1-0 at the interval. The second half saw both sides put on an attacking show. **Bertie Black** scored for Killie but the star of the show was a newcomer.

Jim McFadzean was a local lad who had played for **Hearts, St Mirren** and **Raith Rovers** before joining Killie less than a month before this tournament started. He had scored on his debut and in this - his second outing – he scored twice in this thriller which ended **3-3**, preserving Killie's unbeaten record.

The versatile McFadzean played at inside-left in this tournament. In his Rugby Park career he played in every position bar outside-right and in goal.

OUR BOYS

Our Boys were a **Dundee** team (*and not to be confused with a team of the same name from Blairgowrie*) and their visit to Rugby Park in the fourth round of the **Scottish Cup** in 1881-82 represented a significant step forward for Kilmarnock.

Not because of the quality of the Tayside team but simply because they were there at all. After the first three Scottish Cup tournaments the huge increase in the number of teams taking part persuaded the SFA to regionalise the draw in the initial rounds. This was the first time since then that Kilmarnock had managed to progress beyond Ayrshire and reach the *'all-in'* stage of the draw.

Our Boys made a bright start and led 2-1 at half-time. But the second half was one-way traffic as Killie bore down on the Tayside goal time after time. By the final whistle Killie had ran up a **9-2** scoreline. Even then they had their critics, the ***Kilmarnock Standard*** describing Our Boys as *"not being able to play the game much better than eleven old ladies."*

One of the best players to ever appear in a Kilmarnock jersey. **Ian Durrant** celebrates a goal.

PAISLEY ACADEMICALS

What's Kilmarnock's record victory? Some say the **15-0** win over **Lanemark** in the Ayrshire Cup. But if that competition is excluded there are those who say it was the **13-2** triumph over **Saltcoats Victoria** in a Scottish Cup Qualifying match. There are no hard and fast rules on what constitutes a record. But it can be safely said that as far as competitions which are recognised as first-class are concerned then the game against **Paisley Academicals** on **January 18th 1930** is a record score.

This was the first time the little Paisley team had qualified for the **Scottish Cup** and their first round game at Rugby Park was an eventful affair. Kilmarnock were the trophy holders and they were determined there would be no slip-ups against non-League opposition. Goals rattled in from all parts as Killie reached a 7-0 lead after the first 45 minutes.

By time up the tally had reached eleven, although the gallant little Accies did manage to score one themselves. Cup Final heroes from 1929, **John Aitken (2)** and **Jimmy Williamson** both got on the scoresheet. As did **Willie Connell** and **Jimmy Ramsay**.

But the *'Man of the Match'* was undoubtedly **Jimmy Weir**. 'Peerie' Cunningham's understudy came in for only his fourth appearance of the season and scored *six* goals.

It was also his last appearance in a Kilmarnock jersey. A month later, frustrated by lack of first team action, he had signed for **Queen of the South**. As for the poor old Accies, they managed to qualify again a few seasons later only to suffer a 7-0 beating from **Albion Rovers**. That, understandably, was their last appearance in the Scottish Cup.

PARTICK THISTLE

Games	208	
League	173	1895-97, 1900-01, 02-47, 54-70, 71-73, 74-77, 79-81,
		83-89, 90-92, 93-96
Scottish Cup	13	1888, 1902, 14, 68, 70, 80, 83, 2001
League Cup	16	1947, 54, 63, 65, 66, 68, 70, 76
Other	6	1940, 46
Top Scorer	Eddie Morrison 10	5 SL 3 LC 2 SC
Top Home Crowd	20,244 Sep 12th 1953 LC	
Top Away Crowd	21,688 Sep 16th 1953 LC	

Apart from county rivals **Ayr United** and the **Old Firm**; Killie fans have long regarded **Partick Thistle** as their biggest rivals. The reasons for this are not hard to find. Up to the start of the 2001-02 season Killie had played the *Jags* in more League matches than any other side. In all first class games only **Rangers** have been more frequent opponents.

And that rivalry has been there right from Kilmarnock's first League season in 1895-96 when Killie let slip a 2-1 lead to lose 3-2 at Rugby Park. Such was the ferocity of feeling

among the fans that close on fifty of them attacked the Thistle players with stones, sand and mud. An object lesson to those who think that hooliganism is a modern problem. *This violence was perpetrated by our grandfathers grandfathers.*

Games against Thistle were usually hard and close-fought encounters. With the *'Harry Wraggs'* just edging the greater share. After Thistle had moved to their present **Maryhill** headquarters their **Firhill** ground represented a virtual fortress. Killie managed just two wins in over twenty years – a **3-0** success with goals from **Willie Culley (2)** and **Mattha Smith** in January 1918 and a **4-2** upset in November 1925 thanks to **Jimmy Weir (2)**, **Mattha Smith** again and **Bobby Walker**.

If we ignore Killie's 1908-09 'away' win (which was actually played at Rugby Park while Thistle were homeless) then these were the only victories between 1901-33. So you can understand the joy of the support when back-to-back victories were recorded in 1932-33 and 33-34. It's a measure of how difficult Kilmarnock have found Firhill over the years that on only two other occasions have they managed to win twice in succession there. Once at the start of the sixties and again in the late eighties.

At home 1932-33 also sparked off a great run as Killie won five in a row at home for the loss of just one goal. That has never been equalled. Not even by the great sixties team. Surprisingly the best run since then was four in a row in the eighties – a time when both teams were in the doldrums.

One of the most important matches in Kilmarnock's history was a League game at Firhill in 1947. Killie's First Division future was on the line. They were four points ahead of second bottom **Queen's Park** but the **Hampden** team had three games in hand. Even victory in this, their last match of the season, might not be good enough but anything else spelled certain doom.

Dougie McAvoy put Killie ahead and on track for safety just after the half hour mark. The Jags equalised but a free kick from **'Swig' Turnbull** took a deflection off a Thistle defender and landed in the back of the net. Killie were 2-1 up after the first 45 minutes.

With thirty minutes remaining, **Bob Thyne** gave away a penalty which Thistle converted. Kilmarnock seemed to give up the ghost after that and conceded a further three goals to lose 5-2.

With Queen's Park winning, Killie supporters were forced to go through agony over the next fortnight as the **Spiders** first caught them then overtook them and consigned Kilmarnock to Division Two after nearly fifty years in the top flight.

Killie's next League visit to Firhill wasn't until April 1955. In their last away match of the season the Rugby Parkers inflicted humiliation on their hosts as they avenged the disaster of 1947. **Willie Harvey, Willie Jack** and **Gerry Mays** all scored as Killie won 3-0 to equal their biggest win there.

And while Thistle remained awkward foes, there were occasions when Killie really established their authority in the fixture. **Jackie McInally** scored a hat-trick as Killie won **5-1** in February 1960 and the following year the Ayrshire team raced to a **4-1** interval lead. That game could have been a crucial one but as news arrived that **Rangers** were comfortably beating **Ayr** at Ibrox the same afternoon, it meant that Killie were destined to finish runners-up in the League again that season. The second half fizzled out. Normally 4-1 over Thistle would be an occasion for rejoicing. This time it felt a bit flat. The same season saw **Andy Kerr** become the only Kilmarnock player to score a hat-trick at Firhill in a 3-2 win and the following year Killie scored four goals there for the first (and to date last) time in a 4-2 thriller.

But Thistle could still frustrate Kilmarnock. The Championship-winning season got off to a great start with six wins on the trot. Then Thistle turned up at Rugby Park and came away with a 0-0 draw – Killie's first dropped point. The Jags won at Firhill that season and were the only team Kilmarnock failed to score against in the entire League campaign.

Killie could bite back though. **Eddie Morrison**, top scorer against the Jags, fired in a hat-trick in a 4-2 win in February 1970 against a Thistle team doomed to relegation. Morrison scored six goals against the Jags that season as Killie beat Thistle four times in five matches – the other being drawn.

By the mid-70s the fortunes of both clubs were closely entwined. Both teams narrowly missed out on a place in the inaugural Premier Division and both were favourites to go up in 1975-76. But this time it was 1970 in reverse as Thistle won all four games the teams played, including two in the League. That was the difference between the title and the runners-up spot Killie eventually settled for.

By 1983 though, both clubs had lost their Premier ambitions and were resigned to a lengthy spell outside the top flight. And things looked even worse for Killie in 1984-85 as they battled against the drop into the lowest division. When they lined up against Thistle on April 13th 1985 it had been *fifteen years* and *sixteen games* in all competitions since they had last beaten

them at Rugby Park. Fewer than 2,000 were in the ground to see **Lawrie McKinna** and **Scott Cuthbertson** score the first half goals which finally ended that miserable run. Not only that, it was the spark Kilmarnock needed, going on to win their next three games and escape relegation.

The following season saw a rejuvenated Killie make a determined promotion bid which was ultimately unsuccessful. But they got off to a fine start even if a bad defeat at **Ayr** a week before they faced Thistle at Rugby Park kept the crowd down to just 1,944. With the monkey off their backs, Killie tore into the Jags right from the word go. There were just six minutes played when **McKinna** slung over a tempting cross for **Ian Bryson** to knock in the opener. Next, **Jim**

A typically fearless **Eddie Morrison** is just off-target against Partick Thistle keeper **Alan Rough** in this 1975 Rugby Park match. The statuesque Thistle defender is **Alan Hansen.**

Cockburn provided the pass which **Cuthbertson** took to make it 2-0 just after the twenty minute mark.

Just before the half-hour Killie were awarded a penalty which was despatched with aplomb by **Stuart McLean** to make it 3-0. But Killie weren't finished yet. **Paul Clarke** sent over the ball which allowed **Sammy McGivern** to score the fourth a minute before the break. A satisfied Kilmarnock team left the field to a deserved standing ovation. **Paul Clarke** added a fifth with a header twelve minutes from time to round off Kilmarnock's biggest-ever League win over Thistle. Five goals. Five different scorers. When Killie went on to win the two Rugby Park League games the next season it looked now that it was Kilmarnock who were Partick's bogey side.

But 1987-88 brought a return to fighting against relegation. Just like 1947 Killie's last match was at Firhill. And just like that sad day Killie needed to win to avoid the drop. But it was an edgy Kilmarnock side that started the game. **Allan McCulloch** was in top form however and the keeper kept Killie in the match in the early stages when the loss of a goal would have been disastrous. Killie reached the interval with the match goalless.

At that stage a draw would have been good enough. But Killie knew they couldn't rely on the failings of relegation rivals **East Fife** and **Dumbarton**. If they were to be saved they would have to save themselves.

The second half saw a piece of good fortune that Kilmarnock could only have dreamed of. Thistle saw a sound claim for a penalty turned down then had a man sent off for protesting to the referee. The game was now there for the taking and Killie seized the moment. Awarded a free kick midway through the half, **Jimmy Gilmour** hit a low, hard shot past the keeper to give Killie the lead.

That was enough. The fight drained out of Thistle and Killie kept their nerve until the final whistle. The end of the game brought scenes of celebration from the supporters which would have fooled a passer-by into thinking they had won the League title, not avoided relegation to the lowest flight.

Twelve months later it all turned to dust. In their last home game of the season a 0-0 draw with Thistle kept Killie deep in the relegation mire in what was an ultimately unsuccessful bid to stay up.

The clubs renewed their rivalry in the 1990s in the Premier Division. With the teams back at the top of the Scottish game crowds improved, reaching levels not seen for over thirty years. And the game could still provide excitement too. Hogmanay 1994 is a case in point. Killie arrived at Firhill in fine form, having lost only to **Rangers** in their last seven outings. New keeper **Dragoje Lekovic** had won the fans over instantly. But within seven minutes of this game kicking off he nearly lost them as comical errors from the keeper and his defence gave Thistle a two goal start. But the resilience of this Kilmarnock team showed as **Steve Maskrey** reduced the deficit before half-time then **Gus MacPherson** equalised after the break. It was Killie who finished the stronger but had to settle for a 2-2 draw.

The 1995-96 season saw Killie reap a rich reward in points with three wins and a draw giving them ten and Thistle just one. But that year also saw the Maryhill team lose their place in the top division. At some stage they will return and one of Scottish football's oldest duels will recommence.

The clubs history in the **Scottish Cup** is even older than in the League. The first meeting was a fourth round contest in 1887-88 which saw Killie draw away then lose the replay at Rugby Park. A **4-0** home win in the opening round in 1902 made up for that loss but Killie were again beaten at Rugby Park when they next clashed in the third round in 1914.

Surprisingly the teams didn't meet again until

1968. The first round tie at Firhill ended goalless. Once again, home advantage counted for nothing in the replay as Thistle scored twice before Killie pulled a goal back. Two years later Killie finally managed to win a home tie beating Thistle 3-0 in the first round.

Ten years later the third round in 1980 produced another Rugby Park defeat as Killie went down 1-0. Three years after that came a marathon affair at the same stage. **Ian Bryson's** goal looked to be good enough for Killie at Firhill but the Jags equalised with just four minutes left to play. The Rugby Park replay produced two hours of boredom as neither side looked likely to score. So it was off to Firhill again where an early goal from the home side was cancelled out by **Brian Gallacher** just after the restart. At 1-1 there was another thirty minutes extra time. **Sammy McGivern** struck for Killie straight away in the extra period but Thistle equalised to take the tie to Rugby Park again.

It was goalless at half-time but Thistle's promising young striker **Maurice Johnston** put his side ahead after the break. It was Johnston's third goal in the tie and it proved to be the last. After four games and seven hours Killie were out.

The teams were probably glad of a break after that. Their next meeting wasn't until 2001 and again it was a third round game at Rugby Park. But although Thistle fancied their chances of creating an upset, Killie held firm. **Ally Mitchell's** 27th minute goal booked their place in the next round.

Having been in Killie's group in the **Southern League Cup** in 1945-46 the Jags returned the next season as the first visitors to Rugby Park in the **Scottish League Cup**. Killie won both games that season. When they next met, in 1953-54 Killie were a 'B' Division side and they did well to battle back from 3-1 down at home in their quarter-final tie to win **4-3** before a crowd of **20,244** – the most to ever watch a game against Thistle. Four days later Thistle returned the compliment. The **21,688** at the second leg being the biggest for a Firhill fixture between the two clubs. Killie couldn't hold their lead, going down 4-0 on the night, 7-4 on aggregate.

The teams then met five times between 1962-70. The 1962-63 clash was a quarter-final tie which saw two superb performances from Kilmarnock. They won 2-1 at Firhill and 3-1 at Rugby Park for a 5-2 aggregate victory. What made these results extra special was that, at the time, Partick were the League leaders.

Killie rehearsed for their League campaign in 1964-65 with a 4-0 home win and a 0-0 draw at Firhill in their League Cup section. And as reigning champions, they beat Thistle twice the next season in their way to winning the section. Killie were also section winners in 1967-68.

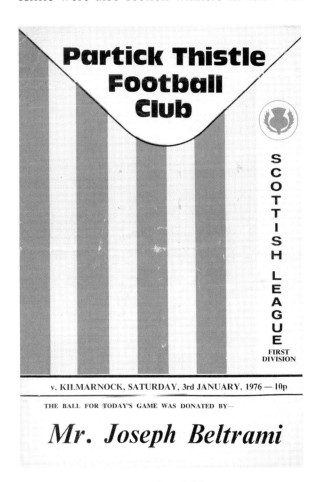

Partick Thistle Football Club

SCOTTISH LEAGUE

FIRST DIVISION

v. KILMARNOCK, SATURDAY, 3rd JANUARY, 1976 — 10p

THE BALL FOR TODAY'S GAME WAS DONATED BY—

Mr. Joseph Beltrami

The teams meet in the new First Division.
There is no truth in the rumour that the reason **Mr Beltrami** sponsored the ball was as a gesture to his many clients in the Firhill support!

Kenny Cameron netted a hat-trick in the **4-0** home win with **Tommy McLean** scoring the other goal but Killie lost 1-0 at Firhill.

The 1969-70 season was the one Killie won four out of five against Thistle and it started in the first game of the season as **John Gilmour** and **Eddie Morrison** scored the goals which brought a 2-0 win at Firhill in their League Cup clash. But it was the Rugby Park game two weeks later which had the fans in raptures. Three up at the break, Killie doubled that in the second half to finish winning 6-0 – their best result ever against Thistle in any competition. **Ross Mathie** and **Willie Waddell** both scored a pair and **Eddie Morrison** and **Tommy McLean** grabbed the others.

Killie lost both games in the 1975-76 League Cup. More than a quarter of a century later the clubs still await their next paring in the tournament.

PEEBLES ROVERS

Peebles Rovers arrived at Rugby Park for their first round Scottish Cup game in January 1927 with a point to prove. The Borders team had been members of the ill-fated **Third Division** and when that division collapsed in 1926 they felt aggrieved at their loss of status. They weren't thought of as potential giant-killers but they had held **Albion Rovers** to a draw in the previous year's tournament and had also drawn with **Hibernian** at **Easter Road** a few seasons before that.

Killie had been going through a difficult time and still faced the threat of relegation when this tie was played. The Board had taken the club into debt by signing new players in a calculated (and successful) attempt to keep top League status. It seemed a recipe for a possible upset.

It didn't turn out that way but it was a far from comfortable day for Kilmarnock. They led 1-0 at the break thanks to a goal from '**Peerie Cunningham**. The striker added a penalty in the second half and **Jimmy Ramsay** also scored but Peebles found the net themselves to make the final score 3-1. It was a nervous performance but the unbeaten run put together since the turn of the year continued. Even so this wasn't destined to be one of Killie's better Cup years – they lost at Dens Park in the next round.

PETERHEAD

Of the 41 other teams playing League football in Scotland, **Peterhead** are the only one Kilmarnock have never met in League, Scottish Cup, League Cup or any other recognised first class competition.

POLONIA BYTOM

Polonia Bytom were in Killie's section in the **1965 New York** tournament. They had a reasonable pedigree, having been Polish champions as recently as 1962. It was really a tournament too far for Kilmarnock this season – their games against the Poles being the 57th and 59th of 60 played. And with the new season just over three weeks away by the time they played the second game against Polonia, thoughts were starting to drift to that brief pause that is laughingly termed the *close season*.

Killie didn't play badly in their first game and a **Davie Sneddon** goal ensured a point in a match they might have won. But by the next match it was clear that Killie's hopes of adding this tournament to their League title had gone. Although they held up fairly well, they lost a goal in each half to go down 2-0.

PORT GLASGOW ATHLETIC

Games	29	
League	25	1895-99, 1902-10
Scottish Cup	4	1906
Top Scorer	Davie Howie 4	All SL
Top Home Crowd	4,200 Nov 9th 1907 SL	
Top Away Crowd	5,000 Feb 17th 1906 SC	
Highest Overall	6,000 Feb 24th 1906	(Cathkin)

It may be more than 90 years since they were last in the League, but **Port Glasgow Athletic's** place in the history of Kilmarnock is secure. They were one of the original opponents back in 1895-96 and the first few games between the clubs went with home advantage. By 1898 though Killie had established themselves as contenders for the top League.

After playing in their first **Scottish Cup Final** in March 1898 Killie still had two League games outstanding. Both of them against Port Glasgow, their nearest rivals in the table. Their Rugby Park fixture was a close match in which goals from **Davie McPherson** and **Bobby Muir** handed Killie a narrow 2-1 victory. **That was enough to secure the Second Division championship.** With nothing at stake Killie lost the return 4-2.

That should have put Kilmarnock into Division One. But there was no automatic promotion and relegation in Scotland until 1922. Killie's name went forward for election to the top flight. Promised support from the big boys never materialised. In a straight fight for the third and last place, Killie lost out to a **Clyde** team that had won only one game all season! The *Standard* suggested that the only reason for Clyde's success was that they *"had a ground in Glasgow."*

So they had one more season with Port Glasgow in which Killie won there for the first time in a thrilling game. 2-0 up at the break it ended **5-4** in Killie's favour. Somewhat surprisingly the Renfrewshire amateurs were themselves elected to Division One in 1902, so the rivalry was soon renewed.

The question of re-election reared its head again. This time it was the other end of the equation. The two teams had to play off in 1906. The winner definitely stayed up, the loser finished third bottom and had to apply for re-election. Killie were only a goal behind at the interval but collapsed in the second half of the game which was played at **Third Lanark's Cathkin Park. 6-0** was the final score. It was a sign of the changing times at Rugby Park that the left-back that day, **Dan Aitken,** was the only one of the starting eleven who had played in the first match of the season as well as the last. Fortunately for Killie they were easily re-elected.

Those footballers of the Edwardian era would have laughed at the suggestion that teams meet each other too often nowadays. The re-election game was the *seventh* time Killie and Port Glasgow had clashed this season.

Two years later came a game which made history. By kick-off on January 4th 1908 there were only *seven* Kilmarnock players stripped and ready to face their opponents. After a 25-minute delay the referee ordered the match to go ahead. Killie put left-half **Willie Shaw** in goal and awaited the inevitable onslaught.

Port Glasgow took the lead and even missed a penalty shortly afterwards. Amazingly, one of Killie's six outfield players, **Davie Howie,** somehow managed to make space for himself and equalised. It couldn't last of course and Port scored again. But at half-time the eleven men were still only leading the seven 2-1.

Deciding they wouldn't have much call for a winger in the second half, **Robert Barton** took over from Shaw in goal. Killie fought as bravely as they could and it was a worthy performance. They lost just two more goals. But it didn't go down well with the Port spectators who felt cheated of a proper contest. One newspaper of the time even stated the obvious by saying there was *"just one side in the game."*

The four missing players had arrived in **Glasgow** for their connection in good time – so they claimed. They said that fog had prevented them from getting to **Port Glasgow** before the game ended. There was a press furore before the affair became quietly forgotten. But not before Kilmarnock entered the record books for having the smallest number to start and finish a first class match.

It was always a struggle for a team like Port Glasgow to survive though and in 1910 they failed to be re-elected. Their final appearance against Kilmarnock was at Rugby Park in March 1910 in a game Killie won **4-0**. Twelve months after that, they failed to win re-election to the Second Division and vanished from the senior ranks forever.

The teams met just once in the **Scottish Cup** but it was one of those marathon ties. The second round game at Rugby Park finished in a 2-2 draw and the replay at Port Glasgow ended goalless so the clubs journeyed to Cathkin where, despite thirty minutes of extra time, again no goals were scored. Back at Cathkin for a second time, Port Glasgow scored the only goal of the game in the first half. After four games it was finally over for Killie. It meant that of seven games they had played against Port Glasgow during the season, Killie had won only one.

PREUSSEN MUNSTER

Killie's second opponents in the **New York** tournament in **1963** were **West German** team **Preussen Munster**. This game was played just three days after Killie's opener and they had to travel to **Chicopee, Massachusetts** for the match. Making his debut for Killie at inside-left was **Jim McFadzean** and he marked the occasion with the opening goal. **Jackie McInally** added another before the Germans pulled one back thanks to a penalty near half-time.

Eric Murray restored the two-goal lead before **Frank Beattie** was sent off. On his way to

protest to the referee about the fouling going on, he slipped and ran right into him. The referee took umbrage and sent Beattie off. The Germans scored shortly afterwards but Killie rallied and a **Bertie Black** penalty made it 4-2 after 77 minutes. Black scored from another penalty near the end and the German team also finished with ten men as their penalty taker **Tybusek** was sent off for arguing with the referee.

Common sense prevailed when the tournament organisers cleared Beattie of any blame and Big Frank went on to play in every game in the section.

QUEEN OF THE SOUTH

Games	76	
League	57	1933-47, 50-51, 54-59, 62-64, 73-74, 75-76, 77-79,
		81-82, 86-90
Scottish Cup	9	1956, 58, 63, 73, 89
League Cup	4	1957, 64
Other	6	1940, 46, 64
Top Scorer	Brien McIlroy 8	5 SL 3 Oth
Top Home Crowd	24,300 Feb 18th 1956 SC	
Top Away Crowd	14,500 Jan 1st 1947 SL	

Queen of the South were comparative latecomers to the Kilmarnock story – the teams not meeting until the **Dumfries** side's arrival in the First Division in 1933. But a keen rivalry soon developed, particularly during times when **Ayr United** were in the lower division. Queens provided Killie with an alternative southern opponent

For a brief spell after the war they were even New Year opposition and the **14,500** who saw a 1-1 draw at **Palmerston Park** on New Year's Day 1947 is the biggest to watch the teams at that ground. Queens were dogged foes but gradually Killie gained the upper hand in their meetings. They were always well on top at Rugby Park but Palmerston Park was a tricky venue for some time. By the early sixties Killie were rattling in goals with abandon. **7-0** at Rugby Park in January 1963, **4-0** at Palmerston the following November.

The mid-seventies saw the teams meet regularly with Killie again well on top. But there was generally little at stake in the encounters. Until May 1982. Killie lined up at home against the *Doonhamers* in their last game of the season. They lay in third place one point behind **Hearts** in the race for promotion to the Premier. But they were playing a Queens side already condemned to relegation while Hearts had to face leaders **Motherwell**. So there was everything still to play for.

But the constant see-sawing from First to Premier and back again had affected support. There were fewer than 2,500 watching at kick-

off. The missing fans had only themselves to blame for not being there to witness what happened that day.

Killie went for the jugular right from kick-off. They knew that if Hearts drew then they would need to win this one by *five* clear goals to overhaul them on goal difference. A **Kenny Armstrong** header was blocked but the ball fell to **Brian Gallacher** who opened the scoring after six minutes. Just two minutes later and Gallacher got on the end of a **Sammy McGivern** cross to make it 2-0. An own goal made it three near the half-hour mark. Then Armstrong had another header blocked seven minutes from half-time. He seized on the rebound himself this time to score the fourth. Just before the whistle **Derrick McDicken** latched on to a **Stuart McLean** free kick to make it 5-0 at the break.

Those few fans in the ground went wild when news came through that Hearts were a goal down. **John Bourke** added a sixth goal, then came a heart-stopping moment. **Ian Bryson** pulled down a Queens attacker eleven minutes from the end. Penalty! As if he was determined not to let the forwards have all the glory, **Allan McCulloch** pulled off a super save from the spot-kick. **6-0** it finished. Hearts lost their game. Killie were back in the Premier with a point to spare.

Seven years later Kilmarnock again faced an already relegated Queen of the South in the last First Division game of the season. But this time circumstances were radically different. Killie were second bottom and seemingly destined to join Queens in the Second Division. They were level on points with **Clyde** but worse off on goal difference. If Clyde won - whatever the margin – Killie would need to win by five more goals to go above them.

It looked like mission impossible. And after 45 minutes little had happened to revise that opinion. A **Willie Watters** goal was all that Killie had to show for their efforts. But news that Clyde were only drawing gave the team renewed hope, Watters scored his second with a shot through the keeper's legs early in the second half then completed his hat-trick in 54 minutes. **Robert Reilly** scored a fourth seven minutes later.

With just over twenty minutes to go, Watters seized on a loose ball and punished the hesitant defence to score Killie's fifth. But the supporters cheers were muted when they heard that Clyde had gone ahead. As nails were bitten down to the quick, the seconds drained away. Then with three minutes left, it was Watters again. He burst through the defence to score his fifth and Killie's sixth.

The final whistle sounded and jubilant Kilmarnock supporters invaded the pitch. They danced, sang, and cheered their team off the park. As things stood Killie were level on both points and goal difference with Clyde but Killie had scored more goals. They were safe. *So the supporters thought.*

But Clyde's game against St Johnstone wasn't over. An amazing seven minutes of injury time had elapsed when they were awarded a penalty. They scored. Now it was Clyde who were a goal to the good and Killie were down. Willie Watters' incredible scoring feat had been to no avail. And Kilmarnock would have to rebuild from the bottom echelon of the Scottish League.

Killie won their two home games against Queens in the bottom division the next season but lost away. It was the last time the teams met in the League as Killie began the long haul back to the top.

Scottish Cup games against Queens do not have a lot of happy memories for Kilmarnock. The biggest crowd to assemble at Rugby Park for this game – **24,300** - did so on February 18th 1956 for the first meeting of the sides in the competition. All the goals in the 2-2 draw came in the first half and the sixth round tie was settled 2-0 in Queens favour four days later at Palmerston.

Queens next provided the Cup opposition two years later in a third round tie (*this was exactly the same stage as the sixth round meeting in 1956 but the SFA's history of changing the names of rounds is too long and complex to go into here*). This was **Willie Waddell's** first season as Kilmarnock manager but the change of boss had no effect on the outcome of the tie. Once again it

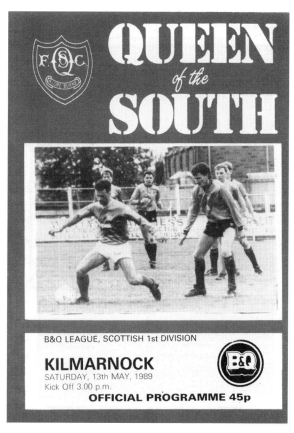

Heartbreak! Despite winning this game **6-0** Killie still ended up relegated.

finished 2-2. And once again Killie lost the replay, this time by 3-0. Oddly enough Queen of the South were the only team Killie managed to beat in the League from the end of November to the middle of March. And they did so twice.

When Queens were again drawn to travel to Rugby Park in a second round tie in 1963 there were few who thought lightning could strike a third time. For Kilmarnock were riding high in the League and Queens were struggling near the foot of the table. But the match ended in a draw yet again, though there were no goals scored on this occasion. It was the first 0-0 draw at Rugby Park in any competition since April 1957.

This was the year of the great freeze and the replay didn't take place until more than six weeks after the first game. It made no difference. Queens won 1-0.

Jim McSherry and **Eddie Morrison** finally ended the hoodoo with the goals in a 2-1 third round victory at Rugby Park in 1973. But at the same stage in 1989 Queens again won after a replay although this time they drew at Palmerston before winning at Rugby Park.

Theirs is not a name that Kilmarnock look forward to seeing come out of the hat.

There have been few meetings in the **League Cup**. Each club won the away fixture when they first met in 1956-57 but Killie won both games easily in their next – and to date last - meeting in 1963-64. Killie also won both **Summer Cup** meetings later that season. Indeed, taking in the League as well, they played Queens six times in all and won every single game, with a goal differential of 19-3.

QUEEN'S PARK

Games	127	
League	102	1900-22, 23-47, 48-54, 56-58, 73-74, 81-82, 89-90
Scottish Cup	6	1887, 93, 1920, 28, 71
League Cup	14	1949, 50, 58, 74, 75, 83, 84
Other	5	1940, 46, 49
Top Scorer	Willie Culley 10	All SL
	Mattha Smith 10	8 SL 2 SC
Top Home Crowd	21,267 Feb 18th 1928 SC	
Top Away Crowd	36,000 Feb 22nd 1928 SC	

The debt owed by Kilmarnock – indeed *all* of Scottish football – to **Queen's Park** is incalculable. The Glasgow club are the oldest in Scotland and it was their letter to Killie in March 1873 asking for a donation of £1 to help buy a trophy called the **Scottish Cup** which was the catalyst in determining that Kilmarnock became an Association Football club. Prior to that they had played mainly as a rugby team – as the name of the ground indicates.

And in the very early days visits from Queen's Park were great occasions. When Killie first played them in the Scottish Cup in 1886-87 they were still the biggest attraction in Scotland.

2,500 – a large crowd for the time - turned up to watch the quarter-final tie. It was the first time Kilmarnock had progressed to that stage but they were to go no further. Queen's won easily. They were four up at half-time and scored again in the second half to win 5-0.

Hopes were high in 1892-93 that Killie would do better when Queen's came visiting in a second round match. But after a valiant first half in which they restricted their opponents to a single goal, Killie were overwhelmed by the sheer power of the Hampden side. It finished 8-0 as Queen's strode on to win the Scottish Cup for the tenth – and last – time.

Times had changed when Queen's next arrived at Rugby Park in the Cup. By 1920 they were just an ordinary team, if still proudly amateur. The third round tie was level at 1-1 after 45 minutes but Killie stepped up the pace in the second half and a new record crowd of 20,000 saw their favourites win 4-1 to take another step on the road to Cup glory that year.

An even bigger crowd – 21,267 – was in attendance at Rugby Park for the third round match in 1928. An enthralling game saw both sides put in a storming performance in a 4-4 draw. Queen's edged the replay 1-0 in front of

36,000. The *Spiders* reached the last four that season - the last time they really had a chance of winning the Cup again.

The only other Scottish Cup tie featuring the pair saw Killie sent to Hampden in a third round tie in 1971 which they won 1-0.

Despite only meeting in three seasons over more than forty years there have been over 100 **League** meetings between the sides. Queen's Park finally gave up the aloof stance they had maintained from the establishment of the Scottish League and joined its ranks in 1900. In

Eddie Morrison in action against Queen's Park.

recognition of their place in the game's development they were admitted straight into the First Division. And Killie's first League trip to the second **Hampden Park** on December 15th 1900 was a classic.

The opening twenty minutes passed quietly enough before Killie opened the scoring. That opened the floodgates and Killie found themselves 5-0 up at half-time and unlucky not to have added to that total. The second period couldn't have been more different. Ten minutes into the half and all was well until Queen's pulled a couple back in quick succession. They then hit Killie with three goals in two minutes to level the game. It finished an incredible **5-5**. Two of Queen's goals came from a name now more familiar in the high street than in the stands – **RS McColl.**

The amateurs found League football a struggle though and in November 1905 Kilmarnock tore them apart once again, leading 4-0 at Rugby Park at half-time. There was no second half comeback this time and Killie ran in three more goals for an emphatic 7-0 victory. Two players – **Jock Young** and **Tom Galloway** – bagged hat-tricks with **Willie Banks** scoring the seventh.

Killie continued to find a rich haul of goals and points at Rugby Park. In 1909-10 they hammered a hapless Queen's **6-1** after leading only 2-1 at the break. In 1928-29 they ripped the *Spiders* defence apart taking a 5-0 lead in just 30 minutes and despite a plucky fightback by the amateurs won **7-4** with **Mattha Smith** scoring four times. **'Peerie' Cunningham (2)** and **Jimmy Ramsay** completed the scoring. Yet after winning 4-1 at Hampden the following season they lost inexplicably at home 5-1. A **Bobby Beattie** hat-trick was the inspiration behind a **5-0** home win in 1934-35 when they also won 4-1 away.

Hampden was one of Kilmarnock's favourite away venues in the inter-war period with several fine victories. None more so than on their last visit before the outbreak of war. On December 10th 1938 **Sammy Ross**, a fine left-half but converted to centre-forward by manager **Jimmy McGrory** bagged a hat-trick there with winger **Benny Thomson** scoring twice as Killie won 5-1.

Their last away game before Rugby Park was taken over by the army and Killie closed down during wartime was a 1-0 win in a Western League game at Hampden in May 1940 and they started back where they had left off with a visit to Hampden in August 1945 their first competitive match for over five years. Technically it wasn't a post-war game, as the Japanese surrender was still three days away.

Killie scored three times against the 14-year old keeper **Ronnie Simpson** before Queen's pulled two back. It looked as though Killie hadn't been too badly affected by the wartime closure but that was, alas, a mirage. The opposition they had beaten were one of the weakest sides around as became apparent the next season.

1946-47 was the first 'official' post-war season and Killie kicked off with a 2-2 draw at home to Queen's Park. They won 1-0 in the Hampden return but by the end of the term Killie had amassed one point less than the Hampden men and were relegated. Twelve months later Queen's Park joined them in the 'B' Division.

That set the scene for some epic encounters in front of big crowds between Scotland's two oldest clubs as they strove to regain top flight status. January 1950 was a fine example. Killie took more than 10,000 supporters with them to Hampden for the League game. A right-footed shot from left-winger **Alex Donaldson** gave Killie the lead in a closely-contested affair. **Tommy Johnston** put the Ayrshiremen two ahead with nearly an hour played but Queen's pulled one back within three minutes. Queen's fought like furies to protect their unbeaten home record but **Sam Cowan** scored a third for Killie in the dying seconds to secure a famous win.

There were **27,205** spectators present – *the largest recorded crowd for any Scottish League game outside the top flight.*

On April 24th (a significant date in Killie's history) 1954 Queen's Park lined up at Rugby Park in what was a celebratory affair. Killie had already won promotion and the match saw them wave goodbye to the lower League with a 2-0 win.

Two years later Queen's Park rejoined them in Division One. But this was the *Spiders* last attempt to live with the elite. Although they survived the first season their second was a disaster. Killie's final match of the 1957-58 campaign was a visit to a ghostly Hampden. Just 500 fans bothered to watch as Killie won 2-1 with goals from **Frank Beattie** and **Vernon Wentzel.**

Since then the only League fixtures against Queen's Park have come in seasons when Killie have been escaping the clutches of a lower division. In 1974 Queen's were the seventh in a run of ten successive Killie victories as they powered to promotion from the old Division Two. The deadly duo of **Ian Fleming** and **Eddie Morrison** despatched the *Spiders* that day. Fleming with a hat-trick and Morrison with two as Killie won 5-0.

In 1981-82 Queen's Park reached the First Division and while they took a point from Rugby Park in a goalless encounter, Killie won twice at Hampden on their way to promotion. And in 1989-90 while Killie lost at Hampden they took full points from the two Rugby Park matches as they bade adieu to the Second Division.

In the **League Cup** the teams have been drawn together seven times. Neither side impressed in their 'B' Division encounters. The first significant pairing was in 1957-58 when three out of the four points available were won by Killie as they topped the group. Killie repeated

that performance in 1973-74 then took all four points the next season as they again won the section. Hapless Queen's were beaten 6-0 at Rugby Park with **Ian Fleming** scoring twice as **Eddie Morrison, Jimmy Cook, Gordon Smith** and **Brian Rodman** all found the net as well.

There was another easy win in 1982-83. **John Bourke** scored two and was joined on the scoresheet by **Stuart McLean, Brian Gallacher** and **Ally Mauchlen** in a **5-1** win. Killie also won at Hampden on their way to topping the section.

The next year they met in a two-legged clash. Two goals from **Jim Clark** gave Killie a 2-1 lead at Hampden at half-time but they lost 3-2. The situation was eventually retrieved in a hard-fought game at Rugby Park as a brace from **Sammy McGivern** and another from **Derrick McDicken** saw Killie edge past Queen's 3-1 to win 5-4 on aggregate.

John Bourke is foiled on this occasion by Queen's Park's Atkins.

RAITH ROVERS

Games	114	
League	103	1910-17, 19-26, 27-29, 38-39, 47-49, 54-63, 67-70, 73-74,
		78-79, 81-82, 83-84, 87-89, 90-94, 95-97
Scottish Cup	3	1929, 72, 93
League Cup	7	1955, 62, 63, 95
Other	1	1949
Top Scorer	Andy Kerr 13	9 SL 4 LC
Top Home Crowd	18,129 Aug 14th 1954 LC	
Top Away Crowd	15,000 Sep 24th 1921 SL	

Raith Rovers were a welcome sight to Ayrshire eyes when they were elected to the First Division in 1910. For the **Kirkcaldy** team were poor travellers and Killie won their first *nine* home League matches against them. Away from home it was tougher. It took until 1916-17 for Killie to claim the points at **Stark's Park** when they registered an emphatic 4-0 triumph. Raith (along with Aberdeen and Dundee) dropped out of the League for the next two seasons).

They were tougher opposition when they came back and the next away win wasn't until Boxing Day 1925 when Killie won a high-scoring affair **5-4**. Rovers were relegated that season and spent little time in the top flight for the remainder of the inter-war period. What few games there were often provided a spectacle. Killie won **7-1** at Rugby Park in 1928-29 with **'Peerie' Cunningham** scoring four. Yet at Stark's Park the same season Killie threw away a 3-0 half-time lead, losing 5-3.

After Killie's relegation in 1947, Raith Rovers were the first side to visit Rugby Park in the 'B' Division. Killie must have thought life in the lower orders was going to be easy as they demolished Rovers **7-1** with both **Allan Collins** and **Frank Walsh** scoring hat-tricks. **'Swig' Turnbull** was the other marksman in this Rugby Park rout.

Of course it was to take seven years for Killie to rejoin the big time. And they found Stark's Park a difficult venue when they did. They recorded their first post-war win on that ground in April 1960 thanks to goals from **Bertie Black** and **Vernon Wentzel.**

At home Killie were generally far superior to their Fife opponents. Such was the case in January 1961 when they ran up a **6-0** scoreline with **Andy Kerr** claiming a hat-trick. October 1968 witnessed one of the most remarkable games ever played at Rugby Park. Killie were 4-0 down to Rovers at half-time and many supporters left the ground at that point. They missed an incredible second half fightback, led by **Tommy McLean**. The little winger scored twice, including a last-minute equaliser, as Killie rose from the dead to force a draw. **Eddie Morrison** and **Brien McIlroy** were also on target that day.

In January 1970 Killie were two down at Stark's Park with just six minutes remaining when **Allan 'Chopper' MacDonald** pulled a goal back. Morrison and **Ross Mathie** then both found the net to conjure up an amazing victory. MacDonald had been signed from Hearts as a replacement for broken leg victim **Frank Beattie** and this was his Killie debut. His goal that day was the only one he ever scored for the club.

Games against Rovers were infrequent after that and usually inconsequential too. But the 1992-93 season was of a different order as both teams battled for a place in the Premier. Rovers quickly established themselves at the top but Killie were more than a match for them when the sides clashed. Even Rovers boss **Jimmy Nicholl** was forced to admit his team had been second best when they scraped a lucky point at home against Killie in October. There was no such luck for his side when they visited Rugby Park in January 1993 as **Ian Porteous (2)** and **Billy Stark** gave Killie a 3-0 victory.

Both sides were promoted that season but it was Kilmarnock who had the strength to survive in the top flight. Their fighting spirit was exemplified by a game at Stark's Park the following season when Killie found themselves two down at half-time. A terrific fightback in the second half earned them a point thanks to goals from **Bobby Williamson** and **Ally Mitchell**. Every point was vital in a season which saw Killie survive and Rovers go down.

Rovers came back up but they couldn't live with the elite. In 1995-96 Killie destroyed them 5-1 at Rugby Park. **John Henry** and **Paul Wright** scored two apiece with **Tom Brown** claiming the other.

An excellent victory for Kilmarnock in this cup-tie and a magnificent goal from **Eddie Morrison**.

There have been only three **Scottish Cup** meetings but all have been significant. In a 1929 quarter-final tie Raith provided awkward opposition at Stark's Park as goals from **'Peerie' Cunningham, Danny Paterson** and **Mattha Smith** gave Kilmarnock a 3-2 win and put them a step closer to Hampden.

1972 brought another visit to Kirkcaldy in the last eight as Killie won 3-1 thanks to goals from **Jimmy Cook, George Maxwell** and **Eddie Morrison**. Morrison's strike was a classic – a twenty yard shot that was praised by manager **Walter McCrae** as one of the best he'd ever seen.

In 1993 the teams met at Rugby Park for the first time, in a third round tie. And Kilmarnock put Rovers to the sword as a **Bobby Williamson** hat-trick helped them to a 5-0 rout. **George**

Paul Wright scores in the 5-1 victory at Rugby Park.

McCluskey and **Gus MacPherson** notched the others.

Similarly, there haven't been that many meetings in the **League Cup**. Killie's 3-2 win in **August 1954** was doubly significant though. It was their first match in their first season back at the top and it brought a crowd of **18,129** to watch the fixture - the highest for a match against Raith. Killie also won the Stark's Park tie. In 1961-62 **Brien McIlroy** scored his first hat-trick for the club in a **7-1** demolition of Rovers. Killie won

4-1 away but still didn't top the section that season.

They did the next season as they again beat Rovers twice. There has only been one clash since. 1994-95 took Killie to a third round tie in Kirkcaldy where, despite goals from **Ray Montgomerie** and **Bobby Williamson**, they were beaten 3-2 thanks to a **Colin Cameron** hat-trick. It cost Killie their 100% record over Rovers and put the Fifers a step further along the road to winning the trophy that season.

Pic 79

Ready to party. Killie fans await the start of the Cup Final in 1997.

RANGERS

Games	210	
League	170	1899-1947, 54-73, 74-75, 76-77, 79-81, 82-83, 93-2001
Scottish Cup	22	1892, 98, 1902, 03, 11, 25, 29, 32, 33, 38, 54, 60, 62,
		78, 79, 94
League Cup	13	1953, 58, 61, 63, 64, 66, 67, 83, 91
Other	5	1940, 46, 80
Top Scorer	Tommy McLean 7	4 SL 3 LC
Top Home Crowd	35,995 Mar 10th 1962 SC	
Top Away Crowd	66,000 Sep 14th 1957 LC	
Highest Overall	114,708 Apr 6th 1929 SC	

Queen Victoria may have been on the throne when Kilmarnock joined Division One but even then there was no bigger club in the Scottish game than **Rangers**. The pattern of the earliest games would be familiar to modern supporters – heavy defeats away and tightly contested matches at Rugby Park which Rangers edged, often as a result of dubious refereeing decisions.

So when the teams assembled at Rugby Park on **August 17th 1901** – six years to the day since Killie's first game in League football – there were few who though that Kilmarnock's third season in the top flight would see any difference. But history was to be made that day as Killie's right-winger **John Graham** evaded the Gers defence to put the home team ahead. On the opposite flank was debutant **Arthur Norwood** and he marked the occasion with the second goal. **Jim Howie** added a third to send the home fans into a frenzy. A minute from half-time a suspiciously offside-looking strike from Rangers was allowed to stand and it was 3-1 at the break.

Killie had lost after holding the interval lead in both their previous home games against Rangers so nothing was being taken for granted as the second half got under way. But Rangers were also up against driving rain and a fierce wind as well as a determined Killie. Graham stole the ball, beat two defenders and lashed it home off the underside of the bar. Although Rangers pulled a goal back, the game was over. 4-2 to Killie – **their first victory over Rangers in any competitive match.**

That was the start of a good little spell against the **Ibrox** giants. A 0-0 draw followed the next year then a 2-2 tie in which Killie – at the foot of the table - more than matched the leaders. But more often than not the Glasgow side had the upper hand. Especially on their own Ibrox turf. But in December 1908 Killie grabbed a shock lead before Rangers drew level, somewhat luckily. With the game heading for a draw Rangers were awarded a penalty. No great surprise in itself. What happened next though is not an everyday Ibrox occurrence. Rangers 'scored' with the spot-kick, only for the referee to insist it be re-taken, as he hadn't blown his whistle. Keeper **Aitken** made a marvellous save and Killie took a point from Ibrox for the first time.

Back at Rugby Park Killie beat Rangers 3-2 near the end of the 1911-12 season in a game which saw the remarkable **Willie Culley** make his debut. There were other victories to savour - 4-1 in 1916-17 and 1-0 two seasons later. And at the dawn of the 1930s Killie won two in succession for the first time. But there were still embarrassing defeats, **7-1** at home in 1919-20 being particularly hard to bear.

And Ibrox was still a no-go area as far as a Killie victory was concerned. After the draw in 1908-09 Killie suffered *fifteen* successive defeats, including an **8-0** slaughter in 1918-19. And a draw in 1924-25 was followed by another *eight* straight losses. The run was stopped with a 2-2 draw in 1933-34.

So when Killie lined up at Ibrox the following season there was little for Rangers to fear. The Ibrox team were in their usual position – top of the table. They were heading for their **eighth** championship in nine seasons and it had been more than **three years** since they had last been beaten at Ibrox. What threat did a mid-table Kilmarnock side with an Ibrox record of Played 35 W0 D3 L32 pose?

But the Ibrox legions knew something was amiss when **James Black** put Killie ahead with less than a minute played. With just seven minutes gone **Jimmy Williamson** found himself in space in the penalty area and he scored the goal which put Killie in a position they had never before experienced at Ibrox – two goals ahead.

The inevitable Rangers onslaught was met with a stiff Killie rearguard. Their defence was breached just once by the break. In the second half Killie's **John Keane** found himself surrounded by Rangers players in the Ibrox penalty area yet managed to keep possession and turn and score to make it 3-1 to Killie.

No one will find it a great surprise that Rangers were then awarded a penalty. The referee had ignored their claims for handball but surrounded by pleading Rangers players he wavered and pointed to the spot. Up stepped the renowned **Torry Gillick** who missed - the ball going past the post.

Gillick scored with five minutes to go but Killie hung on to claim a famous victory, their first at Ibrox. Even the Glasgow press was generous in its praise of the Ayrshire side. As for the local press, well, the *Standard* had wondered on the day of the game if Killie were due a win at Ibrox, the one ground in the country where they had yet to record a victory.

Rangers recovered sufficiently to give Killie an 8-0 beating two seasons later but at Rugby Park it was a different story as Killie won the final two home games before the outbreak of war.

After the conflict Rangers' first visit to Rugby

Park attracted a new League record crowd of **32,325** to see the Ibrox side win 2-0. Their next trip to Ayrshire wasn't until 1955 when Killie recorded their first post-war triumph, courtesy of a **Bobby Flavell** goal.

Kilmarnock now had a team capable of challenging the best and in 1956-57 they reached new heights. They controlled the League clash at Ibrox and **Davie Curlett's** goal brought their second victory on that ground. Three days before Christmas an outstanding performance from **Gerry Mays** – who scored two goals – helped them to a 3-2 win over Rangers. **Willie Harvey** was the other scorer as they recorded a 'double' over the Gers for the first time ever.

The next season saw both teams go goal-crazy. Killie won again at Ibrox. They raced into a 3-1 half-time lead and emerged 4-3 ahead by time up. Curlett and Mays were again on the scoresheet as was **Frank Beattie** who hit two. And at Rugby Park the goals rained down again in a 3-3 thriller.

In 1960-61 there was another Ibrox triumph and it was earned the hard way. Killie were two down after 35 minutes play but **Andy Kerr** and **Jackie McInally** brought them level by the interval. **Hugh Brown** hit a second half winner to give Kilmarnock their third win at Ibrox out of the last five played. It would be more than 30 years later before they won there again. Kerr was one of the scorers again, alongside **Billy Muir** as Killie won 2-0 at Rugby Park late in the season to record another 'double' and keep up the pressure on Rangers at the top of the table. The season finished with Killie just losing out on the title to Rangers by a single point.

In both 1962-63 and 63-64 Killie again finished runners-up to Rangers. In the latter season just two points separated the top two with six games to play but a 2-0 defeat at Ibrox effectively killed off Killie's chances. The championship season saw both games drawn 1-1 though the rumour that the headline *"Mason scores against Rangers"* was used by one Sunday paper when Killie's **Joe Mason** did precisely that at Ibrox, sadly, cannot be substantiated. There were more

30,000 plus crowds too. Firstly in a 1-1 draw in the championship season then in 1966-67 when the visiting **Premier** of the **Soviet Union Alexei Kosygin** saw the match. It was an exciting encounter narrowly lost 2-1.

The 1968-69 term brought another goal frenzy as Killie took the lead at Ibrox; scored again in the second half then fell 3-2 behind before equalising. Two strikes from **Eddie Morrison** and a goal from **Gerry Queen** gave Killie a deserved point. The return at Rugby Park on January 4th 1969 was a ferocious encounter.

The attendance of **32,893** was a new high for a League match at Rugby Park and is destined to remain an all-time record. Killie lay fifth in the table, one point behind Rangers and just four off leaders Celtic. But when Rangers went ahead after only seven minutes the Rugby Parkers

chances looked dead and buried. But after fifteen minutes play, a **Tommy McLean** free kick was met by an unmarked **Billy Dickson** and Killie were level. An unfortunate own goal from **Frank Beattie** put Rangers back in front before Gers skipper **John Greig** brought down **Eddie Morrison** in the box.

Unsurprisingly Rangers felt hard done by when the referee awarded a penalty. They always do. But Tommy McLean was lethal from the spot and made it 2-2 at half-time. Rangers took the lead for the third time after an hour but **Brien McIlroy** was on hand to make it 3-3 shortly afterwards. Then Rangers' **Colin Stein** assaulted McLean. That was the signal for **Billy Dickson** to come to the winger's defence. Stein and Dickson were both sent off as trouble erupted on the terracing and an otherwise magnificent game was marred by its ugly ending.

Ross Mathie powers a header towards the Rangers goal at a packed Rugby Park.

Eddie Morrison scored twice to give Killie their first home victory for nearly a decade in 1972-73 but the season ended in the disappointment of relegation. It was much worse when Killie returned to the top flight in 1974-75 going down **6-0** at home to Rangers. So when Killie travelled to Ibrox later that season many were expecting a stroll for the home side. It turned out totally different. Killie had the temerity to take the lead before settling for a 3-3 draw thanks to goals from **Derrick McDicken, Davie Provan** and **Ian Fallis.**

Killie's first foray into the Premier Division ended in relegation but even so there were some good performances like the one which saw **Alan Robertson's** goal bring a victory over Rangers.

In their first season back in the First Division the whole club was shocked by the tragic death of **Ian Fallis** in a road crash at the age of 23. Immediately Kilmarnock made arrangements to assist his teenage widow and Rangers were eager to help. The Ibrox side agreed to play in a benefit match and also loaned out **Colin Stein** to Killie until the end of the season. Rangers chief **Willie Waddell** clearly still had affection for his old club.

When Killie returned to the Premier under **Davie Sneddon** the part-time team put on some sterling shows. **Jim Clark** and **Joe Cairney's** goals gave Killie a 2-1 win over Rangers in September 1979 and near the end of the season a **Bobby Street** goal made it a home 'double' and virtually guaranteed Killie another season in the Premier as well.

1980-81 was a horror story though as injury-ravaged Killie lost **8-1** at home to the Gers, restoring some pride with a 1-1 draw later in the season. **John Bourke** was the scorer in both matches.

When Killie returned to the Premier Division in 1993 they faced Rangers at Ibrox in the fourth game of the season. This was a Rangers team which had drawn twice with European champions **Marseilles** and indeed had been

within 90 minutes of the European Cup Final themselves. They had been undefeated at home for nearly *eighteen months.* You had to back to 1981 for Killie's last away win in the Premier Division let alone Ibrox. That particular honour hadn't been achieved since 1960.

But Killie were equal to the task. They took the game to Rangers, reasoning that if they packed their defence and awaited the onslaught then they would surely lose, and heavily too. The Killie tactics paid off. Rangers weren't used to teams having a go at them. And when **Mark Roberts** headed Killie in front after just over an hour, the Killie fans were in raptures. Rangers managed to equalise ten minutes later and it began to look like a draw. Even that would have been a tremendous result but the game went past the allotted 90 minutes. Some cynics in the Killie support predicted an injury time penalty for Rangers, They were wrong. **Ian Porteous** robbed Gers goalscorer **Steven Pressley** and fired in a shot. Keeper **Ally Maxwell** managed to block but the ball rolled only as far as the waiting **Bobby Williamson**. The striker tapped the ball into the net and the 3,600 Kilmarnock fans behind the goal went absolutely crazy. 94 minutes on the clock and no way back for Rangers.

Killie had pulled off one of the biggest shocks of the season and it echoed around the football world *"Rangers stunt bij Kilmarnock"* was the headline in the Dutch magazine *International Voetbalnieuws*. No one needed to be a linguist to understand what that meant.

Killie's last home match that season was against Rangers and victory was absolutely vital as the Rugby Parkers occupied a relegation spot. Killie attacked from the start but that precious goal kept eluding them. There were only eleven minutes left when they won a free kick, 25 yards from goal. **Tom Black** took the kick and struck it sweetly through a forest of legs into the corner of the net. 1-0 to Killie and coupled with results elsewhere meant they were out of the bottom three and could travel to the last match at Easter Road with renewed heart.

That game was also the end of an era. The 18,012 spectators were the last to ever stand on the Rugby Park terracing. The very next day the bulldozers moved in, ready to begin the transition to a ground fit for the 21st century. Rugby Park was rebuilt without any interruption to the fixture list – an amazing feat – and twelve months later with the last stands built Rangers were visitors on League duty as a cheque from the Football Trust was handed over. Doing the honours that night was the late trade union leader **Jimmy Knapp**, a lifelong Kilmarnock supporter. On the pitch it was **Brian Laudrup** who stole the show scoring the only goal of the game.

But even as the 21st century dawned some of the suspicions that had always attached themselves to Scottish football lingered on. Two goals to the good in under ten minutes thanks to **Andy McLaren**, Killie lost 4-2 at home in 2000-2001 after they had a man sent off and Rangers had been awarded a penalty.

But the myth of *'Fortress Ibrox'* has been well and truly demolished. Kilmarnock managed just four wins in almost 100 years then doubled that tally in eight. The 1993-94 win was followed by another in March 1997 as **Jim McIntyre** and **Paul Wright** gave Killie a crucial victory in their successful bid to avoid the play-offs and also gave them a foretaste of what was to come in the **Scottish Cup Final** on the same ground a couple of months later.

Then, in the second last game of the following season an **Ally Mitchell** goal in the last minute kept Killie on course for Europe and destroyed Rangers *'ten in a row'* chances at the same time.

But the most impressive of the lot was the most recent. Killie travelled to Ibrox in October 2000 on the back of an eight-game unbeaten run so were hardly likely to be intimidated by the prospect of facing a Rangers side that had lost the last two games played. Even so nobody was prepared for what happened next.

Christophe Cocard gave Killie the lead in just five minutes. And with just over half an hour gone **Gary Holt** added a second. As the game wore on the expected Rangers fightback failed to materialise and it was Killie who were still controlling the game. When **Arthur Numan** put through his own goal midway through the second half, thousands of disgruntled Rangers supporters made for the exits as the contingent of Kilmarnock supporters sang and danced in the Broomloan stand.

Rangers 0 Kilmarnock 3. There has never been such an emphatic victory at Ibrox ever. All of Killie's previous wins had been by the odd goal. This was a victory on a truly epic scale.

Kilmarnock have played more **Scottish Cup** games against Rangers than against any other side. And some have been among the most important in the club's history. The first contest took place back in the **1891-92** season when non-league Killie took the reigning joint-champions of Scotland to three games before being narrowly beaten at neutral Westmarch, then St Mirren's ground.

Their next meeting was truly historic. In 1898 Kilmarnock, then in the Second Division, reached the **Scottish Cup Final** for the first time. Opponents Rangers were a side packed with experience at the highest levels of the game but the raw Kilmarnock side took the game to their illustrious opponents. It was halfway through the second half before they fell behind to a suspiciously offside-looking goal. Even when they went two behind Killie still pressed forward.

Defeat was no disgrace. In fact Kilmarnock had made a name for themselves against the cosmopolitan sneering that had accompanied their presence in the Final. The local press reminded their city brethren that there had been *fifteen* Ayrshire-born players on the pitch proving the ability of the county to provide the best in the game.

Killie lost several times to the Ibrox side; in **1902, 1903,** and **1911** and again in **1925** when a

Celebration. Kilmarnock fans salute their team's historic 3-0 win at Ibrox in October 2000.

record crowd (for the time) of **31,502** watched a quarter-final tie dominated by two veteran thirtysomethings. **Walter Bird** of Kilmarnock who scored the opener and the former Rugby Park hero **Andy Cunningham** who scored the winner for Rangers fifteen minutes from time as Killie lost 2-1.

So when they clashed again in the Final in 1929 few outside Ayrshire gave Killie much hope. And not without reason. Apart from their 100% record against Kilmarnock in cup ties, so much else was in Rangers favour. They were the holders. They had just won the League for the third year in succession. Ten of their starting eleven were full internationals, including all-time greats such as **Alan Morton** – *'The Wee Blue Devil'* – **Davie Meiklejohn** and **Bob McPhail** (whose older brother **Malcolm** won a winner's medal with Killie in 1920). They were a team assembled at a cost of around £10,000 (a massive figure for the 1920s) as opposed to Killie's £800. Killie were also forced to field two

reserves – **Jimmy Williamson** and **John Aitken** - as their left wing pairing and in **Hugh McLaren** they had a centre-half who was only on loan from **Aberdeen** to play in the semi and the Final. No cups no caps, no hope seemed to be the summing-up.

But the supporters disagreed. There was a massive contingent from Ayrshire among the **114,708** present. *It was the largest attendance to ever watch a Kilmarnock match.* Killie, captained by **Mattha Smith** – the only survivor from the 1920 team – were up against blazing sunshine and a strong wind in the first half as they prepared to withstand the Rangers assault. They survived the first fifteen minutes and were beginning to look good when Killie's **Hugh Morton** brought down Rangers' **Jock Buchanan**. The penalty was heading unerringly for the top corner of the net when keeper **Sam Clemie** made the save of his career, leaping to catch the ball and smother it beneath him as he returned to the ground. Clemie had a deserved reputation for saving spot-kicks and this was the most important one he ever made.

Rangers, naturally, appealed for another penalty but referee **Tom Dougray** ignored their pleas. Clemie was still the busier keeper but Killie managed to reach the dressing room with the score 0-0. Early in the second half Rangers keeper **Hamilton** met **Willie Connell's** shot with a miskicked clearance. The ball veered unsteadily to **John Aitken** who blasted a first-time effort bang into the net. Now it was Killie who laid siege to the Rangers goal. Connell hit the post and Mattha Smith also came close. With twelve minutes remaining Connell sent **Williamson** through and he put the chance away to make it **2-0** to Kilmarnock.

Rangers' frustration began to show and Buchanan was sent off – *the first player to be dismissed in a Scottish Cup Final.* The Cup was Kilmarnock's and it was a deserved victory as even the Glasgow press was forced to acknowledge.

Thousands lined the streets to greet the victors on their return. Inside the Grand Hall, the Provost was howled down by the fans who wanted to hear Sam Clemie speak. Sam disarmingly told the audience *"I can save penalty kicks but I canna mak a speech."* That was eloquence enough for the fans. Poignantly, one of those present was **Ex-Provost Wilson** who had played in the very first cup tie against **Renton** back in 1873.

It was a glorious occasion. The two reserves had scored the goals which won the Cup. And Mattha Smith achieved something which no other player has achieved wearing Kilmarnock colours to this day; *he won a second Scottish Cup winner's medal.*

Drama such as that isn't meant to occur more than once in a lifetime but the Killie and Rangers Scottish Cup show was destined to run and run. Three years later **Jock McEwan** led Killie out at Hampden in front of **111,982** spectators to face Rangers in the Scottish Cup Final again. He had four others of the 1929 team with him so inexperience wasn't a charge that could be levelled at Kilmarnock this time. And there were new heroes too. **Tom Smith** at centre-half and '**Bud' Maxwell** up front being the most prominent.

Again it was Killie who took the lead. An undignified scramble three minutes from half-time ended up with **Maxwell** prodding the ball home. Eight minutes after the break **Bob McPhail's** 20 yarder beat **Willie Bell** in the Kilmarnock goal to level at 1-1. McPhail netted again but was given offside. Killie struck back and Maxwell saw a shot cleared off the line. The teams were forced to return the following Wednesday.

The replay drew another massive crowd – **105,695** but it was a disappointing day for Kilmarnock. They fell behind in just ten minutes but managed to stay in contention until twenty minutes from the end when Rangers scored again. The Gers added a third for good measure five minutes later.

Revenge was gained less than twelve months later. A new Rugby Park record gate of **32,745** saw Killie knock out Rangers in a third round tie. **Willie Liddell**, who was only playing because **Connell** was injured, seized on a cross from **McEwan** to score in 37 minutes. This was the only defeat Rangers suffered in the Scottish Cup between 1931-37 so it was little surprise that thousands of supporters invaded the pitch when the final whistle blew.

Five years later Killie took on Rangers at Hampden again. But this meeting, in April 1938, was in the semi-finals. There was a crowd of **70,833** who saw a thrilling match in which both sides gave it their all. In the end it was the relegation-threatened Killie who took Rangers scalp to add to the previously collected head of Celtic by winning 4-3 with two goals each from **Allan Collins** and **Benny Thomson.**

In their last year in the 'B' Division Killie clashed with Rangers at Ibrox in a second round tie and came away with a superb 2-2 draw. The replay attracted yet another record crowd to Rugby Park. **33,545** saw Killie put up a tremendous fight before losing 3-1.

In **1960** Kilmarnock reached their seventh Scottish Cup Final and for the fourth time their opponents were Rangers. And for once they weren't raging underdogs. For Killie were certain to finish second in the League with Rangers a distant third. There was a 1-1 League draw at Rugby Park a week before the Final so it was a confident Killie who took the field in front of **108,017** fans. *It was the last time Kilmarnock would play in front of a six-figure crowd.*

An injury to centre-half **Willie Toner** disrupted Kilmarnock's game plan and midway through the half constant Rangers pressure paid off when **Jimmy Millar** beat Killie keeper **Jimmy Brown** to the jump to put Rangers ahead. Right at the start of the second half a **Matt Watson** foul on **Alex Scott** just outside the area saw referee **Bobby Davidson** award a penalty as the Rangers player fell inside the box. **Eric Caldow** blasted the ball over the bar and Killie fans with long memories began to wonder if it might be 1929 all over again.

Alas, it was not to be. Midway through this period Millar scored with another header and the Cup was on its way to Ibrox. Killie had finished as 'double' runners-up. Second in both League and Cup. **It would be nearly 40 years later before a Kilmarnock side again played in a Scottish Cup Final.**

But no one could foretell that future in **March 1962** when the clubs met again. Rugby Park was the setting for a quarter-final tie. 36,500 tickets were printed and every single one was snapped up. The **35,995** who turned up was yet another new record for the ground. Thanks to changes firstly in licensing arrangements and latterly to all-seater criteria *it will remain the ground record in perpetuity.*

The game itself was a thriller. After just eight minutes Killie's **Hugh Brown** robbed **Jim**

Baxter of possession and sent in a cross for **Andy Kerr** to nod Killie in front. Killie had other chances but couldn't add to their lead. Rangers fought back and right on the stroke of half-time the otherwise immaculate **Davie Sneddon** put in a tackle on **Ian McMillan** on the edge of the box. As the Rangers player tumbled, inevitably a penalty was given. This time **Eric Caldow** made no mistake. The Cumnock-born defender sent keeper **Sandy McLaughlan** the wrong way and Rangers were level.

Just after an hour Rangers were ahead with a goal which took just four touches from keeper **Ritchie** until it was in the back of the Killie net. But with twelve minutes to go hope was restored as **Bertie Black** cracked home the equaliser. With seven minutes left McMillan's solo run took him past the Killie defence before he unleashed an unstoppable shot to put Rangers ahead again. Rangers added a fourth two minutes from time to put the final result at odds with the play. Killie may have lost **4-2** but they had played a full part in a tremendous game. The record crowd deserved a stupendous match. And they got it.

The teams took a rest from each other after that, the next meeting not coming until **1978**. Rangers had already printed tickets for the visit of Celtic in a quarter-final tie and were a bit surprised when Killie spoiled the party by knocking out the other half of the Old Firm to take their place. But having beaten Celtic on the Monday it was asking too much of the part-time Killie to do the same to Rangers five days later. The 4-1 defeat was no disgrace though and the sight of **Colin Stein** playing against Rangers must have unsettled a few among the Ibrox faithful.

Drawn again to visit Ibrox in the fourth round in 1979 a small crowd of only 17,000 saw the part-time First Division side stun Rangers when **Derrick McDicken's** equaliser brought them back to Rugby Park for a replay. The ground safety limit at Rugby Park was now **18,500** but **19,493** turned up to see Killie fight all the way before going down **1-0.**

Andy McLaren shakes off the attentions of Lorenzo Amoruso at Ibrox.

The clubs didn't meet again until the semi-finals in **1994.** It was the first time in 22 years that Kilmarnock had reached that stage of the competition and they were fighting against relegation too. But this was a confident Killie team and, having won at Ibrox earlier in the season, nothing overawed them. Centre-half **Craig Paterson** put the much-vaunted **Mark Hateley** into his hip pocket at the start of the match and kept him there for 90 minutes. Even with other attacking options in the shape of **Ally McCoist, Gordon Durie** and **Duncan Ferguson**, Rangers couldn't penetrate the Killie defence. Indeed, Kilmarnock were the better team on the day and had an **Ally Mitchell** attempt been struck with his right foot rather than his left it could have been all over there and then.

The 1929 team had been compared unfavourably in terms of transfer fees to Rangers. The gap was even greater now. *In this game Rangers fielded two substitutes whose value on the transfer market exceeded the cost of transforming Rugby Park into an all-seated ground!*

The replay brought yet more of the controversy which has dogged meetings with Rangers for more than a century. **Tom Black** gave Killie a deserved first half lead and **Ally Mitchell** nearly made it two after the break. But a minute later a **Hateley** header bounced down off the bar and referee **Les Mottram** awarded a goal. Killie were furious. They protested vehemently that the ball had not crossed the line and TV evidence seemed to bear that out. But to no avail.

Four minutes later Hateley added a second goal and Killie were out. Killie's dream of Cup glory was dashed. But Rangers hopes turned to dust too when Dundee United beat them in the Final.

The first meeting of the sides in the **League Cup** was a sensational affair. 'B' Division Kilmarnock faced Rangers at **Hampden** in a semi-final tie in **October 1952** as rank outsiders.

Killie fought magnificently. **Bob Thyne** was outstanding in defence, marshalling his side with authority. And when their ranks were breached keeper **John Niven** repelled all attempts on goal. Killie had their chances as well but the game was heading for a 0-0 draw when an attempted clearance hit off **Willie Jack's** backside and into the net. 1-0 to Kilmarnock and no time for Rangers to reply. The 'B' Division team had won the right to play Dundee in the Final.

In 1957-58 Kilmarnock, with new manager **Willie Waddell** at the helm, met Rangers in the quarter-finals. Killie took a 2-1 lead to Ibrox and played admirably in the second leg in front of a crowd of **66,000.** At half-time it was 1-1 on the night and Killie maintained their aggregate lead until the final fifteen minutes when Rangers scored twice to win 3-1 on the night and 4-3 overall.

In October 1960, just six months after losing to them in the Scottish Cup Final Kilmarnock met Rangers in the **League Cup Final** at Hampden. The sides were basically the same though Rangers had added the incomparable **Jim Baxter** to their line-up. It was an evenly contested game until eight minutes from the interval when **Ralph Brand** put Rangers ahead. Both teams had chances in the second period but the game was settled when **Alex Scott** spotted Killie keeper **Jimmy Brown** off his line and sent in an in-swinger which went in off the post. *It was Kilmarnock's fourth runners-up prize in six months.*

When Killie were drawn against Rangers in the 1962-63 competition few were confident of victory. Since beating Rangers at the same stage ten years previously Killie had lost five times in all to Rangers in knockout competitions. But this night was different. If it wasn't quite *"the greatest ever game in League Cup history"* as **Hugh Taylor** put it in the *Daily Record* the next day, it must have come pretty close.

76,000 witnessed this epic match and Killie got off to a bright start when **Brien McIlroy** headed them in front after sixteen minutes. But within minutes Rangers were 2-1 ahead. **Andy Kerr** brought Killie level just before half-time. The second half saw Killie at their finest as **Frank Beattie** made **Jim Baxter** look average. Injured **Matt Watson** saw off the threat from **Willie Henderson** and **Jackie McGrory** was outstanding in defence. With ten minutes to go a **Davie Sneddon** corner was met by a leaping **Bertie Black** who headed home the winner. Kilmarnock were in the League Cup Final for the third time. And they had beaten Rangers twice in the last four to get there.

The next season saw the teams drawn together in the same section. Killie lost 4-1 at home in front of a massive crowd of **34,246.** For many years this was quoted as the ground record and even today some publications, lax in their research, still cite this match rather than the Cup quarter-final of 1962 as providing the ground record. Killie partially redeemed their defeat with a 2-2 draw at Ibrox.

Two years later it was yet another semi-final at Hampden. There were **54,702** present as Kilmarnock, the reigning Champions of Scotland, were outclassed for long periods by Rangers. It was 3-1 at half-time and Killie were down **6-1** with just twenty minutes remaining before staging an astonishing fightback, scoring three times to make it **6-4** by the close. Rangers were relieved to hear the whistle. But even the hardest of hearts must have felt something for **Tommy McLean** that night. The winger had scored a hat-trick yet had left the ground on the losing side.

Drawn in the same section the following year both games were tight affairs. 0-0 at Ibrox and a 1-0 win for Rangers at Rugby Park.

There were more goals when the teams next met, in a quarter-final tie in 1982-83. Sadly for Killie they were on the receiving end of all but one of them. Having lost a League game **5-0** at Ibrox four days before meeting Rangers at Rugby Park in the first leg, it would be true to say that it wasn't exactly a confident Kilmarnock side that took the field. Yet few could have expected it to turn out quite as badly as it did. Two down at the break Killie were eventually beaten **6-1**. **Stuart McLean** scored Killie's lone goal. There were under 8,000 watching that night and with the tie effectively over, just over 5,000 bothered to turn up at Ibrox where Killie were beaten **6-0** for an embarrassing **12-1** aggregate scoreline.

The last meeting was a third round tie in **1990-91** at Ibrox and Kilmarnock, just newly-promoted to the First Division gave a good account of themselves. Although Rangers were always on top, Killie defended superbly, going down just 1-0 to a late goal from **Maurice Johnston.**

A rare goal from skipper **Ray Montgomerie** as he outjumps Paul Gascoigne
to put Killie ahead at Ibrox in December 1996.

REAL MADRID

"They all laughed at Christopher Columbus when he said the world was round", sang **Frank Sinatra.** And the same sort of scoffing went on in Scottish football's journalistic circles when Kilmarnock made their first title bid in 1960. Newspapers fell over themselves in the rush to conjure up a comic image of **Real Madrid** ever paying a visit to **Rugby Park** in the **European Cup**.

Scribes from the same papers were in another rush in November 1965. The scramble for places in the press box to watch **Kilmarnock versus Real Madrid** in the **European Cup**. Or, as *Francis Albert* crooned later in the same song: *"Ho ho ho. Who's got the last laugh now?"*

Real were packed with some of the biggest names in the game. Outside-left **Francisco Gento** had played in every one of their *five* European Cup triumphs. **Santamaria** had played in three. The biggest star of all was **Ferenc Puskas** – *the Galloping Major* – Now in his late thirties and somewhat portly round the middle, but still indisputably the genius who had inspired firstly the fabulous **Hungarian** team of the 1950s and then Real.

There were new faces too. Like striker **Amancio** and central defender **Zoco**. Both stars in their own right. Both members of the **Spanish** team which had won the **European Championship** in **1964.**

It had been only two years since Real had beaten Rangers 7-0 on aggregate in the European Cup so Kilmarnock were expected to be a mere stepping stone on their way to a sixth European Cup.

But Killie had other ideas and in less than ten minutes the near-25,000 crowd was filling the night sky with cheers as **Brien McIlroy** had the ball in the Spaniards net. The cheers soon subsided as he was ruled offside. But still Killie pressed forward and after twenty minutes won a penalty when **Jackie McInally** was brought down in the box.

The awesome responsibility of the penalty kick was placed on the shoulders of a player aged just 18. **Tommy McLean** stepped forward and with all the coolness of a battle-scarred veteran knocked the ball into the net to put Kilmarnock one up.

The lead lasted just four minutes. The hitherto anonymous **Puskas** suddenly found a burst of speed, reminiscent of his prime, and set up a pass to **Martinez** for the equaliser.

The game turned on two incidents early in the second half. McInally was again impeded inside the area, being brought down by **Zoco**. As an irate Killie made fruitless appeals to the referee for a second penalty, the side briefly lost concentration and allowed **Gento** space on the left. His cross was met by **Amancio** who fired Real ahead.

But this Kilmarnock team never gave up. Just seven minutes later as the hour mark approached **Ronnie Hamilton's** cross was headed firmly between the posts by Jackie McInally. Killie searched for the winner often making Real look ordinary in the process. Gento was even booked for fouling McLean. But at the end of a titanic struggle the Scots had to settle for a 2-2 draw. They were applauded off the pitch by their fans. Kilmarnock had matched Real Madrid. **It was another night when Killie made all of Scotland feel proud.**

In the second leg Killie held out in the **Bernabeau** against a stream of Spanish attacks. Then they silenced the supporters in that famous stadium in 27 minutes when Brien McIlroy fired the Scots into the lead.

But the Spaniards were stung by this shock and scored twice within the next four minutes. Even then Killie had their chances. McInally rounded the keeper and with the goal at his mercy somehow contrived to shoot wide. When Real scored again to make it 3-1 at half-time the tide was turning against Kilmarnock.

Gento added a fourth for Real before Killie spurned their last chance to get back into the game. They were awarded a penalty. But for the first time in his career, McLean failed from the spot. A fifth goal from Real made the final score look a lot more comfortable than it had actually been.

Kilmarnock could look back on their foray into the European Cup with pride. For long periods they had equalled the best the continent had to offer. And this was a superb Real Madrid, make no mistake. They went on to defeat **Anderlecht, Inter Milan** and **Partizan Belgrade** to win their **sixth** European Cup. It would be more than 30 years later before a Real Madrid side ever won it again. **That was the measure of the team that conquered Europe but couldn't win at Rugby Park.**

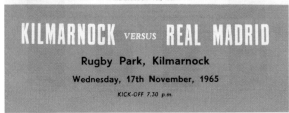

The Champions of Scotland prepare to take on the best in Europe.

RECIFE

After the antics of Mantova, Killie's last opponents in the **1963 New York** tournament were **Brazilian** team **Recife**. Killie's chances of winning their group were gone but they still wanted to go out on a high note.

Willie Waddell's team had to be rejigged slightly for this, their 53rd and final game of the season. **Pat O'Connor** made his first appearance of the tournament, but on the left side of midfield rather than his accustomed right. He took **Frank Beattie's** slot with Beattie moved to centre-half to replace **Jackie McGrory. Andy King**, who had featured in only the Mantova

match kept his place at right-back.

But despite the changes, the weariness and the weather Killie soon found out that Recife were not up to the standard of Bangu and took a 1-0 lead back to the dressing room.

A solid second half performance allowed then to dominate the rest of the game and run out victors by 3-1 with **Bertie Black, Eric Murray** and **O'Connor** the goalscorers. It enabled them to finish a creditable third in the seven-team group, having lost only once.

RENTON

Games	6	
League	5	1895-97
Scottish Cup	1	1874
Top Scorer	'Bummer' Campbell 3	All SL
Top Home Crowd	3,000 Aug 15th 1896 SL	

The history of Kilmarnock might not start with **Renton.** But the history of the **Scottish Cup** does. On **October 18th 1873** the first ever Scottish Cup tic took place and it featured Killie and Renton. The match was played at Queen's Park's **Crosshill** ground – the original Hampden Park - but for Killie it ended in a 2-0 defeat.

That wasn't at all surprising. The Ayrshire side turned up with only ten players and were constantly pulled up by the referee for using their hands. Some of their players clearly still had difficulty in discerning the difference between Association and Rugby football. And considering that cach half lasted for 40 minutes who could fault them?

The game was still in its infancy, witness Killie playing seven of their nine outfield players as

forwards. By all accounts it was an intriguing episode with the play improving the longer the game went on. But, unsuccessful though they were, Kilmarnock had helped make history that day. And, alongside **Queen's Park** and **Dumbarton** they can claim to have contested every Scottish Cup ever since.

They never met Renton in the Cup again but the Dunbartonshire side – 'Champions of the World' in 1888 – were in the Second Division when Killie joined the League in 1895. They may have declined from their peak but Renton were still capable of giving Killie a hard time. Killie won the home fixture 4-2 but lost 3-0 away. They were forced to meet the Dunbartonshire team for a third time at the end of the season.

Both teams finished with 21 points and although Renton were superior both in terms of goal

History is made. The very first Scottish Cup tie in 1873 featured Kilmarnock and Renton.

average and goal difference, Scottish League rules decreed a play-off for third place.

Third was a vital spot in the division as the top three put their names forward for election to Division One. The game took place at **Cathkin Park** but Killie missed out, losing narrowly 2-1.

They opened up their second League season by beating Renton **5-1** at home with **'Bummer' Campbell** claiming a hat-trick and won the away fixture for the first time by 2-1.

Killie were scheduled to play Renton again in 1897-98 but after four games the Dunbartonshire side dropped out of League football forever and Hamilton stepped in to take their place.

REYKJAVIK KR

In the early days of European football a trip to **Iceland** meant an easy win away and the chance for some shooting practice at home. By the end of the 20th century that perception was no longer true. At a national level Iceland were capable of taking points off anybody at home and of creating the odd shock away. And in club football too Icelandic teams were getting better.

Strongest of all were **KR Reykjavik.** The team drawn to play Kilmarnock in the **Qualifying Round** of the **1999-2000 UEFA Cup** were record League and Cup winners in their country and on their way to yet another domestic 'double' when this tie took place.

The Icelandic side included their country's 'Player of the Year' – the much-travelled **David Winnie.** The former **Ayr United** man was no stranger to the Killie side and his warnings of a tough game proved correct in the first leg in Reykjavik. Even so, Killie made a real effort to win the match – to the extent of bringing on striker **Paul Wright** as a substitute with five minutes to go when many teams would have settled for an extra defender.

In fact Killie's adventurous approach cost them dearly when **Hinriksson** scored in 87 minutes to give the home team a 1-0 lead to protect at Rugby Park.

And they protected it well. The frustrated Kilmarnock team threw everything at Reykjavik without success. An ignominious exit loomed until Killie were awarded a penalty in the last minute of the second leg. As usual Paul Wright was totally nerveless as he slotted home the spot-kick to take the game into extra time.

After just two minutes **David Bagan** cheered the 11,760 fans when he put Killie two up and 2-1 ahead on aggregate. But the loss of a goal would have eliminated the Ayrshire team on away goals and it was a pretty nervous half hour until the final whistle sounded and Kilmarnock could claim their place in the first round.

Goal hero **Paul Wright** in action against Reykjavik.

ROSS COUNTY

Nowadays they are a respected force in the Scottish League but back in **1962** when **Ross County** visited Rugby Park in a third round **Scottish Cup** match they were just an average Highland League side.

In reaching this stage of the competition they had equalled their previous best and in winning away to Dumbarton in the previous round, they had knocked out a League team for the first time.

So the **Dingwall** outfit travelled to Ayrshire with nothing to lose. And for the first 45 minutes they kept things pretty tight, going in at the interval just 2-0 down. The second half saw Kilmarnock's superiority come through as time after time the Highland defence was breached. Andy Kerr, Brien McIlroy and Ernie Yard all got on the scoresheet. As did defender Jim Richmond. But the scoring honours went to Joe Mason who notched up a hat-trick as Killie won easily 7-0.

ROYAL ANTWERP

Kilmarnock manager **Malcolm MacDonald** had his work cut out at the start of the **1966-67** season as he also took on the role of **Scotland** boss on a temporary basis. So he was probably glad when the club was given a bye in the first round of that season's **Fairs Cup**.

The second round draw sent Kilmarnock to a new country – **Belgium** – to face **Royal Antwerp**. They had been Belgian champions four times, most recently in 1957, and were regarded in their own country a bit like Kilmarnock were in Scotland. Just behind the big two (in this case **Anderlecht** and **Standard Liege**) and capable of challenging the best. Also like Killie they had played once in the European Cup and lost to Real Madrid.

There the similarities ended. For Kilmarnock were a far more disciplined side than Antwerp. **Jackie McInally** gave Killie a first half lead in Belgium and they defended it to the end despite provocation from the Belgians. Killie returned to Scotland with their first ever away win in Europe under their belts.

The second leg took place just seven days later and Killie were in top form. After losing the opening League game of the season they had won five and drawn the other in the six played since. They were in no mood to let the Belgians disrupt that run.

And it turned into a stroll for Kilmarnock. They led 3-0 at half-time and the goals kept on coming after the break, even if the Belgians did manage a couple of their own. That was of little account as Killie ended up winning **7-2** – *their biggest win in Europe* – and 8-2 on aggregate. **Jackie McInally, Tommy McLean** and **Gerry Queen** all scored two each with **Craig Watson** also registering. The crowd of nearly 12,000 left the ground happy in the knowledge that Killie were about to make an impression on Europe this season.

Mattha Smith. Grandfather of 70s star Gordon and the only player to win two Scottish Cup winners medals while with Kilmarnock. So far.

ST BERNARD'S

Games	4	
League	2	1899-1900
Scottish Cup	2	1894, 95
Top Scorer	All 1: Brodie, Campbell,	SC
	Anderson, Ferguson, Howie	SL
Top Home Crowd	3,500 Sep 16th 1899 SL	
Top Away Crowd	3,000 Nov 25th 1893 SC	

Kilmarnock were drawn against **Edinburgh** side **St Bernard's** two years in succession in the **Scottish Cup**. In the first round in 1893-94 the Edinburgh team visited Rugby Park. Killie put up a spirited fight but St Bernard's were top-drawer opposition. They finished third in the First Division this season so their 3-1 win – all the goals coming in the first half – was no great surprise.

1894-95 was Kilmarnock's last season as a non-league club. And it was a successful one too with 25 wins from 40 games played and 140 goals scored. But when they came up against the Saints again, this time in Edinburgh in a second round match, the gulf in class was apparent. Killie were beaten again and by the same score

3-1. Although not up to the quality of their opponents it was still a good performance from the Ayrshire club which stood them in good stead when up for election to the League at the end of the season. Their conquerors went on to win the Scottish Cup that year.

The clubs met in only one League season. In September 1899 Killie finally beat the Edinburgh side with a 2-1 Rugby Park victory. They drew 1-1 in Edinburgh in November. St Bernard's failed to gain re-election to the top flight at the end of the season. Although they continued to play League football up until the outbreak of the Second World War, Killie were destined never to play them again.

ST JOHNSTONE

Games	120	
League	100	1924-30, 32-39, 47-54, 60-62, 63-73, 74-75, 77-79, 81-82,
		84-85, 88-89. 93-94, 97-2001
Scottish Cup	3	1982, 93
League Cup	14	1950, 53, 66, 70, 74, 76, 93, 2001
Other	3	1940, 50
Top Scorer	Eddie Morrison 7	All SL
Top Home Crowd	15,086 May 15th 1999 SPL	
Top Away Crowd	8,800 Feb 25th 1961 SL	

Killie had nearly 30 League seasons under their belt before they ever played **St Johnstone**. And they found the **Perth** club to be a welcome addition to the fixture card. Between their first meeting in 1924-25 and the start of the 1970s they lost just *twice* at Rugby Park. Nor did St Johnstone's **Muirton Park** hold any fears for Kilmarnock either. They put together a ten-game unbeaten run right throughout the 1950s and 60s

on that ground.

There were some pretty spectacular high-scoring games too. **5-4** to Killie in October 1932 for example. In 1954 as Killie put together an eight-match unbeaten run which powered them to promotion Saints were crushed **5-0** at Rugby Park. And there was a **5-3** victory towards the end of the 1966-67 season. Away from home

Killie won several times by three goals. Yet there was one inexplicable blemish on their record. In 1927-28 after trailing just 1-0 at the interval, Kilmarnock were beaten **7-1** on their own turf.

As Kilmarnock declined generally after 1970 so too did their results against Saints and there were few encounters between the clubs until Killie regained their place in the Premier in 1993-94.

That season saw both Kilmarnock and St Johnstone engaged in a desperate struggle to avoid relegation and Killie's games against the Perth team went a long way to determining the outcome. Both Rugby Park matches were dour 0-0 draws. Games at St Johnstone's new all-seated **McDiarmid Park** were just as tight but Killie held the edge. **Bobby Williamson's** goal won the points in November 1993 and a **Gus MacPherson** strike did likewise the following March.

Those victories were absolutely essential to survival. At the end of the season Killie finished on the same points as Partick Thistle and St Johnstone. They were two goals better off than Thistle and three to the good on St Johnstone. It was the Perth team that went down but it was a close-run thing.

When St Johnstone returned to the top division three years later they were a transformed team, spending more time in the top half of the table than at the foot. They battled with Killie all the way in 1997-98 for 4th place in the League and the European spot that came with it. In the end Killie held off the Perth challenge to claim the coveted Euro-spot but twelve months later the battle was renewed.

In 1998-99 Killie had a tremendous season. They held second place in the table until mid-February and as the season neared its finish were engaged in another battle royal with St Johnstone. Again there was a European place at stake. But this time only the team finishing third was guaranteed a place in continental competition.

As Killie's last match was at Ibrox while Saints had a home game with Dundee, then the meeting of the clubs at Rugby Park on the second last day of the season became a potential decider. Killie went into it a point ahead, knowing that victory would secure the European place and third place in the League for the first time since 1966.

There was a crowd of **15,086**, the biggest ever to watch this fixture. And when **Mark Roberts** put the home team ahead after just eight minutes, Killie were looking good. But St Johnstone were feisty fighters and **Gary Bollan** brought them

John Bourke puts Killie into the next round of the Cup.

back into it with an equaliser midway through the second half.

There were no more goals so it went down to the last day. The Saints duly got their home win over Dundee and while Killie put up a terrific performance at Ibrox to gain a draw after falling behind, it wasn't quite enough. They finished in fourth – the lowest they'd been since the end of August – one point behind St Johnstone.

But the matter didn't finish there. Scotland finished top of UEFA's *'Fair Play'* League that season and Kilmarnock had the best disciplinary record of any Scottish club. So they were awarded entry to the UEFA Cup via the place reserved for the winners of that contest. **Justice had been done.**

It was **1982** before the teams met in the **Scottish Cup** when two goals from **John Bourke** and another from **Sammy McGivern** gave Killie 3-1

victory in a fourth round clash at Rugby Park. The clubs only other meeting was also in the fourth round, in 1993. After a goalless draw at Rugby Park, Killie were desperately unlucky in the replay. **Tommy Burns** tried to lob the keeper from just inside the Saints half and watched in agony as the ball bounced inches over the bar. Killie eventually lost 1-0 in extra time.

The **League Cup** on the other hand, has produced fourteen games against St Johnstone. Both sides won their home games in 1949-50 but in 1952-53 Killie won both matches as they marched towards the Final. They repeated that in 1965-66 when they won the section but it was Saints turn to win both games in 1969-70 when they reached the Final.

Killie came back from a first leg deficit to win after extra time at Rugby Park in a second round game in 1973-74 and the honours were even with a win apiece in 1975-76. St Johnstone's

Blair Millar scores against St Johnstone in 1985, one of only three League meetings in the 1980s.

158

quarter-final Rugby Park win in 1992-93 gave them a cup 'double' over Killie that season. The most recent meeting was a third round clash at McDiarmid Park in 2000-2001 when the game was decided in Killie's favour by a goal from **Ally McCoist**. It was not only McCoist's last ever goal in the competition; it was also his final appearance.

St Johnstone also appear in a curious footnote to the Kilmarnock story. In 1949-50 the teams met in the semi-finals of the **'B' Division**

Supplementary Cup. Killie came back from two down at Muirton to force a draw. The replay didn't take place until the following August by which time the new season was well underway. Killie won 2-1 after extra time to reach the Final. But the Final was never played. Nor did the competition take place at all that season. And when it did emerge from hibernation in 1951-52 it was as a fresh tournament and Kilmarnock's name went into the hat along with all the others.

ST MIRREN

Games	162	
League	135	1899-1935, 36-47, 54-67, 68-71, 73-74, 75-76, 79-81,
		82-83, 92-93, 2000-01
Scottish Cup	6	1899, 1908, 22, 33, 78
League Cup	16	1955, 56, 57, 62, 71, 77, 78, 86, 2001
Other	5	1918, 40, 46
Top Scorer	Andy Cunningham 8	All SL
	Brien McIlroy 8	6 SL 2LC
Top Home Crowd	27,992 Jan 1st 1955 SL	
Top Away Crowd	20,000 Apr 11th 1908 SC	
	20,000 Jan 2nd 1928 SL	
	20,000 Sep 18th 1954 SL	
	20,000 Jan 2nd 1956 SL	

Rivalry with **St Mirren** was intense right from the clubs first meeting. Killie believed (not without justification) that the **Paisley** side had been among those who had delayed the Ayrshire team's entry into the top flight.

Kilmarnock had an early opportunity to prove that they were worthy of a place at the top table for their very first match in Division One was away to St Mirren. **Bob Findlay** scored the only goal of the game to get Killie off to a flying start in the top League in August 1899. And that **Love Street** victory was one to cherish for it was twelve years before Killie took full points from there again. That was in a game which was goalless at the break but finished 4-2 to Kilmarnock.

At home, Killie found the *Buddies* difficult to beat. But once they did manage to win (at the fifth time of asking) Rugby Park became a

fortress as Killie embarked on a thirteen match unbeaten run there.

There were some fine performances too. In 1905-06 it stood at 3-3 at half-time before Killie won **5-3**. In 1907 the fixture was played on New Year's Day for the first time – the start of a decades-long tradition. And Kilmarnock's 1-0 win that day ended a spell of fourteen games without a win. And even when St Mirren finally managed to win at Rugby Park, Killie roared back the next season (1917-18) with a **5-1** victory.

1918-19 brought even greater satisfaction when they repeated that scoreline at Love Street. After the change in the offside law in 1925 there were goals a-plenty in this fixture. The game at Rugby Park in October 1927 saw Killie win **6-2** while at Love Street the next season Killie lost **5-4** away.

On Hogmanay 1929 fire broke out at the Glen cinema in Paisley. Sixty-nine children aged between 18 months and 14 years old died in the rush to escape the building. Firemen reported seeing a mound of bodies breast-high just ten feet away from safety. It was Britain's worst ever cinema disaster.

Naturally, both St Mirren and Kilmarnock begged the Scottish League to call off the scheduled Ne'erday game at Love Street. They refused. The town of Paisley ushered in 1930 in a sea of anguish but the Scottish League were unbending. They ordered the game to go ahead. Under protest, and fearful of sanctions, both teams acquiesced.

The result is immaterial. The whole affair is an example of the insensitivity of the football authorities to the world around them. Even today their reactions to disaster vary tremendously. The SFA called off an international in 1997 after a woman was killed in a car crash in Paris. Yet UEFA in 2001 only pulled back at the last minute from sending Rangers into a war zone.

The same UEFA showed more sensitivity in calling off European games after the loss of thousands of lives in terrorist attacks in the USA. But, on the same evenings as the UEFA postponements, both the English and Scottish Leagues went ahead with domestic games.

Gordon Cramond is Killie's lone scorer as they go down to a heavy defeat at Rugby Park.

The Rugby Park fixture in **April 1947** was one of the most significant in Killie's history. Just a couple of weeks earlier Killie looked like they had climbed clear of the relegation zone leaving Saints and Queen's Park to fight it out for second bottom spot. But after losing to Celtic, Killie still had some work to do. Victory over St Mirren would have saved them from the drop. But it was a game in which nothing went right for Kilmarnock. Trailing 2-1 at the interval, the second half was one long tale of woe. The Buddies won **5-1** to virtually ensure their own safety and send Kilmarnock off to Firhill for their last match with their time in the top flight fast ebbing away.

Killie's return to the First Division saw the first Ne'erday game against St Mirren since before the war. And there was a massive crowd of **27,992** there to witness the occasion at Rugby Park. **Bobby Flavell** made his debut for Kilmarnock that day but it was **Tommy Henaughan** who scored for Killie in a 1-1 draw.

Kilmarnock firmly established themselves as superior to Saints. At Love Street they won *seven out of eight* between 1958-66, the first three without losing a goal. The last match of the sequence was an amazing affair. A pitifully small Ne'erday crowd of under 4,000 was all that Love Street could attract to see a sensational game in which Killie led **5-1** at half-time. The *Buddies* came more into it in the second period but Killie still won by an incredible **7-4** scoreline.

Killie's goals came from their *'M'-men*. **Brien McIlroy** and **Jackie McInally** both hit two and **Joe Mason, Tommy McLean** and **Eric Murray** all scored as well A *'double-M'* – boss **Malky MacDonald** took to a shine to one of the opposing players that day and bought **Gerry Queen** from Saints for £4,000 with **Ronnie Hamilton** heading to Paisley. Queen gave sterling service to Kilmarnock before being transferred to **Crystal Palace**. It was while with that club he was sent off for fighting on the pitch which inspired one of the most famous football headlines ever:

"QUEEN IN BRAWL AT PALACE"

Killie were usually in charge at Rugby Park as well but there was an inexplicable lapse in the first home game of the 1959-60 season when they were beaten **5-0** by Saints. But St Mirren were finding it harder to stay in Division One and games between the clubs became fewer in number. By 1973-74 both teams were in the Second Division and although Killie reached the Premier before St Mirren, the Paisley team proved to have the greater staying power. They had a spell of fifteen years in the top flight and had the better of things on the rare occasions the clubs met. The worst result came in October 1980 when **Gordon Cramond** got Killie's only counter in a **6-1** Rugby Park defeat.

St Mirren were back in the First Division just as Killie were escaping it. In the 1992-93 season honours were even. Both clubs won one and lost one at home. Killie's 2-1 defeat at Love Street late in the season after leading for much of the match through an **Ally Mitchell** goal was their only loss in their last nine matches. It came too late for St Mirren to make up lost ground.

The Paisley Saints didn't return to the top until **2000-2001** when they were promoted to the SPL. Killie's first fixture of the season was at Love Street and a **Gary Holt** goal sent all three points to Ayrshire. Killie won at home then met Saints on Boxing Day for their third clash of the season.

The struggling *Buddies* led 1-0 for most of the match and less than 25 minutes remained when **Paul Wright** grabbed the equaliser. The same player popped up five minutes from time to put Killie ahead then sealed a virtuoso performance with a third in the dying seconds to secure his hat-trick. St Mirren were relegated at the end of the season.

Kilmarnock's first competitive match against St Mirren was a quarter-final **Scottish Cup** tie at Rugby Park in **March 1899** – just months before Killie joined the top flight. There was a record crowd of **11,129** to see St Mirren take a 2-0 first half lead leaving too much for Killie to do after the break. It finished 3-1 in Saints favour and, having remained undefeated throughout the League campaign, was the only game Killie lost all season

In 1908 Kilmarnock reached the last four in the Cup for the first time in a decade and a new record gate of **15,000** saw them take on St Mirren at Rugby Park in the semi-final. But it was a drab encounter with few chances from either side and after it petered out in a 0-0 draw, the teams headed for Love Street a fortnight later. The replay was little better from Kilmarnock's point of view as Saints made home advantage tell, winning 2-0 with a goal in each half.

Killie also lost a second round game at Rugby Park 2-1 in 1922 before finally recording a win over St Mirren with a 1-0 triumph at Love Street in the second round in 1933. In 1978 First Division Killie travelled to Love Street to face Premier side Saints in a third round tie. Despite having lost there earlier in the season in the League Cup, Killie were more than a match for the *Buddies*. They won 2-1 thanks to goals from **George Maxwell** and **Donnie McDowell** who had joined Killie from St Mirren earlier in the season. A decision that St Mirren manager **Alex Ferguson** must have regretted that day.

The **League Cup** found the teams drawn together in the same section for three successive seasons from **1954-57** and they weren't happy times for Killie as they failed to win any of the six matches played. Drawn together again in 1961-62 Killie lost at Love Street before finally beating Saints at the eighth attempt. It was only

1-1 at half-time in the Rugby Park game but Killie put in a five-star performance in the second period winning **6-1**. **Bertie Black** and **Brien McIlroy** both scored two and **Frank Beattie** and **Joe Mason** completed the scorers.

Killie won both games in 1970-71 but failed to progress from the section. And they only took one point from the two games in 1976-77. They lost a two-legged tie 2-1 on aggregate the next season. Killie's goal was scored by **Ian Fallis**. Sadly, it was to be his last.

Saints won a second round tie easily enough 3-1 in 1985-86. For fifteen years after that the teams didn't meet. Then came the semi-final in **2001**. It was a cold February night at **Hampden** with fewer than 10,000 in attendance. Most attention was focused on the Old Firm semi taking place the following evening but for Killie and Saints

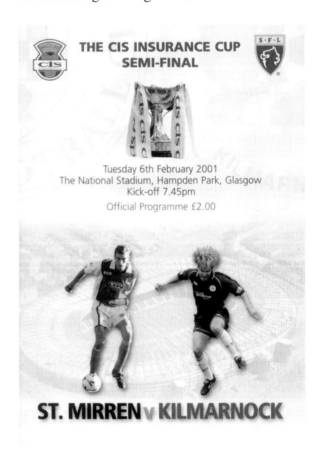

A convincing win for Kilmarnock and a wonder goal from **Craig Dargo** in this League Cup semi-final at Hampden in 2001.

this was a rare chance to appear in a national Cup Final.

Although few in number, both sets of fans were highly vocal, managing to create a cup-tie atmosphere despite the fact that the stands behind the goals were closed. Killie ran the show and it was no surprise when **Andy McLaren** put them ahead six minutes from the interval.

But no cup tie is over when there's just a goal between the teams. St Mirren must have thought they were still in with a chance when Killie's

Craig Dargo received the ball inside his own half midway through the second period. But Dargo had thoughts of his own. He ran like a man possessed, shrugging off his challengers and shooting home from the edge of the penalty area. It was a magnificent solo goal, worthy of winning any competition.

It certainly knocked whatever fight St Mirren still possessed right out of them and **Peter Canero** wrapped things up with twelve minutes to go. 3-0 to Kilmarnock and they were back in the **League Cup Final** after a gap of 38 years.

SHELBOURNE

August 14th 1997 was an important date in the Kilmarnock story. It marked the club's first match in European competition since September 1970 and Irish Cup holders **Shelbourne** were the opposition in the **European Cup-Winners' Cup**. They were an experienced side in European terms –this was their ninth season in Europe. Many of the Kilmarnock players weren't even born the last time the club played in Europe but even so, it was generally agreed that a Scottish team should beat an Irish team with little difficulty.

Naturally Shelbourne and their large and enthusiastic band of supporters in the crowd of 9,041 at Rugby Park disagreed with that analysis. And the Irish team made a strong start to the game, stunning the home supporters not only with the quality of their play but also with a goal after twelve minutes.

From that moment on Kilmarnock knew they had a fight on their hands to secure a place in the next round. But Shelbourne were sound in defence as well and gave little away. They reached the sanctuary of the dressing room with their lead intact.

After ten fruitless minutes in the second half,

manager **Bobby Williamson** made a double substitution. On came new French signing **Jerome Vareille** and experienced Scottish international **Pat Nevin**. Both were making their home debuts and both were skilful ball players who could take on and beat opponents.

The move was a success as Killie upped the tempo and won a penalty after 65 minutes. **Paul Wright** stepped up to the mark and blasted the ball home to become the first player to score for Killie in Europe since **Eddie Morrison**. But the winner still proved elusive. The game had ran past the 90th minute and the fans were heading for the exits when a loose ball fell to Wright. Without hesitation he shot instantly into the net to give Killie a 2-1 lead. It was the last kick of the match.

Dublin is renowned as one of the great entertainment cities of the world and Kilmarnock fans travelled there in vast numbers for the second leg, determined to enjoy themselves yet aware that, under the away goals rule, a 1-0 defeat would end their team's hopes.

But after a cagey opening twenty minutes, those fans were singing and dancing. From an impossible-looking angle, **Jim McIntyre** looked up and hit a marvellous shot into the net. Killie had a breathing space. Shelbourne didn't lie down though. They came back to equalise on the night six minutes from the interval.

Chances were few and far between in the second period and there were no more goals. Killie had done enough to go through 3-2 on aggregate and the Dublin bars experienced a night of the *craic* – Ayrshire style.

"In Dublin's fair city."
Killie fans celebrated the return to Europe by travelling in large numbers to get behind the team.

SIGMA OLOMOUC

Most Kilmarnock supporters didn't know much about **Sigma Olomouc** when Killie were drawn against them in the **UEFA Cup** in **1998-99**. And the little they did know wouldn't have helped them a lot. They had finished third in the **Czech** League to qualify for Europe. Only one of their players – defender **Martin Kotulek** – was a full international. But their European pedigree was impressive. In four previous appearances they had been beaten three times by teams ranked among the very best; **Gothenburg, Real Madrid** and **Juventus**. The fourth occasion had seen them lose to a Polish club. They had reached the last eight on one occasion and among their victories was a 7-1 thrashing of Turkish cracks **Fenerbache**.

That was enough to let Killie know they were in for a hard time in the Czech Republic when they visited the **Ander Stadium** in the first leg. And it was a gruelling experience for the Scots.

Sigma may have had only the one full international but their squad was laced with Czech under-21 stars and it was one of these – **Jiri Krohmer** – who gave the home side the lead in 26 minutes just as it looked like Killie had weathered the storm.

Killie continued to be put under the cosh but with twelve minutes left they were still just that single goal down when another Czech under-21 player – **Radim Konig** – struck to leave the Ayrshire side facing an uphill task at Rugby Park.

Killie's hopes of retrieving the situation were killed off at home inside twenty minutes. With thirteen minutes played, another of the Czech's side's talented youngsters – **Marek Heinz** – put Sigma further ahead. And six minutes later veteran **Josef Mucha** made it 2-0. Kilmarnock's unbeaten record against continental opposition at Rugby Park had gone.

Gus MacPherson prepares to skipper Killie in the second leg against Sigma Olomouc.

6TH GRV

6th GRV or **Galloway Rifle Volunteers** to give them their full name made fairly frequent appearances in the Scottish Cup proper. But the first decent opposition they faced usually dismissed them. Such was the case in 1898 when the **Dalbeattie** team travelled to Rugby Park for a first round Scottish Cup tie.

Killie were in no mood for an upset and though the Volunteers kept the score down to 2-1 at half-time, Kilmarnock piled on the pressure in the second half to run out winners by 5-1. This was the first step in their march to the Final.

SLAVIA SOFIA

Slavia Sofia had reached the semi-finals of the Cup-Winners' Cup in 1967 where they were narrowly beaten by Rangers. So Killie knew this **Bulgarian** team posed a threat to their **Fairs Cup** prospects in this second round tie in **1969-70**.

But the Scots got off to a dream start. With only ten minutes played. **Ross Mathie** and **Jimmy Cook** had given them a 2-0 lead. Near the half-hour mark though, they lost playmaker **Jim McLean** to injury. It didn't seem to faze Killie. In the second half the 5'4" winger Cook actually headed into the net but Mathie was offside.

The striker made up for that lapse fifteen minutes from the end when the keeper parried away a Morrison shot and Mathie seized the chance to make it 3-0. Less than a minute later a dreadful clearance by the Slavia keeper fell to **John Gilmour** who lobbed the ball over the stopper's head from 40 yards out. At 4-0 Kilmarnock supporters were delirious. Even when Slavia pulled a goal back with two minutes to go, it did nothing to dent their belief that the tie was over.

But the Bulgarians thought differently, as Killie found out in Sofia. They conceded a goal in the first minute and another after 24 minutes. At 2-0 down and over an hour to play they had to avoid a further loss. One more goal and they would be out on the away goals rule. **Billy Dickson** was the captain that night and he played the role to perfection, steadying the troops, barking out orders and leading by example.

Thanks in large part to Dickson, Killie came through the rest of the match unscathed to take their place in the next round.

STENHOUSEMUIR

Games	24	
League	19	1947-54, 73-74, 89-90
Scottish Cup	3	1952, 76
League Cup	2	1973
Top Scorer	Willie Jack 5	4 SL 1 SC
Top Home Crowd	11,649 Jan 26th 1952 SC	
Top Away Crowd	2,500 Apr 3rd 1954 SL	

Stenhousemuir were another latecomer to Killie's history. The clubs didn't meet until Killie were relegated to the 'B' Division. And their first meeting at **Ochilview**, in October 1947, ended with Killie losing 1-0. They eased the pain of that loss with a **7-2** home win later in the season. But the next season Killie knew what it was like to be on the end of a hiding as they crashed **6-2** away. In 1950-51 tiny *Stenny* even did the 'double' over them.

Kilmarnock improved greatly after that and in the promotion-winning season of 1953-54 they obtained two crucial victories over Stenhousemuir. At Rugby Park they were a goal down at half-time to a Stenhousemuir side that lay in second place. Killie – fresh from a win over leaders Motherwell – turned it on in the second half as **Tommy Henaughan** scored a hat-trick. Goals from **Jimmy Middlemass, Davie Curlett** and **Matt Murray** helped them to a **6-2** win. And in the third last game of the season it was Middlemass who broke the deadlock at Ochilview. His goal set Killie up for the decider with Third Lanark.

Since then Killie have only met 'Muir in two other seasons - both promotion-winning campaigns. In 1973-74 when Killie won both matches and in 1989-90 when Killie won two and lost one to a Stenhousemuir team that harboured hopes of going up themselves.

The **Scottish Cup** has drawn the teams together twice. In January 1952 **Willie Jack** and **Willie Harvey** scored the first half goals against a seasoned cup-fighting Stenhousemuir team in a first round tie which brought Kilmarnock their first Scottish Cup victory since 1939. Then in 1976 Killie were fortunate to escape from Ochilview with a 1-1 draw in a third round clash. A second half goal from **Gordon Smith** saw them safely through at Rugby Park.

In the **League Cup** in 1972-73 two sides qualified from the four in the section. Despite taking three points out of four against *Stenny*,

Killie were beaten into third place by the *Warriors*.

This Scottish Cup tie finished 1-1 in 1976 and Stenhousemuir's goalscorer **Billy Murdoch** was signed by Killie as soon as the replay was over, making his debut three days later.

STEWARTON

There are no riveting tales told by greybeards of the days when **Stewarton** took on the might of Kilmarnock. And the reason for this is simple. Stewarton were drawn to play Killie at Rugby Park in the first round of the 1880-81 **Scottish Cup.**

But the Stewarton men simply didn't turn up and Killie were awarded a walkover. *"An ungentlemanly practice"* as the *Standard* described it. Given Stewarton's Scottish Cup record – they won one game in a dozen years and took several heavy beatings – maybe it was just as well that they didn't appear.

STIRLING ALBION

Games	55	
League	43	1947-49, 50-51, 52-53, 54-56, 58-60, 61-62, 65-68,
		73-74, 77-79, 89-90, 91-93
Scottish Cup	3	1950, 86
League Cup	7	1948, 60, 67, 98
Other	2	1948, 91
Top Scorer	Jackie McInally 5	3 SL 2 LC
Top Home Crowd	22,734 Jan 28th 1950 SC	
Top Away Crowd	9,400 Feb 1st 1950 SC	

Although they have played them more than fifty times, Kilmarnock have never been in the same division as **Stirling Albion** for more than three consecutive years. Killie found them to be awkward opponents at first. They didn't manage a home win until February 1953 but what a win it was. Stirling were certainties for promotion but Killie destroyed them **6-0** with **Tommy Henaughan, Gerry Mays** and **Jimmy Middlemass** all scoring twice.

On returning to the 'A' Division in 1954, Killie struggled to begin with. The only team they beat in their first twelve games was Albion. It was also Killie's first win at their Annfield home. After that Kilmarnock had the best of it when the teams met, though the games were generally close.

When did Kilmarnock get a draw at Annfield when Shankly was in charge? Like so many 'trick' questions the answer is easier than it at first appears. The **Annfield** in question was Stirling's ground and the **Shankly** was **Bill's** brother **Bob** who was general manager of Albion when Killie met them in the old Second Division in 1973-74.

Bob Shankly was a distinguished manager in his own right - winning the league with Dundee in 1962. But the team boss at Stirling was a newcomer to the ranks of management – one **Francis Whitfield Beattie**. After nineteen years at Rugby Park, **Big Frank** had taken over as manager of Albion Rovers for a year before moving on to Stirling.

So what thoughts must have entered his mind on April 27th 1974? Killie were looking for promotion back to Division One. A draw or a win over Albion and they were there. Defeat and they would have to face promotion rivals Hamilton away in their last match.

Killie were on a roll. They had won their last nine matches so the fans expected nothing less than victory this day. But it was a nervous start and Albion capitalised on it by taking the lead after just six minutes. Killie hardly threatened for the rest of the first half and at the interval were still a goal behind.

Kilmarnock hadn't won any game this season when they had trailed at the interval. That knowledge and the news that Hamilton were winning increased the nervousness in the terracing and on the pitch. Halfway through the second period with the game running away from his team, manager **Willie Fernie** sent on substitute **Ian McCulloch.**

McCulloch soon made his robust presence felt, challenging for everything. Three minutes after he came on Killie won a corner. **Gordon Smith's** flag-kick was met by the soaring **Ian Fleming** who headed the equaliser. The next twenty minutes weren't easy on anyone's nerves as everyone in the ground was all too aware that one mistake could mean failure. But with three minutes to go the familiar figure of **Eddie Morrison** smashed the ball home to give Killie a 2-1 victory and send a signal to the exuberant fans to invade the pitch when the final whistle blew.

The teams haven't met often since then. In 1978-79 there was a **5-0** win at Rugby Park and a **4-1** triumph at Annfield in another promotion year for Kilmarnock. And in 1989-90 it was the *Binos* who pushed Killie to the wire in the promotion race that season. Despite losing 2-1 at home, Killie won both other games 1-0, once at home and once away. And in 1992-93 Killie won three of the four League games, including one at Stirling's temporary home at Ochilview. They lost the other match – also at Ochilview – 2-0 with ex-Killie striker **Willie Watters** scoring both goals. Shades of **Ross Mathie** in 1973.

But the crucial game that season turned out to be the last of the four. In the 40th game of the campaign, Killie turned Albion over 3-0 with **George McCluskey, Ally Mitchell** and **Dugald McCarrison** doing the damage. With St Mirren beating Dunfermline the same day, it meant that Killie were back in a promotion spot and back in charge of their own destiny.

There have been just two **Scottish Cup** meetings. In 1950 Killie could only manage a 2-2 draw at home in the first round and lost the replay 3-1. And they won a third round tie 1-0 in 1986. The decline in support between these games is astonishing. **22,734** watched the first tie. **2,199** attended the second.

In the **League Cup** the teams met three times in sectional matches with little at stake but their most recent meeting was a shocker for Kilmarnock. The Scottish Cup holders visited Stirling's new **Forthbank** ground in a third round tie in August 1997. After 37 minutes the game was still scoreless. Then Killie were rocked by two goals in three minutes. Before Killie could get back into the game, ex-Rugby Parker **Tommy Tait** added a third ten minutes after the interval. **Jerome Vareille** pulled one back shortly afterwards but Killie were hit by another two goals in three minutes before **Paul Wright** added a second for the visitors. The *Binos* scored again a minute before the end to make it **6-2** at the finish.

A dreadful night for Kilmarnock but it gave the Albion fans something with which to taunt their deadly rivals Falkirk as they reminded Bairns fans of their defeat in the Scottish Cup Final.

Tommy Burns drives Killie to victory over Stirling Albion and a step closer to the Premier Division.

STRANRAER

Games	12	
League	5	1973-74, 89-90
Scottish Cup	5	1953, 60, 90, 98
League Cup	2	1975
Top Scorer	Ian Fleming 5	2 SL 3 LC
Top Home Crowd	8,506 Jan 30th 1960 SC	
Top Away Crowd	4,468 Jan 24th 1998	

Kilmarnock are the second oldest club in Scotland, **Stranraer** the third oldest. Yet the two teams have met on only a dozen occasions. They have been in the same division in just two seasons, Killie taking three points out of four in 1973-74 but losing all three games in 1989-90.

In the **Scottish Cup** Killie won 4-0 at **Stair Park** in a first round tie in 1953 and triumphed **5-0** in the same round at Rugby Park in 1960. When they next met, in a second round tie in 1990, it created an unwanted piece of history.

The teams drew 1-1 at Stair Park and the Rugby Park replay finished goalless after 120 minutes.

Tom Black scored a vital winner against Rangers to help keep Killie in the Premier in 1994 and played for Stranraer against Killie in the Cup.

Killie were beaten 4-3 on penalties. **It was the first Scottish Cup tie to ever be decided by penalty kicks**. It also meant that Killie had played Stranraer five times this season and failed to win a single match.

So Kilmarnock were well aware of the potential pitfalls when they visited Stranraer to begin their defence of the Scottish Cup in 1998. After a tricky opening period, **Jerome Vareille** gave Killie the lead ten minutes from the break. A second from **Mark Roberts** four minutes after the restart wrapped up the third round tie for Killie.

The only **League Cup** meetings came in 1974-75 when Killie won both games easily, 5-0 at home and 2-0 at Stranraer.

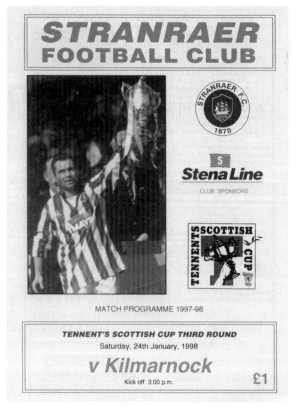

MATCH PROGRAMME 1997-98

TENNENT'S SCOTTISH CUP THIRD ROUND
Saturday, 24th January, 1998
v Kilmarnock
Kick off 3.00 p.m.   £1

Killie made a successful start to their defence of the Scottish Cup at Stair Park.

THIRD LANARK

Games	99	
League	88	1899-1925, 28-29, 31-34, 35-47, 53-54, 57-65
Scottish Cup	4	1897, 1904, 10
Other	7	1940, 46, 65
Top Scorer	Willie Culley 14	All SL
Top Home Crowd	21,663 Apr 17th 1954 SL	
Top Away Crowd	16,000 Aug 29th 1932 SL	

Third Lanark were one of the founding fathers of Scottish football. Like Kilmarnock they were competitors in the first **Scottish Cup** back in 1873. So it's no great surprise to find that the teams met in that competition before they ever clashed in the League. What is unusual is that in almost 100 years they were drawn together only three times.

In a quarter-final tie at Rugby Park in 1897 the teams were locked together at 1-1 for much of the match before Killie struck with two late goals to take them into the last four for the first time. In 1904 Killie travelled to **Cathkin Park** for another quarter-final tie but Thirds were too strong, winning easily 3-0. In 1910 Thirds left Rugby Park with a 0-0 draw in a first round match. Owing to poor weather the replay was postponed but the teams played a friendly instead which Killie lost 6-1. The let-off did them little good. For when the replay took place the following week, they were beaten 2-0.

In the League Killie found Third Lanark to be difficult opponents. Especially at Cathkin. They lost by **5-0** in 1905-06 and **6-3** in the final League game of the season two years later. This game witnessed one of football's rarities – a player who scores a hat-trick yet finishes on the losing side. That was the misfortune that befell **Willie Hunter**, a loan signing from Airdrie.

Things got even worse for Killie two years after that when they were hammered **7-0**, five of these goals coming in the first half. Yet in their next game at Cathkin they won 2-0 with goals from **Andy Cunningham** and **Davie Howie**. It was their first League win there at the twelfth time of asking.

The home record was much better but before that mould-breaking win at Cathkin, Killie had gone down 5-1 at Rugby Park the same season.

Killie's performances against Thirds improved greatly after the First World War. The Glasgow side were no longer the force they had been in the game and spent several seasons in the Second Division.

Killie's first home game in 1932-33 saw them demolish Thirds **6-0** with **'Bud Maxwell'** scoring a hat-trick. This was an amazing season for Maxwell. He had also scored a treble against reigning Champions **Motherwell** away in a 3-3 draw the week before the Thirds game. He missed the next match through injury but came back after that to score in all the next five games. By the end of that period he had played *seven* matches and scored *thirteen* goals. In total he scored 32 times from 33 played. Only injury prevented him from breaking **'Peerie' Cunningham's** record of 34 League goals in a season.

Third Lanark won 1-0 at Rugby Park on August 26th 1939. *It was the last match to be played in peacetime until the visit of Aberdeen six years later.*

Deep in relegation trouble after the war, Killie faced a vital game away to Thirds who at the time were using Hampden as their base. Killie arrived an hour late, during which time the crowd turned angry, demanding a refund and attacking police and photographers with snowballs. It was the middle of March but the winter of 1947 was one of the worst – and longest – ever recorded. The authorities managed to thwart a pitch invasion and the game eventually kicked off – at 4.15pm.

The delay didn't seem to bother Killie as they turned on the style in the second half, scoring three times to win 4-1. Unfortunately it was too late to save their season and the next time the teams met it was in the 'B' Division.

It was also the most important match Kilmarnock would ever play against Thirds. On **April 17th 1954** Killie lined up at home to Thirds in their second last match of the season knowing that a win would end their seven-years exile in the 'B' Division. A draw and Killie would still be favourites. But defeat would leave the Cathkin club four points behind them with two games in hand.

A massive crowd of **21,663** turned up with the vast majority expecting and desiring a Killie victory. The first 45 minutes saw a series of fruitless attacks by Kilmarnock with nothing to show for them. Midway through the second half, **Bob Thyne** gave away a penalty which Thirds converted. All of a sudden the top flight seemed as far away as ever.

Killie attacked *en masse*. All finesse was forgotten as they surged forward time after time. Finally, the Thirds defence cracked as **Gerry**

Mays knocked in the equaliser with just thirteen minutes remaining. Then it was Kilmarnock's turn to be awarded a penalty. With nearly 22,000 pairs of eyes and the burden of seven long years on him, **Jimmy Middlemass** took the kick. *And blasted the ball wide.* It finished 1-1. Killie would have to wait.

The wait wasn't long. 48 hours later Killie manager **Malky MacDonald** phoned the sports desk of a Glasgow paper to be told that **Third Lanark** had only drawn with **Dunfermline** that afternoon. The exile was over. Kilmarnock had won promotion.

Kilmarnock's championship season was also Third Lanark's last in Division One. And the campaign started with a 3-1 win over Thirds at Rugby Park. On Boxing Day Killie won 4-0 at Cathkin. But that wasn't the last time the teams met. In the **Summer Cup** in 1965, Killie won 3-0 away before a paltry crowd of just **667**. And on May 14th that year fewer than 4,000 were at Rugby Park to see a comprehensive **6-2** win for Kilmarnock.

No one present had any inkling it would be the last time these two ancient standard bearers of Scottish football would ever play each other. **Two years later Third Lanark were dead.**

THORNLIEBANK

Kilmarnock travelled to play **Thornliebank** in the third round of the Scottish Cup in **1883-84**. Their opponents had a good Cup pedigree, having reached the Final in 1880. Killie were beaten 2-1 but lodged a successful protest with the match being replayed two weeks later.

Nothing had changed in the interim, other than that Thornliebank were even more violent than in the first match. Killie again lost 2-1, with **Sandy Higgins** getting the goal. But four Kilmarnock players needed medical treatment after the game. Little wonder that Thornliebank were labelled as *"most unmanly and brutal"* in the press.

VALE OF LEITHEN

Vale of Leithen had been competing in the Scottish Cup since 1919 but they had never beaten a League team in the competition when they were drawn to play at Rugby Park in the second round in **1958**.

Killie had been going through a rough patch in the League however, so the **Innerleithen** side travelled with hope of causing an upset. But, in **Willie Waddell's** first Cup game as Kilmarnock manager his team performed professionally. 4-0 up at the break, Kilmarnock completed the job in the second half, winning **7-0** before a crowd of just under 10,000.

The highlight for Killie was the form of **Joe McBride**. The striker had only made his debut at Christmas, less than two months beforehand, and in this match scored his first hat-trick. **Willie Harvey** and **Vernon Wentzcl** with two goals apiece completed the scoring.

VALE OF LEVEN ROVERS

Ah, the complexities of the early days of Scottish football. The **Vale of Leven Rovers** team that Kilmarnock faced at home in the first round of the **Scottish Cup** in **1874-75** were **NOT** the same team as the famous **Vale of Leven** side that won the Scottish Cup three times. Nor were they the Glasgow-based side with the same name.

They were though the first team Kilmarnock ever defeated in the Scottish Cup. Little is known of the game but we do know that Killie won **4-0** and that one of the goalscorers was **Peter Brown**, scorer of the club's first ever goal in a friendly match against Paisley in December 1873. Another was **David Sturrock,** who would score the first hat-trick against Ayr Eglinton a year later. Scoring too was **John Wallace**, the club's founder. It was Wallace, the club secretary, who was the main force in founding the club in **1869.**

VALENCIENNES

Having won one and drawn two in their first three games in the **1963 New York** tournament, Kilmarnock took on **French** team **Valenciennes** in good heart, though the effects of a long season and the travelling involved in this tourney were beginning to have an effect.

From **New York to Chicopee, Massachusetts,** back to **New York** and then to **Chicago** for this game, it was little wonder that Killie were feeling tired. They held out against a strong French team until the second half but ended up losing 2-1. **Ernie Yard** scored Killie's goal.

It was the only game they lost in the competition but it was enough to prevent them from winning their group.

VIKING STAVANGER

Norwegian team **Viking Stavanger** were the seeded side in their **UEFA Cup** first round contest with Kilmarnock in **2001-02** but Killie still thought it was a tie they could win.

UEFA's decision to postpone all matches as a mark of respect to the thousands who perished in the terrorist attacks on America in September 2001 meant that both legs had to be played within seven days. The first leg, at Rugby Park, saw a tentative opening half which was nearing its conclusion when Viking's **Sanne** sped into the penalty area and smashed home past **Gordon Marshall.**

Killie were well on top in the second half but struggled to find the equaliser. When **Paul Di Giacomo** hit the post it looked like all the home team's efforts would be in vain. But with 72 minutes played, **Ally Mitchell** sent over a cross which was headed down by **Alan Mahood** to **Craig Dargo.** The quick-thinking striker reacted instantly to level the tie on the night. Try as they might, Killie couldn't find a way through again and were left facing an uphill task in Norway.

Around 700 Kilmarnock supporters made the short hop over the North Sea. As they flew over the fjords they also glimpsed the mountain range protecting Stavanger. A clear sign of the task awaiting their team. For Stavanger were an experienced side. **Barcelona, Sporting Lisbon** and **Werder Bremen** had all been beaten in their (to Scottish eyes) strange-looking stadium. Just one stand, a running track around the perimeter, no turnstiles and plenty of opportunity for people in nearby houses to watch their football for free.

Yet the Scottish contingent – management, players, press and supporters alike – were all confident that Killie could win. And the supporters were enjoying themselves in unseasonably warm weather in the picturesque town. Nothing, it seemed could spoil their stay.

And then the match kicked off.

Less than a minute had elapsed before poor defending set up a chance for Sanne who promptly scored. Viking piled on the pressure and in 17 minutes the former Manchester United player **Erik Nevlund** added a second. Killie now needed to score twice to go through but a third for Viking looked more likely. Early in the second half, the Norwegians missed a gilt-edged opportunity to finish the game off but shot wide when it looked easier to score.

Killie came more into it in the second period and Alan Mahood was denied by a fine save from the keeper. But it was too little too late. Manager **Bobby Williamson** freely admitted that his side had let themselves and the supporters down. Those same supporters bade their farewells to the fjords with a last defiant rendition of *'Paper Roses'* as they awaited their flight back to Prestwick.

But although this was the first time a Norwegian team had eliminated a Scottish side in European competition, the result of the tie simply confirmed the UEFA rankings. When details of shock results were posted on UEFA's website the next day, this match wasn't among them. Kilmarnock's performance was no better than expected but nor was it any worse. Neither that nor the surprising knowledge that this had actually been Killie's *third best* European season statistically did anything to assuage the fans' hurt. Kilmarnock's ninth venture into Europe was over.

WEST BROMWICH ALBION

West Bromwich Albion were a mid-table side from the old English First Division (today's Premiership) when Killie met them in the **1965 New York** tournament. They had quite a few players of proven ability. **Jeff Astle, Tony Brown** and **Clive Clark** were all established goalscorers and in defence they could rely on Welsh international **Graham Williams** and Eaglesham-born **Doug Fraser**. Midfield creativity came from another Scot, the unfortunately named **Bobby Hope** (*whatever were his parents thinking of?*).

But in the first game in America it was the newly crowned Champions of Scotland who called the shots. **Bertie Black** gave Killie the half-time lead and **Ronnie Hamilton** added another after the break to give Killie a comfortable 2-0 victory.

But Killie struggled with the heavy schedule towards the end of their American trip. Three games in a week was too much for the Ayrshire side as they ended their 60-game season and the scores were reversed in the second meeting as Albion won 2-0.

WEST HAM UNITED

Games	3	
Other	3	1963, 69
Top Scorer	Eddie Morrison 2	All Oth
Highest Overall	14,532 Oth	(New York)

First opponents for Kilmarnock in their trip to the states for the **1963 New York** tournament were **West Ham United**. At first glance the *Hammers* seemed to be just a run-of-the-mill mid-table team from England's top flight. But they had a fair amount of skill in their ranks and were being slowly transformed into one of the English game's top teams.

Geoff Hurst was already a goalscorer of note and in **Bobby Moore**, they possessed one of the finest defenders British football has ever produced. Given that Killie had scored **120** goals in **46** domestic matches it was no surprise that their meeting became a free-scoring affair. The crowd of **14,532** was the best Kilmarnock ever played in front of in the States with the exception of the Final against Bangu. And the punters left the ground full of praise for both teams after an entertaining **3-3** draw. **Black, Richmond** and **Yard** netting the Killie goals.

When they met again in America in **1969** things were totally different. Only **Jackie McGrory, Frank Beattie** and **Brien McIlroy** remained from the touring party of 1963. And the Hammers too had changed. Moore and Hurst were still there but they now also included players like **Billy Bonds, Trevor Brooking, Martin Peters** and a certain **Bobby Ferguson**. They had also added the **FA Cup** and the **European Cup-Winners' Cup** to their trophy cabinet since last facing Kilmarnock.

So when **Gerry Queen** and **Eddie Morrison** provided the goals that gave Killie a 2-1 win in **Seattle,** it was rightly seen as a great result for the Scottish team. But Killie couldn't repeat this success when the teams met again. They went under 4-1 in front of only 3,000 fans with Eddie Morrison grabbing Killie's goal.

WOLVERHAMPTON WANDERERS

Games	4	
Other	4	1969, 73
Top Scorer	Eddie Morrison 1	Oth
	Tommy McLean 1	Oth
Top Home Crowd	3,721 Sep 26th 1972	
Top Away Crowd	8,734 Sep 12th 1972	

Wolverhampton Wanderers were another of Killie's opponents in the **1969 USA** tournament. **Wolves** had some fine players in their ranks like **Phil Parkes, Peter Knowles, Mike Bailey, Dave Wagstaffe** and Scottish international **Hugh Curran**. They also had one of the undoubted superstars of that era – the incomparable **Derek Dougan**.

So losing 3-2 in **Kansas City** with **Eddie Morrison** and **Tommy McLean** scoring for Killie was no disgrace. Five days later, in their 'home' match in **St Louis**, Killie never got going and slumped to a 3-0 defeat.

When the teams met again in the **Texaco Cup** in 1972-73 their fortunes had both changed radically. While Killie were heading for relegation later that season, Wolves were on the way up. They had won the first Texaco Cup – *a competition for teams in the UK and Ireland that had just missed out on European qualification and later renamed the Anglo-Scottish Cup* – in 1971 and had reached the Final of the **UEFA Cup** in 1972. They would go on to win the **League Cup** in England in 1974.

And in addition to the talent they possessed in 1969 they had added players of top quality like **Kenny Hibbett**, Scottish internationals **Jim McCalliog** and **Frank Munro** and goal machine **John Richards**. They also still had Dougan.

It should have been no contest. But for the first 45 minutes at **Molineux**, Killie gave their hosts a fright. An own goal sent the Ayrshire team into the dressing room 1-0 up. Wolves came roaring back after the break to score five without reply and kill off the tie.

Little wonder that fewer than 4,000 bothered to attend the second leg at Rugby Park. Those that did must have wondered why they'd made the effort when the floodlights failed, leaving the ground in darkness for twenty minutes. When the power was restored, two players making their debuts that evening played leading roles in helping Killie to a 0-0 draw –their first clean sheet of the season. For goalkeeper **Jim Stewart** and defender **Alan Robertson** it was an impressive start to their illustrious Kilmarnock careers.

Killie's introduction to the Texaco Cup produced a painful defeat but unearthed two new stars in **Jim Stewart** and **Alan Robertson.**

ZELJEZNICAR SARAJEVO

Bosnia wasn't the most attractive destination for Kilmarnock supporters in the **1998-99 UEFA Cup**. Torn apart by years of civil war, the country was slowly rebuilding itself. As a consequence of the Balkan Wars in the 1990s teams from the former **Yugoslavia** had been absent from European competition for several years. Therefore, when their clubs returned to European football they had no ranking points and were classified alongside teams from **Luxembourg, Liechtenstein** and **Andorra** when the draw took place for this season's competitions.

Given that pre-war Yugoslav teams were among the strongest on the continent – **Red Star Belgrade** were European Champions in 1991 – this was a palpable absurdity. In being sent to play **Zeljeznicar** in **Sarajevo**, Kilmarnock had drawn the short straw in more ways than one.

To make matters worse the first leg was played in Bosnia on July 22nd 1998, *just ten days after the World Cup Final officially drew season 1997-98 to a close.* Under the prevailing circumstances it turned out to be one of Kilmarnock's finest performances and best results in continental football.

Killie held the line firmly in the first half and started to carve out their own opportunities after the break. **Kevin McGowne** scored in 55 minutes to give Killie the lead and a precious away goal. Zeljeznicar equalised eleven minutes later but Killie were still playing for the win. The only substitution to take place was **Mark Roberts** coming on for **Paul Wright** with eleven minutes to play. A straight swap – striker for striker. A second goal wasn't forthcoming but a 1-1 draw was an excellent result.

The fans felt so too. The second leg took place at Rugby Park just seven days later and a crowd of **14,512** turned up for the occasion. It was Killie's best since facing Leeds in 1967. Teams like **Anderlecht, CSKA Sofia, Gothenburg** and **Red Star Belgrade** all had home ties the same evening but the only crowd bigger than Rugby Park's was at **Ibrox!**

And those fans were rewarded when **Alan Mahood** scored shortly after the half-hour mark to put Killie ahead 2-1 on aggregate. Even now, one goal lost would mean extra time and the last hour was tense. Manager **Bobby Williamson** resisted the temptation to simply defend Killie's lead. His substitutions – **Pat Nevin** for **Alex Burke** and **John Henry** for Mahood – were both like-for-like.

Kilmarnock held on to register a fine victory over difficult opposition

State of the Ark? The old half-time scoreboard may have been decidedly low-tech but it was a much-loved feature of the old Rugby Park.

ZURICH

Kilmarnock journeyed to **Switzerland** for their first round tie in the **1969-70 Fairs Cup**. Opponents **Zurich** had a fair record in continental competition but were considered to be not quite as good as Killie. In those days Scottish sides took part in Europe expecting – as opposed to hoping – to do well.

The first leg started like a dream for Killie as goals from **Jim McLean** and **Ross Mathie** put them 2-0 ahead. But the Swiss team didn't lie down. They won a penalty which they converted and then scored again to make it 2-2 at half-time. Killie were under constant pressure in the second half and conceded another goal. But even at 3-2 down they remained the favourites to progress.

The second leg at Rugby Park started brightly as Killie got the goal they needed to nudge ahead

on the away goals rule. But the identity of the scorer was a surprise. **Jackie McGrory** played for Kilmarnock for *thirteen* seasons. He turned out in the club colours *476* times. Only *four* players have made more appearances. He won *three* full caps for Scotland. **But his header against Zurich was the only occasion in his entire career that he scored a goal!**

When **Tommy McLean** added a second after the break, Killie looked home and dry. But Zurich pulled one back. At 2-1 on the night Killie were still ahead on away goals but the tie was delicately poised. Step forward, as he did so often when needed, **Eddie Morrison**. The striker's first European goal secured a 3-1 victory, and booked Killie's place in the second round.

40 years of hurt? Killie's 1997 Cup Final victory against Falkirk avenged defeat in 1957.

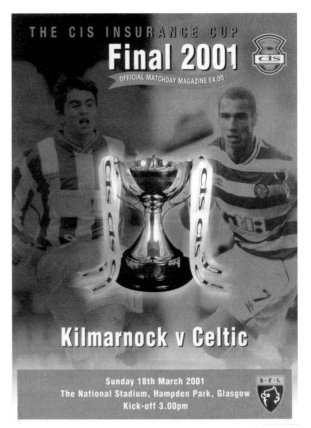

The first Cup Final of the third millennium. And Killie are there.

STATISTICS

STATISTICS

Explanation of abbreviations

P = Played, W = Won, D = Drawn, L = Lost, F = Goals For, A = Goals Against, Pts = Points. HT = Half-time, Res = Result. Att = Attendance. AET = After Extra Time, W/O = Walkover, Scr = Scratched, NK = Not Known, P/O = Play-off. QF = Quarter-Final. SF = Semi-Final. F = Final. Pos = Position. " = first player taken off. Replaced by No 12 throughout. * = second player taken off. Replaced by No 14 until end of 1994-95. Replaced by No 13 from 1995-96 onwards. x = third player taken off. Replaced by No 14. GA = Goal Average. GD = Goal Difference. HOME matches in capitals. Away matches in lower case.

Substitute numbers are listed as 12 and 14 as was the tradition when there were only two substitutions allowed. Since the introduction of three possible substitutions these are listed as 12,13, and 14. Since the establishment of the SPL in 1998 squad numbers have been used by players. To accommodate these it would be necessary to list players numbers from 1-40 making this section difficult to read. I have therefore continued to list players as 1-11.

The Divisions of the Scottish League have been given different names at different times. For the reader's convenience I have referred to Divisions One and Two until the major re-organisation of 1975. Thereafter I have listed the divisions as Premier, First and Second until 1998 when the Scottish Premier League was established.

Where a division has been known by any other names (eg 'B' Division) this has been mentioned in the text wherever relevant. Please also note that the terms Division One/First Division etc. are interchangeable in the text section until the 1975 reorganisation.

Attendance figures for Home matches from 1947 onwards are taken from the club records as researched by club historian John Livingston. Away figures from 1961 are from the Scottish Football League. All other attendances are based on newspaper reports.

Any errors in this section must be attributed solely to myself.

LEGENDS

These are the legends. Those Kilmarnock players who have either made over 300 appearances, scored 50 goals or played for Scotland. One player - **Tommy McLean** - has all three achievements to his credit. The dates given are for the period a player was registered with Kilmarnock, e.g. 1964-74 = from 1964-65 - 1973-74. Substitute appearances are **included** in the totals but listed in brackets. Competitions included in the 'other' category include all recognised first class matches outwith the main three Scottish competitions which are featured in this book. All figures are correct to the end of season 2000-2001.

Appearances. The '300' club.

No	Player	Service	Total	League	Scottish Cup	League Cup	Other (1st class)
1	Alan Robertson	1972-89	607 (4)	481 (3)	28	76 (1)	22
2	Frank Beattie	1953-72	602 (2)	422 (1)	40	80	59 (1)
3	Stuart McLean	1973-91	572 (38)	478 (34)	30	50 (3)	14 (1)
4	Alan McCulloch	1972-91	523	440	29	47	7
5	Jackie McGrory	1960-73	476	336	35	59	46
6	Matt Watson	1954-68	474 (2)	323 (2)	35	74	42
7	Derrick McDicken	1972-85	454 (28)	345 (24)	25 (2)	67	17 (2)
8	Paul Clarke	1974-86	452 (8)	362 (5)	25 (1)	49 (1)	16 (1)
9	Mattha' Smith	1916-31	440	415	24	-	1
10	Jamie Mitchell	1900-04, 06-21	435	410	23	-	2
11	Gus MacPherson	1990-2001	422 (2)	356 (2)	31	19	16
12	George Maxwell	1968-82	404 (29)	309 (24)	21	54 (4)	20 (1)
13	Jock McEwan	1923-35	395	353	42	-	-
14	Hugh Morton	1922-32, 33-37	382	340	42	-	-
15	Ally Mitchell*	1991-2001	379 (44)	321 (38)	23 (3)	21 (2)	14 (1)
16	Ray Montgomerie	1988-99	366 (24)	313 (21)	25 (1)	16 (2)	12
17	Eddie Morrison	1966-76	352 (10)	268 (7)	21 (1)	45 (2)	18
18=	Bertie Black	1952-67	347	234	29	59	25
18=	Andy King	1960-72	347 (3)	224 (3)	24	51	48
20	Brien McIlroy	1960-70	332 (3)	218 (2)	24	51 (1)	39
21	Ralph Collins	1949-59	330	246	21	58	5
22	Jackie McInally	1959-68	328 (1)	212 (1)	24	48	44
23	Freddie Milloy	1932-40, 45-48	322	266	22	4	30
24	Jimmy Brown	1953-61	321	231	29	55	6
25	Willie Culley	1911-23	317	301	13	-	3
26	Mark Reilly*	1991-98, 98-2001	316 (21)	266 (17)	24	15 (2)	11 (2)
27	Tommy McLean	1962-71	313	216	22	34	41 (1)

* Both Ally Mitchell and Mark Reilly were still with Kilmarnock when this book was printed.

The Hotshots. 50 goals or more.

No	Player	Service	Total	League	Scottish Cup	League Cup	Other (1st class)
1	Willie Culley	1911-23	159	149	8	-	2
2	Eddie Morrison	1966-76	154	121	9	19	5
3	Brien McIlroy	1960-70	152	105	8	22	17
4	Jackie McInally	1959-68	137	86	15	20	16
5	Bertie Black	1952-67	129	85	10	21	13
6	'Bud' Maxwell	1929-34, 39-40	124	103	19	-	2
7	Andy Kerr	1959-63	119	90	4	19	6
8	Mattha' Smith	1916-31	115	109	6	-	-
9	Gerry Mays	1952-59	111	79	9	23	-
10	'Peerie' Cunningham	1925-31	110	102	8	-	-
11	Allan Collins	1936-40, 45-48	91	60	4	5	22
12	Andy Cunningham	1909-15	81	75	6	-	-
13	Tommy McLean	1962-71	73	48	5	12	8
14	Paul Wright	1994-2001	72	58	6	4	4
15	'Bummer' Campbell*	1887-1901	68	48	20	-	-
16	George Maxwell	1968-82	67	53	4	8	2
17=	Ian Fleming	1970-76	65	51	-	14	-
17=	Willie Harvey	1951-58	65	42	7	15	1
19	Willie Connell	1927-34	62	49	13	-	-
20=	John Bourke	1978-83, 87-89	59	44	6	7	2
20=	Malcolm McPhail	1915-24	59	55	2	-	2
20=	Ross Mathie	1969-73	59	41	6	7	5
23	Jimmy Robertson	1934-38	58	54	4	-	-
24	Ronnie Hamilton	1961-66	56	38	1	4	13
25	Jimmy Ramsay	1920-24, 26-33	54	44	10	-	-
26	Benny Thomson	1934-40	53	39	12	-	2
27	Davie Curlett	1949-58	52	40	3	9	-
28	Jimmy Williamson	1927-37	51	48	3	-	-

* These are minimum figures. It is impossible to say exactly how many goals Campbell scored.

At the time of going to print, Ally Mitchell needed two more goals to join this company.

They played for Scotland. The Internationalists.

Figures in brackets represent total number of caps won. Scotland career figures are for time spent with Kilmarnock only.

Player	Killie Career	Scotland Career	Caps
William Agnew	1900-08	1906-08	3
Geordie Anderson	1896-1909	1900-01	1
James 'Bummer' Campbell	1887-1901	1890-92	2
Billy Dickson	1962-74	1969-70	5
Ian Durrant*	1998-2001	1998-2000	9 (20)
Bobby Ferguson	1963-67	1965-67	7
Bob Findlay	1896-1905	1897-98	1
Campbell Forsyth	1960-66	1963-65	4
Sandy Higgins	1882-88, 94-95	1884-85	1
Gary Holt	1995-2001	2000-01	2
Ally Hunter	1968-73	1971-74	4
John 'Jocky' Johnston	1889-1901	1893-94	1
Ally McCoist	1998-2001	1998-99	2 (61)
Jackie McGrory	1960-73	1964-66	3
Andy McLaren*	2000-01	2000-01	1
Tommy McLean	1962-71	1968-71	6
Davie McPherson	1890-1904	1891-92	1
John McPherson	1885-88	1887-88	1 (9)
Jamie Mitchell	1900-04, 06-21	1907-10	3
Hugh Morton	1922-37	1928-29	2
Joe Nibloe	1924-33	1928-32	11
James 'Duster' Orr	1890-92	1891-92	1
George Robertson	1936-39	1937-38	1
Tom Smith	1927-37	1933-34	1 (2)
Jim Stewart	1971-78	1976-79	1 (2)
Bob Templeton	1907-13	1907-13	6 (11)
Willie Toner	1954-63	1958-59	2

* Ian Durrant and Andy McLaren were current Kilmarnock players at the time of writing.

In addition to the above, David Lyner was capped for Northern Ireland V Wales in 1923, Malcolm McPhail won an unofficial cap for Scotland against Ireland in a victory international in 1919 and Dragoje Lekovic was capped twice for Yugoslavia during his spell at Rugby Park.

BASIC SEASONAL STATISTICS

Season	Av Home Lg Att	Top League Scorer	Most Appearances
1895-96	2200	9 Fisher	19* Johnstone, McPherson
1896-97	1333	12 Campbell	18* McLean
1897-98	2000	11 Campbell	18* Busby
1898-99	2643	12 Campbell, Reid	18* Findlay
1899-1900	4689	6 Howie	18* Craig, Anderson
1900-01	4200	7 A Reid	20* Craig, Muir, A Reid
1901-02	4611	5 Graham, Morton	18* Craig, Busby, Agnew, McPherson, Anderson, Mitchell
1902-03	3727	5 R Findlay	22* Anderson
1903-04	3440	5 Blair	26* Gunzeon
1904-05	4545	8 Blair	26* Aitken, Blair
1905-06	3929	12 J Young	30/31 (possible) Aitken
1906-07	3911	5 Agnew, Maxwell, Skillen	27/34 Mitchell
1907-08	6247	7 Templeton	33/34 Mitchell, Howie
1908-09	5459	12 Douglas	34* D Armour
1909-10	4882	18 Cunningham	32/34 Mitchell
1910-11	5575	14 Cunningham	34* Kirkwood
1911-12	4453	14 Cunningham	30/34 Templeton
1912-13	5121	11 Cunningham	31/34 Blair, Cunningham
1913-14	5263	12 Neil	37/38 Cunningham
1914-15	4300	20 Neil	37/38 Mackie
1915-16	4368	23 Culley	37/38 Blair, Mackie
1916-17	3474	16 Culley	38* McPhail
1917-18	5000	16 Culley	33/34 Blair
1918-19	5353	20 Culley	34* McPhail
1919-20	5857	14 Culley	42* Gibson
1920-21	7143	24 JR Smith	42* Gibson
1921-22	6952	20 Culley	40/42 Culley, Gibson
1922-23	7816	15 Jackson	38* Jackson
1923-24	7318	19 Gray	38* Borland, Gibson, J Morton
1924-25	6632	14 M Smith	38* Hood
1925-26	7158	26 Weir	37/38 Hood
1926-27	6632	19 H Cunningham	38* Nibloe
1927-28	6734	34 H Cunningham	38* Nibloe, Ramsay
1928-29	7516	23 H Cunningham	37/38 Connell
1929-30	6895	18 McGowan	37/38 McEwan, M Smith
1930-31	6895	18 Maxwell	38* Clemie
1931-32	7053	20 Maxwell	37/38 Connell
1932-33	6316	32 Maxwell	38* McEwan
1933-34	7553	33 Maxwell	38* Milloy
1934-35	6158	23 J Robertson	38* Kelvin
1935-36	6289	19 Beattie	38* Beattie, Leslie
1936-37	6158	12 J Robertson	38* Thomson
1937-38	8447	14 Collins	38* Ross
1938-39	8059	17 Reid	38* Hunter, Reid
1939-40§	2962	20 Collins	30* Gallacher
1945-46	11267	21 Walsh	29/30 Walsh
1946-47	13622	9 Collins	28/30 Downie
1947-48	6717	24 Collins	30* Collins
1948-49	8477	21 McLaren	29/30 McLaren
1949-50	10338	13 Johnston	29/30 Thyne
1950-51	8016	10 Jones	29/30 Benson

Season	Av Home Lg Att	Top League Scorer	Most Appearances
1951-52	9776	16 Mathie	30* Niven
1952-53	9122	20 Mays	30* Niven
1953-54	11643	17 Harvey	30* Brown, Henaughan, Russell
1954-55	15504	8 Jack	30* Brown
1955-56	12600	12 Curlett	33/34 Brown
1956-57	12593	18 Mays	31/34 Brown, Harvey
1957-58	11636	15 Mays	34* Toner
1958-59	10330	13 Black, Wentzel	34* Black, Watson
1959-60	13158	16 McInally	34* Watson
1960-61	12451	34 Kerr	34* Kerr, Richmond
1961-62	10478	23 Kerr	34* Richmond
1962-63	8777	25 Kerr	34* Beattie, McGrory, Watson
1963-64	8891	24 McIlroy	34* Forsyth, McGrory, McIlroy
1964-65	10476	15 Hamilton	34* Murray
1965-66	8706	20 McIlroy	34* Ferguson
1966-67	8439	16 McIlroy	34* McGrory
1967-68	5694	14 Queen, Morrison	34* McGrory, T McLean
1968-69	8294	13 McIlroy, Morrison	34* McGrory, McLaughlan
1969-70	6724	21 Mathie	34* McLaughlan, Mathie, Morrison, Cook+
1970-71	5933	10 T McLean	34* Dickson
1971-72	5717	15 Mathie	34* Cook, Hunter, Maxwell
1972-73	4489	16 Morrison	34* Morrison, Smith
1973-74	3639	33 Fleming	36* Rodman, Sheed
1974-75	7022	11 Fleming, Morrison	34* Rodman
1975-76	4239	10 Fallis	26* Fallis, Robertson, Stewart
1976-77	5849	10 Fallis	36* Robertson
1977-78	2834	13 McDowell	39* Stewart
1978-79	3033	21 Bourke	39* McCulloch
1979-80	6990	9 Street	36* McCulloch
1980-81	4507	5 Bourke	34/36 McLean+
1981-82	2609	14 Bourke	39* Armstrong, McCulloch, Robertson+
1982-83	3463	9 Gallacher	36* J Clark
1983-84	1358	11 R Clark, Gallacher	39* McCulloch
1984-85	1351	12 B Millar	39* P Clarke+
1985-86	1949	14 Bryson	38/39 Bryson , P Clarke+, McCulloch
1986-87	1899	10 Bryson	44* McGuire+
1987-88	1846	15 Harkness	44* McLean
1988-89	2487	12 Watters	39* McCulloch
1989-90	3247	23 Watters	38/39 Tait+, Watters+
1990-91	4939	14 Williamson	38/39 Geddes
1991-92	4388	10 Campbell, Mitchell	43/44/ MacPherson+
1992-93	4694	11 McCluskey	44* Geddes
1993-94	9161	7 Williamson	44* Black, Geddes, Millen
1994-95	9530	6 McKee	35/36 Mitchell+
1995-96	8719	13 Wright	36* Wright+
1996-97	9125	15 Wright	33/36 MacPherson, Reilly+
1997-98	9955	10 Wright	36* Reilly
1998-99	11533	7 McCoist	36* Durrant, Marshall
1999-2000	9419	8 Cocard	35/36 Holt
2000-01	8224	8 Wright	35/38 Dindeleux

* Indicates ever-present   + Includes appearances as a substitute   § 1939-40 Western League

1879 ~ Back: A. Robertson, J. Dunlop, J. Black, R. Rankin, M. Robertson, R. Norval, J. Wallace.
Seated: J.B. Wilson, W. Millar, D. Gilmour, R. Millar.

1891-92

Scottish Cup: 1873 - 1895

Season	Rd	Date	Opposition	H.	Res	Att	Goalscorers	1	2	3	4	5	6	7	8	9	10	11	Notes
1873-74	1	18 Oct	Renton	0-0	0-2		Brown, Wallace, Sturrock, NK	R. Rankin	R. Railton	R. Lipscomb	J.E. Wilson	W. Drennan	J. Wallace	C. Cowie	D. Sturrock	G. Blair	G. Paxton	J. Wallace	1
1874-75	1	17 Oct	VALE OF LEVEN ROV	4-0	4-0			"	J.W. Railton	G.H. Lipscomb	G. Paxton	W. Mitchell	D. Sturrock	J.B. Wilson	F. Reid	P. Brown	D. Brown	J. Wallace	
	2	21 Nov	Eastern (Glasgow)	0-3	0-3			"			W. Thomson	J. Paxton	D. Brown	P. Brown	J. Wallace	J.B. Wilson	D. Sturrock	A. Ferguson	2
1875-76	1	9 Oct	AYR EGLINTON	3-0	8-0		A.Ferguson, NK 7 goals	"			W. Thomson	W. Thomson	D. Brown	P. Brown	J. Wallace	J.B. Wilson	D. Sturrock		
	2	6 Nov	Clydesdale	0-2	0-6			"				J. Paxton							
1876-77	1		BYE																
1877-78	1	21 Oct	MAUCHLINE	0-1	1-2		Thomson	"	W. Thomson	G.H. Lipscomb	T. Ferguson	G. Paxton	J.B. Wilson	A. Ferguson	R. Hamilton	J. Ferguson	D. Brown	P. Brown	3
	2	29 Sep	HURLFORD		5-1		NK												
1878-79	1	20 Oct	Ayr Academical	0-0	0-1														
1879-80	1	28 Sep	KILBIRNIE		0-2														
	2	20 Sep	AYR ACADEMICAL		W/O														
			Mauchline		2-6		NK												
		11 Oct	Mauchline		W/O														
1880-81	1	11 Sep	STEWARTON	4-1	6-3		NK	Cumming	Bone	McLean	Cunningham	Wallace	Hamilton	Andrews	W. Miller	R. Miller	Barclay	Black	
	2	9 Oct	AYR F.C.	3-3	3-3		NK	"	Whiteside	Whiteside	Whiteside	Cuthbertson		Plumtree	Wallace				4
	3r	13	MAUCHLINE		0-3			"											
1881-82	1	10 Sep	LARGS ATHLETIC	1-1	6-0		Hay(2), NK 4 goals	"	Whiteside	Walker	Young	Burnett	Morton	Wallace	Hay	Kirkland	Robertson		
	2	8 Oct	AUCHINLECK BOSWELL	1-1	7-1		Burnett, Robertson, Hamilton, Morton, NK 3	"	Walker	Whiteside						Hamilton			5
	3	22	KILBIRNIE	1-0	2-0		Wallace, Hay	"											
	4	19 Nov	OUR BOYS DUNDEE	0-0	9-2		NK	"											
	5	10 Dec	Arthurlie	0-0	1-4	2000	Hamilton	"											
1882-83	1	16 Sep	MAUCHLINE	1-0	2-0		McSkimming, Hay	Cumming	Cunningham	Lucas	Burnett	Black	McCartney	Wark	Hamilton	Hay	Howat	McSkimming	
	2	30	HURLFORD	1-1	2-6		Hamilton, NK	"	Lucas	Walker	Young	McCartney	Burnett			McSkimming	Hay	Black	
1883-84	1	8 Sep	KILBIRNIE		W/O														
	2	29	HURLFORD	1-0	3-0	1000	Grier, McLaughland, Wark	McCall	Lucas	Young	Grier	Burnett	Wark	Wallace	Ramsay	Higgins	G. Black	McLaughland	
	3	3 Nov	Thorniebank	0-1	1-2		Higgins	"			Burnet	Grier	A. Black	G. Black	Wark	Walker	Higgins	Wallace	6
1884-85	1	27 Sep	Hurlford	1-3	1-3		NK	Cumming	Young	Ramsay	Grier	Jas McPherson	Burnett	Cox	Wallace			Black	7
	2	4 Oct	Annbank		1-4		NK	"											
1885-86	1	12 Sep	ANNBANK	3-0	7-1		NK												
	2	17 Oct	HURLFORD	1-1	1-1	2000	Higgins												
	2r	14	Hurlford	0-3	1-5	2000	Smith, NK												8
1886-87	1	11 Sep	CUMNOCK		W/O		Smith												
	2	2 Oct	LANEMARK	6-1	10-2		NK	Richmond	Miller	Porteous	Sawers	Dunn	Mitchell	Smith	Higgins	Walker	McGuinness	John McPherson	9
	3	23	LUGAR BOSWELL	2-1	7-2		Walker(2), Higgins, NK 4 goals	"	Porteous	West	Stewart	A. Young	Jas McPherson	Lyle	Smith	Taylor			
	4		BYE																
	5	4 Dec	DUNBLANE	2-0	6-0		NK												
1887-88	QF	25	QUEENS PARK	0-4	0-5	2500		Richmond	Porteous	A. Young	Mason	Dunn	Mitchell	Taylor	Smith	Higgins	McGuinness	John McPherson	
1887-88	1	3 Sep	AYR THISTLE	5-0	8-2		McGuinness(2), Taylor(2), NK 4 goals	"			Dunn	Mitchell	W. Young						
	2		BYE																
	3	15 Oct	Dykebar	1-2	2-2	3000	McGuinness, Smith												
	3r	22	DYKEBAR	6-0	9-1	3000	Higgins(3), Taylor(2), McGuinness(2), NK 2 goals												
	4	5 Nov	Partick Thistle	1-1	2-2	4000	McPherson(2)												
	4r	12	PARTICK THISTLE	0-1	1-4	5000	McGuiness												
1888-89	1	1 Sep	Lugar Boswell	1-0	5-0	5000	Forbes(2), Russell, J.Campbell, Lyle	Gray	Porteous	Stevenson	Mitchell	Dunn	A. Campbell	Gardiner	Lyle	Forbes	Russell	J. Campbell	
	2	22	KILBIRNIE	1-2	1-3	5000	Brodie	"				Russell	J. Campbell	Tannahill	Brodie	Brodie	J. Campbell	Taylor	
1889-90	1	7 Sep	ANNBANK	2-3	2-3	4000	J.Campbell, NK	"	Stevenson	Smith	Paterson	A. Campbell	J. Campbell		Brodie	A. Campbell	Reid	Kelvin	
1890-91	1	6 Sep	ANNBANK	3-2	4-4		Porter(2), Kelvin, Cunningham	"	Paterson	Orr	Porter	J. Campbell	Johnstone		Brodie	Reid	Cunningham		
	1r	13	Annbank	1-4	2-6		Kelvin(2)		Porter		Paterson								
1891-92	1	28 Nov	East Stirling	4-0	6-1	3000	Tannahill(2), McAvoy, Campbell, O.G., NK	Henderon	Hunter						D. McPherson	Brodie	McAvoy		
	2	19 Dec	Rangers	0-0	0-0	2000													
1892-93	1r	28	Rangers	1-0	1-1	3000	Brodie												
1892-93	1	28 Jan	Rangers	2-1	2-3	4000	McPherson, Kelvin	Cochrane	Watson	R. Brown	Broadhurst		A. Campbell		Cook	Trodder	Todd	McAvoy	10
	2	26 Nov	Albion Rovers	0-1	2-1		Todd(2)	"							Richardson	Cook	McAvoy	Todd	
1893-94	1	28 Jan	QUEENS PARK	0-1	0-8														
1893-94	1	25 Nov	ST. BERNARDS	1-3	1-3	3000	Brodie	McMillan	Hunter		Ghee			Louden	D. McPherson	Brodie		Kelvin	11
1894-95	1	24 Nov	EAST STIRLING	2-1	5-1		Higgins(3), Campbell, McLean	Cochrane	Busby		D. McPherson	Miller		Brode	Higgins	J. Campbell		McLean	12
	2	15 Dec	St. Bernards	0-1	1-3	2000	Campbell												

NOTES:

1. Played at Crosshill (Queens Park F.C. Ground) - Kilmarnock fielded only 10 men. 2. Kilmarnock fielded only 10 men. 3. Mauchline's second goal (84 mins.) disputed by Killie - game ended at that time. SFA adjudicated in Mauchline's favour.

4. Originally played 23/10/80. Mauchline won 2-1. Killie successfully protested that full 90 minutes not played. 5. Kilbirnie walked off after Killie's second goal, with 20 minutes left to play. Result stood. 6. Originally played 20/10/83 - Also 2-1 to Thorniebank, but Kilmarnock protest successful. 7. Originally played 20/9/84 - Killie won 6-1. Hurlford successful protest 'breach of registration rules) - Kilmarnock made similar protest prior to kick-off on 27/9/84. Hurlford disqualified, Kilmarnock reinstated to competition.

8. Originally played 3/10/85. Kilmarnock 3 Hurlford 4. Killie protested successfully re. breach of registration. Kilmarnock failed to appear for scheduled replay on 24/10/85. On 31/10/85, replay at Ayr was abandoned after 80 mins., score 1-1. 7/11/85, 2-2 AET.

9. 'Kilmarnock Herald' lists no.2, Watson not Millar. 10. At Westmarch (St. Mirren F.C. Ground). 11. Kilmarnock played in qualifying competition: 2/9 Kilmarnock 5 Morton 3. 23/9 Kilmarnock 1 Newmilns 0. 14/10 Kilmarnock 3 Motherwell 3.

21/10 Motherwell 1 Kilmarnock 3. 12. Kilmarnock played in qualifying competition: Away to Pollokshaws - W/O. 22/9 Carfin 4 Kilmarnock 4. 29/9 Kilmarnock 4 Carfin 2. 13/10 Dykehead 1 Kilmarnock 3.

SEASON 1895-96   Division Two

No.	Date	Opposition	H.T.	Res.	Att.	Goalscorers	Gordon	Busby	Maxwell	McPherson	J.Brown	Johnstone	Watson	Fisher	McAvoy	Cox	R.Brown	McLean	Harrow	Sawers	Ralston	Smith	"Richards"
1	17 Aug	Leith Athletic	1-1	1-3	1500	McAvoy	1	2	3	4	5	6	7	8	9	10	11						
2	24	MOTHERWELL	2-1	7-1	2000	Watson,McAvoy,Cox(3),McPherson,Fisher	1		2	6	5	4	7	8	9	10	11	3					
3	31	MORTON	2-0	5-1	1000	Cox(2), Fisher, Campbell, McAvoy	1		3	6	5	4	11	10	9	8	7	2					
4	7 Sep	Partick Thistle	2-1	2-2	2000	J.Brown, McAvoy	1	2	3	4	5	6	7	8	9	10	11						
5	14	RENTON	3-2	4-2	2000	Fisher(2), Watson, Cox	1	3	2	6	5	4	10	8	9		11		7				
6	28	Port Glasgow Athletic	0-3	1-6		Fisher	1	3	2	4	5	6		8	9	10	7		11				
7	19 Oct	Renton	0-1	0-3			1			2	4	6	7	9	5	8	10	3	11				
8	26	Morton	1-1	3-2	1500	McAvoy, McLean, McPherson	1	2		4	5	6	7	8	9	10		3	11				
9	9 Nov	Airdrieonians	2-2	3-5		Harrow(2), Campbell	1	2		4	5	6	7	8	9	10		3		11			
10	16	Motherwell	1-2	4-2*		Campbell(2), McLean, Not known	1	3		6	5	4	8		9		7	2	11				
11	21 Dec	Linthouse	0-0	3-1		Campbell, McLean, Watson	1	2		4		6	8	10	5	9		3	11				7
12	1 Feb	LINTHOUSE	0-2	3-2	2000	Fisher(2), McLean	1	2		4	5	6	8	10		9	7	3	11				
13	22	AIRDRIEONIANS	4-2	6-4		McAvoy(2), McLean(2), Watson, Fisher	1	3		6	5	4	10	9		8	11	2	7				
14	7 Mar	ABERCORN	0-3	2-4		Watson, McAvoy	1	3		6	5	4	11		9	8		2	7		10		
15	14	PORT GLASGOW ATH.	1-0	2-1		Fisher, Campbell		3		6	5	4		9	7	10	11	2		8	1		
16	21	LEITH ATHLETIC	0-0	1-0	3000	McLean		3		6	5	4		9			10	11	2	7	8	1	
17	11 Apr	PARTICK THISTLE	2-1	2-3		Not known(2)		3		6	5	4		9			10	11	2	7	8	1	
18	18	Abercorn	0-2	2-3		Campbell(2)		3		6	5	4			10	9	8	7	2		11	1	
19	20 May	Renton+	1-2	1-2		McLean		3		6	5	4			9	8		7	2			1	10
						Apps.	14	16	6	19	18	19	14	17	15	17	14	15	12	2	4	5	1	1
						Goals				2	1		5	9	8	8	6		7	2			

* Abandoned after 73 minutes. Result allowed to stand, Kilmarnock fielded only 10 men.

+ Play-off for 3rd/4th place at Cathkin Park.

Pos	P.	W.	D.	L.	F.	A.	Pts.
4th	18	10	1	7	51	45	21

Scottish Cup

| 1 | 18 Jan | Annbank | 1-3 | 2-3 | | Campbell, McLean | 1 | 2 | | 4 | | 6 | 7 | 5 | 9 | 10 | 8 | 3 | 11 | | | | |

SEASON 1896-97   Division Two

No.	Date	Opposition	H.T.	Res.	Att.	Goalscorers	Ralston	H.Smith	Busby	Johnstone	J.Brown	McPherson	McLean	Richmond	Campbell	McAvoy	Watson	R.Brown	Fulton	Baillie	Muir	Paterson	McArthur	Cochran	Dowdles	Revie	Anderson	Edgar	Findlay	McLatchie	Reid	Scott	Miller
1	15 Aug	RENTON	1-1	5-1	3000	Campbell(3), Richmond, McAvoy	1	2	3	4	5	6	7	8	9	10	11																
2	22	Leith Athletic	0-1	1-4	2000	Campbell	1	3	2		5	4	11	10	9	7	8		6														
3	5 Sep	DUMBARTON	3-0	5-1	1000	Campbell,J.Brown,McLean,Watson,Fulton	1		2		5	4	11	10	9	8	7	3	6														
4	10 Oct	Morton	1-2	2-3		R.Brown, Campbell	1		2	6		4	11	10	9	8	7	3	5														
5	17	LEITH ATHLETIC	1-0	1-0	2000	Watson	1		2		5	4	11	10	9	8	7	3	6														
6	2 Jan	Airdrieonians	2-3	5-4		McLean,Richmond,Campbell,N.K.,McPherson			2	6		4	11	10	9	8	7	3	5	1													
7	6 Mar	Renton	1-0	2-1		McArthur(2)	3	2				11			8			6		1	10	9	4	7		5							
8	20	Port Glasgow Athletic	1-3	2-5		Richmond, Campbell			2	4		6	7	8	9			11	3	5	1	10											
9	27	PARTICK THISTLE	1-1	1-3	2500	McLean			2	5		4	11	10	9		8	3	6	1		7											
10	10 Apr	Dumbarton	1-0	6-0		Revie(2),McArthur,Campbell,Dowdles,McLean			2	4		7		5			3		1	9	8	10	11									
11	17	Partick Thistle	0-1	0-2	5000				2	6		4	11		5	8		3	1	9	10	7										
12	27	Linthouse	1-0	1-1	1000	Findlay	2			4	7		9	8			3	6	1		10			5	11							
13	1 May	Motherwell	0-1	2-1	3000	McLean, Campbell			2	6		11	9	8			3	4	1		10	5	7									
14	6	MOTHERWELL	0-0	4-0	500	McLean(2), Campbell(2)			2	6		4	7	9	8		3		1		10	5	11									
15	8	LINTHOUSE	0-0	0-3	500		2			4	7		9	8			3	6	1		10	5			11							
16	11	PORT GLASGOW ATH.	2-0	3-0	1000	Reid(2), McLean			2	6		4	7	5	8		3		1		9							11	10			
17	13	AIRDRIEONIANS	1-1	1-2	500	Cochran			2		4	7		5	8		3		1		9			6					11	10			
18	15	MORTON	2-1	3-2	1000	McLean(2), Findlay			2	6		4	7		8		3		1		9				5				11		10		
						Apps.	5	5	16	10	4	17	18	8	16	14	9	15	11	1	12	2	4	9	2	3	6	1	6	1	3		
						Goals				1	1	10	3	12	1	2	1	1					3	1	1	2			2		2		

Pos	P.	W.	D.	L.	F.	A.	Pts.
3rd	18	10	1	7	44	33	21

Scottish Cup

No.	Date	Opposition	H.T.	Res.	Att.	Goalscorers																											
1	9 Jan	Motherwell	3-2	3-3	1000	Campbell, McAvoy, Richmond	1		2	6		4	11	10	9	8	7	3	5														
1R	16	MOTHERWELL	2-1	5-2	2000	McLean(2), Campbell, McAvoy, Watson			2	4		6	7	8	9	10	11	3	5		1												
2	6 Feb*	FALKIRK	6-2	7-3		Campbell(3),Richmond(2),McAvoy,McPherson			2	4		6	7	8	9	10	11	3			1	5											
QF	13	THIRD LANARK	1-1	3-1	7000	Campbell, Richmond, Scott			2	6		4	11	10	9	8		3			1											7	5
SF	13 Mar	Dumbarton	1-1	3-4	6000	Campbell(3)			2	6		4	11	10	9	8	7	3			1												5

* Originally played 23 January. Kilmarnock 3 - Falkirk 1 (Scorers: McLean, Richmond, Watson). Falkirk successfully appealed over pitch markings.

Kilmarnock played in the Qualifying Competition this season, results as follows:

	Date	Opposition		Res.	Goalscorers
	29 Aug	Lugar Boswell		6-2	Campbell(3), J.Brown, Not known(2)
	12 Sep	SALTCOATS VICTORIA		13-2	Campbell(8),McAvoy,McLean,Richmond,N.K.(2)
	26	Ayr		7-1	Campbell(3),McAvoy,Richmond,Watson,McLean
	24 Oct	HURLFORD		4-2	Campbell(2), J.Brown, Watson
	7 Nov	Partick Thistle		5-2	McAvoy,McLean,Campbell,Richmond,McPherson
	21	DUNBLANE		2-0	Watson(2)
	5 Dec	MOTHERWELL*		4-1	Richmond, Campbell, McAvoy, McPherson

* Played at Hampden Park

Back row (l-r): J.Q. McPherson (Trainer), T. Busby, A. Alexander (Treasurer), J. Ralston, J. Taylor (Secretary), R. Brown, R. Thomson (Vice-President).
Middle row: D. Watson, C. Smith (Match Secretary), J. Campbell, J.W. Somerville (Hon. Vice-President), R. Richmond, A. McLean, R. Gibson.
Front row: D. McPherson, A. Paterson, J. Johnstone.

SEASON 1897-98 — Division Two

No.	Date	Opposition	H.T.	Res.	Att.	Goalscorers
1	4 Sep	Motherwell	0-1	2-1	2000	Campbell(2)
2	11	ABERCORN	4-1	7-1		Campbell(2),McAvoy(3),McPherson,Findlay
3	25	Morton	2-2	4-3	3000	Campbell(2), McPherson, Findlay
4	9 Oct	LEITH ATHLETIC	2-1	3-1	3000	McAvoy, Reid, Maitland
5	16	AYR	4-1	5-2		Findlay(2), Maitland(2), McPherson
6	23	MORTON	5-0	5-2	1500	Reid(3), Campbell, McLean
7	30	Abercorn	0-2	1-4	2500	Findlay
8	6 Nov	Hamilton Acas.	1-0	3-2	1200	Findlay, Maitland, Watson
9	13	LINTHOUSE	4-0	5-0		Maitland(3),Findlay,Watson
10	20	Leith Athletic	1-1	2-2		McAvoy, McLean
11	27	AIRDRIEONIANS	4-1	5-2	1000	Anderson,Johnstone,McLean,Reid,Maitland
12	18 Dec	MOTHERWELL	4-0	6-2	2500	Anderson(2),Muir(2),Campbell,Maitland
13	12 Feb	Airdrieonians	1-2	1-2		Anderson
14	5 Mar	HAMILTON ACAS.	2-0	5-0		McPherson,McLean,McAvoy,Muir,Campbell
15	12	Ayr	1-0	3-0	2500	McPherson, McAvoy, Muir
16	19	Linthouse	1-0	3-0	2000	Anderson, Campbell, Maitland
17	2 Apr	PORT GLASGOW ATH.	0-0	2-1	2000	McPherson, Muir
18	9	Port Glasgow	1-1	2-4		Findlay, Campbell

Pos	P.	W.	D.	L.	F.	A.	Pts.
1st	18	14	1	3	64	29	29

Player appearances — columns: McCowan, Busby, Brown, McPherson, Anderson, Johnstone, McLean, McAvoy, Campbell, Reid, Findlay, McAllan, Maitland, Muir, Watson, Baillie, Cochran, Doig, Gordon

McCowan	Busby	Brown	McPherson	Anderson	Johnstone	McLean	McAvoy	Campbell	Reid	Findlay	McAllan	Maitland	Muir	Watson	Baillie	Cochran	Doig	Gordon
1	2	3	4	5	6	11	8	9	10			7						
1	2	3	4	5	6	7	8	9	10	11						1		
	2	3	4		6	7	8	5		10	11	1	9					
	2	3	4		6	7	8	5		10	11	1	9					
	2	3	6		4	7	8			10	11	1	9	5				
	3	2	6	5		11	10	9		8	7	1				4		
	2	3	4	5	6	11				8	7	1		10				
	2	3	4	5	6			8		10	11	1	9	7				
	2	3	4	5	6			8		10	11	1	9	7				
	2	3	4	5	6	7	8	9					10	11	1			
	2		4	5	6	7	8			10	11	1	9				3	
	3	2	6	5	4			9	8	7	1	11	10					
	2	3	4	5		9				8	7	1	11	10				
	2	3	6	5	4		9			10	11	1	7	6				1
	2	3	6	5	4		10	9					10	11		8		1
	2	3	6	5	4		10	9		7			11			8		1
	2	3	4	5	6	11		9	10			8	7					1
	2	3		5	6			10	9			11	8	7		4		

Apps.	2	18	17	17	16	16	11	13	15	14	15	12	11	10	2	1	4	1	3
Goals				6	5	1	4	7	11	5	8		10	5	2				

Scottish Cup

	Date	Opposition	H.T.	Res.	Att.	Goalscorers
1	6 Jan	6th GRV	2-1	5-1		Muir(2), Campbell, Maitland, Reid
2	22	LEITH ATHLETIC	4-1	9-2	3500	Muir(2),Andrsn(2),Reid(2),McPhrsn,Mtlnd,Cpbll
QF	5 Feb	Ayr Parkhouse	5-2	7-2	6000	Reid(3),Findlay(2),Campbell,Muir,Maitland
SF	19	DUNDEE	1-2	3-2	11000	Reid, Findlay, Maitland
F	26 Mar	Rangers*	0-0	0-2	1300	

* Played at Hampden Park

McCowan	Busby	Brown	McPherson	Anderson	Johnstone	McLean	McAvoy	Campbell	Reid	Findlay	McAllan	Maitland	Muir	Watson	Baillie	Cochran	Doig	Gordon
	2	3	4	5	6			9	10	11	1	7	8					
	2	3	4	5	6			9	10	11	1	8	7					
	2	3	6	5	4			9	8	7	1	10	11					
	2	3	4	5	6			9	10	11	1	8	7					
	2	3	6	5	4			9	8	7	1	10	11					

SEASON 1898-99 — Division Two

No.	Date	Opposition	H.T.	Res.	Att.	Goalscorers
1	27 Aug	AIRDRIEONIANS	2-0	5-0	4000	Reid(2), McPherson, Howie, Findlay
2	3 Sep	Abercorn	1-1	2-1	1500	Findlay, Maitland
3	10	PORT GLASGOW ATH.	2-1	4-1	4000	Muir(2), McPherson, Findlay
4	24	Morton	2-1	2-1	3000	Reid, Maitland
5	8 Oct	LEITH ATHLETIC	3-2	5-3	4000	Reid(3), Findlay, Maitland
6	15	MORTON	1-0	2-0	2000	Reid, Young
7	22	Airdrieonians	2-3	4-4		Campbell(2), Anderson, Reid
8	5 Nov	LINTHOUSE	5-0	8-0	1500	Howie(4),Maitland(2),Campbell,Findlay
9	19	Ayr	1-0	1-1		Reid
10	26	ABERCORN	2-0	3-0	1500	Muir, Howie, N.K.
11	3 Dec	Hamilton Acas	1-1	7-1	1000	Campbell(2),Findly(2),Andrsn,Jhnstne,Mtlnd
12	10	HAMILTON ACAS	2-1	7-1		Campbell(3),Maitland(2),Muir,Findlay
13	17	Port Glasgow Athletic	2-0	5-4	2500	Howie(3), Findlay, Maitland
14	7 Jan	AYR	2-1	5-1		McPherson,Muir,Reid,Findlay,Maitland
15	18 Mar	Motherwell	2-0	3-3	2000	Muir, Campbell, Maitland
16	8 Apr	Linthouse	1-0	2-0		Howie, O.G.
17	15	Leith Athletic	2-2	3-3		Campbell(2), Findlay
18	22	MOTHERWELL	4-0	5-0	1500	Reid(2), McPherson, Howie, Campbell

Pos	P.	W.	D.	L.	F.	A.	Pts.
1st	18	14	4	0	73	24	32

Player appearances — columns: Paterson, Busby, Brown, McPherson, Anderson, Carr, Muir, Howie, Campbell, Reid, Findlay, Johnstone, Maitland, Craig, Young, McAvoy, Hewitt, Aitken

Paterson	Busby	Brown	McPherson	Anderson	Carr	Muir	Howie	Campbell	Reid	Findlay	Johnstone	Maitland	Craig	Young	McAvoy	Hewitt	Aitken
1	2	3	4	5	6	7	8	9	10	11							
1	2	3	4	5		7		9	10	11	6	8					
1	2	3	4	5		7			10	11	6	8					
	2	3	4			7	8	5	10	11	6	9	1				
	2	3	4		5	7		9	10	11	6	8	1				
	2	3	4	5		7	8		10	11	6		1	9			
	3	2	4	5		8		9	10	11	6		1		7		
	2	3		5	4		8	9	10	11	6	7	1				
	2	3	4	5		7		9	10	11	6	8	1				
	2	3	4	5	6	7	9		10	11		8	1				
	2	3		5	4	7		9	10	11	6	8	1				
	2			5	4	7		9	10	11	6	8	1			3	
	3	2	4	5		7	10			9	11	6	8	1			
	2	3	4	5		7	10		9		11	6	8	1			
		3	4	5		7	10	9			11	6	8	1		2	
	2	3	4	5		7	10	9			11	6	8	1			
	2	3	4	5		7	10	9	8		11	6		1			
	2	3	4	5			8	9	10	11	6	7	1				

Apps.	3	17	17	15	16	6	16	11	14	16	18	16	14	15	1	1	2	
Goals				4	2		6	11	12	12	11	1	11		1			

Scottish Cup

	Date	Opposition	H.T.	Res.	Att.	Goalscorers
1	14 Jan	Orion	2-0	2-0	5000	Findlay(2)
2	11 Feb	East Stirling	0-0	1-1	6500	Reid
2R	18	EAST STIRLING	0-0	0-0	8000	
2R	25	East Stirling*	3-1	4-2	8000	Muir(3), Campbell
QF	11 Mar	ST. MIRREN	0-2	1-2	11129	McPherson

* Played at Cathkin Park

Paterson	Busby	Brown	McPherson	Anderson	Carr	Muir	Howie	Campbell	Reid	Findlay	Johnstone	Maitland	Craig	Young	McAvoy	Hewitt	Aitken
	2	3	4	5		7		9	10	11	6	8	1				
	2	3		5		7	10	4	9	11	6	8	1				
	2	3		5		7	10	4	9	11	6	8	1				
	2	3		5		7		9	10	11	6	8	1				4
		3	4	5		8		9	10	11	6	7	1				2

Back row (l-r): J.Q. McPherson (Trainer), D. McPherson, T. Busby, G. Anderson, R. Brown, J. Johnstone. Front row: R. Muir, D. Maitland, J. Campbell (on floor), J. McAllan, W. Reid, R. Findlay.

SEASON 1899-1900 — Division One

No.	Date	Opposition	H.T.	Res.	Att.	Goalscorers	Craig	Busby	Brown	McPherson	Anderson	McCrone	Muir	Howie	Campbell	Reid	Findlay	Johnstone	Maitland	Morton	Terras	Duncanson	Ferguson	Hewitt	Young
1	19 Aug	St. Mirren	1-0	1-0	5000	Findlay	1	2	3	4	5	6	7	8	9	10	11								
2	26	CELTIC	0-2	2-2	11500	Howie(2)	1	2	3		5	4	7	8	9	10	11	6							
3	2 Sep	Hibernian	0-2	1-3	7400	Howie	1	2	3		5	4	7	8	9		11	6	10						
4	9	RANGERS	2-1	2-4	11000	Howie, Johnstone	1	2	3	4	5		7	8		10	11	6	9						
5	16	ST. BERNARD'S	1-1	2-1	3500	Anderson, Howie	1	2	3	4	5		7	10	9		11	6	8						
6	23	Hearts	0-0	0-1	4000		1	2	3	4	5		7	10	9			6	8	11					
7	30	THIRD LANARK	1-0	1-1	2700	Morton	1	2	3	4	5			8	9	10		6	7	11					
8	7 Oct	CLYDE	1-0	3-1	3000	Campbell(2), Maitland	1	2	3	4	5			10	9			8	11	6	7				
9	14	HIBERNIAN	0-1	0-3	4500		1	2	3	4	5		7	8	9	10	11	6							
10	21	DUNDEE	1-0	2-1	3000	Campbell(2)	1	2	3	4	5		7		9	10		6	8				11		
11	4 Nov	St. Bernard's	1-0	1-1	600	Ferguson	1	2	3	4	5		7	8		10		6		11			9		
12	11	ST. MIRREN	1-1	2-2	1500	McPherson, Findlay	1	2	3	4	5		7			10	11	6	8				9		
13	25	Third Lanark	1-1	1-2	3000	Findlay	1	2	3	4	5		7	10			11	6	8				9		
14	9 Dec	Rangers	1-2	1-6	5000	Findlay	1		3	4	5		7	10	9		11	6	8				2		
15	16	Celtic	1-1	3-3	2000	Howie, Maitland, Reid	1	2	3	4	5		7	10		9	11	6	8						
16	30	Clyde	3-1	3-2	2000	Young(3)	1	2		4	5		7	8			11	6	9					3	10
17	6 Jan	Dundee	3-1	3-3	4000	Ferguson, Muir, Reid	1	2		4	5		7		9	10		6	8				11	3	
18	17 Mar	HEARTS	1-1	2-1	4500	Reid, Muir	1	2	3	4	5		7			10	11	6	9				8		
Apps.							18	17	16	16	18	3	16	14	11	11	12	16	14	4	1	1	6	3	1
Goals										1	1		2	6	4	3	4	1	2	1			2		3

Scottish Cup

Pos P. W. D. L. F. A. Pts.
5th 18 6 6 6 30 37 18

No.	Date	Opposition	H.T.	Res.	Att.	Goalscorers	Craig	Busby	Brown	McPherson	Anderson	McCrone	Muir	Howie	Campbell	Reid	Findlay	Johnstone	Maitland	Morton	Terras	Duncanson	Ferguson	Hewitt	Young
1	13 Jan	EAST STIRLING	0-0	2-0	1000	Howie, Maitland	1	2		4	5		7	10	9			6	8	11			3		
2	27	ORION	4-0	10-0	3000	Maitland(5),Howie(2),Campbell,Mortn,Terrs	1	2	3		5		7	10	9			6	8	11	4				
QF	17 Feb	Celtic	0-2	0-4	8000		1		3		5		7	10	9			6	8	11	4		2		

SEASON 1900-01 — Division One

No.	Date	Opposition	H.T.	Res.	Att.	Goalscorers	Craig	Busby	Muir	McPherson	Anderson	Johnstone	A.Reid	Howie	Campbell	W.Reid	Ferguson	Maitland	Crerar	Brown	Jas Wyllie	Graham	Hewitt	Morton	Woodburn	Agnew	Mitchell	Robertson
1	18 Aug	Partick Thistle	0-0	2-1	5000	A.Reid, Campbell	1	2	3	4	5	6	7	8	9	10	11											
2	22	Third Lanark	0-2	2-3	2000	Anderson, Crerar	1	2	3	4	5	6	7	8		10	11		9									
3	25	DUNDEE	1-0	2-0	3500	McPherson, Maitland	1	2	3	4	5	6	7	10	9		11	8										
4	1 Sep	Rangers	1-5	1-5	9500	Crerar	1	2	3	4	5	6	7	8		10	11		9									
5	8	HIBERNIAN	2-2	2-2	4000	McPherson, Ferguson	1	2	8	4	5		7			10	11		9	3	6							
6	15	Dundee	0-1	0-3	10000		1	2		4	5		7	8		10	11		10	3	6	9						
7	22	PARTICK THISTLE	2-1	2-1	3500	Muir(2)	1	2		4	5		7			10			8	3	6	9						
8	6 Oct	QUEENS PARK	0-1	2-1	2000	Busby, A.Reid	1	2	8	4	5					10	11				6	9	3	7				
9	13	St. Mirren	0-2	1-3	3000	W.Reid	1		8	4	5	6				10	11			2		9	3	7				
10	20	MORTON	1-1	4-1	4000	Crerar(2), Graham, A.Reid	1	2		4	5		7			10	11		8	3	6	9						
11	27	Celtic	0-1	0-1	5000		1	2		4	5		7			10	11		8		6	9	3					
12	3 Nov	CELTIC	1-0	2-1	6500	Graham, A.Reid	1	2		4	5		7			10	11		8		6	9	3					
13	10	HEARTS	1-1	1-3	4000	Graham	1	2		4	5	6	7			10	11		8			9	3					
14	24	Hibernian	2-2	2-2	3000	Busby, Maitland	1	2			5		7			10	11		8		6	9	3		4			
15	1 Dec	RANGERS	1-0	1-2	10000	Graham	1	2		4	5		7			10	11		8		6	9	3	8				
16	8	Hearts	0-5	0-7	3000		1	2			5					10	11		8			9		7	6	3	4	
17	15	Queens Park	5-0	5-5	4500	Graham(2), A.Reid(2), Maitland	1	2		4			7			10	11		8		5	9		6	3			
18	22	ST. MIRREN	1-2	2-2	2500	Howie, A.Reid	1	2		4			7			10	11	5	8			9		6	3			
19	29	Morton	0-2	2-3	4000	Busby, Muir	1	2		4			7			10	11					9	3	8	6		5	
20	1 Jan	THIRD LANARK	2-1	2-1	3500	Howie(2)	1	2		4			7			10	11					9		6	3	5	2	
Apps.							20	16	20	18	16	6	20	9	4	14	6	9	6	5	9	15	8	5	6	4	3	1
Goals								3	3	2	1		7	3	1	1	1	3	4			6						

Scottish Cup

Pos P. W. D. L. F. A. Pts.
5th 20 7 4 9 35 47 18

No.	Date	Opposition	H.T.	Res.	Att.	Goalscorers	Craig	Busby	Muir	McPherson	Anderson	Johnstone	A.Reid	Howie	Campbell	W.Reid	Ferguson	Maitland	Crerar	Brown	Jas Wyllie	Graham	Hewitt	Morton	Woodburn	Agnew	Mitchell	Robertson
1	12 Jan	AIRDRIEONIANS	3-1	3-2	3000	Maitland(3)	1	2		4	5		7			10	11		8			9		6	3			
2	9 Feb*	Celtic	0-3	0-6	12000		1	2		4	5		7			10	11		8			9		3	6			

* Match was scheduled for 26/1/01 but the referee failed to appear. The clubs played a friendly instead, Celtic winning 2-1; Kilmarnock team was exactly the same as appeared in the cup-tie, Muir scored for Killie.

Opening of ground - August 1899

SEASON 1901-02   Division One

No.	Date	Opposition	H.T.	Res.	Att.	Goalscorers
1	17 Aug	RANGERS	3-1	4-2	6000	Graham(2), Howie, Norwood
2	24	Dundee	0-0	0-0	10000	
3	31	HIBERNIAN	0-0	0-0	5500	
4	7 Sep	Rangers	0-2	2-3	16000	Howie(2)
5	14	MORTON	0-0	2-0	5000	Anderson, Morton
6	21	Hearts	0-1	0-3	7000	
7	28	CELTIC	0-0	0-1	8000	
8	5 Oct	Morton	0-1	1-1		Wyllie
9	12	ST. MIRREN	1-0	1-2	3000	Wyllie
10	19	HEARTS	1-0	1-0	4000	Morton
11	2 Nov	Third Lanark	0-0	0-0	4500	
12	9	DUNDEE	3-0	4-0	3500	Graham(2), Howie, Morton
13	16	Hibernian	0-3	0-5		
14	7 Dec	THIRD LANARK	0-2	1-2	2000	T.Findlay
15	21	St. Mirren	0-1	1-1		Morton
16	28	Celtic	1-2	2-4	3000	Graham, Morton
17	18 Jan	QUEENS PARK	0-0	1-1	4500	McPherson
18	15 Mar	Queens Park	0-0	1-0	4000	McPherson

Player appearances (shirt numbers):

No.	Craig	Busby	Agnew	McPherson	Anderson	Mitchell	A.Reid	John Wyllie	Graham	Howie	Norwood	Maitland	Morton	T.Findlay	R.Findlay	Brown	Chapman
1	1	2	3	4	5	6	7	8	9	10	11						
2	1	2	3	4	5	6	7	8	9	10	11						
3	1	2	3	4	5	6	7	8	9	10	11						
4	1	2	3	4	5	6			9	8			10	7	11		
5	1	2	3	4	5	6			9	8			10	7	11		
6	1	2	3	4	5	6	7		9	10		8			11		
7	1	2	3	4	5	6			9	8			10	7	11		
8	1	2	3	4	5	6			9	8		11	10	7			
9	1	2	3	4	5	6			9	8		11	10	7			
10	1	2	3	4	5	6			9	7		11	8	10			
11	1	2	3	4	5	6			9	8			7	10		11	
12	1	2	3	4	5	6			9	8			11	10		7	
13	1	2	3	4	5	6		8	9				11	10		7	
14	1	2	3	4	5	6			9			8	11	10		7	
15	1	2	3	4	5	6			9	8			7	10			11
16	1	2	3	4	5	6			9	8			7	10			11
17	1	2	3	4	5	6			9	10		8	7				11
18	1	2	3	4	5	6			9	8		10		11		7	
Apps.	18	18	18	18	18	18	4	12	17	17	3	7	15	7	1	4	3
Goals				2	1			2	5	4	1	1	5	1			

Pos P. W. D. L. F. A. Pts.
7th 18 5 6 7 21 25 16

Scottish Cup

No.	Date	Opposition	H.T.	Res.	Att.	Goalscorers
1	11 Jan	PARTICK THISTLE	2-0	4-0	4000	Graham(2), Chapman, Maitland
2	25	DUNDEE	1-0	2-0	6200	Howie, Mitchell
QF	22 Feb*	Rangers	0-0	0-2	11600	

No.	Craig	Busby	Agnew	McPherson	Anderson	Mitchell	Graham	Howie	Maitland	Morton	T.Findlay	Chapman
1	1	2	3	4	5	6	9	10	8	7		11
2	1	2	3	4	5	6	9	8		7	11	10
QF	1	2	3	4	5	6	9	8		7	11	10

* The match was scheduled for February 8th, because of bad weather conditions, the game played on this day was classed as a friendly. Rangers won 3-0.

SEASON 1902-03   Division One

No.	Date	Opposition	H.T.	Res.	Att.	Goalscorers
1	16 Aug	Partick Thistle	1-0	1-2	4500	G.Young
2	23	MORTON	0-2	4-2	3000	Mair, T.Findlay, R.Findlay, Morton(?)
3	30	Dundee	0-1	0-2	8500	
4	6 Sep	HIBERNIAN	1-2	1-4	4000	T.Findlay
5	13	Morton	0-0	1-0	5500	R.Findlay
6	20	CELTIC	0-2	1-3	7000	Wyllie
7	27	St. Mirren	0-3	0-4	4000	
8	4 Oct	PORT GLASGOW ATH.	1-0	1-0	2500	Wilson
9	11	QUEENS PARK	0-0	1-1	4500	Crichton
10	18	Third Lanark	0-1	0-2	4000	
11	25	PARTICK THISTLE	1-0	2-0	3000	G.Young, R.Findlay
12	1 Nov	Celtic	0-2	1-3	4000	Gibson
13	8	THIRD LANARK	2-1	2-2	3500	G.Young, T.Findlay
14	15	Hibernian	1-1	1-2	5000	G.Young
15	22	HEARTS	1-3	1-3	3000	O.G.
16	29	Rangers	0-4	0-5	4500	
17	6 Dec	Hearts	1-0	1-1	6000	McPherson
18	13	DUNDEE	0-1	0-2	4000	
19	20	RANGERS	0-0	0-0	4000	
20	27	ST. MIRREN	0-3	2-3	2500	McKay, Wilson
21	31 Jan	Queens Park	2-1	3-2	3500	R.Findlay(2), Gibson
22	14 Feb	Port Glasgow Athletic	0-0	1-0	2000	T.Findlay

Player appearances (shirt numbers):

No.	Craig	Busby	Morton	McPherson	Anderson	Mitchell	Morton	G.Young	Mair	T.Findlay	R.Findlay	Wyllie	Wilson	McConnell	Crichton	Gibson	McKay	R.Young
1	1	2	3	4	5	6	7	8	9	10	11							
2	1	2	3	4	5		7	8	9	10	11	6						
3	1	2	3	4	5	6	7	8	9	10	11							
4	1	2	3	4	5	6		9		10	11	7	8					
5	1	2	3	4	5	6	7			10	11	9	8					
6	1	2	3	4	5	6	7			10	11	9	8					
7	1	2	3	4	5	6	7		8	10	11	9						
8	1		3	4	5	7	11			10			9	8	2	6		
9	1		2	4	5	6	11	9		10				8	3	7		
10	1		2	4	5	6	7	9		10	11			8	3			
11	1	2		4	5	6	7	9			11			10	3		8	
12	1		2	4	5		7	9			11			10	3	6	8	
13	1		2	4	5	6	7	9		10	11				3		8	
14	1	2			5	6	7	9			11				3	4	8	10
15	1		2		5	6	7	9			11				3	4	8	10
16	1	2	3	4	5	6	7			10	11						8	9
17	1		3	4	5	6	11	7		10			2				8	9
18	1		3	4	5	6		7		10	11	2					8	9
19	1		2	4	5		11				7		10	3	6	8	9	
20			2	4	5	6	7						10	3	6	8	9	1
21	1		2		5	6	7			10	11	9		3	4	8		
22	1		2		5	6	7			10	11	9		3	4	8		
Apps.	21	10	20	18	22	19	20	12	5	16	17	11	10	12	9	12	7	1
Goals				1				4	1	4	5	1	2		1	2	1	

Pos P. W. D. L. F. A. Pts.
9th 22 6 4 12 24 43 16

Scottish Cup

No.	Date	Opposition	H.T.	Res.	Att.	Goalscorers
1	17 Jan	Arbroath	3-0	3-1	3000	McKay(2), T.Findlay
2	24	Rangers	0-1	0-4	7500	

No.	Craig	Morton	McPherson	Anderson	Mitchell	T.Findlay	Crichton	Gibson	McKay	R.Young
1	1	2	4		6	11	10	7	3	5
2	1	2	4	5	6	11	10	7	3	

Robert Templeton.

One of the greatest players of his day, later labelled the "Stanley Matthews" of his generation. Templeton once stuck his head in a lion's mouth. For a bet! He was a victim of 'flu epidemic in 1919.

SEASON 1903-04 — Division One

No.	Date	Opposition	H.T.	Res.	Att.	Goalscorers
1	15 Aug	QUEENS PARK	0-1	2-1	3500	Blair, O.G.
2	22	Morton	2-2	2-4	4000	Graham, Blair
3	29	PARTICK THISTLE	0-2	1-3	4000	McLeod
4	5 Sep	Dundee	0-1	0-4	6000	
5	12	HIBERNIAN	0-0	0-0	3000	
6	19	MORTON	1-0	1-1		McPherson
7	26	Hearts	1-1	1-2	6000	Blair
8	3 Oct	PORT GLASGOW ATH.	0-0	0-4	3500	
9	10	Airdrieonians	1-1	2-1	4000	Banks, R.Findlay
10	17	ST. MIRREN	0-0	2-0	3200	McPherson, R.Findlay
11	24	Motherwell	0-2	0-2	3000	
12	31	THIRD LANARK	0-0	1-2	4300	R.Findlay
13	7 Nov	Dundee	0-1	0-1	3800	
14	14	CELTIC	1-4	1-6	4500	McPherson
15	21	Partick Thistle	0-1	0-4	2000	
16	28	AIRDRIEONIANS	0-0	0-2	3000	
17	5 Dec	RANGERS	1-1	2-2	6000	Banks, Gibson
18	12	Port Glasgow Athletic	0-1	1-4	3000	Banks
19	19	St. Mirren	0-2	0-3	1800	
20	26	Queens Park	1-0	1-1	3000	Blair
21	9 Jan	MOTHERWELL	2-0	2-1	1800	Blair, Morton(No.11)
22	16	Rangers	0-1	0-3	4000	
23	5 Mar	HEARTS	1-3	2-3	2000	Gibson, Morton(No.11)
24	12	Hibernian	2-2	2-2		Morton(No.11), Wyllie
25	26	Third Lanark	2-1	2-3	4500	Gibson(2)
26	23 Apr	Celtic	1-1	1-6	4000	Banks

Pos P. W. D. L. F. A. Pts.
14th 26 4 5 17 26 65 13

Player appearances 1903-04

	Craig	Morton	Gunzeon	McPherson	Anderson	Wyllie	Graham	Gibson	Blair	McKay	McGimpsey	Morton	Crichton	McLeod	Banks	R.Findlay	Young	Fairgray	T.Findlay	Mitchell	W.McDonald	J.McDonald	Davidson
Apps.	23	20	26	18	20	21	8	17	24	11	8	17	17	4	21	9	3	1	3	10	2	3	
Goals				3			2	4	5			3		1	4	3							

Scottish Cup

No.	Date	Opposition	H.T.	Res.	Att.	Goalscorers
1	23 Jan	Nithsdale Wands	2-1	2-2	900	Blair(2)
1R	30	NITHSDALE WANDS	1-1	1-1	2500	McKay
1R	6 Feb	NITHSDALE WANDS	1-1	2-1*	4000	Davidson, Gibson
2	13	ALBION ROVERS	2-1	2-2		R.Findlay, Gibson
2R	20	Albion Rovers	0-0	1-0	4000	Blair
QF	27	Third Lanark	0-2	0-3	12000	

* After extra time.

SEASON 1904-05 — Division One

No.	Date	Opposition	H.T.	Res.	Att.	Goalscorers
1	20 Aug	HEARTS	1-0	3-2	4500	Banks, Blair, Gibson
2	27	MOTHERWELL	0-2	0-2	4000	
3	3 Sep	PORT GLASGOW ATH.	0-0	1-1	3000	W.McDonald
4	10	Morton	1-1	1-2	4000	Morton
5	17	THIRD LANARK	0-0	0-0	4000	
6	24	Dundee	0-2	0-3	5000	
7	1 Oct	HIBERNIAN	1-0	2-1	4000	Blair(2)
8	8	QUEENS PARK	2-1	2-1	4500	Banks, Blair
9	15	Port Glasgow Athletic	1-1	1-1		Blair
10	22	Airdrieonians	1-0	1-1		Currie
11	29	ST. MIRREN	1-0	1-0	5000	Banks
12	5 Nov	CELTIC	0-3	0-3	8000	
13	12	Third Lanark	1-0	1-3	4500	Wyllie
14	19	Motherwell	0-1	1-2	3500	Wyllie
15	26	Hibernian	1-0	1-2	2500	Blair
16	3 Dec	RANGERS	0-1	0-4	6500	
17	10	Partick Thistle	0-2	0-2	5000	
18	17	Queens Park	0-1	1-1	2000	Maxwell
19	24	MORTON	0-0	1-0	2000	Fairfoul
20	31	Celtic	0-2	1-3	4000	Maxwell
21	2 Jan	PARTICK THISTLE	0-2	3-2	5000	Banks(3)
22	7	Hearts	2-1	3-1	4000	Graham(3)
23	14	AIRDRIEONIANS	1-0	1-0	4500	Maxwell
24	21	Rangers	2-4	2-6	8000	Maxwell(2)
25	11 Feb	DUNDEE	1-0	2-1	4000	Blair(2)
26	18	St. Mirren	0-1	0-1		

Pos P. W. D. L. F. A. Pts.
9th 26 9 5 12 29 45 23

Player appearances 1904-05

	Young	Battles	Aitken	Johnstone	Crichton	W.McDonald	Currie	Gibson	Banks	Blair	Morton	W.Monteith	J.McDonald	Anderson	Fairfoul	McQueen	Wyllie	Hendron	Maxwell	Graham
Apps.	5	23	26	18	20	23	14	4	25	26	18	21	3	17	16	7	2	4	9	5
Goals						1	1	1	6	8	1				1		2		5	3

Scottish Cup

No.	Date	Opposition	H.T.	Res.	Att.	Goalscorers
1	28 Jan	BEITH	1-2	2-2	3000	Morton(2)
1R	4 Feb	Beith	1-1	1-3	4000	Maxwell

SEASON 1905-06   Division One

No.	Date	Opposition	H.T.	Res.	Att.	Goalscorers
1	19 Aug	Rangers	1-2	2-3	10000	Fairfoul, A.Graham
2	26	CELTIC	2-3	2-4	8500	Banks, Maxwell
3	2 Sep	Aberdeen	0-1	0-2	5000	
4	9	MORTON	1-1	3-1	3000	Banks, A.Graham, J.Young
5	16	Hearts	0-1	0-3	7000	
6	30	MOTHERWELL	0-0	1-0	3000	J.Young
7	7 Oct	Dundee	0-2	1-2	4000	A.Graham
8	14	ST. MIRREN	3-3	5-3	3000	A.Graham(2), J.Young(2), McDonald
9	21	PARTICK THISTLE	1-2	1-2	3000	Brown
10	28	Airdrieonians	1-1	1-1	4000	A.Graham
11	4 Nov	FALKIRK	0-1	2-1	3500	Cameron, W.Shaw
12	11	QUEENS PARK	4-0	7-0	3500	J.Young(3), Galloway(3), Banks
13	18	HEARTS	1-0	1-1	5000	Fairfoul
14	25	Port Glasgow Athletic	1-0	2-3	1700	Morton, Brown
15	2 Dec	Third Lanark	0-2	0-5	4000	
16	9	HIBERNIAN	0-1	0-2	3500	
17	16	DUNDEE	1-2	2-2	3000	A.Graham, J.Young
18	23	Queens Park	0-1	1-4	4000	Fairfoul
19	30	ABERDEEN	1-0	2-0	3000	A.Graham, Maxwell
20	2 Jan	Celtic	0-0	0-2	6500	
21	6	RANGERS	1-2	1-3	6000	Fairfoul
22	13	Partick Thistle	0-1	1-2	2800	J.Young
23	20	THIRD LANARK	1-0	2-0	4000	A.Graham, W.Shaw
24	3 Feb	AIRDRIEONIANS	0-0	0-0	4000	
25	10 Mar	Motherwell	0-0	1-5	3000	Fairfoul
26	17	Falkirk	1-2	3-2	3000	Brown, Fairfoul, J.Young
27	31	Hibernian	0-1	1-2	2500	J.Young
28	7 Apr	Morton	0-2	0-3	2000	
29	28	PORT GLASGOW ATH.	2-0	3-2	3000	Brown, J.Young, Maxwell
30	12 May	St. Mirren	1-0	1-2	2000	Wishart
31	15	Port Glasgow Athletic*	0-1	0-6		

* Cathkin Park Play-off for 3rd last place.

Appearances / Goals

Player	Apps	Goals
W.Monteith	19	
Duncan	13	
Aitken	30	
Banks	15	3
W.Shaw	23	2
McDonald	20	1
Maxwell	17	3
Fairfoul	26	6
A.Graham	21	9
J.Young	26	12
Morton	14	1
Crichton	18	
R.Young	10	
Grant	3	
Galloway	8	3
Brown	21	4
Watson	13	
Cameron	1	1
Bridges	1	
Fullarton	12	
Wishart	8	1
McLounie	3	
McQueen	2	
Black	4	
Gibson	2	
McKeown	1	
NcCallum	2	
Moffat	2	
Drain	2	
S.Graham	2	
H.C.Shaw		
H.Monteith	2	

Pos	P	W	D	L	F	A	Pts
15th	30	8	4	18	46	68	20

Scottish Cup

	Date	Opposition	H.T.	Res.	Att.	Goalscorers
1	27 Jan	CLYDE	2-0	2-1	6000	Crichton, Fairfoul
2	10 Feb	PORT GLASGOW ATH	1-2	2-2	4000	J.Young(2)
2R	17	Port Glasgow Athletic	0-0	0-0	5000	
2R	24	Port Glasgow Athletic* +	0-0	0-0	6000	
2R	3 Mar	Port Glasgow Athletic*	0-1	0-1	5000	

* Played at Cathkin Park   + After Extra Time

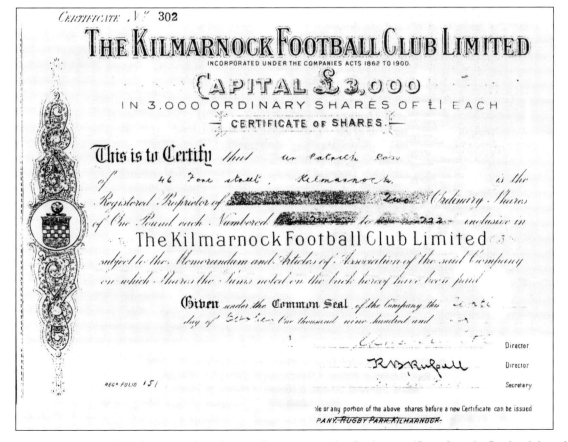

CERTIFICATE Nº 302

THE KILMARNOCK FOOTBALL CLUB LIMITED
INCORPORATED UNDER THE COMPANIES ACTS 1862 TO 1900.

CAPITAL £3,000
IN 3,000 ORDINARY SHARES OF £1 EACH
CERTIFICATE OF SHARES.

This is to Certify that Mr Patrick Ross of 46 Fore Street, Kilmarnock, is the Registered Proprietor of Two Ordinary Shares of One Pound each Numbered ... to ... inclusive in

The Kilmarnock Football Club Limited
subject to the Memorandum and Articles of Association of the said Company on which Shares the Sums noted on the back hereof have been paid

Given under the Common Seal of the Company this ... day of ... One thousand nine hundred and ...

Director
Director
Secretary

REGⁿ FOLIO 151

...ble or any portion of the above shares before a new Certificate can be issued
PANY. RUGBY PARK. KILMARNOCK.

Kilmarnock became a Limited Company in 1906. Here is a rare example of a share certificate from the first batch issued.

SEASON 1906-07 Division One

No.	Date	Opposition	H.T.	Res.	Att.	Goalscorers	Monteith	McCallum	McKeown	Fullarton	Moffat	Black	Maxwell	Wishart	T. Brown	Graham	Linward	Williams	Crichton	Drain	Shaw	Agnew	Morton	Howie	Mitchell	W. Johnstone	Skillen	Anderson	R Barton	Young	Neill	Livingstone	H Wilson	A. Brown
1	18 Aug	AIRDRIEONIANS	0-1	0-1	6000		1	2	3	4	5	6	7	8	9	10	11																	
2	25	Celtic	0-3	0-5	14000			2	3		5	6	7	8		10	11	1	4	9														
3	1 Sep	PARTICK THISTLE	2-1	3-1	4000	Maxwell, Graham, Drain	1	2	3	4		6	7	8		10	11			9	5													
4	8	CLYDE	0-2	1-2	3000	Shaw	1	3	2	4		6	7	8		10	11			9	5													
5	15	Hibernian	0-1	0-1	5000		1	2		4		6	7	8		10	11				5	3	9											
6	22	HAMILTON A.	0-0	1-0	3500	Moffat	1	2				6	7	8	9	10	11		4		5	3												
7	29	St. Mirren	0-0	0-3	4500		1	2		4		6	7		9	10	11				5	3			8									
8	6 Oct	Queens Park	0-0	1-1	3000	Maxwell	1	2			5	6	7	8	9		11					3	10	4										
9	13	RANGERS	0-3	1-5	7000	Moffat	1	2			5	6	7	8	9		11					3	10	4										
10	20	Port Glasgow Athletic	1-1	2-3	1500	Howie, Wishart	1	2		4			7	8			11				5	3	10	6	9									
11	27	ABERDEEN	0-1	1-3	2500	Linward	1	2					7	8			11		4		5	3	10	6	9									
12	3 Nov	Dundee	2-1	2-4	5000	Brown, Skillen					5			8				1	6		4	3	7	10	2		9							11
13	10	Motherwell	0-2	0-3	2500								7	8				1	6		4	3		10	2		9	5						11
14	17	HEARTS	0-1	2-2	3000	Skillen(2)						6		8				1			4	3		10	2		9	5	7						11
15	24	FALKIRK	0-2	1-4	3000	Agnew						6		8				1			4	3		10	2		9	5	7						11
16	1 Dec	HIBERNIAN	1-2	1-3	3000	Linward						6		8			11	1			4	3		10	2		9	5	7						
17	8	Third Lanark	0-1	1-2	1500	Barton		2				6		8			11	1	4			3	9	10				5	7						
18	15	Morton	2-0	2-2	2500	Maxwell, Morton		2				6		8			11	1	4			3	9	10				5	7						
19	22	Airdrieonians	0-1	0-1	1000			2				6		8			11		4			3	9	10				5	7	1				
20	29	CELTIC	0-2	2-2	5000	Drain, Maxwell		2				6		8			11		4			3	9	10				5	7	1				
21	1 Jan	ST. MIRREN	1-0	1-0	6000	O.G.		2				6		8			11		4			3	9	10				5	7	1				
22	5	Partick Thistle	0-2	0-3	3000			2				6		8	9		11		4			3	7	10				5		1				
23	12	THIRD LANARK	2-3	3-3	3000	Agnew(2), Drain						6		8	9		11		4			3		10	2			5	7	1				
24	19	Aberdeen	0-0	0-3	4000							6		8	9				4			3	7	10	2			5		1				11
25	9 Feb	Clyde	0-2	0-2	5000			2				6	7	8			11		4			3		10				5		1		9		
26	2 Mar	QUEENS PARK	2-0	3-1	3000	Barton, Howie, Livingstone		2				6		8			11		4			3		10				5	7	1		9		
27	9	DUNDEE	1-2	1-3	4000	Maxwell						6		8			11		4			3		10	2			5	7	1		9		
28	16	Hearts	0-1	0-1	2000									8			11		4			3		10	2			5	7	1	2	9	6	
29	23	MOTHERWELL	3-0	3-2	3000	Barton, Graham, Howie						6		8			11		4			3		10	2			5	7	1		9		
30	30	Hamilton A.	2-0	2-0	2500	Graham, Howie						6		8	9		11		4			3	7	10	2			5		1				
31	6 Apr	MORTON	1-0	3-0	2500	Agnew, Barton, Skillen						6		8		10	11		4		5	3			2				7	1		9		
32	13	Falkirk	1-1	1-2	3000	Agnew						6		8		10	11		4			3			2			5	7	1		9		
33	20	Rangers	0-1	0-3	2000							6		8		10	11		4			3			2			5	7	1		9		
34	27	PORT GLASGOW ATH.	0-0	2-1	4000	Morton, Skillen						6		8			11		4			3	10		2			5	7	1		9		
					Apps.		10	20	4	6	9	15	24	14	1	17	19	8	16	15	21	26	19	20	27	3	11	22	18	16	2	5	1	6
					Goals						2		5	1		3	2			3	1	5	2	4			5		4			1		1

Pos	P	W	D	L	F	A	Pts
17th	34	8	5	21	40	72	21

Scottish Cup

No.	Date	Opposition	H.T.	Res.	Att.	Goalscorers	McCallum	Black	Maxwell	Wishart	T. Brown	Graham	Linward	Crichton	Agnew	Morton	Howie	Mitchell	Skillen	Anderson	R Barton	Young	Livingstone
1	2 Feb*	CLACHNACUDDIN	3-0	4-0	3000	Drain, Graham, Maxwell, Morton	2	6		8	9		11		10		3	7		4		5	1
2	16	HEARTS	0-0	0-0	8000			6	7	8				4	10		3	11	2		5	1	9
2R	23	Hearts	0-1	1-2	15000	Agnew		6	7	8				4	10		3	11	2		5	1	9

* Originally scheduled for 26/1. Ground declared unsafe but a friendly took place, Kilmarnock winning 1-0. Scorer: Linward.

Standing (l-r): G. Fullarton, W. Shaw, F. Frew (Secretary), D. McCallum, W. Agnew.
Seated (l-r): J. Maxwell, D. Howie, H. Monteith, S. Graham, W. Linward.
Kneeling (l-r): T. Drain, H. Black.

No.	Date	Opposition	H.T.	Res.	Att.	Goalscorers
1	17 Aug	Hearts	0-1	0-1	9000	
2	24	THIRD LANARK	1-1	2-2	5500	Howie, Skillen
3	31	Partick Thistle	0-2	2-2	3000	Morton, Skillen
4	7 Sep	Rangers	0-0	0-1	14000	
5	14	CELTIC	0-0	0-0	15000	
6	21	Queens Park	1-1	1-1	8000	H.Wilson
7	28	CLYDE	0-1	2-2	5000	Livingstone(2)
8	5 Oct	Aberdeen	0-1	0-1	7000	
9	12	MORTON	1-1	1-1	4500	Howie
10	19	Hibernian	0-2	1-3	3500	Agnew
11	26	FALKIRK	0-3	1-6	7000	Agnew
12	2 Nov	Motherwell	0-0	2-1	4500	A.Armour, Barton
13	9	PORT GLASGOW ATH.	1-0	1-1	4200	H.Wilson
14	16	AIRDRIEONIANS	0-0	0-1	4000	
15	23	Dundee	0-2	0-4	8500	
16	30	Clyde	0-0	0-0	2800	
17	7 Dec	HAMILTON A.	1-0	2-0	3500	Howie, Templeton
18	14	HIBERNIAN	2-0	3-0	4500	H.Wilson, Templeton(2)
19	21	Celtic	1-1	1-4	9000	A.Armour
20	28	MOTHERWELL	0-0	2-0	3500	A.Armour, Templeton
21	1 Jan	ST. MIRREN	1-2	2-2	6500	Agnew, Templeton
22	2	Falkirk	0-3	0-5	7500	
23	4*	Port Glasgow Athletic	1-2	1-4	3000	Howie
24	11	PARTICK THISTLE	0-0	0-1	6000	
25	18	St. Mirren	0-0	0-0	5000	
26	1 Feb	HEARTS	0-0	2-0	5000	Barton, Walker
27	15	QUEENS PARK	1-1	2-2	6000	Agnew, Templeton
28	29	ABERDEEN	0-0	1-0	6500	Templeton
29	7 Mar	RANGERS	0-1	0-2	8000	
30	14	Airdrieonians	0-0	0-1	3000	
31	21	DUNDEE	0-1	1-1	5500	Hunter
32	4 Apr	Hamilton A.	3-2	3-3	3000	A.Armour, Crichton, T.Findlay
33	22	Morton	0-0	2-2	2000	Agnew, Barton
34	25	Third Lanark	2-4	3-6	3000	Hunter(3)

* Kilmarnock fielded only seven players.

Pos	P	W	D	L	F	A	Pts
15th	34	6	13	15	38	61	25

Player appearances (shirt numbers):

No.	R.Young	Mitchell	A.Wilson	Anderson	Shaw	Barton	Howie	Skillen	H.Wilson	Morton	Walker	Nisbet	Livingstone	Strachan	McAllister	Allison	Templeton	A.Armour	McCallum	Halley	Doolan	J.Young	Crichton	Hunter	T.Findlay	Neilson	Johnstone	Murray
1	1	2	3	4	5	6	7	8	9	10	11																	
2	1	2	3	4	5	6	7	8	9	10	11																	
3	1	2	3	4	5	6	7	8	9	10	11	6																
4	1	2	3	4	5	6	7	8		10	9		11															
5	1	2	3	4	5	6	7	8	9	10	11																	
6	1	2	3	4	5	6	7	8	9	10	11																	
7	1	2			5	6	7	8		10	11	4			9													
8	1	2	3	4	5	6	7	8	9	10	11																	
9	1	2	3	4	5	6	7	8		10	11	9																
10		2	3	4	5	6			9		10			1	7	8	11											
11		2	3	4		5				10	9		7		1		11									6		
12		2	3	4		6	7	8		10				5			11	9										
13		2	3			6	7	4		10		11	5		1		8	9										
14	4	3	6				7	8		10	11	5		1			9	2										
15		2	3	4		6	7	8		10	9	5		1			11											
16		2	3	4				8		10	11	5	9	1				7										
17		2	3	4		6				10		5		1			11	9	7									
18	6	3	4			8				10		5		1			11	9	2	7	7							
19		2	3	4		6				10		5		1			11	9	7									
20		2	3	4		0		0		10		5		1			11	0	7									
21		2	3	4		6				10		5		1			11	9	7									
22		2	3	4	5	6	10	8						1			11	9	7									
23		2			10	5	6*	7**		8		4					11	9	7									
24	1	6	2	4	5		10	8						9			11			7	3							
25	1	2	3	10	5	6	7	8				4					11	9										
26	1	2	3		5	6	10	8				4			7		11		9									
27	1	2	3	4	5		10	8				6			7		11	9										
28	1	2		8	5							6			7		11	9		3	10					4		
29	1	2		4	5			8				6			7		11	10	3		9							
30	1			4	5	6	7	8							10			11	9	3								2
31	1	2	3	4	5	6		8				7					10	11			9							
32	1	2	3		5			8			6						11	7					4	9	10			
33	1	2	3		5	6	8	4				7					11							9	10			
34	1	2	3		5	6	8	4									11	7						9	10			
Apps	20	33	30	28	23	26	22	33	6	21	14	20	2	3	13	7	2	19	17	3	11	2	3	2	4	3	1	1
Goals		5				3	4	2	3	1	1				2			7	4					1	4	1		

* No.1 for first 45 minutes
" No.1 for second 45 minutes

Scottish Cup

No.	Date	Opposition	H.T.	Res.	Att.	Goalscorers	R.Young	Mitchell	A.Wilson	Anderson	Shaw	Barton	Howie	Skillen	H.Wilson	Morton	Walker	Nisbet	Livingstone	Strachan	McAllister	Allison	Templeton	A.Armour	McCallum	Halley	Doolan	J.Young	Crichton	Hunter	T.Findlay
1	23 Jan	HAMILTON A.	1-1	2-1	4000	A.Wilson, Shaw	1	2	3	10	5	6	7	8				4					11	9							
2	8 Feb	DUNBLANE	3-0	3-0	4000	A.Wilson, Templeton, Walker	1	2	3	10	5	6	9	8				4			7		11								
QF	22	Hibernian	1-0	1-0	11000	McAllister	1	2	3	4	5			8				6			7		11	10		9					
SF	28 Mar	ST. MIRREN	0-0	0-0	15000		1	2	3		5	6		8				4			7		11							9	10
SFR	11 Apr	St. Mirren	0-1	0-2	20000		1	2	3	4	5			8				6					11	7						9	10

Bob Templeton makes his debut. Three Kilmarnock players, Agnew, Mitchell and Templeton play for Scotland v Ireland. Only seven players turn up for match at Port Glasgow. League crowds total over 100,000 for the first time.

SEASON 1908-09 — Division One

No.	Date	Opposition	H.T.	Res.	Att.	Goalscorers
1	15 Aug	PARTICK THISTLE	1-0	4-1	5000	D.Armour, Barton, Boyd, Templeton
2	19	Clyde	2-2	2-5	5000	D.Armour, Barton
3	22	Celtic	0-4	1-5	11000	D.Armour
4	29	AIRDRIEONIANS	0-1	0-1	4000	
5	5 Sep	Hamilton A.	0-0	0-0	2500	
6	12	RANGERS	0-2	0-5	9000	
7	19	MOTHERWELL	1-0	4-1	3500	Mitchell(2), Halley, Young
8	26	Aberdeen	0-1	0-2	7000	
9	3 Oct	St. Mirren	0-3	0-3	8000	
10	10	Hearts	0-0	0-0	7500	
11	17	FALKIRK	2-0	3-1	4800	Douglas(2), Howie
12	24	QUEENS PARK	1-0	1-1	6300	Douglas
13	31	PORT GLASGOW ATH.	0-0	1-0	3800	A.Ramsay
14	7 Nov	CLYDE	2-0	2-1	5800	Douglas, A.Ramsay
15	14	Dundee	0-2	0-5	8000	
16	21	HIBERNIAN	0-0	0-1	3500	
17	28	THIRD LANARK	3-1	4-2	3800	Howie, Mitchell, D.Armour, Douglas
18	12 Dec	MORTON	0-0	2-1	3500	Douglas, A.Ramsay
19	19	Rangers	1-1	1-1	8000	A.Ramsay
20	26	DUNDEE	2-0	2-0	5500	Howie, Templeton
21	1 Jan	ST. MIRREN	1-0	1-1	8500	A.Ramsay
22	2	CELTIC	1-0	3-1	13000	Douglas, Howie, Mitchell
23	4	Third Lanark	0-1	0-4	11500	
24	9	Hibernian	1-1	1-2	5500	O.G.
25	6 Feb	Morton	0-0	1-1	3000	Bulloch
26	13	Airdrieonians	0-0	1-1	4000	McDermott
27	20	HEARTS	1-3	2-5	5500	Douglas, McDermott
28	27	Partick Thistle*	0-0	1-0	2900	Halley
29	6 Mar	Queens Park	2-0	2-0	2500	Douglas, Barrie
30	13	ABERDEEN	3-2	3-2	4000	Douglas, Howie, Templeton
31	20	HAMILTON A.	1-1	3-1	3300	Douglas(2), A.Ramsay
32	27	Motherwell	0-0	1-2	2000	Bulloch
33	3 Apr	Falkirk	1-2	1-3	3000	Glass
34	17	Port Glasgow Athletic	0-0	0-2	3000	

* Played at Rugby Park

Pos P W D L F A Pts.
10th 34 13 7 14 47 61 33

Player appearances (shirt numbers worn)

No.	Aitken	D.Armour	Mitchell	Howie	Barrie	Shaw	A.Armour	A.Ramsay	Barton	Boyd	Templeton	Halley	Black	Douglas	Young	Gray	Crichton	Glass	McAllister	Kirkcaldy	Anderson	Stevenson	Bulloch	McDermott
1	1	2	3	4	5	6	7	8	9	10	11													
2	1	2	3	4	5	6	7	8	9	10	11													
3	1	2	3	8	5	6	7		9	10	11	4												
4	1	2	3	4	5		7	8		10	11				6	9								
5	1	2	3	10	5	6	8	7			11	4			9									
6	1	2	3	8	5	6	9				7	4				10	11							
7	1	2	3	10	5	6	7				11	4			9	8								
8	1	2	3	10	5		7		6		11	4			9	8								
9	1	2		10	5	6	7	8			11	4			9		3							
10	1	2	3	10	5		7	8			11	4			9	6								
11	1	2	3	10	5		7	8			11	4		9				6						
12	1	2	3	10	5		7	8				4		9				6	11					
13	1	2	3	10	5		7	8				4		9				6	11					
14	1	2	3	10	5		7	8			11	4		9				6						
15	1	3	2	10	5			8			11	4		9			7	6						
16	1	2	3	10	5		7	8			11	4		9				6						
17	1	2	3	10	5		7	8			11			9				6			4			
18	1	2	3	10	5		7	8			11			9			4	6						
19	1	2	3	10	5		7	8			11			9			4	6						
20	1	2	3	10	5		7	8			11	4		9				6						
21	1	2	3	10	5		7	8			11	4		9				6						
22	1	2	3	10	5		7	8				4		9				6	11					
23	1	2		10	5			8				4		9			7	6	11	3				
24	1	2	3	10	5		7	8				4		9				6	11					
25		2	3		5		7	8			11	4						6		1			9	10
26	1	2	3		5		7	8			11	4						6					9	10
27	1	2	3		5		7	8			11	4		9				6						10
28	1	2		10	5			8			11	4		9			3	6	7					
29	1	2	3	10	5		7	8			11	4		9				6						
30	1	2	3	10	5		7	8			11	4		9				6						
31	1	2	3	10	5		7	8			11	4		9				6						
32	1	2	3	10	5			8			11	4					7	6					9	
33	1	2	3	10	5	4	7				11			9				6						
34	1	2	3		5	6		8							10	7		4					9	
Apps	33	34	30	32	31	9	30	26	5	5	29	28	1	25	3	6	5	25	5	2	1	1	5	3
Goals		4	5	1			4	6	2	1	3	2		12	1			1					2	2

Scottish Cup

	Date	Opposition	H.T.	Res.	Att.	Goalscorers	Aitken	D.Armour	Mitchell	Howie	Barrie	A.Armour	A.Ramsay	Templeton	Halley	Douglas	Glass
1	23 Jan	Hearts	0-1	1-2	18000	Howie	1	2	3	10	5	7	8	11	4	9	6

George Halley.

A product of the famous Glenbuck Cherrypickers junior team, Halley played for the Scottish League and made the trials for the Scotland side without ever being selected. He left Rugby Park for Bradford Park Avenue before going on to win Championship and FA Cup winners medals with Burnley.

SEASON 1909-10 Division One

No.	Date	Opposition	H.T.	Res.	Att.	Goalscorers
1	16 Aug	Rangers	0-1	0-3	12000	
2	21	St. Mirren	0-2	1-2	6000	Barrie
3	28	AIRDRIEONIANS	2-1	3-3	5000	Cunningham(2), Chalmers
4	4 Sep	Third Lanark	0-5	0-7	6000	
5	11	QUEENS PARK	2-1	6-1	5000	Ramsay(3),A.Armour,Cunningham,Hastie
6	18	Hibernian	0-2	1-2	4000	Hastie
7	25	HAMILTON A.	1-0	1-0	4000	Douglas
8	2 Oct	Hearts	0-2	0-3	5000	
9	9	MOTHERWELL	2-0	2-1	4000	Cunningham(2)
10	16	Dundee	0-1	2-2	7500	Cunningham(2)
11	23	RANGERS	0-0	0-2	9500	
12	30	Port Glasgow Athletic	0-1	1-1	3000	A.Armour
13	6 Nov	CLYDE	2-1	6-3	4000	Cunningham(2),Halley(2),Barrie,Anderson
14	13	Falkirk	0-2	0-4	7000	
15	20	HIBERNIAN	1-0	4-0	5000	A.Armour, Cunningham, Howie, Ramsay
16	27	Airdrieonians	1-0	2-2	**3000**	Halley, Ramsay
17	4 Dec	Celtic	1-1	1-2	6000	Howie
18	11	MORTON	0-0	2-0	2000	A.Armour, Howie
19	25	CELTIC	0-1	0-1	10000	
20	1 Jan	ST. MIRREN	1-0	2-1	10500	Cunningham, Howie
21	3	Motherwell	1-2	1-3	6000	Cunningham
22	8	Partick Thistle	0-1	0-3	5000	
23	15	THIRD LANARK	0-0	0-0	3000	
24	12 Feb	Hamilton A.	3-1	7-1	3000	Cunningham(3), Howie(2), McAllister(2)
25	19	PARTICK THISTLE	1-1	2-1	4000	Anderson, Cunningham
26	26	ABERDEEN	0-1	0-2	4000	
27	5 Mar	Morton	0-2	0-4	4000	
28	12	PORT GLASGOW A.	1-0	4-0	3000	Howie(2), Hastie, McAllister
29	19	FALKIRK	0-1	0-2	3000	
30	26	Aberdeen	1-0	2-1	6000	Howie
31	2 Apr	Clyde	0-0	0-0	2000	
32	9	Queens Park	1-0	1-1	3000	Howie
33	26	DUNDEE	1-1	2-1	3000	Howie, Cunningham
34	30	HEARTS	0-1	1-1	4000	Cunningham

Pos P. W. D. L. F. A. Pts.
11th 34 12 8 14 53 59 32

Player appearances and goals

Player	Apps	Goals
Aitken	16	
D.Armour	10	
Mitchell	32	
Glass	9	
Barrie	31	2
R.Anderson	29	2
A.Armour	24	4
Ramsay	15	5
Douglas	4	1
Cunningham	24	18
Gray	1	
Howie	29	11
Templeton	24	
Halley	29	3
Chalmers	13	1
Stevenson	6	
Kirkwood	23	
Hastie	23	3
Glover	12	
McNeill	1	
"Mack"	3	
Ewing	2	
Doolan	3	
McAllister	9	3
Allan	1	
Neilson	1	

Scottish Cup

No.	Date	Opposition	H.T.	Res.	Att.	Goalscorers
1	22 Jan	THIRD LANARK	0-0	0-0	8500	
1R	5 Feb*	Third Lanark	0-1	0-2	6000	

* Scheduled for 29/1. Owing to poor weather, the game was played as a friendly. Thirds won 6-1, Hastie scored for Killie.

James Mitchell, shown here on a 1909/10 Gallaher's Cigarettes card.

His Kilmarnock career spanned from November 1900 to April 1921 less two years spent with Hurlford after recovering from a career-threatening injury. Jamie's rehabilitation was so completed that he played for Scotland and became the first player to appear for Killie in over 400 matches. A century later only five others have played more League games for Kilmarnock.

SEASON 1910-11 — Division One

No.	Date	Opposition	H.T.	Res.	Att.	Goalscorers	Rennie	Kirkwood	Mitchell	Allan	Barrie	Anderson	A.Armour	Gilchrist	Cunningham	Howie	Templeton	Chalmers	Johnstone	Glover	Halley	Cameron	Train	Gray	Shortt	Dunlop	Doolan	Burnett
1	15 Aug	Clyde	0-0	0-0	10000		1	2	3	4	5	6	7	8	9	10	11											
2	20	AIRDRIEONIANS	0-1	0-1	6000		1	2	3	4	5	6	7	8	9		11	10										
3	27	St. Mirren	0-0	1-1	6500	Mitchell	1	2	3	9	5	6	7	8		10	11		4									
4	3 Sep	CELTIC	1-0	1-0	8500	Gilchrist	1	2	3		5	6	7	9	10	8	11		4									
5	10	Morton	0-0	0-0	6000		1	2	3		5	6	7	9	10	8	11		4									
6	17	HEARTS	2-0	3-1	7500	Allan(2), Cunningham	1	2	3	9	5	6	7		10	8	11		4									
7	24	Partick Thistle	0-0	0-1	5500		1	2	3	9	5	6	7		10	8	11		4									
8	1 Oct	THIRD LANARK	1-2	1-5	7000	Gilchrist	1	2	3		5	6	7	9	10	8	11		4									
9	8	Dundee	1-1	1-2	6000	Gilchrist		2	3		5	6	7	9	10	8	11			1	4							
10	15	Aberdeen	0-1	0-1	7000		1	2	3		5	6	7	8			11	10			4							
11	22	MOTHERWELL	1-0	1-0	3000	Cunningham	1	2	3		5	6	7	8	9	10	11				4							
12	29	Falkirk	0-1	2-2	6000	Howie, Mitchell	1	2	3		5	6	7	8	9	10	11				4							
13	5 Nov	HAMILTON A.	1-0	3-0	4000	Cunningham(2), Howie	1	2	3		5	6	7	8	9	10	11				4							
14	12	Rangers	0-1	0-3	6000		1	2	3		5	6	7		9	10	11				4		8					
15	19	CLYDE	1-0	5-2	6000	Howie(3), Anderson, Cunningham	1	2	3		5	6	7	8	9	10	11				4							
16	26	Hibernian	0-0	1-0	4000	Gilchrist	1	2	3			6	7	8	9	10	11				4	5						
17	3 Dec	DUNDEE	1-0	2-0	7000	Allan, Cunningham	1	2	3	9	5	6	7	8	10		11				4							
18	10	Raith Rovers	1-0	1-1	5000	Allan	1	2	3	9	5	6	7	8			11				4			10				
19	17	Celtic	0-2	0-2	6000		1	2	3		5	6	7	8	9	10	11				4							
20	24	QUEENS PARK	1-1	2-1	2000	Cunningham, Gray	1	2	3			6	7	8	9	10					4	5		11				
21	31	RANGERS	0-2	0-2	12000		1	2	3		5	6	7	8	9	10	11				4							
22	2 Jan	ST. MIRREN	2-0	2-2	9000	Barrie, Cunningham	1	2	3	9	5	6	7		10		11				4		8					
23	7	Airdrieonians	1-1	1-3	2000	Shortt	1	2	3	9	5	6	7		10		11				4				8			
24	14	HIBERNIAN	2-1	3-1	3200	Cunningham, Gilchrist, Halley	1	2	3		5	6	7	9	10		11				4				8			
25	21	Third Lanark	1-0	2-0	6000	Cunningham, Howie	1	2	3		5	6	7	8	9	10	11				4							
26	4 Feb	MORTON	1-1	2-3	4000	Cunningham, Dunlop	1	2	3		5	6	7		10		11				4				8	9		
27	11	Hearts	0-1	0-5	6000			2	3		5	6	7	10			11				4				8	9		1
28	18	Aberdeen	1-0	1-1	10000	Cunningham	1	2	3		5	6	7	8	9	10	11				4							
29	25	Queens Park	0-1	1-1	4000	Cunningham	1	2	3		5	6	7	8	9	10	11				4							
30	4 Mar	PARTICK THISTLE	0-0	0-0	3000	Barrie	1	2	3		5	6	7	8	9	10	11				4							
31	25	RAITH ROVERS	0-0	1-0	3000	Howie	1	2			5	6	7	8	9	10	11				4						3	
32	1 Apr	Motherwell	0-1	0-1	2000		1	2	3		5	6	7	8		10	11				4				9			
33	8	FALKIRK	1-1	2-2	4000	Barrie, Cunningham	1	2	3		5	6	7		9	10	11				4		8	7				
34	10	Hamilton A.	1-0	2-0	2000	Allan, Howie	1	2	3	9	5	6			10	8	11				4			7				
Apps.							32	34	33	10	32	32	29	26	29	27	33	4	6	1	24	2	8	2	6	2	1	1
Goals									2	5	3	1		5	14	8					1				1	1	1	

Pos P. W. D. L. F. A. Pts.
10th 34 12 10 12 42 45 34

Scottish Cup

No.	Date	Opposition	H.T.	Res.	Att.	Goalscorers	Rennie	Kirkwood	Mitchell	Allan	Barrie	Anderson	A.Armour	Gilchrist	Cunningham	Howie	Templeton	Chalmers	Johnstone	Glover	Halley
1	28 Jan	Rangers	0-1	1-2	40000	A.Armour	1	2	3		5	6	7	8	9	10	11				4

A. Cunningham.

Mattha' Shortt makes his debut. Geordie Anderson plays his last game in an Ayrshire Cup match against Beith and emigrates to Canada a month later. Pitch invasions, crowd trouble and street disorder mar the season.

SEASON 1911-12 — Division One

No.	Date	Opposition	H.T.	Res.	Att.	Goalscorers	Smart	Kirkwood	Mitchell	Steel	Barrie	Anderson	Armour	J.Cunningham	Mackay	A.Cunningham	Templeton	Thomson	Shortt	Train	Clark	Orr	Allan	Carson	Johnstone	Hannigan	Hastie	Lynch	Wilkinson	Davidson	Burnett	W.Cunningham	Dunlop	Wilson	Logan	Ballantyne	Buchan	Gray	Culley	Blair	Watson	McBean
1	16 Aug	Clyde	0-1	1-3	6000	J.Cunningham	1	2	3	4	5	6	7	8	9	10	11																									
2	19	Airdrieonians	0-1	0-1	3500		1		3	4	5	6		8	9	10	11	2	7																						
3	26	St. Mirren	0-0	4-2	7000	J + A Cunningham, Clark(2)	1		3		5	6		8		9	11	2	10	4	7																					
4	2 Sep	Third Lanark	0-1	0-2	6000		1		3		5	6		8		9	11	2	10	4	7																					
5	9	HAMILTON A.	1-2	2-3	5500	A.Cunningham, Templeton	1	2			5	6	7	8		9	11	3	10	4																						
6	16	Hearts	0-0	1-1	10000	A.Cunningham	1	2	3		5		7	8		9	11		10			4	6																			
7	23	CELTIC	0-1	0-2	6000		1	2	3		5		7	8		9	11		10			4	6																			
8	30	Aberdeen	1-0	2-1	4000	J.Cunningham, Carson		2	3		5		7	8			11	1			10	4	6	9																		
9	7 Oct	RAITH ROVERS	2-1	3-1	4000	Armour, J.Cunningham(2)	1	2	3		5		7	8		10	11					4	6	9																		
10	14	Morton	0-1	0-2	7000		1	2	3		5		7	8		10	11					6	4	9																		
11	21	QUEENS PARK	1-0	1-2	3200	A.Cunningham	1	2	3		5		7	8		9	11		10			4	6																			
12	28	Motherwell	0-0	1-0	5000	A.Cunningham	1	2	3		5		7	10		9	11	8				4	6																			
13	4 Nov	PARTICK THISTLE	0-1	0-1	4000		1	2	3		5			10		9	11	8	7			6	4																			
14	11	Raith Rovers	0-2	2-3	5200	Kirkwood, Hannigan	1	2	3		5	6		8			11	10				4	9			7																
15	18	HEARTS	0-1	1-3	4500	A.Cunningham	1	2	3		5	6	7	8		10	11					4	9																			
16	25	DUNDEE	1-0	1-0	4500	A.Cunningham	1	2	3				7			10	11					4	6	9	5		8															
17	2 Dec	Hibernian	0-0	1-0	4500	J.Cunningham	1	2	3					7		9	11	8				4	6		5		8															
18	9	THIRD LANARK	0-0	0-0	3000		1	2	3	4			7		9	10	11						6		5		8															
19	16	FALKIRK	0-0	1-0	5000	A.Cunningham	1	2	3	4						9	11		10						5		8	6	7													
20	23	CLYDE	0-1	1-3	4500	A.Cunningham	1	2	3	4						9	11		10						5		8	6	7													
21	30	Rangers	1-5	1-6	10000	A.Cunningham	1	2			5	6		8		10	11					4		9					7	3												
22	1 Jan	ST. MIRREN	1-1	1-1	9000	Wilkinson			3		5	6			9	10	11	8				4							7				1	2							
23	6	AIRDRIEONIANS	1-0	2-1	4000	A.Cunningham, Clark			3		5	6		11		10					9	4		8					7				1	2							
24	13	Hamilton A.	0-0	0-4	4000				3		5	6		11							9	4		8					7		10		1	2							
25	20	HIBERNIAN	0-2	1-2	4000	A.Cunningham					5	6		11		10						4							7				1	2			2	9			
26	3 Feb	Queens Park	0-1	0-1	4000				3		5	6		11		10	7				9						4					2			8						
27	2 Mar	Partick Thistle	1-1	1-3	8000	A.Cunningham	1	2	3		5	6		9			11		4				10												8	7					
28	9	MOTHERWELL	1-0	1-1	3500	A.Cunningham	1	2	3		5	6		9			11		4				10												8	7					
29	16	MORTON	0-0	1-0	3000	Ballantyne		2	3							10						4					8							1		7	5	11			
30	23	Dundee	1-5	2-5	3000	Logan(2)		2	3			6							4								8					1	10	9	7	5	11			
31	30	RANGERS	2-1	3-2	4000	Logan, Shortt, O.G.		2	3			6					11		4								8					1	10	7	5		9			
32	6 Apr	Falkirk	0-1	0-2	6000			2	3						6		11		4								8		7			1	10		5		9			
33	13	Celtic	0-1	0-2	2500				3		5	6				10	11		4												2		8	7		9	1		
34	27	ABERDEEN	2-0	3-0	4000	Logan(2), Shortt		2	3		5					10	11		4													8		6	9	1	7	
					Apps.		23	28	28	3	27	18	13	25	2	29	30	4	20	3	8	11	15	9	8	1	11	3	8	1	8	6	2	1	9	6	5	2	4	2	1
					Goals			1					1	6		14	1		2		3			1		1			1						5	1					

Pos P. W. D. L. F. A. Pts.
16th 34 11 4 19 38 60 26

Scottish Cup

	Date	Opposition	H.T.	Res.	Att.	Goalscorers	Smart	Kirkwood	Mitchell	Steel	Barrie	Anderson	Armour	J.Cunningham	Mackay	A.Cunningham	Templeton	Thomson	Shortt	Train	Clark	Orr	Allan	Carson	Johnstone	Hannigan	Hastie	Lynch	Wilkinson	Davidson	Burnett	W.Cunningham	Dunlop	Wilson	Logan	Ballantyne	Buchan	Gray	Culley	Blair	Watson	McBean
1	27 Jan	HAMILTON A.	1-0	1-0	10000	A.Cunningham		2			5	6		11		10	7				9	4							1						8							3
2	10 Feb	Leith Athletic	1-0	2-0	6000	A.Cunningham(2)		2	3		8					10	11		5	9		4					7		1						8							
QF	24	CLYDE	0-2	1-6	19564	Logan		2	3			6		9		10	11		5			4							1						8	7						

Willie Culley.

All-time record scorer Willie Culley makes his debut. New record crowd for cup-tie v Clyde. Mattha' Shortt has to play in goal in win at Pittodrie.

SEASON 1912-13   Division One

No.	Date	Opposition	H.T.	Res.	Att.	Goalscorers
1	17 Aug	PARTICK THISTLE	2-0	2-1	6000	Culley(2)
2	24	St. Mirren	0-2	0-4	10000	
3	31	CELTIC	0-1	0-2	9000	
4	7 Sep	Hamilton A.	1-1	1-3	4000	Watson
5	14	MORTON	1-1	1-1	6000	Armstrong
6	21	THIRD LANARK	0-0	2-0	5000	Armstrong, Kirsop
7	28	Raith Rovers	0-0	0-0	4000	
8	30	Rangers	0-2	0-3	14000	
9	5 Oct	DUNDEE	0-0	2-0	4000	A.Cunningham, Duff
10	12	Clyde	0-0	0-0	4000	
11	19	AIRDRIEONIANS	0-0	0-1	4050	
12	26	Hearts	0-3	0-5	10000	
13	2 Nov	QUEENS PARK	0-0	2-1	4000	Culley, Watson
14	9	Aberdeen	0-0	0-0	7000	
15	16	HIBERNIAN	0-1	0-1	4000	
16	23	Falkirk	0-0	0-0	3000	
17	30	Partick Thistle	0-2	1-4	5000	Logan
18	7 Dec	Airdrieonians	0-3	2-3	4000	A.Cunningham, Duff
19	14	MOTHERWELL	0-0	0-1	6000	
20	21	Third Lanark	0-0	0-0	2000	
21	28	HEARTS	0-0	2-2	4000	A.Cunningham, Duff
22	1 Jan	ST. MIRREN	1-1	2-1	10000	A.Cunningham, Dickie
23	4	Morton	2-1	3-1	7000	Culley, Dickie(2)
24	11	CLYDE	1-1	3-2	4000	A.Cunningham, Dickie
25	18	HAMILTON A.	1-1	1-1	5000	Duff
26	1 Feb	Dundee	0-0	0-0	5000	
27	1 Mar	RANGERS	1-2	2-3	6000	A.Cunningham, Maxwell
28	8	ABERDEEN	2-0	3-1	3000	Culley, A.Cunningham, Templeton
29	15	RAITH ROVERS	1-3	4-3	4000	Dickie(2), Culley, A.Cunningham
30	22	Queens Park	1-1	1-1	6000	Duff
31	29	Celtic	1-1	1-4	8000	A.Cunningham
32	12 Apr	Motherwell	0-0	1-0	4000	A.Cunningham
33	19	Hibernian	0-1	0-4	4000	
34	30	FALKIRK	1-1	1-1	3000	O.G.

Pos P. W. D. L. F. A. Pts.
11th 34 10 11 13 37 54 31

Player appearance grid (shirt numbers by match):

No.	Blair	Mitchell	Trialist	Brown	Aitken	Duff	Buchan	Kirsop	Logan	Culley	A. Cunningham	Templeton	Kirkwood	Watson	Shortt	W. Cunningham	Law	Dickie	Armstrong	Goodwin	Bond	Clark	Steel	Maxwell	Murray	McKay	Burnett	Neil	Trialist
1	1	2	3	4	5	6	7	8	9	10	11																		
2	1	3		4	5	6		8	9	10	11		2	7															
3	1	3			5	6		8	9	10	11		2	7	4														
4	1	3			5	6		8	9	10				7	4	2	11												
5	1	3				6	7		9	10					4	2	11	5	8										
6	1	3				5	7		9	10					4	2		6	8										
7	1	3				5	7	8	9	10	11				4	2		6											
8	1	3				5	7	8	9	10	11				4	2		6											
9	1	3			5			8	9	10	11			7	4	2		6											
10	1	3			5			8	9	10	11			7	4	2		6											
11	1	3			5			8	9	10	11			7	4	2		6											
12	1	3				5		8	9	10	11			7	4	2		6											
13	1	3			5	6			9					7	4	2				8									
14	1	3			5	6				10	9	11	2		4					8	7								
15	1				5	6	7			10	9	11	3		4	2				8									
16	1	3			4	5	10	7	9			11	2							6	8								
17	1	3			4	5		7	9			10	11	2						6	8								
18	1	3				5		7	9			10	11	2	4					6	8								
19	1	3				5					9	10	11	2	7	4				8		6							
20	1	3			4	5					9	10	11	2		7				6	8								
21	1	3				6					9	11	2		4			10		8			5	7					
22	1	3			6	5					9	11			4	2		10		8				7					
23	1	3				5					9	11			4	2		10		8		6	7						
24	1			3		5		8	9			11			4	2		10		7		6							
25	1	3				5		8	9			11			4	2		10		7		6							
26	1					5			9			11			4	2		8		6			7	3	10				
27	1			3		5					9	8	11		4			10		6			7	2					
28	1				2	5					9	8	11		4			10		7		6		3					
29	1					5					9	8	11		4	2		10		7		6		3					
30	1					5					9	8	11	2	4			10		7		6		3					
31	1		5			2					11	8			4			10		7		6		3					9
32		3				5					11	8			4			10		7		6		2		1	9		
33		3				5					11	8			4	2		7		6			9	10	1				
34		3				5					8	11			4			10		7		6		2		1	9		
Apps	31	26	1	3	8	26	15	9	14	27	31	29	11	9	30	18	2	24	2	21	1	2	12	5	9	2	3	2	1
Goals						5		1	1	6	11	1		2				6	2					1					

Scottish Cup

No.	Date	Opposition	H.T.	Res.	Att.	Goalscorers
1	25 Jan	NITHSDALE W.	1-0	3-0	6000	A.Cunningham, Maxwell, Steel
2	8 Feb	ABERCORN	1-1	5-1	8000	Dickie(3), A.Cunningham, Maxwell
QF	22	HEARTS	0-1	0-2	16000	

No.	Blair	Mitchell	Duff	Culley	A.Cunningham	Templeton	Kirkwood	Shortt	W.Cunningham	Dickie	Goodwin	Clark	Steel	Maxwell
1	1		5		8	9	11	3	4	2	10		6	7
2	1		5		8	9	11		4	2	10		6	7, 3
QF	1	3	5		9	11		4	2	10		8	6	7

Left to right: Back row - W.S. Kirsop, Wm. Cunningham, J. Mitchell, M. Shortt, T. Blair, H. Duff, J. Buchan
Front row - A. Logan, G. Watson, W. Dickie, W. Culley, A. Cunningham, R. Templeton.

SEASON 1913-14   Division One

No.	Date	Opposition	H.T.	Res.	Att.	Goalscorers
1	16 Aug	RANGERS	0-2	1-6	9000	Goodwin
2	23	Dumbarton	1-1	1-1	7000	Culley
3	30	CLYDE	1-0	2-2	6000	A.Cunningham(2)
4	6 Sep	Queens Park	0-3	1-3	9000	Duff
5	13	AYR UNITED	0-1	0-1	6000	
6	20	Airdrieonians	0-1	1-3	4000	Neil
7	27	HIBERNIAN	0-1	0-3	4000	
8	4 Oct	Third Lanark	1-0	1-1	5000	Culley
9	11	RAITH ROVERS	1-1	3-1	5000	Dickie, Neil, Waddell
10	18	Morton	0-1	0-2	7000	
11	25	HAMILTON A.	3-2	5-2	4000	A.Cunningham(2), McCurdie(2), Goodwin
12	1 Nov	Celtic	0-1	0-4	12000	
13	8	Motherwell	0-1	0-4	6000	
14	15	FALKIRK	0-3	2-3	4000	Culley, Neil
15	22	Partick Thistle	2-2	2-4	12000	Culley, A.Cunningham
16	29	DUNDEE	0-0	0-0	5000	
17	6 Dec	Aberdeen	1-1	2-1	7000	Culley, Neil
18	13	HEARTS	0-2	0-3	6000	
19	20	Hamilton A.	0-3	0-6	3000	
20	27	PARTICK THISTLE	1-0	2-0	3000	Neil, Whittle
21	1 Jan	ST. MIRREN	1-0	3-1	9000	Whittle(2), A.Cunningham
22	3	Clyde	0-0	0-0	6000	
23	6	St. Mirren	0-1	1-1	4000	A.Cunningham
24	10	THIRD LANARK	1-0	1-1	4000	A.Cunningham
25	17	Hibernian	1-0	1-0	7000	Whittle
26	24	DUMBARTON	3-0	6-0	5000	Neil(3), Whittle(3)
27	31	Falkirk	1-2	1-4	3000	Whittle
28	14 Feb	Raith Rovers	1-1	1-1	5000	Neil
29	28	AIRDRIEONIANS	2-1	3-2	4000	A.Cunningham, Neil, Watson
30	7 Mar	Hearts	1-0	1-0	8000	Goldie
31	14	Ayr United	0-0	0-0	6000	
32	21	Rangers	0-1	0-1	12000	
33	28	QUEENS PARK	3-0	5-0	5000	Whittle(3)
34	8 Apr	CELTIC	0-1	0-1	5000	
35	11	Dundee	1-1	1-3	7000	Neil
36	18	MORTON*	0-1	0-1	8000	
37	22	ABERDEEN	1-2	1-2	4000	Culley
38	25	MOTHERWELL	0-0	2-0	4000	Culley, Neil

* Played away owing to agricultural show at Rugby Park

Pos	P.	W.	D.	L.	F.	A.	Pts.
12th	39	11	9	18	48	68	31

Player appearances (columns: Blair, Murray, Mitchell, Shortt, Duff, Steel, Goodwin, A.Cunningham, Whittle, Dickie, Neil, Burnett, Culley, Grant, Mackie, W.Cunningham, Clark, Fulton, McCurdie, Smith, Waddell, Hamilton, Watson, G.Goldie, Vickers)

Apps.	Goals
Blair 9	
Murray 28	
Mitchell 34	
Shortt 22	
Duff 6	1
Steel 4	
Goodwin 11	2
A.Cunningham 37	9
Whittle 24	11
Dickie 15	1
Neil 32	12
Burnett 1	
Culley 21	7
Grant 28	
Mackie 23	
W.Cunningham 11	
Clark 8	
Fulton 25	
McCurdie 5	2
Smith 1	
Waddell 30	1
Hamilton 1	
Watson 13	1
G.Goldie 19	1
Vickers 7	

Scottish Cup

No.	Date	Opposition	H.T.	Res.	Att.	Goalscorers
1		Bye				
2	7 Feb	HAMILTON A.	1-1	3-1	11000	A.Cunningham, Goldie, Neil
3	21	PARTICK THISTLE	1-3	1-4	12000	Whittle

The last peacetime season. No fewer than 21 Kilmarnock players and 3 Directors served in the armed forces during the First World War. Seven players failed to return, having made the supreme sacrifice:
David Simmon, Alex McCurdie, Charles Vickers, John Rollo, Alexander Barrie, James Maxwell and Daniel McKellar.

SEASON 1914-15 — Division One

No.	Date	Opposition	H.T.	Res.	Att.	Goalscorers	Blair	W.Cunningham	Mitchell	Shortt	Campbell	Mackie	G.Goldie	Neil	Culley	A.Cunningham	McKellar	McCurdie	Millar	Morton	Hamilton	Armour	Vickers	Fulton	Slimmon	Dickie	Armstrong	Goodwin	Howie
1	15 Aug	Morton	0-1	1-3	7000	Culley	1	2	3	4	5	6	7	8	9	10	11												
2	22	CLYDE	0-2	0-3	5000		1	2	3	4	5	6	7	8		10	11	9											
3	29	Rangers	0-2	1-2	15000	Neil		2	3	4		6	7	8		5	11	9	1	10									
4	5 Sep	HEARTS	0-1	0-2	4000			2	3	4		6	7	8		5	11	9	1	10									
5	12	Motherwell	0-3	2-3	5000	Campbell(2)			3	4	9	6	7	8		5			1	10	2								
6	19	AYR UNITED	1-2	1-2	8500	Campbell			3	4	9	6	11	8		5			1	10	2	7							
7	26	Airdrieonians	1-0	2-0	3000	Armour, Vickers		2	3	4		6	7			10	8		1		5	9	11						
8	3 Oct	FALKIRK	0-0	1-0	5000	Armour		2	3	4		6	7			10	8		1		5	9	11						
9	10	Third Lanark	0-2	2-3	6000	Armour, Culley		2	3			6	7			10	8		1		5	9	11	4					
10	17	Partick Thistle	0-0	0-0	10000			2	3	4		6		8	9	10	11		1		5	7							
11	24	HIBERNIAN	2-1	5-1	6000	Culley(2), Neil(2), Hamilton		2		4		6		8	9	10	11		1		5	7			3				
12	31	Dundee	1-0	1-0	4000	Neil		2		4		6		8	9	10	11		1		5	7			3				
13	7 Nov	CELTIC	0-2	1-3	6200	Hamilton		2		4		6		8	9	10	11		1		5	7			3				
14	14	Raith Rovers	0-1	0-3	3000			2		4		6	7	8	9	10	11		1		5				3				
15	21	St. Mirren	1-1	3-2	3000	Neil(2), A.Cunningham		2		4		6	7	8	9	10	11		1		5				3				
16	28	ABERDEEN	4-0	5-2	2000	Neil(2), Armour, Culley, A.Cunningham		2		4		6		8	9	10			1		5	7	11		3				
17	5 Dec	Queens Park	0-0	0-1	4000			2		4		6		8	9	10			1		5	7	11		3				
18	12	RANGERS	0-0	0-1	3000			2	11	4		6	7	8		10		9	1		5				3				
19	19	Aberdeen	0-1	0-3	4000		1	2	11	4		6					8	9			5	7			3	10			
20	26	AIRDRIEONIANS	2-0	2-1	3000	Goldie, Neil	1	2		4		6	7	8		10	11	9			5				3				
21	1 Jan	ST. MIRREN	0-0	2-1	5000	Culley, A.Cunningham	1	2		4		6	7	8	9	10	11				5				3				
22	2	Hibernian	0-1	1-3	3000	A.Cunningham	1	2			4	6		8	9	10	11				5	7			3				
23	4	Celtic	0-1	0-2	8000		1	2			4	6		8	9	10	11				5	7			3				
24	9	RAITH ROVERS	3-0	3-1	2000	Culley(2), Neil	1	2		4		6		8	9	10					5	7	11		3				
25	16	DUMBARTON	3-0	4-0	5000	Neil(4)	1	2		4		6		8	9	10					5	7	11		3				
26	23	Clyde	0-0	0-1	1800		1	2		4		6		8	9	10					5	7	11		3				
27	30	HAMILTON A.	0-0	1-0	4000	A.Cunningham	1	2	3	4		6		8	9	10	11				5	7							
28	6 Feb	Hearts	0-2	1-3	8000	Neil	1	2	3			6		8	9	10	11				5	7		4					
29	13	PARTICK THISTLE	0-0	2-0	4000	A.Cunningham, Neil	1	2	3	4		6		8	9	10	11				5	7							
30	20	Ayr United	0-1	0-2	10000		1	2	3	4		6		8	9	10					5	7	11						
31	27	QUEENS PARK	0-0	3-0	1500	Armour, Culley, A.Cunningham	1	2	3	4		6		8	9	10	11				5	7							
32	6 Mar	MOTHERWELL	1-2	2-2	4000	Culley, Neil	1	2	3	4		6		8	9	10					5	7						11	
33	13	Hamilton A.	0-0	0-0	4000			2	3	4		6		8	9	10	11		1			7				5			
34	20	DUNDEE	2-2	3-2	4000	A.Cunningham(2), McKellar		2	3	4		6		8	9	10	11		1			7				5			
35	27	THIRD LANARK	1-1	2-1	4000	Culley, Neil	1	2	3	4		6		8	9	10	11					7				5			
36	3 Apr	Dumbarton	0-0	0-1	2000		1	2	3	4		6			9	10	11					7				5	8		
37	10	Falkirk	1-2	2-3	2000	Culley, Neil	1	2	3	4		6		8	9		11					7				5	10		
38	24	MORTON	1-1	2-2	3000	Howie, Neil	1	2	3	4		6		8		10	11					7				5			9
Apps							20	36	24	36	6	37	14	33	31	34	24	6	18	4	30	27	9	2	16	7	2	1	1
Goals											3		1	20	12	9	1					2	5	1					1

Pos P. W. D. L. F. A. Pts.
12th 38 15 4 19 55 59 34

Tom Blair.

Killie's first cup-winning keeper. Blair later played in England, the USA and Northern Ireland. He even made an emergency appearance, aged 45, for Dundee United in 1937-38.

SEASON 1915-16   Division One

No.	Date	Opposition	H.T.	Res.	Att.	Goalscorers	Blair	Hamilton	Mitchell	Shortt	Dickie	Mackie	G.Goldie	Fulton	Culley	Armstrong	McKellar	Murray	Armour	Goodwin	Anderson	Burnett	McAlpine	Slimmon	McPhail	Neil	McKnight	J.Goldie
1	21 Aug	ABERDEEN	3-0	5-0	3000	Culley(3), Armstrong, G.Goldie	1	2	3	4	5	6	7	8	9	10	11											
2	28	Falkirk	0-0	0-0	4000		1	2	3	4	5	6	7	8	9	10	11											
3	4 Sep	RANGERS	0-2	0-3	8000		1	5	3	4		6	7	8	9	10	11	2										
4	11	Hearts	0-0	1-0	5000	Culley	1	2	3	4	5	6	7	8	9	10	11											
5	18	MOTHERWELL	0-0	1-0	4000	Culley	1	2	3	4	5	6		8	9	10	11	7										
6	25	DUMBARTON	3-1	5-1	4000	Culley(2), Armour, Murray, Shortt	1	2	3	4	5	6		8	9		11	10	7									
7	2 Oct	Hamilton A.	1-4	2-5	5000	Culley, G.Goldie	1	2	3	4	5	6	7	8	9		11				10							
8	9	HIBERNIAN	0-0	0-0	3000		1	2	3	4	5	6		8	9	10	11	7										
9	16	Airdrieonians	0-0	0-0	4000		1	2	3	4	5	6		8	9		11					10	7					
10	23	AYR UNITED	0-1	0-1	6000		1	2	3	4	5	6		8	9	10	11	7										
11	30	PARTICK THISTLE	1-0	1-1	4000	Dickie	1	2	3	4	5	6		8	9	10	11	7										
12	6 Nov	Raith Rovers	0-1	1-1	3000	Culley		2	3	4	5	6		8	9	7	11	10			1							
13	13	DUNDEE	2-0	2-0	3000	Armstrong, Fulton	1	2	3	4	5	6		8	9	10	11	7										
14	20	Celtic	0-1	0-2	4000		1	2	3	4		6		5	9	10	11	7			8							
15	27	QUEENS PARK	3-0	4-0	3000	Culley(3), Armour	1	5	3	4		6		8	9		11	2	7		10							
16	4 Dec	St. Mirren	0-0	0-3	3000		1	5	3	4		6		8	9		11	2	7		10							
17	11	Morton	0-0	0-2	4000		1	5	3	4		6	7	8	9		11	2			10							
18	18	THIRD LANARK	1-1	1-1	4000	Culley	1	2	3	4	5	6		8	9	10		7							11			
19	25	Ayr United	0-1	0-2	5000		1		3		5	10		4	9	8		2	7				6		11			
20	1 Jan	ST. MIRREN	0-1	1-1	5000	Dickie	1	2		4	5						8		7				6	3	11	9	10	
21	3	RAITH ROVERS	1-0	2-0	4000	Culley, McKnight	1	2	3	4	5	6		8	9				7						11		10	
22	8	Aberdeen	0-0	0-2	4000		1	2	3	4	5	6	7	8											11	9	10	
23	15	CLYDE	0-0	0-1	3000		1	2	3	4						10	8		7				5		11	9		
24	22	Rangers	1-0	1-3	4000	McKnight	1	2			5	6	7		9										11	8	10	4
25	29	HAMILTON A.	1-0	3-0	3000	Anderson, Culley, McPhail	1	2			5	6	7	8	9						10				11			4
26	5 Feb	Queens Park	1-1	2-1	3000	Culley, Dickie	1	2			5	6	7	8	9		10								11			4
27	12	Partick Thistle	0-3	0-4	5000		1	2			5	6		8	9						10				11	7		4
28	19	AIRDRIEONIANS	1-0	4-0	5000	Culley(3), Fulton	1	2			5	6	7	8	9						10				11			4
29	26	Hibernian	0-0	0-1	3000		1	2			5	6	7	8	9						10				11			4
30	4 Mar	CELTIC	0-2	0-3	10000		1	2	3			5	7	8	9	6									11			4
31	11	Motherwell	1-1	1-1	3500	Dickie	1		3		5	6	7	8	9	10		2							11			4
32	18	MORTON	0-1	1-1	5000	Armstrong	1	2	3		5	6	7	8	9	10									11			4
33	1 Apr	FALKIRK	1-2	1-3	3000	Culley	1	2	3		5	6	7	8	9	10									11			4
34	8	Dundee	0-2	0-2	5000		1	9	3	4		6	7	8				2			10				11			5
35	15	HEARTS*	1-1	3-1	3000	Culley(2), G.Goldie	1	2	3	4		6	7	8	9	10									11			5
36	18	Clyde	1-0	1-1	1000	McPhail	1	2		4		6	7	8	9	10				3					11			5
37	22	Third Lanark	1-1	2-1	3000	Armstrong, Culley	1	2		4		6	7	8	9	10				3					11			5
38	29	Dumbarton	1-0	1-1	3000	G.Goldie	1	2	3	4		6	7	8	9	10									11			5
						Apps.	37	36	35	27	26	37	22	34	36	26	13	12	14	2	11	1	3	1	21	5	4	15
						Goals			1		4		4	2	23	4		1	2		1				2		2	

* Played at Ayr, owing to agricultural show at Rugby Park.

Pos	P.	W.	D.	L.	F.	A.	Pts.
10th	38	12	11	15	46	49	35

Malcolm McPhail.

Even today Malcolm McPhail is still in the Top 20 of Kilmarnock goalscorers and as far as League games are concerned, only thirteen players have scored more. Remarkable, considering he was an out-and-out winger. His younger brother Bob was a legend for Airdrie, Rangers and Scotland. Malky earned an unofficial cap in a victory international against Ireland in 1919.

SEASON 1916-17   Division One

No.	Date	Opposition	H.T.	Res.	Att.	Goalscorers	Blair	T.Hamilton	Patrick	Henderson	J.Goldie	Johnstone	G.Goldie	Smith	Culley	Rutherford	McPhail	Mitchell	Armstrong	Fulton	Mackie	"Burnett"	"Brown"	Dorbie	Lock	R.Hamilton	Hempsey	Sinclair	Harris	Gordon	"Goldie"
1	19 Aug	Falkirk	0-0	0-1	3000		1	2	3	4	5	6	7	8	9	10	11														
2	26	MORTON	3-1	3-2	4000	G.Goldie, McPhail, Smith	1	2	3	4	5	6	7	8	9	10	11														
3	2 Sep	Clyde	1-0	1-1	6000	Culley	1	2	3	4	5	6	7	8	9	10	11														
4	9	AYR UNITED	1-2	1-2	6500	Culley	1	2		4	5		7	8	9	10	11	3			6										
5	16	Rangers	0-3	0-3	10000		1	2		4	5	6			9	10	11	3		7	8										
6	23	HIBERNIAN	0-1	1-3	4000	T.Hamilton	1	2	3	4	5	6		8	9	10	11				7										
7	30	Motherwell	0-0	1-0	5000	McPhail	1	2	3	4	5	6	7	8	9	10	11														
8	7 Oct	Partick Thistle	0-1	1-1	8000	Armstrong	1	2	3	4	5	6	7	8		10	11				9										
9	14	HEARTS	1-0	3-0	1000	McPhail, Patrick, Rutherford	1	2	9	4	5			8		10	11	3		7	6										
10	21	Aberdeen	1-0	1-1	4000	Rutherford			3	4	5			8	9	10	11	2		7	6	1									
11	28	DUNDEE	2-0	3-0	4000	Culley(2), Henderson		2		4	5			8	9	10	11	3		7	6	1									
12	4 Nov	Raith Rovers	2-0	4-0	2000	Armstrong(2), Fulton(2)		2		4	5			8		10	11	3	9	7	6	1									
13	11	THIRD LANARK	1-1	2-1	3000	McPhail, Rutherford	1	2		4	5			8	9	10	11	3		7	6										
14	18	AIRDRIEONIANS	1-1	1-3	3500	Culley	1	2		4	5			8	9	10	11	3		7	6										
15	25	Dumbarton	1-0	1-1	3000	McPhail	1	2	3	4	5			8		10	11		9	7	6										
16	2 Dec	Queens Park	0-0	2-0	2000	McPhail	1	2	3	4	5			8		10	11		9	7	6										
17	9	HAMILTON A.	2-0	4-0	2000	Culley(3), T.Hamilton	1	2	3		5			8	9	10	11			7	6		4								
18	16	Ayr United	1-0	2-0	4000	Fulton, Smith	1	2	3	4	5			8	9	10	11			7	6										
19	23	RAITH ROVERS	1-0	3-0	2000	Culley(2), McPhail		2	3	4	5			8	9	10	11			7	6	1									
20	30	Dundee	0-0	2-0	4000	Mitchell, Smith		2	3	4	5			8		10	11	9		7	6			1							
21	1 Jan	ST. MIRREN	1-1	1-4	6000	Rutherford	1	2	3	4	5			8	9	10	11			7	6										
22	2	Morton	0-2	1-2	2000	Fulton	1		3	4			7	8	9	10	11	2		5	6										
23	6	PARTICK THISTLE	0-0	0-1	3000		1	2		4	5			8	9	10	11	3		7	6										
24	13	St. Mirren	1-2	1-2	5000	Smith	1	2		7	4			8	9	10	11	3		5	6										
25	20	Hibernian	0-2	1-2	4000	Fulton	1		3	4	5			8		10	11	2	9	7	6										
26	27	ABERDEEN	4-0	7-0	2000	McPhail(2),Armstrng,Cully,Fltn,J.Gldie,Smth	1	2		4	5	6		8	9		11	3	10	7											
27	3 Feb	Hamilton A.	0-1	0-3	4000		1	2	3	4	5	6		8			11	9	7												
28	10	QUEENS PARK	2-0	4-2	3500	Smith(2), McPhail(2)		2			5		9	8		10	11	3		4	6					1	7				
29	17	Airdrieonians	1-0	2-3	2500	Armstrong, T.Hamilton		2		4	5			8		10	11	3	9	7	6				1						
30	24	CELTIC	1-1	2-2	6000	Fulton, T.Hamilton		2	3	4	5			8	9	10	11			7	6							1			
31	3 Mar	CLYDE	0-0	2-0	2000	Smith, McPhail		2	3	4	5			8	9	10	11			7	6							1			
32	10	MOTHERWELL	1-0	3-0	2500	Culley, Rutherford, Smith		2		4	5			8	9	10	11	3			6							1			7
33	17	Third Lanark	0-0	0-3	5000		1	2	3	4	5		7			10	11		9	8	6										
34	24	DUMBARTON	0-0	0-0	3000		1	2	3		5	4		8		10	11	9			6										7
35	31	RANGERS	2-0	4-1	5000	Rutherford(3), McPhail	1	2		4	5			8	9	10	11	3		7	6										
36	7 Apr	Hearts	0-0	0-0	3000		1	2	8	4	5					10	11	3											9	10	
37	14	FALKIRK	3-1	4-1	3000	Culley(3), Smith	1		3	4	5	6		8	9	10	11	2		7											
38	21	Celtic	2-0	2-0	18000	Culley, Smith	1		3	4	5			8	9	10	11	2		7	6										
					Apps.		28	33	25	35	37	11	9	35	25	36	38	21	12	29	28	4	1	1	1	1	1	3	1	1	2
					Goals			4	1	1	1		1	11	16	8	13	1	5	7											

Pos P. W. D. L. F. A. Pts.
6th 38 18 7 13 69 45 43

Mattha Smith.

First victory at Celtic Park ends home team's record undefeated run. Mattha' Smith makes his debut. Smith is also the first Killie player to score at Somerset Park. Alex McCurdie and James Maxwell killed in action. Bobby Beattie born.

SEASON 1917-18   Division One

No.	Date	Opposition	H.T.	Res.	Att.	Goalscorers
1	18 Aug	RANGERS	0-0	0-1	10000	
2	25	Hibernian	1-0	3-0	7000	Culley, A.Goldie, Rutherford
3	1 Sep	AYR UNITED	2-0	2-0	5000	Culley, Smith
4	8	Falkirk	0-1	0-1	3000	
5	15	ST. MIRREN	3-0	5-1	5000	A.Goldie(2), Culley, McPhail, Smith
6	22	Motherwell	1-1	1-1	5000	Fulton
7	29	MORTON	2-0	4-0	5000	Culley(2), A.Goldie, T.Hamilton
8	6 Oct	HEARTS	1-0	4-3	4000	McPhail(2), Fulton, Rutherford
9	13	Celtic	2-1	3-2	18000	McPhail(2), Smith
10	20	THIRD LANARK	2-0	3-1	5000	Culley(2), Smith
11	27	Dumbarton	2-1	4-1	3000	Culley(2), A.Goldie, T.Hamilton
12	3 Nov	PARTICK THISTLE	0-0	0-0	5000	
13	10	Airdrieonians	0-0	1-0	5000	Culley
14	17	MOTHERWELL	2-0	4-0	4000	Fulton(2), J.Goldie, Smith
15	24	Ayr United	1-0	2-0	5000	Fulton, G.Hamilton, McPhail
16	1 Dec	HAMILTON A.	1-2	2-3	4000	Rutherford(2)
17	8	Hearts	0-2	0-3	6000	
18	15	Clyde	2-0	2-1	4000	McPhail, Smith
19	22	CLYDEBANK	2-0	4-2	4000	Fulton(3), A.Goldie
20	29	Queens Park	0-1	0-3	8000	
21	1 Jan	St. Mirren	0-0	0-2	12000	
22	5	HIBERNIAN	1-1	3-1	4000	Culley(2), Young
23	12	Morton	1-0	2-2	3000	A.Goldie(2)
24	26	Partick Thistle	2-0	3-0	10000	Culley(2), Smith
25	2 Feb	DUMBARTON	0-0	0-0	5000	
26	9	FALKIRK	1-0	3-0	4000	T.Hamilton, McPhail, Smith
27	16	Third Lanark	1-1	1-1	6000	Smith
28	23	CLYDE	2-0	4-0	5000	Smith(3), Culley
29	2 Mar	Rangers	0-2	0-3	20000	
30	16	QUEENS PARK	2-0	3-1	5000	G.Hamilton, McPhail, Smith
31	23	Clydebank	0-0	0-1	9000	
32	30	CELTIC	0-2	1-3	8000	McPhail
33	6 Apr	Hamilton A.	0-0	1-4	5000	Culley
34	13	AIRDRIEONIANS	2-0	3-0	3000	Fulton, A.Goldie, McPhail

Pos	P.	W.	D.	L.	F.	A.	Pts.
3rd	34	19	5	10	69	41	43

Player appearances (shirt numbers):

No.	Blair	T.Hamilton	Mitchell	Henderson	J.Goldie	Mackie	Fulton	Smith	Culley	Rutherford	McPhail	G.Hamilton	A.Goldie	Johnstone	Miller	Patrick	M.Thom	Hopecroft	A.Thom	Young	Neave	Dickie	Farrell	Thomson	Lees
1	1	2	3	4	5	6	7	8	9	10	11														
2	1	2	3	4	5	6			9	10	11	7	8												
3	1	2	3	4	5	6		8	9		10	11	7												
4	1	2	3	4	5	6		8	9		10	11	7												
5	1	2	3	4	5	6	7	8	9		11		10												
6	1	2	3	4	5		7	8	9		11		10	6											
7	1	2	3		5	6	7	8	9		11		10	4											
8		2			5	6	7		9	10	11		8	4	1	3									
9	1	2	3	4	5	6	7	8	9	10	11														
10	1	2	3	4	5	6	7	8	9	10	11														
11	1	2	3	4	5				9	10	11	7	8	6											
12	1	2	3	4	5	6	7	8	9	10	11														
13	1	2	3	4	5	6	7	8	9		11		10												
14	1	2	3	4	5	6	9	8			11	7	10												
15	1	2	3	4	5	6	9	8			10	11	7												
16	1	2		4	5	6	7		9	10	11		8			3									
17	1	2	3			6	5	8	9	10	11	7		4											
18	1	2	3	4			6	9	8		11	7		10	5										
19	1				5	6		9	8		11	7	10		4				3						
20	1	2	3	4			6	9	8		11	7		10	5										
21	1	2		4		6			8		10			9	5		3	7	11						
22	1	2	3	4		6		8	9		10	7		5						11					
23	1	2	3	4		6		8	9	5	11		10						7						
24	1	2	3	4		6	7	8	9	5	11			10											
25	1	2	3	4		6	7	8	9	5	11			10											
26	1	2					7	8	9		11			10	6		3				5				
27	1	2	3	4				9	8		11			10	6			7			5				
28	1	2		4				8	9		11	7		10	6		3				5				
29	1	2	3	4		6	7	8	9		11			10							5				
30	1	2	3	4				8	9		11	7		6								10	5		
31	1	2	3	4				8	9		11	7		10	6						5				
32	1	2	3	4							9	11		7	10	6					5		8		
33	1	2	3	4		6		9	8	10	11	7									5				
34	1	2	3	4		6	8				9	11	7	10							5				
Apps	33	32	30	30	17	26	23	29	27	16	32	17	23	16	1	2	5	1	1	2	9	1	1		
Goals		3			1		9	13	16	4	11	2	9							1					

Scottish War Funds Cup

No.	Date	Opposition	H.T.	Res.	Att.	Goalscorers
1	9 Mar	St. Mirren	2-1	3-2*		Culley(2), McPhail
2	20 Apr	Morton	0-2	1-7	5000	McPhail

Cup player appearances:

No.	Blair	T.Hamilton	Mitchell	Henderson	J.Goldie	Mackie	Fulton	Smith	Culley	Rutherford	McPhail	G.Hamilton	A.Goldie	Johnstone	Miller	Patrick	M.Thom	Hopecroft	A.Thom	Young	Neave	Dickie	Farrell	Thomson	Lees
1	1		2	4				9	8	10	11	7		6		3									5
2	1	2	3			6	9				11	7		8			10				5		4		

* after extra time

T. Hamilton.

Kilmarnock top of the League for the first time in October 1917. They finish third, their best position since joining the League. Death of club founder and first Secretary John Wallace in Australia in November 1917. Future striker Alan Collins born.

SEASON 1918-19   Division One

No.	Date	Opposition	H.T.	Res.	Att.	Goalscorers
1	17 Aug	Motherwell	0-0	2-1	**6000**	Culley, A.Goldie
2	24	QUEENS PARK	1-0	1-0	5000	Culley
3	31	Clydebank	0-1	1-3	5000	Culley
4	7 Sep	HIBERNIAN	3-1	7-1	5000	Culley(4), A.Goldie(2), Guthrie
5	14	Morton	1-0	2-2	7000	Culley, Shortt
6	21	AIRDRIEONIANS	2-1	3-1	3000	A.Goldie(2), Fulton
7	28	DUMBARTON	0-0	0-0	3000	
8	5 Oct	St. Mirren	1-1	5-1	6000	Culley(2), McPhail(2), A.Goldie
9	12	CELTIC	1-0	1-1	10000	Culley
10	19	Third Lanark	0-1	4-3	4000	Culley(2), A.Goldie, Howie
11	26	PARTICK THISTLE	0-1	0-3	5000	
12	2 Nov	Hearts	0-0	4-1	6000	Turner(2), Gray, McPhail
13	9	Falkirk	1-0	1-0	4000	"Fulton"
14	16	AYR UNITED	0-2	2-3	6000	Fulton, Turner
15	23	Clyde	0-0	1-1	6000	Turner
16	30	MOTHERWELL	0-0	0-2	6000	
17	7 Dec	HAMILTON A.	3-0	5-0	4000	McPhail(3), Mackie, Turner
18	14	Ayr United	1-2	1-3	7000	Dickie
19	21	Rangers	0-4	0-8	10000	
20	28	FALKIRK	0-0	0-0	3000	
21	1 Jan	ST. MIRREN	0-2	1-3	8000	Howie
22	4	Hibernian	3-0	4-1	5000	Culley(3), McHallum
23	11	RANGERS	0-0	1-0	10000	McPhail
24	18	Airdrieonians	0-1	2-2	4000	Dickie, Mackie
25	25	CLYDE	3-0	5-3	4000	McPhail, Culley, Dickie(2), Gray
26	1 Feb	Celtic	1-1	1-2	25000	Culley
27	8	THIRD LANARK	0-1	0-1	6000	
28	15	Partick Thistle	0-1	0-4	6000	
29	22	HEARTS	2-0	2-2	5000	Fulton, McHallum
30	8 Mar	Dumbarton	0-0	1-0	3000	Culley
31	15	CLYDEBANK	1-1	2-3	**4000**	McPhail, Shankland
32	22	MORTON	0-1	0-1	4000	
33	29	Queens Park	1-1	2-1	8000	Culley, Gray
34	5 Apr	Hamilton A.	0-1	0-2	4000	

Pos 9th **P** 34 **W** 14 **D** 7 **L** 13 **F** 61 **A** 59 **Pts** 35

Player appearances / shirt numbers:

No.	Hamilton	Shortt	Neave	Mackie	A.Goldie	Culley	Howie	McPhail	Blair	Turner	Gray	Dickie	McHallum	J.Goldie	Johnstone	Lock	Potts	Murray	Mitchell	Fulton	Shankland	Guthrie	McAllister	Riddell	Rundell	Landells	Stevenson	McGregor	Neil	Burnett
1	2	4	5	6	8	9	10	11											3			7								1
2	2	4	5	6	8	9	10	11	1	7									3											
3	2	4	5	6	8	9	10	11	1										3			7								
4	2	4	5		10	9		11	1	7						6			3			8								
5		4	5	6	10	9	8	11	1							3			2											
6	2	4	5	6	10	9	8	11	1											7										
7	2	4	5	6	10	9	8	11	1							3				7										
8	2	4	3	6	10	9	8	11									1			7				5						
9	2	4	3	6	10	9	8	11	1	7							1							5						
10	2	5	3	6	10	9	8	11				7					1			4										
11	2	5	3	6	10		8	11						9			1	4		7										
12	2	5	3	6			8	11				9	7				1	4						10						
13	2	5	3	6			8	11				7					1	4						10						
14	2	4		6				11				9	7	5			1			3	8			10						
15	2	5	3	6				11				1	10	7			4	8												
16	2	4		6				11				9	7					8						10	5	3				
17	2	5		10				11				9	7			6		8							.	4				
18	2	5	3		9			11	1	8	7	10				6										4				
19		5		10	9	8	1	11	1			7						6	4							2			3	
20	2	4		6	9		8	11	1			7		10															3	
21	2	4		6	9	8		11	1			7	5	10															3	
22	2	8	3	6	9			11	1			7	5	10		4														
23	2	4		6	9			11	1			7	8	10	5				3											
24	2	4		10				11	1			7	9	8	5	6			3						4					
25		2	4	7	6			9		11	1			7	8	10			3					4						
26	2	4	7	6				9		11	1			8	10	5			3											
27	2	4	6					9		11	1			7	8	10	5		3											
28	2	4		6				9		11	1				8		5		3		10			7						
29	2	4		6				9		11	1			7	8	10	5		3	9										
30	2		3	6				9		11	1			7		10	5			8				4						
31	2		3	6				9		11	1			7	10	5				8				4					7	
32	2		3	6				9		11	1			7	10		5			8										
33	2			6			10			11	1			7			5			8				4					9	
34		4	2	10						11	1			7	5	3				8									9	
Apps.	30	29	24	30	11	24	14	34	26	9	22	14	12	11	8	7	8	7	6	7	6	5	2	3	5	2	2	2	3	1
Goals				1		2	7	20	2	9		5	3	4	2					3	1	1								

Victory Cup

No.	Date	Opposition	H.T.	Res.	Goalscorers
1	1 Mar	Albion Rovers	0-0	1-1*	Hamilton
1R	5	ALBION ROVERS	0-0	0-1	

Victory Cup appearances:

No.	Hamilton	Shortt	Neave	Mackie	Culley	Blair	Turner	Gray	J.Goldie	Johnstone	Potts	Mitchell	Riddell	Burnett
1	2	4	8	6	9		1		7	10	5	3		11
1R	2	8	3	6	9	11	1			10	5		4	7

* A.E.T.
The following players made one appearance each (match number/position):
Ford (6/3), Hart (15/9), McQueen (17/3), McLean (20/5), McNeill (20/8), Henderson (32/4), Lees (33/3), Campbell (34/6), "Fulton" (13/9), "McAllister" (5/7)

M. Shortt.

End of the First World War. Malcolm McPhail capped in unofficial "Victory" international. Sandy Goldie dies of influenza. Killie celebrate their 50th anniversary in October 1918.

SEASON 1919-20   Division One

No.	Date	Opposition	H.T.	Res.	Att.	Goalscorers
1	16 Aug	CLYDE	0-1	2-1	5000	McLean, McPhail
2	23	Raith Rovers	0-1	1-5	7000	McLean
3	27	Celtic	0-0	0-1	10000	
4	30	ALBION ROVERS	0-0	1-0	5000	Donnelly
5	1 Sep	Dumbarton	0-1	2-2	4000	Clark, Higgins
6	6	Hamilton A.	0-1	2-5	4000	Higgins, Mackie
7	9	Partick Thistle	0-0	0-1	7000	
8	13	DUMBARTON	2-1	3-1	5000	Clark(2), McHallum
9	15	RANGERS	0-3	1-7	15000	McHallum
10	20	Ayr United	0-2	0-5	8000	
11	4 Oct	Rangers	0-2	0-5	6000	
12	11	MORTON	0-1	0-1	4000	
13	18	FALKIRK	0-0	3-0	4000	Culley(2), McLean
14	25	Motherwell	1-1	1-1	6000	Culley
15	1 Nov	ST. MIRREN	2-1	3-2	5000	McNaught, McPhail, M.Smith
16	8	Airdrieonians	0-0	0-0	4000	
17	15	Aberdeen	0-0	0-1	10000	
18	22	HEARTS	1-1	2-1	6000	McNaught, McPhail
19	29	CLYDEBANK	0-0	2-4	5000	Higgins, McPhail
20	6 Dec	Third Lanark	1-0	1-0	5000	Culley
21	13	Hibernian	0-3	1-4	11000	McPhail
22	20	PARTICK THISTLE	1-0	2-0	6000	M.Smith(2)
23	27	Queens Park	1-1	3-1	8000	McPhail(2), Culley
24	1 Jan	St. Mirren	0-0	2-1	7000	J.R. Smith, M.Smith
25	3	AYR UNITED	1-1	2-1	13000	Culley, J.R. Smith
26	5	Falkirk	0-0	0-1	4000	
27	10	Dundee	1-2	2-3	11000	M.Smith, J.R. Smith
28	17	CELTIC	0-2	2-3	10000	Gibson, McPhail
29	24	RAITH ROVERS	0-0	2-0	5000	Culley, J.R. Smith
30	31	AIRDRIEONIANS	3-0	3-2	6000	Culley(2), J.R. Smith
31	14 Feb	THIRD LANARK	1-0	1-0	6000	Culley
32	28	HIBERNIAN	3-0	4-1	5000	J.R. Smith(2), Culley, M.Smith
33	13 Mar	DUNDEE	1-2	2-1	7000	McPhail(2), Culley, O.G.
34	20	HAMILTON A.	2-1	2-1	7000	Culley, McPhail
35	3 Apr	Clyde	0-1	1-2	8000	J.R. Smith
36	7	QUEENS PARK	1-0	1-0	5000	Higgins
37	10	Clydebank	0-0	0-1	6000	
38	19	MOTHERWELL	0-0	0-1	5000	
39	21	ABERDEEN	0-1	0-3	3000	
40	26	Morton*	0-0	0-4	5000	
41	28	Hearts	1-0	1-0	11000	McLean
42	1 May	Albion Rovers	1-0	2-0	6500	Culley, McLean

* Kilmarnock fielded only 10 players

Player columns (across top): Blair, Hamilton, Murray, Shortt, Gibson, Mackie, McNaught, Shankland, McLean, Higgins, McPhail, Neave, Donnelly, McHallum, Clark, Mitchell, Bagan, Maitland, M.Smith, Culley, Playfair, Elliott, J.R.Smith, Cherry, Lambie, Garrity, Houston, Bolland

	Blair	Hamilton	Murray	Shortt	Gibson	Mackie	McNaught	Shankland	McLean	Higgins	McPhail	Neave	Donnelly	McHallum	Clark	Mitchell	Bagan	Maitland	M.Smith	Culley	Playfair	Elliott	J.R.Smith	Cherry	Lambie	Garrity	Houston	Bolland
Apps	40	41	6	37	42	20	32	2	13	26	40	16	3	9	4	1			32	10	30	26	4	2	15	3	1	2
Goals					1	1	2		5	4	11		1	2	3				6	14			8					

Pos P. W. D. L. F. A. Pts.
9th 42 20 3 19 59 74 43

Scottish Cup

	Date		H.T.	Res.	Att.	Goalscorers
1		Bye				
2	7 Feb	Alloa Athletic	1-0	2-0	10000	Culley, Higgins
3	21	QUEENS PARK	1-1	4-1	20000	J.R.Smith(2), Hamilton, McPhail
QF	6 Mar	Armadale	2-0	2-1	8000	Culley, J.R.Smith
SF	27	Morton*	1-2	3-2	50000	J.R.Smith(2), McPhail
F	17 Apr	Albion Rovers*	1-1	3-2	95000	Culley, Shortt, J.R.Smith

* Played at Hampden

Scottish Cup Winners.
Back row: J. McAdam, H. Wilson, H. Spence (Secretary), R.B. Russell, R.H. Thomson. Next row: W.C. Cunningham, P. Carrick. T. Hamilton, T. Blair, D. Gibson, J. McWhinnie, A. Gibson. Seated: J.L. Morison, J. McNaught, M. Smith, J.R. Smith, W. Culley, M. McPhail, C. Smith. On ground: A. Mackie, M. Shortt, R. Neave, J. Bagan.

SEASON 1920-21   Division One

No.	Date	Opposition	H.T.	Res.	Att.	Goalscorers	Cree	Hamilton	Gibson	Bagan	J.Goldie	Neave	McNaught	M.Smith	J.R.Smith	Culley	McPhail	Hillcoat	Shortt	Ramsay	Fullarton	Robertson	Playfair	Garrity	Wilson	Houston	McHallum	McConnell	Cherry	Jackson	Bolland	Walker	Pollock	Frew	Lorimer	Murray
1	18 Aug	Third Lanark	3-2	4-4	8000	J.R.Smith(2), McNaught, M.Smith		2	3	4			6	7	8	9	10	11		5																
2	21	Morton	1-6	2-9	10000	J.R.Smith, McPhail	1	2	3	4	5		6	7	8	9	10	11																		
3	25	RAITH ROVERS	1-0	1-0	5000	McPhail			3	4	5		6	7		9		11	1	10	2	8														
4	28	RANGERS	1-0	1-2	15000	O.G.		2	3	4			6	7	8	9		11	1	5		10														
5	1 Sep	Clydebank	1-1	2-2	6000	J.R.Smith(2)		2	3		4		6	7	9		10	11	1	5		8														
6	4	Hibernian	0-0	0-0	10000			2	3	4			6	7	8	9		11	1	5		10														
7	7	St. Mirren	0-0	2-1	4000	Goldie, J.R.Smith			3		5	2		7	8	9			1	10				4	6	11										
8	11	QUEENS PARK	1-1	1-1	5000	M.Smith		2	3	4	5		6	7	8	9	10		1							11										
9	18	Raith Rovers	0-2	0-2	10000			2	3	4			6	7	8	9	10		1							11	5									
10	22	Morton	1-1	3-1	4000	Ramsay, J.R.Smith, M.Smith		2	3		5		6	7	8	9		11	1	10				4												
11	25	CLYDEBANK	1-1	2-2	7000	Hamilton, McConnell		2	3		5		6	7	8			11	1	10				4				9								
12	2 Oct	Ayr United	0-0	0-0	8000			2	3				6	7	8	9	10	11	1	5				4												
13	9	HAMILTON A.	1-0	5-0	7000	J.R.Smith(3), M.Smith(2)		2	3				6	7	8	9	11		1	5				4												
14	16	Albion Rovers	0-1	0-2	9000			2	3				6	7	8	9	11		1	5	10			4												
15	23	MOTHERWELL	0-2	0-3	10000			2	3				6	7	8	9	10	11	1	5				4												
16	30	Dundee	0-0	1-3	15000	J.R.Smith		2	3		5			7	8	9	10	11	1					4	6											
17	6 Nov	PARTICK THISTLE	0-0	0-1	6000			2	3	4	5		6	7	8	9	10	11	1																	
18	13	Celtic	0-0	0-2	8000			2	3	4	5		6	7	8	9	10	11	1																
19	20	THIRD LANARK	3-2	3-2	7000	Hamilton(2), Ramsay		2	3	4	5	6			8	9		11	1	10									7							
20	27	Hearts	1-2	1-4	17000	Ramsay		2	3	4					8	9		11	1	10			7							6						
21	4 Dec	Clyde	0-1	2-1	8000	J.R.Smith(2)		2	3						8	9		11	1	5		10		4						7		6				
22	11	ABERDEEN	1-0	1-0	7000	J.R.Smith		2	3						8	9		11	1	5		10		4						7		6				
23	18	Dumbarton	0-1	0-1	3000			2	3							9		11	1	5		10		4						7		6	8			
24	25	FALKIRK	2-0	2-0	7000	Ramsay(2)		2	3		4		6						1	10		11								7		5				
25	1 Jan	ST. MIRREN	2-0	3-2	10000	J.R.Smith(2), Goldie		2	3		4			7	8	9		11	1	10		6										5				
26	3	Airdrieonians	0-2	0-3	7000			2	3		4			7	8	9		11	1	10		6										5				
27	8	Rangers	0-1	0-2	15000			2	3		4		6		8	9			1	10		11										5				
28	15	HEARTS	0-1	1-2	7000	Culley		2	3		4	6		7		9		11	1	10		8										5				
29	9 Feb	ALBION ROVERS	2-0	3-1	5000	J.R.Smith(2), Jackson		2	3		4	6			8	9		11	1	5		10								7						
30	12	Hamilton A.	0-0	0-2	10000				3		4	6			8	9		11	1	5		10	7										5		2
31	16	Falkirk	0-2	0-2	4500			2	3		4	6		7	8	9		11	1	5		10													
32	19	AIRDRIEONIANS	1-0	2-0	3000	Ramsay, M.Smith		2	3		4	6		7	8	9		11	1	5		10													
33	23	DUMBARTON	0-0	4-1	2000	Murray, Culley, M.Smith, McPhail			3			6		7	8	9	10	11		5										4			1		2
34	26	Partick Thistle	1-0	1-1	10000	J.R.Smith			3		4	6		7	8	9	10	11	1	5															2
35	5 Mar	AYR UNITED	2-1	2-1	10000	Culley, J.R.Smith			3		4	6		7	8	9	10	11	1	5															2
36	12	Aberdeen	0-0	1-1	10000	M.Smith			3		4	6		7	8	9	10	11	1	5															2
37	19	DUNDEE	3-0	5-0	6000	Culley, McNaught, Murray, J.R.Smith, M.Smith			3		4	6		7	8	9	10	11	1	5															2
38	26	CELTIC	0-1	3-2	12000	Culley, McNaught, M.Smith			3		4	6		7	8	9		11	1	5		10													2
39	2 Apr	HIBERNIAN	0-1	1-3	8000	Murray			3		4	6		7	8	9	10	11	1	5															2
40	9	CLYDE	0-0	0-1	7000		1		3		4	6		7	8	9			5	10		11													2
41	16	Queens Park	0-0	2-1	12000	J.R.Smith(2)	1		3		4	6		7	8	9	10		5			11													2
42	30	Motherwell	0-0	1-0	8000	J.R.Smith	1		3		4			7	8	9	10	11	5													6			2
		Apps.					4	29	42	11	29	34	33	38	38	24	31	37	25	26	1	6	4	9	2	8	1	1	5	3	1	5	2	1	1	11
		Goals						3			2		3	10	24	5	3			6									1	1						3

```
Pos   P.  W.  D.  L.  F.  A.  Pts.
12th  42  17  8   17  62  68  42
```

Scottish Cup

No.	Date	Opposition	H.T.	Res.	Att.	Goalscorers	Cree	Hamilton	Gibson	Bagan	J.Goldie	Neave	McNaught	M.Smith	J.R.Smith	Culley	McPhail	Hillcoat	Shortt	Ramsay	Fullarton	Robertson	Playfair	Garrity	Wilson	Houston	McHallum	McConnell	Cherry	Jackson	Bolland	Walker	Pollock	Frew	Lorimer	Murray
1	22 Jan	Arbroath	1-0	4-2	5000	J.R.Smith(2), Culley, Ramsay		2	3		4	6	7		9	10	11	1		8												5				
2	5 Feb	ABERDEEN	1-1	1-2	12000	Hamilton		2	3		4	6			9	10	11	1		8										7		5				

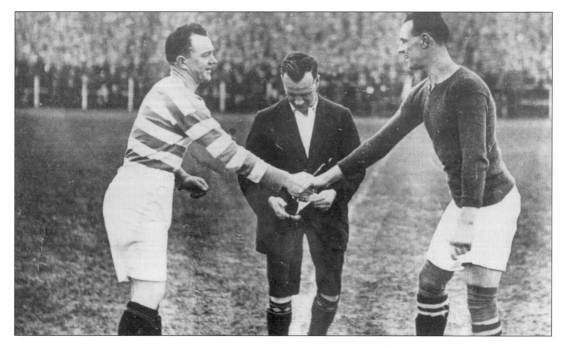

Kilmarnock v Celtic in the 1920s
Celtic Captain J. McStay shakes hands with Kilmarnock Captain J. Dunlop (on right) prior to kick-off with Referee looking on.

SEASON 1921-22 — Division One

No.	Date	Opposition	H.T.	Res.	Att.	Goalscorers	Neil	Murray	Gibson	Gray	Goldie	Pollock	McNaught	M.Smith	Skinner	Ramsay	McPhail	Shortt	Neave	Culley	Gunn	Watson	Garrity	Jackson	Frew	Robertson	Scott	Herron	Hood	Cherry	Good	Howat	Bailey	Cree	Logue
1	15 Aug	Albion Rovers	0-1	0-4	5000		1	2	3	4	5	6	7	8	9	10	11																		
2	20	DUMBARTON	1-0	1-0	10000	Culley,	1	2	3		4		7	8		9		5	6	10	11														
3	23	MORTON	1-0	2-1	9000	Culley, Watson	1	2	3		4		7				10	5	6	9	11	8													
4	27	Clyde	0-0	0-3	8000		1	2	3	7	4						10	5	6	9	11	8													
5	3 Sep	ALBION ROVERS	1-0	1-1	12000	Pollock	1	2	3		4			8	9			5		10	11		6	7											
6	10	Rangers	0-1	0-1	20000		1	2	3		4		7		9		11	5		10		8	6												
7	17	ABERDEEN	1-3	2-3	7000	Skinner, Watson	1	2	3		4		7		9		11	5		10		8	6												
8	21	ST. MIRREN	0-0	1-1	5000	Frew	1	2	3		5		7		9		11			10		8	6		4										
9	24	Raith Rovers	0-1	0-4	15000		1	2	3		5		7			10	11			9		8			4						6				
10	1 Oct	AYR UNITED	0-1	2-2	12000	McPhail, Watson	1	2	3		5			8			11			9		10		7	4						6				
11	8	Hamilton A.	1-4	1-7	9000	Watson	1	2	3		5			8			11			10		9	6	7	4										
12	15	THIRD LANARK	1-0	3-0	10000	Culley(3)	1	2	3		6		7	8			11	5		9		10			4										
13	22	Dundee	0-3	0-5	10000		1	2	3		6		7	8			11	5		9		10			4										
14	29	HIBERNIAN	1-1	1-1	5000	Culley	1		3		6			8			11	5		9		10		7	4	2									
15	5 Nov	Partick Thistle	0-0	0-2	12000		1		3				6	8			11			9		10		7	5	2	4								
16	12	CELTIC	3-1	4-3	10000	Jackson, McNaught, Shortt, Watson	1		3		6		7	8			5			11		10		9	4	2									
17	19	MOTHERWELL	0-0	4-0	8000	Jackson(2), Watson, O.G.	1		3	7	6			8			5			11		10		9	4	2									
18	26	Airdrieonians	0-0	0-2	5000		1		3	7	6			8			5			11		10		9	4	2									
19	3 Dec	QUEENS PARK	1-0	2-0	5000	Jackson(2)	1		3		6		7	8			5			11		10		9	4	2									
20	10	Morton	1-1	1-5	8000	Culley	1		3				7	8		6	5			11		10		9	4	2									
21	17	RAITH ROVERS	0-1	2-2	4000	Gibson, Watson			3				7	8		6	5			11		10		9	4	2									1
22	24	Clydebank	0-1	1-1	3000	Smith	1		3	4			7	8		6	11	5		10		9				2									
23	26	Hearts	0-1	0-1	10000		1		3				7	8		6	11	5		10		9				2	4								
24	31	HEARTS	2-0	3-0	7000	Smith(2), McPhail	1		3	7				8		6	11	5		10		9				2	4								
25	2 Jan	St. Mirren	1-1	1-1	14000	Gray	1		3	7				8		6	11	5		10		9				2	4								
26	3	AIRDRIEONIANS	1-1	2-1	7000	Culley, Smith	1		3	7				8		6	11	5		10		9				2	4								
27	7	Dumbarton	0-3	3-5	4000	Culley, Gray, Smith	1		3	7				8		6	5			11		10		9		2	4								
28	14	Falkirk	1-1	1-2	5000	Bailey	1		3					8				5	6	11		10		7		2	4					9			
29	21	CLYDEBANK	1-1	3-2	6000	Culley(2), Smith	1		3	5			6	8			11			10				7		2	4					9			
30	4 Feb	Hibernian	0-2	0-3	8000		1		3	5				8		10	11			8				7		2	4		9		6				
31	15	DUNDEE	3-0	5-3	3000	Culley(3), Jackson(2)			3	7	5			8	6		11			10				9		2	4	1							
32	18	Ayr United	2-3	2-4	6000	Culley, Jackson			3	7			6	8			11			10			5	9		2	4	1							
33	25	FALKIRK	0-1	1-2	5000	Smith			3		5		7	8			11			10		9				2	4	1		6					
34	1 Mar	Motherwell	0-0	0-3	3000				3		5			8			11			9		10		7			4	1		6	2				
35	4	PARTICK THISTLE	2-0	2-1	8000	Culley, Jackson			3		5		7	8	6		11			10				9		2	4	1							
36	11	Celtic	0-1	0-1	6000				3		5		7	8	9	6	11			10						2	4	1							
37	18	CLYDE	1-0	1-0	5000	Skinner			3		5		7	8	9	6	11			10			4			2		1							
38	25	Queens Park	1-0	1-1	10000	Culley			3		5		7	8	6		11	4		10		9				2		1							
39	1 Apr	HAMILTON A.	0-1	1-1	2000	Culley			3	9	5		7	8			11			10			4			2		1		6					
40	8	Aberdeen	0-0	1-0	11000	Culley			3		5		7	8	6		11	4		9		10				2		1							
41	24	RANGERS	0-1	1-2	12000	Culley			3		5			8	6		11			9		10		7		2	4	1							
42	29	Third Lanark	0-1	0-2	5000				3		5			8	6		11			9		10		7		2	4	1							
Apps.							29	14	40	11	32	2	22	34	7	26	28	25	4	40	4	27	6	27	18	19	12	12	9	4	4	2	2	1	1
Goals								1	2	1		1	1	7	2		2	1		20		7		9	1						1				

	Pos	P	W	D	L	F	A	Pts.
	17th	42	13	9	20	56	83	35

Scottish Cup

No.	Date	Opposition	H.T.	Res.	Att.	Goalscorers	Neil	Murray	Gibson	Gray	Goldie	Pollock	McNaught	M.Smith	Skinner	Ramsay	McPhail	Shortt	Neave	Culley	Gunn	Watson	Garrity	Jackson	Frew	Robertson	Scott	Herron
1	28 Jan	Caledonian	2-0	5-1	1000	Culley(2), Gray, Scott, Watson	1		3	7	5		6				11			10		8	9			2	4	
2	11 Feb	ST. MIRREN	0-2	1-4	15000	Culley			3	7			6	8			11	5		10		9				2	4	1

J. Hood.

Last season for the 22-team Division One. Mattha' Smith's benefit season. Bummer Campbell, now over fifty, scores two in benefit game for the unemployed.

SEASON 1922-23 — Division One

No.	Date	Opposition	H.T.	Res.	Att.	Goalscorers	Herron	Hood	Gibson	Turnbull	Goldie	Ramsay	Jackson	Smith	Brown	McLeavy	Culley	McPhail	H.Morton	Harvey	Watson	McCulloch	Morris	J.Morton	Dunlop	Lyner	Murray	Skillen	Marshall	Rattray
1	16 Aug	ABERDEEN	1-0	1-0	9000	Culley	1	2	3	4	5	6	7	8	9	10	11													
2	19	Albion Rovers	0-0	1-1	7000	Jackson	1	2	3	4	5	6	7	8	9	10	11													
3	26	AYR UNITED	1-0	2-0	12000	Jackson, Ramsay	1	2	3	4	5	6	7	8	9			10	11											
4	2 Sep	Dundee	0-2	0-2	15000		1	2	3	4	5	6	7	8	9			10	11											
5	9	CLYDE	2-0	4-1	10000	Culley(2), Smith(2)	1	2	3	4	5	6	7	8	9		10					11								
6	16	Hamilton A.	3-2	3-3	6000	Brown(2), Ramsay	1	2	3	4	5	6	7	8	9		10					11								
7	23	RAITH ROVERS	1-1	1-2	7000	Brown	1	2	3	4	5	6	7	8	9		10					11								
8	30	Hibernian	0-0	1-1	18000	Brown	1	2	3	4		6	7	8	9		10				5	11								
9	7 Oct	ALLOA ATHLETIC	1-1	2-2	8000	Culley(2)	1	2	3	4	5	6	7	8	9		10					11								
10	14	Morton	2-0	4-1	6000	Culley(3), Smith	1		3	4	5	6	7	8	9		10					11	2							
11	21	HEARTS	1-0	1-2	5000	Culley	1		3	4	5	6	7	8	9		10					11	2							
12	28	St. Mirren	0-2	0-2	11000		1		3	2	4	6	7	8	9		10			5		11								
13	4 Nov	MOTHERWELL	0-2	0-6	6000		1		3	4	6		7	8	9		10			2	5	11								
14	11	AIRDRIEONIANS	0-1	0-1	7000		1	2	3	4	5	6	7	8	9			10	11											
15	18	Aberdeen	0-0	0-5	10000		1	2	3	6	5		7	8	9			10	11	4										
16	25	FALKIRK	0-0	1-0	6000	Culley		2	3	4	5	6	7	8	9		9	10	11					1						
17	2 Dec	Third Lanark	0-0	2-1	7000	McPhail, Morton		2	3	5	4	6	9	8				10	11	7				1						
18	16	PARTICK THISTLE	0-1	1-3	6000	Lyner		2	3	4		6	9	8				10				11		1	5	7				
19	23	Celtic	0-0	2-1	8000	Jackson, Lyner		2	3	6		4	9	8				10				11		1	5	7				
20	27	Alloa Athletic	0-1	3-3	3000	Dunlop, Goldie, McPhail		2	3	6	4		9	8				10				11	7	1	5					
21	30	HIBERNIAN	0-0	1-0	5000	Ramsay		2	3	4		10	9	8				10	11	6				1	5	7				
22	1 Jan	ST. MIRREN	1-2	1-2	14000	McPhail		2	3	4		10	7	8	9				11	6				1	5					
23	2	Ayr United	1-1	1-2	11000	Jackson		2	3		4		9	8					11	6				1	5		10			
24	6	DUNDEE	0-0	2-0	8000	Jackson, Ramsay		2	3	4		10	9	8					11	6				1	5	7				
25	20	RANGERS	1-2	1-2	15000	Jackson		2		4		10	9	8					11	6				1	5	7		3		
26	3 Feb	CELTIC	2-2	4-3	7500	Jackson, McCulloch, Rattray, Smith		2	3	4			9	8						6		11		1	5	7				10
27	7	Raith Rovers	0-1	0-1	4000			2	3	4			9	8						6		11		1	5	7				10
28	10	Hearts	0-4	0-5	13000			3	2	4			9	8						6		11		1	5	7				10
29	17	HAMILTON A.	3-0	3-0	6000	Lyner, McCulloch, Smith		2	3	4			9	8						6		11		1	5	7				10
30	3 Mar	Airdrieonians	1-2	1-4	4000	Jackson		2	3	4			9	8						6		11		1	5	7				10
31	10	Clyde	0-1	0-2	5000			2	3			6	9	8						4		11		1	5	7				10
32	17	ALBION ROVERS	4-0	7-0	6000	Jackson(4), Lyner, McCulloch, Rattray		2	3	4		6	9	8								11		1	5	7				10
33	21	THIRD LANARK	1-0	2-0	4000	Jackson, Dunlop		2	3	4		6	9	8								11		1	5	7				10
34	24	Partick Thistle	0-0	1-1	10000	Jackson		2	3	4		6	9	8						11				1	5	7				10
35	31	MORTON	2-1	3-2	7000	Jackson, Lyner, Rattray		2	3	4		6	9	8						11				1	5	7				10
36	7 Apr	Motherwell	0-1	1-4	3000	Dunlop		2	3	6			9	8						11				1	5	7			4	10
37	21	Rangers	0-1	0-1	10000			2	3			4	6	9	8					11				1	5	7				10
38	28	Falkirk	0-0	0-0	5000			2	3			4	6	9			8			11				1	5	7				10
					Apps.		15	34	35	23	31	29	38	36	19	2	16	18	21	6	1	14	2	23	21	18	1	1	1	13
					Goals						1	4	15	5	4		10	3	1			3			3	5				3

Pos P. W. D. L. F. A. Pts.
15th 38 14 7 17 57 66 35

Scottish Cup

No.	Date	Opposition	H.T.	Res.	Att.	Goalscorers	Hood	Ramsay	Jackson	Smith	Brown	H.Morton	McCulloch	J.Morton	Dunlop	Lyner	Rattray
1	13 Jan	BROXBURN	1-0	5-0	7000	Jackson(4), Smith	2	6	10	9	8	11	4	1	5	7	3
2	27	EAST FIFE	0-0	1-1	8000	Culley	2	4	10	9	8	11	6	1	5	7	3
2R	31	East Fife	0-1	0-1	6000		2	5	4	6	9	8	10	11	1	7	3

Walter Jackson.

Walter Jackson was the younger brother of "Wembley Wizard" Alex. An excellent winger, he was often played at centre-forward and proved to be equally adept in that role as well.

SEASON 1923-24   Division One

No.	Date	Opposition	H.T.	Res.	Att.	Goalscorers	J.Morton	Hood	Gibson	Willis	Dunlop	Ramsay	Lyner	Davidson	Gossman	Rattray	Borland	Skillen	Gray	Smith	Howat	H.Morton	McEwan	Brown	Greig	McPhail	Allison	Adams	Campbell
1	18 Aug	QUEENS PARK	0-1	1-4	17000	Dunlop	1	2	3	4	5	6	7	8	9	10	11												
2	25	Ayr United	0-0	0-0	8000		1	2	3	4	5	6	7		9	8	11	10											
3	1 Sep	HIBERNIAN	0-1	2-1	10000	Ramsay, Skillen	1	2	3	4	5	6	7		9	8	11	10											
4	8	Clyde	1-1	1-1	3000	Borland	1	2	3	4	5	6	7		9	8	11	10											
5	15	HAMILTON A.	0-0	1-0	7000	Gray	1	2	3	4	5	6	7	8			11	10	9										
6	22	Clydebank	1-1	2-1	3000	Gray, Ramsay	1	2	3	4	5	6	7	8			11		9	10									
7	29	DUNDEE	0-1	1-3	6000	Ramsay	1	2	3	4	5	6	7	8			11		9	10									
8	6 Oct	Morton	1-0	2-0	4000	Gray(2)	1	2	3	4	5	6	7				11	10	9	8									
9	13	FALKIRK	2-0	2-1	8000	Gray(2)	1	2	3	4		6	7				11	10	9	8	5								
10	20	Motherwell	0-3	0-4	6000		1	2	3	4		6	7				11	10	9	8	5								
11	27	ST. MIRREN	1-0	2-0	10000	Gray, Skillen	1	2	3	4		6	7				11	10	9	8	5								
12	3 Nov	ABERDEEN	1-0	2-1	5000	Lyner, Willis	1	2	3	4		6	7				11	10	9	8	5								
13	10	Hearts	0-2	1-4	12000	Skillen	1	2	3	4		6	7				11	10	9	8		5							
14	17	RAITH ROVERS	1-1	1-2	5000	Smith	1	2	3	4		6	7				11	10	9	8		5							
15	24	Third Lanark	0-0	1-2	5000	Ramsay	1	2	3	5		10	7				11		9	8		4	6						
16	1 Dec	Airdrieonians	1-1	2-2	7000	Gray, Ramsay	1	2	3	5		10					11		9	8		6	4	7					
17	8	CELTIC	0-0	1-1	12000	Gray	1	2	3	5		10					11		9	8		6	4	7					
18	15	Partick Thistle	0-2	2-2	10000	Gray(2)	1	2	3	5		10	7				11		9	8		6	4						
19	22	HEARTS	1-0	2-1	10000	Gray, Smith	1	2	3	5		10	7				11		9	8		6	4						
20	29	THIRD LANARK	0-0	0-0	5000		1	2	3	5		10	7				11		9	8		6	4						
21	1 Jan	St. Mirren	0-0	1-0	13000	Gray	1	2	3	5		10	7				11		9	8		6	4						
22	2	AYR UNITED	0-1	1-1	12000	Borland	1	2	3	5		10	7				11		9	8		6	4						
23	5	Queens Park	0-2	1-3	12000	Gray	1	2	3	5		10	7				11		9	8		6	4						
24	12	CLYDEBANK	1-1	2-3	5000	Gossman, Willis	1	2	3	5		10	7		8		11		9			6	4						
25	19	Dundee	1-1	2-4	14000	McPhail, Smith	1		3	5		10	7						9	8		4	6		2	11			
26	2 Feb	PARTICK THISTLE	0-1	3-1	5000	Gray(2), Ramsay	1		3	5		10							9	8		4	6	2		11			
27	13	MORTON	1-2	1-3	1000	Gray	1		3	5		6							9	8		4	6	2		11		10	
28	19	Rangers	0-1	0-2	10000		1		3	5		10	7				11		9	8		4	6	2					
29	27	Hibernian	0-2	1-3	4000	Smith	1		3	5		10	7				11		9	8		4	6	2					
30	5 Mar	RANGERS	0-1	1-1	10000	Willis	1		3	9			7				11	10		8		4	6	2			5		
31	8	Celtic	0-2	1-2	16000	Skillen	1		3	9			7				11	10		8		4	6	2			5		
32	15	CLYDE	1-0	3-0	3000	Borland, Smith, Adams	1		3	4			7				11	10		8		2	6				5	9	
33	29	Hamilton A.	1-2	1-2	6000	Campbell	1		3	4			7				11	10		8		2	6				5		9
34	2 Apr	AIRDRIEONIANS	0-2	1-2	4000	Gray	1		3	5							11	10	7	8		2	6	4					9
35	5	Raith Rovers	1-2	1-4	5000	Gray	1		3	4			7				11		9	8		2	6				5	10	
36	12	Falkirk	1-1	1-2	4000	Smith	1	2	3								11	10	9	8		4	6			7	5		
37	19	Aberdeen	0-2	0-2	10000		1	2	3				7			10	11		9	8		4	2				5		
38	26	MOTHERWELL	1-0	1-0	4000	Brown	1	2	3								11	10	9	8		4	6	7			5		
Apps							38	26	38	35	8	28	21	1	8	7	38	30	32	4	19	19	22	1	3	1	8	5	
Goals										3	1	6	1		1		3	4	19	6				1		1		1	1

Pos P. W. D. L. F. A. Pts.
16th 38 12 8 18 48 65 32

Scottish Cup

No.	Date	Opposition	H.T.	Res.	Att.	Goalscorers	J.Morton	Hood	Gibson	Willis	Dunlop	Ramsay	Lyner	Borland	Skillen	Gray	Smith	H.Morton	McEwan	Brown	McPhail
1	26 Jan	CELTIC	1-0	2-0	17200	Gray, Ramsay	1		3	5		10				7		9	8	4	6	2	11
2	9 Feb	Ayr United	0-0	0-1	16562		1		3	5		10				7		9	8	4	6	2	11

Gallaher's Cigarette card from 22nd December 1923
showing Bobby Brown of Kilmarnock taking on Hearts' McMullan, with Killie centre-half Joe Willis looking on.

SEASON 1924-25   Division One

No.	Date	Opposition	H.T.	Res.	Att.	Goalscorers	Gould	Hood	Gibson	H.Morton	Clark	Brown	Walker	Smith	Gray	Bird	Borland	McEwan	Wilson	Nibloe	Weir	J.Morton	Willis	Adams	Lindsay	Rock	Dunlop
1	16 Aug	Morton	1-0	2-2	6000	Borland(2)	1	2	3	4	5	6	7	8	9	10	11										
2	20	Queens Park	1-1	2-1	8000	Gray, Borland	1	2	3	6	5	4	7	8	9	10	11										
3	23	HIBERNIAN	0-1	0-1	8000		1	2	3	6	5	4	7	8	9	10	11										
4	30	Rangers	0-1	1-1	18000	Clark	1	2	3	4	5		7	8	9		11	6	10								
5	6 Sep	AIRDRIEONIANS	2-1	2-3	8000	Brown, Smith	1	2	3	4	5	7		8	9		11	6	10								
6	13	Dundee	0-0	1-3	12000	Wilson	1	2		4	5		7	8			11	6	10	3	9						
7	20	HAMILTON A.	1-2	1-3	8000	Smith		2		4	5		7	8			11	6	10	3	9	1					
8	27	Falkirk	0-0	0-0	7000		1	2		4	5		7	8	9	10	11	6		3							
9	4 Oct	THIRD LANARK	1-2	2-2	7000	Gray, Borland	1	2		4	5		7	8	9	10	11	6		3							
10	11	QUEENS PARK	1-1	3-1	7000	Borland, Gray, Walker	1	2			5	4	7	8	9		11	6	10	3							
11	18	Ayr United	1-0	1-0	8000	Gray	1	2	3		5	4	7	8	9		11	6	10								
12	25	Cowdenbeath	0-3	2-5	7000	Smith(2)	1	2		4	5		7	8	9		11	6	10	3							
13	1 Nov	ST. MIRREN	3-1	3-2	7000	Bird, Gray, Smith	1	2	3		5	4	7	8	9	10	11	6									
14	8	Celtic	0-1	0-6	8000		1	2	3	9	5	4	7	8		10	11	6									
15	15	Raith Rovers	0-2	1-3	7000	Brown	1	2	3			4	7	8			11	6	10		9		5				
16	22	HEARTS	1-0	2-1	3000	Brown, McEwan	1	2	3		5		8	7		9	10	6							4	11	
17	29	Aberdeen	0-0	0-0	12000		1	2	3		5		8	7		9	10	6							4	11	
18	6 Dec	MOTHERWELL	0-1	0-2	6000		1	2	3	11	5		7	8			10	6					4		9		
19	13	St. Johnstone	2-4	2-4	6000	Bird, Smith	1	2	3		5	7		8		10		6					4		11	9	
20	20	RAITH ROVERS	1-0	3-0	7000	Lindsay(2), Smith	1	2	3	4			10	7	8	9		6							11		5
21	27	PARTICK THISTLE	0-0	1-1	5000	Walker	1	2	3	4			10	7	8	9		6							11		5
22	1 Jan	AYR UNITED	2-0	4-1	12000	Gray(2), Brown, Dunlop	1	2	3	4			10	7	8	9		6							11		5
23	3	Hibernian	0-0	0-2	13000		1	2	3	4	5			7	8	9		6							11		
24	5	St. Mirren	0-1	0-3	5000		1	2	3	4			10	7	8	9		6							11		5
25	10	DUNDEE	1-1	4-1	6000	Smith(2), Hood, McEwan	1	2	3				10	7	8	9		6					4		11		5
26	17	Third Lanark	0-1	0-2	6000		1	2	3				10	7	8	9		6					4		11		5
27	31	ABERDEEN	0-0	0-1	6000		1	2		3			10	7	8	9		6					4		11		5
28	11 Feb	Airdrieonians	2-2	2-4	5000	McEwan, Rock	1	2		3			7	8			10	6					4		11	9	5
29	14	Partick Thistle	1-2	1-2	5000	Hood	1	2		3			7	8			10	6					4		11	9	5
30	25	MORTON	2-0	3-1	3000	Smith(2), Dunlop	1	2	3	6			10	7	8								4		11	9	5
31	28	FALKIRK	0-0	1-0	10000	Rock	1	2	3				10	7	8			6					4		11	9	5
32	11 Mar	Hamilton A.	1-2	1-2	5000	Smith	1	2	3	4			7	8		10		6							11	9	5
33	14	Hearts	1-1	1-1	20000	Dunlop	1	2	3	4			7	8		10		6							11	9	5
34	21	COWDENBEATH	0-0	0-0	5000		1	2	3	4			7	8		10	9	6							11		5
35	28	RANGERS	0-0	0-0	12000		1	2	3	4			7	9	8	10		6							11		5
36	4 Apr	Motherwell	0-1	1-2	2000	Walker	1	2	3	4			7	9	8	10		6							11		5
37	15	CELTIC	1-1	2-1	4000	Rock, Smith	1	2	3	4			7	8		10		6							11	9	5
38	22	ST. JOHNSTONE	2-0	4-0	2000	Rock, Gray, Walker, Smith	1	2	3	4			7	8		10		6							11	9	5
						Apps.	37	38	29	28	19	24	36	36	28	14	15	34	8	6	3	1	9	3	22	10	18
						Goals		2			1	4	4	14	8	2	5	3			1				2	4	3

Pos P. W. D. L. F. A. Pts.
12th 38 12 9 17 53 64 33

Scottish Cup

No.	Date	Opposition	H.T.	Res.	Att.	Goalscorers	Gould	Hood	Gibson	H.Morton	Clark	Brown	Walker	Smith	Gray	Bird	Borland	McEwan	Wilson	Nibloe	Weir	J.Morton	Willis	Adams	Lindsay	Rock	Dunlop
1	24 Jan	ARBROATH ATHLETIC	2-0	3-0	6000	Bird, Rock, Smith	1	2				6		8		10				3	7		4		11	9	5
2	7 Feb	HEARTS	2-0	2-1	14000	Lindsay, Rock	1	2	3				7	8			10						4	6	11	9	5
3	21	DYKEHEAD	0-0	5-0	6100	Lindsay(2), Bird, Rock, Weir	1	2	3				7			10	6				8		4		11	9	5
QF	7 Mar	RANGERS	1-0	1-2	31502	Bird	1	2	3				7	8			6	10					4		11	9	5

Robert M. Rock.

Popular rumour ascribes the Rugby Road wall as being built from the proceeds of Bobby Rock's transfer fee.

First New Year's Day Ayrshire derby. Killie beat English giants Everton 3-2 at Goodison Park. Goalkeeping legend Jimmy Brown born.

SEASON 1925-26   Division One

No.	Date	Opposition	H.T.	Res.	Att.	Goalscorers
1	15 Aug	QUEENS PARK	2-0	2-1	10000	Gray, Walker
2	22	Hibernian	0-2	0-8	17000	
3	29	CLYDEBANK	1-1	2-2	5000	Gray, Rock
4	5 Sep	Falkirk	1-2	1-6	8000	Rock
5	12	MORTON	2-0	2-0	7000	Gray, Cunningham
6	19	Hamilton A.	2-2	2-2	6000	Lindsay, Weir
7	26	COWDENBEATH	0-1	1-1	5000	Lindsay
8	3 Oct	Rangers	0-2	0-3	20000	
9	10	AIRDRIEONIANS	2-1	3-2	10000	Lindsay(2), O.G.
10	17	St. Mirren	0-1	2-3	12000	Gray, Weir
11	24	Dundee United	0-0	1-3	8000	Weir
12	31	Aberdeen	1-2	2-3	12000	Hood, Lindsay
13	7 Nov	ST. JOHNSTONE	1-1	3-2	6000	Weir(2), Lindsay
14	14	Partick Thistle	2-1	4-2	8000	Weir(2), Smith, Walker
15	21	RAITH ROVERS	2-0	3-0	3000	Weir(2), Smith
16	28	Hearts	0-1	0-1	16000	
17	5 Dec	RANGERS	1-2	2-2	10000	Hood, Smith
18	12	Dundee	0-1	0-1	9000	
19	19	FALKIRK	1-1	2-3	5000	McCall, Weir
20	26	Raith Rovers	3-3	5-4	3000	Weir(2), Dunlop, Smith, Walker
21	1 Jan	St. Mirren	3-1	4-1	12000	Weir(2), Cunningham, Walker
22	2	DUNDEE UNITED	1-1	2-3	10000	Weir, Morton
23	4	HAMILTON A.	4-1	4-1	7000	Crump(2), Rock, Smith
24	9	Morton	1-1	2-1	4000	Cunningham(2)
25	16	DUNDEE	2-1	5-2	7000	Smith(2), Lindsay, Cunningham, Weir
26	30	St. Johnstone	0-0	2-0	8000	Cunningham, Lindsay
27	10 Feb	CELTIC	1-0	1-0	8000	Cunningham, Weir
28	13	PARTICK THISTLE	2-0	3-3	8000	Weir(2), McCall
29	20	Clydebank	1-2	1-5	4000	Dunlop
30	27	Motherwell	1-1	2-1	6000	McCall, Morton
31	13 Mar	Cowdenbeath	0-0	0-0	5000	
32	17	ABERDEEN	1-0	3-0	4000	Weir(3)
33	20	HEARTS	3-1	5-1	8000	Weir(2), Wishart(2), McCall
34	27	Queens Park	1-1	2-2	10000	Cunningham, Weir
35	3 Apr	Celtic	0-0	0-0	12000	
36	10	MOTHERWELL	0-0	1-2	6000	Dunlop
37	17	Airdrieonians	1-3	2-3	4500	Crump, Weir
38	24	HIBERNIAN	0-1	2-1	5000	Cunningham, Smith

Appearances and goals (shirt numbers worn per match):

No.	Gould	Hood	Gibson	Morton	B.Brown	McEwan	Walker	Smith	Rock	Gray	Crump	Marshall	Lindsay	Reilly	Cunningham	Nibloe	Weir	Dunlop	A.Brown	McCall	Clemie	Mathieson	Ritchie	Wishart
1	1	2	3	4	5	6	7	8	9	10	11													
2	1	2	3	4	5	6	7	8	9	10	11													
3	1	2	3	4		6	7	8	9	10			5		11									
4	1	2	3	4		6	7	8	9	10			5		11									
5	1	2	7	4	3	6			9	10					11	5	8							
6	1	2	5	4				8		10					11	6	7	3	9					
7	1	2	5					4	9	10					11	6	7	3	8					
8	1	2	5					8	9	10					11	6	7	3						
9	1	2	3	4				8		10					11	6	7		9	5				
10	1	2	3	4			7	8		10					11	6			9	5				
11	1	2		4			7			10					11	6	3		9	5	8			
12	1	2		4		10	7	8							11	6	3		9	5				
13	1	2		4		6	7	8					10		11		3	9		5				
14	1	2		4		6	7	8							11		3	9		5	10			
15	1	2		4		6	7	8							11		3	9		5	10			
16	1	2		4		6	7	8							11		3	9		5	10			
17	1	2		4		6	7	8							11		3	9		5	10			
18	1	2		4		6	7	8							11		3	9		5	10			
19	1	2		4		6	7	8							11		3	9		5	10			
20	1	2		4		6	7	8							11	10	3	9		5				
21	1	2		4		6	7	8							11	10	3	9		5				
22	1	2		4		6	7	8							11	10	3	9		5				
23		2		4		6	7	8	9	10	11						3					1		5
24	1	2		4		6	7	8							11							5		
25	1	2		4		6	7	8							11	10	3	9		5				
26	1	2		4		6	7	8							11	10	3	9		5				
27	1	2		4		6	7	8							11	10	3	9		5				
28	1	2		4		6		8							11		7	3		9	10	5		
29	1		2			6	7	8							11	10	3	9		5			4	
30	1	2		4		6		8				11					7	3		9	5	10		
31		2		4		6		8				9			11		7	3		9	5	10	1	
32		2		4		6						11				8	3	9		5	10	1		7
33		2		4		6						11				8	3	9		10	1	5		7
34		2		4		6						11				8	3	9		10	1			7
35		2		4		6		8				11				10	3	9		5		1		7
36		2		4		6		8				11					3	9		5	10	1		7
37		2		4		6		8				11		4		10	3	9			1	5		7
38		2		4		6		8				11				10	3	9		5	1			7
Apps.	29	37	10	36	3	31	22	35	8	14	13	2	25	9	22	31	30	26	1	13	9	4	1	7
Goals		2		2			4	8	3	4	3		8		9		26	3		4				2

Pos P   W   D   L   F   A   Pts.
9th 38 17 7 14 79 77 41

Scottish Cup

No.	Date	Opposition	H.T.	Res.	Att.		Gould	Hood	Morton	McEwan	Walker	Smith	Cunningham	Nibloe	Weir	Dunlop	McCall
1	23 Jan	CELTIC	0-1	0-5	24174		1	2	4	6	7	8	11	10	3	9	5

Back row (l-r): J. McEwan, J. Nibloe, W. Gould, J. McCall, H. Morton.
Front row (l-r): R. Walker, M. Smith, J. Hood, J. Dunlop, J. Weir, T. Lindsay.

SEASON 1926-27 — Division One

No.	Date	Opposition	H.T.	Res.	Att.	Goalscorers
1	14 Aug	CELTIC	1-2	2-3	20000	Cunningham, McEwan
2	21	Motherwell	0-1	0-1	6000	
3	28	DUNFERMLINE	1-2	2-3	10000	Cunningham, R.Walker
4	4 Sep	Dundee United	0-1	2-1	10000	R.Walker, Weir
5	11	ST. JOHNSTONE	1-0	2-0	4000	Weir(2)
6	18	Partick Thistle	0-3	0-5	20000	
7	25	HEARTS	1-2	1-4	6000	McCall
8	27	Aberdeen	0-4	1-5	15000	Crump
9	2 Oct	Airdrieonians	0-1	0-2	3000	
10	9	ABERDEEN	0-0	0-0	4000	
11	16	MORTON	2-0	2-0	3000	Cunningham, D.Walker
12	23	Queens Park	0-1	0-1	10000	
13	30	St. Mirren	0-0	0-1	9000	
14	6 Nov	FALKIRK	1-1	1-1	5000	Cunningham
15	13	DUNDEE	3-0	3-2	5000	Wishart(2), Leitch
16	20	Clyde	0-0	1-1	5000	Brown
17	27	HAMILTON A.	0-0	0-1	5000	
18	4 Dec	Hibernian	1-1	1-5	8000	McCall
19	11	Cowdenbeath	1-0	1-3	4000	Cunningham
20	18	RANGERS	0-0	0-0	12000	
21	25	Celtic	0-1	0-4	12000	
22	1 Jan	ST. MIRREN	1-2	2-2	15000	Mathieson, Murphy
23	3	Dunfermline	3-1	3-2	4000	Cunningham, Leitch, Thomson
24	8	DUNDEE UNITED	2-0	3-0	4000	Cunningham(2), Murphy
25	15	St. Johnstone	2-0	3-3	8000	Cunningham(3)
26	29	PARTICK THISTLE	0-0	2-0	4000	Cunningham, Ramsay
27	12 Feb	AIRDRIEONIANS	2-1	4-2	6000	Cunningham(2), Morton, Reilly
28	19	Hearts	1-0	1-1	10000	Cunningham
29	26	Morton	1-3	2-3	5000	Cunningham, Ramsay
30	5 Mar	QUEENS PARK	1-0	2-2	5000	Murphy, Ramsay
31	12	MOTHERWELL	1-2	1-4	6000	Cunningham
32	19	Falkirk	1-0	1-0	6000	Weir
33	26	Dundee	2-0	2-1	6000	Cunningham, Thomson
34	2 Apr	CLYDE	1-1	4-1	4000	Weir(3), Cunningham
35	9	Hamilton A.	0-1	0-2	4000	
36	20	HIBERNIAN	2-0	4-0	2000	Weir(2), Murphy, Ramsay
37	23	COWDENBEATH	1-1	1-4	5000	Ramsay
38	30	Rangers	0-1	0-1	8000	

Player appearances (shirt numbers)

No.	Clemie	Hood	Nibloe	Morton	Dunlop	McEwan	Smith	Mathieson	Cunningham	Weir	Crump	Wishart	R.Walker	D.Walker	McCall	McLeod	Marshall	Reilly	Leitch	Brown	Gould	Scott	Thomson	Murphy	Ramsay	Paton	Leslie
1	1	2	3	4	5	6	7	8	10	9	11																
2	1	2	3	4		6		5	8			11	7	9	10												
3	1	2	3	4		6			8	9	11		7		10	5											
4	1	2	3			6			8	9			7		10	5	4	11									
5	1	2	3	4		6			8	9			7		10	5		11									
6	1	2	3			6			8	9			7		10	5	4	11									
7	1	2	3			6			10	9			7		11	5	4	8									
8	1	2	3			6				9	11		7		10	5	4			8							
9	1	2	3			6				9	11		7		10	5	4			8							
10		2	3	10	5	6			8			11	7		9		4				1						
11		2	3	10	5	6			8			11	7	9			4				1						
12		2	3	10	5	6			8	7	11				9		4				1						
13		2	3	11		6			8	9			7		10	5	4				1						
14		2	3	4		6			8	9			7			5			11		1		10				
15		2	3	4		6				9		8	7			5			11	10	1						
16		2	3	4		6				9		8	7			5			11	10	1						
17		2	3	4		6				9		8	7			5			11	10	1						
18		2	3	4					9						10	5		6	7	8	1						
19		2	3	4					9	10	11					5		6	7	8	1						
20		2	3	4		6		5	10	9			7						11	8	1						
21		2	3	4		6		5		8				9					7	10	1		11				
22		2	3	4		6		5		9									7		1			11	8	10	
23		2	3	4		6			9						5				7		1			11	8	10	
24		2	3	4		6			9						5				7		1			11	8	10	
25		2	3	4		6			9						5				7		1			11	8	10	
26		2	3	4		6			9						5				7		1			11	8	10	
27		2	3	4					9	8					5			6	7		1			11		10	
28	1	2	3	4					9						5			6	7					11	8	10	
29	1	2	3	4					9						5			6	7					11	8	10	
30	1	2	3	4					9						5			6	7					11	8	10	
31	1		3	2		6			9		11				5			4	7					8	10		
32	1		3	4					8	9					5				6					11	7	10	2
33	1		3	4					8	9					5				6					11	7	10	2
34	1		3	4					8	9					5				6					11	7	10	2
35	1		3	4					8	9					5				6					11	7	10	2
36	1		3	4		6			8	9					5									11	7	10	
37	1		3	4		6			8	9					5									11	7	10	2
38	1		3	4		6			8	9					5									11	7	10	2
Apps	20	30	38	33	4	28	1	5	34	26	11	11	7	3	10	33	2	19	18	9	18	1	17	16	17	5	2
Goals				1		1		1	19	9	1	2	2	1	2			1	2	1			2	4	5		

Pos	P.	W.	D.	L.	F.	A.	Pts.
16th	38	12	8	18	54	71	32

Scottish Cup

No.	Date	Opposition	H.T.	Res.	Att.	Goalscorers
1	22 Jan	PEEBLES ROVERS	1-0	3-1	4000	Cunningham(2), Ramsay
2	5 Feb	DUNDEE	0-1	1-1	13000	Ramsay
2R	9	Dundee	1-2	1-5	12000	Murphy

No.	Hood	Nibloe	Morton	McEwan	Mathieson	Cunningham	McLeod	Leitch	Gould	Murphy	Ramsay	Paton
1	2	3	4	6	5	9		7	1	11	8	10
2	2	3	4	6		9	5	7	1	11	8	10
2R	2	3	4	6		9	5	7	1	11	8	10

Joe Nibloe.

Kilmarnock's most-capped player.

The Rugby Road wall built. Stars of the 40s and 50s Hugh McLaren and Bobby Dougan born. 19th century heroes John McPherson and Bob Findlay die.

SEASON 1927-28   Division One

No.	Date	Opposition	H.T.	Res.	Att.	Goalscorers	Clemie	Hood	Nibloe	Morton	McLeod	Reilly	Murphy	Cunningham	Weir	Ramsay	Thomson	Williamson	Millar	McEwan	Paton	Pirrie	Smith	Mathieson	Cunningham(Celtic)	Robertson	Connell	Hogg	Leslie	R.Walker
1	13 Aug	Hearts	1-0	1-0	22000	Weir	1	2	3	4	5	6	7	8	9	10	11													
2	16	Celtic	1-2	1-6	15000	Ramsay	1		3	4	5	6	7	8	9	10	11				2									
3	20	PARTICK THISTLE	2-2	2-3	10000	Cunningham(2)	1	2	3	4	5	6	7	9		10		8	11											
4	27	Aberdeen	2-0	2-1	12000	Murphy, Weir	1	2	3	4	5		7	9	8	10			11	6										
5	3 Sep	BO'NESS	1-1	3-1	6000	Cunningham(3)	1	2	3	4	5		7	9	8	10			11	6										
6	10	Cowdenbeath	0-0	1-1	3000	Cunningham	1	2	3	4	5		7	9	8	10			11	6										
7	17	MOTHERWELL	1-1	1-3	8000	Millar	1	2	3	4	5		7	9	8	10			11	6										
8	24	St. Johnstone	0-0	1-1	7000	Cunningham		2	3	4	5		7	9	8	10			11	6			1							
9	1 Oct	AIRDRIEONIANS	1-2	2-2	7000	Cunningham, Smith		2	3	4			7	9		10	11			6		1	8	5						
10	8	Bo'ness	1-0	1-2	4000	Cunningham		2	3	4				8	9	10	11			6		1	7	5						
11	15	ST. MIRREN	2-1	6-2	7000	Cunningham(2), Mortn, Mrphy, Rmsy, Thomsn		2	3	4	5		7	9		10	11			6		1	8							
12	22	QUEENS PARK	1-1	1-1	6000	Ramsay		2	3	4	5		7	9		10	11			6		1	8							
13	29	Raith Rovers	0-0	3-1	5000	Thomson, Ramsay, Weir		2	3	4			7		9	10	11			6		1	8	5						
14	5 Nov	Falkirk	0-2	0-6	7000			2	3	4			7		9	10	11			6		1	8	5						
15	12	Dundee	0-1	0-7	7000			2	3	4			7	9		10	11			6		1	8		5					
16	19	CLYDE	1-0	3-0	5000	Cunningham (No.9(2), Cunningham(No.5)	1		3	4		6	7	9		10	11						8		5	2				
17	26	Hamilton A.	1-2	1-3	3000	Cunningham	1		3	4		6	7	9		10	11						8		5	2				
18	3 Dec	HIBERNIAN	0-1	2-1	5000	Cunningham(2)	1		3	4	5	6		9		10	11						8		7	2				
19	10	DUNFERMLINE	2-0	2-1	5000	Cunningham, Ramsay	1		3	4		6	7	9		10	11	8						5		2				
20	17	RANGERS	1-1	1-1	14440	Cunningham	1		3	4	5	6	7	9		10	11						8			2				
21	24	HEARTS	3-0	5-0	6000	Cunningham, Murphy, Morton, Ramsay, Smith	1		3	4	5	6	7	9		10	11						8			2				
22	2 Jan	St. Mirren	1-1	1-1	20000	Morton	1		3	4	5	6	7	9		10	11						8			2				
23	3	COWDENBEATH	0-0	2-1	7500	Thomson, Weir	1		3	4	5		7	9	8	10	11			6						2				
24	7	ABERDEEN	2-0	2-1	3000	Cunningham(2)	1		3	4	5			9	8	10	11			6						2	7			
25	14	Motherwell	2-1	3-3	5000	Murphy(2), Cunningham	1		3	4	5		8	9		10	11			6						2	7			
26	28	CELTIC	1-1	2-2	18000	Cunningham, Murphy	1		3	4	5		11	9		10							8			2	7			
27	8 Feb	Airdrieonians	1-0	2-0	2000	Cunningham(2)	1		3	4	5		11	9		10							8			2	7			
28	11	ST. JOHNSTONE	0-1	1-7	8000	Cunningham	1		3	4	5	6	11	9		10							8			2	7			
29	25	Queens Park	2-2	3-5	15000	Cunningham(2), Ramsay	1		3	4				9		10				6			8			2	7	5		
30	29	RAITH ROVERS	0-0	1-0	3000	Cunningham	1		3	4				9		10	11			6			8				7	5	2	
31	7 Mar	Partick Thistle	0-2	0-2	3000		1		3	4				9		10	11			6			8				7	5	2	
32	10	FALKIRK	1-1	1-1	3000	Ramsay	1	2			5		11	9		10				6			8			3	7	4		
33	17	DUNDEE	1-2	1-2	3000	Ramsay	1		3	4	5		11	9		10				6			8				7	2		
34	24	Clyde	1-0	1-1	4000	McEwan	1		3	4	5		11			10				6			8			2	7			9
35	31	HAMILTON A.	1-1	3-1	3000	Connell, Cunningham, Smith	1		3	4	5			9		10	11			6			8				7	2		
36	7 Apr	Hibernian	0-0	1-3	3000	Millar	1		3	4	5			9		10			11	6			8			2	7			
37	14	Dunfermline	3-0	4-0	1000	Cunningham(3), Ramsay	1		3		5			9		10			11	6			8	2			7	4		
38	21	Rangers	0-3	1-5	28000	Cunningham	1		3		5			9		10			11	6			8			2	7	4		
		Apps.					30	14	38	35	27	11	29	36	11	38	20	2	9	27	1	8	26	6	4	18	15	6	4	1
		Goals								3			6	34	4	10	3		2	1			3		1		1			

Pos	P.	W.	D.	L.	F.	A.	Pts.
8th	38	15	10	13	68	78	40

Scottish Cup

No.	Date	Opposition	H.T.	Res.	Att.	Goalscorers	Clemie	Hood	Nibloe	Morton	McLeod	Reilly	Murphy	Cunningham	Weir	Ramsay	Thomson	Williamson	Millar	McEwan	Paton	Pirrie	Smith	Mathieson	Cunningham(Celtic)	Robertson	Connell	Hogg	Leslie	R.Walker
1	21 Jan	Leith Athletic +	2-1	3-2	7000	Connell, Ramsay, Thomson	1		3	4	5			8	9	10	11			6						2	7			
2	4 Feb	Forfar Athletic	1-1	2-1	3000	Cunningham, Murphy	1		3	4	5		11	9		10				6			8			2	7			
3	18	QUEENS PARK	3-2	4-4	21267	Smith(2), Cunningham, Morton	1		3	4	5			9		10	11			6			8			2	7			
3R	22	Queens Park	0-0	0-1	36000		1		3	4	5		11	9		10				6			8			2	7			

+ Played at Easter Road

Tom Smith.

Joined Killie from a Cumnock juvenile team in December 1927.

SEASON 1928-29   Division One

No.	Date	Opposition	H.T.	Res.	Att.	Goalscorers	Clemie	Robertson	Nibloe	Morton	Hogg	McEwan	Connell	Williamson	Cunningham	Ramsay	Clark	M.Smith	Weir	Dunlop	Paterson	Leslie	Bernard	Aitken	Mathieson	Stewart	T.Smith	McLaren
1	11 Aug	Rangers	0-3	2-4	20000	Cunningham, Ramsay	1	2	3	4	5	6	7	8	9	10	11											
2	18	HIBERNIAN	1-0	1-0	8000	Williamson	1	2	3	4	5	6	7	8	9	10	11											
3	25	Airdrieonians	0-1	1-2	4000	Ramsay	1	2	3	4	5	6	7	8	9	10	11											
4	1 Sep	DUNDEE	2-0	3-1	6000	Cunningham, Morton, Smith	1	2	3	4	5	6	7		9	10			8	11								
5	8	Celtic	0-1	0-3	18000		1	2	3	4	5	6	7		9	10			8	11								
6	15	ABERDEEN	0-1	0-1	6000		1	2	3	4	5	6	7		10	9			8	11								
7	22	THIRD LANARK	2-0	3-0	8000	Cunningham, Paterson, Ramsay	1	2	3	4			7		9	10	6	8			5	11						
8	24	Aberdeen	1-1	1-2	13000	Smith	1		3	4			7		9	10	6	8			5	11		2				
9	29	Clyde	1-1	1-1	7000	Connell	1	2	3	4			7		9	10	6	8			5	11						
10	6 Oct	St. Johnstone	0-1	0-1	6000			2	3	4			7		9	10	6	8			5	11	1					
11	13	PARTICK THISTLE	2-0	2-2	6000	Connell(2)		2	3	4			7		9	10	6	8			5	11	1					
12	20	St. Mirren	2-2	4-5	7000	Connell, Cunningham, Morton, Smith		2	3	4		6	7		9			8			5	11	1					
13	27	COWDENBEATH	2-1	4-2	5000	Cunningham(3), Dunlop		2	3		4	6	7		9			8	10		5	11	1					
14	3 Nov	Motherwell	0-0	3-2	8000	Cunningham(2), Smith	1	2	3	4		6	7		9	10		8			5	11						
15	10	QUEENS PARK	5-0	7-4	5000	Smith(4), Cunningham(2), Ramsay	1	2	3	4		6	7		9	10		8			5	11						
16	17	Ayr United	1-2	4-2	14000	Morton, Ramsay, Paterson, Smith	1	2	3	4		6	7		9	10		8			5	11						
17	24	HEARTS	1-0	3-2	10000	Connell(2), Cunningham	1	2	3	4		6	7		9	10		8			5	11						
18	1 Dec	Falkirk	1-1	2-2	5000	Cunningham, Morton	1	2	3	4		6	7		9	10		8			5	11						
19	8	RAITH ROVERS	3-0	7-1	5500	Cunningham(4), Connell(2), Morton	1	2	3	4		6	7		9	10		8			5	11						
20	15	Hamilton A.	1-0	2-0	4000	Cunningham, Paterson	1	2	3	4		6	7		9	10		8			5	11						
21	22	Hibernian	1-0	1-1	2000	Ramsay	1	2	3	4		6	7		9	10		8			5	11						
22	29	RANGERS	1-2	1-3	30000	Dunlop	1	2	3	4		6	7		9	10		8			5	11						
23	1 Jan	ST. MIRREN	0-2	2-4	15000	Cunningham, Smith	1		3	4		6	7		9	10		8			5			2		11		
24	2	Cowdenbeath	0-2	0-2	2000		1	2	3	4		6	7	8	9						5	11				10		
25	5	AIRDRIEONIANS	0-1	0-2	4000		1	2	3	4		6	7		9	10			8	5				11				
26	12	Dundee	1-1	3-1	8000	Connell, Cunningham, Paterson	1	2	3	4		6	7		9	10		8			5	11						
27	26	HAMILTON A.	0-0	0-0	5000		1	2	3	4		6	7		9	10		8			5	11						
28	9 Feb	Third Lanark	1-2	3-2	6000	Cunningham, Dunlop, Smith	1	2	3	4		6	7		9	10		8			5	11						
29	23	ST. JOHNSTONE	0-1	1-1	4000	Ramsay	1	2		4		6	7		9	10		8			5	11		3				
30	9 Mar	MOTHERWELL	3-1	4-2	5000	Paterson(2), Smith, Weir	1	2	3	4		6	7	10				8	9		5	11						
31	12	Partick Thistle	1-1	1-2	900	Connell	1	2	3	4		6	7	10				8	9		5	11						
32	20	Queens Park	0-1	0-2	4000				3		4	6			9	10					7		1	11	8	5	2	
33	30	Hearts	1-1	3-3	15000	Connell(2), Aitken	1	2	3	4		6	7	10					8	9				11		5		
34	1 Apr	CLYDE	2-0	3-1	4000	Aitken, Cunningham, Ramsay		2		4		6	7		9	10					1			11	8	5	3	
35	9	FALKIRK	0-0	1-1	4000	Smith	1	2		4		6	7	10	9			8						11		5	3	
36	20	Raith Rovers	3-0	3-5	500	Williamson(2), Cunningham	1	2	3	4	5	6	7	10	9			8						11				
37	24	AYR UNITED	0-2	1-2	6000	McEwan	1	2	3	4		6	7	10	9			8						11		5		
38	27	CELTIC	1-1	2-3	6300	Aitken, Williamson	1	2	3	4		6	7	10	9			8						11		5		
						Apps.	32	35	35	35	10	33	37	12	35	28	8	31	8	25	24	3	6	9	3	6	3	6
						Goals				5		1	12	4	23	8		13	1	3	6			3				

Pos P. W. D. L. F. A. Pts.
10th 38 14 8 16 79 74 36

Scottish Cup

No.	Date	Opposition	H.T.	Res.	Att.	Goalscorers	Clemie	Robertson	Nibloe	Morton	Hogg	McEwan	Connell	Williamson	Cunningham	Ramsay	Clark	M.Smith	Weir	Dunlop	Paterson	Leslie	Bernard	Aitken	Mathieson	Stewart	T.Smith	McLaren
1	19 Jan	GLASGOW UNIVERSITY	4-0	8-1	3500	Rmsy(3),Cnnll,Cnninghm,McEwn,Ptrsn,Smth		2	3	4		6	7		9	10		8			5	11	1					
2	2 Feb	BO'NESS	2-1	3-2	4000	Connell, Cunningham, Ramsay	1		3	4		6	7		9	10		8			5	11			2			
3	16	Albion Rovers	0-0	1-0	7000	Connell	1	2	3	4		6	7		9	10	11	8			5							
QF	2 Mar	Raith Rovers	3-1	3-2	11500	Cunningham, Paterson, Smith	1	2	3	4		6	7		9	10		8			5	11						
SF	23	Celtic*	1-0	1-0	40000	Weir	1	2	3	4		6	7	10				8	9		5							5
F	6 Apr	Rangers#	0-0	2-0	114708	Aitken, Williamson	1	2	3	4		6	7	10	9			8						11				5

* Ibrox   # Hampden

Scottish Cup Winners
Back row: H. Spence (Secretary), G. Neil, R.H. Thomson, H. Alexander, T. Robertson, S. Clemie, J. Nibloe, R. Thomson, T. Wylie, J.L. Morison, J. Walker. Middle row: D. Dick (Vice-President), W. Connell, H. Cunningham, J. Weir, M. Smith, J. Ramsay, J. Williamson, J. Aitken, A.S. McCulloch (President).
Front row: T. Wallace (Ass. Trainer), H. Morton, H. McLaren, J. Dunlop, J. McEwan , J. McWhinnie (Trainer).

SEASON 1929-30 Division One

No.	Date	Opposition	H.T.	Res.	Att.	Goalscorers
1	10 Aug	HAMILTON A.	3-0	3-0	7000	Cunningham, Williamson(2)
2	17	Hearts	0-1	1-1	20000	Williamson
3	24	CLYDE	1-0	2-1	8000	Cunningham, M.Smith
4	31	Queens Park	1-1	4-1	18000	Connell(3), Paterson
5	7 Sep	AYR UNITED	1-0	2-0	14000	Cunningham(2)
6	14	Morton	2-2	2-4	10000	Cunningham(2)
7	21	RANGERS	1-0	1-0	23000	Paterson
8	28	Dundee	0-1	2-2	10000	Connell, M.Smith
9	5 Oct	Partick Thistle	1-2	2-3	20000	McGowan, M.Smith
10	12	ST. JOHNSTONE	1-1	3-1	7000	McEwan, M.Smith, Williamson
11	19	Cowdenbeath	0-1	3-2	3000	McEwan, Morton, Williamson
12	26	ST. MIRREN	1-3	2-3	6000	Connell, McGowan
13	2 Nov	ABERDEEN	2-1	4-2	10000	Paterson(2), McGowan, M.Smith
14	9	Airdrieonians	0-1	2-2	3000	McGowan, Paterson
15	16	DUNDEE UNITED	0-2	0-2	5000	
16	23	FALKIRK	2-1	3-2	5500	Connell, Cunningham, Williamson
17	30	Hibernian	0-0	0-0	3500	
18	7 Dec	Motherwell	0-1	0-2	2000	
19	14	CELTIC	1-1	1-1	7000	Williamson
20	21	Hamilton A.	0-1	1-1	3000	Weir
21	28	HEARTS	0-1	2-1	4000	Aitken, O.G.
22	1 Jan	St. Mirren	1-1	1-3	5000	Cunningham
23	2	COWDENBEATH	3-1	3-2	7000	Cunningham(2), Clark
24	4	Clyde	0-0	1-1	7000	Cunningham
25	11	QUEENS PARK	1-4	1-5	4000	Cunningham
26	25	Ayr United	1-1	1-1	11000	M.Smith
27	8 Feb	Rangers	0-3	0-4	25000	
28	15	MORTON	3-0	7-2	3000	McGowan(5), Ramsay, O.G.
29	22	PARTICK THISTLE	0-0	1-1	5000	McEwan
30	1 Mar	St. Johnstone	1-1	3-1	2000	McGowan(2), M.Smith
31	8	Aberdeen	0-2	3-4	12000	Wales(2), M.Smith
32	15	AIRDRIEONIANS	5-0	7-1	5000	McGowan(4), Cunningham, Paterson, M.Smith
33	22	Dundee United	4-2	4-6	5000	McGowan, Ramsay, M.Smith, Wales
34	29	Falkirk	0-0	0-1	2000	
35	5 Apr	HIBERNIAN	0-0	3-1	4500	Morton, McEwan, McGowan
36	12	MOTHERWELL	1-1	2-3	3000	Cunningham, McGowan
37	19	Celtic	0-2	0-4	4000	
38	21	DUNDEE	0-2	0-2	3000	

Player appearances (shirt numbers):

No.	Clemie	Robertson	Nibloe	Morton	Dunlop	McEwan	Connell	M.Smith	Cunningham	Williamson	Paterson	Ramsay	McGowan	T.Smith	Leslie	Hogg	Aitken	Weir	Stewart	Clark	G.B.Wilson	Irvine	McLeod	Wales
1	1	2	3	4	5	6	7	8	9	1U	11													
2	1	2	3	4	5	6	7	8	9	10	11													
3	1	2	3	4	5	6	7	8	9	10	11													
4	1	2	3	4	5	6	7	8	9	10	11													
5	1	2	3	4	5	6	7	8	9	10	11													
6	1	2	3	4	5	6	7	8	9		11	10												
7	1	2	3	4	5	6	7	8	9		11	10												
8	1	2	3	4	5	6	7	8	9		11	10												
9	1	2	3	4	5	6	7	8			11	10	9											
10	1		3	4	5	6	7	8			10	11	9	2										
11	1	2	3	4	5	6	7	8			10	11	9											
12	1	2		4	5	6	7	8			10	11	9		3									
13	1		3	4	5	6	7	8			10	11	9	2										
14	1	2	3	4	5	6	7	8			10	11	9											
15	1	2	3	4	5	6	7	8			10	11	9											
16	1	4	3		5	6	7	8	9	10	11						2							
17	1		3		5	6	7	8	9		10						2							
18	1		3		5	6	7	8	9		10						2	11						
19	1		3	4	5	6	7	8		10							2	11	9					
20	1		3	4	5	6	7	8		10							2	11	9					
21	1		3	4		6	7	8		10							2	11	9	5				
22	1		3	4		6	7	8	9	10							2	11		5				
23	1	2	3	4			7	8	9	10								11		5	6			
24			3			6	7	10	9		11						2	4			1	5	8	
25			3		5	6		8	9		7	10					2	11			1		4	
26	1	2	3	4	5	6		8	9		7	10						11						
27	1	2	3		5	6		8	9	7		10					4	11						
28	1	2	3			6		8	7		11	10	9			4				5				
29	1	2	3	4		6		8	7		11	10	9							5				
30	1	2	3	4		6		8				10	9							5				7
31	1	2	3	4		6		8	9		11	10								5				7
32	1	2	3			6	7	8			11	10	9							5	4			7
33	1	2	3			6		8				10	9					11		5	4			7
34	1	2	3	4		6		8	9		11	10						5						7
35	1	2	3	4		6		8				10	9					5	11					7
36	1	2	3	4		6		8	11			10	9					5						7
37	1	2	3	4		6		8	9	11	10							5						7
38	1		3			6		8				10	9	2				5	11		4			7
Apps.	30	28	30	29	23	37	23	37	24	10	26	20	16	12	1	14	3	6	1	7	4	7	2	8
Goals				2		4	6	10	14	7	6	2	18				1	1		1				3

Pos	P.	W.	D.	L.	F.	A.	Pts.
8th	38	15	9	14	77	73	39

Scottish Cup

No.	Date	Opposition	H.T.	Res.	Att.	Goalscorers
1	18 Jan	PAISLEY ACAS.	7-0	11-1	3000	Weir(6), Aitken(2), Connell, Ramsay, Williamsn
2	1 Feb	Hamilton A.	0-1	2-4	12000	Cunningham, McEwan

Scottish Cup appearances (shirt numbers):

No.	Clemie	Robertson	Nibloe	Morton	Dunlop	McEwan	Connell	M.Smith	Cunningham	Williamson	Paterson	Ramsay	McGowan	T.Smith	Leslie	Hogg	Aitken	Weir	Stewart	Clark
1	1	2	3	4		6	7				8		10				11	9	5	
2	1	2	3	4	5	6		8	9	10	7						11			

Back row: T. Robertson, T. Smith, S. Clemie, H. Morton.
Middle row: W. Clark, J. Aitken, J. Dunlop, J. Nibloe, J. McEwan.
Front row: Hugh Spence (Secretary), W. Connell, M. Smith, H. Cunningham, J. Ramsay, D. Paterson, James McWhinnie (Trainer).

SEASON 1930-31 — Division One

No.	Date	Opposition	H.T.	Res.	Att.	Goalscorers	Clemie	Leslie	Nibloe	Morton	Stewart	Clark	Connell	M.Smith	Cunningham	Ramsay	Aitken	Robertson	McEwan	Nicol	Young	T.Smith	Duncan	Maxwell	Kenmuir	Wales	Napier	Irvine	Muir	Parry	Falconer
1	9 Aug	Celtic	1-2	1-3	20000	Ramsay	1	2	3	4	5	6	7	8	9	10	11														
2	16	PARTICK THISTLE	1-0	2-0	8000	Cunningham, M.Smith	1		3	4	5		7	8	9			2	6	10	11										
3	23	Airdrieonians	1-3	3-4	4000	Connell, Nicol, M.Smith	1		3	4	5		7	8	9			2	6	10	11										
4	30	HEARTS	0-1	0-1	9500		1		3	4			7	8	9		11	2	6			5	10								
5	6 Sep	Motherwell	1-0	1-1	5000	Connell	1		3	4			7	8		10	11	2	6			5		9							
6	13	AYR UNITED	1-1	2-1	8000	Ramsay, M.Smith	1		3	4			7	8		10	11	2	6			5		9							
7	20	St. Mirren	0-2	2-4	10000	Duncan, Maxwell	1		3	4			7	8			11	2	6			5	10	9							
8	27	COWDENBEATH	0-1	0-1	7000		1		3	4			7	8		10		2	6			5	11	9							
9	4 Oct	Leith Athletic	1-0	1-0	7000	Connell	1		3	4			7	8	9		11	2	6			5	10								
10	11	DUNDEE	0-1	1-2	6000	Aitken	1		3	4			7	8	9		11	2	6			5	10								
11	18	RANGERS	1-0	1-0	15000	Connell	1		3	4			7	8			11	2	6			5	10	9							
12	25	Falkirk	2-1	2-4	5000	Maxwell(2)	1		3	4			7	8			11	2	6			5	10	9							
13	1 Nov	HAMILTON A.	2-1	3-1	4000	Wales(2), Morton	1		3	4			7				11	2	6			5	10	9		8					
14	8	Aberdeen	0-1	0-2	13000		1		3	4			7	8			11	2	6			5	10	9							
15	15	EAST FIFE	3-0	5-1	4000	Wales(4), Connell	1		3	4			7	8			11	2	6			5	10			9					
16	22	Hibernian	1-3	2-3	1000	Connell, T.Smith	1		3	4			7				11	2	6			5	10			9	8				
17	29	QUEENS PARK	1-1	2-1	5000	Aitken, Maxwell	1		3	4			7				11	2	6			5	10	9		8					
18	6 Dec	Morton	1-1	2-2	3000	Maxwell(2)	1		3	4			7				11	2	6			5	10	9		8					
19	13	CLYDE	1-0	2-1	4000	Aitken, Maxwell	1		3	4			7				11	2	6			5	10	9			8				
20	20	CELTIC	0-1	0-3	16000		1		3	4			7			10	11	2	6			5		9			8				
21	27	Partick Thistle	1-1	1-3	8000	Irvine	1		3	4			7			10	11	2	6			5					8	9			
22	1 Jan	ST. MIRREN	1-1	2-3	15000	Maxwell(2)	1		3	4			7				11	2	6			5	10	9		8					
23	3	AIRDRIEONIANS	1-0	1-0	5000	Aitken	1	3		4			7				11	2	6			5	10	9			8				
24	5	Cowdenbeath	0-1	1-3	1000	Maxwell	1	3					7			10	11	2	6			5		9			8	4			
25	10	Hearts	2-0	4-1	15000	Connell, Maxwell, Morton, Ramsay	1		3	4			7			10	11	2	6			5		9			8				
26	24	MOTHERWELL	0-2	1-4	5000	McEwan	1		3	4			7			10	11	2	6			5		9			8				
27	7 Feb	LEITH ATHLETIC	1-0	2-1	5000	Aitken(2)	1		3	4			7	8		10	11	2	6			5		9							
28	21	Rangers	0-0	0-1	8000		1		3	2			7			10	11		6			5		9				4	8		
29	7 Mar	Hamilton A.	0-0	0-0	1500		1	2	3										6			5	11	9			10	4	8	7	
30	11	FALKIRK	1-0	1-1	4000	Napier	1	2	3		5		7				11		6					9			10	4	8		
31	18	ABERDEEN	0-0	1-1	4000	Duncan	1		3	2	5		7						6				11	9			10	4	8		
32	21	East Fife	0-3	1-4	2500	Aitken	1		3	2	5		7				11		6					9			10	4	8		
33	28	Dundee	1-0	2-0	4000	Maxwell, Muir	1		3	4			7				11		6			5		9			10		8		2
34	4 Apr	HIBERNIAN	1-0	4-0	4000	Maxwell(3), Aitken	1	2	3	4			7				11		6			5		9			10		8		
35	18	MORTON	2-0	3-0	2500	Maxwell, Aitken	1	2	3	4			7				11		6			5		9			10		8		
36	21	Queens Park	0-2	0-2	2000		1		3	4			7				11	2	6			5		9			10		8		
37	25	Clyde	2-0	3-0	1500	Connell, Maxwell, McEwan	1	2	3	4			7				11		6			5		9			10		8		
38	29	Ayr United	0-0	0-1	12000		1	2	3	4			7				11		6			5		9			10		8		
		Apps.					38	12	33	35	6	1	36	15	6	13	32	26	32	3	2	29	21	27	1	6	18	11	13	1	1
		Goals								2			8	3	1	3	9		2	1		1	2	18		6	1	1	1		

Pos P. W. D. L. F. A. Pts.
11th 38 15 5 18 59 60 35

Scottish Cup

No.	Date	Opposition	H.T.	Res.	Att.	Goalscorers	Clemie	Leslie	Nibloe	Morton	Stewart	Clark	Connell	M.Smith	Cunningham	Ramsay	Aitken	Robertson	McEwan	Nicol	Young	T.Smith	Duncan	Maxwell	Kenmuir	Wales	Napier	Irvine	Muir	Parry	Falconer
1	17 Jan	Inv'ness Citadel	2-0	7-0	3000	Maxwell(3), Muir(2), Aitken, Connell	1		3	4			7			10	11	2	6			5		9					8		
2	31	HEARTS	2-2	3-2	14000	Maxwell, Connell, Ramsay	1		3	4			7			10	11	2	6			5		9					8		
3	14 Feb	Montrose	1-0	3-0	3000	Aitken, Connell, McEwan	1		3	4			7			10	11	2	6			5		9					8		
QF	28	Bo'ness	0-1	1-1	6258	Aitken	1	2	3	4			7				11		6			5		9					8		
QFR	4 Mar	BO'NESS	2-0	5-0	8300	Connell(3), Maxwell(2)	1	2	3	4			7				11		6			5		9					8		
SF	14	Celtic*	0-1	0-3	53973		1	2	3	4			7				11		6			5		9					8		

* Hampden

4th June 1930 v Stratford at Kitchener, Ontario
on Canadian/USA Tour - Killie won 7-0

SEASON 1931-32   Division One

No.	Date	Opposition	H.T.	Res.	Att.	Goalscorers	Clemie	Leslie	Nibloe	Morton	T.Smith	McEwan	Connell	Muir	Maxwell	Napier	Aitken	Falconer	McLeod	Nicholson	Duncan	Sneddon	McDougall	Bell	Gilmour	Irvine	Kelvin	Williamson	Robertson	Nicol
1	8 Aug	AIRDRIEONIANS	3-1	4-2	7000	Connell, Maxwell, Muir, Napier	1	2	3	4	5	6	7	8	9	10	11													
2	15	Hearts	0-3	0-3	25000		1		3	4	5	6	7	8	9	10	11	2												
3	19	Hamilton A.	1-0	3-1	7000	Aitken, Connell, Napier	1		3	4	5	6	7	8	9	10	11	2												
4	22	MOTHERWELL	1-0	1-0	12000	Maxwell	1	2	3	4	5	6	7	8	9	10	11													
5	26	QUEENS PARK	1-1	4-1	7000	Connell(2), Maxwell, McEwan	1		3	4	5	6	7		9	10	11		2	8										
6	29	Third Lanark	1-1	3-1	16000	Maxwell(3)	1		3	4	5	6	7		9		11	2	8				10							
7	2 Sep	MORTON	0-0	1-0	5000	Aitken	1		3	4	5	6			9		11	2	8	7			10							
8	5	ST. MIRREN	1-0	3-0	9000	McEwan(2), Aitken	1	2	3	4	5	6	7	8	9		11						10							
9	9	Dundee United	0-0	0-0	8000		1	2	3	4	5	6	7		9		11		8				10							
10	12	Ayr United	1-1	1-1	10000	McEwan	1	2	3	4	5	6	7		9	8	11						10							
11	19	COWDENBEATH	1-0	3-2	5000	Connell, Maxwell, McEwan	1	2	3	4	5	6	7		9		11						10	8						
12	26	Partick Thistle	2-1	2-4	15000	Connell, McEwan	1	2	3	4		6	7		9	10	11		8				5							
13	3 Oct	CELTIC	2-2	2-3	20000	Duncan, McEwan	1	2	3	4		6	7		9		11				10		5	8	5					
14	10	Dundee	1-1	1-1	10000	Maxwell	1	2	3	4	5	6	7		9		11				10			8						
15	17	Clyde	0-0	0-0	8000		1	2	3	4	5	6	7		9		11				10			8						
16	24	FALKIRK	2-1	2-1	4000	Connell, Maxwell	1	2	3	4	5	6	7	8	9		11				10									
17	31	Leith Athletic	0-1	1-3	3000	McEwan	1	2	3	4	5	6	7	8	9		11				10									
18	14 Nov	Aberdeen	1-0	1-1	9000	Maxwell		2	3	4	5	6	7		9		11		8		10			1						
19	21	HAMILTON A.	0-1	1-1	4000	Maxwell		2	3	4	5	6	7		9		11		8		10			1						
20	28	Queens Park	0-2	0-2	6000				3	4	5	6	7		9		11	2	8		10			1						
21	5 Dec	Morton	1-2	1-3	4000	Connell		2	3	4	5	6	7		9		11		8		10			1						
22	12	DUNDEE UNITED	4-0	5-0	5000	Aitken(5), Maxwell(2), Connell		2	3	4	5	6	7		9		11		8		10			1						
23	19	Airdrieonians	0-0	2-0	2000	Duncan, Gilmour		2	3	4		6	7	8			11				10	5		1	9					
24	26	HEARTS	0-1	2-1	4000	Aitken(2)		2	3	4	5	6	7				11		8		10			1	9					
25	1 Jan	St. Mirren	0-2	0-2	10000			2	3	4		6	7				11		8		10	5		1	9					
26	2	AYR UNITED	2-1	5-1	10000	Maxwell(3), Connell, Duncan		2	3	4	5	6	7		9		11		8		10			1						
27	9	Motherwell	0-2	0-4	6000				3	4	5	6	7		9		11	2	8		10			1						
28	23	THIRD LANARK	1-0	2-1	8000	Aitken, Connell		2	3		5	6	7		9		11		8					1		4	10			
29	6 Feb	PARTICK THISTLE	2-2	3-4	7000	Connell, Maxwell, Nibloe		2	3	4	5	6	7		9		11		8					1			10			
30	20	DUNDEE	0-0	0-0	6000			2	3		5	6	7		9				8					1	11	4	10			
31	27	CLYDE	0-0	1-0	6000	Gilmour		2	3	4	5		7					6	8					1	11		9	10		
32	12 Mar	LEITH ATHLETIC	1-3	6-3	3000	Aitken(2), Connell(2), Maxwell(2)		2	3	4	5	6	7		9		11		8		10			1						
33	19	Rangers	0-1	0-3	16000			2	3	4	5	6	7		9		11		8		10			1						
34	2 Apr	Falkirk	1-2	1-4	5000	Maxwell		2	3		5	6	7	8	9						10			1		11	4			
35	6	ABERDEEN	0-1	0-2	2000				3		5	6	7	8	9		11				10			1		4		2		
36	9	Cowdenbeath	1-1	1-0	1000	Gilmour	1		3	4		7	6				11		8		10	5			9			2		
37	23	Celtic	0-3	1-4	7000	Duncan		2	3		5	6	7				11				9			1	8		10			4
38	30	RANGERS	2-4	2-4	10000	Aitken, Leslie		2	3	4		6	7				5		11		10			1	9			8		
		Apps.					10	30	31	33	32	37	10	31	36	7	10	1	29	5	5	20	9	4	4	?	?	1		
		Goals						1	1			8	14	1	20	2	14				4				3					

Pos P. W. D. L. F. A. Pts.
9th 38 16 7 15 68 70 39

Scottish Cup

	Date		H.T.	Res.	Att.	Goalscorers	Leslie	Nibloe	Morton	T.Smith	McEwan	Connell	Muir	Maxwell	Aitken	McLeod	Duncan	Bell
1	16 Jan	EAST FIFE	2-1	4-1	5700	Aitken, Connell, Duncan, McLeod	2	3	4	5	6	7		9	11	8	10	1
2	30	ALBION ROVERS	1-0	2-0	7593	Connell, McLeod	2	3	4	5	6	7		9	11	8	10	1
3	13 Feb	Dundee United	0-1	1-1	12969	Maxwell	2	3	4	5	6	7		9	11	8	10	1
3R	17	DUNDEE UNITED	2-0	3-0	9410	Aitken, Duncan, Maxwell	2	3	4	5	6	7		9	11	8	10	1
QF	5 Mar	Dunfermline	1-1	3-1	10000	Maxwell(2), Duncan	2	3	4	5	6	7		9	11	8	10	1
SF	26	Airdrieonians*	2-0	3-2	28138	Aitken, Maxwell, McEwan	2	3	4	5	6	7	8	9	11		10	1
F	16 Apr	Rangers#	1-0	1-1	111982	Maxwell	2	3	4	5	6	7	8	9	11		10	1
FR	20	Rangers#	0-1	0-3	105695		2	3	4	5	6	7	8	9	11		10	1

* Firhill # Hampden

Scottish Cup Finalists 1931-32
Back row: J. McKenzie, G. Neil, H. Brown, J. Leslie, W. Bell, J. Nibloe, H. Alexander, T. Wylie. Middle row: J. Walker, R. Thomson (Vice-President), J. McLeod, J. Muir, D. Dick (President), J. Duncan, J. Aitken, J.L. Morison, H. Spence (Secretary).
Front row: Jas. McWhinnie (Trainer), T. Smith, J. McEwan, T. Wallace (Ass. Trainer).
Insets: W. Connell, J. Maxwell, H. Morton.

SEASON 1932-33 Division One

No.	Date	Opposition	H.T.	Res.	Att.	Goalscorers
1	13 Aug	Motherwell	2-2	3-3	11000	Maxwell(3)
2	20	THIRD LANARK	3-0	6-0	9000	Maxwell(3), Kelvin, McEwan, Sneddon
3	24	Aberdeen	0-5	1-7	12000	McEwan
4	27	Cowdenbeath	0-1	1-4	2000	Maxwell
5	3 Sep	PARTICK THISTLE	2-0	3-0	7000	Maxwell(2), Connell
6	10	St. Mirren	2-1	2-3	7000	Maxwell, Williamson
7	14	HAMILTON A.	1-1	3-2	4000	Aitken, Maxwell, McEwan
8	17	AYR UNITED	3-4	3-5	10000	Maxwell(2), Connell
9	24	Celtic	0-0	0-0	6000	
10	1 Oct	EAST STIRLING	1-1	2-1	5000	Connell(2)
11	8	Airdrieonians	1-1	1-2	2000	Maxwell
12	15	DUNDEE	1-2	2-2	5000	Aitken, McEwan
13	22	ST. JOHNSTONE	2-2	5-4	5000	Maxwell(2), Williamson, McEwan, Muir
14	29	Rangers	0-2	0-2	6000	
15	5 Nov	ABERDEEN	1-1	4-3	8000	Connell(2), Aitken, McEwan
16	12	Hamilton A.	0-0	0-0	3000	
17	19	QUEENS PARK	0-0	3-1	10000	Maxwell(2), Sneddon
18	26	MORTON	0-1	1-1	6000	Maxwell
19	3 Dec	Hearts	0-1	0-1	10000	
20	10	CLYDE	1-1	1-2	4000	Sneddon
21	17	Falkirk	0-1	2-2	4000	McEwan, Sneddon
22	24	MOTHERWELL	1-1	1-3	9000	McEwan
23	31	Third Lanark	1-3	2-3	6000	Maxwell(2)
24	2 Jan	ST. MIRREN	0-1	0-1	7000	
25	3	Ayr United	1-1	3-2	10000	Maxwell(2), Napier
26	7	COWDENBEATH	3-1	4-1	4000	Maxwell(2), Aitken, McEwan
27	14	Partick Thistle	2-0	3-1	9000	Maxwell(2), Gilmour
28	28	CELTIC	0-2	2-2	12000	Liddell, Sneddon
29	11 Feb	East Stirling	1-1	3-2	4000	Maxwell(2), Sneddon
30	25	AIRDRIEONIANS	2-0	2-4	3000	Maxwell, Sneddon
31	11 Mar	St. Johnstone	0-4	1-6	6000	Muir
32	18	RANGERS	1-3	2-6	7000	Liddell, O.G.
33	29	Dundee	0-3	0-3	1000	
34	8 Apr	Morton	2-4	2-5	1500	Duncan, Gilmour
35	12	HEARTS	0-0	0-0	2000	
36	22	Clyde	1-0	1-0	4000	McEwan
37	26	Queens Park	1-0	2-1	2000	Gilmour, Maxwell
38	29	FALKIRK	0-1	1-1	3000	Maxwell

Player appearances (shirt numbers):

No.	Milliken	Leslie	Milloy	Glass	Smith	McEwan	Connell	Sneddon	Maxwell	Kelvin	Aitken	Williamson	Duncan	Bell	Muir	MacDougall	Napier	A.D.Turner	Taylor	Kenmuir	"Newman"	Falconer	Liddell	Gilmour	Landsborough	Beattie	McDonald
1		2	3	4	5	6	7	8	9		11	10	1														
2		2	3	4	5	6	7	8	9	10	11		1														
3		2	3	4	5	6	7	8			11	10	1												9		
4		2	3	4	5	6	7	8	9	10	11								1								
5	1	2	3	4	5	6	7	8	9		11	10															
6	1	2	3	4	5	6	7	8	9		11	10															
7	1	2	3	4	5	6	7	8	9		11	10															
8	1	2	3	4	5	6	7	8	9		11			10													
9	1	2	3	4	5	6	7	8	9		11	10															
10	1	2	3	4	5	6	7	8	9		11	10															
11		2	3	4	5	6	7		9		11	10				1	8										
12		2	3	4		6	7		9		11	10				1	8	5									
13		2	3	4		6	7		9		11	10				1	8		5								
14	1	2	3	4		6	7		9		11	10					8	5									
15	1	2	3	4	5	6	7	8	9		11	10															
16	1	2	3	4	5	6		8	9		11	10								7							
17	1	2	3	4	5	6		8	9		11	10								7							
18	1	2	3	4	5	6		8	9		11	10								7							
19	1	2	3	4	5	6		8	9		11	10								7							
20	1	2			5	6		8	9		11	10								7	4						
21	1	2			5	6		8	9		11						10			4	7						
22			3	4	5	6		10	9		11	8						7	2								
23	1	2	3	4	5	6		8	9		11												7				
24	1	2	3	4	5	6			9		11						8						7	10			
25	1	2	3	4		6		8	10	11							5						7	9			
26	1	2	3	4	5	6		8	9		11												7	10			
27		2	3	4	5	6		8	9		11						1						7	10			
28	1	2	3	4		6		8	9		11												7	10	5		
29	1	2	3	4	5	6		8	9		11												7	10			
30	1	2	3	4	5	6		8	9		11												7	10			
31	1	2	3	4		6				10	11				8			5					7	9			
32	1	2	3	4		6			9		11												7	10	5		
33		2		4	5	6		8			11						9	1		10			7				3
34		2	3	4		6		8			11						9	1					5	7	10		
35	1	2	3	4	5	6		8	9	11													7			10	
36	1	2	3	4	5	6		8	9		11												7	10			
37	1	2	3	4	5	6			9		11						8						7	10			
38	1	2	3	4	5	6			9		11						8						7			10	
Apps.	28	37	37	36	30	38	15	30	33	5	36	18	4	9	9	1	6	4	2	4	1	1	16	13	2	2	1
Goals						10	6	7	32	1	4	2	1		2		1						2	2			

Pos	P.	W.	D.	L.	F.	A.	Pts.
14th	38	13	9	16	72	86	35

Scottish Cup

	Date	Opposition	H.T.	Res.	Att.	Goalscorers	Milliken	Leslie	Milloy	Glass	Smith	McEwan	Sneddon	Maxwell	Aitken	Liddell	Gilmour
1	21 Jan	LOCHGELLY	3-0	3-1	3615	Maxwell(2), Gilmour	1	2	3	4	5	6	8	9	11	7	10
2	4 Feb	St. Mirren	1-0	1-0	12000	Aitken	1	2	3	4	5	6	8	9	11	7	10
3	16	RANGERS	1-0	1-0	32745	Liddell	1	2	3	4	5	6	8	9	11	7	10
QF	4 Mar	MOTHERWELL	1-2	3-3	20658	Maxwell(2), McEwan	1	2	3	4	5	6	8	9	11	7	10
QFR	8	Motherwell	0-3	3-8	23000	Glass(2), Maxwell	1	2	3	4	5	6	8	9	11	7	10

Bobby Beattie.

Bobby Beattie made his debut against Hearts near the end of the season.

SEASON 1933-34   Division One

No.	Date	Opposition	H.T.	Res.	Att.	Goalscorers
1	12 Aug	COWDENBEATH	2-0	4-1	7000	Keane, Liddell, Maxwell, Williamson
2	16	THIRD LANARK	1-1	1-2	8000	Maxwell
3	19	Partick Thistle	2-1	3-2	10000	Liddell(2), Maxwell
4	23	ABERDEEN	1-0	2-0	7000	Keane, Maxwell
5	26	CELTIC	3-2	4-3	14000	Liddell(2), Maxwell, Williamson
6	2 Sep	Hibernian	1-1	1-4	15000	Maxwell
7	9	ST. MIRREN	2-0	3-0	6000	Maxwell(2), Liddell
8	13	Hamilton A.	1-1	2-2	3000	Kelvin, Maxwell
9	16	Third Lanark	0-0	1-1	6000	Glass
10	23	AIRDRIEONIANS	2-1	7-1	5000	Maxwell(3), Keane(2), Connell, McEwan
11	30	Ayr United	1-1	1-1	12000	Keane
12	7 Oct	MOTHERWELL	1-1	1-3	15000	Keane
13	14	Dundee	2-0	2-0	10000	Connell, Maxwell
14	21	St. Johnstone	2-0	3-0	4000	Maxwell(3)
15	28	RANGERS	0-2	1-3	16000	Maxwell
16	4 Nov	Aberdeen	0-1	0-2	12000	
17	11	HAMILTON A.	1-0	1-1	6000	Maxwell
18	18	Queens Park	2-0	4-3	6000	Keane, Kennedy, Maxwell, O.G.
19	25	Queen of the South	1-1	1-4	9000	Keane
20	2 Dec	HEARTS	0-2	2-5	8000	Maxwell, Williamson
21	9	Clyde	0-0	1-0	4000	Maxwell
22	16	FALKIRK	0-0	1-1	6000	McEwan
23	23	Cowdenbeath	1-0	1-0	1500	Maxwell
24	30	PARTICK THISTLE	0-0	2-0	7000	Maxwell, Williamson
25	1 Jan	St. Mirren	0-3	1-3	15000	Kennedy
26	2	AYR UNITED	3-1	4-2	12000	Maxwell(2), Keane, Kennedy
27	6	Celtic	0-2	1-4	4000	Landsborough
28	13	HIBERNIAN	0-0	2-0	5000	Landsborough, Maxwell
29	27	Airdrieonians	1-1	1-3	2000	Williamson
30	17 Feb	CLYDE	2-2	2-2	5000	Maxwell(2)
31	24	Motherwell	0-2	0-2	5000	
32	3 Mar	DUNDEE	0-2	1-3	4000	Maxwell
33	10	ST. JOHNSTONE	1-0	1-0	2500	Liddell
34	17	Rangers	0-1	2-2	6000	Keane, Williamson
35	31	QUEEN OF THE SOUTH	0-0	3-0	7000	Keane(2), Maxwell
36	7 Apr	Hearts	1-0	1-1	3500	Keane
37	18	QUEENS PARK	0-1	3-1	3000	Kennedy, Maxwell, Williamson
38	28	Falkirk	1-1	2-2	2000	Maxwell(2)

Pos	P.	W.	D.	L.	F.	A.	Pts.
7th	38	17	9	12	73	64	43

Appearances and Goals by player:

	Miller	Leslie	Milloy	Glass	Smith	McEwan	Liddell	Williamson	Maxwell	Beattie	Keane	Kennedy	Morton	Landsborough	Kelvin	MacDonald	Connell	Kenmuir	Ross	Anderson	Gilmour	Bradley
Appo.	37	3	38	10	34	36	27	34	36	2	37	23	22	13	20	3	15	2	3	12	2	1
Goals				1		2	7	7	33		13	4		2	1		2					

Scottish Cup

No.	Date	Opposition	H.T.	Res.	Att.	Goalscorers
1	20 Jan	Airdrieonians	0-1	1-1	7245	Keane
1R	24	AIRDRIEONIANS	3-1	3-2	6969	Landsborough, Maxwell, McEwan
2	3 Feb	Albion Rovers	0-0	1-2	11665	Williamson

Back row (l-r): J. Glass, T. Smith, H. Morton, J. Miller, F. Milloy, J. McEwan.
Front row (l-r): W. Liddle, J. Williamson, J. Maxwell, W. Kennedy, J. Keane.

SEASON 1934-35 — Division One

No.	Date	Opposition	H.T.	Res.	Att.	Goalscorers	Miller	Anderson	Milloy	Morton	Kelvin	McEwan	Lidell	A.Robertson	J.Robertson	Beattie	Keane	Ross	Kennedy	McCarthy	Glass	Brown	Smith	Williamson	Black	Gilmour	Leslie	Kenmuir	Landsborough	Fyfe	Thomson	Cook	Meechan
1	11 Aug	Celtic	1-1	1-4	15000	O.G.	1	2	3	4	5	6	7	8	9	10	11																
2	18	HIBERNIAN	0-1	0-1	5000		1	2	3	4	5		7			10	11	6	8	9													
3	22	St. Johnstone	1-0	1-2	4000	J.Robertson	1	2	3		5		7		9	10	11	6	8		4												
4	25	Airdrieonians	1-2	2-3	4000	Williamson(2)		2	3	4		6	7			10						1	5	8	9	11							
5	1 Sep	AYR UNITED	3-2	6-3	8000	Keane(2), J.Robertson(2), Beattie, Williamson	1	2	3		4				9	10	11	6					5	8	7								
6	4	RANGERS	0-1	1-3	13000	J.Robertson	1	2	3		4				9	10	11	6					5	8	7								
7	8	St. Mirren	2-0	2-0	5000	Beattie, J.Robertson	1		3		4				9	10	11	6					5	8	7		2						
8	15	FALKIRK	2-0	4-1	5000	J.Robertson(3), Black	1		3		4				9	10	11	6					5	8	7		2						
9	22	Motherwell	1-2	2-3	1500	J.Robertson, Williamson	1		3		4				9	10	11	6					5	8	7		2						
10	24	Aberdeen	1-0	3-1	9000	Keane(2), Black	1		3		4				9	10	11	6					5	8	7		2						
11	29	PARTICK THISTLE	1-0	2-0	6000	Keane, J.Robertson	1		3		4				9	10	11	6					5	8	7		2						
12	6 Oct	Dunfermline	2-1	2-2	3000	Black(2)	1		3		4				9	10	11	6					5	8	7		2						
13	13	DUNDEE	0-0	2-1	6000	Beattie, J.Robertson	1		3		4				9	10	11	6					5	8	7		2						
14	20	ABERDEEN	1-1	1-3	6000	Beattie	1		3		4				9	10	11	6					5	8	7		2						
15	27	Hamilton A.	0-3	2-4	5000	Beattie, Keane	1		3		4				9	10	11	6					5	8	7		2						
16	3 Nov	QUEENS PARK	2-0	5-0	6000	Beattie(3), J.Robertson, Williamson	1		3		4				9	10	11	6					5	8	7		2						
17	10	QUEEN OF THE SOUTH	1-0	3-1	6000	Black, Keane, O.G.	1		3		4				9		11	6	10				5	8	7		2						
18	17	Hearts	2-0	2-2	18000	J.Robertson(2)	1		3		4				9	10	11						5	8	7		2	6					
19	24	CLYDE	0-0	2-0	7000	Black, Keane	1		3		4				9	10	11	6					5	8	7		2						
20	1 Dec	Albion Rovers	0-0	0-0	5000		1		3		4				9	10	11	6					5	8	7		2						
21	8	ST. JOHNSTONE	0-0	1-0	4000	Williamson	1		3		4				9	10	11						5	8	7		2	6					
22	15	Rangers	2-1	3-2	12000	Black, Keane, Williamson	1		3		4				9	10	11						5	8	7		2	6					
23	22	CELTIC	1-2	2-3	15000	Beattie, J.Robertson	1		3		4				9	10	11						5	8	7		2	6					
24	29	Hibernian	0-0	0-0	9000		1		3		4		7		9		11						5	10			2	6	8				
25	1 Jan	ST. MIRREN	1-2	1-4	4000	Kenmuir	1				5		4		9		11	6	8					10	7		2		3				
26	2	Ayr United	1-1	1-2	12000	Landsborough	1	2	3		4				9	10	11	6					5		7				8				
27	5	AIRDRIEONIANS	0-0	0-0	5000		1	2	3		4				9	10	11	6					5							8	7	10	
28	12	Falkirk	1-3	2-5	6000	Beattie, J.Robertson	1	2	3		4				9	10	11	6					5	8							7		
29	19	MOTHERWELL	1-1	3-3	8000	Keane(2), J.Robertson	1		3		4				9	10	11	6					5	8	7		2						
30	2 Feb	Partick Thistle	1-2	2-4	8000	Keane, J.Robertson	1	2	3		4				9	10	11	6					5	8							7		
31	16	DUNFERMLINE	0-3	1-3	3000	J.Robertson	1		3		4		7			10	11	6					5	8			2						9
32	23	Queens Park	2-0	4-1	4000	Beattie(2), Williamson(2)	1		3		4					10	11	6					5	8	9		2				7		
33	2 Mar	Dundee	1-0	2-0	4000	Leslie, O.G.	1		3		4					10	11						5	8	9		2	6			7		
34	9	Clyde	1-0	1-1	4000	Beattie	1		3		4					10	11						5	8	9		2	6			7		
35	16	HAMILTON A.	3-0	4-1	5000	J.Robertson(2), Williamson, Beattie	1	2	3		4				9	10	11	6					5	8							7		
36	30	Queen of the South	0-0	1-0	7000	Williamson	1	2	3		4				9	10	11	6					5	8							7		
37	13 Apr	HEARTS	1-2	3-3	4000	J.Robertson(2), Beattie	1	2	3		4				9	10	11	6					5	8							7		
38	27	ALBION ROVERS	2-1	2-1	2000	Beattie, Williamson		2	3		4					10	11	6				1	5	8	9						7		
Apps.							36	14	37	3	38	2	6	1	34	32	37	29	4	1	1	2	34	31	26	1	24	9	3	1	10	1	1
Goals															23	16	12							12	7		1	1	1				

Pos	P	W	D	L	F	A	Pts
9th	38	16	6	16	76	68	38

Scottish Cup

No.	Date	Opposition	H.T.	Res.	Att.	Goalscorers	Miller	Anderson	Milloy	Morton	Kelvin	McEwan	Lidell	A.Robertson	J.Robertson	Beattie	Keane	Ross	Kennedy	McCarthy	Glass	Brown	Smith	Williamson	Black	Gilmour	Leslie
1	26 Jan	Galston	0-0	1-0	4211	Black	1		3		4				9	10	11	6					5	8	7		2
2	9 Feb	Hearts	0-1	0-2	36863		1		3		4				9	10	11	6					5	8	7		2

John Keane
who scored the winner in
the historic victory at Ibrox.

SEASON 1935-36 Division One

No.	Date	Opposition	H.T.	Res.	Att.	Goalscorers	Miller	Leslie	Milloy	Morton	Smith	Kenmuir	Thomson	Williamson	Robertson	Beattie	Keane	Brown	Ross	Clark	Milliken	Black	McClure	Roberts	Alexander	"Russell"	Fyfe	Gallacher
1	10 Aug	MOTHERWELL	2-0	2-3	9000	Robertson, Williamson	1	2	3	4	5	6	7	8	9	10	11											
2	17	Third Lanark	0-0	2-3	8000	Robertson, Thomson		2	3		5	4	7	8	9	10	11	1	6									
3	24	AIRDRIEONIANS	0-0	2-2	6000	Robertson, Williamson	1	2	3		5	4	7	8	9	10	11		6									
4	28	Queen of the South	1-2	1-2	9500	Beattie	1	2	3	4	5		7	8	9	10	11		6									
5	31	Ayr United	1-1	3-1	17500	Clark, Robertson, Thomson	1	2	3	4	5		7	8	11	10			6	9								
6	7 Sep	DUNFERMLINE	0-1	1-2	6000	Thomson	1	2	3	4	5		7	8	10	11			6	9								
7	14	Partick Thistle	0-1	0-2	7000		1	2	3	4	5		7		8	10	11		6	9								
8	18	ST. JOHNSTONE	2-1	4-1	4000	Beattie, Keane, Ross, Williamson	1	2	3		5		7	8	9	10	11		6		4							
9	21	ARBROATH	3-0	5-0	5000	Beattie(3), Milloy, Williamson	1	2	3		5		7	8	9	10	11		6		4							
10	28	Hibernian	0-1	1-3	5000	Beattie	1	2	3		5		7	8	9	10	11		6		4							
11	5 Oct	CELTIC	0-0	1-1	15000	Robertson	1	2	3		5		7	8	9	10	11		6		4							
12	12	Dundee	0-0	0-0	5500		1	2	3	11	5			8	9	10			6		4		7					
13	19	Hamilton A.	1-0	2-3	3000	Milloy, Williamson	1	2	3				7	8	9	10			6		4		5	11				
14	26	ABERDEEN	1-4	2-5	6000	Beattie, Robertson	1	2	3				7	8	9	10			6				5	11				
15	2 Nov	Albion Rovers	1-1	3-2	4000	Beattie, Robertson, Ross	1	2	3		5		7	8	9	10			6		4			11				
16	9	HEARTS	0-0	2-0	6000	Robertson, Thomson	1	2	3		5		7	8	9	10			6		4			11				
17	16	QUEENS PARK	1-1	1-1	7000	Robertson		2	3		5		7	8	9	10			6		4			11		1		
18	23	Clyde	0-0	0-1	5000		1	2	3		5		7	8	9	10			6		4			11				
19	30	Rangers	1-0	1-2	8000	Thomson	1	2	3		5		7	8	9	10			6		4			11				
20	7 Dec	QUEEN OF THE SOUTH	2-1	4-2	5000	Beattie(2), Robertson(2)	1	2	3		5		7	8	9	10			6		4			11				
21	14	St. Johnstone	0-0	0-0	3500		1	2	3		5		7	8	9	10			6		4			11				
22	28	THIRD LANARK	1-0	1-0	5000	Thomson	1	2	3		5		7	8	9	10			6		4			11				
23	1 Jan	Arbroath	0-0	0-0	4000		1	2	3		5		7	8	9	10			6		4			11				
24	2	AYR UNITED	3-0	7-2	17500	Robertson(4), Beattie, Roberts, Williamson	1	2	3		5		7	8	9	10			6		4			11				
25	4	Airdrieonians	2-1	4-1	3000	Beattie(2), Roberts(2)	1	2	3		5			8	9	10			6		4		7	11				
26	11	Dunfermline	0-0	1-0	4000	Robertson	1	2	3		5			8	9	10			6		4			11				
27	15 Feb	Celtic	0-1	0-4	6000		1	2	3				7	8	9	10			6				5	11	4			
28	22	PARTICK THISTLE	1-1	2-1	4000	Beattie, Thomson	1	2	3				7	8	9	10			6		4		5	11				
29	29	DUNDEE	1-1	4-1	3000	Robertson, Beattie, Williamson, Roberts	1	2	3	4			7	8	9	10			6				5	11				
30	7 Mar	HAMILTON A.	3-2	4-3	3000	Beattie(2), Roberts, Williamson	1	2	3	4			7	8	9	10			6				5	11				
31	14	Aberdeen	1-2	1-2	8000	Robertson	1	2	3	4			7	8	9	10			6				5	11				
32	21	ALBION ROVERS	2-0	2-2	4000	Roberts, Thomson	1	2	3	4			7	8		10			6	9			5	11				
33	1 Apr	Hearts	1-1	2-4	6000	Beattie(2)	1	2	3		5		7	8	9	10			6		4			11				
34	4	Motherwell	1-1	2-3	3000	Roberts, Williamson	1	2	3		5		7	8	9	10			6		4			11				1
35	8	HIBERNIAN	0-1	0-1	4000		1	2			5		7	8	9	10			6		4			11	3			
36	11	Queens Park	0-1	0-1	5000			2		6			7		9	10		1		4			5	11	3		3	8
37	25	RANGERS	0-2	0-3	7000			2	3	4			7		10			1	6				5	11				8
38	29	CLYDE	2-0	2-0	3000	Kenmuir, Williamson		2	3		5	9	7	8		10		1	6		4			11				
Apps.							33	38	32	10	31	4	30	34	30	30	9	4	30	5	20	2	11	25	2	1	6	2
Goals									2			1	8	10	18	19	1		2	1				7				

```
Pos   P.   W.   D.   L.   F.   A.   Pts.
8th   38   14   7    17   69   64   35
```

Scottish Cup

No.	Date	Opposition	H.T.	Res.	Att.	Goalscorers	Miller	Leslie	Milloy	Morton	Smith	Kenmuir	Thomson	Williamson	Robertson	Beattie	Keane	Brown	Ross	Clark	Milliken	Black	McClure	Roberts	Alexander	"Russell"	Fyfe	Gallacher
1	29 Jan	East Stirling	2-1	5-2	4000	Robertson(3), Thomson(2)	1	2	3		5		7	8	9	10			6		4			11				
2	8 Feb	Falkirk	0-1	1-1	20000	Robertson	1	2	3		5		7	8	9	10			6		4			11				
2R	12	FALKIRK	0-0	1-3*	15000	Thomson	1	2	3				7	8	9	10			6		4		5	11				

* A.E.T.

Back row (l-r): T. Smith (Captain), M. Kenmuir, J. Leslie. W. Brown, F. Milloy, S. Ross.
Front row: B. Thomson, J. Williamson, J. Robertson, R. Beattie, J. Keane.

SEASON 1936-37 Division One

No.	Date	Opposition	H.T.	Res.	Att.	Goalscorers	Miller	Leslie	Milloy	Miliken	Smith	Ross	Thomson	Williamson	Clarkson	Beattie	Roberts	J.Robertson	Alexander	G.Robertson	McClure	McAvoy	Anderson	Fyfe	Henry	Gallacher	Collins	Morton	Gillespie	Brown	Brownlie
1	8 Aug	Third Lanark	0-1	1-2	10000	Clarkson	1	2	3	4	5	6	7	8	9	10	11														
2	15	DUNDEE	1-0	1-1	7000	Beattie	1	2	3	4	5	6	7		9	10	11	8													
3	19	THIRD LANARK	0-2	0-3	4500		1	2	3	4	5	6	7	8	9	10	11														
4	22	Dunfermline	3-0	5-0	5500	Clarkson(2), Thomson(2), Williamson	1	2	3		5		7	8	9	10	11		4	6											
5	29	PARTICK THISTLE	1-0	1-0	6000	Clarkson	1	2	3		5	6	7	8	9	10	11		4												
6	5 Sep	Celtic	0-0	4-2	8000	Beattie, J.Robertson, Thomson, Williamson	1	2	3		5	6	7	8		10	11	9	4												
7	9	Dundee	1-2	2-2	6000	Roberts(2)	1	2	3			6	7	8		10	11	9	4	5											
8	12	HIBERNIAN	3-1	3-2	5000	Thomson(2), Beattie	1	2	3			6	7		9	10	11	8	4	5											
9	19	St. Mirren	0-1	2-3	8000	Clarkson, J.Robertson	1	2	3			6	7		9	10	11	8	4	5											
10	26	ARBROATH	2-0	2-0	5000	Beattie, Clarkson	1	2	3			6	7	8	9	10	11		4	5											
11	3 Oct	Motherwell	0-1	1-2	6000	Williamson	1	2	3			6	7	8	9	10	11		4	5											
12	10	FALKIRK	2-1	3-2	6000	Beattie, Roberts, Williamson	1	2	3		5	6	7	8	9	10	11		4												
13	17	ALBION ROVERS	2-1	3-1	4000	Roberts(2), Ross	1	2	3		5	6	7	8	9	10	11		4												
14	24	Hearts	0-2	0-5	9000		1	2	3		5	6	7	8	9	10			4		11										
15	31	Queens Park	1-1	1-2	5000	Thomson	1		3		5	6	7	8	9	10		11	4				2								
16	7 Nov	CLYDE	2-1	3-1	4000	Williamson(2), Roberts	1		3			6	7	8		10	11	9	4	5			2								
17	14	RANGERS	1-2	1-2	15000	J.Robertson	1		3			6	7	8		10	11	9	4	5			2								
18	21	Queen of the South	0-1	0-1	5000		1		3		5	6	7	8		10	11	9	4				2								
19	28	ST. JOHNSTONE	2-1	4-2	4000	J.Robertson(3), Beattie	1				5	6	7	8		10	11	9	4				2	3							
20	5 Dec	HAMILTON A.	2-1	2-2	3000	Beattie, Thomson	1				5	6	7			10	11	9	4				2	3	8						
21	12	Aberdeen	0-2	0-2	14000		1		3			6	7	8		10	11	9	4	5			2								
22	19	DUNFERMLINE	2-0	3-3	3000	Henry(2), J.Robertson	1		3			6	7			10	11	9	4	5			2		8						
23	26	Partick Thistle	0-3	0-4	8000		1		3				7			10	11	9		6	5		2		8	4					
24	1 Jan	ST. MIRREN	1-1	2-1	15000	Ross, O.G.	1		3				7	8		10	11	9		6	5		2			4					
25	2	Falkirk	0-2	0-5	10000		1		3				7			10	11	9		6	5		2			4	8				
26	9	CELTIC	2-1	3-3	12000	Beattie, Collins, J.Robertson	1		3				7			10	11	9		6	5		2			4	8				
27	16	Hibernian	0-0	0-0	5000		1		3				7			10	11	9		6	5		2			4	8				
28	23	MOTHERWELL	0-0	0-1	7000		1		3				7			10	11			6	5		2			4	8		9		
29	6 Feb	Arbroath	0-0	0-0	2000		1	2					7	8	9	10	11			6	5			3		4					
30	20	Albion Rovers	3-0	3-1		Roberts, J.Robertson, Thomson	1		3			6	7	8		10	11	9		4	5		2								
31	27	Rangers	0-3	0-8	10000		1		3			6	7	8		10	11	9		4	5		2								
32	6 Mar	HEARTS	1-0	3-0	8000	J.Robertson, Ross, Thomson			3			6	7			10		9		4	5		2				8			1	11
33	20	Clyde	0-2	0-2	5000				3			6	7			10		9		4	5		2				8			1	11
34	3 Apr	QUEEN OF THE SOUTH	1-0	1-0	3500	Thomson			3			6	7			10	11	9		4	5		2				8			1	
35	10	St. Johnstone	0-1	3-1	3000	Collins, Roberts, J.Robertson			3			6	7			10	11	9		4	5		2				8			1	
36	16	Hamilton A.	1-0	2-2	2000	Thomson, J.Robertson			3			6	7			10	11	9		4	5		2				8			1	
37	23	QUEENS PARK	0-0	0-0					3			6	7							4	5	10	2				8	11	9	1	
38	29	ABERDEEN	1-1	1-2	3000	Collins		2	3			6	7			10	11			4	5						8		9	1	
				Apps.			31	28	23	3	13	35	38	21	14	37	34	26	5	32	25	1	18	2	3	5	11	1	3	7	2
				Goals								3	11	6	6	8	8	12							2		3				

Pos P. W. D. L. F. A. Pts.
11th 38 14 9 15 60 70 37

Scottish Cup

No.	Date	Opposition	H.T.	Res.	Att.	Goalscorers	Miller	Milloy	Thomson	Williamson	Clarkson	Beattie	Roberts	G.Robertson	McClure	Anderson	Gallacher
1	30 Jan	BRECHIN CITY	0-2	1-2	2727	Roberts	1	3	7	8	9	10	11	6	5	2	4

George Robertson.

Later capped for Scotland, he made his debut against Dunfermline in August this season.

SEASON 1937-38   Division One

No.	Date	Opposition	H.T.	Res.	Att.	Goalscorers	Brown	Leslie	Milloy	G.Robertson	McClure	Ross	Thomson	Collins	McGowan	Beattie	Howie	Stewart	J.Robertson	McAvoy	Anderson	Fyfe	Gallacher	Roberts	Hunter	Henry	Gillespie	Marsh	Milliken	Turnbull	Reid	McGrogan	Borthwick	Gillan	McIntyre
1	14 Aug	AYR UNITED	2-1	2-1	10000	Collins, McGowan	1	2	3	4	5	6	7	8	9	10	11																		
2	21	Partick Thistle	0-2	0-3	10000		1	2	3	4	5	6	7	8	9	10	11																		
3	25	Ayr United	1-4	2-4	12000	McGowan, J.Robertson	1	2	3	4		6	7	8	9	10		5	11																
4	28	CELTIC	0-0	2-1	19000	McGowan, Leslie	1	2	3	4	5	6	7	8	9	10			11																
5	4 Sep	Hibernian	0-0	1-1	12000	McGowan	1	2	3	4	5	6	7	8	9	10			11																
6	11	ST. MIRREN	0-1	0-3	10000		1	2	3	4	5	6	7	8	9	10			11																
7	15	PARTICK THISTLE	0-1	1-3	3500	McGowan	1	2	3	4	5	6	7	10	9	8			11																
8	18	St. Johnstone	1-4	2-6	4000	Collins, Thomson	1			4	5	6	7	10	9	8			11	2	3														
9	25	MOTHERWELL	0-1	0-2	4000		1		3	4	5	6	7	10		8				9	11	2													
10	2 Oct	Dundee	2-0	2-1	6000	McGowan, Ross	1	2	3	4	5	8	7	10	9							11	6												
11	9	THIRD LANARK	2-2	4-2	4000	McGowan(2), Collins, Gallacher	1	2	3	4	5	8	7	10	9							11	6												
12	16	Falkirk	2-2	2-2	7500	Collins, Ross	1	2	3	4	5	8	7	10	9							11	6												
13	23	QUEENS PARK	0-1	1-3	4000	Ross	1	2	3	4	5	8	7	10	9							11	6												
14	30	Clyde	1-1	2-2	4000	Thomson(2)	1	2	3	4	5	8	7	10						9			6	11											
15	6 Nov	Rangers	0-3	1-4	10000	Henry		2	3	4	5	8	7							9			6		1	11	10								
16	13	QUEEN OF THE SOUTH	1-0	1-1	5000	Ross			3	4	5	8	7							6	9	2					11	1	10						
17	20	Arbroath	0-1	1-2	3500	Roberts		2	8		5	6	7	10						9	3	4		11				1							
18	27	Hamilton A.	1-3	2-4	3500	Gillespie, Thomson		2		4		6	7	8				5		10	3			11			9	1							
19	4 Dec	ABERDEEN	3-0	3-3	6000	Collins, McAvoy, Thomson		2		4		6	7	8				5		10	3			11			9	1							
20	11	Morton	1-2	2-4	3000	Gillespie, Collins		2		4		6	7	8				5		10	3			11			9	1							
21	25	Celtic	0-6	0-8	6000				3	4		6	7	8				5		10				11				9	1	2					
22	29	HIBERNIAN	0-1	0-3	5000				3	4	5	6	7	8						10		2		11				1	9						
23	1 Jan	St. Mirren	0-0	2-0	10000	Collins(2)			3	4	5	6	7	9						10		2			1						8	11			
24	3	FALKIRK	1-1	2-2	10000	Collins, McAvoy			3	4	5	6	7	9						10		2			1						8	11			
25	8	ST. JOHNSTONE	1-1	2-2	10000	Thomson, McAvoy			3	4	5	6	7	9						10		2			1						8	11			
26	15	Motherwell	1-2	3-4	4000	Collins, McGrogan, Thomson			3		5	6	7	9						10		2			1					4	8	11			
27	29	DUNDEE	1-0	3-1	4000	McGrogan, Ross, Thomson			3	4	5	6	7	9						10		2			1						8	11			
28	5 Feb	Third Lanark	2-0	4-2	5000	Thomson(2), Collins, G.Robertson			3	4		6	7	9				5		10		2			1						8	11			
29	12	HEARTS	1-1	3-1	12000	Collins, McAvoy, Reid			3	4		6	7	9				5		10		2			1						8	11			
30	19	Queens Park	0-0	1-1	10000	Reid			3	4		6	7	9				5		10		2			1						8	11			
31	26	CLYDE	1-0	2-1	10000	Reid, McGrogan			3	4		6	7	9				5		10		2			1						8	11			
32	12 Mar	RANGERS	0-1	2-1	21000	McGrogan, Thomson			3	4		6	7	9				5		10		2			1						8	11			
33	26	ARBROATH	1-0	2-1	7000	Collins, McGrogan			3	4		6	7	9				5		10		2			1						8	11			
34	9 Apr	Aberdeen	1-2	1-2	10000	Thomson			3	4		6	7	9				5		10		2			1						8	11			
35	13	HAMILTON A.	1-1	2-2		McAvoy, McGrogan			3	4	5	6	7	9						10		2			1						8	11			
36	16	Queen of the South	0-2	1-0	8500	Collins			3		5	6	7	9						10		2			1					4	8	11			
37	29	MORTON	1-0	3-0	8000	Gallacher, Henry, Gillespie			3	4		6						5				2	8			10	9					7	11		1
38	30	Hearts	1-2	1-5	14000	Gillespie			3	4		6	7									2				10	9					5	11	8	1
Apps.							14	14	38	38	25	38	36	34	12	9	2	11	11	20	4	21	10	12	16	4	6	7	2	2	14	12	2	1	2
Goals								1		1		5	12	14	8				1	5			2	1		2	4				3	6			

Pos   P.   W.   D.   L.   F.   A.   Pts.
18th 38   12   9   17   65   91   33

Scottish Cup

No.	Date	Opposition	H.T.	Res.	Att.	Goalscorers	Milloy	G.Robertson	Ross	Thomson	Collins	Stewart	McAvoy	Fyfe	Hunter	Reid	McGrogan
1	22 Jan	DUMBARTON	2-0	6-0	9000	McAvoy, Reid(2), Fyfe, Thomson(2)	3	4	6	7	9		10	2	1	8	11
2	12 Feb	BYE															
3	5 Mar	Celtic	2-0	2-1	39839	Collins, McGrogan	3	4	6	7	9	5	10	2	1	8	11
QF	19	AYR UNITED	1-0	1-1	27442	Thomson	3	4	6	7	9	5	10	2	1	8	11
QFR	23	Ayr United	1-0	5-0	23785	Thomson(2), Collins, McAvoy, McGrogan	3	4	6	7	9	5	10	2	1	8	11
SF	2 Apr	Rangers*	1-1	4-3	70833	Collins(2), Thomson(2)	3	4	6	7	9	5	10	2	1	8	11
F	23	East Fife*	1-1	1-1	80091	McAvoy	3	4	6	7	9	5	10	2	1	8	11
FR	27	East Fife*	2-1	2-4#	92716	McGrogan, Thomson	3	4	6	7	9	5	10	2	1	8	11

* Hampden   # After Extra Time

Scottish Cup Finalists
Back row: J.A. Herries, N.D. Robinson, A. Fyfe, J. Hunter, F. Milloy, J. Henderson (Chairman), T. Wylie.
Middle row: J. McGrory (Manager), B. Thomson, G. Reid, A. Collins, D. McAvoy, F. McGrogan, J. McWhinnie (Trainer).
Front row: G. Robertson, J. Stewart, S. Ross.

No.	Date	Opposition	H.T.	Res.	Att.	Goalscorers	Hunter	Fyfe	Milloy	G.Robertson	Stewart	Ross	Thomson	Reid	Collins	McAvoy	Borthwick	Drysdale	Turnbull	McGrogan	Harvey	Gallacher	Henry	Davidson	Wyllie	Cahill
1	13 Aug	Celtic	1-3	1-9	15000	McAvoy	1	2	3	4	5	6	7	8	9	10	11									
2	20	HIBERNIAN	0-0	0-1	8000		1		3	4	5	6	7	8	9	10	11	2								
3	24	CELTIC	0-0	0-0	20000		1	2	3		5	6	7	8		10			4	9	11					
4	27	Motherwell	1-2	2-5	8000	Turnbull(2)	1	2	3		5	6	7	8		10	11		4	9						
5	3 Sep	ST. JOHNSTONE	1-0	1-0	8000	McGrogan	1	2	3			6	7	8		10		5	4	9	11					
6	10	St. Mirren	0-0	1-0	7000	Turnbull	1	2	3		5			8		10			4	9	11		7			
7	14	Hibernian	1-0	1-0	8000	Reid	1		3		5	6		8	9	10		2	4		11		7			
8	17	ARBROATH	0-0	0-0	3000	McAvoy	1		3		5	6		8	9	10		2	4		11		7			
9	24	Third Lanark	3-1	3-3	7000	Harvey, Henry, Reid	1	2	3		5	6	7	8					4	9	11		10			
10	1 Oct	PARTICK THISTLE	2-1	4-2	7000	Borthwick, Drysdale, Henry, McGrogan	1		3		5			8	9		11	4			7	6	10	2		
11	8	Ayr United	1-1	2-2	12000	Collins, Drysdale	1	2	3		5		7	8	9			4			11	6	10			
12	15	FALKIRK	1-0	1-1	7000	Henry	1	2	3		5			8	9		11	4			7	6	10			
13	22	RANGERS	1-0	3-1	18000	McGrogan, Reid, Thomson	1	2	3		5		7	8		10		4			11	6			9	
14	29	Queen of the South	0-2	0-2	7700		1	2	3		5		7	8	9	10		4			11	6				
15	5 Nov	RAITH ROVERS	3-2	4-2	7000	Collins, McAvoy, Reid, Thomson	1	2	3		5		7	8	9	10		4			11	6				
16	12	HAMILTON A.	2-0	2-2	5500	Ross, Thomson	1	2	3		5	9	7	8		10		4			11	6				
17	19	Aberdeen	1-0	2-1	12000	McGrogan, Thomson	1		3		5	9	7	8		10		4	2		11	6				
18	26	ALBION ROVERS	1-1	4-2	6000	Ross(2), McAvoy, Reid	1		3		5	9	7	8		10		4	2		11	6				
19	3 Dec	Hearts	1-1	1-2	16000	Thomson	1		3		5	9	7	8		10		4	2		11	6				
20	10	Queens Park	2-0	5-1	8000	Ross(3), Thomson(2)	1		3		5	9	7	8		10		4	2		11	6				
21	17	CLYDE	1-2	1-4	5000	Reid	1		3		5	9	7	8		10		4	2		11	6				
22	28	MOTHERWELL	0-1	1-3	3000	McAvoy	1	3				9	7	8		10		4	2		11	6			5	
23	31	St. Johnstone	1-1	3-1	4000	McAvoy(2), Borthwick	1	3			5	9		8		10	11	4	2			6			7	
24	2 Jan	ST. MIRREN	2-1	3-2	18000	Reid(3)	1	3			5	9	7	8		10	11	4	2			6				
25	3	Falkirk	0-1	0-4	12000		1	3			5	9	7	8	10			4	2			6				
26	7	THIRD LANARK	2-1	5-2	8000	Borthwick(2), Thomson, Milloy, Reid	1	3			5	9	7	8		10	11	4	2			6				
27	28	AYR UNITED	2-0	2-2	14500	Reid(2)	1	3		4	9			8		10	11	5	2			6			7	
28	11 Feb	Arbroath	1-1	1-4	3500	Reid	1	3		4			7	8	9	10		5	2		11	6				
29	18	Partick Thistle	0-2	3-4	6000	Ross(2), Drysdale	1	3				9	7	8		10		4	2		11	6			5	
30	25	Rangers	2-0	2-2	10000	McGrogan(2), Ross	1	3				9		8		10		4	2		11	6			5	7
31	8 Mar	QUEEN OF THE SOUTH	1-1	1-1	2500	Ross	1	3				9		8		10		4	2		11	6			5	
32	11	Raith Rovers	2-1	3-2	5000	McGrogan(2), Ross	1	3				9		8		10		4	2		11	6			5	7
33	18	Hamilton A.	1-2	1-3	3000	Reid	1	3				9	7	8		10		4	2		11	6			5	
34	1 Apr	Albion Rovers	1-3	1-6	3000	Reid	1	3				9	7	8		10		4	2		11	6			5	
35	5	ABERDEEN	0-1	0-3	4000		1	2	3		5			8		11					7	6	10		9	4
36	8	HEARTS	3-0	4-1	6000	Collins(3), Reid	1	3			5		7	8	9	10		4	2		11	6				
37	22	QUEENS PARK	2-0	3-0	5000	McGrogan(2), Harvey	1	3			5		7	8	9	10		4	2		11	6				
38	29	Clyde	0-3	1-5	10000	Collins	1	3			5		7	8	9	10		4	2		11	6				
		Apps.					38	18	33	4	28	25	27	38	16	32	9	36	26	31	34	3	5	1	11	3
		Goals						1				10	8	17	6	7	4	3	3	9	2		3			

Pos P. W. D. L. F. A. Pts.
10th 38 15 9 14 73 86 39

Scottish Cup

No.	Date	Opposition	H.T.	Res.	Att.	Goalscorers	Hunter	Fyfe	Milloy	G.Robertson	Stewart	Ross	Thomson	Reid	Collins	McAvoy	Borthwick	Drysdale	Turnbull	McGrogan	Harvey
1	21 Jan	BERWICK RANGERS	2-0	6-1	6439	Barthwick(2), Ross(2), McAvoy, Thomson	1		3	4		9	7	8		10	11	5	2		6
2	4 Feb	Hibernian	1-0	1-3	32394	Ross	1		3	6		9	7	8		10	11	5	2		4

Looking smart in the last pre-war season.

SEASON 1939-40 — Division One

No.	Date	Opposition	H.T.	Res.	Att.	Goalscorers
1	12 Aug	MOTHERWELL	2-0	3-3	14000	Collins(2), McAvoy
2	19	St. Johnstone	2-0	3-0	3500	Collins, McAvoy, McGrogan
3	23	Motherwell	2-2	2-4	8000	McGrogan, Reid
4	26	THIRD LANARK	0-0	0-1	8000	
5	2 Sep	Arbroath	0-1	2-1	4000	Collins, Reid

Player grid (Hunter, Turnbull, Milloy, Drysdale, Stewart, Harvey, Thomson, Reid, Collins, McAvoy, McGrogan, McClure, Bell, Dornan, Wylie, Rodman, Gallacher):

Match	Hunter	Turnbull	Milloy	Drysdale	Stewart	Harvey	Thomson	Reid	Collins	McAvoy	McGrogan	McClure	Bell	Dornan	Wylie	Rodman	Gallacher
1	1	2	3	4	5	6	7	8	9	10	11						
2	1	2	3	4		6	7	8	9	10	11	5					
3	1	2	3	4		6	7	8	9	10	11	5					
4	1	2	3	4		6	7	8	9	10	11	5					
5		2		4		6		8	9		11		1	3	5	7	10
Apps.	4	5	4	5	1	5	4	5	5	4	5	3	1	1	1	1	1
Goals								2	4	2	2						

Fixtures abandoned · 2nd World War

Western League

No.	Date	Opposition	H.T.	Res.	Att.	Goalscorers
1	21 Oct	Third Lanark	1-0	2-3		Gallacher, McGrogan
2	28	DUMBARTON	2-0	5-0	3000	Collins(4), Thomson
3	4 Nov	Airdrieonians	0-2	0-3		
4	11	MOTHERWELL	1-0	1-1	3000	McGrogan
5	18	Celtic	0-0	1-1	3000	Turnbull
6	25	PARTICK THISTLE	1-1	5-2	2000	Collins(2), Reid, Gallacher(2)
7	2 Dec	Rangers	0-0	1-4	5500	Collins
8	9	MORTON	3-1	4-2	1000	Collins(3), Maxwell
9	16	Queen of the South	1-4	2-4		Collins, Turnbull
10	23	QUEENS PARK	0-0	2-1	3000	McAvoy(2)
11	30	Albion Rovers	2-1	3-2		Collins, McGrogan, Reid
12	1 Jan	St. Mirren	1-0	3-3		Collins(2), Turnbull
13	2	AYR UNITED	1-0	3-1	5000	Collins(2), Gallacher
14	6	HAMILTON A.	1-3	1-4	3000	Collins
15	13	CLYDE	1-2	1-2		Collins
16	10 Feb	Motherwell	1-0	1-2	3000	Reid
17	17	CELTIC	2-1	3-2	5500	Collins(2), Kirkpatrick
18	16 Mar	QUEEN OF THE SOUTH	0-2	1-3	4000	Maxwell
19	30	ALBION ROVERS	2-0	6-2	3000	Rodman(2), 'Newman'(2), Gallacher, Reid
20	2 Apr	THIRD LANARK	0-1	1-2	2000	Gillespie
21	6	ST. MIRREN	0-1	3-1	2000	Gallacher, McGrogan, Rodman
22	10	Dumbarton	1-2	2-2		Gallacher, 'Newman'
23	13	Ayr United	1-1	3-2	2500	Rodman(2), Gardiner
24	20	Hamilton A.	0-0	0-0	2500	
25	24	Partick Thistle	0-4	2-5		Gillespie, Newman
26	27	Clyde	0-1	2-1	3000	McGrogan, Rodman
27	11 May	Morton	0-0	0-2		
28	15	RANGERS	1-1	3-1		Gillespie(2), Gallacher
29	18	Queens Park	1-0	1-0		Reid
30	25	AIRDRIEONIANS	0-5	1-5	2000	McGrogan

Apps. 18, 11, 22, 26, 24, 20, 2, 23, 17, 4, 23, 12, 26, 10, 7, 1, 29, 4, 10, 1, 6, 1, 8, 5, 7, 7, 2, 1, 3

Goals 3 … 1, 5, 20, 2, 6 … 16, 8, 2, 1, 1, 4, 4

Pos	P.	W.	D.	L.	F.	A.	Pts.
8th	30	13	5	12	63	63	31

War Cup

Rnd	Date	Opposition	H.T.	Res.	Att.	Goalscorers
1	24 Feb	AYR UNITED	0-0	1-0	8631	Gallacher
1	2 Mar	Ayr United (Agg: 3-2)	0-1	2-2	9941	Collins, Thomson
2	9	ALBION ROVERS	1-0	2-1	7586	Collins, McGrogan
QF	23	Dundee United	0-2	0-3	10000	

The legendary "Bud" Maxwell, scorer of over 100 goals, came back for one final season during wartime.

Players (columns): Walsh, Turnbull, Bradford, Milloy, M.McDonald, Jenkins, Geddes, M.McLaren, Ballantyne, Johnstone, Horton, Harrison, Dornan, Harvey, McIntyre, Drury, McAvoy, King, Wilson, Davie, Cavin, Downie, J.Taylor, A.Taylor, Whyte, Burns, Shufflebottom, Sinclair, Scott, McClure, Hood, Mitchell, Stevenson, Devlin, D.McDonald, Dougan

No.	Date	Opposition	H.T.	Res.	Att.	Goalscorers
1	11 Aug	Queens Park	2-0	3-2	5000	Turnbull(2), McLaren
2	18	ABERDEEN	0-3	1-4	12000	O.G.
3	25	Morton	0-4	1-6	9000	Scott
4	1 Sep	RANGERS	0-5	0-7	17000	
5	8	Queen of the South	0-1	1-2	8000	Ballantyne
6	15	CLYDE	0-0	0-0	5000	
7	22	Hamilton A.	2-3	4-4	4000	Walsh(2), Harrison, McLaren
8	29	HEARTS	2-0	2-2	12000	Walsh, Redmond
9	6 Oct	MOTHERWELL	2-3	2-5	12000	Harrison, Walsh
10	13	HIBERNIAN	1-2	3-4	10000	McAvoy, McLaren, Walsh
11	20	Falkirk	1-1	4-3	9000	Walsh(2), Harrison, Turnbull
12	27	Partick Thistle	2-2	3-5	4000	Henry, Horton, Walsh
13	3 Nov	ST. MIRREN	5-2	6-4	15000	McIntyre(2), Ballant'e, Bradford, Turnbull, Walsh
14	10	Third Lanark	0-1	1-4	3000	McLaren
15	17	CELTIC	2-0	2-1	20000	Walsh(2)
16	24	QUEENS PARK	1-0	2-2	15000	McAvoy, McLaren
17	1 Dec	Aberdeen	0-1	0-2	14000	
18	8	MORTON	1-1	1-1	6000	Harrison
19	15	Rangers	0-3	1-5		Walsh
20	22	Clyde	0-1	0-3	6000	
21	29	HAMILTON A.	0-1	0-2	7000	
22	1 Jan	QUEEN OF THE SOUTH	1-0	1-1	10000	Walsh
23	2	Hearts	0-1	4-1	15000	Walsh(3), McLaren
24	5	Motherwell	2-1	2-2	8000	Walsh(2)
25	12	Hibernian	1-0	1-4	11000	McLaren
26	26	PARTICK THISTLE*	1-0	2-1	11000	McLaren, Walsh
27	2 Feb	St. Mirren	0-2	1-4	7000	Walsh
28	9	THIRD LANARK	0-1	1-3	9000	Davie
29	16	Celtic	1-1	1-1	20000	Walsh
30	6 Apr	FALKIRK	2-1	6-2	8000	Devlin(2), Davie, Sinclair, J.Taylor Turnbull

* Played at Somerset Park

Pos P. W. D. L. F. A. Pts.
15th 30 7 8 15 56 87 22

The following players made one League appearance each, their position ('P') in the corresponding match ('M') was as follows:
Bell (P1 M9): Cox (P6 M21): Henry (P10 M12, 1 goal): Hunter (P1 M8): Jessop (P11 M3): Loneskie (P3 M5): Marshallsay (P7 M2): Melia (P7 M6): Pattison (P7 M12): Quinn (P2 M17): Also Redmond made 2 appearances (P8 M3 & P7 M8). A total of 47 players used in League matches.

Southern League Cup

No.	Date	Opposition	H.T.	Res.	Att.	Goalscorers
1	23 Feb	ABERDEEN	0-1	1-1	16000	Turnbull
2	2 Mar	Partick Thistle	0-1	0-3	15000	
3	9	HIBERNIAN	1-0	1-0	12000	Devlin
4	16	Aberdeen	0-0	0-1	15000	
5	23	PARTICK THISTLE	1-1	2-2	12000	D.McDonald, J.Taylor
6	30	Hibernian	0-2	0-4	20000	

Pos P. W. D. L. F. A. Pts.
4th 6 1 2 3 4 11 4

Victory Cup

No.	Date	Opposition	H.T.	Res.	Att.	Goalscorers
1	20 Apr	East Fife	0-1	0-2	9000	
1	27	EAST FIFE	1-0	3-0*	9000	Devlin(2), Walsh
2	4 May	Aberdeen	1-1	1-1	15000	Walsh
2	13	ABERDEEN (Agg: 1-4)*	0-0	0-3	20000	

* After extra time, Agg: 3-2 † Player 7 was A.Collins

Bobby Ferguson was born in 1945.

Killie's custodian on that historic day at Tynecastle was the most expensive keeper in the world when he left Rugby Park to join West Ham.

SEASON 1946-47 — Division One

No.	Date	Opposition	HT	Res.	Att.	Goalscorers	Downie	Hood	Landsborough	Turnbull	McClure	McDonald	Sinclair	Reid	Walsh	Devlin	Kirkpatrick	Davie	Cavin	McAvoy	Milloy	McLeish	Collins	Bradford	Drury	Hunter	Geddes	Thyne	Stevenson	Dornan	Henry	McCulloch	Cox	Harkness
1	10 Aug	QUEENS PARK	0-1	2-2	14000	Devlin, Turnbull	1	2	3	4	5	6	7	8	9	10	11																	
2	14	Aberdeen	0-0	0-1	18000		1	2	3	4	5		7	8	9	10		6		11														
3	17	Rangers	2-1	2-3	25000	Devlin, Walsh	1	2	3	4	5			8	9	10		6	7	11														
4	21	HAMILTON A.	0-1	1-1	14000	McLeish	1	2		4	5	10		8	9		11	6				3	7											
5	24	MORTON	1-1	2-3	15000	Devlin, Turnbull	1	2		4	5	11		8		10		6				3	7	9										
6	28	Clyde	1-0	3-3	6000	Turnbull(3)	1	2	3	8				4		10		6					7	9	5	11								
7	31	FALKIRK	0-1	2-1	12000	Collins, Devlin	1	2	3	8				4		10		6					7	9	5	11								
8	4 Sep	Hibernian	0-2	0-6	20000		1	2	3	8				4	9			6					7		5	11				10				
9	7	QUEEN OF THE SOUTH	0-0	1-3	10000	Turnbull		2	3	8				4			11	6		10			7	9	5		1							
10	14	Hearts	0-0	0-2	25000		1	2	3	8							11	6		10			7	9	5		4							
11	2 Nov	PARTICK THISTLE	3-0	3-1	15000	McAvoy(2), O.G.	1	2	3	6				8	9	4	11			10								5	7					
12	9	St. Mirren	0-0	1-3	10000	McAvoy	1		2	6				8	9	4	11			10	3							5	7					
13	16	Motherwell	1-0	1-2	8000	Collins	1	2	3					8		4	11	6		10			9					5	7					
14	23	THIRD LANARK	0-0	0-2	8000		1		3					8		4	11	6		10			9					5	7	2				
15	30	Celtic	0-3	2-4	15000	Collins(2)	1		3	8						4	11	6		10			9					5	7	2				
16	7 Dec	Queens Park	0-0	1-0	8000	Kirkpatrick	1		3	4					9	10	11	6					8					5	7	2				
17	14	ABERDEEN	1-0	2-1	10000	Stevenson(2)	1		3	4					9	8		6		11								5	7	2	10			
18	21	Hamilton	1-1	2-2	3500	Stevenson, Walsh	1		3	4					9		11	6		10						2		5	7		8			
19	28	CLYDE	1-1	2-2	15000	Henry(2)	1	2	3	4					9	10	11	6										5	7		8			
20	1 Jan	Queen of the South	1-1	2-2	14500	Walsh	1	2	3					8	9	4	11	6		10								5	7					
21	2	RANGERS	0-2	0-2	32325		1	2	3					8	9	4		6		10			11					5	7					
22	4	HEARTS	0-0	0-0	10000		1	2	3					8	9	4		6		10								5	7			11		
23	18	HIBERNIAN	1-1	3-5	15000	Henry(2), Collins	1		3	2				8		4		6					9					5	7		10			11
24	1 Feb	Falkirk	1-2	3-3	9000	Collins(2), McLeish	1		3	2				8		4		6				7	9					5			10			11
25	8	Morton	0-0	0-0	5000		1		3	2				8		4		6				7	9					5			10		11	
26	15 Mar	Third Lanark*	1-1	4-1	12000	Collins(2), Drury, Reid	1		3	2				8		4		6		10		7	9		11			5						
27	22	MOTHERWELL	1-0	2-0	16000	Drury, McAvoy	1		3	2				8		4		6		10		7	9		11			5						
28	29	CELTIC	0-2	1-2	12000	McLeish	1	2	3	4				8				6		10		7	9		11			5						
29	5 Apr	ST. MIRREN	1-2	1-5	8000	Devlin	1	2	3	4						8		6		10			9		11			5	7					
30	12	Partick Thistle	2-1	2-5	15000	Turnbull, McAvoy			3	2				8	9	4		6		10								5	7		8			
Apps.							28	21	23	27	5	8	2	17	13	27	12	25	1	17	3	12	19	5	9	2	3	20	15	4	8	1	1	2
Goals										7				1	3	5	1			5		3	9		2				3		4			

* at Hampden

Pos	P.	W.	D.	L.	F.	A.	Pts.
15th	30	6	9	15	44	66	21

Pos	P.	W.	D.	L.	F.	A.	Pts.
3rd	6	3	0	3	12	11	6

League Cup Section AA

No.	Date	Opposition	HT	Res.	Att.	Goalscorers	Downie	Hood	Landsborough	Turnbull	McClure	McDonald	Sinclair	Reid	Walsh	Devlin	Kirkpatrick	Davie	Cavin	McAvoy	Milloy	McLeish	Collins	Bradford	Drury	Hunter	Geddes	Thyne	Stevenson	Dornan	Henry	McCulloch	Cox	Harkness
1	21 Sep	PARTICK THISTLE	3-1	3-2	12000	Collins, Kirkpatrick, McAvoy	1	2	3	7				8		4	11	6		10			9		5									
2	28	Hearts	1-1	1-3	25757	McAvoy	1	2	3	7				8		4	11	6		10			9		5									
3	5 Oct	Clyde	0-1	2-3	12000	Walsh, O.G.	1	2	3	7	5			8	9	4	11	6		10														
4	12	Partick Thistle	0-0	3-1	15000	McAvoy(3)	1	2	3	7				8		4	11	6		10			9						5					
5	19	HEARTS	1-0	2-0	20000	Collins, Reid	1	2	3	7				8		4	11	6		10			9						5					
6	26	CLYDE	1-1	1-2	20000	McAvoy	1	2	3	7				8		4	11	6		10			9						5					

Scottish Cup

No.	Date	Opposition	HT	Res.	Att.	Goalscorers	Downie	Hood	Landsborough	Turnbull	McClure	McDonald	Sinclair	Reid	Walsh	Devlin	Kirkpatrick	Davie	Cavin	McAvoy	Milloy	McLeish	Collins	Bradford	Drury	Hunter	Geddes	Thyne	Stevenson	Dornan	Henry	McCulloch	Cox	Harkness
1	25 Jan	Falkirk	0-1	0-2	12522		1		3	2						4		6		10			9					5	7		8			11

Dougie McAvoy.
One of the few experienced pre-war players
available in this relegation season.

Division Two — Match Details

No.	Date	Opposition	H.T.	Res.	Att.	Goalscorers
1	13 Aug	St. Johnstone	1-1	2-2	6000	Collins, Cox
2	27	RAITH ROVERS	3-0	7-1	8655	Collins(3), Walsh(3), Turnbull
3	20 Sep	Ayr United	3-2	3-2	12000	Drury(2), Turnbull
4	27	DUNDEE UNITED	1-1	5-2	7870	Collins(3), Walsh(2)
5	4 Oct	Stenhousemuir	0-1	0-1	2300	
6	11	HAMILTON A.	2-0	3-0	9633	Collins(2), McAvoy
7	18	Leith Athletic	1-1	1-3	4000	Drury
8	25	DUNFERMLINE	3-0	3-0	8644	Devlin(2), Drury
9	1 Nov	Cowdenbeath	0-0	0-1	7000	
10	8	EAST FIFE	0-0	0-2	7337	
11	15	ARBROATH	1-0	2-1	6571	Collins(2)
12	22	Albion Rovers	1-1	1-2	6000	Collins
13	29	ALLOA ATHLETIC	2-1	5-1	5707	Collins(2), McAvoy, Stevenson, Turnbull
14	6 Dec	DUMBARTON	1-0	2-2	6080	Collins, McAvoy
15	13	Stirling Albion	0-1	1-2	6000	Turnbull
16	20	ST. JOHNSTONE	1-0	1-0	7264	Turnbull
17	27	Raith Rovers	1-0	3-4	4500	Cavin(2), Turnbull
18	1 Jan	AYR UNITED	3-2	4-4	6390	Collins, Drury, Mennie, Pattison
19	3	Dundee United	1-2	3-2	11000	Cavin, Collins, McLaren
20	10	STENHOUSEMUIR	2-1	7-2	6467	Turnbull(3), McLaren(2), Collins, Drury
21	17	Hamilton A.	1-2	1-3	3500	Drury
22	31	LEITH ATHLETIC	3-1	6-2	4609	Collins(2), Cavin, Drury, McLaren, Turnbull
23	14 Feb	Dunfermline	1-2	1-3	3000	Cavin
24	21	COWDENBEATH	0-2	1-3	5049	Turnbull
25	28	East Fife	1-0	3-1	8000	Collins, Drury(2)
26	6 Mar	Arbroath	0-3	1-5	3000	Collins
27	13	ALBION ROVERS	1-2	1-4	6011	Collins
28	20	Alloa Athletic	0-3	1-4	5000	Collins
29	26	Dumbarton	0-1	2-1	2000	Henderson, Stevenson
30	3 Apr	STIRLING ALBION	1-1	2-2	4476	Davie, Drury

Pos P. W. D. L. F. A. Pts.
6th 30 13 4 13 72 62 30

Division Two — Player Appearances

No.	Hunter	Turnbull	Hood	Devlin	Thyne	Davie	McLeish	Collins	Walsh	Cavin	Drury	Mennie	Morrison	McAvoy	Freckleton	Stevenson	McLaren	Archibald	Henderson	Cox	J.Lamont	Maxwell	Pattison	Murdoch	W.Lamont	Healy	McCulloch	White	Geddes
1	1	2	3	6	5	4		9			11			10		7				8									
2	1	2	3	4	5	6	7	8	9		11			10															
3	1	2	3	4	5	6	7	8	9	10	11																		
4	1	2	3	4	5	6	7	8	9	10	11																		
5	1	2	3	4	5	6	7	8	9	10	11																		
6	1	5	3	4		6	7	8		10	11	2		9															
7	1	5	3	4		6	7	8		10	11	2		9															
8	1	6	3	9	5		7	8			11	2	4		10														
9	1	5	3	9		6	7	8			11	2	4		10														
10	1	4	3	9	5	6	7	8			11	2		10															
11	1	4	3	6	5		7	8			11	2		9	10														
12	1	4	3	6	5			8	9		11	2			10	7													
13	1	4	3	6	5			8	9		11	2		10		7													
14	1	4	3		5	6		8	9		11	2		10		7													
15	1	4	3		5	6		8	9		10	2			7		11												
16	1	4	3		5	6		8		7		2			10		11	9											
17	1	4	3		5	6				9	7	2			10		11		8										
18		4	3		5			9		8	11	2			10						1	6	7						
19		4	3		5			9		8	11	2			10						1	6	7						
20	1	8	3		5	4	7	9			11	2			10							6							
21	1	8	3		5	4		9			11	2			10		7					6							
22	1	4	3		5	8		9		7	11	2			10							6							
23	1	4	3		5	8		9		7	11	2			10							6							
24		2	3		5	8		9		7	11	4			10							6		1					
25		4	3		5	8		9		7	11	2			10							6		1					
26			3		5	8		9			11	2	4		10							6	7	1					
27			3		5	8		9			11	2	4		10		11					6	7	1					
28	1		3		5	4		9		8	11				10							6	7		2				
29	1	4	3		5	6					10	2		9		7	11		8										
30	1		3		5	4		8			11	2			10							6	7						9
Apps	24	26	29	13	27	24	15	30	4	16	27	25	4	10	6	6	15	1	2	1	2	12	5	4	1	1			
Goals		11		2		1		24	5	5	11	1		3		2	4		1	1			1						

League Cup Section BD

Pos P. W. D. L. F. A. Pts.
3rd 6 2 2 2 12 12 6

No.	Date	Opposition	H.T.	Res.	Att.	Goalscorers
1	9 Aug	Ayr United*	1-2	2-2	13500	Stevenson, Turnbull
2	16	EAST FIFE	0-0	0-0	9606	
3	23	Stirling Albion	3-2	3-5	5535	Collins(2), McLaren
4	30	AYR UNITED	1-0	1-2	12285	Turnbull
5	6 Sep	East Fife	2-1	3-1	7000	Cavin, Collins, Drury
6	13	STIRLING ALBION	2-1	3-2	7660	Walsh(2), Drury

*Kilmarnock were numbered for the first time.

No.	Hunter	Turnbull	Hood	Devlin	Thyne	Davie	McLeish	Collins	Walsh	Cavin	Drury	Mennie	Morrison	McAvoy	Freckleton	Stevenson	McLaren	Archibald	Henderson	Cox	J.Lamont	Maxwell	Pattison	Murdoch	W.Lamont	Healy	McCulloch	White	Geddes
1	1	2	3	6	5	4			9		11			10		7													8
2	1	2	3	6	5	4			9					10		7	11	8											
3	1	8	3	4	5	6	7	9				2			10		11												
4	1	2	3	4	5	6	7		9		11			10															8
5	1	2	3	4	5	6	7	8	9	10	11																		
6	1	2	3	4	5	6	7	8	9		11			10															

Scottish Cup

No.	Date	Opposition	H.T.	Res.	Att.	Goalscorers
1	24 Jan	East Fife	0-1	0-2	12000	

Hunter	Turnbull	Hood	Thyne	Davie	Collins	Cavin	Drury	Mennie	Freckleton	Maxwell
1	8	3	5	4	9	7	11	2	10	6

B Division Supplementary Cup

No.	Date	Opposition	H.T.	Res.	Att.	Goalscorers
1	5 Jan	STIRLING ALBION	0-2	1-2	5184	McLaren

Turnbull	Hood	Thyne	Collins	Cavin	Drury	Mennie	Freckleton	McLaren	J.Lamont	Maxwell
4	3	5	8	9	11	2	10	7	1	6

Plenty of ads but no room for comment in Killie's post-war programme.

SEASON 1948-49   Division Two

No.	Date	Opposition	H.T.	Res.	Att.	Goalscorers
1	14 Aug	EAST STIRLING	3-1	3-2	12211	Brown, Clive, McLaren
2	18	Queens Park	1-1	3-2	10000	McLaren(2), Clive
3	21	AYR UNITED	0-2	1-2	13049	Drury
4	28	Arbroath	0-0	1-1	5000	Drury
5	1 Sep	HAMILTON A.	3-1	3-1	10346	Bowman, Clive, Hamill
6	4	Dundee United	0-3	1-4	8000	Hamill
7	23 Oct	Stirling Albion	0-2	1-3	4574	McLaren
8	30	DUNFERMLINE	1-0	1-2	7042	Clive
9	6 Nov	Cowdenbeath	0-1	0-1	3500	
10	13	STENHOUSEMUIR	0-0	1-0	5977	McLaren
11	20	Airdrieonians	0-1	0-5	6000	
12	27	DUMBARTON	1-1	4-2	7236	McLaren(2), Clive, Smith
13	4 Dec	ST. JOHNSTONE	2-1	3-1	9219	McLaren(3)
14	11	Raith Rovers	2-1	2-3	8000	McLaren, Aitken
15	18	ALLOA ATHLETIC	4-0	6-0	7888	Clive(3), Bowman, McLaren, McLeish
16	25	QUEENS PARK	1-0	1-1	12522	McLaren
17	1 Jan	Ayr United	1-1	1-1	13422	Clive
18	3	ARBROATH	3-0	8-0	10467	McLaren(3), Sinclair(3), Clive(2)
19	8	East Stirling	0-1	0-3	2500	
20	15	DUNDEE UNITED	2-0	3-3	6347	Hunter(2), McLaren
21	29	Hamilton A.	0-3	1-3	4000	Gordon
22	5 Feb	STIRLING ALBION	0-2	0-2	6331	
23	12	Dunfermline	0-2	2-3	5000	Clive, McCulloch
24	19	COWDENBEATH	0-0	2-2	6832	Fitzsimmons, McCulloch
25	26	Stenhousemuir	1-4	2-6	1500	Aitken, McCulloch
26	5 Mar	AIRDRIEONIANS	1-2	3-3	5657	Brown, Hunter, McLaren
27	12	Dumbarton	2-1	2-2	2500	Hunter, McLaren
28	19	St. Johnstone	0-0	0-1	4000	
29	26	RAITH ROVERS	2-0	3-1	6033	McLaren(2), Smith
30	2 Apr	Alloa Athletic	0-1	0-1	4000	

Pos	P.	W.	D.	L.	F.	A.	Pts.
11th	30	9	7	14	58	61	25

Player appearances (Division Two) — Apps / Goals

	Purdie	Mennie	Hood	Gordon	Thyne	Miller	Hunter	Hamill	Clive	Brown	McLaren	Bowman	McCulloch	Drury	Murdoch	Lamont	Smith	McMahon	Anderson	Maxwell	McLeish	Sinclair	Lambie	Aitken	McFarlane	Hamilton	Fitzsimmons	Saddington	Sherry	Boyd	Black	Archibald
Apps	10	7	28	18	23	16	13	7	22	11	29	8	8	8	4	7	19	2	1	5	6	7	5	15	14	7	9	5	5	5	2	2
Goals				1			4	2	12	2	21	2	3	2			2				1	3		2			1					

Additional League appearances: McSkimming (Position 7, Game 30) and Dalziel (Position 8, Game 9).

League Cup Section BB

	Date	Opposition	H.T.	Res.	Att.	Goalscorers
1	11 Sep	East Stirling	1-1	1-2	4000	Bowman
2	18	QUEENS PARK	1-3	3-3	9365	Clive, Lambie, McLaren
3	25	ALLOA ATHLETIC	2-1	4-3	8209	Bowman, Lambie, McLaren, Miller
4	2 Oct	EAST STIRLING	2-1	4-1	8332	Bowman, Hunter, Lambie, McLaren
5	9	Queens Park	1-0	2-2	15000	Clive, McLaren
6	16	Alloa Athletic	0-2	0-2	6000	

Pos	P.	W.	D.	L.	F.	A.	Pts.
3rd	6	2	2	2	14	13	6

Scottish Cup

	Date	Opposition	H.T.	Res.	Att.	Goalscorers
1	22 Jan	Dumbarton	1-2	2-5	10090	Hunter, McLaren

B Division Supplementary Cup

	Date	Opposition	H.T.	Res.	Att.	Goalscorers
1	25 Aug	Queens Park	1-1	2-1	7500	McLaren(2)
QF	25 Apr	ALLOA ATHLETIC	4-0	5-1	3247	McLaren(2), Lambie(2), Aitken
SF	4 May	Raith Rovers	0-1	1-5		McLaren

Brian Rodman, born this season, was a superb
defender unlucky not to have been capped.
He was on the Scotland bench at
Wembley in 1975.

SEASON 1949-50 — Division Two

No.	Date	Opposition	H.T.	Res.	Att.	Goalscorers
1	10 Sep	Albion Rovers	0-1	1-3	4000	Hardy
2	17	ARBROATH	2-0	2-2	7689	McSkimming(2)
3	24	Ayr United	1-0	1-2	16000	McLaren
4	1 Oct	DUNDEE UNITED	0-1	2-3	6383	Hardy, Paton
5	8	Morton	1-1	1-3	10000	McKay
6	15	QUEENS PARK	2-2	3-3	9043	Clive, McGill, Paton
7	22	FORFAR ATHLETIC	1-1	3-1	8167	Clive, McKay, McGill
8	5 Nov	COWDENBEATH	1-0	2-0	7690	Donaldson, Reid
9	12	Stenhousemuir	2-0	2-0	2000	Reid(2)
10	19	AIRDRIEONIANS	0-1	1-1	10354	O.G.
11	26	Dumbarton	1-0	1-0	2000	Donaldson
12	3 Dec	St. Johnstone	0-2	0-2	6000	
13	10	HAMILTON A.	1-0	2-0	9402	Johnston(2)
14	17	Alloa Athletic	0-2	3-2	1200	Johnston(2), Donaldson
15	24	ALBION ROVERS	1-0	2-1	7706	Johnston, Donaldson
16	31	Arbroath	1-0	2-1	3500	Johnston(2)
17	2 Jan	AYR UNITED	3-0	4-0	23520	Cowan(2), Johnston, Paton
18	3	Dundee United	0-1	0-3	8000	
19	7	MORTON	0-0	2-0	19245	Cowan, Donaldson
20	14	Queens Park	1-0	3-1	27205	Cowan, Donaldson, Johnston
21	21	Forfar Athletic	0-1	0-1	3600	
22	4 Feb	DUNFERMLINE	2-0	3-2	11926	Johnston(2), Middlemass
23	18	STENHOUSEMUIR	3-2	3-2	10902	Donaldson, Johnston, Paton
24	25	Airdrieonians	0-1	0-2	16000	
25	4 Mar	DUMBARTON	1-0	1-1	8689	Johnston
26	11	ST. JOHNSTONE	1-1	1-1	8521	McDowell
27	18	Hamilton A.	0-1	0-1	3000	
28	25	ALLOA ATHLETIC	1-0	3-0	5834	J.W.McGhee(2), Cowan
29	1 Apr	Cowdenbeath	2-2	2-3	4000	Davidson, Donaldson
30	29	Dunfermline	0-1	0-2	5000	

Player columns (left to right): J.Brown, Hood, Lamont, Doig, Thyne, Middlemass, Hardy, Cowan, Reid, Paton, McLaren, Black, J.McGhee, J.W.McGhee, McSkimming, Finlay, Norwood, G.Brown, Boyd, Clive, Benson, McKay, Collins, McKenzie, McGill, Donaldson, Aitken, Rae, McDowell, Johnston, Davidson, Hamilton

Pos	P	W	D	L	F	A	Pts
8th	30	14	5	11	50	43	33

Apps: 1 19 10 28 29 24 10 13 5 19 5 1 2 3 3 2 1 1 11 26 24 23 2 1 24 2 2 6 15 4 1

Goals: 1 2 5 3 4 1 2 2 2 2 2 8 1 13 1

Additional League appearance: Wyllie (Position 6, Match 25).

League Cup Section BD

Pos	P	W	D	L	F	A	Pts
4th	6	2	0	4	10	15	4

No	Date	Opposition	H.T.	Res.	Att.	Goalscorers
1	13 Aug	St. Johnstone	2-2	2-3	7000	Clive, Middlemass
2	17	QUEENS PARK	2-0	2-0	12219	Aitken, Clive
3	20	Dunfermline	0-2	1-5	8000	Middlemass
4	27	ST. JOHNSTONE	2-0	2-0	9950	McLaren, Reid
5	31	Queens Park	1-0	1-3	8000	Paton
6	3 Sep	DUNFERMLINE	1-1	2-4	8401	Middlemass, Paton

Additional League Cup appearances: Calder (Position 1, Matches 4, 5 & 6), Feeney (Position 7, Match 2).

Scottish Cup

No	Date	Opposition	H.T.	Res.	Att.	Goalscorers
1	28	STIRLING ALBION	1-1	1-1	22734	Johnston
1R	1 Feb	Stirling Albion	0-2	1-3	9400	Donaldson

B Division Supplementary Cup

No	Date	Opposition	H.T.	Res.	Att.	Goalscorers
1	12 Sep	DUNDEE UNITED	2-0	4-3	5712	McLaren(3), Finlay
QF	25 Apr	AIRDRIEONIANS	2-0	2-1	3610	Middlemass, Paton
SF	10 May	St. Johnstone	0-2	2-2	5000	Davidson, Johnston
SFR	23/8/50	ST. JOHNSTONE *	1-1	2-1+	8911	J.W.McGhee, Donaldson #

+ After extra time # Russell played at No.4 and Wilson played at No.8. * Played in season 1950-51. Final never played. Competition abandoned for 1950-51.

Team v Stirling Albion in Scottish Cup, 28th January 1950
Back row: J. Brown (Trainer), J. Hood, R. Collins, J. Benson, R. Thyne, E. Doig, J. Middlemass.
Front row: W. McKay, G. Paton, T. Johnston, S. Cowan, A. Donaldson.

SEASON 1950-51 Division Two

League matches

No.	Date	Opposition	H.T.	Res.	Att.	Goalscorers
1	9 Sep	QUEEN OF THE SOUTH	0-1	0-1	11567	
2	16	Arbroath	0-0	2-0	3000	Johnston, McKay
3	23	AYR UNITED	0-1	0-1	14306	
4	30	Dundee United	1-3	2-5	5000	Jones(2), McKay
5	7 Oct	ALBION ROVERS	2-2	3-2	8088	Jones(2), McKay
6	14	Queens Park	1-1	1-2	13000	Irving
7	21	Forfar Athletic	0-0	0-0	2400	
8	28	DUNFERMLINE	0-1	1-1	9154	Jones
9	4 Nov	Cowdenbeath	0-3	0-3	3000	
10	11	ALLOA ATHLETIC	2-2	2-2	5962	Hood, Johnston
11	18	Hamilton A.	2-0	3-2	5000	Aitken, McGhee, Menzies
12	25	DUMBARTON	0-1	1-3	7844	McGhee
13	2 Dec	ST. JOHNSTONE	0-2	2-2	7857	McKay, Menzies
14	9	Stirling Albion	0-0	0-1	9000	
15	16	STENHOUSEMUIR	0-2	1-2	4921	Bootland
16	23	Queen of the South	1-0	1-0	6500	Menzies
17	30	ARBROATH	1-1	1-1	5553	Menzies
18	1 Jan	Ayr United	0-0	0-1	14000	
19	2	DUNDEE UNITED	1-0	2-0	9705	Bootland, Thyne
20	13	QUEENS PARK	0-1	3-1	8542	Bootland, Johnston, McDonald
21	20	FORFAR ATHLETIC	1-0	1-1	6078	Menzies
22	3 Feb	Dunfermline	1-3	2-4	4000	Hood, Johnston
23	10	COWDENBEATH	1-0	4-0	4276	Hood(2), Jones, Donaldson
24	17	Alloa Athletic	0-1	4-1	3000	Borland(2), Donaldson, Hood
25	24	HAMILTON A.	1-1	1-1	7926	Doig
26	3 Mar	Dumbarton	1-1	1-2	3000	Jones
27	10	St. Johnstone	0-1	0-1	6000	
28	17	STIRLING ALBION	0-0	1-1	8382	Jones
29	24	Stenhousemuir	0-2	1-4	1000	Doig
30	7 Apr	Albion Rovers	1-1	3-1	4000	Jones(2), O.G.

Appearances (per player): Benson 29, Collins 28, Hood 13, Russell 25, Thyne 24, Middlemass 19, McKay 21, Clive 9, Menzies 11, Irving 16, Donaldson 9, Kelly 17, Johnston 4, Doig 17, Jones 15, Davidson 2, Bootland 13, McGill 5, Paton 6, Borland 17, Anderson 1, Caldwell 3, Cowan 7, Aitken 7, McGhee 3, Wilson 5, McDonald 2, Neil 1, Apsley 1

Goals (per player): Hood 5, Thyne 1, McKay 4, Menzies 5, Irving 1, Donaldson 2, Johnston 4, Doig 2, Jones 10, Bootland 3, Borland 2, Aitken 1, McGhee 2, McDonald 1

Pos	P	W	D	L	F	A	Pts
12th	30	8	8	14	44	49	24

League Cup Section BA

Pos	P	W	D	L	F	A	Pts
3rd	6	1	2	3	9	10	4

No.	Date	Opposition	H.T.	Res.	Att.	Goalscorers
1	12 Aug	DUNFERMLINE	2-1	3-1	12761	Donaldson, Johnston, McGill
2	16	Ayr United	2-2	2-2	16000	Donaldson, Thyne
3	19	Dumbarton	0-1	0-1	5500	
4	26	Dunfermline	4-2	4-5	7000	Clive(2), Donaldson, McKay
5	30	AYR UNITED	0-1	0-1	17779	
6	2 Sep	DUMBARTON	0-0	0-0	7568	

Scottish Cup

No.	Date	Opposition	H.T.	Res.	Att.	Goalscorers
1	27 Jan	East Stirling	0-1	1-2	2500	McKay

Hampshire may not be the most exciting location Killie have ever travelled to but they were happy to provide the opposition to Aldershot in a benefit match at the end of this season.

SEASON 1951-52   Division Two

No.	Date	Opposition	H.T.	Res.	Att.	Goalscorers	Niven	Collins	Hood	Stewart	Thyne	Middlemass	Donaldson	Henaughan	Mathie	Harvey	Clark	Bunten	Doig	Russell	McKay	Caldwell	Borland	Anderson	Clive	Jack	Cowan	Grant	Henderson	McLachlan	Kelly	Boyd
1	8 Sep	Clyde	2-1	3-1	12000	Donaldson(2), Harvey	1	2	3		5		7	8	9	10	11		4	6												
2	15	DUMBARTON	1-0	2-1	11652	Donaldson, Russell	1	2	3		5		7	8	9	10	11		4	6												
3	22	Ayr United	1-1	2-3	18000	Hood, Harvey	1	2	3		5		7	8	9	10	11		4	6												
4	29	ALBION ROVERS	0-0	3-1	10526	Donaldson(2), Henaughan	1	2	3		5	6	11	8	9	10			4					7								
5	6 Oct	Dunfermline	1-2	2-5	7000	O.G., Mathie	1	2	3		5	6	11	8	9	10			4					7								
6	13	STENHOUSEMUIR	0-1	0-2	9524		1	2	3	4		6	11	8	9	10					7	5										
7	20	Forfar Athletic	0-1	0-1	2500		1	2	3		5	6	11	8	9	10				4	7											
8	27	ST. JOHNSTONE	1-0	3-0	8377	Mathie(2), Borland	1	2	3		5	6	11	8	9	10				4			7									
9	3 Nov	ARBROATH	1-0	4-0	7798	Mathie(2), Henaughan, Thyne	1	2	3		5	6		8	9	10	11			4			7									
10	10	Dundee United	0-1	0-1	2200		1	2	3		5	6	11	8	9	10				4			7									
11	17	ALLOA ATHLETIC	0-0	1-0	7752	Harvey	1	2	3		5	6	11	8	9	10				4			7									
12	24	Cowdenbeath	0-3	1-3	3000	Thyne	1	2	3		5	6	11	8						4			7			10						
13	1 Dec	Queens Park	0-1	0-1	7000		1		3		5	6	11			10		8	4				7			9						
14	8	HAMILTON A.	2-1	3-2	6516	Mathie(2), Donaldson	1	2	3		5	6	11	8	9	10				4			7									
15	15	Falkirk	2-1	3-3	9000	Mathie(2), Henaughan	1	2	3		5	6	11	8	9	10				4			7									
16	22	CLYDE	0-0	1-0	14910	Donaldson	1	2	3		5	6	11	8	9	10				4			7									
17	29	Dumbarton	1-2	2-4	4000	Anderson, Harvey	1	2	3		5	6	11	8	9					4				7		10						
18	1 Jan	AYR UNITED	3-0	4-0	13756	Donaldson(2), Anderson, Harvey	1	2	3		5	6	11	8	9					4				7		10						
19	5	DUNFERMLINE	3-0	5-3	9039	Mathie(2), Clark, Harvey, Middlemass	1	2	3		5	6		8	9		11			4				7		10						
20	9	Albion Rovers	0-0	0-0	400		1		3		5	6		8	9		11			4				7		2	10					
21	12	Stenhousemuir	1-1	2-1	1500	Harvey, Thyne	1		3		5	6	11	8						4				7		2	9	10				
22	19	FORFAR ATHLETIC	1-0	3-0	9044	Cowan, Jack, Harvey	1	2	3		5	6	11	8						4				7			9	10				
23	13 Feb	Arbroath	0-1	1-2	1000	Mathie	1	2	3		5				9					6	4		8	7								
24	16	DUNDEE UNITED	2-2	2-6	10116	Henderson, Mathie	1	2	3		5	6	11		9					4				7		10			8			
25	20	St. Johnstone	1-0	2-0	1500	Anderson, Cowan	1	2	3			6	11		9						8			7			10			4		5
26	23	Alloa Athletic	1-1	2-1	3500	Cowan, Mathie	1	2	3	6			11		9				4			5		7			10				8	
27	1 Mar	COWDENBEATH	3-0	5-1	7204	Jack(2), Middlemass(2), Mathie	1	2	3		5	6	11		9					4				7		8	10					
28	8	QUEENS PARK	2-0	3-1	8936	Jack, Mathie, O.G.	1	2	3		5	6	11		9					4				7		8	10					
29	15	Hamilton A.	0-1	1-2	3000	Clark	1	2	3		5	6			9		11			4				7		8	10					
30	22	FALKIRK	1-1	2-1	11496	Anderson, Cowan	1	2			5	6	11	8	9					4				7			10					3
				Apps.			30	28	29	2	27	25	26	16	27	21	7	1	7	25	4	2	6	19	4	9	9	2	1	1	1	1
				Goals				1			3	3	9	3	16	8	2			1			1	4		4	4	1				

Pos	P.	W.	D.	L.	F.	A.	Pts.
5th	30	16	2	12	62	48	34

League Cup Section BB

Pos	P.	W.	D.	L.	F.	A.	Pts.
2nd	6	4	0	2	9	4	8

No.	Date	Opposition	H.T.	Res.	Att.	Goalscorers	Niven	Collins	Hood	Stewart	Thyne	Middlemass	Donaldson	Henaughan	Mathie	Harvey	Clark	Doig	Russell
1	11 Aug	AYR UNITED	0-0	3-0	15604	Mathie(3)	1	2	3	4	5	6	7	8	9	10	11		
2	15	Forfar Athletic	0-1	1-2	3000	Clark	1	2	3	4	5	6	7	8	9	10	11		
3	18	Dumbarton	0-1	0-1	5000		1	2	3	4	5		7	8	9	10	11	6	
4	25	Ayr United	0-1	2-1	8500	Hood, Mathie	1	2	3		5		7	8	9	10	11	4	6
5	29	FORFAR ATHLETIC	1-0	1-0	11983	Harvey	1	2	3		5		7	8	9	10	11	4	6
6	1 Sep	DUMBARTON	0-0	2-0	12173	Harvey, Mathie	1	2	3		5		7	8	9	10	11	4	6

Scottish Cup

No.	Date	Opposition	H.T.	Res.	Att.	Goalscorers	Niven	Collins	Hood	Thyne	Middlemass	Donaldson	Henaughan	Russell	Anderson	Jack	Cowan	Grant
1	26 Jan	STENHOUSEMUIR	2-0	2-0	12000	Harvey, Jack	1	2	3	5	6	11	8	4	7	9	10	
2	9 Feb	Aberdeen	1-1	1-2	11649	Harvey	1	2	3	5	6	11	8	4	7	9	10	

B Division Supplementary Cup

No.	Date	Opposition	H.T.	Res.	Att.	Goalscorers	Niven	Collins	Hood	Thyne	Middlemass	Donaldson	Harvey	Henaughan	Russell	Anderson	Jack	Boyd
1	29 Mar	FALKIRK	0-0	1-0	8961	Harvey	1	2		5	6	11	10	8	4	7	9	3
QF	12 Apr	Hamilton A.	0-0	1-0	5000	Jack	1	2	3	5	6	11	10	8	4	7	9	
SF	19	CLYDE	0-2	1-3	11256	Middlemass	1	2	3	5	6	11	10	8	4	7	9	

The year Jim McSherry, the present Commercial Manager, was born.

The first post-war testimonial, for Bob Thyne, sees Killie beat Celtic. Killie win their first cup-tie since 1939.

SEASON 1952-53 — Division Two

No.	Date	Opposition	H.T.	Res.	Att.	Goalscorers	Niven	Collins	Hood	Russell	Thyne	Middlemass	Anderson	Harvey	Mays	Jack	Murray	Clive	Kelly	Donaldson	Mathie	Henaughan	McDonald	Imrie	Stewart	Milloy	McCorkindale	Lee	Mackay	Curlett
1	6 Sep	ALLOA ATHLETIC	0-0	1-2	10683	Middlemass	1	2		4	5	6	7	8	9	10	11		3											
2	20	AYR UNITED	0-1	0-1	12204		1	2		4	5	6	7	8	9	10				3		11								
3	27	Queens Park	0-2	3-2	10000	Henaughan, Mathie, Middlemass	1	2	3	4	5	6		8	7	10					9	11								
4	11 Oct	Dunfermline	0-0	1-2	5000	Harvey	1	2	3	4	5	6		8	9	10	11					7								
5	18	MORTON	1-1	3-2	11128	Henaughan(2), Middlemass	1	2	3	4	5	6		8	9	10	11					7								
6	1 Nov	Stirling Albion	0-2	1-3	8000	Mays	1	2	3	4	5	6	11	8	9	10						7								
7	8	DUMBARTON	1-0	2-1	11160	Mays, O.G.	1	2	3	4	5	6		10	7		11					8	9							
8	15	ST. JOHNSTONE	1-1	2-3	9885	Middlemass, Thyne	1	2	3	4	5	6		10	7		11					8	9							
9	22	Hamilton A.	0-0	2-2	6000	Thyne, Mays	1	2	3		5	6		8	9	10	11								7					
10	29	STENHOUSEMUIR	2-0	4-1	7256	Jack(2), Mathie, Murray	1	2	3	6	5				7	10	11				9	8			4					
11	6 Dec	COWDENBEATH	0-0	2-0	8223	Murray, Stewart	1	2	3	6	5				7	10	11				9	8			4					
12	13	Arbroath	1-1	2-2	3200	Murray(2)	1	2	3	6	5				7	10	11				9	8			4					
13	20	Alloa Athletic	2-0	2-1	2500	Jack, Mathie	1	2	3	6	5				7	10	11				9	8			4					
14	27	DUNDEE UNITED	0-0	1-0	9192	Mathie	1	2	3	6	5				7	10	11				9	8			4					
15	1 Jan	Ayr United	0-0	2-0	18500	Mays(2)	1	2	3	6	5			8	9	10	11					7			4					
16	3	QUEENS PARK	0-1	0-1	12880		1	2	3	6	5			8	9	10	11					7			4					
17	10	Albion Rovers	1-0	1-2	1500	Mays	1	2	3	6	5			8	9	10	11					7			4					
18	17	DUNFERMLINE	2-0	2-3	8088	Mays, Thyne	1	2	3	4	5	6		7			11					9	10	8						
19	31	Morton	1-0	4-1	5000	Jack(2), Murray, Thyne	1	2	3	4	5	6		8	9	10	11					7								
20	21 Feb	STIRLING ALBION	3-0	6-0	8466	Henaughan(2), Mays(2), Middlemass(2)	1		3	4	5	6		8	9	10	11	2				7								
21	28	Dumbarton	2-3	2-4	1800	Harvey, Mays	1		3	4	5	6		8	9	10	11	2				7								
22	7 Mar	St. Johnstone	0-0	2-1	3200	Jack(2)	1	2	3	4		6		8	9	10	11					7							5	
23	14	HAMILTON A.	1-0	6-1	10570	Mays(2), Harvey, Henaughan, Jack, Murray	1	2		4	5	6		8	9	10	11					7				3				
24	21	Stenhousemuir	1-0	4-0	2000	Harvey, Jack(2), Murray	1	2		4	5	6		8	9	10	11					7				3				
25	28	Cowdenbeath	1-2	3-2	1500	Mays(3)	1	2		4	5	6		8	9	10	11					7				3				
26	4 Apr	ARBROATH	2-0	4-0	7238	Jack(2), Mays, Middlemass	1	2		4	5	6		8	9	10	11					7				3				
27	11	ALBION ROVERS	3-0	4-0	5473	Jack, Mays, Middlemass, Murray	1	2		4	5	6		8	9	10	11					7				3				
28	18	Dundee United	2-1	4-5	2000	Mays(3), Russell	1	2		4	5	6		8	9	10	11					7				3				
29	22	Forfar Athletic	0-4	0-6	1400		1	2	3	4	5		7		9							8				11		6		10
30	25	FORFAR ATHLETIC	2-0	4-0	4386	Harvey(2), Jack, McCorkindale	1	2	3	4	5	6		9		10						7					11			
					Apps.		30	28	22	29	29	21	4	24	29	25	26	2	2	1	7	27	3	1	9	7	1	1	1	1
					Goals					1	4	8		6	20	14	8				4	6			1		1			

Pos	P	W	D	L	F	A	Pts
4th	30	17	2	11	74	48	36

League Cup Section BA

Pos	P	W	D	L	F	A	Pts
1st	6	5	0	1	15	8	10

No.	Date	Opposition	H.T.	Res.	Att.	Goalscorers	Niven	Collins	Hood	Russell	Thyne	Middlemass	Anderson	Harvey	Mays	Jack	Murray	Clive	Kelly	Donaldson	Mathie	Henaughan
1	9 Aug	ALLOA ATHLETIC	3-1	3-1	8542	Anderson, Harvey, Mays	1	2	3	4	5	6	7	8	9	10	11					
2	13	Dunfermline	2-1	4-3	7500	Anderson, Jack, Murray, O.G.	1	2	3	4	5	6	7	8	9	10	11					
3	16	Arbroath	0-1	0-2	3100		1	2	3	4	5	6	7	8	9	10	11					
4	23	Alloa Athletic	0-0	1-0	3000	Mays	1		3	4	5	6	7	8	9	10	11	2				
5	27	DUNFERMLINE	2-2	3-2	12268	Jack, Mays, Middlemass	1		3	4	5	6	7	8	9	10	11	2				
6	30	ARBROATH	2-0	4-0	10190	Mays(2), Harvey, Jack	1	2	3	4	5	6	7	8	9	10	11					
QF	13 Sep	St. Johnstone	3-1	3-1	8600	Donaldson(2), Mays	1	2		4	5	6		8	9	10	11			3	7	
QF	17	ST. JOHNSTONE (Agg 7-2)	1-1	4-1	11597	Jack(2), Harvey, Mays	1	2		4	5	6		8	9	10				3		11
SF	4 Oct	Rangers*	0-0	1-0	45715	Jack	1	2	3	4	5	6		8	9	10	11					7
F	25	Dundee*	0-0	0-2	51830		1	2	3	4	5	6		8	9	10	11					7

* Played at Hampden Park

Scottish Cup

No.	Date	Opposition	H.T.	Res.	Att.	Goalscorers	Niven	Collins	Hood	Russell	Thyne	Middlemass	Harvey	Mays	Jack	Murray	Henaughan
1	24 Jan	Stranraer	2-0	4-0	4100	Murray, Henaughan, Jack, Mays	1	2	3	4	5	6	8	9	10	11	7
2	7 Feb	Hamilton A.	1-1	2-2	19210	Middlemass, Murray	1	2	3	4	5	6	8	9	10	11	7
2R	11	HAMILTON A.	0-2	0-2	13620		1	2	3	4	5	6	8	9	10	11	7

Scottish League Cup Finalists 1952-53
Back row (l-r): J. Brown (Trainer), J. Middlemass, R. Thyne, J. Russell, J. Niven, R. Collins, J. Hood, D. Mathie (Reserve).
Front row (l-r): T. Henaughan, W. Harvey, G. Mays, W. Jack, M. Murray.

SEASON 1953-54   Division Two

No.	Date	Opposition	H.T.	Res.	Att.	Goalscorers	Brown	McLachlan	Hood	Russell	Thyne	Middlemass	Henaughan	Harvey	Mays	Curlett	McCorkindale	Stewart	Murray	Collins	Jack	Milloy	Black	McFarlane	Baillie
1	5 Sep	Dunfermline	0-1	0-1	7500		1		3	4	5	6	7	8		10	11			2	9				
2	19	Ayr United	0-1	0-1	15000		1	6	3	4	5		7	8	9	10	11			2					
3	26	ALBION ROVERS	0-2	0-3	10209		1	6		4	5		11	8	9	10				2		3	7		
4	3 Oct	Morton	4-1	6-4	8000	Harvey(2), Mays(2), Curlett, Henaughan	1	6		4	5		11	8	9	10				2		3	7		
5	10	DUNDEE UNITED	0-2	3-2	9168	Henaughan, Mays, McLachlan	1	6		4	5		11	8	9	10				2		3	7		
6	17	Alloa Athletic	0-0	0-1	3500		1	6	3	4	5		11	8	9	10				2			7		
7	24	FORFAR ATHLETIC	3-0	6-0	7908	Harvey(3), Curlett, Henaughan, Jack	1	6	3	4	5		11	8		10	7			2	9				
8	31	ARBROATH	1-0	4-0	7597	Harvey(2), Curlett, Jack	1	6	3	4	5		11	8		10	7			2	9				
9	7 Nov	Third Lanark	0-0	0-2	7000		1	6	3	4	5		11	8		10				2	9		7		
10	14	Dumbarton	2-1	5-2	2500	Harvey(2), Jack(2), Hood	1	6	3	4	5		11	8		10	7			2	9				
11	21	COWDENBEATH	0-0	1-0	9006	Jack	1		3	4	5	6	11	8		10	7			2	9				
12	28	St. Johnstone	4-0	4-1	7500	Curlett(2), Harvey, Henaughan	1		3	4	5	6	11	8		10	7			2	9				
13	5 Dec	Motherwell	0-0	2-0	14500	Harvey(2)	1		3	4	5	6	11	8		10	7			2	9				
14	12	STENHOUSEMUIR	0-1	6-2	10287	Henaughan(3), Curlett, Middlemass, Murray	1		3	4	5	6	11	8		10	7			2	9				
15	19	DUNFERMLINE	1-1	2-2	13290	Curlett, Jack	1		3	4	5	6	11	8		10	7			2	9				
16	26	Queens Park	1-0	1-1	7143	Harvey	1		3	4	5	6	11	8		10	7			2	9				
17	1 Jan	AYR UNITED	0-2	0-3	19917		1		3	4	5	6	11		9	8			7	2	10				
18	2	Albion Rovers	1-0	1-1	9000	Harvey	1	5	3	4		6	11	8	9				7	2	10				
19	9	MORTON	2-0	2-0	11071	Henaughan, Jack	1	5	3	4		6	11	8			7			2	9				
20	16	Dundee United	0-0	2-0	6500	Curlett, Harvey	1	5	3	4		6	11	8			7			2	9				
21	23	ALLOA ATHLETIC	2-0	2-0	9791	Jack, Russell	1		3	4	5	6	11	8			7			2	9				
22	30	Cowdenbeath	0-1	0-6	2500		1	6	3	4	5		11	8			7			2	9				
23	6 Feb	Forfar Athletic	2-1	3-2	2500	Curlett, Harvey, Middlemass	1		3	4	5	6	11	8			7			2	9				
24	20	Arbroath	0-0	1-0	3450	Henaughan	1	2		4	5	6	11	8			7				9		3		
25	6 Mar	DUMBARTON	2-1	7-2	9159	Curlett(2), Mddlemss(2), Hnaughn, Jack, Mays	1			4	5	6	11	8			7			2	9	3			
26	20	ST. JOHNSTONE	3-0	5-0	10751	Mays(2), Harvey, Henaughan, Jack	1			4	5	6	11	8			7			2	9	3			
27	31	MOTHERWELL	2-1	4-2	15133	Henaughan(2), Curlett, Mays	1	3		4	5	6	11	8			7			2	9				
28	3 Apr	Stenhousemuir	0-0	1-0	2500	Middlemass	1	3		4	5	6	11	8			7			2	9				
29	17	THIRD LANARK	0-0	1-1	21663	Mays	1	3		4	5	6	11	8			7			2	9				
30	24	QUEENS PARK	1-0	2-0	9698	Curlett, Jack	1	3		4	5	6	11	8			7				9				2
						Apps.	30	18	20	30	27	20	20	30	29	19	29		13	28	25	6	4	1	1
						Goals		1	1	1		5	13	17	8	13			1		11				

Pos	P.	W.	D.	L.	F.	A.	Pts.
2nd	30	19	4	7	71	39	42

League Cup Section BC

Pos	P.	W.	D.	L.	F.	A.	Pts.
1st	6	5	0	1	14	5	10

No.	Date	Opposition	H.T.	Res.	Att.	Goalscorers	Brown	McLachlan	Hood	Russell	Thyne	Middlemass	Henaughan	Harvey	Mays	Curlett	McCorkindale	Stewart	Murray	Collins	Jack	Milloy	Black	McFarlane	Baillie
1	8 Aug	Motherwell	0-2	0-3	13400		1	2	3	4	5		7	8	9	10	11	6							
2	12	MORTON	0-0	1-0	11473	Harvey	1	2	3	4	5	6	7	8	9	10				11					
3	15	DUNDEE UNITED	3-0	4-1	10948	Curlett, Harvey, Mays, Russell	1	2	3	4	5	6	7	8	9	10				11					
4	22	MOTHERWELL	2-0	4-1	17653	Curlett(2), Mays(2)	1		3	4	5	6	7	8	9	10				11	2				
5	26	Morton	2-0	2-0	7000	Jack, Mays	1	5	3	4		6	7		9	8				11	2	10			
6	29	Dundee United	2-0	3-0	8000	Curlett, Middlemass, Murray	1	5	3	4		6	7	8		10				11	2	9			
QF	12 Sep	PARTICK THISTLE	1-3	4-3	20244	Mays(2), Harvey, Middlemass	1		3	4	5	6	7	8	9	10				11	2				
QF	16	Partick Thistle (Agg: 4-7)	0-2	0-4	21688		1	6	3	4	5		7	8	9					11	2	10			

Scottish Cup

No.	Date	Opposition	H.T.	Res.	Att.	Goalscorers	Brown	McLachlan	Hood	Russell	Thyne	Middlemass	Henaughan	Harvey	Mays	Curlett	McCorkindale	Stewart	Murray	Collins	Jack	Milloy	Black	McFarlane	Baillie
1		Bye																							
2	13 Feb	Rangers	1-0	2-2	40000	Henaughan, Murray	1		3	4	5	6	11	8		10			7	2	9				
2R	17	RANGERS	0-2	1-3	33545	Jack	1			4	5	6	11	8		10			7	2	9	3			

John Bourke, born this year.

Promotion after seven years in the "B" Division.
Frank Beattie and Matt Watson both sign for Killie.
Bertie Black makes his debut. Hugh Spence,
manager of the 1920 and 1929 cup-winning teams
dies.

SEASON 1954-55 — Division One

No.	Date	Opposition	H.T.	Res.	Att.	Goalscorers	Brown	Collins	Rollo	Russell	Thyne	Middlemass	Murray	Harvey	Mays	Curlett	Henaughan	McLachlan	Black	Beattie	Hood	Imrie	Newbiggin	Toner	Jack	Dougan	Mackay	Flavell	Baillie	Watson	Clark
1	11 Sep	EAST FIFE	0-0	0-0	14594		1	2		4	5	6	7	8	9	10	11			3											
2	18	St. Mirren	0-0	0-2	20000		1	2		4	5	6	7	8	9	10	11			3											
3	25	DUNDEE	0-2	0-2	15166		1	2		4	5	6	10	8	9		11	7		3											
4	2 Oct	Celtic	1-3	3-6	30000	Curlett, Mays, Henaughan	1	2	3	4	5	6	8		7	10	11				9										
5	9	PARTICK THISTLE	1-0	1-2	12806	Beattie	1	2	3	4	5	6	7		9	10	11			8											
6	16	Stirling Albion	1-0	2-1	7000	Curlett(2)	1	2		4	5		11	8	7	9				3	10		6								
7	30	Hibernian	1-0	2-3	27500	Mays, Hood	1	2	6	4	5		11	8	7	9				3	10										
8	6 Nov	Rangers	0-3	0-6	40000		1	2	6	4	5		11	8	7	10				3					9						
9	20	Falkirk	2-4	3-5	12000	Toner(2), Hood	1	2	6		5		11	8	7					3	10			4	9						
10	24	HEARTS	0-2	1-3	7689	Beattie	1	2	3		5	6	7	8			11			10				4	9						
11	27	Clyde	1-0	1-1	10000	Toner	1	2	3		5	6	7			4	11			8				9	10						
12	4 Dec	ABERDEEN	0-2	0-4	13219		1		3		5	6	7			4	11			8			2	9	10						
13	11	QUEEN OF THE SOUTH	4-1	4-1	11998	Harvey, Jack, Mackay, Murray	1	2	3				7	8		4	11							9	10	5	6				
14	18	Raith Rovers	0-0	0-0	6000		1	2	3				7	8	9	4	11								10	5	6				
15	25	East Fife	1-1	5-1	5000	Jack(2), Henaughan, Imrie, Mays	1	2	3				8	7		4	11					9			10	5	6				
16	1 Jan	ST. MIRREN	1-1	1-1	27992	Henaughan	1	2	3				7	8	9	4	11								10	5	6				
17	3	Dundee	3-1	5-2	13000	Jack(2), Harvey, Henaughan, Murray	1	2	3				7	8	9	4	11								10	5	6				
18	8	CELTIC	0-0	1-2	24518	Murray	1	2	3				7	8	9	4	11								10	5	6				
19	29	Motherwell	1-0	1-0	12000	Henaughan	1	2	3	4			7	8	9		11								10	5	6				
20	12 Feb	HIBERNIAN	0-2	1-3	19059		1		3				7	8	9		11							10		5	6	9	2		
21	26	RANGERS	1-0	1-0	24201	Flavell	1		3				7			4	11			8				10		5	6	9		2	
22	5 Mar	Queen of the South	0-0	0-1	10000		1		3				7			4	11			8				10		5	6	9		2	
23	12	FALKIRK	0-0	2-0	15132	Flavell, Toner	1		3				7			4	11			8				10		5	6	9		2	
24	19	CLYDE	0-1	2-1	15005	Beattie, Murray	1		3				7			4	11			8				10		5	6	9		2	
25	30	Aberdeen	0-3	1-4	17000	Mackay	1		3				7			4	11			8				10		5	6	9		2	
26	6 Apr	Hearts	2-0	2-2	15000	Murray, O.G.	1		3				7			4	8							10		5	6	9		2	11
27	9	RAITH ROVERS	2-0	2-2	12627	Clark, Flavell	1	2	3				7			4	8							10		5	6	9			11
28	13	MOTHERWELL	1-1	1-2	10498	Mays	1	2	3				8	7	4									10		5	6	9			11
29	16	Partick Thistle	2-0	3-0	18000	Harvey, Jack, Mays	1	2	3	4		6	8	7	9										10	5					11
30	30	STIRLING ALBION	1-0	2-1	8055	Jack(2)	1	2	3	4		6	7	8	9									10	10	5					11
						Apps.	30	22	25	11	12	8	26	18	14	26	23	1		15	9	2	3	12	12	18	16	15	2	5	5
						Goals							5	3	5	3	5			3	2	1		4	8		2	3			1

Pos	P	W	D	L	F.	A.	Pts.
10th	30	10	6	14	46	58	26

League Cup Section AA

Pos	P	W	D	L	F.	A.	Pts.
3rd	6	2	1	3	8	11	5

No.	Date	Opposition	H.T.	Res.	Att.	Goalscorers	Brown	Collins	Rollo	Russell	Thyne	Middlemass	Murray	Harvey	Mays	Curlett	Henaughan	Beattie	Hood	Imrie
1	14 Aug	RAITH ROVERS	1-0	3-2	18129	Curlett, Harvey, Middlemass	1	2	3	4	5	6	7	8	9	10	11			
2	18	Motherwell	0-2	0-3	17000		1	2	3	4	5	6	7	8	9	10	11			
3	21	ST. MIRREN	2-0	2-2	19749	Harvey, Mays	1	2	3	4		6	11	8	9	10		5	7	
4	28	Raith Rovers	1-0	1-0	12000	Mays	1	2	3	4		6	7	8	9	10	11	5		
5	1 Sep	MOTHERWELL	0-1	0-1	21567		1	2	3	4		6	7	8	9	10	11	5		
6	4	St. Mirren	1-0	2-3	15000	Beattie, Curlett	1	2	3	4	5		11		9	10		6	7	8

Scottish Cup

No.	Date	Opposition	H.T.	Res.	Att.	Goalscorers	Brown	Collins	Rollo	Murray	Harvey	Curlett	Henaughan	Toner	Dougan	Mackay	Flavell	Baillie
5	5 Feb	East Fife	2-0	2-1	11000	Flavell, Harvey	1	2	3	7	8	4	11	10	5	6	9	
6	19	CELTIC	0-1	1-1	32887	Henaughan	1	2	3	7	8	4	11	10	5	6	9	
6R	23	Celtic	0-0	0-1	41000		1		3	7	8	4	11	10	5	6	9	2

Back row (l-r): R. Collins, A. Rollo, J. Brown, J. Russell, R. Thyne, J. Middlemass.
Front row (l-r): G. Mays, M. Murray, A. Imrie, D. Curlett, T. Henaughan.

SEASON 1955-56 — Division One

No.	Date	Opposition	H.T.	Res.	Att.	Goalscorers
1	10 Sep	AIRDRIEONIANS	1-0	2-1	12500	Catterson, Lawlor
2	17	East Fife	1-0	1-2	5800	Catterson
3	24	ST. MIRREN	1-0	1-1	10000	Lawlor
4	1 Oct	Hibernian	1-1	1-2	20000	Catterson
5	8	PARTICK THISTLE	0-0	0-1	12000	
6	15	Stirling Albion	2-1	2-1	7000	Flavell, Harvey
7	22	DUNDEE	0-0	0-0	12000	
8	29	Motherwell	0-0	1-2	12000	Curlett
9	5 Nov	QUEEN OF THE SOUTH	1-1	2-2	15000	Flavell(2)
10	12	Raith Rovers	1-1	1-2	8000	Mackay
11	19	RANGERS	0-1	1-2	25600	Beattie
12	26	Clyde	1-0	3-1	9000	Beattie, Harvey, Mays
13	3 Dec	FALKIRK	3-1	4-4	10500	Beattie(2), Flavell, Mays
14	10	Celtic	2-0	2-0	15000	Curlett(2)
15	17	ABERDEEN	0-0	1-0	14000	Curlett
16	24	HEARTS	0-2	2-4	17000	Mays(2)
17	31	Dunfermline	1-0	3-0	7000	Beattie, Curlett, Mays
18	2 Jan	St. Mirren	2-1	2-2	20000	Beattie, Mays
19	7	EAST FIFE	2-0	3-0	10000	Beattie(2), Fletcher
20	14	Airdrieonians	1-2	2-3	8000	Curlett(2)
21	21	HIBERNIAN	0-0	0-1	14000	
22	28	Partick Thistle	0-1	1-1	12000	Mays
23	11 Feb	STIRLING ALBION	1-1	3-2	10000	Flavell(3)
24	25	Dundee	1-0	1-1	11000	Flavell
25	3 Mar	MOTHERWELL	2-0	2-0	10600	Flavell, Mays
26	10	Queen of the South	0-0	0-2	7000	
27	17	RAITH ROVERS	1-1	1-1	10000	Beattie
28	24	Rangers	1-2	2-3	30000	Curlett, Fletcher
29	31	CLYDE	1-0	1-0	10000	Murray
30	7 Apr	Falkirk	0-0	0-0	7000	
31	13	CELTIC	0-0	0-0	13000	
32	21	Aberdeen	1-1	2-3	15000	Beattie, Flavell
33	25	Hearts	2-0	2-0	13000	Curlett(2)
34	28	DUNFERMLINE	0-0	3-0	8000	Curlett(2), Mays

Appearance / team grid (shirt numbers)

No.	Brown	Collins	Rollo	Curlett	Dougan	Newbiggin	Mays	Murray	Flavell	Jack	Henaughan	Toner	Russell	Black	Taggart	Catterson	Lawlor	Clark	Harvey	Beattie	Bowie	Watson	Mackay	Fletcher	Stewart	Bunten
1	1	2	3	4								5	7	6	9	10	11	8								
2	1	2	3	4								5	7	6	9	10	11		8							
3		5	3	4									7	6	9	10	11	8				1	2			
4	1	5	3	4									7	6	9	10	11	8					2			
5	1	5	3	4					11				7	6	9					8	10		2			
6	1	5	3	4			11	9					7	6						8	10		2			
7	1	5	3	4			11	9					7	6						8	10		2			
8	1		3	9			7		11				5		4					8	10		2	6		
9	1		3	4			7	11	9				5							8	10		2	6		
10	1		3	9			7		11				5		4					8	10		2	6		
11	1		3	4			7		9		11			6						8	10		2	5		
12	1		3	9			7		11					4	6					8	10		2	5		
13	1		3	9			7		11					4	6					8	10		2	5		
14	1		3	9			7						5		4					8	10		2	6		11
15	1		3	9			7						5		4			8			10		2	6		11
16	1		3	9			7						5		4						10		2	6		11
17	1		3	9			7						5		4					8	10		2	6		11
18	1		3		5		7		9		11	4								8	10		2	6		
19	1	5	3	9			7		11			4								8	10		2	6		
20	1	5	3	9			7		11											8	10		2	6	4	
21	1	5	3	9			7		11											8	10		2	6	4	
22	1	5	3	9			7		11											8			2	6	4	
23	1	5	3	9			7		11											8			2	10	4	6
24	1	5	3	9			7		11											8	10		2	6	4	
25	1	5	3	9			7		11						6					8	10		2		4	
26	1	2		5				11	9						7					8	10		3	6	4	
27	1	2		9	5			11							7					8	10		3	6	4	
28	1	2		9	5		7	11													10		3	6	4	8
29	1	2		9	5		7	11													10		3	6	4	8
30	1	2		9	5		7	11												8	10		3	6	4	
31	1	2		9			7		11				5					10					3	6	4	8
32	1	2		9			7		11				5								10		3	6	4	8
33	1	2		9			7		11				5								10		3	6	4	8
34	1	2		9			7		11				5								10		3	6	4	8
Apps	33	23	25	32	6		25	9	23			3	15	2	8	17	5	6	4	20	29	1	32	25	15	15
Goals				12			9	1	10							3	2		2	10			1	2		

Pos	P	W	D	L	F	A	Pts
8th	34	12	10	12	52	45	34

League Cup Section AA

Pos	P	W	D	L	F	A	Pts
2nd	6	2	3	1	7	7	7

No.	Date	Opposition	H.T.	Res.	Att.	Goalscorers
1	13 Aug	ST. MIRREN	0-0	0-0	20000	
2	17	Dundee	2-0	2-1	16000	Jack, Murray
3	20	AIRDRIEONIANS	1-0	2-0	18000	Murray, Rollo
4	27	St. Mirren	0-1	0-3	15000	
5	31	DUNDEE	0-0	0-0	16000	
6	3 Sep	Airdrieonians	1-2	3-3	8000	Catterson, Clark, Harvey

League Cup team grid (shirt numbers):

No.	Brown	Collins	Rollo	Curlett	Dougan	Newbiggin	Mays	Murray	Flavell	Jack	Henaughan	Toner	Russell	Black	Taggart	Catterson	Lawlor	Clark
1	1	2	3	4	5	6	7	8	9	10	11							
2	1	2	3	4	5	6	7	8	9	10	11							
3	1	2	3	4		6	7	8	9	10	11	5						
4	1	2	3	4		6	7	8	9	10	11	5						
5	1	2	3	8	6				9	10	11	5	4		7			
6	1	2	3	4								5	7	6	9	10	11	8

Scottish Cup

No.	Date	Opposition	H.T.	Res.	Att.	Goalscorers
5	4 Feb	Falkirk	1-0	3-0	10808	Beattie(2), Curlett
6	18	QUEEN OF THE SOUTH	2-2	2-2	24300	Harvey, Flavell
6R	22	Queen of the South	0-1	0-2	14000	

Scottish Cup team grid (shirt numbers):

No.	Brown	Collins	Rollo	Curlett	Mays	Flavell	Beattie	Bowie	Mackay	Fletcher	Stewart
5	1	5	3	9	7	11	8	10	2	6	4
6	1	5	3	9	7	11	8	10	2	6	4
6R	1	5	3	9	7	11	8	10	2	6	4

Walter McCrae's decades-long service at Rugby Park began this season.

SEASON 1956-57 — Division One

No.	Date	Opposition	H.T.	Res.	Att.	Goalscorers	Brown	Collins	J.Stewart	R.Stewart	Toner	Mackay	Muir	W.Harvey	Curlett	Beattie	Burns	T.Harvey	Baillie	Dougan	Mays	Taggart	Fletcher	Lawlor	Watson	Black	Campbell	Falls	Malloy	Catterson	Caven	Neil	Milloy	Hill	McBain
1	8 Sep	Dundee	0-0	1-1	14000	Curlett	1	2	3	4	5	6	7	8	9	10	11																		
2	15	Rangers	1-0	1-0	30000	Curlett	1	2	3	4		6	7	8	9	10	11					5													
3	22	St. Mirren	0-1	0-2	10000		1	2	3	4		6	7	8	9	10	11					5													
4	29	EAST FIFE	0-1	1-1	10000	Curlett	1	2	3	4		6	7	8	9	10	11					5													
5	6 Oct	Dunfermline	1-1	1-2	7000	Muir	1	2	3			6	7	8	4		11				9	5		10											
6	13	AYR UNITED	3-0	4-1	18000	Burns, W.Harvey, Mays, Muir	1	2		4	5	6	7	8			11				9		10		3										
7	20	Partick Thistle	1-1	1-2	12000	Collins	1	2		4	5	6	11	8							9		10		3	7									
8	27	Hibernian	0-0	0-0	14000		1	2		4	5	6	7	8		10					9				3	11									
9	3 Nov	FALKIRK	0-0	1-1	10500	Beattie	1	2			5	6	7	8		10	11				9				3	4									
10	10	Aberdeen	0-1	3-1	11000	Fletcher, Beattie, Mays	1	2			5		7	8		10					9		11		3	6	4								
11	17	Hearts	1-2	2-3	14000	Black, Mays	1	2			5	6		8		10	11				9				3	7	4								
12	24	RAITH ROVERS	2-0	3-0	9246	Beattie(2), Mays	1	2			5	6	7	8		10					9				3	11	4								
13	1 Dec	MOTHERWELL	2-0	2-2	14873	Black, Beattie	1	2			5	6	7	8		10					9				3	11	4								
14	8	Queen of the South	0-0	3-0	6500	Black(2), Mays		2			5	6	7	8		10					9				3	11	4		1						
15	15	AIRDRIEONIANS	0-2	3-4	8037	Beattie, Mays, Muir		2			5	6	7	8		10					9				3	11	4		1						
16	22	RANGERS	1-0	3-2	22436	Mays(2), W.Harvey	1	2		4	5	6	7	8		10					9				3	11									
17	29	Queens Park	0-0	2-1	9000	Black, Muir	1	2		4	5	6	7	8		10					9				3	11									
18	1 Jan	ST. MIRREN	1-1	3-2	18055	Burns, Mays, Muir	1	2		4	5	6	7	8			11				9				3	10									
19	2	Celtic	0-1	1-1	14000	Mays	1	2		4	5	6	7	8			11				9				3	10									
20	5	DUNDEE	2-0	4-0	13788	Mays(2), Beattie, Mackay	1	2		4	5	6		8		10	11				9				3	7									
21	12	East Fife	0-0	0-0	6000		1	2		4	5	6		8		10	11				9				3	7									
22	19	DUNFERMLINE	0-0	0-0	11160		1		3	4	5	6		8		10	11				9				2	7									
23	26	Ayr United	1-0	2-0	15000	Black, W.Harvey	1		3	4	5	6	7	8		10					9				2	11									
24	9 Feb	PARTICK THISTLE	0-1	1-1	13776	Mays	1		3		5	6	7	8		10					9				2	11	4								
25	23	HIBERNIAN	1-1	2-1	9297	Caven, Muir	1		3	4	5	6	7	8			11								2	10					9				
26	6 Mar	Falkirk	0-1	0-2	15000		1		3	4	5	6	7	8			11								2	10					9				
27	9	ABERDEEN	2-0	2-1	13859	Curlett, Mays	1	2	3	4	5	6	7		8		11				9					10									
28	16	HEARTS	1-0	4-1	18598	Mays(2), Curlett, W.Harvey	1	2	3	4	5	6		8	9		11				7					10									
29	30	Motherwell	1-0	1-0	—	Black, Curlett	1	2	3	4	5	6	7	8	9		11									10									
30	3 Apr	QUEEN OF THE SOUTH	0-0	1-3	9159	Black	1	2	3	4		6	11			10					5	7				8					9				
31	13	Airdrieonians	1-0	1-0	8000	W.Harvey	1	2	3	4	5	6	7	8			11				9					10									
32	15	Raith Rovers		0-2	6000	Mays(2)											11			10	9	6	8			2	4					1	3	5	7
33	26	CELTIC	0-0	0-0	6917		1	2	3	4	5		11	8	9						7	6				10									
34	27	QUEENS PARK	0-0	1-0	6388	Curlett	1	2	3	4	5		11	8	9						7	6				10									
						Apps.	31	28	17	24	27	30	29	31	10	21	19			6	27	3	4	1	21	25	9	2	2		3	1	1	1	1
						Goals		1				1	6	5	7	7	2				18		1			8					1				

Pos P. W. D. L. F. A. Pts.
3rd 34 16 10 8 57 39 42

League Cup Section 3

Pos P. W. D. L. F. A. Pts.
4th 6 1 2 3 8 14 4

No.	Date	Opposition	H.T.	Res.	Att.	Goalscorers	Brown	Collins	J.Stewart	R.Stewart	Toner	Mackay	Muir	W.Harvey	Curlett	Beattie	Burns	T.Harvey	Baillie	Dougan	Mays	Taggart	Fletcher	Lawlor	Watson	Black	Campbell	Falls	Malloy	Catterson	Caven
1	11 Aug	DUNFERMLINE	0-0	0-0	12000		1	2			5	6		8	9	10	11						7	4		3					
2	15	St. Mirren	0-1	2-2	10000	Curlett, Mays	1	2				6		8	9	10	11					5	7	4		3					
3	18	QUEEN OF THE SOUTH	0-2	2-3	10000	W.Harvey, Mays	1	2				6		8	9	10	11					5	7	4		3					
4	25	Dunfermline	0-1	1-5	7000	Mays		2		4		6		8	9	10	11	1	3	5	7									
5	29	ST. MIRREN	1-3	1-4	12000	Catterson		2		4		6	7			10	11	1	3	5			8							9	
6	1 Sep	Queen of the South	1-0	2-0	7000	Curlett, W.Harvey		2		4	5		7	8	9		11		3			6	10			3					

Scottish Cup

No.	Date	Opposition	H.T.	Res.	Att.	Goalscorers	Brown	Collins	J.Stewart	R.Stewart	Toner	Mackay	Muir	W.Harvey	Curlett	Beattie	Burns	Dougan	Mays	Watson	Black
5	2 Feb	AYR UNITED	0-0	1-0	22192	Beattie	1		3	4	5	6	7	8		10			9	2	11
6	16	East Fife	0-0	0-0	8716		1		3	4	5	6	7	8		10			9	2	11
6R	20	EAST FIFE	0-0	2-0	18856	Black, Mays	1		3	4	5	6	7	8			11		9	2	10
QF	2 Mar	AIRDRIEONIANS	2-0	3-1	23509	Mays(2), W.Harvey	1		3	4	5	6	7	8			11		9	2	10
SF	23	Celtic *	1-0	1-1	109145	Mays	1	2	3	4		6		8	9		11	5	7		10
SFR	27	Celtic *	2-1	3-1	76963	Mays(2), Black	1	2	3	4	5	6		8	9		11		7		10
F	20 Apr	Falkirk *	1-1	1-1	81375	Curlett	1	2	3	4	5	6		8	9		11		7		10
FR	24	Falkirk *	0-1	1-2#	79960	Curlett	1	2	3	4	5	6		8	9		11		7		10

* Played at Hampden Park # After extra time, at 90 minutes 1-1

Back row (l-r): J. Stewart, R. Collins, W. Toner, R. Dougan, J. Brown, F. Beattie, A. Mackay, R. Stewart, M. Watson.
Front row (l-r): W. McCrae (Trainer), W. Muir, G. Mays, W. Harvey, D. Curlett, R. Black, D. Burns, M. MacDonald (Manager).

SEASON 1957-58 — Division One

No.	Date	Opposition	H.T.	Res.	Att.	Goalscorers	Brown	Collins	J.Stewart	R.Stewart	Toner	Mackay	Curlett	Beattie	Mays	Black	Burns	Taggart	Muir	Harvey	Neil	Henaughan	Jamieson	Kennedy	Hill	McBride	Milloy	Lawlor	Falls	Wentzel	Watson	Chalmers	Ross
1	7 Sep	AIRDRIEONIANS	1-0	3-1	10740	Beattie, Burns, Mays	1	2	3	4	5	6	7	8	9	10	11																
2	21	ST. MIRREN	3-0	4-2	11954	Mays(2), Burns, R.Stewart	1	2	3	4	5	6			9	10	11		7	8													
3	5 Oct	THIRD LANARK	0-2	2-4	8414	Mays(2)	1		3		5	6	7	8	9					11			10	2	4								
4	12	East Fife	1-1	2-1	5000	Henaughan, Mays	1			4	5	3		8	9	10			7			11		6	2								
5	19	CLYDE	1-1	3-2	13937	Beattie, Burns, Mays	1	2		4	5			8	9	10	11		7					6									
6	26	QUEENS PARK	1-0	3-1	11821	Black, Beattie, Mays	1	2		4	5			8	9	10	11		7					6									
7	2 Nov	Celtic	0-2	0-4	33915		1		2	4	5	3		8	9	10	11		7					6									
8	9	Rangers	3-1	4-3	45000	Beattie(2), Curlett, Mays	1	2	3	4	5		8	10	9			11	7					6									
9	16	MOTHERWELL	0-0	0-1	13748		1	2	3	4	5		8	10	9		11		7					6									
10	23	Aberdeen	0-1	2-1	15000	Curlett(2)	1	2	3	4	5		8		9		11		7					6	10								
11	30	PARTICK THISTLE	2-0	4-1	12590	Mays(2), Black, Curlett	1	2	3	4	5		8		9		11		7					6	10								
12	7 Dec	Falkirk	1-1	1-1	10000	Mays	1	2	3	4	5		8	10	9				7					6	11								
13	14	Hearts	0-2	1-2	25000	Mays	1	2	3	4	5		8	10	9		11		7					6									
14	21	HIBERNIAN	0-3	1-4	12562	Mays	1	2	3	4	5		8	10	9				7					6	11								
15	25	Dundee	0-1	0-2	9000		1	2	3	4	5		7	8				11						6	10	9							
16	28	Raith Rovers	0-0	1-1	8000	McBride	1	2	3	4	5		7	8			11							6	10	9							
17	1 Jan	St. Mirren	1-2	1-2	10000	Beattie	1	2	3	6	5		4	8			11		7						10	9							
18	2	QUEEN OF THE SOUTH	2-0	2-0	12040	Beattie, O.G.	1	2		4	5		7	10	9									8	6				3	11			
19	4	Airdrieonians	0-1	1-1	8500	Harvey	1	2		4	5		7	10	9									8	6				3	11			
20	11	DUNDEE	1-0	1-1	10312	Curlett	1	2		4	5		7	10	9		11							8	6				3				
21	18	Third Lanark	0-0	1-2	12000	McBride	1	2			5		7		9		11							8	6	10	3		4				
22	1 Feb	Queen of the South	1-0	2-1	6500	Mays, Muir	1	2	3		5				9		11	7	8						6	10			4				
23	22	CELTIC	0-1	0-1	21897	McBride	1	2	3								11	7	8						6	10			4	9			
24	8 Mar	Motherwell	1-1	2-2	10000	Burns, Chalmers	1	2	3	4	5					10	11	7							6	8						9	
25	10	RANGERS	2-1	3-3	15335	McBride(2), Burns	1	2	3							10	11					7			6	8			4			9	
26	15	EAST FIFE	3-0	4-0	7844	Black(3), Chalmers	1		3		5					10	11					7			6	8			4		2	9	
27	19	ABERDEEN	1-0	2-0	7809	Black(2)	1		3		5					10	11					7			6	8			4		2	9	
28	22	Partick Thistle	0-0	0-2	10000		1		3		5					10	11					7			6	8			4		2	9	
29	29	FALKIRK	1-1	1-1	6457	McBride			3		5					10	11					7			6	8			4		2	9	1
30	5 Apr	HEARTS	0-1	1-1	15865	O.G.	1		3		5	6			9	10	11					7			4	8				2			
31	12	Hibernian	1-0	2-1	18000	Black, McBride	1	2			5	6				10	11							8	7	4				9			
32	16	Clyde	1-0	2-3	6000	Black, McBride	1	2			5	6		8		10	11								7	4				9		3	
33	26	RAITH ROVERS	1-0	1-1	4478	Black		2			5	6		8		10	11	7							4					9		3	1
34	30	Queens Park	1-1	2-1	500	Beattie, Wentzel		2		4	5	6		8		10	11	7												9		3	1
		Apps.					31	24	25	21	34	12	16	20	22	26	17		18	7		19	1	30	1	15	4	2	8	3	9	6	3
		Goals						1					5	8	15	10	5		1	1		1		8					1			2	

Pos P. W. D. L. F. A. Pts.
5th 34 14 9 11 60 55 37

League Cup Section 4

Pos P. W. D. L. F. A. Pts.
1st 6 3 3 0 12 6 9

No.	Date	Opposition	H.T.	Res.	Att.	Goalscorers	Brown	Collins	J.Stewart	R.Stewart	Toner	Mackay	Curlett	Beattie	Mays	Black	Burns	Taggart	Muir	Harvey	Henaughan	Jamieson
1	10 Aug	HEARTS	1-0	2-1	19806	Harvey, Mays	1	2	3	4	5				9	10	11	6	7	8		
2	14	Dundee	0-0	3-0	15000	Beattie, Burns, Mays		2	3	4	5				10	9			11	6	7 8	1
3	17	QUEENS PARK	1-1	3-1	13587	Beattie, Harvey, Taggart		2	3	4	5				10	9			11	6	7 8	1
4	24	Hearts	0-1	1-1	25000	Mays	1	2	3	4	5		7	8	9	10	11	6				
5	28	DUNDEE	0-0	1-1	13535	Mays	1	2	3	4	5		7	8	9	10	11	6				
6	31	Queens Park	1-1	2-2	5500	Curlett, Mays	1	2	3	4	5		7	8	9	10	11	6				
QF	11 Sep	RANGERS	1-0	2-1	26803	Muir, O.G.	1	2	3	4	5	6		8	9	10	11		7			
QF	14	Rangers (Agg: 3-4)	1-1	1-3	66000	Black	1	2	3	4	5	6		8	9	10	11		7			

Scottish Cup

No.	Date	Opposition	H.T.	Res.	Att.	Goalscorers	Brown	Collins	J.Stewart	R.Stewart	Toner	Mackay	Curlett	Beattie	Mays	Black	Burns	Taggart	Muir	Harvey	Henaughan	Jamieson	Kennedy	Hill	McBride	Milloy	Lawlor	Falls	Wentzel	Watson
2	15 Feb	VALE OF LEITHEN	4-0	7-0	9795	McBride(3), Harvey(2), Wentzel(2)	1	2	3		5						11		7	8					6	10			4	9	
3	1 Mar	QUEEN OF THE SOUTH	0-1	2-2	20477	Black, McBride	1		3		5						7		11	8					6	10			4	9	2
3R	5	Queen of the South	0-0	0-3	11000		1	2	3	4	5				9	7			11	8					6	10					

Back row: McKay, McBride, R. Stewart, Higginson, J. Stewart, Brown, Neil, Campbell, McBain, Taggart, Mays, Henaughan. Middle: Jamieson, Falls, Davidson, Toner, Dougan, Beattie, Hill, Kennedy, Watson, Curlett. Front: Cowan, Harvey, McPike, Collins, Muir, Black, Horn, Burns.

SEASON 1958-59 — Division One

Player columns (left to right): J.Brown · Watson · J.Stewart · R.Stewart · Toner · Mackay · H.Brown · Henaughan · McBride · Black · Burns · Collins · Kennedy · Chalmers · Muir · Beattie · O'Connor · Ross · Dougan · Mays · Wentzel · Grant · McPike · T.Brown

No.	Date	Opposition	H.T.	Res.	Att.	Goalscorers
1	20 Aug	HIBERNIAN	1-0	1-1	9955	Black
2	6 Sep	St. Mirren	2-0	2-0	11000	Black, Henaughan
3	13	CELTIC	1-2	1-4	22286	McBride
4	20	Dundee	0-1	0-1	12000	
5	27	STIRLING ALBION	1-1	3-3	9974	Henaughan(2), H.Brown
6	4 Oct	Airdrieonians	0-0	0-3	7500	
7	11	DUNFERMLINE	0-0	1-1	8391	O.G.
8	18	QUEEN OF THE SOUTH	3-0	5-0	7770	R.Stewart(3), McBride, Muir
9	25	Raith Rovers	0-0	0-1	8000	
10	29	Partick Thistle	1-1	1-1	10000	Black
11	1 Nov	ABERDEEN	2-0	2-0	6791	Black, McBride
12	8	Falkirk	0-0	0-0	10000	
13	15	Motherwell	1-0	1-0	13000	Black
14	22	RANGERS	0-1	0-3	25672	
15	29	HEARTS	2-1	3-2	15269	Wentzel(2), Black
16	13 Dec	RAITH ROVERS	0-0	2-0	6743	McBride(2)
17	20	Clyde	3-1	4-2	10000	Black(2), Mays, McBride
18	27	Hibernian	1-1	3-4	12000	Wentzel(2), R.Stewart
19	1 Jan	ST. MIRREN	0-0	1-0	10860	Mays
20	10	DUNDEE	0-0	1-0	8726	Wentzel
21	17	Stirling Albion	1-0	1-3	4000	Wentzel
22	21	Celtic	0-0	0-2	8000	
23	24	AIRDRIEONIANS	1-1	4-2	9594	Wentzel(4)
24	7 Feb	Dunfermline	3-0	3-0	6000	Black, McBride, R.Stewart
25	18	Queen of the South	1-1	2-2	6500	Mays, McBride
26	21	PARTICK THISTLE	1-2	1-2	8897	Wentzel
27	4 Mar	Aberdeen	2-1	2-2	5000	Black, Burns
28	7	FALKIRK	1-1	4-1	7491	Muir(2), Black, Wentzel
29	18	MOTHERWELL	1-2	1-3	7298	Wentzel
30	21	Rangers	0-1	0-1	25000	
31	24	Third Lanark	0-0	0-2	2500	
32	28	Hearts	1-0	1-3	18000	Black
33	18 Apr	CLYDE	3-0	4-1	5799	Black, Mays, McBride, McPike
34	21	THIRD LANARK	1-0	4-0	4086	Black, Burns, McPike, O.G.

Appearances: J.Brown 33 · Watson 34 · J.Stewart 2 · R.Stewart 26 · Toner 19 · Mackay 22 · H.Brown 12 · Henaughan 11 · McBride 29 · Black 34 · Burns 12 · Collins 14 · Kennedy 4 · Chalmers 2 · Muir 20 · Beattie 27 · O'Connor 3 · Ross 1 · Dougan 27 · Mays 16 · Wentzel 18 · Grant 5 · McPike 2 · T.Brown 1

Goals: R.Stewart 5 · H.Brown 1 · Henaughan 3 · McBride 10 · Black 13 · Burns 2 · Muir 3 · Mays 4 · Wentzel 13 · McPike 2

Pos	P	W	D	L	F	A	Pts
8th	34	13	8	13	58	51	34

League Cup Section 4

Pos	P	W	D	L	F	A	Pts
1st	6	4	0	2	12	6	8

No.	Date	Opposition	H.T.	Res.	Att.	Goalscorers
1	9 Aug	ABERDEEN	0-1	1-2	8758	Kennedy
2	13	Falkirk	1-0	3-1	8000	McBride(2), R.Stewart
3	16	Hibernian	1-0	3-0	17000	Black, Henaughan, McBride
4	23	Aberdeen	2-0	2-0	14000	McBride(2)
5	27	FALKIRK	1-1	1-2	10463	Black
6	30	HIBERNIAN	2-0	2-1	15700	Burns, McBride
QF	10 Sep	DUNFERMLINE	2-0	4-1	14275	Black, H.Brown, Kennedy, McBride
QF	16	Dunfermline (Agg: 7-4)	2-2	3-3	10000	H.Brown, Henaughan, McBride
SF	1 Oct	Hearts*	0-1	0-3	41527	

*Played at Easter Road

Scottish Cup

No.	Date	Opposition	H.T.	Res.	Att.	Goalscorers
1		Bye				
2	14 Feb	Dumbarton	4-1	8-2	8804	McBride(3), Wentzel(3), Burns, Mays
3	28	Hamilton A.	0-0	5-0	10391	Black(2), Wentzel(2), Burns
QF	14 Mar	Aberdeen	1-2	1-3	19000	Mays

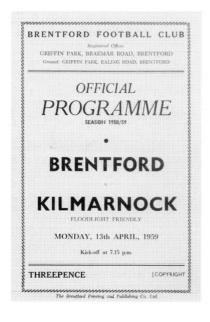

BRENTFORD FOOTBALL CLUB
Registered Office:
GRIFFIN PARK, BRAEMAR ROAD, BRENTFORD
Ground: GRIFFIN PARK, EALING ROAD, BRENTFORD

OFFICIAL
PROGRAMME
SEASON 1958/59
•
BRENTFORD
v
KILMARNOCK
FLOODLIGHT FRIENDLY
MONDAY, 13th APRIL, 1959
Kick-off at 7.15 p.m.

THREEPENCE   COPYRIGHT

The Brentford Printing and Publishing Co. Ltd.

Rhodesian born Vernon Wentzel scored the only goal in the 1959 friendly win over ex-boss Malky McDonald's new club.

SEASON 1959-60   Division One

No.	Date	Opposition	H.T.	Res.	Att.	Goalscorers	J.Brown	Watson	Cook	Stewart	Toner	Kennedy	Copeland	McInally	McBride	Black	McPike	Baillie	Dougan	MacKay	Wentzel	O'Connor	Henaughan	Muir	Burns	Beattie	Horn	H.Brown	Anton	T.Brown	Richmond	Kerr	Bryceland
1	19 Aug	Celtic	0-1	0-2	18000		1	2	3	4	5	6	7	8	9	10	11																
2	5 Sep	ST. MIRREN	0-2	0-5	12276		1	2	3				7	8	9						5	6		10	11	4							
3	12	Airdrieonians	2-1	3-1	5000	Wentzel, Black(2)	1	2	3				7		8	10					5	9	6	11		4							
4	19	STIRLING ALBION	2-0	2-0	7672	Black, Wentzel	1	2	3					8	10						5	9	6	7		4	11						
5	26	Hibernian	1-3	2-4	20000	McBride, Wentzel	1	2	3				7	10	8						5	9	6			4	11						
6	3 Oct	DUNDEE	1-1	2-2	8206	McBride, McInally	1	2	3				7	8	9	10					5		6			4	11						
7	10	Partick Thistle	2-2	2-3	15000	McBride, Watson	1	2	3				7	8	9	10					5		6			4	11						
8	17	ABERDEEN	1-0	2-0	7149	Black(2)	1	2		5					9	10				3		6	8			4	11	7					
9	24	Arbroath	2-0	3-0	4000	McBride, Wentzel	1	2		5					9	10				3	7	6	8			4	11						
10	31	MOTHERWELL	1-0	2-0	11478	Beattie, Muir	1	2		5				8	9	10				3		6		11		4							
11	7 Nov	THIRD LANARK	0-1	3-2	9927	Black, O'Connor, Wentzel		2		5				8	9	10				3	7	6		11		4			1				
12	14	Hearts	0-2	1-3	18000	McInally	1	2		5				8	9	10				3	7	6		11		4							
13	21	AYR UNITED	0-0	0-0	19355	McBride, Wentzel	1	2		5				8	9	10				3	7	6		11		4							
14	28	DUNFERMLINE	1-2	3-2	9047	Black, T.Brown, Muir	1	2		5				8		10				3	7	6		11		4				9			
15	5 Dec	Rangers	0-2	0-5	20000		1	2		5				8		10				3	7	6		11		4				9			
16	12	RAITH ROVERS	0-0	1-0	8897	McInally	1		3		5	6		8		10							7	11		4					2	9	
17	19	Clyde	0-1	2-1	8000	McInally(2)	1		3		5	6		8		10							7	11		4					2	9	
18	26	CELTIC	1-1	2-1	15948	Black, Kerr	1		3		5	6		8		10							7	11		4					2	9	
19	1 Jan	St. Mirren	3-0	3-0	18000	Kerr, Muir, Wentzel	1		3		5	6		8		10							7	11		4					2	9	
20	2	AIRDRIEONIANS	1-0	1-0	13971	Kerr	1		3	2	5	6		8		10							7	11		4						9	
21	9	Stirling Albion	1-0	1-0	5316	Kerr	1		3	2	5	6		8		10							7	11		4						9	
22	16	HIBERNIAN	0-0	3-1	17448	Kerr, McInally, Muir	1		3		5	6		8		10							7	11		4					2	9	
23	23	Dundee	1-0	4-0	15000	Muir(2), Black, McInally	1		3		5	6		8		10							7	11		4					2	9	
24	6 Feb	PARTICK THISTLE	3-0	5-1	13132	McInally(3), Muir, Wentzel	1		3		5	6		8		10							7	11		4					2	9	
25	1 Mar	ARBROATH	2-0	3-2	8337	McInally(2), Kerr	1		3	7	5	6		8		10								11		4					2	9	
26	5	Motherwell	1-0	2-1	16000	Black, McInally	1		3	7	5	6		8		10								11		4					2	9	
27	14	Third Lanark	0-2	4-3	10000	Muir(2), McInally, Stewart	1		3	7	5	6		8		10								11		4					2	9	
28	19	HEARTS	0-0	2-1	26584	McInally, Muir	1		3	7	5	6		8		10								11		4					2	9	
29	22	Aberdeen	0-0	1-0	13000	Black	1		3	7	5	6		8		10							11			4					2	9	
30	26	Ayr United	2-0	3-1	19000	Kerr(2), McInally	1		3	7	5	6		8		10								11		4					2	9	
31	4 Apr	Dunfermline	0-0	0-1	14000		1		3	7	5	6		8		10								11		4					2	9	
32	16	RANGERS	1-1	1-1	26925	Black	1		3	7	5	6		8		10								11		4					2	9	
33	27	Raith Rovers	1-0	2-0	6000	Black, Wentzel	1		3	2		6		8		10							7	11		4					5	9	
34	30	CLYDE	0-1	0-2	6986		1		3	2		6		8		10							7	11		4					5	9	
Apps.							33	34	8	13	26	20	6	29	13	33	1			4	10	22	14	5	24	1	33	6	1	1	3	17	17
Goals								1		1				16	6	13					9	1		10		1				1		8	

Pos P. W. D. L. F. A. Pts.
2nd 34 24 2 8 67 45 50

League Cup Section 3

Pos P. W. D. L. F. A. Pts.
3rd 6 2 1 3 13 13 5

No.	Date	Opposition	H.T.	Res.	Att.	Goalscorers	J.Brown	Watson	Cook	Stewart	Toner	Kennedy	Copeland	McInally	McBride	Black	McPike	Baillie	Dougan	MacKay	Wentzel	O'Connor	Henaughan	Muir	Burns	Beattie
1	8 Aug	HEARTS	0-0	0-4	16378		1		3			8		4	7					10	11	2	5	6	9		
2	12	Stirling Albion	1-0	2-2	4500	Wentzel(2)	1	2	3	4			7	8						10	11	5	6	9			
3	15	ABERDEEN	2-1	2-3	10427	McInally, Wentzel	1	2	3	4	6	7	8		10	11				5	9						
4	22	Hearts	0-1	0-2	30000		1	2	3	4			7	8	9	11				5		6	10				
5	26	STIRLING ALBION	3-0	5-0	8118	McInally(2) Copeland, McBride, O'Connor	1	2	3	4			7	8	9					5		6	10	11			
6	29	Aberdeen	2-0	4-2	8000	Burns, Henaughan, McBride, McInally	1	2	3	4			7	8	9					5		6	10	11			

Scottish Cup

No.	Date	Opposition	H.T.	Res.	Att.	Goalscorers	J.Brown	Cook	Stewart	Toner	Kennedy	McInally	Black	Henaughan	Muir	Beattie	Richmond	Kerr
1	30 Jan	STRANRAER	2-0	5-0	8506	Wentzel(2), Black, McInally, Muir	1	3	5	6	—	8	10	7	11	4	2	9
2	22 Feb	Hearts	0-1	1-1	33869	Muir	1	3	7	5	6	8	10	—	11	4	2	9
2r	24	HEARTS	1-0	2-1	24359	Muir, Stewart	1	3	7	5	6	8	10	—	11	4	2	9
3	27	MOTHERWELL	0-0	2-0	29412	McInally(2)	1	3	7	5	6	8	10	—	11	4	2	9
QF	12 Mar	Eyemouth United	2-1	2-1	2900	Black, McInally	1	3	7	5	6	8	10	—	11	4	2	9
SF	2 Apr	Clyde*	2-0	2-0	43900	Kerr, Muir	1	3	7	5	6	8	10	—	11	4	2	9
F	23	Rangers+	0-1	0-2	108017		1	3	7	5	6	8	10	—	11	4	2	9

* Played at Ibrox   + Played at Hampden

New York Int. Tourn.

Pos P. W. D. L. F. A. Pts.
1st 5 4 1 0 11 2 9

No.	Date	Opposition	H.T.	Res.	Att.	Goalscorers	J.Brown	Cook	Stewart	Toner	Kennedy	McInally	Black	Henaughan	Muir	Beattie	Richmond	Kerr	Bryceland
1	25 May	Bayern Munich	0-1	3-1	10444	Bryceland, Kerr, McInally	1	3	5	6		8		7	11	4	2	9	10
2	30	Glenavon	0-0	2-0	6000	Muir, Watson	1	3	5	6		8		7	11	4	2	9	10
3	1 Jun	Burnley	1-0	2-0	13000	Kerr, Wentzel	1	3	5	6		8		7	11	4	2	9	10
4	8	Nice	0-0	1-1	12861	McInally	1	3	5	6		8		7	11	4	2	9	10
5	18	New York Americans	1-0	3-1	11704	McInally, Muir, O.G.	1	3	5	6		8		7	11	4	2	9	10
F	6 Aug	Bangu	0-1	0-2	25044		1	3	5	6	8	10		9	11	4	7	2	

Glenavon and New York Americans matches played at Roosevelt Stadium, Jersey City. All other games played at Polo Grounds, New York

Scottish Cup Finalists and League Runners-up
Back row: M. Watson, J. Richmond, F. Beattie, W. Toner, R. Kennedy, A. Kerr.
Front row: R. Stewart, J. McInally, J. Brown, R. Black, W. Muir.

SEASON 1960-61 — Division One

No.	Date	Opposition	H.T.	Res.	Att.	Goalscorers	J.Brown	Richmond	Watson	Beattie	Toner	Kennedy	Muir	McInally	Kerr	Black	McIlroy	Wentzel	H.Brown	Stewart	O'Connor	Davidson	McGrory	McLaughlan	Cook	King
1	24 Aug	CELTIC	0-1	2-2	23745	McInally(2)	1	2	3	4	5	6	7	8	9	10	11									
2	10 Sep	St. Mirren	0-0	1-0	15000	Muir	1	2	3	4	5	6	7	8	9	10	11									
3	17	HIBERNIAN	1-0	3-2	11995	Black, Kerr, Wentzel	1	2	3	4	5	6		8	9	10	11	7								
4	24	Ayr United	1-2	2-2	17500	Kerr, Richmond	1	2	3	4	5	6		8	9	10	11		7							
5	1 Oct	Raith Rovers	1-0	1-1	5000	McIlroy	1	2	3		5	6		8	9	10	11		7	4						
6	8	CLYDE	0-0	1-0	11657	Kerr	1	5	3	4				8	9	10	11		7		2					
7	15	Dundee	0-0	0-1	16000		1	2	3	4	5				9	10	11		7	8	6					
8	22	ST. JOHNSTONE	2-1	2-2	9409	Black, Kerr	1	2	3	4	5	6		8	9	10	11		7							
9	2 Nov	THIRD LANARK	1-0	3-0	4361	H.Brown, Kerr, Muir	1	2	3		5	6	11		9	10			7	4						
10	5	Airdrieonians	0-0	1-1	8000	McIlroy	1	2	3			6	11	8	9	10			7	4		5				
11	12	HEARTS	1-1	2-1	13393	Kerr(2)		2	3		5	6	11		9	10			7			8	4	1		
12	19	Dundee United	1-0	4-2	12000	Kerr(3), McIlroy		2	3		5	6		10	9		11		7			8	4	1		
13	26	Rangers	2-2	3-2	55000	H.Brown, Kerr, McInally		2	3		5	6	11	10	9		7		7			8	4	1		
14	3 Dec	MOTHERWELL	3-2	5-3	11533	Kerr(4), McInally		2	3		5	6	11	10	9		7					8	4	1		
15	10	Aberdeen	1-2	2-3	14000	Kerr, McInally		2	3		5	6	11	10	9		7					8	4	1		
16	17	DUNFERMLINE	0-1	1-1	8783	Kerr		2	3		5	6	11	10	9		7					8	4	1		
17	24	Partick Thistle	1-2	3-2	20000	Kerr(3)		2	3		5	6	10	11	8	9			7				4	1		
18	31	Celtic	1-0	2-3	26000	H.Brown, Kennedy		2	3		5	6	10	11	8	9			7				4	1		
19	2 Jan	ST. MIRREN	1-1	1-2	18240	Kerr		2	3		5	6		4	11	8	9		10					1		
20	7	Hibernian	0-0	0-4	18000			2		4	5	6	11	8	9				10					1	3	
21	14	AYR UNITED	2-0	5-1	14907	McInally(2), Davidson, Kerr, Muir		2	3	4	5	6	11	10	9				7			8		1		
22	21	RAITH ROVERS	3-0	6-0	9841	Kerr(3), H.Brown, Davidson, McInally		2	3	4	5	6	11	10	9				7			8		1		
23	4 Feb	Clyde	1-1	3-1	8000	Black, Kerr, McInally		2	3	4	5	6	11	10	9	8			7					1		
24	18	DUNDEE	1-0	2-1	10191	Davidson, McInally		2	3	4	5	6	11	10	9				7			8		1		
25	25	St. Johnstone	0-1	1-1	8800	Kerr		2	3	4	5	6	11		9	10			7			8		1		
26	4 Mar	Third Lanark	1-0	1-0	8500	Kerr		2	3	4		6	11	10	9				7			8	5	1		
27	11	ABERDEEN	1-0	4-1	8360	McInally(2), Davidson, Kerr		2		4	5	6	11	10	9				7			8		1		3
28	15	AIRDRIEONIANS	1-0	1-0	7841	Kerr		2	3	4	5	6	11	10	9				7			8		1		
29	18	Hearts	1-0	1-0	17000	Kerr		2	3	4	5	6	11	10	9	8			7					1		
30	25	DUNDEE UNITED	0-0	1-0	8012	Muir		2	3	4	5	6	11	10	9	8			7					1		
31	1 Apr	RANGERS	2-0	2-0	29528	Kerr, Muir		2	3	4	5	6	11	10	9	8			7					1		
32	8	Motherwell	3-0	3-1	17000	Black(2), Kerr		2	3	4	5	6	11	10	9	8			7					1		
33	29	PARTICK THISTLE	4-1	4-1	9865	H.Brown(2), Black, Kerr		2	3	4	5	6	11	10	9	8			7					1		
34	1 May	Dunfermline	1-1	4-2	10917	Black(2), McInally(2)		2	3	4	5	6	11	10	9	8			7					1		
Apps.							10	34	32	28	31	31	28	28	34	23	14	1	31	3	1	17	2	24	2	
Goals								1				1	5	14	34	8	3	1	6			4				

Pos	P	W	D	L	F	A	Pts.
2nd	34	21	8	5	77	45	50

League Cup Section 3

Pos	P	W	D	L	F	A	Pts.
1st	6	4	1	1	12	7	9

No.	Date	Opposition	H.T.	Res.	Att.	Goalscorers	J.Brown	Richmond	Watson	Beattie	Toner	Kennedy	Muir	McInally	Kerr	Black	McIlroy	Wentzel	H.Brown	Stewart
1	13 Aug	HIBERNIAN	1-1	4-2	15451	Black(3), Kerr	1	2	3	4	5	6	11	8	9	10			7	
2	17	Airdrieonians	1-0	2-0	7000	Beattie, Kerr	1	2	3	4	5	6	11	8	9	10			7	
3	20	DUNFERMLINE	2-1	2-1	13251	Kerr, Muir	1	2	3	4	5	6	11	8	9	10			7	
4	27	Hibernian	1-2	2-2	23000	Black, O.G.	1	2	3	4	5	6		8	9	10	11			
5	31	AIRDRIEONIANS	2-0	2-0	11661	Black, Muir	1	2	3	4	5	6	7	8	9	10	11			
6	3 Sep	Dunfermline	0-1	0-2	6919		1	2	3	4	5	6		8	9	10	11		7	
QF	14	Clyde	0-0	2-1	18000	Kerr, Wentzel	1	2	3	4	5	6		8	9	10	11	7		
QF	21	CLYDE (Aggregate: 5-2)	2-0	3-1	15990	McIlroy(2), Kerr	1	2	3	4	5	6		8	9	10	11		7	
SF	12 Oct	Hamilton A.*	1-0	5-1	15000	Black(2), Kerr(2), McInally	1	2	3	4	5	6		8	9	10	11		7	
F	29	Rangers+	0-1	0-2	82063		1	2	3	4	5	6	11	8	9	10			7	

* Played at Ibrox   + Played at Hampden

Scottish Cup

No.	Date	Opposition	H.T.	Res.	Att.	Goalscorers	Richmond	Watson	Beattie	Toner	Kennedy	Muir	McInally	Kerr	H.Brown	Davidson	McLaughlan
1		Bye															
2	11 Feb	HEARTS	0-2	1-2	18383	Davidson	2	3	4	5	6	11	10	9	7	8	1

New York Tournament

Pos	P	W	D	L	F	A	Pts.
5th	7	2	2	3	12	13	6

No.	Date	Opposition	H.T.	Res.	Att.	Goalscorers	Richmond	Watson	Beattie	Toner	Kennedy	Muir	McInally	Kerr	Black	H.Brown	Davidson	McGrory	McLaughlan	King
1	25 May	Everton	0-2	1-2	5000	Kerr	2	3	4	5	6	11	10	9	8	7			1	
2	30	Karlsruhe	1-1	2-3	10000	Kennedy, Muir	2	3	4	5	6	11	10	9	8	7			1	
3	1 Jun	New York Americans	2-0	4-0	7000	Black, H.Brown, Kerr, Watson	2	3	4	5	6	11		9	8	7	10		1	
4	6	Montreal Concordia	1-1	4-2	4000	Kerr(2), Black, McInally	2	3	4	5	6	11	10	9	8	7			1	
5	10	Besiktas	0-1	1-1	2000	Muir	2	3	4	5	6	11	10	9	8	7			1	
6	14	Dynamo Bucharest	0-0	0-0	3000			3	4	5	6	11	10	9	8	7			1	2
7	18	Bangu	0-2	0-5	4000		2	3		5	6	11	10	9	8	7		4	1	

Karlsruhe, Dynamo Bucharest and Bangu matches played in New York. All other games played in Montreal.

Ray Montgomerie.
Killie's cup-winning captain
was born this year.

SEASON 1961-62   Division One

No.	Date	Opposition	H.T.	Res.	Att.	Goalscorers
1	23 Aug	CELTIC	2-1	3-2	19215	Black, McInally, Muir
2	9 Sep	Airdrieonians	1-0	2-0	4029	McIlroy(2)
3	16	ST. MIRREN	3-0	4-3	11492	Hamilton(2), Davidson, McIlroy
4	23	Hibernian	1-1	2-3	13181	McInally, Mason
5	30	ST. JOHNSTONE	1-0	2-0	11848	Mason, Muir
6	7 Oct	Dundee	2-2	3-5	12677	Black, McIlroy, McInally
7	14	THIRD LANARK	2-1	2-2	12681	Black, Hamilton
8	21	Dundee United	0-1	2-1	8975	Black, Yard
9	28	FALKIRK	1-0	2-0	9630	Richmond, Yard
10	4 Nov	Partick Thistle	3-2	4-2	11614	McInally(2), Yard(2)
11	11	RAITH ROVERS	2-0	2-3	8252	Black, McInally
12	18	Stirling Albion	0-1	2-2	4231	Black, Kerr
13	25	DUNFERMLINE	0-0	1-1	9391	McInally, Watson
14	2 Dec	ABERDEEN	3-1	4-2	6885	Kerr, Muir, Sneddon, Yard
15	16	Hearts	1-1	3-3	11225	Black, Richmond, Yard
16	23	MOTHERWELL	0-1	1-2	11525	Beattie
17	30	RANGERS	0-1	0-1	21992	
18	6 Jan	Celtic	1-1	2-2	33940	Kerr, McIlroy
19	10	AIRDRIEONIANS	2-1	4-2	5488	Kerr(2), Sneddon, Yard
20	13	HIBERNIAN	1-1	4-2	8599	Kerr(2), McIlroy, Yard
21	17	St. Mirren	0-1	1-2	5547	McIlroy
22	20	St. Johnstone	2-0	2-0	7133	Mason, O.G.
23	3 Feb	DUNDEE	0-0	1-1	14314	Kerr
24	10	Third Lanark	1-2	1-3	8760	Yard
25	21	DUNDEE UNITED	2-0	5-3	5584	Kerr(4), McIlroy
26	24	Falkirk	1-0	1-0	4910	Kerr
27	3 Mar	PARTICK THISTLE	1-0	1-1	9805	Kerr
28	14	Raith Rovers	0-1	2-2	2021	Kerr(2)
29	17	STIRLING ALBION	0-1	2-1	4671	Kerr, McIlroy
30	21	Dunfermline	0-1	0-2	7528	
31	31	Aberdeen	1-2	3-3	3269	Kerr(2), McInally
32	7 Apr	HEARTS	0-0	2-0	6750	Kerr(2)
33	21	Motherwell	0-0	2-0	4236	Black, Kerr
34	28	Rangers	0-0	1-1	39848	Kerr

Player appearances (shirt numbers by match — best reading):

No.	McLaughlan	Richmond	Watson	Davidson	Toner	Beattie	McIlroy	Mason	Black	McInally	Muir	Brown	Hamilton	McGrory	Kerr	Yard	Sneddon	Forsyth	Murray	King	O'Connor
1	1	2	3	4	5	6	7	8	9	10	11										
2	1	2	3	4	5	6	7	8	9	10				11							
3	1	2	3	4	5	6	7	8		10	11		9								
4	1	2	3	4	5	6	7	8	11	10				9							
5	1	2	3	4		6	7	8	9	10	11				5						
6	1	2	3	4		6	7	8	9	10	11				5						
7	1	2	3	4		6		8	9	10	11		7		5						
8	1	2	3	4		6			9	10	11		7		5	8					
9	1	2	3	4		6			9	10	11		7		5	8					
10	1	2	3	4		6			9	10	11		7		5	8					
11	1	2	3	4		6			9	10	11		7		5	8					
12	1	2	3	4	5	6		8			11		7		9	10					
13	1	2	3	4	5	6		8		10	11		7		9						
14	1	2	3	6	5	4					11		7		10	8	9				
15	1	2	3	6	5	4			9		11		7			8	10				
16	1	2	3	6	5	4			9		11		7			8	10				
17	1	2	3	4	5	6					11		7		10	8	9				
18		2	3	4	5	6	11						7		10	8	9			1	
19		2	3	4		6	11					5	7		9	8	10			1	
20		2	3	4		6	11					5	7		9	8	10			1	
21		2	3	4		6	11					5	7		9	8	10			1	
22	1	2	3	4	5	6	11	10					7			9	8				
23	1	2	3	4	5	6	11	10					7		9	8					
24	1	2	3		5	6		10					11	7	9	8					
25	1	2	3	4	5	6	11	8					7		9		10				
26	1	2	3		5	6	11	8					7		9		10		4		
27	1	2	3		5	6	11	8					7		9		10		4		
28	1	2	3	4	5		11	8					7		9		10		6		
29	1	2	3	4	5	6	11	8					7		9		10				
30	1	2	3	4	5	6	11	8					7		9		10				
31	1	4	3		5	6	11	8		10			7		9				2		
32	1		3		5		11	8					7		9		10		4	2	6
33	1		3		5		11	8					7		9		10		4	2	6
34	1		3				11	8					7		5		9		4	2	6
Apps	30	34	32	28	22	30	19	13	22	21	18	18	4	6	26	15	19	4	6	4	3
Goals		2	1	1		1	9	3	8	8	3		3		23	9	2				

Pos	P.	W.	D.	L.	F.	A.	Pts.
5th	34	16	10	8	74	58	42

League Cup Section 4

Pos	P.	W.	D.	L.	F.	A.	Pts.
2nd	6	3	0	3	18	8	6

No.	Date	Opposition	H.T.	Res.	Att.	Goalscorers
1	12 Aug	St. Mirren	0-0	0-1	16149	
2	16	HEARTS	1-0	1-2	13841	Beattie
3	19	Raith Rovers	3-0	7-1	3837	McIlroy(3), Kerr(2), McInally, O.G.
4	26	ST. MIRREN	1-1	6-1	15838	Black(2), McIlroy(2), Beattie, Mason
5	30	Hearts	0-0	0-2	17035	
6	2 Sep	RAITH ROVERS	2-0	4-1	7359	McInally(2), McIlroy, O.G.

Scottish Cup

No.	Date	Opposition	H.T.	Res.	Att.	Goalscorers
1		Bye				
2	27 Jan	Brechin City	4-1	6-1	1834	Yard(4), Kerr, O.G.
3	17 Feb	ROSS COUNTY	2-0	7-0	8568	Masson(3), Kerr, McIlroy, Richmond, Yard
QF	10 Mar	RANGERS	1-1	2-4	35995*	Black, Kerr

* Record attendance for Rugby Park, 36,500 tickets sold.

Davie Sneddon signs for a club record £17,000. Ground admission rises to 3/- (15p). Work commences on a new stand (now the West Stand). And a record 35,995 watch the cup-tie against Rangers.

SEASON 1962-63 Division One

No.	Date	Opposition	H.T.	Res.	Att.	Goalscorers
1	22 Aug	PARTICK THISTLE	1-2	1-2	9522	Muir
2	8 Sep	St. Mirren	4-1	4-2	11342	Black, Brown, O'Connor, Sneddon
3	15	THIRD LANARK	1-1	2-2	8448	Kerr, O.G.
4	22	Queen of the South	0-1	1-1	7600	Kerr
5	29	AIRDRIEONIANS	5-0	8-0	7317	Kerr(5), O'Connor(2), Sneddon
6	6 Oct	Celtic	0-0	1-1	36407	Kerr
7	13	HEARTS	2-1	2-2	19057	Black, Sneddon
8	20	Dundee	0-1	0-1	14863	
9	31	MOTHERWELL	2-1	7-1	5951	Blck,Brwn,Kerr,McIlry,Msn,O'Cnnr,Rchmnd
10	3 Nov	Clyde	4-0	5-0	4559	Mason(3), Hamilton, Kerr
11	10	RAITH ROVERS	1-1	3-1	7522	Beattie, Brown, Kerr
12	17	Hibernian	0-0	2-0	3867	Kerr, Mason
13	24	Dundee United	1-1	3-3	10934	Kerr(3)
14	1 Dec	DUNFERMLINE	2-0	3-0	9055	Hamilton(2), Kerr
15	8	Rangers	1-4	1-6	40319	Black
16	15	FALKIRK	3-0	3-1	5707	Mason(2), McIlroy
17	22	Aberdeen	0-0	0-1	11945	
18	29	Partick Thistle	1-2	2-3	12481	Black, O.G.
19	1 Jan	ST. MIRREN	2-1	2-1	7980	Hamilton, Mason
20	2	Third Lanark	0-0	1-0	7493	Black
21	5	QUEEN OF THE SOUTH	5-0	7-0	7718	Hamilton(2), Kerr(2), Black, McIlroy, Mason
22	9 Mar	CLYDE	0-1	3-2	7350	Black, Mason, Sneddon
23	16	Raith Rovers	1-0	4-1	1851	Kerr(3), O'Connor
24	18	Hearts	2-1	3-2	15591	Kerr(2), O.G.
25	23	HIBERNIAN	1-0	2-0	7692	Black, Mason
26	27	CELTIC	2-0	6-0	16002	Black(2), Kerr(2), Mason, Sneddon
27	6 Apr	Dunfermline	0-1	1-1	5336	Mason
28	13	Motherwell	0-2	1-2	4553	Black
29	20	Falkirk	3-0	5-0	4492	McIlroy(2), Yard(2), Black
30	24	Airdrieonians	0-0	3-0	2600	Yard(2), Black
31	27	ABERDEEN	1-1	2-2	6436	Yard(2)
32	1 May	DUNDEE UNITED	1-0	2-0	4505	McIlroy, O.G.
33	11	DUNDEE	1-0	1-0	6147	McInally
34	13	RANGERS	0-0	1-0	12801	Yard

	Pos	P.	W.	D.	L.	F.	A.	Pts.
	2nd	34	20	8	6	92	40	48

League Cup Section 3

	Pos	P.	W.	D.	L.	F.	A.	Pts.
	1st	6	5	1	0	20	0	11

	Date	Opposition	H.T.	Res.	Att.	Goalscorers
1	11 Aug	AIRDRIEONIANS	1-0	4-0	9797	Kerr(2), Davidson, McInally
2	15	Dunfermline	0-2	3-3	7404	Brown(2), Beattie
3	18	Raith Rovers	1-2	3-2	4870	Brown, Kerr, Sneddon
4	25	Airdrieonians	2-0	4-0	3721	Kerr(2), Black, Brown
5	29	DUNFERMLINE	2-2	3-2	10901	Black, Kerr, McIlroy
6	1 Sep	RAITH ROVERS	2-1	3-1	6540	Kerr, McIlroy, O.G.
QF	12	Partick Thistle	1-0	2-1	21404	Brown, McIlroy
QF	19	PARTICK THIS. (Agg. 5-2)	1-0	3-1	14920	Kerr(2), Black
SF	10 Oct	Rangers*	2-2	3-2	76043	Black, Kerr, McIlroy
F	27	Hearts*	0-1	0-1	51280	

* Hampden

Scottish Cup

	Date	Opposition	H.T.	Res.	Att.	Goalscorers
1		Bye				
2	26 Jan	QUEEN OF THE SOUTH	0-0	0-0	10812	
3	11 Mar	Queen of the South	0-0	0-1	10370	

U.S. Tournament

	Pos	P.	W.	D.	L.	F.	A.	Pts.
	3rd	6	2	3	1	17	13	7

	Date	Opposition	H.T.	Res.	Att.	Goalscorers
1	30 May	West Ham United	1-1	3-3	14532	Black, Richmond, Yard
2	2 Jun	Preussen Munster*	2-1	5-2	6000	Black(2), McFadzean, McInally, Murray
3	5	Oro (Mexico)	0-1	3-3	7138	McFadzean(2), Black
4	12	Valenciennes+	0-0	1-2	7000	Yard
5	19	Mantova	2-0	2-2	7473	Black, McFadzean
6	23	Recife	1-0	3-1	5826	Black, Murray, O'Connor

* Played at Chicopee, Massachussetts   + Played at Chicago   All other games - New York

Andy Kerr.

A goalscoring legend at Rugby Park. And no wonder. This season alone he plundered 25 League goals even though he played in only 24 matches!

SEASON 1963-64   Division One

No.	Date	Opposition	H.T.	Res.	Att.	Goalscorers	Forsyth	King	Richmond	Murray	McGrory	O'Connor	Brown	McFadzean	Yard	Black	McIlroy	Watson	Beattie	Mason	Sneddon	McInally	Layburn	Hamilton	McLaughlan	Dickson	McLean
1	21 Aug	East Stirling	0-0	2-0	4656	Brown, McIlroy	1	2	3	4	5	6	7	8	9	10	11										
2	7 Sep	ST. MIRREN	0-0	2-0	7247	Black(2)	1	2		4	5		7		9	10	11	3	6	8	10						
3	14	Airdrieonians	3-1	5-4	3607	McIlroy(2), Murray, O'Connor, Sneddon	1	2		4	5	7	8		9		11	3	6		10						
4	21	DUNFERMLINE	0-0	0-3	8285		1	2		4	5	7			9		11	3	6		10	8					
5	28	Hibernian	0-0	2-0	11030	Murray(2)	1	2		9	5	4	7				11	3	6		10	8					
6	5 Oct	PARTICK THISTLE	3-0	3-0	6470	King, McIlroy, McInally	1	2		9	5	4	7				11	3	6		10	8					
7	12	Falkirk	0-1	1-1	4843	McIlroy	1	2		9	5	4	7				11	3	6		10	8					
8	19	ABERDEEN	1-0	2-0	5685	McIlroy, Murray	1	2		9	5	4	7				11	3	6		10	8					
9	26	HEARTS	2-1	3-1	8469	McInally(2), McIlroy	1	2		9	5	4	7				11		6		10	8			3		
10	2 Nov	Queen of the South	1-0	4-0	5089	McIlroy(2), Murray, Brown	1	2		9	5	4	7				11	3	6		10	8					
11	9	DUNDEE UNITED	1-0	2-0	7214	McIlroy, Sneddon	1	2		9	5	4	7				11	3	6		10	8					
12	16	RANGERS	0-0	1-1	27548	McIlroy	1	2			5	4	7	9			11	3	6		10	8					
13	23	Celtic	0-2	0-5	27548		1	2			5	4	7	9			11	3	6		10	8					
14	30	MOTHERWELL	3-0	5-2	6679	Murray(2), McIlroy, McInally, Sneddon	1	2		9	5	4	7				11	3	6		10	8					
15	7 Dec	DUNDEE	1-1	1-1	10166	Murray	1	2		9	5	4	7				11	3	6		10	8					
16	14	St. Johnstone	1-0	2-0	6126	Brown, Murray	1	2		9	5	4	7				11	3	6		10	8					
17	21	Third Lanark	0-1	2-1	2909	McInally(2)	1	2		9	5	4	7				11	3	6		10	8					
18	28	EAST STIRLING	2-0	4-1	7566	Brown, McIlroy, McInally, Mason	1	2		9	5	4	7				11	3	6	10		8					
19	1 Jan	St. Mirren	1-0	3-1	10225	McIlroy, Mason, Murray	1	2		9	5	4	7				11	3	6	10		8					
20	2	AIRDRIEONIANS	3-1	4-1	10642	McInally(2), Murray, Sneddon	1	2		9	5	4	7				11	3	6		10	8					
21	4	Dunfermline	1-2	3-2	7663	McIlroy(3)	1	2		9	5	4	7				11	3	6		10	8					
22	18	HIBERNIAN	1-1	2-1	9554	King, Murray	1	2		9	5	4	7				11	3	6		10	8					
23	1 Feb	Partick Thistle	0-2	0-2	18165		1	2		9	5	4	7				11	3	6		10	8					
24	8	FALKIRK	6-0	9-2	7758	McIlroy(4), McInally(3), Beattie, Brown	1			9	5		7	4			11	3	6		10	8			2		
25	19	Aberdeen	0-0	0-0	6165		1	2		9	5	4	7	8			11	3	6		10						
26	22	Hearts	0-0	1-1	13639	King	1	2		9	5		7	4			11	3	6		10				8		
27	29	QUEEN OF THE SOUTH	2-1	2-1	8340	McIlroy(2)	1	2		9	5		7	4			11	3	6		10				8		
28	11 Mar	Dundee United	1-2	1-2	7916	McIlroy	1	2		9	5		7	4			11	3	6		10	8					
29	14	Rangers	0-2	0-2	45870		1	2		9	5		7	4			11	3	6		10	8					
30	21	CELTIC	1-0	4-0	11459	McInally(2), Murray(2)	1	2		9	5			4		9	11	3	6		10	8					
31	1 Apr	Motherwell	0-0	0-2	3663		1	2		9	5		7	4			11		6		10	8			3		
32	4	Dundee	1-1	1-2	11796	McIlroy	1	2		9	5		7	4			11		6		10	8			3		
33	18	ST. JOHNSTONE	2-0	4-1	4321	Hamilton(3), McInally	1				5		7	4			11	3	6		10	8		9	2		
34	25	THIRD LANARK	1-0	2-0	3672	Hamilton(2)	1	2			5		7	4			11	3	6	8	10			9			
						Apps.	34	32	1	29	34	23	31	14	1	7	34	30	33	4	31	27	5	4			
						Goals		3		14		1	5			2	24	1	2		4	16		5			

Pos	P.	W.	D.	L.	F.	A.	Pts.
2nd	34	22	5	7	77	40	49

League Cup Section 3

Pos	P.	W.	D.	L.	F.	A.	Pts.
2nd	6	2	2	2	9	9	6

No.	Date	Opposition	H.T.	Res.	Att.	Goalscorers	Forsyth	King	Richmond	Murray	McGrory	O'Connor	Brown	McFadzean	Yard	Black	McIlroy	Watson	Beattie	Mason	Sneddon	McInally	Layburn	Hamilton
1	10 Aug	Queen of the South	0-0	4-1	7787	McInally(3), Hamilton	1	2		4	5	6	7		9		11	3				8		10
2	14	CELTIC	0-0	0-0	20246		1	2		4	5	6	7		9		11	3				8		10
3	17	RANGERS	1-1	1-4	34246	McInally	1	2	3	4	5	6	7	10			11					8		9
4	24	QUEEN OF THE SOUTH	1-0	2-0	6851	Sneddon(2)	1	2	3	4	5		7		9	10	11		6			8		
5	28	Celtic	0-1	0-2	11104		1	2	3	4	5		7	10	9		11		6			8		
6	31	Rangers	0-1	2-2	34570	Beattie, Brown	1	2	3	4	5		7		9		11		6	8	10			

Scottish Cup

No.	Date	Opposition	H.T.	Res.	Att.	Goalscorers	Forsyth	King	Richmond	Murray	McGrory	O'Connor	Brown	McFadzean	Yard	Black	McIlroy	Watson	Beattie	Mason	Sneddon	McInally	Layburn	Hamilton	McLaughlan
1	11 Jan	GALA FAIRYDEAN	1-0	2-1	8717	McInally, Murray	1	2		9	5	4	7				11	3	6		10	8			
2	25	Hamilton A.	1-1	3-1	9378	McIlroy(2), O.G.	1	2		9	5	4	7				11	3	6		10	8			
3	15 Feb	ALBION ROVERS	1-0	1-0	10238	Beattie, Murray	1	2		9	5		7	4			11	3	6		10	8			
QF	7 Mar	Falkirk	1-1	2-1	14000	McIlroy(2)	1	2		9	5		7	4			11	3	6		10	8			3
SF	28	Dundee*	0-1	0-4	32664		1	2		9	5			7			11		6		10	8			

* Ibrox

Summer Cup

Pos	P.	W.	D.	L.	F.	A.	Pts.
1st	6	5	1	0	19	5	11

No.	Date	Opposition	H.T.	Res.	Att.	Goalscorers	Forsyth	King	Richmond	Murray	McGrory	O'Connor	Brown	McFadzean	Yard	Black	McIlroy	Watson	Beattie	Mason	Sneddon	McInally	Layburn	Hamilton	McLaughlan	Dickson	McLean
1	2 May	MOTHERWELL	1-1	2-2	4519	Hamilton, Sneddon	1	2			5		7	4			11	3	6	8	10			9			
2	6	Queen of the South	0-1	3-1	2466	McIlroy(2), Hamilton		2			5		7	4			11	3	6		10	8		9	1		
3	9	AIRDRIEONIANS	1-0	4-0	4120	McIlroy(2), Hamilton, McFadzean		2			5		7	4			11	3	6		10	8		9	1		
4	13	Motherwell	2-1	4-1	3811	Hamilton(3), Sneddon		2			5		7	4			11	3	6		10	8		9	1		
5	15	QUEEN OF THE SOUTH	1-0	4-0	4310	Hamilton(2), McIlroy, Sneddon		2			5		7	4			11	3	6		10	8		9	1		
6	20	Airdrieonians	2-0	2-1	1034	Mason(2)				4			7	5			11	3	6	9	10	8			1	2	
SF	27	HIBERNIAN	3-3	4-3	8716	Hamilton, McIlroy, McInally, O.G.		2			5			4			11	3	6		10	8		9	1		7
SF	30	Hibernian (Agg. 4-6)	0-2	0-3	17273			2		4	5						11	3	6		10	8		9	1		7

Back row (l-r): R. Hamilton, B. Shepherd, J. Richmond, C. Forsyth, T. Brown, F. Malone, J. Mason. Middle row: W. Dickson, R. Alexander, J. McGrory, F. Beattie, B. Ferguson, J. McFadzean, J. McInally, S. Layburn, T. Taylor. Front row: T. McLean, D. Sneddon, H. Brown, B. Black, M. Watson, A. McLaughlan, A. King, P. O'Connor, E. Yard, E. Murray, B. McIlroy.

SEASON 1964-65 — Division One

Player columns (left→right): Forsyth, King, Watson, O'Connor, McGrory, Beattie, Murray, McInally, Hamilton, Sneddon, McIlroy, McFadzean, McLean, Ferguson, Brown, Malone, Mason, Dickson, Black, McDonald, Shepherd

No.	Date	Opposition	H.T.	Res.	Att.	Goalscorers
1	19 Aug	THIRD LANARK	0-0	3-1	5197	Watson, O'Connor, Hamilton
2	5 Sep	St. Mirren	0-0	2-0	4636	McIlroy, Hamilton
3	12	AIRDRIEONIANS	1-0	2-0	5299	Hamilton, McInally
4	19	St. Johnstone	0-0	1-0	4829	McInally
5	26	DUNFERMLINE	0-0	1-0	10755	Hamilton
6	3 Oct	Hibernian	1-0	2-1	15471	Hamilton(2)
7	10	PARTICK THISTLE	0-0	0-0	8379	
8	17	Dundee	0-1	3-1	13171	Murray, Sneddon, McInally
9	28	CELTIC	3-0	5-2	19122	McInally(2), McFadzean(2), Hamilton
10	31	Dundee United	0-0	1-0	8567	McInally
11	7 Nov	MOTHERWELL	1-0	1-1	9698	Hamilton
12	14	RANGERS	0-0	1-1	32021	Beattie
13	21	Aberdeen	0-1	1-1	9101	McInally
14	28	Clyde	2-0	2-1	4863	McFadzean, McInally
15	5 Dec	FALKIRK	2-0	2-0	5535	McInally, Sneddon
16	12	Morton	0-2	1-5	10306	Hamilton
17	19	HEARTS	2-1	3-1	18285	McIlroy, Sneddon, Hamilton
18	26	Third Lanark	2-0	4-0	2549	McLean(2), McInally, McIlroy
19	1 Jan	ST. MIRREN	2-0	4-0	12039	Hamilton(2), Sneddon, Murray
20	2	Airdrieonians	0-0	1-2	7808	Hamilton
21	9	ST. JOHNSTONE	0-0	0-0	6694	
22	16	Dunfermline	0-0	0-1	9766	
23	30	Partick Thistle	0-1	0-1	6560	
24	13 Feb	DUNDEE	1-1	1-4	7158	Hamilton
25	16	HIBERNIAN	1-1	4-3	10535	Black(2), Murray, King
26	27	Celtic	0-1	0-2	21875	
27	10 Mar	DUNDEE UNITED	1-1	4-2	5756	Black(2), McIlroy, McLean
28	13	Motherwell	0-0	2-0	4096	McIlroy, Mason
29	20	Rangers	0-0	1-1	30574	Mason
30	27	ABERDEEN	2-0	2-1	5193	Murray, McIlroy
31	3 Apr	CLYDE	2-0	2-1	5816	McInally, Hamilton
32	7	Falkirk	1-0	1-0	2569	McIlroy
33	17	MORTON	0-0	3-0	10605	Black(2), McIlroy
34	24	Hearts	2-0	2-0	36346	Sneddon, McIlroy

Player appearances (shirt numbers):

No.	Fo	Ki	Wa	OC	McG	Be	Mu	McI	Ha	Sn	McIl	McF	McL	Fe	Br	Ma	Mas	Di	Bl	McD	Sh
1		2	3	4	5	6	7	8	9	10	11										
2	1	2	3		5	6	4	8	9	11	7	10									
3	1	2	3		5	6	4	8	9	11	7	10									
4	1	2	3		5	6	4	8	9	11	7	10									
5	1	2			5	6	4	8	9	10	11	3	7								
6		2	3		5	6	4	8	9	11	7	10		1							
7	1		3		5	6	4	8	9	10	11	2	7								
8	1	2	3		5	6	4	8	9	11	7	10									
9	1	2	3		5	6	4	8	9	11	7	10									
10	1	2	3		5	6	4	8	9	11	7	10									
11	1	2	3		5	6	4	8	9	11	7	10									
12	1	2	3		5	6	4	8	9	11		10	7								
13	1	2	3		5	6	4	8	9	11		10	7								
14	1	2	3		5	6	4	8	9	11	7	10									
15	1	2	3			6	4	8	9	10	11	5	7								
16	1	2	3			6	4	8	9	10	11	5		7							
17	1	2	3		5	6	4		9	10	11	8	7								
18	1	2	3		5		4	8	9	10	11	6	7								
19	1	2	3		5	6	4	8	9	10	11		7								
20	1	2	3		5	6	4	8	9	11		10	7								
21	1	2	3		5	6	4	8	9		11		7				10				
22	1	2	3		5	6	4	8	9	10	11		7								
23	1	2	3		5	6	4	7		10	11								9		
24	1	2	3		5	6	4	8	9	10	11		7								
25	1	2			5	6	4	8	9	10			7						3	11	
26	1	2	3		5	6	4	8	9	11	7	10									
27	1	2	3		5		4	8			11	6		7			10		9		
28		2			5		4	8			11	6	7	1				10	3	9	
29		2			5	6	4	8			11			3	7	1				9	
30		2			5	6	4			10	11		3	7	1			8		9	
31		2	3		5	6	4	7	10		11		8		1					9	
32		2	3		5	6	4	7	10		11		8		1					9	
33		2	3		5	6	4	8		10	11			7	1					9	
34		2	3		5	6	4	8		10	11			7	1					9	
Apps	26	33	29	1	32	31	34	32	28	28	29	26	19	8	1	2	4	2	9		
Goals		1	1	1			1	4	11	15	5	9	3	3			2		6		

Pos	P	W	D	L	F	A	Pts
1st	34	22	6	6	62	33	50

League Cup Section 3

No.	Date	Opposition	H.T.	Res.	Att.	Goalscorers
1	8 Aug	HEARTS	0-0	1-1	8832	McIlroy
2	12	Partick Thistle	0-0	0-0	7767	
3	15	Celtic	0-1	1-4	22017	Watson
4	22	Hearts	0-0	1-0	10391	McInally
5	26	PARTICK THISTLE	2-0	4-0	6344	Hamilton(2), Murray, McInally
6	29	CELTIC	0-0	2-0	10834	Hamilton, McIlroy

Pos	P	W	D	L	F	A	Pts
2nd	6	3	2	1	9	6	8

Scottish Cup

No.	Date	Opposition	H.T.	Res.	Att.	Goalscorers
1	6 Feb	COWDENBEATH	1-0	5-0	6276	McInally(3), McLean(2)
2	20	East Fife	0-0	0-0	9003	
2R	24	EAST FIFE	1-0	3-0	10201	McInally(2), Hamilton
QF	6 Mar	Celtic	0-1	2-3	47000	McInally(2)

Inter-Cities Fairs Cup

No.	Date	Opposition	H.T.	Res.	Att.	Goalscorers
1	2 Sep	Eintracht F.	0-0	0-3	35000	
1	22	EINTRACHT F. (Agg. 5-4)	2-1	5-1	14930	Hamilton(2), McIlroy, McFadzean, McInally
2	11 Nov	EVERTON	0-0	0-2	23561	
2	23	Everton (Agg. 1-6)	1-2	1-4	30730	McIlroy

Summer Cup

Pos	P	W	D	L	F	A	Pts
2nd	6	4	1	1	17	9	9

No.	Date	Opposition	H.T.	Res.	Att.	Goalscorers
1	1 Mar	AIRDRIEONIANS	2-0	3-1	3904	Sneddon, McInally, Murray
2	5	Third Lanark	0-0	3-0	667	Black(2), McIlroy
3	8	MOTHERWELL	0-0	1-0	5061	McInally
4	12	Airdrieonians	0-0	4-2	861	McIlroy, McIlroy, Sneddon, Murray
5	15	THIRD LANARK	3-1	6-2	3718	McIlroy(2), Murray(2), Black, McInally
6	19	Motherwell	0-1	0-3	6519	

New York Int. Tourn.

Pos	P	W	D	L	F	A	Pts
4th	6	1	1	4	5	11	3

No.	Date	Opposition	H.T.	Res.	Att.	Goalscorers
1	4 Jul	Ferencvaros	1-0	1-2	6000	O.G.
2	7	West Bromwich Albion	1-0	2-0	5000	Black, Hamilton
3	11	Polonia Bytom	1-1	1-1	5000	Sneddon
4	18	West Bromwich Albion	0-2	0-2	4000	
5	21	Polonia Bytom	0-1	0-2	4000	
6	25	Ferencvaros	1-1	1-4	5000	McIlroy

SEASON 1965-66 Division One

No.	Date	Opposition	H.T.	Res.	Att.	Goalscorers	Ferguson	King	Watson	Murray	Beattie	McFadzean	McLean	Hamilton	Black	Sneddon	McIlroy	McInally	McGrory	O'Connor	Malone	Dickson	Mason	Brown	Queen	Layburn	Bertelsen
1	25 Aug	PARTICK THISTLE	0-0	2-1	7806	McIlroy(2)	1	2	3	4	5	6	7	8	9	10	11										
2	11 Sep	Hibernian	2-0	3-3	13385	McIlroy(3)	1	2	3	4	5	6	7		9	10	11	8									
3	18	ST. MIRREN	2-0	3-1	6538	McFadzean, McLean, Hamilton	1	2	3	4	6	10	7	9			11	8	5								
4	25	Dunfermline	0-0	0-1	7104		1	2	3		6		7	9		10	11	8	5	4							
5	2 Oct	HAMILTON A.	2-1	3-1	5155	McIlroy, McLean, King	1	2	3		6		7	10	9		11	5	4	8							
6	9	Stirling Albion	1-1	3-2	3985	Hamilton(2), McIlroy	1	2		4	6	10	7	9			11	8	5				3				
7	16	DUNDEE	2-2	5-3	7829	Hamilton(2), McFadzean(2), McLean	1	2		4	6	10	7	9			11	8	5				3				
8	23	Morton	2-0	4-1	8458	McIlroy(3), Hamilton	1	2		4	6	10	7	9			11	8	5				3				
9	30	CLYDE	0-0	1-2	6362	Hamilton	1	2		4	6	10	7	9			11	8	5				3				
10	6 Nov	Aberdeen	0-0	0-1	8907		1	2	3	4	6		7	9	8		11		5								
11	13	MOTHERWELL	1-0	5-0	6689	McIlroy(2), McInally, Murray, Hamilton	1	2	3	4		6	7	9			10	11	8	5							
12	20	Rangers	0-3	0-5	33225		1	2		4			7	9			10	11	8	5	6		3				
13	27	Celtic	0-0	1-2	21131	McIlroy	1	2	3	4		6	7	9			11	8	5	10							
14	11 Dec	Falkirk	1-1	2-3	2617	McLean, McFadzean	1	2		4		6	7				11	8	5	10			3	9			
15	18	Dundee United	0-0	0-0	7170		1	2		4	6	10					11	8	5				3	9	7		
16	25	ST. JOHNSTONE	2-0	3-1	4493	McLean, McIlroy, Hamilton	1	2			6	4	7	9			11	8	5				3	10			
17	1 Jan	St. Mirren	5-1	7-4	3906	McIlroy(2),McInally(2),Mason,McLean,Murry	1		3	4	6	10	7				11	8	5				2	9			
18	3	HIBERNIAN	1-0	1-0	11298	Mason	1	2		4	6		7				10	11	8				3	9			
19	8	Partick Thistle	0-1	0-1	6310		1	2	3	4	6	10	7				11	8	5					9			
20	15	DUNFERMLINE	0-0	1-0	8526	McInally	1	2	3	4	6		7				10	11	8	5				9			
21	22	Hamilton A.	2-0	4-1	2573	Queen(2), Mason, McInally	1	2	3	4	6		7				11	8	5				9		10		
22	29	STIRLING ALBION	1-0	2-1	5651	Queen, O.G.	1	2	3	4	6		7				11	8	5				9		10		
23	12 Feb	Dundee	2-0	2-0	8782	Black(2)	1	2	3	4	6		7		9		11	8	5						10		
24	26	Clyde	1-1	4-1	5137	Queen, Murray, Black, McLean	1	2	3	4	6		7		9		11	8	5						10		
25	28	MORTON	2-0	4-0	7148	McInally(2), Queen, Murray	1	2		4	6		7		9	11		8	5						10	3	
26	9 Mar	ABERDEEN	0-0	1-3	5592	McLean	1	2		4	6	3	7		11			8	5						10		9
27	12	Motherwell	2-0	3-0	4383	McInally(2), McIlroy	1	2		4	6	3	7				11	8	5						10		9
28	19	RANGERS	0-0	1-1	25372	McLean	1	2		4	5	3	7				11	8		6					10		9
29	29	CELTIC	0-2	0-2	25035		1	2		4	5	3	7		9		11	8		6					10		
30	4 Apr	HEARTS	0-2	2-2	5026	McInally, Bertelsen	1	2		4	6		7				11	8	5						10		9
31	9	Hearts	1-2	3-2	6209	McIlroy(2), Bertelsen	1	2	3	4	6		7				11	8	5						10		9
32	16	FALKIRK	1-0	1-0	3773	McIlroy	1	2	3	4	6		7				11	8	5						10		9
33	23	DUNDEE UNITED	0-0	1-0	5711	Queen	1	2	3	4	6		7				11	8	5						10		9
34	30	St. Johnstone	0-0	1-1	2441	Bertelsen	1	2	3	4	6		7				11	8	5						10		9
		Apps					34	33	19	31	30	19	33	13	9	9	32	31	30	7	1	10	9	1	14	1	8
		Goals						1		4		4	9	9	3		20	10					3		6		3

Pos P. W. D. L. F. A. Pts.
3rd 34 20 5 9 73 46 45

League Cup Section 3

Pos P. W. D. L. F. A. Pts.
1st 6 5 0 1 11 3 10

No.	Date	Opposition	H.T.	Res.	Att.	Goalscorers	Ferguson	King	Watson	Murray	Beattie	McFadzean	McLean	Hamilton	Black	Sneddon	McIlroy	McInally	McGrory	O'Connor	Malone	Dickson	Mason	Brown	Queen	Layburn	Bertelsen
1	14 Aug	St. Johnstone	1-0	1-0	5810	McIlroy	1	2	3	4	5	6	7		9	10	11	8									
2	18	PARTICK THISTLE	1-0	2-0	9756	McIlroy, Black	1	2	3	4	5	6	7		9	10	11	8									
3	21	Dunfermline	0-1	3-1	9073	McLean, Sneddon, McIlroy	1	2	3	4	5	6	7		9	10	11	8									
4	28	ST. JOHNSTONE	0-0	3-0	7309	Black(2), Sneddon	1	2	3	4	5	6	7		9	10	11	8									
5	1 Sep	Partick Thistle	1-1	2-1	3926	McIlroy, McInally	1	2	3	4	5		6		9	10	11	8					7				
6	4	DUNFERMLINE	0-0	0-1	6858		1	2	3	4	5		6		9	10	11	8					7				
QF	15	AYR UNITED	0-0	2-0	10728	McIlroy, Black	1	2	3	4	6	8	7		9	10	11		5								
QF	22	Ayr United (Agg: 4-2)	1-2	2-2	8495	Murray, McIlroy	1	2	3	4	6	8	7	9		10	11		5								
SF	6 Oct	Rangers *	1-3	4-6	54702	McLean(3), McInally	1	2	3	4	6		7	10	9		11	8	5								

* Hampden

Scottish Cup

No.	Date	Opposition	H.T.	Res.	Att.	Goalscorers	Ferguson	King	Watson	Murray	Beattie	McFadzean	McLean	Hamilton	Black	Sneddon	McIlroy	McInally	McGrory	O'Connor	Malone	Dickson	Mason	Brown	Queen	Layburn	Bertelsen
1	5 Feb	Morton	0-1	1-1	9735	Queen	1	2	3	4	6		7				11	8	5					9	10		
1R	9	MORTON	2-0	3-0	11109	Beattie, Black, Queen	1	2	3	4	6			9			11	8	5						10		
2	21	MOTHERWELL	2-0	5-0	13209	McIlroy, Queen, Black, McInally, O.G.	1	2	3	4	6			9			11	8	5						10		
QR	5 Mar	Dunfermline	1-0	1-2	19363	McInally	1	2		4	6	3	7				11	8	5						10		

European Champions Cup

No.	Date	Opposition	H.T.	Res.	Att.	Goalscorers	Ferguson	King	Watson	Murray	Beattie	McFadzean	McLean	Hamilton	Black	Sneddon	McIlroy	McInally	McGrory	O'Connor	Malone	Dickson	Mason	Brown	Queen	Layburn	Bertelsen
1	8 Sep	17 Nentori	0-0	0-0	30000		1	2	3	4	5	6	7		9	10	11	8									
1	29	17 NENTORI (Agg: 1-0)	0-0	1-0	15717	Black	1	2	3		5	6	7	10	9		11	8		4							
2	17 Nov	REAL MADRID	1-1	2-2	24325	McLean, McInally	1	2	3	5		6	7	9			10	11	8	4							
2	1 Dec	Real Madrid (Agg: 3-7)	1-3	1-5	35000	McIlroy	1	2	3	5		6	7	9			10	11	8	4							

1965-66. Apart from departed manager Willie Waddell, this squad set out in defence of the League Championship. Back row: Smillie, Shepherd, Malone, Forsyth, T. Brown, McDonald, O'Connor. Middle row: N. McNeill (2nd XI Manager), H. Brown, Bitten, Murray, McGrory, Ferguson, McFadzean, McInally, Dickson, Layburn, J. Murdoch (Ass. Trainer). Front: W. Waddell (Manager), McLean, Mason, Black, Watson, Beattie (Capt.), King, Sneddon, Hamilton, McIlroy, W. McCrae (Trainer).

SEASON 1966-67 — Division One

No.	Date	Opposition	H.T.	Res.	Att.	Goalscorers	Dick	King	M.Watson	O'Connor	McGrory	Beattie	C.Watson	McFadzean	Bertelsen	Queen	McIlroy	Dickson	McInally	Ferguson	Murray	McLean	Sneddon	Brown	Rodman	Morrison
1	10 Sep	St. Mirren	0-1	2-3	3769	Bertelsen, McFadzean	1	2	3	4	5	6	7	8	9	10	11									
2	17	AYR UNITED	1-0	1-0	9094	C.Watson	1	2		4	5	6	7		9	10	11	3	8							
3	24	Clyde	2-1	3-1	2823	McIlroy, McInally, C.Watson		2		4	5	6	7	12		10"	11	3	8	1	9					
4	1 Oct	STIRLING ALBION	0-0	2-1	3689	McInally (2)		2		4	5	6"		12		10	11	3	8	1	9	7				
5	8	Dundee	1-0	1-1	9082	C. Watson		2		4	5	6	9	3		10	11		8	1		7				
6	15	HIBERNIAN	1-0	2-1	8341	Bertelsen, C.Watson		2		4	5	6	11	3	9	10			8	1		7				
7	29	AIRDRIEONIANS	0-0	1-0	5881	Bertelsen		2		4	5	6	11"	3	9	10		12	8	1		7				
8	5 Nov	PARTICK THISTLE	0-0	0-0	5132			2		4	5	6	11	3	9				8	1		7	10			
9	9	Rangers	0-1	0-3	28839			2	3	4	5		12		9	10"		6	8	1		7	11			
10	12	Dundee United	1-1	1-1	6278	O'Connor		2		4	5	6	10	3	9				8	1		7	11			
11	19	FALKIRK	1-0	3-0	4601	McInally, McLean, Bertelsen		2		4	5	6	10	3	9"			12	8	1		7	11			
12	26	St. Johnstone	3-0	3-1	3849	Murray (2), McIlroy		2		4	5	6	10	3			11	12	8	1	9	7"				
13	3 Dec	CELTIC	0-0	0-0	27136			2		4	5	6	10	3			11		8	1	9	7				
14	10	DUNFERMLINE	1-0	1-1	6921	McIlroy		2		4	5	6	10	3			11		8	1	9	7				
15	17	Motherwell	0-1	0-2	2601			2		4	5	6	10	3			11		8	1	9	7				
16	24	HEARTS	1-1	1-2	5039	McIlroy		2		4	5	6		3	9	10	11		8	1		7				
17	31	Aberdeen	0-0	0-4	12673			2		4	5	6		3	9	10	11		8	1		7				
18	2 Jan	ST. MIRREN	1-0	3-0	6626	Beattie, Queen, McInally		2		4	5	6	10	3		9			8	1		7	11			
19	3	Ayr United	2-1	3-2	7899	C.Watson (3)		2		4	5	6	10	3		9			8	1		7	11			
20	7	CLYDE	1-2	1-3	5885	McLean		2		4	5	6	10	8	9			3		1		7	11"	12		
21	14	Stirling Albion	0-0	4-1	3077	McIlroy, McInally, McLean, Queen		2		4	5	6	10	3		9	11		8	1		7				
22	21	DUNDEE	2-2	4-4	4685	McIlroy (2), C.Watson, McInally		2		4	5	6	10	3		9	11		8	1		7				
23	4 Feb	Hibernian	1-2	1-3	10862	Morrison	1	2	3	4	5		10				11		8			7		6		9
24	11	RANGERS	0-0	1-2	31551	McIlroy		2			5	6	10	3	9		11		8	1	4	7				
25	25	Airdrieonians	0-0	4-1	2595	Bertelsen (3), McIlroy		2		4	5	6	10	3	9		11		8	1		7				
26	4 Mar	Partick Thistle	1-0	2-1	4196	Queen, McLean		2	12	4	5	6	10"	3		9	11		8	1		7				
27	18	Falkirk	0-0	1-0	3241	McLean		2		4	5	6		3	9		11		8	1	10	7				
28	20	DUNDEE UNITED	1-0	4-0	4719	McIlroy (2), McInally, Bertelsen		2		4	5			3	9		11		8	1	6	7	10			
29	25	ST. JOHNSTONE	3-0	5-3	3948	McIlroy (3), McLean, Bertelsen		2		4"	5			3	9		11		8	1	10	7	12			
30	8 Apr	Dunfermline	1-0	1-1	4812	McIlroy		2			5	6	10	3	9		11		8	1	4	7				
31	12	MOTHERWELL	1-0	3-0	4994	McIlroy, Bertelsen, McLean		3			5	6	12	2	9	10	11"		8	1	4	7				
32	22	Hearts	0-1	0-1	5809					6	5		3		9	10	11	2	8	1	4	7				
33	1 May	ABERDEEN	0-0	1-1	5229	McLean		2		6	5		11	3	9	10			8	1	4	7				
34	15	Celtic	0-1	0-2	19077			2			5	6	11	3	9	10			8	1	4	7				
Apps.							3	32	3	29	34	29	26	29	17	22	23	8	32	31	15	31	5	3	1	1
Subs									1						2	2					3			1	1	
Goals								1			1		8	1	10	3	16		8		2	8				1

Pos	P.	W.	D.	L.	F.	A.	Pts.
7th	34	16	8	10	59	46	40

League Cup Section 2

No.	Date	Opposition	H.T.	Res.	Att.	Goalscorers	Dick	King	M.Watson	O'Connor	McGrory	Beattie	C.Watson	McFadzean	Bertelsen	Queen	McIlroy	Dickson	McInally	Ferguson	Murray	McLean	Sneddon
1	13 Aug	STIRLING ALBION	2-0	2-0	5292	Bertelsen, Queen	1	2	3		5	6		8	9	10	11				4	7	
2	17	Hibernian	1-0	1-2	11159	Queen		2	3		5	6			9	10	11			1	4	7	8
3	20	Rangers	0-0	0-0	51765			2	3	4	5	6		8	9	10	11			1		7	
4	27	Stirling Albion	0-0	0-0	3375		1	2	3	4	5	6		8	9	10	11					7	
5	31	HIBERNIAN	2-0	3-0	12285	McIlroy (2), Queen	1	2	3	4	5	6		8	9	10	11					7	
6	3 Sep	RANGERS	0-0	0-1	29743		1	2	3	4	5	6		8	9	10	11					7	

Pos	P.	W.	D.	L.	F.	A.	Pts.
3rd	6	2	2	2	6	3	6

Scottish Cup

No.	Date	Opposition	H.T.	Res.	Att.	Goalscorers	King	O'Connor	McGrory	Beattie	C.Watson	McFadzean	Bertelsen	Queen	McIlroy	McInally	Ferguson	McLean
1	28 Jan	DUNFERMLINE	0-2	2-2	12847	McInally, King	2	4	5	6	10	3	9		11	8	1	7
1R	1 Feb	Dunfermline	0-1	0-1	19000		2	4	5	6	10	3		9	11	8	1	7

Inter-Cities Fairs Cup

No.	Date	Opposition	H.T.	Res.	Att.	Goalscorers	King	O'Connor	McGrory	Beattie	C.Watson	McFadzean	Bertelsen	Queen	McIlroy	McInally	Ferguson	Murray	McLean
1		Bye																	
2	25 Oct	Royal Antwerp	1-0	1-0	10000	McInally	2	4	5	6	11	3	9	10		8	1		7
2	2 Nov	ROYAL ANTWERP (Agg: 8-2)	3-0	7-2	11963	McInally (2), McLean (2), Queen (2), C.Watson	2	4	5	6	11	3	9	10		8	1		7
3	14 Dec	LA GANTOISE	1-0	1-0	8612	Murray	2	4	5	6	10	3			11	8	1	9	7
3	21	La Gantoise (Agg: 3-1)	0-0	2-1*	9500	McInally, McLean	2	4	5	6		3	9	10	11	8	1		7
QF	19 Apr	Lokomotiv Leipzig	0-1	0-1	30000		3		5	6			9	10	11	8	1	4	7
QF	26	LOKOMOTIV LEIP. (Agg: 2-1)	1-0	2-0	15595	Murray, McIlroy	2		5	6	10	3	9		11	8	1	4	7
SF	19 May	Leeds United	2-4	2-4	43189	McIlroy (2)	2	8	5	6	7	3	9	10	11		1	4	
SF	24	LEEDS UNITED (Agg: 2-4)	0-0	0-0	24831		2		5	6		3	9	10	11	8	1	4	7

* After Extra Time. 90 minutes 0-1.

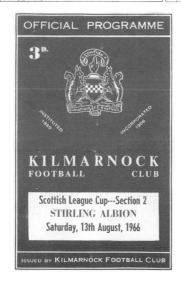

OFFICIAL PROGRAMME
3 D.
KILMARNOCK FOOTBALL CLUB
INSTITUTED 1869 — INCORPORATED 1906
Scottish League Cup---Section 2
STIRLING ALBION
Saturday, 13th August, 1966
ISSUED BY KILMARNOCK FOOTBALL CLUB

Killie get the season under way against Stirling Albion.

SEASON 1967-68 — Division One

No.	Date	Opposition	H.T.	Res.	Att.	Goalscorers
1	9 Sep	MORTON	2-0	3-1	7508	Murray(2), McInally
2	16	Stirling Albion	0-0	0-0	2636	
3	23	AIRDRIEONIANS	1-2	2-2	4452	Cameron(2)
4	30	Dunfermline	1-0	2-1	3987	McInally, McIlroy
5	7 Oct	DUNDEE	0-0	0-0	4640	
6	14	Falkirk	1-1	1-1	3227	McIlroy
7	21	RAITH ROVERS	1-1	1-2	3286	Cameron
8	28	Clyde	0-0	1-2	1663	McIlroy
9	11 Nov	PARTICK THISTLE	0-1	0-3	2719	
10	15	Celtic	0-1	0-3	26727	
11	18	Motherwell	0-1	2-1	2270	Cameron, Morrison
12	25	Dundee United	0-1	2-3	5144	Morrison, McLean
13	2 Dec	HEARTS	2-2	5-2	5558	Morrison(2), Queen
14	9	ABERDEEN	1-0	3-0	4834	Morrison(2), Queen
15	16	St. Johnstone	1-0	1-0	2439	Cameron
16	23	Rangers	0-3	1-4	33239	Cameron
17	30	HIBERNIAN	0-0	1-0	6460	McLean
18	1 Jan	Morton	0-1	2-3	3762	Queen, Morrison
19	2	STIRLING ALBION	2-0	5-2	4743	Morrison(2), Queen, McIlroy, O.G.
20	20	Dundee	2-2	5-6	6310	Morrison(2), Cameron(2), McIlroy
21	3 Feb	FALKIRK	1-0	3-0	2400	Morrison, Queen, Cameron
22	6	DUNFERMLINE	0-0	1-1	3056	Queen
23	10	Raith Rovers	0-0	2-1	2836	Queen, Cameron
24	21	Airdrieonians	1-0	2-3	2322	Queen, Gilmour
25	28	CLYDE	1-0	5-1	2968	Queen(2), McLean, Cameron, Gilmour
26	2 Mar	CELTIC	0-3	0-6	18591	
27	13	Partick Thistle	0-0	0-1	1700	
28	16	MOTHERWELL	1-0	1-1	2333	Queen
29	6 Apr	Aberdeen	1-1	1-1	5465	Morrison
30	10	Hearts	0-0	0-1	6000	
31	13	ST. JOHNSTONE	1-0	1-0	2939	Morrison
32	17	DUNDEE UNITED	1-0	4-0	3020	Queen(2), McFadzean, Dickson
33	20	RANGERS	1-1	1-1	17286	McFadzean
34	27	Hibernian	1-1	3-3	4688	McLean, Queen, McFadzean

Player appearances (columns: McLaughlan, King, M.Watson, Murray, McGrory, Beattie, McLean, McInally, Cameron, Queen, McIlroy, C.Watson, McFadzean, Dickson, Gilmour, Coghill, Arthur, Morrison, Sinclair, Brown, Rodman, Dick, Sneddon)

No.	McLaughlan	King	M.Watson	Murray	McGrory	Beattie	McLean	McInally	Cameron	Queen	McIlroy	C.Watson	McFadzean	Dickson	Gilmour	Coghill	Arthur	Morrison	Sinclair	Brown	Rodman	Dick	Sneddon
1	1	2	3	4	5	6	7	8	9	10	11												
2	1	2	3	4	5	6	7	8	9	10		11											
3	1	2"	12	4	5	6	7	8	9	10		11		3									
4	1		2	4	5	6	7	8	9"	10	11			3	12								
5	1		2	4	5	6	7		9	10	11			3		8							
6	1	2		4	5	6	7		9	10	11			3		8							
7	1	2		4	5	6	7		9	10	11			3		8							
8	1	2		4	5	6	7	8	9		11			3		10							
9	1	2		4"	5	6	7	8	9		11			3		10							
10	1				5	6	7		8	10	11			3	4			2	9				
11	1				5	6	7		8					3	4	10	11	2	9				
12	1			4	5	6	7							3				2	9		10	11	
13	1			4	5	6	7	12			11		8	3				2	9		10"		
14	1			4	5	6	7				11		8	3				2	9		10		
15	1			4	5	6"	7				11		8	12				2	9		10		
16	1			4	5	6	7				11		8	3				2	9		10		
17	1				5	6	7		9				8	11	3	4		2			10		
18	1				5	6	7			11"			8	12	3	4		2	9		10		
19	1				5	6	7				11		8	3	4			2	9		6		
20	1			4	5	6"	7				10		8	11	3	12		2	9				
21	1		3		5		7				11		8		4	10		2	9		6		
22	1	12	3		5		7				11		8		6			2	9"		4		
23	1		3		5		7				11		8		6			2	9		4		
24	1				5	6	7				11		8		3			2	9		4		
25	1				5	6	7				11		8		3			2	9		4		
26	1				5	6	7				11		8		3			2	9		4		
27	1				5	6	7				11		8		3			2	9		4		
28		3			5	6	7				11		8		4			2	9				1
29	1	3		4	5	6	7						8		11		10	2	9				
30	1	3		4	5		7					12	8		11		10	6			2	9"	
31	1	3		4	5		7						8		11		10	6			2	9	
32	1	3		4	5		7						8		11		10	6			2	9	
33		3		4	5		7						8		11		10	6			2	9	1
34		3		4	5"		7						8		11		10	6			2	9	12 1
Apps	31	14	7	21	34	25	34	6	27	30	17	2	30	9	15	4	25	24	7	1	8	3	
Subs		1	1									1	1	1	2			1	1			1	
Goals				2			4	2	11	14	5		3	1	2			14					

Pos	P	W	D	L	F.	A.	Pts.
7th	34	13	8	13	59	57	34

League Cup Section 1

Pos	P	W	D	L	F.	A.	Pts.
1st	6	3	2	1	11	5	8

No.	Date	Opposition	H.T.	Res.	Att.	Goalscorers
1	12 Aug	DUNFERMLINE	1-1	2-2	7269	Cameron, McInally
2	16	Airdrieonians	1-1	2-1	2596	Cameron, McInally
3	19	PARTICK THISTLE	2-0	4-0	5892	Cameron(3), McLean
4	26	Dunfermline	2-0	3-1	8155	Cameron(3)
5	30	AIRDRIEONIANS	0-0	0-0	5687	
6	2 Sep	Partick Thistle	0-0	0-1	3432	
QF	13	Morton	2-2	2-3	8777	Queen, McLean
QF	27	MORTON (Agg: 3-5)	0-0	1-2	14344	McInally

League Cup appearances:

No.	McLaughlan	King	M.Watson	Murray	McGrory	Beattie	McLean	McInally	Cameron	Queen	McIlroy	C.Watson	McFadzean	Dickson	Gilmour	Coghill	Arthur	Morrison	Sinclair	Brown	Rodman	Dick	Sneddon
1	1	2		4	5	6		8	9	10	11	7	3"										12
2	1	2	3	4	5	6		8	9	10	11	7											
3	1	2	3	4	5	6"	7	8	9	10	11	12											
4	1	2	3	4	5		7	8	9	10	11				6								
5	1	2	3	4	5		7	8	9	10	11				6								
6	1	2	3	4	5	6	7	8	9	10	11												
QF	1	2	3	4	5	6	7	8	9	10	11												
QF	1		2	4	5	6	7	8	9	10	11			3									

Scottish Cup

No.	Date	Opposition	H.T.	Res.	Att.	Goalscorers
1	27 Jan	Partick Thistle	0-0	0-0	9800	
1R	31	PARTICK THISTLE	0-2	1-2	9191	Morrison

Scottish Cup appearances:

No.	McLaughlan	King	M.Watson	Murray	McGrory	Beattie	McLean	McInally	Cameron	Queen	McIlroy	C.Watson	McFadzean	Dickson	Gilmour	Coghill	Arthur	Morrison	Sinclair	Brown	Rodman	Dick	Sneddon
1	1		3	4	5		7			10			8		11			6			2	9	
1R	1		3	4	5		7			10			8		11			6			2	9	

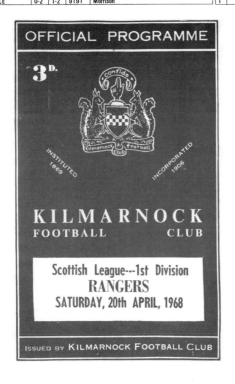

OFFICIAL PROGRAMME

3D.

KILMARNOCK FOOTBALL CLUB

INSTITUTED 1869 — INCORPORATED 1906

Scottish League---1st Division
RANGERS
SATURDAY, 20th APRIL, 1968

ISSUED BY KILMARNOCK FOOTBALL CLUB

The last of its kind.
This match against Rangers was
the last issue of the "blue-cover"
programme.

SEASON 1968-69 Division One

No.	Date	Opposition	H.T.	Res.	Att.	Goalscorers	McLaughlan	King	Dickson	Gilmour	McGrory	Beattie	T.McLean	Queen	Morrison	J.McLean	Cook	McIlroy	Arthur	Rodman	McFadzean	Evans	Sinclair	McKellar	Miller	Dick	Waddell
1	7 Sep	St. Mirren	1-1	1-1	5204	Queen	1	2	3	4	5	6	7	8	9	10	11										
2	14	MORTON	0-0	1-0	5812	Morrison	1	2	3	4	5	6	7	8	9	10		11									
3	21	Rangers	1-0	3-3	39407	Morrison(2), Queen	1	2	3	4			7	8	9	10	11			6							
4	28	DUNFERMLINE	0-1	0-1	6507		1	2	3	4	5		7	8	9	10	11			6							
5	5 Oct	Arbroath	1-1	2-1	3015	J.McLean(2)	1	2	3	4	5		7	8	9	10		11		6							
6	12	DUNDEE UNITED	3-0	3-0	5151	Morrison, T.McLean, J.McLean	1		3	4"	5	6	7	8	9	10			2	12							
7	19	Hibernian	0-0	0-1	8653		1	2	3	4	5		7	8	9	10	11			6							
8	26	RAITH ROVERS	0-4	4-4	4565	T.McLean(2), Morrison, McIlroy	1	2	3	4	5	12	7		9	10	8	11	6"								
9	2 Nov	Hearts	0-0	1-0	6943	T.McLean	1	2	3	4	5	6	7	8	9	10		11									
10	9	FALKIRK	1-1	5-1	4340	McIlroy(3), J.McLean, Morrison	1	2	3	4	5	6	7	8	9	10		11									
11	16	Partick Thistle	0-0	2-0	4400	McIlroy, Queen	1	2	3	4	5	6	7	8	9	10		11									
12	23	DUNDEE	1-0	1-0	6594	Morrison	1	2	3	4	5	6	7	8	9	10		11									
13	30	Clyde	1-0	1-2	3824	Morrison	1	2	3	4	5	6	7		9	10		11	12		8"						
14	7 Dec	Airdrieonians	0-0	2-0	2759	Morrsion, McIlroy	1	2	3	4	5	6"	7	8	9	10		11					12				
15	14	ST. JOHNSTONE	1-0	2-0	5154	Morrsion, J.McLean	1	2	3	4	5	6	7	8	9	10		11									
16	21	Celtic	0-1	1-1	37321	McIlroy	1	2	3	4	5	6	7	8	9	10		11									
17	28	ABERDEEN	1-0	2-1	7128	McIlroy, Morrison	1	2	3	4	5	6	7	8	9	10		11									
18	1 Jan	ST. MIRREN	0-0	0-0	12082		1	2	3	4	5	6	7	8	9"			11			12						
19	2	Morton	1-0	2-3	7300	McIlroy(2)	1	2	3	4	5		7	8	9	10"		11	6	12							
20	4	RANGERS	2-2	3-3	32893	Dickson, T.McLean, McIlroy	1	2	3	4	5	6	7	8	9	10		11									
21	11	Dunfermline	1-0	1-1	8662	O.G.	1	2	3	4	5	6	7		9	8		11	10								
22	18	ARBROATH	0-0	1-0	5544	J.McLean	1	2	3	4	5	6	7		9	8		11	10								
23	1 Feb	Dundee United	1-0	2-2	5076	Queen, Morrison	1	2		4	5	6"	7	8	9			11	3	10	12						
24	19	HIBERNIAN	1-0	2-1	5673	McIlroy, Queen	1	2	3	4	5	6	7	8	9			11	10								
25	22	HEARTS	0-0	1-0	7025	McIlroy	1	2	3	4	5	6	7		9			11					10				
26	26	Raith Rovers	0-0	0-0	2246		1	2	3	4"	5	6	7	8	9	10		11					12				
27	8 Mar	PARTICK THISTLE	0-1	1-1	4541	McFadzean	1	2	3	4	5		7		9			11	6	8							
28	12	Falkirk	1-1	1-1	2838	Dickson	1	2	3	4	5	6	7		9	10		11	12		8"						
29	15	Dundee	0-0	0-0	4345		1	2	3	4	5	6	7	8	9	10		11									
30	22	CLYDE	0-0	0-0	5042		1	2	3	4	5	6	7	8	9	10		11									
31	29	AIRDRIEONIANS	1-0	2-1	4069	Gilmour, McKellar	1	2	3	4	5	6	7	8	9"			10	11					12			
32	5 Apr	St. Johnstone	0-0	0-1	3748		1	2	3	4	5	6	7	8		10	11"						12	9			
33	19	Aberdeen	1-0	1-0	7502	Cook	1	2	3		5	6	4	9	8	7		11					10				
34	21	CELTIC	2-0	2-2	18873	Morrison, Queen	1	2	3		5	6	7	8	9	10		11		4							
					Apps.		34	33	33	32	34	27	33	28	33	31	7	28	6		6		7	1	1		
					Subs									1					1	1	2	3	2	1			
					Goals			2	1				5	6	13	6	1	13			1			1			

Pos	P	W	D	L	F	A	Pts.
4th	34	15	14	5	50	32	44

League Cup Section 2

Pos	P	W	D	L	F	A	Pts.
4th	6	0	3	3	5	14	3

No.	Date	Opposition	H.T.	Res.	Att.	Goalscorers
1	10 Aug	Dundee	0-4	0-4	7648	
2	14	AIRDRIEONIANS	0-2	0-3	5446	
3	17	HEARTS	3-1	3-3	7213	Queen(2), Cook
4	24	DUNDEE	0-0	2-2	5435	T.McLean, Morrison
5	28	Airdrieonians	0-1	0-2	3692	
6	31	Hearts	0-0	0-0	6283	

Scottish Cup

No.	Date	Opposition	H.T.	Res.	Att.	Goalscorers
1	25 Jan	GLASGOW UNIVERSITY	2-0	6-0	7771	Queen(3), McIlroy(2), O.G.
2	8 Feb	Montrose	0-1	1-1	2600	Morrison
2R	12	MONTROSE	3-0	4-1	7385	T.McLean(3), Morrison
QF	1 Mar	Aberdeen	0-0	0-0	22601	
QFR	5	ABERDEEN	0-1	0-3	18128	

USA Tournament (Representing St. Louis)

Pos	P	W	D	L	F	A	Pts.
5th	8	2	1	5	11	18	26

No.	Date	Opposition	H.T.	Res.	Att.	Goalscorers
1	3 May	Aston Villa	1-0	1-2	8171	J.McLean
2	9	West Ham United	1-1	2-1	7764	Queen, Morrison
3	11	Wolves	1-2	2-3	3000	Morrison, T.McLean
4	14	Dundee United	1-0	3-3	1200	Queen(2), T.McLean
5	16	Wolves	0-2	0-3	5000	
6	23	Dundee United	0-0	0-1	5000	
7	25	Aston Villa	2-0	2-1	5000	J.McLean, Queen
8	30	West Ham United	0-2	1-4	3008	Morrison

Venues in order: Atlanta, Seattle, Kansas City, Dallas, St.Louis, St.Louis, St. Louis Baltimore

Centenary Match

No.	Date	Opposition	H.T.	Res.	Att.	Goalscorers
1	12 Apr	EINTRACHT FRANKFURT	1-0	1-1	10513	Queen

Players and officials assemble at Centenary match v Eintracht in April 1969.
Match finished 1-1, Gerry Queen scoring for Killie.

No.	Date	Opposition	H.T.	Res.	Att.	Goalscorers	McLaughlan	King	Dickson	Gilmour	McGrory	Beattie	T.McLean	Mathie	Morrison	J.McLean	W.Waddell	Cook	Strachan	Rodman	Maxwell	Arthur	Sheed	MacDonald	R.Waddell
1	30 Aug	Motherwell	0-0	0-1	6762		1	2	3	4	5	6	7	8	9	10	11"	12							
2	3 Sep	CELTIC	1-2	2-4	23821	Mathie, Morrison	1	2	3			6	7	8	9	10	4	11	5						
3	6	RAITH ROVERS	0-0	1-0	3978	Mathie	1	2	3	4		6	7	8			10	11	5						
4	13	Hearts	1-0	1-4	8227	Morrison	1	2	3	4		5"	7	8	9	10	12	11	6						
5	20	AYR UNITED	2-1	4-1	10087	Cook(2), T.McLean, Mathie	1	2	3	4	5		7	9	8	10		11	6						
6	27	St. Mirren	1-0	2-0	5342	Mathie, Morrison	1	2	3	4	5		7	9	8	10		11	6						
7	4 Oct	Partick Thistle	1-0	2-2	4025	Gilmour, Strachan	1	2	3	4	5		7	9	8	10		11	6						
8	11	DUNDEE	2-0	3-0	4895	Morrison, Mathie	1	2	3	4	5		7	9	8	10		11	6						
9	18	Dunfermline	0-1	1-2	7974	O.G.	1	2	3	4	5		7	9	8	10		11	6						
10	25	HIBERNIAN	1-1	2-2	7608	Gilmour, Mathie	1	2	3	4	5		7	9	8	10		11	6						
11	1 Nov	Clyde	3-2	3-2	1944	Cook, Mathie, Morrison	1	2	3	4			7	9	8	10		11	6	5					
12	8	MORTON	1-0	5-2	4141	T.McLean(2), Mathie(2), Dickson	1	2	3	4	5	6	7	9	8"		10	12	11						
13	15	Rangers	1-2	3-5	35499	Morrison(2), Mathie	1	2	3	4"	5	6	7	8	9	10	12	11							
14	29	ABERDEEN	0-0	0-2	5396		1	2	3	4	5	6	7	9	8		11	10							
15	2 Dec	ST. JOHNSTONE	3-0	4-1	3795	Mathie(2), Gilmour, Morrison	1	2	3	4	5		7	9	8		10	11	6						
16	6	Dundee United	1-1	2-2	5639	Mathie, Morrison	1	2	3	4	5		7	9	8		10	11	6						
17	13	MOTHERWELL	1-1	2-2	5027	Cook, T.McLean	1	2	3	4	5		7	9	8		10	11	6						
18	20	Celtic	1-2	1-3	31459	Morrison	1	2	3	4	5	6"	7	9	8		10	11	12						
19	1 Jan	ST. MIRREN	0-0	1-1	7587	T.McLean	1	2"	3	4	5		7	9	8		10	11	6		12				
20	3	Ayr United	0-1	2-3	12722	Mathie(2)	1		3	4	5		7	9	8		10	11	6			2			
21	17	HEARTS	0-0	0-0	5593		1	2	3	12	5		7	9	4	10		11	6				8"		
22	31	Raith Rovers	0-2	3-2	1713	MacDonald, Mathie, Morrison	1	2	3		5		7	9	8	10		11	6					4	
23	11 Feb	DUNDEE UNITED	1-0	3-1	4647	Cook, Mathie, Morrison	1	2	3	4	5		7	9	8	10		11						6	
24	25	PARTICK THISTLE	2-0	4-2	5173	Morrison(3), Mathie	1	2	3	4	5		7	9	8	10		11						6	
25	28	Dundee	0-2	0-3	7666		1	2	3	4	5		7	9	8	10		11						6	
26	7 Mar	DUNFERMLINE	1-0	1-0	5391	Mathie	1	2	3	4	5		7	9	8	10		11						6	
27	21	CLYDE	1-0	2-1	3811	T.McLean, Morrison	1	2	3	4	5		7	9	8	10		11						6	
28	25	Hibernian	1-1	1-2	7100	T.McLean	1	2	3	4			7	9	8	10		11	5					6	
29	28	Morton	0-0	1-1	2680	Mathie	1	2	3		6		7	9	8	10		11	5					4	
30	1 Apr	Airdrieonians	0-0	0-1	1431		1	2	3	4	5		7	9	8	10		11	5						
31	4	RANGERS	0-1	2-2	11135	J.McLean, T.McLean	1	2	3	4	6		7	9	8	10		11	5						
32	6	Aberdeen	1-0	2-2	6155	Mathie, Morrison	1	2	3	4	6		7	9	8			11	5					10	
33	11	AIRDRIEONIANS	1-0	1-0	2223	T.McLean	1	2	3	4"	6		7	9	8	12		11	5					10	
34	18	St. Johnstone	1-1	1-1	1954	Morrison	1		2		12	6		9	8			10	11"	7		5	3		4
						Apps.	34	33	33	32	29	8	33	34	34	24	10	33	18	8	1	1	1	11	
						Subs				2									1	3	1	1		1	
						Goals		1	3		9			21	19	1		5	1					1	

Pos	P.	W.	D.	L.	F.	A.	Pts.
6th	34	13	10	11	62	57	36

League Cup Section 3

Pos	P.	W.	D.	L.	F.	A.	Pts.
2nd	6	3	1	2	12	5	7

No.	Date	Opposition	H.T.	Res.	Att.	Goalscorers	McLaughlan	King	Dickson	Gilmour	McGrory	Beattie	T.McLean	Mathie	Morrison	J.McLean	W.Waddell	Cook	Strachan	Rodman	Maxwell	Arthur	Sheed	MacDonald	R.Waddell
1	9 Aug	Partick Thistle	1-0	2-0	4915	Gilmour, Morrison	1	2	3	8	5	6	7		9	10	11								4
2	13	ST. JOHNSTONE	1-2	2-3	5603	Gilmour, T.McLean	1	2	3	8	5	6	7		9	10	11								4
3	16	Dundee	0-0	0-0	9207		1	2	3	8	5		7		9	10	6	11							4
4	20	St. Johnstone	0-1	1-2	7313	J.McLean	1	2	3	4	5	6	7	8	9	10	11								
5	25	PARTICK THISTLE	3-0	6-0	3472	Mathie(2), W.Waddell(2), T.McLean, Morrison	1	2	3	4	5	6	7	8	9	10	11								
6	27	Dundee	1-0	1-0	3971	King	1	2	3	4	5	6	7	8	9	10	11								

Scottish Cup

No.	Date	Opposition	H.T.	Res.	Att.	Goalscorers	McLaughlan	King	Dickson	Gilmour	McGrory	Beattie	T.McLean	Mathie	Morrison	J.McLean	W.Waddell	Cook	Strachan	Rodman	Maxwell	Arthur	Sheed	MacDonald	R.Waddell
1	24 Jan	PARTICK THISTLE	2-0	3-0	7763	Cook, Mathie, Morrison	1	2	3	4	5		7	9	8	10		11	6						
2	7 Feb	HEARTS	1-0	2-0	14782	Cook, Mathie	1	2	3		5		7	9	8	10		11	6					4	
QF	21	Motherwell	0-0	1-0	16514	Mathie	1	2	3	4	5		7	9	8	10		11						6	
SF	14 Mar	Aberdeen *	0-1	0-1	25812		1	2	3	4	5		7	9	8	10		11						6	

* Muirton Park, Perth

Inter-Cities Fairs Cup

No.	Date	Opposition	H.T.	Res.	Att.	Goalscorers	McLaughlan	King	Dickson	Gilmour	McGrory	Beattie	T.McLean	Mathie	Morrison	J.McLean	W.Waddell	Cook	Strachan	Rodman	Maxwell	Arthur	Sheed	MacDonald	R.Waddell
1	16 Sep	Zurich	2-2	2-3	13500	J.McLean, Mathie	1	2	3		4	5	6	7	11	9	10			8					
1	30	ZURICH (Agg: 5-4)	1-0	3-1	9593	McGrory, T.McLean, Morrison	1	2	3	4	5	12	7	9	8	10"		11	6						
2	19 Nov	SLAVIA SOFIA	2-0	4-1	9535	Mathie(2), Cook, Gilmour	1	2	3	4	5	6	7	9	8	10"	12	11							
2	26	Slavia Sofia (Agg: 4-3)	0-2	0-2	12000		1	2	3	4	5	6	7	9	8		11	10							
3	17 Dec	DINAMO BACAU	0-0	1-1	7749	Mathie	1	2	3	4	5	6	11	9	8			10	7						
3	13 Jan	Dinamo Bacau (Agg: 1-3)	0-1	0-2	20000		1	2	3	4"	5		7	9	8	10		6				12	11		

Back row: W. Dickson, R. Arthur, E. Morrison, J. Gilmour, J. McGrory, A. McDonald, R. Mathie, J. McLean.
Front row: T. McLean, W. Waddell, A. McLaughlan, A. King, J. Cook.

SEASON 1970-71   Division One

Match results

No.	Date	Opposition	H.T.	Res.	Att.	Goalscorers
1	29 Aug	Motherwell	0-2	1-4	5661	Cook
2	5 Sep	ST. MIRREN	0-0	1-2	4256	Mathie
3	12	Ayr United	1-1	1-1	8488	McLean
4	19	ABERDEEN	0-4	0-4	5056	
5	26	Cowdenbeath	2-1	2-1	3148	Morrison, Gilmour
6	3 Oct	HEARTS	2-0	3-0	5365	McLean, Cook, Dickson
7	10	Falkirk	0-1	0-3	4018	
8	17	DUNDEE UNITED	1-1	2-1	3644	McCulloch, Mathie
9	24	MORTON	0-1	2-2	3743	Mathie, Cook
10	31	Dundee	0-1	0-3	3578	
11	7 Nov	ST. JOHNSTONE	1-2	2-4	3910	McLean, Mathie
12	14	Celtic	0-2	0-3	24410	
13	21	Hibernian	0-1	0-1	6364	
14	28	AIRDRIEONIANS	2-2	2-3	3912	Graham, McLean
15	5 Dec	Dunfermline	0-0	1-0	4164	Gilmour
16	12	CLYDE	1-0	1-1	3805	Morrison
17	19	Rangers	0-1	2-4	19450	McLean, Maxwell
18	26	MOTHERWELL	0-0	0-0	5323	
19	1 Jan	St. Mirren	1-0	3-2	5934	McLean(2), Maxwell
20	2	AYR UNITED	1-0	1-1	15240	McLean
21	9	Aberdeen	0-1	0-3	19032	
22	16	COWDENBEATH	1-1	2-1	4015	Gilmour, Waddell
23	30	Hearts	0-1	0-2	8823	
24	6 Feb	FALKIRK	2-2	3-2	4712	McCulloch, Morrison, O.G.
25	20	Dundee United	1-1	2-3	3852	McCulloch, Cook
26	27	Morton	0-2	0-3	2324	
27	9 Mar	DUNDEE	0-1	1-1	3003	McLean
28	13	St. Johnstone	1-2	3-2	8513	McCulloch, Morrison, O.G.
29	20	CELTIC	1-0	1-4	17075	Morrison
30	27	HIBERNIAN	3-0	4-1	4209	McCulloch, Gilmour, McLean, Cook
31	10 Apr	DUNFERMLINE	0-0	0-0	5050	
32	14	Airdrieonians	1-1	1-1	2064	Cook
33	17	Clyde	0-0	1-0	1537	Waddell
34	24	RANGERS	1-1	1-4	8544	McCulloch

Pos P. W. D. L. F. A. Pts.
13th 34 10 8 16 43 67 28

Appearances (shirt numbers worn)

No.	Hunter	Swan	Dickson	Morrison	Rodman	MacDonald	T.McLean	Sheed	Mathie	Maxwell	Cook	J.McCulloch	King	Gilmour	McGrory	Arthur	Johnston	McSherry	Gillespie	Leckie	Wylie	I.Fleming	Cairns	Graham	W.Waddell	McLaughlan	Whyte
1	1	2	3	4	5	6	7	8"	9	10	11	12															
2	1		3	8					9	10	11		2	4	5	6	7										
3	1		3	9"	6		7		12	10	11			4	5	2		8									
4	1	3	2"	8			7		9	4	11"	12			5	6		10									
5	1		3	9		6	7		11	8				4	5	2		10									
6	1		3	8	10	6	7		9	2	11			4	5												
7	1		3	8"		6	7		9	2	11			4	5				12	10							
8	1		3				7		9	6	11	8		2	5			10	4"	12							
9	1		3		6		7		9	10	11		2	4	5			8									
10	1		3		6	8	7		9"		11		2	4	5			12									
11	1		3	8	6	10	7		12	2	11			4	5				9"								
12	1		3	9	2	6	7		12	8"	11			4	5								10				
13	1		3	8	2	6	7		9"	12	11			4	5								10				
14	1		3	9	2	6	7			12	11			4	5								10	8"			
15	1		3	9	8	6	7			2	11			4	5								10				
16	1		3	9	8	6	7			2	11			4	5								10				
17	1		3	9		6	7			8	11			4	5								10				2
18	1		3	9		6	7			8	11			4	5								10				2
19	1		3	9		6	7			8	11			4	5								10				2
20	1		3	9		6	7			8	11			4	5								10				2
21	1		3	9		6	7			8	11			4	5								10				2
22	1		3	12		6"	7			9				4	5								10	8	11		2
23			3	12		6	7		9					4	5				8"		10	1					2
24			3	8		6	7				11	9		4	5						10					1	2
25			3	8			7			2	11	9		4	5						10					1	6
26			3	8			7				11	9		4	5			6			12		10"			1	2
27	1		3	12		6	7			8	11	9		4	5						10"						2
28	1		3	8		6	7		12		11	9		4"	5								10				2
29	1		3	8	12	6	7				11	9		4	5						10"						2
30	1		3	8		6	7			8	11	9		4	5						10"			12			2
31	1		3	8"		6	7				11	9		4	5						10			12			2
32	1		3	8		6	7				11	9		4	5								10				2
33	1		3			6	7				11	9		4	5				8				10				2
34	1		3	12		6	7				11	9		4	5						10"						2
Apps	30	2	34	26	11	27	33	1	16	17	32	12	3	32	33	4	1	7	2	1		1	16	2	9	4	18
Subs				4	1				1	2		2				2			1			1		1	1	2	
Goals		1	5				10		4	1	6	6		4										1	2		

League Cup Section 3

Pos P. W. D. L. F. A. Pts.
2nd 6 4 1 1 8 4 9

No.	Date	Opposition	H.T.	Res.	Att.	Goalscorers
1	8 Aug	AYR UNITED	0-0	1-0	7073	Mathie
2	12	St. Mirren	2-0	3-1	4488	Gilmour, Cook, Mathie
3	15	Dundee	0-1	0-2	7644	
4	19	ST. MIRREN	1-0	2-0	4931	McLean(2)
5	22	Ayr United	0-0	0-0	7911	
6	26	DUNDEE	2-0	2-1	3280	Mathie, McLean

No.	Hunter	Swan	Dickson	Morrison	Rodman	MacDonald	T.McLean	Sheed	Mathie	Maxwell	Cook	J.McCulloch	King	Gilmour	McGrory	Arthur	Johnston	McSherry	Gillespie	Leckie	Wylie	I.Fleming	Cairns	Graham	W.Waddell	McLaughlan	Whyte
1			3	8	6				9	10	11		2	4	5		7										1
2	1		3	8	6	12			9	10	11		2	4	5								7"				
3	1		3"	7	6	8			9	10	11	12	2	4	5												1
4		3		8	6		7		9	10	11		2	4	5												1
5		3		8"	5	6	7		9	10	11	12	2		4												1
6		2	3		5	6	7	8	9	10	11	12		4"													

Scottish Cup

No.	Date	Opposition	H.T.	Res.	Att.	Goalscorers
3	23 Jan	Queens Park	1-0	1-0	5923	Waddell
4	13 Feb	Morton	1-0	2-1	6840	McCulloch, Waddell
QF	6 Mar	AIRDRIEONIANS	0-3	2-3	11572	Dickson, Gilmour

No.	Hunter	Swan	Dickson	Morrison	Rodman	MacDonald	T.McLean	Sheed	Mathie	Maxwell	Cook	J.McCulloch	King	Gilmour	McGrory	Arthur	Johnston	McSherry	Gillespie	Leckie	Wylie	I.Fleming	Cairns	Graham	W.Waddell	McLaughlan	Whyte
3	1		3	12		6			9					7					4	5			10	8"	11		2
4			3	8		6	7				11	9		4	5						10			1			2
QF			3	8			7				11	9		4	5			6			10				1		2

European Fairs Cup

No.	Date	Opposition	H.T.	Res.	Att.	Goalscorers
1	15 Sep	Coleraine	0-0	1-1	5000	Mathie
1	29	COLERAINE (Agg: 3-4)	2-0	2-3	5911	McLean, Morrison

No.	Hunter	Swan	Dickson	Morrison	Rodman	MacDonald	T.McLean	Sheed	Mathie	Maxwell	Cook	J.McCulloch	King	Gilmour	McGrory	Arthur	Johnston	McSherry	Gillespie	Leckie	Wylie	I.Fleming	Cairns	Graham	W.Waddell	McLaughlan	Whyte
1	1		3	8	6		7		9	10	11			4	5	2											
1	1	12	3	9		6	7		11"	8	14			4"	5	2		10									

Back row (l-r): I. Welsh, A. McDonald, G. Maxwell, J. McGrory, J. Stewart, F. Beattie, E. Gillespie, J. Gilmour, B. Rodman, R. Mathie, W. Dickson. Front row (l-r): R. Arthur, A. King, G. Smith, W. Waddell, A. McLaughlan, I. Doherty, E. Morrison, T. McLean, J. Cook.

No.	Date	Opposition	H.T.	Res.	Att.	Goalscorers	Hunter	Whyte	Dickson	MacDonald	Rodman	McGrory	McSherry	Gilmour	J.McCulloch	Maxwell	Cook	J.Fleming	Beattie	Morrison	Cairns	I.Fleming	Mathie	King	Sheed	Lee	Stevenson
1	4 Sep	Falkirk	0-2	1-3	5897	Gilmour	1	2	3	4	5	6	7	8	9	10	11										
2	11	AYR UNITED	1-1	1-2	7774	Cook	1	2	3		5	6	7	8	9	4	11	10									
3	18	Motherwell	0-2	0-3	3774		1	2			5	6	7	8	9	3	11		4	10							
4	25	DUNDEE UNITED	1-0	2-0	3012	Cook, McSherry	1	2			5	6	10	8	9	4	11			7	3						
5	2 Oct	Partick Thistle	1-1	2-2	7491	Cook, Maxwell	1	2		5		6	10	8	9	4	11			7	3						
6	9	ABERDEEN	0-0	0-3	5963		1	2			5	6	10	8	9	4	11			7	3						
7	16	East Fife	0-1	0-2	3495		1	2			5	6	10	8	9"	4	11			12	3	7					
8	23	HEARTS	1-2	2-2	4536	Mathie, Morrison	1	2			5	6	7	8		4	11			10	3		9				
9	30	Rangers	1-1	1-3	25442	Mathie	1	2			5	6	7	8	10	4	11				3		9				
10	6 Nov	CLYDE	0-1	2-1	3714	Maxwell, Mathie	1	2			5	6	7	8		4	11			10	3		9				
11	13	Dunfermline	0-0	1-0	4344	Morrison	1	2			5	6	7	8		4	11			10	3		9				
12	20	AIRDRIEONIANS	1-0	5-2	3095	Mathie(2), Morrison, Cook, Maxwell	1	2			5	6	7	8		4	11			10	3		9				
13	27	Hibernian	2-1	2-3	7950	Mathie, Maxwell	1	2			5	6	7	8	12	4	11			10"	3		9				
14	4 Dec	Celtic	0-1	1-5	26824	Mathie	1	2			5	6	7	8		4	11			10	3		9				
15	11	ST. JOHNSTONE	1-0	2-0	3634	Cook, Maxwell	1	2"	12		5	6	7	8		4	11			10	3		9				
16	18	Dundee	0-0	0-2	4646		1		2		5	6	7	8"		4	11			10	3		9	12			
17	25	MORTON	2-1	4-2	4093	Cook(2), Gilmour, Mathie	1		2		5	6	7	8		4	11			10	3		9				
18	1 Jan	FALKIRK	0-0	2-0	5860	Cook, Mathie	1		2		5	6	7	8		4	11			10	3		9				
19	3	Ayr United	0-0	0-0	15265		1		2		5	6	7	8		4	11			10	3		9				
20	8	MOTHERWELL	0-0	1-0	5017	Mathie	1		2		5	6	7			4	11			10	3		9	12	8"		
21	15	Dundee United	1-1	2-1	3255	Morrison, Mathie	1		2		5	6	7	8		4	11			10	3		9				
22	22	PARTICK THISTLE	1-1	1-4	7056	Mathie	1	2	3		5	6	7	8		4	11					10	9				
23	29	Aberdeen	1-2	2-4	13823	I.Fleming, Cook	1	2	3		5	6	7	8		4	11					10	9				
24	12 Feb	EAST FIFE	2-2	2-2	3414	Maxwell	1	2	3		5	6	7	8		4	7			10	11		9				
25	19	Hearts	1-2	1-2	8503	Morrison	1		2		5	6	7	8		4	11			10	3		9				
26	4 Mar	RANGERS	0-0	1-2	14707	Mathie	1		2		5	6	7	8		4	11			10	3		9				
27	11	Clyde	2-0	3-0	1987	Morrison(2), Mathie	1		2		5	6	7	8		4	11			10	3		9				
28	21	DUNFERMLINE	0-0	0-0	3944		1		2		5	6	7	8		4	11			10	3		9				
29	25	Airdrieonians	2-0	4-0	4065	Morrison, Cook, Mathie, Gilmour	1	2	3		5	6	7	8		4	11			10			9				
30	3 Apr	HIBERNIAN	0-0	1-1	6118	O.G.	1	2	3		5	6	7	8		4	11			10			9				
31	8	CELTIC	0-1	1-3	12620	Morrison	1	2"	3		5	6	7	8		4	11			10	12		9				
32	15	St. Johnstone	0-2	1-5	2290	Maxwell	1		2		5	6	7	8		4	11			10	3		12	9"			
33	22	DUNDEE	0-1	0-3	2625		1		2		5	6	7	8		4	11			10	3		9				
34	29	Morton	1-1	1-1	2692	Morrison	1	2	3		5	6	7	8		4				9		10				6	

						Apps.	34	22	21	2	33	33	33	33	8	34	34	1	1	28	25	4	26		1	1	
						Subs		1								1					1	1		2			
						Goals						1	3			8	10			10		1	15				

Pos P. W. D. L. F. A. Pts.
11th 34 11 6 17 49 64 28

League Cup Section 1

Pos P. W. D. L. F. A. Pts.
2nd 6 2 1 3 7 9 5

							Hunter	Whyte	Dickson	MacDonald	Rodman	McGrory	McSherry	Gilmour	J.McCulloch	Maxwell	Cook	J.Fleming	Beattie	Morrison	Cairns	I.Fleming	Mathie	King	Sheed	Lee	Stevenson
1	14 Aug	Dundee United	0-0	0-1	6223		1	2	3	10		5			9	4	7	11	6	8							
2	18	MOTHERWELL	1-1	2-1	5138	Morrison, McCulloch	1	2	3	10"		5			9	4	11		6	8	12						7
3	21	Hibernian	0-1	1-3	12515	Beattie	1	2	3			5	10		9	4	11		6	8							7
4	25	Motherwell	0-0	0-2	3284		1	2	3		5	6	7	8	9	10	11"		4	12							
5	28	DUNDEE UNITED	2-1	4-2	3053	McSherry(2), McCulloch, Gilmour	1	2	3		5	6	7	8	9	10	11		4								
6	1 Sep	HIBERNIAN	0-0	0-0	4168		1	2	3		5	6	7	8	9	4	11			10							

Scottish Cup

							Hunter	Whyte	Dickson	MacDonald	Rodman	McGrory	McSherry	Gilmour	J.McCulloch	Maxwell	Cook	J.Fleming	Beattie	Morrison	Cairns	I.Fleming	Mathie	King	Sheed	Lee	Stevenson
3	5 Feb	ALLOA ATHLETIC	3-0	5-1	4415	Mathie(2), Maxwell, Morrison, Cook	1	2	3		5	6	7	8		4	11			10			9				
4	26	Elgin City	2-0	4-1	10506	Maxwell, Mathie, Cook, O.G.	1	12	2		5	6	7	8		4	11			10	3"		9				
QF	18 Mar	Raith Rovers	1-0	3-1	10815	Cook, Maxwell, Morrison	1		2		5	6	7	8		4	11			10	3		9				
SF	12 Apr	Celtic*	0-1	1-3	48398	Cook	1		2		5	6	7	8		4	11			10	3		9				

* Hampden

Back row (l-r): G. Maxwell, R. Mathie, G. SMith, J. Stewart, R. Sheed, B. Rodman, J. Cook. Middle row: H. Allan (Physio), J. Whyte, A. McDonald, J. McCulloch, J. Gilmour, A. Hunter, F. Beattie, A. Lee, J. McGrory, E. Morrison, J. Murdoch (Trainer). Front row: W. McCrae (Manager), R. Stevenston, A. Cairn, J. Fleming, W. Dickson, I. Welsh, J. McSherry, I. Flexney, A. King, N McNeil (Ass. Manager).

SEASON 1972-73   Division One

No.	Date	Opposition	H.T.	Res.	Att.	Goalscorers	Hunter	Whyte	Dickson	Gilmour	McGrory	Lee	Smith	Maxwell	Morrison	McSherry	Cook	I.Fleming	Cairns	Rodman	Cameron	J.McCulloch	Stewart	Robertson	Stevenson	McGovern	Sheed	Mathie
1	2 Sep	Celtic *	1-4	2-6	11661	Cook, Morrison	1	2	3	4	5"	6	7	8	9	10	11	12										
2	9	AYR UNITED	0-0	0-1	5425		1		2	4		6	7	5	9		10	11	8	3								
3	16	Motherwell	0-0	0-2	4451		1	2	3	8		4	11	6	9	7			10	5								
4	23	EAST FIFE	0-2	1-3	2542	Maxwell	1	2	3"	4		6	7	10	9				11		5	8	12					
5	30	RANGERS	1-1	2-1	10643	Morrison(2)		2		4			8	6	9	10	11				5		1	3	7			
6	7 Oct	Arbroath	2-2	3-3	2662	Cook(2), J.McCulloch		2		4			8	6	9	10	11				5	12	1	3	7"			
7	14	ST. JOHNSTONE	1-0	1-4	3061	Maxwell	1	2		8		4	7	6	9	10	11			5					3			
8	21	Dundee	0-1	0-1	5588		1	2		4		8	7	6	9	10	11			5					3			
9	28	AIRDRIEONIANS	1-1	3-1	2776	Morrison, Smith, Maxwell	1	2		4		8	7	6	9	10	11			5					3			
10	4 Nov	Hibernian	1-3	1-4	11172	Morrison	1	2		4		8	7	6	9	10	11			5					3			
11	11	DUMBARTON	0-0	2-2	3039	Morrison, Cook	1	2		4"		8	10	6	9	7	11			5		12			3			
12	18	Aberdeen	0-1	0-3	11054		1	2	8			6	10	4	9	7	11"		12	5					3			
13	25	Morton	0-2	1-2	3043	Morrison	1	2	6				8	4	9	7	11			5						10		
14	2 Dec	PARTICK THISTLE	2-0	2-3	3490	Morrison, O.G.	1	2		4			8	6	9		11			5		7"			3	10	12	
15	9	Hearts	0-0	0-0	6568			2		4			8	6	9		11			5		7		1	3	10		
16	16	DUNDEE UNITED	0-0	0-1	2536			2		4			8	6	9		11			5		7		1	3	10"	12	
17	23	Falkirk	0-1	2-3	3114	Smith, Maxwell		2		4			8	6	9		11			5		7		1	3	10		
18	1 Jan	Ayr United	1-0	1-1	8507	Morrison		2		4		12	8	6	9		11			5"		7		1	3	10		
19	0	MOTHERWELL	0-0	1-0	4083	Cameron		2		4	5"		8	6	9		11					7		1	3	10	12	
20	13	East Fife	0-1	0-3	3622			2		4		5	8		9	10	11							1	3	7	6	
21	20	Rangers	0-3	0-4	14515			2		4			8	5	9	10	11							1	3	7	6	
22	27	ARBROATH	1-0	2-0	2869	McSherry, Smith		2		4			8	6	9	7	11			5				1	3	10		
23	7 Feb	CELTIC	0-2	0-2	11185			2		4			8	6	9	7	11			5				1		10		
24	10	St. Johnstone	2-2	2-2	2124	McSherry, Smith		2		4			8	6	9	7	11		3	5				1		10"	12	
25	27	DUNDEE	0-1	1-2	2323	Fleming		2		4			10	6	8"	7	11	9		5				1	3		12	
26	3 Mar	Airdrieonians	0-0	1-0	4026	Morrison		2		4			10	6	8	7	11	9		5				1	3			
27	10	HIBERNIAN	0-0	1-0	6700	Morrison, Dickson		2		4			10	6	8	7	11	9		5				1	3			
28	17	Dumbarton	2-1	2-4	4141	Morrison, McSherry		2		4			10	6	8	7	11	9		5				1	3			
29	24	ABERDEEN	0-0	0-2	3908			2		4			10	6	8	7	11	9		5				1	3			
30	31	MORTON	1-0	2-0	2380	Morrison, Whyte		2		4			10	6	8	7	11	9		5				1	3			
31	7 Apr	Partick Thistle	0-0	1-1	5240	McSherry		2		4			10	6	8	7	11	9		5				1	3			
32	14	HEARTS	1-0	2-1	4036	Morrison, Rodman		2		4			10	6	8	7	11	9		5				1	3			
33	21	Dundee United	1-1	1-2	3634	Morrison		2		4			10	6	8	7		9		5				1			11	
34	28	FALKIRK	2-0	2-2	5314	Morrison, Sheed		2	3				10	6	8	7		9		5				1			11	
Apps.							12	33	27	11	1	12	34	33	34	27	30	12	4	29	7		22	27	3	12	4	
Subs															1					1	1		1	2			5	
Goals								1	1				4	4	16	4	4	1		1	1	1					1	

* Played at Hampden Park

Pos	P.	W.	D.	L.	F.	A.	Pts.
17th	34	7	8	19	40	71	22

League Cup Section 4

Pos	P	W.	D.	L.	F.	A.	Pts.
3rd	6	2	1	3	9	9	5

No.	Date	Opposition	H.T.	Res.	Att.	Goalscorers	Hunter	Whyte	Dickson	Gilmour	Lee	Smith	Maxwell	Morrison	McSherry	Cook	I.Fleming	Rodman	Cameron	Stewart	Robertson	Stevenson	McGovern	Mathie
1	12 Aug	Stenhousemuir	0-0	1-1	1046	Mathie	1	2	10	4	6		8	7		11		3	5					9
2	16	DUNDEE UNITED	2-0	2-3	3548	Gilmour, Cook	1	2	10	4	6	12	8	7"		11		3	5					9
3	19	DUNFERMLINE	2-0	2-1	3066	Morrison, Mathie	1	2	10	4	6		8	7		11		3	5					9
4	23	Dundee United	1-1	1-2	4012	Morrison	1	2	10	4	6		8	7		11		3	5					9
5	26	STENHOUSEMUIR	1-0	3-1	2478	Morrison(3)	1	2	3	4	6	12	8	7"		11	9	10	5					
6	30	Dunfermline	0-0	0-1	2024		1	2		4	6	7		9	10	11	8	3	5					

Scottish Cup

No.	Date	Opposition	H.T.	Res.	Att.	Goalscorers	Whyte	Gilmour	Lee	Smith	Maxwell	Morrison	McSherry	Cook	Rodman	Robertson	Stevenson	McGovern
3	3 Feb	QUEEN OF THE SOUTH	1-0	2-1	4378	McSherry, Morrison	2	4		8	6	9	7	11	5	1	3	10
4	24	AIRDRIEONIANS	0-1	0-1	5828		2	4	6	8	10	9	7	11	5	1	3	

Texaco Cup

No.	Date	Opposition	H.T.	Res.	Att.	Goalscorers	Hunter	Whyte	Dickson	Gilmour	Lee	Smith	Maxwell	Morrison	McSherry	Cook	Rodman	Cameron	Stewart	Robertson	Stevenson	McGovern
1	12 Sep	Wolves	1-0	1-5	8734	O.G.	1	12	2	4	6	10	8	9	7	11"	3	5				
1	26	WOLVES (Agg: 1-5)	0-0	0-0	3721			2		4		11	6	9	10		5		8	1	3	7

Back row - A. Robertson, A. Cairns, R. Sheed, J. Stewart, E. Morrison, G. Maxwell, J. White;
Middle row - R. Mathie, G. Smith, J. Gilmour, D. McDicken, A. Hunter, A. Lee, J. McGrory, J. McCulloch, B. Rodman;
Front row - B. Stevenson, D. Frye, A. Christie, I. Fleming, B. Dickson, J. McSherry, J. Cook.

SEASON 1973-74 Division Two

No.	Date	Opposition	H.T.	Res.	Att.	Goalscorers	Stewart	Whyte	Robertson	McDicken	Rodman	Gilmour	McSherry	Smith	Morrison	Sheed	Stevenson	Dickson	Maxwell	McGovern	Fleming	Cook	Ferguson	A.McCulloch	I.McCulloch	Cameron	Kerr	J.McCulloch
1	1 Sep	CLYDEBANK	2-2	3-2	2848	Stevenson(2), Morrison	1	2	3	4	5	6	7	8	9"	10	11	12										
2	5	Berwick Rangers	0-2	1-4	917	Morrison	1	2	3	4	5		7	8	9	10	11"			6	12							
3	8	St. Mirren	1-1	3-1	4768	Fleming(2), Cook	1	2	3		5		7	8	10	4				6		9	11					
4	15	MONTROSE	1-0	2-1	2607	Fleming, O.G.	1	2	3		5"		4	8	10	7				6		9	11	12				
5	19	Queen of the South	0-1	0-1	2463		1	2	3		5		4	8	10	7				6		9	11					
6	29	COWDENBEATH	2-2	4-3	2222	Morrison, Sheed, Maxwell, Smith	1	2			5		4	7"	10	9	8	12	3	6			11					
7	2 Oct	BERWICK RANGERS	1-2	2-3	2213	Gilmour, Morrison	1	2			5	4		7	10	9	8		3	6			12	11"				
8	6	Alloa Athletic	0-0	1-0	2004	Smith	1	2	3	6	5		7	11	9	10			4		8							
9	13	AIRDRIEONIANS	1-0	4-0	4281	Maxwell, Fleming, McSherry, Morrison	1	2	3		5		7	11	9	10			6		8	7						
10	20	Queens Park	0-0	2-0	1446	Fleming, Morrison	1	2	3		5	12	4	11"	9	10			6		8	7						
11	27	RAITH ROVERS	0-1	1-1	4181	Maxwell	1	2	3		5	12	4	11"	9	10			6		8	7						
12	10 Nov	Stranraer	1-1	2-2	1558	Fleming, Maxwell	1	2	3		5		7		9	10		6	4		8	7						
13	17	FORFAR ATHLETIC	2-0	5-1	2730	Fleming(2), Morrison(2), McSherry	1		3	5	2		4	11	9	10			6		12	8	7"					
14	21	Albion Rovers	3-0	4-3	295	Morrison(2), Smith(2)	1		3	5	2		4	7	9	10			6		11"	8	12					
15	1 Dec	BRECHIN CITY	1-1	3-1	2769	Fleming(2), Morrison		2	3		5		4	11	9	10			6		8	7		1				
16	22	Stirling Albion	0-0	1-0	1192	Cook	1	2	3		5		4	11	9	10			6		8	7						
17	29	Clydebank	0-0	2-1	1611	Fleming, Smith	1	2	3		5		4	11	9"	10			6		8	7				12		
18	1 Jan	ST. MIRREN	0-1	1-1	4599	Fleming	1	2	3		5		4		9	10	11		6		8	7"				12		
19	5	Montrose	2-0	2-0	914	Morrison, Sheed	1	2	3		5		4	11	9	10	7"		6		8					12		
20	12	HAMILTON	2-1	3-1	4927	Morrison, Smith, Fleming	1	2	3		5		4	11	9	10			6		8	7						
21	19	Cowdenbeath	3-0	4-2	788	Smith(2), Morrison, McSherry	1	2	3	12	5		4	11	9	10"			6		8	7						
22	2 Feb	ALLOA ATHLETIC	4-0	8-2	3515	I.McClch(2),Flmng(2),Smth(2),Sheed,Mxwll	1	2	3	12	5				11	9*	10	14	6"		8	7		4				
23	9	Airdrieonians	0-0	0-0	7824		1	2	3		5			12	11	9	10		6		8	7		4"				
24	16	Stenhousemuir	0-0	1-0	978	Smith	1	2"	3	12	5		4	11	9	10			6		8	7						
25	2 Mar	Raith Rovers	1-2	1-3	2081	Cook	1		3		5		4	11	9	10"			6		8	7	2			12		
26	16	STRANRAER	3-1	4-1	3168	Morrison(3), Fleming	1		3		5		4"	11	9				6		8	7	2					12
27	23	Forfar Athletic	3-3	5-3	697	Fleming(3), McDicken, Maxwell	1		3	14	5			11		10"			6		8	7	2	4	9			12*
28	30	ALBION ROVERS	2-1	3-1	3067	Maxwell(2), Morrison	1		3	12	5			11	9	10			6		8	7	2"	4				
29	6 Apr	Brechin City	3-0	4-0	497	Fleming(2), Morrison(2)	1	2	3		5		4	11	9	10			6		8	7						
30	9	EAST STIRLING	1-0	4-0	3787	Fleming(2), Morrison, Robertson	1	2	3		5		4	11"	9	10			6		8	7				12		
31	13	STENHOUSEMUIR	2-0	3-1	3813	Fleming(2), Morrison	1	2	3		5		4	11	9	10			6		8	7						
32	16	QUEENS PARK	2-0	5-0	4225	Fleming(3), Morrison(2)	1	2	3		5		4	11	9	10			6		8	7						
33	20	East Stirling	1-1	3-1	1250	Maxwell, Cook, Fleming	1	2	3		5		4	11	9	10			6		8	7						
34	24	QUEEN OF THE SOUTH	0-0	1-0	4880	Fleming	1	2	3		5		4"	11	9	10			6		8	7				12		
35	27	STIRLING ALBION	0-1	2-1	5675	Fleming, Morrison	1	2	3		5		4"	11	9	10			6		8	7				12		
36	30	Hamilton	1-1	2-2	2852	Fleming(2)	1	2	3		5		4	11	9	10			6		8	7	2					
						Apps.	35	29	34	5	36	3	32	34	35	36	4	3	35	1	32	31	5	4	1			
						Subs				5		2	1				2	1		2	1	1		5	2	2		
						Goals		1	1	1		1	3	11	25	3	2		9		33	4			2			

Pos	P.	W.	D.	L.	F.	A.	Pts.
2nd	36	26	6	4	96	44	58

League Cup Section 5

Pos	P.	W.	D.	L.	F.	A.	Pts.
1st	6	3	2	1	13	4	8

No.	Date	Opposition	H.T.	Res.	Att.	Goalscorers	Stewart	Whyte	Robertson	McDicken	Rodman	Gilmour	McSherry	Smith	Morrison	Sheed	Stevenson	Dickson	Maxwell	McGovern	Fleming	Cook	Ferguson	A.McCulloch	I.McCulloch	Cameron	Kerr	J.McCulloch
1	11 Aug	East Stirling	1-1	2-3	1060	Smith, Cameron	1	2	3		5	4		8	9"	14	7		10"	6						12		11
2	15	HAMILTON	0-0	0-0	3169		1	2	3	4	5		7	8	9				6							10		11
3	18	QUEENS PARK	1-0	2-0	2591	Morrison, Smith	1	2	3	4	5		7	8	9	11			6							10"		12
4	22	Hamilton	3-0	4-0	2450	Smith, Morrison, McSherry, Stevenson	1	2	3	4	5		7	8	9	10	11		6									
5	25	Queens Park	1-0	1-1	1292	Sheed	1	2	3	4	5		7	8	9	10			6									
6	29	EAST STIRLING	1-0	4-0	2805	Morrison(2), Maxwell(2)	1	2	3	4	5	12	7*	8	9	10"	11		6	14								
2	12 Sep	St. Johnstone	0-0	0-1	3600		1	2	3		5		7	8	10	4			6		9	11						
2	10 Oct	ST. JOHNSTONE (Agg: 3-2)	2-0	3-1"	3478	Maxwell, Fleming, McSherry	1	2	3	6"	5		7	11	9	10		12	4		8							
QF	30	Albion Rovers	0-1	0-2	2821		1	2	3		5	4"		7	11	9	10		6		8					12		
QF	24 Nov	ALBION ROVERS (Agg 5-4)	4-1	5-2	5287	Robertson,Morrison,Cook,Fleming,Maxwell	1		3	5	2		4	7	9	10			6		8	11						
SF	5 Dec	Dundee *	0-0	0-1	4682		1	2	3		5		4	11	9	10			6		8	7						

" After Extra Time - 90 minutes 2-1.   * Hampden.

Scottish Cup

No.	Date	Opposition	H.T.	Res.	Att.	Goalscorers	Stewart	Whyte	Robertson	McDicken	Rodman	Gilmour	McSherry	Smith	Morrison	Sheed	Stevenson	Dickson	Maxwell	McGovern	Fleming	Cook	Ferguson	A.McCulloch	I.McCulloch	Cameron	Kerr	J.McCulloch
3	26 Jan	Hibernian	2-3	2-5	14241	Morrison(2)	1	2	3	12	5		4	11	9				6		8	7			10"			

Back row (l-r): J. Whyte, A. Robertson, D. McDicken, A. McCulloch, R. Sheed, G. Maxwell, D. Fryc. Middle row: A. Ferguson, J. Gilmour, G. SMith, J. Stewart, J. McCulloch, M. Wilson, R. Stevenston. Front row: H. Cameron, W. Dickson, P. McGovern, B. Rodman, I. Fleming, E. Morrison, J. McSherry.

SEASON 1974-75　Division One

Player columns (left to right): Stewart, Maxwell, Robertson, I.McCulloch, Rodman, McDicken, Cook, Fleming, E.Morrison, Sheed, Smith, McSherry, Fallis, Kerr, Provan, McLean, A.McCulloch, Whyte, D.Morrison

No.	Date	Opposition	H.T.	Res.	Att.	Goalscorers	Stewart	Maxwell	Robertson	I.McCulloch	Rodman	McDicken	Cook	Fleming	E.Morrison	Sheed	Smith	McSherry	Fallis	Kerr	Provan	McLean	A.McCulloch	Whyte	D.Morrison
1	31 Aug	Celtic	0-1	0-5	26482		1	2	3	4	5	6	7	8	9	10	11								
2	7 Sep	AYR UNITED	0-0	3-0	7279	Sheed(2), Fleming	1	2	3	4	5	6		8	9	10	11	7							
3	14	Hearts	1-1	1-1	7306	Fleming	1	2	3	4	5	6		8	9	10	11	7							
4	21	ABERDEEN	0-0	1-0	5727	McDicken	1	2	3	4	5	6		8	9	10	11	7							
5	28	RANGERS	0-2	0-6	19609		1	2	3	4	5	6		8	9"	10	11	7	12						
6	5 Oct	St. Johnstone	1-1	2-2	2579	E.Morrison, Sheed	1	2	3	4	5	6		8	9	10	11	7"	12						
7	12	DUNDEE	1-1	1-1	4951	Smith	1	2	3	4	5	6		8	9	10	11	7							
8	19	Motherwell	0-1	0-2	3628		1	2	3	4	5	6		8	9	10	11	7							
9	2 Nov	Partick Thistle	0-2	2-2	3676	E.Morrison, Sheed	1	2	3	4	5	6		8	9	10	7"	11	12						
10	9	Morton	2-0	3-2	2155	Sheed, McDicken, Smith	1	2	3	4	5	6		8	9	10	7	11							
11	13	HIBERNIAN	1-0	1-1	5240	McDicken	1	2	3	4	5	6		8	9	10	7	11							
12	16	DUNFERMLINE	2-1	2-4	5327	Fleming(2)	1	2	3	4	5	6		8	9	10		11		7					
13	23	Clyde	1-3	2-4	1605	E.Morrison(2)		2"	3	4	5	6		8*	9	10	7	11		14	12				
14	30	ARBROATH	0-2	2-2	3426	Sheed, E.Morrison	1		4	5	6		8	9	10	11			7	3		2			
15	14 Dec	AIRDRIEONIANS	2-2	3-3	3931	Maxwell(2), Fleming	1	6	3	8	4	5		11	9	10"	12			7	2				
16	21	Dundee United	2-0	4-3	4415	E.Morrison, Maxwell, Fleming, Sheed	1	11	3	4	5"	6		8	9	10	12			7	2				
17	28	CELTIC	0-1	0-1	17646		1	10	3	4	5	6		8	9		11			7	2				
18	1 Jan	Ayr United	2-2	2-3	9968	Smith, Fleming	1		3	4	5	6		8	9"	10	11		12	7	2				
19	4	HEARTS	1-0	1-1	7233	Fleming		11	3	4	5	6		8		10	9		12	7"	2	1			
20	11	Aberdeen	0-2	0-4	8462		6	3	4"	5			9*	10	8		11		7	2	1	12	14		
21	1 Feb	ST. JOHNSTONE	1-1	1-1	3938	E.Morrison		12	3	4"	5	6		8	9*	10	11	14		7	2	1			
22	8	Dundee	1-2	1-4	4835	Sheed		3	4	5	6		8	9"	10	11		12	7	2	1				
23	15	Rangers	2-1	3-3	27151	McDicken, Provan, Fallis	12	3	4"	5	6		8	9*	10	11	14		7	2	1				
24	22	MOTHERWELL	2-0	3-1	6097	E.Morrison(2), Maxwell		2	3	12	5"	6			9	10	11		8	7	4	1			
25	26	Dumbarton	1-0	1-1	4069	Sheed		2	3		5	6			9	10	11		8	7	4	1			
26	1 Mar	Hibernian	1-0	2-0	7866	E.Morrison, Fallis		2	3		5	6			9	10	11		8	7	4	1			
27	8	PARTICK THISTLE	0-0	1-1	6676	Maxwell		2	3		5	6		12	9	10	11		8	7"	4	1			
28	15	MORTON	2-1	2-1	4155	Smith, Fleming		2	3		5	6		8	9"	10	11		12	7	4	1			
29	22	Dunfermline	1-1	1-1	2594	E.Morrison		2	3	12	5	6		8	9	10	11		7		4"	1			
30	29	CLYDE	0-0	2-0	5054	Smith, Maxwell		2	3		5	6		8	9	10	11			7		1			
31	5 Apr	Arbroath	0-0	0-0	1439			2	3	4	5	6			9		11		8	7	10	1			
32	12	DUMBARTON	0-2	1-2	5489	Fleming		2	3	4	5	6		12	9	10	11		8	7"		1			
33	19	Airdrieonians	2-1	2-2	3827	Fallis, McLean		2	3	4	5	6		8	9	10	11		7	12	4	1			
34	26	DUNDEE UNITED	2-3	2-4	7589	Fallis, Fleming		2	3		5	6		8	12	10	11		9	7"	4	1			
						Apps.	18	29	33	26	34	33	1	27	32	32	31	12	10		20	19	16	1	
						Subs	2		2					2	1		2	1	6	2	2	1		1	1
						Goals		6				4		11	11	9	5		4		1	1			

Pos P. W. D. L. F. A. Pts.
12th 34 8 15 11 52 68 31

Pos P. W. D. L. F. A. Pts.
1st 6 5 1 0 18 1 11

League Cup Section 5

No.	Date	Opposition	H.T.	Res.	Att.	Goalscorers	Stewart	Maxwell	Robertson	I.McCulloch	Rodman	McDicken	Cook	Fleming	E.Morrison	Sheed	Smith	McSherry	Fallis	Kerr	Provan	McLean	A.McCulloch	Whyte	D.Morrison
1	10 Aug	MONTROSE	1-0	2-0	3264	I.McCulloch, Fleming	1	6	3	4		5	7	8		10	11		9					2	
2	14	Strenraer	1-0	5-0	1338	Fleming(3), Smith(2)	1	6	3	4		5	7	8		10	11		9					2	
3	17	Queens Park	2-0	2-0	1559	Fleming(2)	1	2	3	4	5	6	7	8		10"	11	12	9						
4	21	STRANRAER	2-0	2-0	3358	Maxwell, E.Morrison	1	2	3	4	5	6	7	8	9	10	11								
5	24	QUEENS PARK	3-0	6-0	3300	Fleming(2),E.Morrison,Cook,Smith,Rodman	1	2	3	4	5	6	7	8	9	10	11								
6	28	Montrose	1-0	1-1	1179	Fleming	1	2	3	4	5	6	7	8		10	11		9						
QF	11 Sep	HIBERNIAN	2-1	3-3	10022	Fleming(2), E.Morrison	1	2	3	4	5	6		8	9	10	11	7"	12						
QF	25	Hibernian (Agg: 4-7)	1-1	1-4	15694	E.Morrison	1	2	3	4	5	6		8	9	10	11	7							

Scottish Cup

No.	Date	Opposition	H.T.	Res.	Att.	Goalscorers	Stewart	Maxwell	Robertson	I.McCulloch	Rodman	McDicken	Cook	Fleming	E.Morrison	Sheed	Smith	McSherry	Fallis	Kerr	Provan	McLean	A.McCulloch	Whyte	D.Morrison
1	29 Jan	Hearts	0-0	0-2	21054				3	4	5	6		8	9	10	11			7	2	1			

Drybrough Cup

| QF | 27 Jul | Hibernian | 0-1 | 1-2 | 13272 | Fallis | 1 | 2 | 3 | 4 | 5 | 6 | 7 | 8 | 9" | 10 | | | 12 | 11 | | | | | |

A. Robertson, P. Clarke, D. McDicken, J. Stewart, G. Smith, R. Sheed, G. Maxwell. Middle row: H. Allan (Physio), A. Ferguson, S. McLean, I. Kerr, A. McCulloch, I. McCulloch, D. Frye, D. Provan, R. Stewart (Trainer). Front row: W. Fernie (Manager), J. Cook, I. Fallis, I. Fleming, B. Rodman, E. Morrison, J. McSherry, D. Matthews, D. Sneddon (Ass. Manager).

SEASON 1975-76 — First Division

Match Record

No.	Date	Opposition	H.T.	Res.	Att.	Goalscorers
1	30 Aug	HAMILTON	4-2	4-2	3917	Smith, Fallis, Provan, E.Morrison
2	6 Sep	Airdrieonians	2-3	4-3	3683	E.Morrison(2), Fallis, Smith
3	13	PARTICK THISTLE	0-0	0-1	6375	
4	20	East Fife	2-2	4-2	2344	Smith(2), I.Fleming, Fallis
5	27	CLYDE	1-0	3-0	3610	I.Fleming(2), E.Morrison
6	4 Oct	ST. MIRREN	3-1	3-1	3577	E.Morrison(2), McLean
7	11	Montrose	0-1	0-2	1724	
8	18	ARBROATH	1-0	2-1	3801	Fallis, Smith
9	25	Morton	2-1	3-1	2137	I.Fleming(2), Smith
10	1 Nov	Falkirk	0-0	1-0	3862	Smith
11	8	QUEEN OF THE SOUTH	0-0	2-0	4345	Provan, Fallis
12	15	Dunfermline	0-0	0-1	2673	
13	22	DUMBARTON	1-0	1-0	4532	Fallis
14	29	Clyde	1-0	2-0	2662	McDicken, Fallis
15	6 Dec	St. Mirren	0-0	0-0	5800	
16	13	MONTROSE	0-0	1-1	3992	McLean
17	20	Arbroath	0-1	0-2	1838	
18	27	MORTON	3-0	3-2	4344	E.Morrison, Fallis, Smith
19	1 Jan	AIRDRIEONIANS	0-1	2-1	5010	Provan, Smith
20	3	Partick Thistle	0-1	0-2	11507	
21	10	DUNFERMLINE	3-0	4-0	3831	Fallis, Sheed, O.G 2
22	17	Dumbarton	0-1	0-3	2611	
23	31	EAST FIFE	1-1	1-1	4003	Clarke, McCulloch
24	7 Feb	Hamilton	0-0	1-1	3000	Rodman
25	21	FALKIRK	1-0	1-0	3773	Fallis
26	28	Queen of the South	0-2	1-2	4557	Rodman

Pos	P.	W.	D.	L.	F.	A.	Pts.
2nd	26	16	3	7	44	29	35

Player columns (left → right): Stewart, McLean, Robertson, I.McCulloch, Rodman, McDicken, Provan, Fallis, E.Morrison, Sheed, Smith, Clarke, I.Fleming, Maxwell, Jenkins, Wilson, D.Morrison, Sharp, Murdoch, C.Fleming, Matthews, Ferguson, A.McCulloch.

League appearances / goals summary

	Stewart	McLean	Robertson	I.McCulloch	Rodman	McDicken	Provan	Fallis	E.Morrison	Sheed	Smith	Clarke	I.Fleming	Maxwell	Jenkins	Wilson	D.Morrison	Sharp	Murdoch	C.Fleming	Matthews
Apps	26	20	26	23	20	16	23	26	14	25	18	9	15						4	4	1
Subs	2			2	1	1			1			2	4	3	1	2	3	1			
Goals		2		1	2	1	3	10	7	1	9	1	5								

League Cup Section 4

Pos	P.	W.	D.	L.	F.	A.	Pts.
3rd	6	2	0	4	5	9	4

No.	Date	Opposition	H.T.	Res.	Att.	Goalscorers
1	9 Aug	PARTICK THISTLE	1-2	1-3	4724	Sheed
2	13	St. Johnstone	1-1	1-2	2293	I.Fleming
3	16	Dundee United	0-1	0-2	4050	
4	20	ST. JOHNSTONE	0-0	1-0	2383	McCulloch
5	23	DUNDEE UNITED	0-0	1-0	2795	Fallis
6	27	Partick Thistle	0-2	1-2	5211	E.Morrison

Scottish Cup

No.	Date	Opposition	H.T.	Res.	Att.	Goalscorers
3	24 Jan	Stenhousemuir	1-1	1-1	1870	Sheed
3R	28	STENHOUSEMUIR	0-0	1-0	4926	Smith
4	14 Feb	FALKIRK	1-0	3-1	6454	McDicken(2), O.G.
QF	6 Mar	Dumbarton	0-0	1-2	7796	Fallis

Spring Cup Section 2

Pos	P.	W.	D.	L.	F.	A.	Pts.
3rd	6	1	3	2	5	6	5

No.	Date	Opposition	H.T.	Res.	Att.	Goalscorers
1	10 Mar	Berwick Rangers	0-0	0-0	345	
2	13	ALLOA ATHLETIC	0-0	0-0	2568	
3	20	FALKIRK	0-0	0-1	2072	
4	27	Alloa Athletic	1-0	2-2	928	Maxwell, C.Fleming
5	3 Apr	BERWICK RANGERS	2-0	3-1	1445	Murdoch(2), Smith
6	10	Falkirk	0-2	0-2	2257	

Back row: Ronnie Sheed, Ian McCulloch, Brian Rodman, Jim Stewart, Paul Clarke, Derrick McDicken, George Maxwell.
Front row: Stuart McLean, Davie Provan, Gordon Smith, Ian Fallis, Alan Robertson, Ian Fleming.

SEASON 1976-77 Premier Division

No.	Date	Opposition	H.T.	Res.	Att.	Goalscorers	Stewart	S McLean	Robertson	Murdoch	Clarke	Welsh	Provan	I McCulloch	Fallis	Sheed	Smith	Sharp	Maxwell	Jardine	McDicken	A.McCulloch	Doherty	Ward	A.McLean	C.Fleming
1	4 Sep	MOTHERWELL	1-1	1-1	5163	Clarke	1	2	3	4	5	6	7		9"	10	11	12								
2	11	Rangers	0-0	0-0	24800		1	2	3	4	5	6	7	8	9	10	11									
3	18	Aberdeen	0-0	0-2	9566		1	2	3	4	5	6	7	8	9	10	11									
4	25	CELTIC	0-2	0-4	14615		1	2	3	4	5	6	7	8	9		11		10							
5	2 Oct	Hearts	2-1	2-2	9333	McCulloch, McDicken	1	2"	3	4	5	6		7	9	10	11		12		8					
6	23	Partick Thistle	0-1	1-2	4749	Fallis	1	2	3	4	5	6	7	8"	9	10			12		11*					
7	26	HIBERNIAN	1-0	1-1	4202	Smith	1	2	3	4	5	6	7		9	10	11				8					
8	30	AYR UNITED	4-0	6-1	6422	Fallis(3), Sheed, McDicken, Murdoch	1	2	3	4	5	6	7		9	10"	11		12		8					
9	3 Nov	Dundee United	0-2	0-3	4886		1	2	3	4	5	6	7		9	10	11	12			8"					
10	6	Motherwell	2-0	4-5	4754	Fallis(2), Maxwell, Smith	1	2	3	4*	5	6	7		9	10	11		12		8"				14	
11	13	RANGERS	0-3	0-4	14717			2*	3	4	5	6	7		9	10	11		12		8"	1			14	
12	20	ABERDEEN	1-0	1-0	4212	Smith	1	8	3	4	5	6	7		9	10	11		2							
13	27	Celtic	1-2	1-2	20337	McCulloch	1		3	4	5	6	7	8	9	10"	11		2		12					
14	18 Dec	DUNDEE UNITED	0-0	1-0	3529	Fallis	1		3	4	5	6	7	8	9		11"		2		10	12				
15	27	PARTICK THISTLE	0-0	0-0	5018		1	14	3	4	5	6	7	8	9"		11		2		10*	12				
16	1 Jan	Ayr United	1-1	1-3	7938	Smith	1		3	4	5	6	7	8	9		11		2		10					
17	3	MOTHERWELL	1-2	2-2	6309	Fallis, Maxwell	1		3	4	5	6	7	8	9		11		2		10					
18	8	Rangers	0-1	0-3	18189		1		3	4"	5	6	7	8	9	12	11		2		10					
19	22	CELTIC	1-1	1-1	14363	Fallis	1		3	4	5	6	7	8	9	12	11"		2		10					
20	5 Feb	Hearts	0-4	0-4	7226		1		3	4	5	6"	7	8	9	12	14		2		10	11*				
21	7	Aberdeen	0-0	0-2	8477		1		3	4	5		7	8	9	10			2		6				11	
22	12	HIBERNIAN	0-0	0-0	3397		1	2	3	4	5		7	8	9	10			6			12			11"	
23	15	HEARTS	1-1	2-1	3182	Robertson, McDicken	1		3	4	5	6	7	8	9	10	11		2							
24	19	Dundee United	0-3	0-4	5096		1	12	3	4	5	6"	7	8	9"	10	11		2	14						
25	5 Mar	Partick Thistle	1-2	1-3	3147	Smith	1	14	3	4"	5		7	8		10	11*		2	12	6	9				
26	9	Hibernian	0-2	0-2	3158		1		3	4	5		7	8		10			2	12	6	9				11"
27	12	AYR UNITED	0-0	0-1	4124		1		3	4	5		7	8		10		11	2	12	6	9"				
28	19	Motherwell	0-1	0-2	4080		1	12	3	4	5"		7	8	9	10	11*		2	14	6					
29	26	RANGERS	0-0	1-0	8037	Robertson	1		3	12	5	4	7	8		10"	11		2		6					
30	2 Apr	ABERDEEN	1-1	1-2	2330	McCulloch	1		3	10	5	4	7	8	9"		11		2	12	6					
31	9	Celtic	0-0	0-1	18759		1		3	10	5	4	7	8	9		11		2		6					
32	13	Ayr United	0-1	1-1	5046	Smith	1	12	3	10	5	4	7	8	9"		11		2		6					
33	16	HEARTS	2-0	2-2	2471	McDicken, Smith	1		3	10	5	4	7	8	9		11		2		6					
34	20	PARTICK THISTLE	1-1	1-3	1543	Provan	1	12	3	10	5	4	7	8	9*		11		2	14	6"					
35	23	Hibernian	0-0	0-0	3457		1	2	3	10		4	7"	8		12	11			14	6					
36	30	DUNDEE UNITED	1-1	1-2	1643	Fallis	1	2	3	10		4	7	8	9		11				6			5		
				Apps.			35	15	36	34	33	24	34	27	32	18	32	4	25	9	29	1	4	1	2	1
				Subs			6		1							1	3	2	4	5	3	1		5		2
				Goals					2	1	1		1	3	10	1	7		2		4					

Pos	P.	W.	D.	L.	F.	A.	Pts.
10th	36	4	9	23	32	71	17

League Cup Section 2

Pos	P.	W.	D.	L.	F.	A.	Pts.
3rd	6	2	1	3	6	8	5

No.	Date	Opposition	H.T.	Res.	Att.	Goalscorers	Stewart	S McLean	Robertson	Murdoch	Clarke	Welsh	Provan	I McCulloch	Fallis	Sheed	Smith	Sharp	Maxwell	Jardine	McDicken
1	14 Aug	Aberdeen	0-2	0-2	11758		1	2	3	4	5	6	7	8		10	11	12			9"
2	18	AYR UNITED	0-0	2-0	6408	Provan, Murdoch	1	2	3	4	5	6	7	8	9	10	11				
3	21	ST. MIRREN	0-0	1-1	4242	Fallis	1	2	3	4	5	6	7	8	9	10	11				
4	25	Ayr United	1-1	1-3	5173	McCulloch	1	2	3	4	5	6	7	8	9	10	11				
5	28	St. Mirren	0-0	0-1	3712		1	2	3	4	5	6	7	8	9	10	11				
6	1 Sep	ABERDEEN	1-0	2-1	2536	Smith, Welsh	1	2	3	4	5	6	7	8	9	10"	11				12

Scottish Cup

No.	Date	Opposition	H.T.	Res.	Att.	Goalscorers	Stewart	Robertson	Murdoch	Clarke	Welsh	Provan	I McCulloch	Fallis	Smith	Maxwell	McDicken	A.McCulloch
3	29 Jan	Motherwell	0-3	0-3	8355		1	3	4	5	6	7	8	9	11"	2	10	12

Anglo Scottish Cup

No.	Date	Opposition	H.T.	Res.	Att.	Goalscorers	Stewart	S McLean	Robertson	Murdoch	Clarke	Welsh	Provan	I McCulloch	Fallis	Sheed	Smith	McDicken	A.McCulloch
1	7 Aug	Motherwell	1-0	1-1	4706	Smith	1	2	3	4	5	6	7	8	9	10	11		
1	11	MOTHERWELL (Agg: 5-1)	2-0	4-0	5216	Fallis, P.Clarke, McDicken, O.G.	1	2	3	4"	5	6	7	8	9	10	11	12	
QF	14 Sep	Nottm Forest	0-0	1-2	8911	Smith	1	2	3	4	5	6	7	8	9	10	11		
QF	28	NOTTM FOREST (Agg: 3-4)	1-0	2-2*	4503	Fallis(2)	1	2	3	4	5"	6	7	8	9		11	12	10

* After extra time. 90 mins. 2-1

Back row (l-r): Wilson, A. McLean, Provan, I McCulloch, S. McLean, Kelly, Murdoch, Hynds, Doherty. Middle row: Allan (Physio), Fallis, Robertson, Sharp, A. McCulloch, McDicken, J. Stewart, Clarke, Welsh, Jenkins, R. Stewart (Trainer). Front row: Fernie (Manager), Fleming, Dixon, McQueen, Smith, Sheed, Gray, Rodman, Murray, Baird, Sneddon (Coach), Maxwell not in line-up.

No.	Date	Opposition	H.T.	Res.	Att.	Goalscorers	Stewart	Hynds	Robertson	Murdoch	Welsh	Maxwell	Provan	Jardine	Fallis	McLean	Smith	Doherty	Clarke	McGillivray	McDicken	McDowell	McCulloch	Arkison	Stein	Gray	Baird
1	13 Aug	MORTON	0-0	0-3	3462		1	2	3	4	5	6	7	8"	9	10	11	12									
2	20	Stirling Albion	1-0	1-2	2100	Murdoch	1		3	4	5	2"	7	8	9	12				6	11	10					
3	27	HEARTS	1-0	1-1	5003	Doherty	1		3	4"	2	10	8	12	7				9	5	11	6					
4	10 Sep	Queen of the South	0-0	0-1	2563		1		3	4	2		8			7"			12	5	11	6	10	9			
5	14	Hamilton	0-1	1-2	1748	Arkison	1		3			2	10	8	7"					5	11	6	9	4	12		
6	17	ARBROATH	1-0	3-0	2195	McDowell(2), McGillivray	1		3	10	2		8	12						5	11	6	9	4	7"		
7	24	AIRDRIEONIANS	0-0	0-0	2565		1		3	10	2		8"	7	12					5	11	6	9	4			
8	28	Montrose	0-0	0-0	989		1	12	3		2	6	7	10"						5	11	8	9	4			
9	1 Oct	Dundee	1-1	1-2	4719	McCulloch	1	10"	3	14	2	6	7		12					5	11"	8	9	4			
10	8	DUMBARTON	1-0	2-2	3186	Stein, McCulloch	1		3	10	2		7	11						5		6	9	4	8		
11	15	Alloa Athletic	0-1	2-1	1382	Murdoch, McCulloch	1		3	12		6	7	10					2	11"5		8	4		9		
12	19	ST. JOHNSTONE	0-0	0-0	1905		1		3	11"									2	5	12	6	8	4	9		
13	22	Morton	1-0	2-0	4256	Maxwell, McDowell	1		3			2	10	7		4			5		6	8	11		9		
14	29	STIRLING ALBION	1-0	2-3	2896	Stein, Maxwell	1		3			2	10	7		4			5		6	8	11		9		
15	5 Nov	Hearts	0-1	2-1	7703	McDowell(2)	1		3			2	10	7		4			5		6	8	11		9		
16	12	QUEEN OF THE SOUTH	1-0	1-1	2494	Provan	1		3	12			10	7		4"			5		6	8	11		9		
17	19	Arbroath	1-1	2-2	1192	Maxwell, McDowell	1		3			2	10	7		4			5		6	8	11		9		
18	25	Airdrieonians	1-0	2-1	1636	Stein, Provan	1		3			2	10	7		4			5		6	8	11		9		
19	3 Dec	DUNDEE	1-0	1-0	3549	McDowell	1		3	12			10	7		4			2"		5	6	8		9		
20	10	Dumbarton	1-1	2-2	2174	McDowell, Maxwell	1			3			10	7		4			2		5	6	8		9		
21	17	ALLOA ATHLETIC	1-0	3-1	2795	Stein(2), McDowell	1			3			10	7		4			2		5	6	8		9		
22	24	East Fife	3-0	3-2	1391	Stein, Maxwell, Robertson	1		3			12	10	7		4"			2		5	6	8		9		
23	31	Hearts	0-2	0-3	13063		1		3				10	7		4			2		5	6	8		9		
24	2 Jan	QUEEN OF THE SOUTH	1-0	2-0	5154	Stein, Maxwell	1		3				10	7		4			2		5	6	8		9		
25	7	Stirling Albion	0-0	0-0	2137		1		3				10	7		4			2	12	5	6	8"		11	9	
26	14	HAMILTON	1-0	1-1	3548	McDowell	1		3	12	6		10	7		4			2"		5	6	8		11	9	
27	21	AIRDRIEONIANS	0-1	1-1	3370	Stein	1		3		6		10	7		4			2		5	6	8		11	9	
28	11 Feb	DUMBARTON	0-1	0-1	3649		1		3	11	2		10	7					4	12	5	6	8			9"	
29	25	ALLOA ATHLETIC	1-0	4-0	2005	Maxwell, Provan, Doherty, McDowell	1		3	11*	14		10	7		4		2	12	5	6	8"			9		
30	4 Mar	Morton	0-1	0-2	4036		1		3	11"	12		10	7		4		2	14	5	6	8			9*		
31	15	MONTROSE	1-1	5-1	1402	McCulloch(3), Jardine, McDowell	1		11	3			10	4		2			12	5	6	8"	7		9"	14	
32	18	St. Johnstone	0-1	0-2	1584		1		11	3			10	4		2			12	5	6	8"	7		9"	14	
33	22	Dundee	0-1	2-5	5295	McCulloch, Maxwell	1		11	3			10	4		2			9	5	6	8	7				
34	25	ST. JOHNSTONE	1-0	2-0	1997	McDowell, McCulloch	1		3				10	7		4			2	9	5	6	8		11		
35	1 Apr	Arbroath	0-0	0-1	921		1		11	3			10	7		4			2	9"	5	6	8		12		
36	8	East Fife	0-0	0-0	741		1		11	3			10	7		4			2		5	6	9		8		
37	15	MONTROSE	0-0	1-0	1337	Maxwell	1		11				10	7		4			2	9	5	6	8				3
38	22	Hamilton	1-0	3-1	1385	Doherty(2), Jardine	1		12				10	7		4			2	9	5"	6	8		11		3
39	29	EAST FIFE	0-0	0-0	1328		1		12				10	7		4			2	9	5	6	8"		11		3
		Apps.					39	2	28	17	20	35	36	34	4	30	1	7	37	9	36	36	28	4	23		3
		Subs						1							7	3				2	2	1			8	1	1	2
		Goals							1	2		9	3	2				4		1		13	8	1	8		

Pos P. W. D. L. F. A. Pts.
6th 39 14 12 13 52 48 40

League Cup

No.	Date	Opposition	H.T.	Res.	Att.	Goalscorers	Stewart	Hynds	Robertson	Murdoch	Welsh	Maxwell	Provan	Jardine	Fallis	McLean	Smith	Doherty	Clarke	McGillivray	McDicken	McDowell	McCulloch	Arkison	Stein	Gray	Baird
1		Bye																									
2	31 Aug	ST. MIRREN	0-0	0-0	5119		1		3	4	2	10	8	12	7				9"	5	11	6					
2	3 Sep	St. Mirren (Agg: 1-2)	0-0	1-2	9458	Fallis	1		3	4	2	10	8		7					5	11	6	9				

Scottish Cup

No.	Date	Opposition	H.T.	Res.	Att.	Goalscorers	Stewart	Hynds	Robertson	Murdoch	Welsh	Maxwell	Provan	Jardine	Fallis	McLean	Smith	Doherty	Clarke	McGillivray	McDicken	McDowell	McCulloch	Arkison	Stein	Gray	Baird
3	6 Feb	St. Mirren	1-1	2-1	10010	Maxwell, McDowell	1		3	11	12		10	7		4"			2		5	6	8		9		
4	27	Celtic	1-0	1-1	16000	McDowell	1		3	11			10	7		4			2	9	5	6	8				
4R	6 Mar	CELTIC	0-0	1-0	14137	McDicken	1		3				10	7		4			2	12	5	6	8"	11	9		
QF	11	Rangers	0-2	1-4	28000	McCulloch	1		3	14			10	7"		4			2	12	5	6	8*	11	9		

Back row (l-r): J. Doherty, J. Cockburn, R. Hamilton, E. Gray, W. Murray, D. Hynds, I. Baird, H. Arkinson.
Middle row: H. Allan (Physio), J. McNeil, A. Ward, D. McDicken, A. McCulloch, J. Stewart, A. Robinson, P. Clarke, K. Armstrong, G. Wilson, R. Stewart (Trainer). Front row: W. Fernie (Manager), F. Welsh, S. McLean, D. Provan, I. Jardine, A. Robertson, G. Maxwell, I. Fallis, I. McCulloch, W. Murdoch, D. Sneddon (Ass. Manager).

SEASON 1978-79   First Division

No.	Date	Opposition	H.T.	Res.	Att.	Goalscorers
1	12 Aug	Clydebank	0-0	1-2	1854	Cairney
2	19	AIRDRIEONIANS	0-0	2-0	2707	Cairney, Maxwell
3	26	Ayr United	0-0	0-0	4974	
4	6 Sep	DUMBARTON	0-0	0-0	2420	
5	9	DUNDEE	1-0	1-1	3113	Cairney
6	13	St. Johnstone	0-0	0-0	1292	
7	16	Stirling Albion	2-1	4-1	1325	McDicken, Provan, Doherty, Maxwell
8	23	MONTROSE	1-0	2-2	2447	Maxwell, Street
9	26	Clyde	0-0	1-1	1301	McDowell
10	30	Queen of the South	0-1	1-2	1423	Street
11	7 Oct	ABROATH	2-1	3-1	2556	McDowell, Maxwell, Jardine
12	14	RAITH ROVERS	2-0	3-0	2621	Cairney, Hughes, Bourke
13	21	Hamilton	0-2	3-2	2601	Cairney, Maxwell, Bourke
14	28	Airdrieonians	0-3	1-4	2505	Bourke
15	4 Nov	AYR UNITED	0-0	1-2	5946	Hughes
16	11	Dundee	0-0	0-0	5620	
17	18	STIRLING ALBION	1-0	5-0	2739	Bourke(2), Gibson, Doherty, Maxwell
18	25	Montrose	3-0	4-0	874	Maxwell(2), Hughes, Jardine
19	2 Dec	QUEEN OF THE SOUTH	0-0	0-0	2791	
20	9	Arbroath	0-2	2-3	880	Street, J.Clark
21	16	Raith Rovers	1-1	3-1	1843	Bourke(2), Maxwell
22	23	HAMILTON	1-0	4-0	2850	Bourke(3), Gibson
23	20 Jan	MONTROSE	3-0	4-1	1906	Gibson(2), Bourke, P.Clarke
24	3 Feb	ST. JOHNSTONE	3-0	3-2	3200	Bourke, J.Clark, O.G.
25	10	Arbroath	0-0	1-0	1284	Gibson
26	24	RAITH ROVERS	0-1	2-1	3267	Maxwell, Street
27	3 Mar	CLYDEBANK	0-0	0-0	3518	
28	7	Ayr United	0-0	1-2	5693	J.Clark
29	13	Dumbarton	1-0	3-0	1345	Bourke, Cairney, Maxwell
30	17	ST. JOHNSTONE	1-1	3-1	2315	Gibson(2), Cairney
31	24	CLYDE	2-0	2-1	2517	Bourke(2)
32	31	Clydebank	2-0	2-1	2519	Bourke, Gibson
33	4 Apr	Stirling Albion	0-0	0-0	1252	
34	7	Clyde	1-0	1-0	2509	Bourke
35	11	AIRDRIEONIANS	1-0	1-0	2665	Bourke
36	14	QUEEN OF THE SOUTH	2-1	3-1	2978	Bourke, Street, Cairney
37	21	Hamilton	0-0		2897	
38	25	DUNDEE	0-0	2-1	5072	Bourke, McDicken
39	28	Dumbarton	1-0	3-1	2278	Bourke, Cairney, Gibson

Player columns: McCulloch, McLean, Robertson, Jardine, P.Clarke, McDicken, Provan, Maxwell, Cairney, J.Clark, Doherty, Welsh, McDowell, Street, Hughes, Baird, Bourke, Mauchlen, Gibson, Murdoch, Armstrong, Taylor

Apps: McCulloch 39, McLean 38, Robertson 37, Jardine 26, P.Clarke 37, McDicken 36, Provan 4, Maxwell 33, Cairney 26, J.Clark 32, Doherty 8, Welsh 9, McDowell 5, Street 12, Hughes 8, Bourke 27, Mauchlen 21, Gibson 24, Murdoch 1, Armstrong 4, Taylor 2

Subs: Jardine 4, Cairney 1, J.Clark 6, Doherty 6, Welsh 4, McDowell 3, Street 6, Hughes 3, Mauchlen 2, Armstrong 2

Goals: Jardine 2, P.Clarke 1, McDicken 2, Provan 1, Maxwell 11, Cairney 9, J.Clark 3, Doherty 2, McDowell 2, Street 5, Hughes 3, Bourke 21, Gibson 9

Pos	P	W	D	L	F	A	Pts.
2nd	39	22	10	7	72	35	54

League Cup

No.	Date	Opposition	H.T.	Res.	Att.	Goalscorers
1		Bye				
2	30 Aug	ALLOA ATHLETIC	2-0	2-0	2080	McDowell, Street
2	2 Sep	Alloa Athletic (Agg: 3-1)	1-0	1-1	1301	Cairney
3	4 Oct	MORTON	2-0	2-0	3967	Cairney, Maxwell
3	11	Morton (Agg: 4-5)	1-1	2-5*	5623	McDicken, Welsh

* After Extra Time, 90 minutes 2-4.

Scottish Cup

No.	Date	Opposition	H.T.	Res.	Att.	Goalscorers
3	27 Jan	Clyde	1-0	5-1	2509	Bourke(2), Street, Gibson
4	21 Feb	Rangers	0-1	1-1	17500	McDicken
4R	26	RANGERS	0-1	0-1	19493	

Back row: I. Jardine, D. McDicken, K. Armstrong, A. McCulloch, P. Clarke, J. Bourke, F. Welsh, A. Robertson. Middle row: H. Allan (Physio), A. Mauchlen, J. Hughes, J. Clark, J. Cairney, G. Maxwell, S. McLean, R. Street, I. Gibson, J. Doherty, R. Stewart (Coach). Seated: D. Sneddon (Team Manager), A.D. Leggate (Director), D. Faulds (Director), T.M. Lauchlan OBE (Chairman), W. McIvor (Director/Secretary), R. Lauchlan (Director), G. Ralston FRCS(E) (Medical Officer).

SEASON 1979-80 — Premier Division

No.	Date	Opposition	H.T.	Res.	Att.	Goalscorers	McCulloch	McLean	Robertson	J.Clark	P.Clarke	McDicken	Doherty	Maxwell	Gibson	Mauchlen	Street	Bourke	Jardine	Hughes	Cairney	Houston	Cockburn	Welsh	Armstrong	Cramond
1	11 Aug	St. Mirren	0-1	2-2	7449	Doherty, P.Clarke	1	2	3	4	5	6	7	8	9	10	11									
2	18	DUNDEE UNITED	0-0	1-0	5882	Street	1	2	3	4	5	6	12	8	7	10	11*	9								
3	25	Celtic	0-3	0-5	24584		1	2	3	10	5				9"					4	14					
4	8 Sep	HIBERNIAN	0-0	1-0	4654	Jardine	1	2	3	4	5	6		10	8	11	7		9"			12				
5	15	Partick Thistle	0-0	0-0	5078		1	2	3	4	5	6		10	8	11"		12			9	7				
6	22	Morton	1-1	1-3	6618	Gibson	1	2	3	4	5	6		10*	8	7				14	9	12	11*			
7	29	RANGERS	1-0	2-1	15479	J.Clark, Cairney	1	2	3	4	5	6		8	10	9	11				7					
8	6 Oct	DUNDEE	2-1	3-1	4674	Maxwell(2), Bourke	1	2	3	4	5	6		10	8	11	9	7								
9	13	Aberdeen	1-2	1-3	12791	Houston	1	2	3	4	5	6		8	7	10"	12	9			14	11*				
10	20	ST. MIRREN	1-0	1-1	6377	Houston	1	2	3	4	5	6		8	11	10	9"				12	7				
11	27	Dundee United	0-2	0-4	6403		1	2	3	4	5	6		14	12	8	10	11			9"	7*				
12	3 Nov	CELTIC	1-0	2-0	16918	Street, Gibson	1	2	3	4	5	6		8	7	10	11	9								
13	10	Hibernian	0-1	1-1	5269	Maxwell	1	2	3	4	5	6		8	7	10	11	9								
14	17	PARTICK THISTLE	0-1	0-1	4951		1	2	3	4	5	6		8	7*	10	11"	9			14	12				
15	1 Dec	Rangers	1-1	1-2	16557	Houston	1		3	4	5	6		8	11	10	14	12			9"	7*		2		
16	15	Dundee	1-1	1-3	6016	O.G.	1		3	4	5	14		8	9*	10	12	11"			7			2	6	
17	29	DUNDEE UNITED	0-0	0-0	4515		1		3	4		6		8	10	11	9	12			7"			2	5	
18	5 Jan	HIBERNIAN	2-0	3-1	6092	Street(3)	1		3	4	5	6		8	11	9	7							2		10
19	12	Partick Thistle	0-0	1-1	4543	Street	1		3	4	5	6		8	9	11	7							2		10
20	19	Morton	0-0	2-1	5352	P.Clarke, Cramond	1		3	4	5			8	9	12	11"				7			2	6	10
21	9 Feb	DUNDEE	1-1	1-1	4432	Houston	1		3	4	5	6		8	11	10	9	12				7"		2		10
22	23	Aberdeen	2-0	2-1	9567	Street, O.G.	1		3	4	5	6		9	8		11"	12				7		2		10
23	1 Mar	ST. MIRREN	0-0	1-1	6800	Mauchlen	1		3	4	5	6		9	8	11		12			7			2		10"
24	8	Dundee United	0-0	0-0	6497		1		3	4	5	6		12	9"	8	11				7			2		10
25	12	MORTON	0-0	1-1	4905	Mauchlen	1		3	4	5	6		14	12	9	8	11*			7			2		10"
26	15	CELTIC	1-0	1-1	14965	Street	1		3	4	5	6		9"	12	8	11				7			2		10"
27	29	PARTICK THISTLE	0-0	0-1	3814		1		3		5	6	12	4	9	8	11				7"			2		10
28	1 Apr	ABERDEEN	0-1	0-4	5020		1		3		5	6	9	4	12	8	11				7			2		10"
29	5	MORTON	0-1	0-2	4309		1	2	3	4	5	6		7	8	11	9				12					10"
30	12	St. Mirren	1-0	1-1	6740	P.Clarke	1	8	3	4	5	6		14	7"	11	9	12						2		10"
31	16	Celtic	0-1	0-2	16695		1	10	3	4	5	6		12	8	11"	9				14	7*		2		
32	19	ABERDEEN	1-3	1-3	3533	Gibson	1	10	3	4	5	6		7	8	11	9							2		
33	21	Hibernian	1-0	2-1	2659	Houston(2)	1	2	3	4	5	6		8	11	9						7				10
34	23	RANGERS	1-0	1-1	8504	Street	1	2	3	4	5	6		10	8		11	9				7				
35	26	Dundee	0-0	2-0	4003	McDicken, Cairney	1	2	3	4	5	6		8*	11	12	9				7"				14	10
36	30	Rangers	0-1	0-1	7655		1	2	3	4	5	6		11"	12	9	7							2		10
				Apps.			36	34	24	34	35	34	2	19	31	30	26	30	2		9	24	1	17	3	15
				Subs									8	3	2	1		5	3	2	2	9		1		1
				Goals						1	3	1	1	3	3	2	9	1	1		2	6				1

Pos	P.	W.	D.	L.	F.	A.	Pts.
8th	36	11	11	14	38	52	33

League Cup

	Date	Opposition	H.T.	Res.	Att.	Goalscorers	McCulloch	McLean	Robertson	J.Clark	P.Clarke	McDicken	Doherty	Maxwell	Gibson	Mauchlen	Street	Bourke	Jardine	Hughes	Cairney	Houston
1	15 Aug	ALLOA ATHLETIC	1-0	2-1	2491	Jardine, Doherty	1	2	3	8	5"	6	14	12	7	10			4	11	9*	
1	22	Alloa Athletic (Agg: 3-2)	0-0	1-1*	1696	Doherty	1	2	3	11	5	6		8	10	7"	9		4	12		
2	29	FORFAR ATHLETIC	0-0	2-0	2220	P.Clarke, Gibson	1	2	3	4	5	6	12	10	8	11	7				9	
2	1 Sep	Forfar Athletic (Agg: 3-1)	1-0	1-1	1565	Maxwell	1	2	3	4	5	6		10	8	11	7				9	
3	26	Hibernian	1-0	2-1	4241	Cairney, Bourke	1	2	3	4	5	6		8	7"	10	12	9			11	
3	10 Oct	HIBERNIAN (Agg: 4-2)	2-1	2-1	5353	Maxwell, Bourke	1	2	3	4	5	6		8	7	10		9			11	
QF	31	Morton	1-1	1-2	6846	McLean, Street	1	2	3	4	5	6		8	7	10	11	9				
QF	24 Nov	MORTON (Agg: 5-5)#	0-0	3-2*	8407	P.Clarke, Gibson, Cairney	1	2	3	4	5*	6	14	8	7	10	11	9"			12	

* After extra time x 90 minutes 0-1
\# 90 mins - 1-0, Morton won on penalties 5-3

Scottish Cup

	Date	Opposition	H.T.	Res.	Att.	Goalscorers	McCulloch	McLean	Robertson	J.Clark	P.Clarke	McDicken	Doherty	Maxwell	Gibson	Mauchlen	Street	Bourke	Jardine	Hughes	Cairney	Houston	Cockburn	Welsh	Armstrong	Cramond
3	30 Jan	PARTICK THISTLE	0-0	0-1	7677		1		3		5	6		8	7		9				12	11"		2		10

Drybrough Cup

	Date	Opposition	H.T.	Res.	Att.	Goalscorers	McCulloch	McLean	Robertson	J.Clark	P.Clarke	McDicken	Doherty	Maxwell	Gibson	Mauchlen	Street	Bourke
QF	28 Jul	ABERDEEN	0-0	1-0	4548	Street	1	2	3	4	5	6		8	7	10	11	9
SF	1 Aug	RANGERS	0-0	0-2	10035		1	2	3	4	5	6		8	7	10	11	9

Anglo-Scottish Cup

	Date	Opposition	H.T.	Res.	Att.	Goalscorers	McCulloch	McLean	Robertson	J.Clark	P.Clarke	McDicken	Doherty	Maxwell	Gibson	Mauchlen	Street	Bourke	Jardine	Hughes	Cairney	Houston	Cockburn	Welsh
1	6 Aug	Dundee	1-0	1-1	3832	P.Clarke	1	10	3		5	6	12	8	7		11	9"	4					2
1	8	DUNDEE (Agg: 4-4*)	2-1	3-3	3719	Street(2), Gibson	1	2	3	10	5	6	12	8	7"		11	9	4					

* (Agg: 4-4 Dundee won on away goals)

Back row - D. Kilpatrick, I. Gibson, J. McBride, A. Morrison, J. Brown, G. Wilson, J. McClurg, S. Black, J. Cockburn;
Middle row - H. Allan (Physio/Trainer), I. Jardine, J. Bourke, D. McDicken, P. Clarke, A. McCulloch, K. Armstrong, F. Welsh, K. Robin, S. McLean, R. Stewart (Ass. Trainer); Front row - D. Sneddon (Manager), J. Doherty, J. Clark, J. Hughes, G. Maxwell, A. Robertson, A. Mauchlen, R. Street, G. McCready, R. Hamilton.

SEASON 1980-81 — Premier Division

No.	Date	Opposition	H.T.	Res.	Att.	Goalscorers
1	9 Aug	Dundee United	0-1	2-2	5788	Street, A.Mauchlen
2	16	CELTIC	0-3	0-3	13810	
3	23	Partick Thistle	0-0	1-0	3197	McBride
4	6 Sep	HEARTS	0-0	0-1	3995	
5	13	Morton	0-1	0-2	6049	
6	20	RANGERS	0-3	1-8	15021	Bourke
7	27	Airdrieonians	0-0	0-1	2736	
8	4 Oct	ST. MIRREN	0-4	1-6	3897	Cramond
9	11	Aberdeen	0-0	0-2	11164	
10	18	DUNDEE UNITED	0-0	0-1	2719	
11	25	Celtic	1-2	1-4	16537	Cramond
12	1 Nov	PARTICK THISTLE	0-0	0-1	2417	
13	8	AIRDRIEONIANS	1-0	1-1	2230	Houston
14	15	Rangers	0-1	0-2	15791	
15	22	ABERDEEN	1-0	1-1	3319	Street
16	29	St. Mirren	0-1	0-2	5300	
17	6 Dec	Hearts	0-0	0-2	5183	
18	13	MORTON	2-1	3-3	2483	Armstrong, Bourke, Hughes
19	20	RANGERS	1-0	1-1	9172	Bourke
20	1 Jan	CELTIC	1-2	1-2	7625	Hughes
21	3	Dundee United	0-2	0-7	6474	
22	10	ST. MIRREN	1-0	2-0	4385	A.Mauchlen, Doherty
23	31	Morton	0-1	0-1	3497	
24	21 Feb	Partick Thistle	1-0	1-1	1601	Bourke
25	28	DUNDEE UNITED	0-0	0-1	2102	
26	7 Mar	St. Mirren	0-1	1-1	4203	Bourke
27	11	Airdrieonians	0-3	0-3	2084	
28	14	ABERDEEN	0-0	1-0	2415	Doherty
29	21	Rangers	0-1	0-2	8488	
30	24	HEARTS	1-0	2-0	1445	A.Mauchlen, McLean
31	28	AIRDRIEONIANS	0-1	0-1	1849	
32	4 Apr	Hearts	0-1	0-1	1866	
33	15	MORTON	0-0	0-0	973	
34	18	PARTICK THISTLE	0-1	0-1	1262	
35	25	Celtic	0-1	1-1	23050	Eadie
36	2 May	Aberdeen	0-0	2-0	7002	McDicken, McCready

Player columns (left to right): McCulloch, McLean, Robertson, A.Mauchlen, P.Clarke, McDicken, Houston, Gibson, Cairney, Cramond, Street, Doherty, Bourke, Maxwell, McBride, Morrison, Hughes, Cockburn, McCready, Armstrong, Brown, G.Wilson, A.Wilson, Black, McClurg, Bryce, J.Clark, Robin, Eadie, S.Mauchlen

Apps: 19 32 18 31 24 33 14 10 5 16 13 8 26 9 17 1 9 24 4 21 9 4 8 3 3 23 8 4
Subs: 2 1 1 1 3 2 5 1 7 5 4 2 1 1 1 5 3 1
Goals: 1 3 1 1 2 2 5 5 1 2 1 1 1

Pos	P.	W.	D.	L.	F.	A.	Pts.
9th	30	5	3	22	23	65	19

League Cup

No.	Date	Opposition	H.T.	Res.	Att.	Goalscorers
1	13 Aug	AIRDRIEONIANS	1-0	1-0	2986	Cramond
1	20	Airdrieonians (Agg: 2-0)	0-0	1-0	2983	Cramond
2	27	DUNFERMLINE	0-0	0-0	2273	
2	30	Dunfermline (Agg: 2-1)	1-0	2-1	3084	P.Clarke, McBride
3	3 Sep	Dundee	0-0	0-0	4317	
3	24	DUNDEE	0-0	0-0*	2401	

* After extra time, Dundee won 5-3 on penalties.

Scottish Cup

No.	Date	Opposition	H.T.	Res.	Att.	Goalscorers
3	24 Jan	AYR UNITED	1-0	2-1	8185	McDicken, Hughes
4	14 Feb	CLYDEBANK	0-0	0-0	3741	
4R	18	Clydebank	0-0	1-1*	3400	Bourke
4R	23	Clydebank #	0-1	0-1	2340	

* After extra time   # At Love Street

Anglo-Scottish Cup

No.	Date	Opposition	H.T.	Res.	Att.	Goalscorers
1	30 Jul	EAST STIRLING	0-1	1-3	1563	A.Mauchlen
1	6 Aug	East Stirling (Agg: 4-3)	0-0	3-0	1000	McDicken, Cairney, Houston
QF	9 Sep	Blackpool	0-0	1-2	4904	Cramond
QF	14 Oct	BLACKPOOL (Agg: 5-4)	4-1	4-2	2656	Cramond(2), Bourke, Maxwell
SF	4 Nov	NOTTS COUNTY	1-2	1-2	2865	McBride
SF	18	Notts County (Agg: 3-7)	0-2	2-5	4314	Street, McBride

Back row - J. Cockburn, J. Hughes, T. Bryce, S. McLean, G. Maxwell, A. Wilson, J. McLurg, J. McBride, S. Black, J. Cairney, D. Kilpatrick; Middle row - H. Allan, G. Wilson, R. Houston, J. Bourke, P. Clarke, A. McCulloch, K. Armstrong, D. McDicken, F. Welsh, A. Morrison, R. Stewart; Front row - D. Sneddon, J. Doherty, G. Cramond, I. Gibson, A. Robertson, A. Mauchlen, R. Street, J. Clark, G. McCready, R. Hamilton.

SEASON 1981-82   First Division

No.	Date	Opposition	H.T.	Res.	Att.	Goalscorers	McCulloch	McLean	Robertson	J.Clark	Armstrong	P.Clarke	Gallacher	Mauchlen	Bourke	Cockburn	McCready	McGivern	Eadie	McBride	McLeod	McDicken	Wilson	Bryce	Bryson	Robin	Cramond
1	29 Aug	MOTHERWELL	1-0	2-0	2694	Gallacher, O.G.	1	2	3	4	5	6	7	8	9	10	11"	12									
2	5 Sep	Hearts	1-0	1-0	4796	Robertson	1	2	3	4	5	6	7	8		10	11			9"	12						
3	8	Clydebank	0-0	0-0	1042		1	2	3	4	5	6		8		10	11	12	9	7"							
4	12	AYR UNITED	0-0	1-1	5477	Gallacher	1	2	12	4	5	6	7	8	9		11	3"			10						
5	16	Queen of the South	1-1	1-1	1722	P.Clarke	1	2	12	4	5	6	7	8	9*		11	3"		14	10						
6	19	QUEENS PARK	0-0	0-0	2337		1	2	3	4	5	6	7	8	9		11"	12			10						
7	23	St. Johnstone	2-0	2-0	1734	Bourke, J.Clark	1	2	3	4	5	6	7	8	9		11				10						
8	29	East Stirling	1-2	1-2	707	McCready	1	2	3	4	5	6	7	8	9		11"		12		10						
9	3 Oct	DUNFERMLINE	0-1	0-1	2137		1	2	3	4	5	6	7	8	9	12			14	11"	10"						
10	10	FALKIRK	1-0	2-2	1801	Eadie(2)	1		3	4"	5	6	7	8	9		11				10	12					
11	17	Hamilton	0-0	2-1	1247	Gallacher, Bourke	1		2	4"	5	6	7	12	14	3			9*	11	10	8					
12	24	Dumbarton	0-0	2-0	799	Mauchlen, J.Clark	1		2	4	5	6	7	12	9	3	11*		14		10"	8					
13	31	RAITH ROVERS	1-0	1-1	1859	Gallacher	1		2	4	5		7	8	9	3			11		10"6	12					
14	7 Nov	HEARTS	0-0	0-0	3348		1		2	4	5		7	8	9	3			12	11"	10	6					
15	14	Motherwell	0-0	0-2	5068		1		2	4	5		7	8	9	3			12	11"	10	6					
16	21	QUEEN OF THE SOUTH	0-0	0-0	1591		1	14	2	4*	5		7"	8	9	3			12	11	10	6					
17	28	EAST STIRLING	1-0	2-0	1391	Eadie, Gallacher	1	8		2		5	6	7		3			11	9"	12	10	4*		14		
18	5 Dec	Dunfermline	2-1	2-1	1665	McBride, McDicken	1	8		2		5	6	7	14	3			11"	9	10*	4		12			
19	12	ST. JOHNSTONE	0-1	0-2	1811		1	8		2		5	6	7	12	3			11*14	9	10*4						
20	16 Jan	HAMILTON	2-2	2-2	1480	Mauchlen, Bryson	1	12	2		5	6	7	10	9	3				8	4"				11		
21	30	DUMBARTON	0-0	0-0	1346		1	12	2		5	6"	7	10	9	3			14	8	4				11*		
22	17 Feb	Falkirk	2-1	2-1	1115	Bourke(2)	1	14	2	4	5	6	7	10	9	3*			11	8					11"		
23	20	Queens Park	1-0	2-0	1253	P.Clarke, Gallacher	1	2	3		5	6	7	10	9		11"			8				4	12		
24	27	AYR UNITED	0-0	1-1	4687	McGivern	1	2	3	4	5	6	7	10	9		11			8"	12						
25	10 Mar	DUNFERMLINE	0-0	0-0	1356	Bryson, Bourke	1		2	4	5	6	7*	10	9	3"			11	8	12				14		
26	13	Raith Rovers	1-0	3-0	1220	Mauchlen, McDicken, Bourke	1	2	3		5	6	7	10"9					11	7	8				12		
27	17	Ayr United	0-1	1-1	3663	McDicken	1	2	3	4"	5	6	7	10	9		11			8	12						
28	20	FALKIRK	1-1	4-1	1905	McLeod, Bourke, Armstrong, McDicken	1	2	3		5	6	7	10	9		11			8	4						
29	27	Motherwell	0-0	0-1	4816		1	2	3		5	6	7	10	9		11			8	4						
30	30	Queens Park	1-2	3-2	1197	Gallacher(2), McDicken	1	2	3	10	5	6	7				11"			8	4				12		
31	3 Apr	CLYDEBANK	0-0	0-0	2087		1	2	3	10	5	6	7	12	9		11*			8	4"				14		
32	6	Raith Rovers	2-3	3-3	1401	Bryson, P.Clarke, Bourke	1	2	3	10	5	6	7	12	9		14			8	4"				11*		
33	10	St. Johnstone	0-1	3-1	2209	Mauchlen, P.Clarke, Bourke	1	2	3	4	5	6	7	8	9		11			8							
34	17	HAMILTON	0-0	0-0	1878		1	2	3	4	5	6		10"9			7*	14		8	12			11			
35	21	CLYDEBANK	1-0	2-0	1308	Bourke(2)	1	8	2	4"	5	6		10	9	3			7			12		11			
36	24	Dumbarton	0-0	0-2	715	McDicken(2)	1	4"	3			5	6	14	8	9			7		12	10*	11	2			
37	1 May	East Stirling	4-0	5-1	482	Bourke(2), McGivern, McLean, Robertson	1	8	3		5	6	7"	10	9		11			4			12	2			
38	8	HEARTS	0-0	0-0	9997		1	8	3		5	6	7	10	9		11				12	4"		2			
39	15	QUEEN OF THE SOUTH	5-0	6-0	2363	Gallacher(2), Armstrng, McDickn, Burke, O.G.	1	4	3	12	5	6	7	10"9			11*			8		14					
		Apps.					39	28	37	27	39	35	34	31	33	20	10	18	9	5	32	20		2	7	3	
		Subs					4	2	1			1	6	1	1		10	5	2	1	7	1		2	7		
		Goals					1	2	2	2	4	10	4	4			1	2	3	1	1	8			3		

Pos P. W. D. L. F. A. Pts.
2nd 39 17 17 5 60 29 51

League Cup Section 3

Pos P. W. D. L. F. A. Pts.
2nd 6 2 2 2 5 8 6

No.	Date	Opposition	H.T.	Res.	Att.	Goalscorers	McCulloch	McLean	Robertson	J.Clark	Armstrong	P.Clarke	Gallacher	Mauchlen	Bourke	Cockburn	McCready	McGivern	Eadie	McBride	McLeod	McDicken	Wilson	Bryce
1	8 Aug	Aberdeen	0-2	0-3	8414		1	2		4"	5		7	8	9	3	11			12	6		10	
2	12	AIRDRIEONIANS	0-0	1-1	1901	Bourke	1	2		4	5		7	8	9	3	11			12	6		10"	
3	15	Hearts	0-1	1-1	7746	Wilson	1	2		4	5		7	8	9	3	12			11"	6	10		
4	19	Airdrieonians	1-0	1-0	1380	Bourke	1	2		4	5		7		9	3	11			12	6	10"		8
5	22	ABERDEEN	0-2	0-3	3118		1	2	12	4	5		7	8	9	3	11				6			10"
6	26	HEARTS	2-0	2-0	1388	J.Clark, McLean	1	2	3	4	5		7	8	9	10	11"*14				6"	12		

Scottish Cup

No.	Date	Opposition	H.T.	Res.	Att.	Goalscorers	McCulloch	McLean	Robertson	J.Clark	Armstrong	P.Clarke	Gallacher	Mauchlen	Bourke	Cockburn	McCready	McGivern	Eadie	McBride	McLeod	McDicken	Wilson	Bryce
3	6 Feb	MONTROSE	0-0	1-0	1418	Bourke	1	4	2		5		7	10*9		3	11			8"	6		12	14
4	13	ST. JOHNSTONE	1-0	3-1	2693	Bourke(2), McGiven	1	2	4	5	6	7"	10	9	3	12			8			11		
QF	6 Mar	Aberdeen	2-2	2-4	9000	McGiven, Gallacher	1	2	3	4	5"	6	7	10	9		11			8*	12		14	

Back row: B. Gallacher, K. Robin, P. Clarke, J. Bourke, A. McCulloch, K. Armstrong, D. McDicken, A. Robertson, J. McBride.
Front: G. McCready, G. Maxwell, T. Bryce, J. Cockburn, K. Eadie, A. Mauchlen, J. Clark, G. Cramond.

Player columns (left to right): McCulloch, McDicken, Robertson, J.Clark, Armstrong, McClurg, Bryson, McLeod, Bourke, McLean, Gallacher, P.Clarke, Eadie, R.Clark, McKinna, McGivern, Cockburn, Mauchlen, Simpson, Clinging, Wilson, Cuthbertson, Muir

No.	Date	Opposition	H.T.	Res.	Att.	Goalscorers
1	4 Sep	Morton	0-0	0-0	2349	
2	11	HIBERNIAN	0-1	1-1	2800	P.Clarke
3	18	Rangers	0-2	0-5	17350	
4	25	DUNDEE	0-0	0-0	2105	
5	2 Oct	St. Mirren	2-2	2-3	3564	McLean, Mauchlen
6	9	DUNDEE UNITED	1-0	1-1	2446	Gallacher
7	16	Celtic	0-0	1-2	11063	P.Clarke
8	23	ABERDEEN	0-1	0-2	3402	
9	30	Motherwell	1-1	1-3	3016	McLean
10	6 Nov	MORTON	1-0	3-1	1854	J.Clark, Gallacher, Bourke
11	13	Hibernian	1-1	2-2	4192	Bryson, McDicken
12	20	RANGERS	0-0	0-0	9194	
13	27	Dundee	0-3	2-5	4311	J.Clark, McLeod
14	4 Dec	ST. MIRREN	1-0	2-2	2209	P.Clarke(2)
15	11	Dundee United	0-1	0-7	7259	
16	18	CELTIC	0-1	0-4	9024	
17	27	Aberdeen	0-1	0-2	14411	
18	1 Jan	MOTHERWELL	0-1	0-2	3314	
19	3	Morton	0-1	0-1	2015	
20	8	HIBERNIAN	0-2	0-2	2142	
21	15	Rangers	0-0	1-1	11223	McGivern
22	22	DUNDEE	1-0	2-0	1891	Gallacher, R.Clark
23	5 Feb	St. Mirren	0-1	0-2	3303	
24	12	DUNDEE UNITED	0-2	0-5	1834	
25	26	Celtic	0-1	0-4	10691	
26	5 Mar	ABERDEEN	0-2	1-2	2436	Gallacher
27	12	Motherwell	0-2	1-3	2895	McGivern
28	19	MORTON	2-0	4-0	1230	Gallacher(2), McGivern, P.Clarke
29	26	RANGERS	0-1	0-1	6648	
30	2 Apr	Hibernian	1-2	1-8	4065	Gallacher
31	9	Dundee	0-0	0-0	3376	
32	23	Dundee United	0-4	0-4	7516	
33	27	ST. MIRREN	0-2	2-2	1049	Gallacher(2)
34	30	CELTIC	0-2	0-5	7560	
35	4 May	Aberdeen	0-2	0-5	12002	
36	14	MOTHERWELL	1-1	1-1	1203	Simpson

Apps. 35 27 13 36 20 10 18 34 10 19 33 34 6 21 — 32 20 2 17 3 1 1 4
Subs 4 — — 3 11 1 9 2 1 — 1 2 3 2 1 — 1 — — 1 3
Goals 1 — 2 — 1 1 1 2 9 5 — 1 — 3 1 1

	Pos	P.	W.	D.	L.	F.	A.	Pts.
	10th	36	3	11	22	28	91	17

League Cup Section 8

	Pos	P.	W.	D.	L.	F.	A.	Pts.
	1st	6	4	1	1	13	3	9

No.	Date	Opposition	H.T.	Res.	Att.	Goalscorers
1	14 Aug	BERWICK RANGERS	2-0	4-0	1517	McLean, P.Clarke, Mauchlen, O.G.
2	18	Hamilton	0-0	0-0	1472	
3	21	Queens Park	0-0	2-0	1005	McLean, McGivern
4	25	HAMILTON	0-0	1-0	1582	Bourke
5	28	Berwick Rangers	0-1	1-2	672	McLean
6	1 Sep	QUEENS PARK	1-0	5-1	1200	Bourke(2), McLean, Gallacher, Mauchlen
PO	6	COWDENBEATH	1-0	1-0	1091	McLean
PO	8	Cowdenbeath (Agg: 1-1)	0-1	0-1*	686	
QF	22	RANGERS	0-1	0-0	7903	McLean
QF	6 Oct	Rangers (Agg: 1-12)	0-3	0-6	5342	

* After extra time, Kilmarnock won 4-3 on penalties

Scottish Cup

No.	Date	Opposition	H.T.	Res.	Att.	Goalscorers
3	29 Jan	Partick Thistle	0-0	1-1	4398	Bryson
3R	2 Feb	PARTICK THISTLE	0-0	0-0*	3884	
3R	7	Partick Thistle	0-1	2-2*	4809	Gallacher, McGivern
3R	9	PARTICK THISTLE	0-0	0-1	3745	

* After extra time, 7/2/83 game: 1-1 after 90 mins.

Back row (l-r): L. McKinna, J. McClurg, K. Armstrong, P. Clarke, J. Bourke, A. Morrison, A. Robertson.
Middle row: H. Allan (Physio), S. McLean, K. Eadie, I. Bryson, A. Wilson, A. McCulloch, R. McLaughlan, J. Haswell, B. Gallacher, R. Stewart (Trainer).
Front row: D. Wilson (Ass. Manager), J. Clark, S. McGivern, D. McDicken, A. MacLeod, J. Cockburn, J. Clunie (Manager).

SEASON 1983-84   First Division

No.	Date	Opposition	H.T.	Res.	Att.	Goalscorers	McCulloch	Robertson	Cockburn	McLeod	P.Clarke	R.Clark	McGivern	McDicken	Gallacher	Simpson	Bryson	J.Clark	McLean	Lowe	McKinna	Cuthbertson	McClurg	Walker	Brown	Holland
1	20 Aug	Ayr United	2-0	2-0	3129	Bryson, McDicken	1	2	3	4	5	6	7	8	9	10	11									
2	3 Sep	Partick Thistle	0-1	0-2	2252		1	2	3	8"	5	6	7	12	9	10	11	4								
3	10	FALKIRK	0-1	2-1	1485	R.Clark(2)	1	2	3	8"	5	6	7	4	9	10*11		12	14							
4	14	MEADOWBANK	1-0	3-1	1028	McGivern, McLeod, Gallacher	1	2	3	10	5	6	7	4	9		11	8								
5	17	Hamilton	1-0	1-0	1407	R.Clark	1	2	3	10	5	6	7	4	9	12	11"	8								
6	24	ALLOA ATHLETIC	1-0	2-0	1475	McDicken, Gallacher	1	2"	3	10	5	6	7	4	9		11	8	12							
7	28	Clydebank	0-2	0-4	855		1		2	3	5	6	7	4	9	10*11		8		12						
8	1 Oct	Clyde	1-0	1-0	791	R.Clark	1	2	3	10	5	6	7		9	8	11	4								
9	8	BRECHIN CITY	2-0	4-1	1420	McGivern(2), McKinna, McLeod	1	2	3	10	5	6	7		9	8"	11	4			9	12				
10	15	Airdrieonians	0-0	0-1	1317		1	2	3	10	5	6	7	12		8"	11	4			9					
11	22	DUMBARTON	0-0	2-2	1464	McDicken, Bryson	1	2	3	10	5	6	7"	8	9		11	4			12					
12	29	RAITH ROVERS	0-0	2-1	1397	R.Clark, P.Clarke	1	2	3	10	5	6	12	8	9		11"				7	4*	14			
13	5 Nov	Morton	1-0	2-2	1902	McKinna(2)	1	2	3	10	5	6		8"	9		11	4			7		12			
14	12	Meadowbank	1-1	1-2	836	Bryson	1	2"	3	10	5*	6	12	8	9		11	4			7		14			
15	19	HAMILTON	1-1	2-1	1257	Bryson, Gallacher	1	2	3	10	5	6	7"	8	9		11	4			12					
16	26	Brechin City	0-1	2-3	799	Gallacher, McKinna	1	2	3	10	5	6	7	8	9		11"	4			12					
17	3 Dec	CLYDE	0-1	0-1	1317		1	2	3	10	5	6	7	8	9"	14	11"4				12					
18	10	Alloa Athletic	3-0	4-0	574	McGivern(2), McDicken, McKinna	1	2	3		5	6	7	8		10"11		4	12		9					
19	17	CLYDEBANK	0-0	0-1	1149		1	2	3	12	5	6		8		7	10	11	4"		9					
20	26	Falkirk	0-0	3-1	3198	McDicken, Gallacher, O.G.	1	2	3	10	5	6	7	4	9	11				8						
21	31	PARTICK THISTLE	1-1	1-2	3111	R.Clark	1	2		3	5	6	7		9	10	11"			8			12	4		
22	3 Jan	AYR UNITED	0-0	1-0	2890	Cuthbertson	1	2	3	10	5	6	7		9	11				8			12	4"		
23	7	Dumbarton	1-3	3-4	907	McClurg(2), McGivern	1	2	3	10	5	6	7		9	11	12			8*			4"	14		
24	14	AIRDRIEONIANS	1-1	4-1	1310	McDicken(2), R.Clark(2)	1	3		8	5	6	7	4	9	10"11				2			12			
25	4 Feb	MORTON	0-1	0-1	1313		1	3		8	5	6	7	4	9	10	11			2						
26	11	BRECHIN CITY	0-0	1-1	910	R.Clark	1	3		8	5	6	7	4	9	10	11			2						
27	25	Clydebank	0-0	0-3	766		1	3	12	8	5	6	7	4	9	10				2	11"					
28	29	Raith Rovers	0-0	1-2	768	Gallacher	1	3	12	8	5	6	7	4	9	10"				2	11					
29	3 Mar	Hamilton	1-0	1-0	874	McGivern	1	3	10	8	5		11	6	9"					2	12		4	7		
30	10	DUMBARTON	0-0	0-0	1140		1	3	12	8	5	6	11	4	9	10*				2	14			7"		
31	17	Airdrieonians	0-0	0-3	727		1	3		8		6	11"4	12	10					2	9		5	7		
32	24	RAITH ROVERS	1-1	1-2	680	Brown	1	3			6	11	5		10					8	2	9			7	4
33	31	Falkirk	0-2	0-2	1203		1	3		10		11	5	7						2"	9	4	6	12	8	
34	7 Apr	MEADOWBANK	1-0	1-1	539	Gallacher	1	3	10	8		12	11	5	7					2	9	4*	6"	14		
35	14	Partick Thistle	1-0	2-1	1854	Gallacher, O.G.	1	3	10			6	11	12	7	8				2	9		5"		4	
36	21	Clyde	0-2	1-2	633	R.Clark	1	3	10			6	11	12	7	8*				2	9	14	5"		4	
37	28	ALLOA ATHLETIC	1-0	2-0	460	R.Clark, McKinna	1	3	10			6	11	5	7					2	9	8			4	
38	5 May	AYR UNITED	0-0	3-0	1495	Gallacher(2), McKinna	1	3	10			6	11	5	7					2	9	8			4	
39	12	Morton	0-1	2-3	4547	Gallacher, McKinna	1	3	10"			6	11	5	7			12		2	9	8			4	
						Apps.	39	38	29	31	30	36	35	30	34	23	16	19	2	18	7	8	4	7		
						Subs			3	1		1	2	4	1	2	2	1	3	1	6	5	4	2		
						Goals			2	1	11	7	7	11	4			8			1	2			1	

Pos	P	W.	D.	L.	F.	A.	Pts.
6th	39	16	6	17	57	53	38

League Cup Section 4

Round 3

Pos	P	W.	D.	L.	F.	A.	Pts.
2nd	6	3	1	2	9	6	7

	Date	Opposition	H.T.	Res.	Att.	Goalscorers	McCulloch	Robertson	Cockburn	McLeod	P.Clarke	R.Clark	McGivern	McDicken	Gallacher	Simpson	Bryson	J.Clark	McLean	Lowe	McKinna	Cuthbertson	McClurg	Walker	Brown	Holland
2	24 Aug	Queens Park	2-1	2-3	702	J.Clark(2)	1	2	3	8	5	6	7	10	9	12	11"	4								
2	27	QUEENS PARK (Agg: 5-4)	1-1	3-1	1506	McGivern(2), McDicken	1	2	3	8	5	6	7	10	9		11	4								
3	31	Hibernian	0-0	0-2	2681		1	2	3	8	5	6	7	10	9		11	4								
3	7 Sep	AIRDRIEONIANS	2-0	3-0	1046	Gallacher(3)	1	2	3	8	5	6	7	4	9	10	11	4								
3	5 Oct	Celtic	0-0	1-1	5435	Gallacher	1	2	3	10	5	6	7	4	9		11	4								
3	26	Airdrieonians	0-1	2-1	829	P.Clarke, Robertson		2	3	10	5	6	14	8"	9		11"4				7			12		
3	9 Nov	HIBERNIAN	2-0	3-1	2001	McDicken(2), P.Clarke	1	2	3	10	5	6	7"	8	9			4			11		12			
3	30	CELTIC	0-1	0-1	8793		1	2	3	10	5	6	7"	8	9	4	11				12					

Scottish Cup

	Date	Opposition	H.T.	Res.	Att.	Goalscorers	McCulloch	Robertson	Cockburn	McLeod	P.Clarke	R.Clark	McGivern	McDicken	Gallacher	Simpson	Bryson	J.Clark	McLean	Lowe	McKinna	Cuthbertson	McClurg	Walker	Brown	Holland
3	13 Feb	Aberdeen	0-0	1-1	15000	Gallacher	1	3	12	8	5	6	7	4*	9	10	11"			2		14				
3R	15	ABERDEEN	0-2	1-3	6106	McKinna	1	3	4	8	5	6	7		9	10				2	11					

An anxious Jim Clunie, flanked by Davie Wilson (left) and Hugh Allan (right), checks his watch.

SEASON 1984-85 — First Division

No.	Date	Opposition	H.T.	Res.	Att.	Goalscorers
1	11 Aug	Motherwell	0-1	0-2	2384	
2	18	AYR UNITED	0-0	0-0	2013	
3	25	Clyde	0-0	1-4	749	Cuthbertson
4	1 Sep	BRECHIN CITY	0-1	1-1	855	McGivern
5	8	FORFAR ATHLETIC	0-0	2-1	809	McEachran, McKinna
6	15	Clydebank	0-1	0-5	837	
7	22	HAMILTON	0-1	1-2	805	Bryson
8	29	AIRDRIEONIANS	0-3	0-5	1115	
9	6 Oct	Meadowbank	0-1	0-4	419	
10	13	FALKIRK	0-1	3-1	1210	Robertson, Bryson, McKinna
11	20	East Fife	0-0	1-0	1006	Cuthbertson
12	27	St. Johnstone	0-0	1-0	1513	P.Clarke
13	3 Nov	PARTICK THISTLE	0-0	0-0	1834	
14	10	Forfar Athletic	0-2	1-4	1060	McLean
15	17	CLYDEBANK	0-0	1-1	1184	P.Clarke
16	24	Hamilton	0-0	0-1	889	
17	1 Dec	Airdrieonians	0-1	1-2	1483	McGivern
18	8	MEADOWBANK	0-1	2-1	847	McLean, Millar
19	15	Brechin City	1-1	2-3	668	McGivern(2)
20	22	CLYDE	2-0	2-0	1303	Millar(2)
21	29	MOTHERWELL	0-0	0-0	2042	
22	2 Jan	Ayr United	0-0	0-1	4136	
23	5	EAST FIFE	0-0	1-1	1296	McKinna(2), Millar
24	19	ST. JOHNSTONE	2-2	3-2	1451	McKinna(2), Millar
25	2 Feb	Partick Thistle	0-0	0-1	1776	
26	23	Motherwell	1-1	2-2	2288	Millar, McKinna
27	26	CLYDEBANK	0-0	0-0	1336	
28	2 Mar	Brechin City	0-1	1-2	621	Millar
29	9	HAMILTON	1-0	1-1	1225	Millar
30	13	Falkirk	0-2	2-3	1532	Cuthbertson, Millar
31	16	Meadowbank	1-1	1-2	492	McGivern
32	23	FORFAR ATHLETIC	0-0	1-0	1082	Millar
33	30	Ayr United	0-0	0-0	2404	
34	6 Apr	FALKIRK	0-0	0-3	1632	
35	13	PARTICK THISTLE	2-0	2-0	1803	McKinna, Cuthbertson
36	20	East Fife	2-0	2-0	875	Millar(2)
37	27	St. Johnstone	3-2	4-2	781	Millar, Cormack, Cuthbertson, Pelosi
38	4 May	CLYDE	0-0	2-0	1692	Cuthbertson, P.Clarke
39	11	AIRDRIEONIANS	1-2	1-4	1103	Bryson

Player appearances (shirt numbers; * / " denote substitute appearances):

No.	McCulloch	Cockburn	Robertson	Brown	McDicken	R.Clark	McGivern	McConville	McKinna	Bryson	McEachran	P.Clarke	Cuthbertson	McLean	Lowe	Cormack	Martin	Millar	McLeod	Melville	Felosi	Sarwar	Cruickshanks	Houston
1	1	2"	3	4	5	6	7	8	9	10*	11	12	14											
2	1		3	4	5*	6	7	8	9		11"	12	10	2		14								
3	1		3	8	4	6	7	10"	9*	11	5	12	2	14										
4	1		3	8	4	6	7	10	12	11	9"	5		2										
5	1		3	8"	4	6	7	10	12	11	9	5		2										
6	1	14	3	9	4	6"		10*	11	7	8	5		2	12									
7	1	9	3	8	6			11	7	10	5	12	4"	2										
8	1	14	3		6		7	11	10*	9	5	4"	12	2	8									
9	1	10	3	6*		7		12	11	9"	5	14	2	4	8									
10	1	12	3	6*	7			10	9"	11	5	4	2		8									
11	1		3	7	6		12	10	9"	11	5	4	2		8									
12	1		3	7	6		12	10	9	11	5	4	2		8"									
13	1	14	3	7	6		12	10	9"	11	5	4"	2		8									
14	1	10	3		6		4	8*	9	11"	12	5	7	2	14									
15	1	14	3		6		7	4	9	10	11"	5	12	2	8*									
16		12	3"	10	6*		11	8	9		7	5	4	2	14								1	
17	1		3			7	11	9"	10	12	5		6	2	4	8	6							
18	1		3			8	4"	9	11		6		2		7	5	10	12						
19	1		3			0		10	11		5	4	2		7"	6	9	12						
20	1		3			10	4	12	11		5	7"	2			6	9	8						
21	1		3			8	4	10	11		6		2			5	9	7						
22	1		3			8	4	11*	10	14	6		2"	12		5	9	7						
23	1		3			8		10*	11	14	6		2	4		12	5	9	7"					
24	1		3			8		10	11		6		2	4			5	9	7					
25	1		3		12	8		10	11		6"		2	4			5	9	7					
26	1		3	4"		7	8	10	11		6		2				5	9	12					
27	1		3			8	4"	10	11		6		2		12		5	9	7					
28	1		3			8		10	11		6"		4	2		12	5	9	7					
29	1	3	2	6		8*	4"	10	11		5				12	14		9	7					
30	1	3	2	6		8		10	11		5		4					9	7					
31	1	3	2	6				10	11		5	4"	12		14			9	7*					
32	1	3	6			4	8"	10	11		12		2			5	9				7			
33	1	3	2		12				11		6		4		7"	5	9			10				
34	1	3	2	6			8	12	11		6		4		10		9"		7*					14
35	1	3	2					10	11		6	8	4			5	9							
36	1	3	2		12			10*	11"		6	8	4			5	9	14			7			
37	1	3	2					10*	11		6	8	4		10	5	9	12			7"			
38	1	3	2					10	11		0	0	4		6	5					7			
39	1	3	2			10*			11		6	4	14			5"	9	12			7	8		
Apps.	38	24	30	12	22	6	28	22	31	36	11	36	18	33	7	13	19	22	11	1	8	1		
Subs		6				2		4		5		4	3	5	3	7		5			6			1
Goals		1			5		7	3	1	3	6	2				1		12			1			

Pos. P. W. D. L. F. A. Pts.
12th 39 12 10 17 42 61 34

League Cup

No.	Date	Opposition	H.T.	Res.	Att.	Goalscorers																								
2	22 Aug	ALLOA ATHLETIC	1-0	1-1*	849	Cuthbertson	1	3*	4	5	6	7		9		11"	12	10	2		8								14
3	29	Dundee	1-0	1-1#	3367	McDicken	1	3	8*	4	6	7	11	9			12	5	10"	2	14								

* After extra time, Kilmarnock won 3-2 on penalties
# After extra time, Dundee won 3-2 on penalties

Scottish Cup

No.	Date	Opposition	H.T.	Res.	Att.	Goalscorers																								
3	9 Feb	Inverness Thistle	0-1	0-3	2500		1	6	3		4		9		11*	10	8		2	7"	12	5			14					

Back row - A. Robertson, R. Clark, P. Clarke, B. Holland, A. McCulloch, D. McDicken, T. Brown, I. Bryson;
Middle row - G. Johnston, S. McGivern, H. Houston, S. McLean, L. McKinna, P. Martin, B. McConville, J. Clark,
S. Cuthbertson, R. Stewart (Ass. Trainer); Front row - H. Allan (Trainer), J. Cockburn, G. Millar, A. Kerr, J. McEachran,
L. Lowe, S. Johnston, J. Clunie (Manager).

Match Record

No.	Date	Opposition	H.T.	Res.	Att.	Goalscorers
1	10 Aug	ALLOA ATHLETIC	0-0	3-0	1439	McLean, B.Millar, McGivern
2	17	Forfar Athletic	0-0	0-0	967	
3	24	HAMILTON	0-0	1-0	1754	B.Millar
4	31	Ayr United	0-1	0-3	2749	
5	7 Sep	PARTICK THISTLE	4-0	5-0	1944	Bryson, Cuthbertson, McLean, McGivern, Clarke
6	14	Morton	0-0	0-3	1434	
7	21	CLYDE	1-0	1-1	2005	B.Millar
8	28	Brechin City	1-1	4-2	662	Bryson, Sarwar, McKinna, O.G.
9	5 Oct	FALKIRK	1-0	1-0	1937	McLean
10	12	MONTROSE	0-0	0-0	1498	
11	19	Dumbarton	0-1	0-1	1559	
12	26	Airdrieonians	0-0	2-1	1573	Clarke(2)
13	2 Nov	EAST FIFE	1-1	2-2	1425	Cuthbertson(2)
14	9	Partick Thistle	0-1	1-1	2441	Bryson
15	16	MORTON	2-0	3-0	1837	Cockburn, Martin, Cuthbertson
16	23	Clyde	1-1	3-1	1102	McGivern(2), Clarke
17	30	BRECHIN CITY	1-0	3-1	2787	Bryson, B.Millar, Cuthbertson
18	7 Dec	Falkirk	0-0	1-0	2542	McGivern
19	14	Montrose	0-1	1-4	616	McKinna
20	21	DUMBARTON	1-2	1-4	2311	Bryson
21	28	Hamilton	0-2	1-4	3271	Bryson
22	1 Jan	AYR UNITED	0-0	1-2	4119	Bryson
23	4	FORFAR ATHLETIC	1-0	1-0	1679	B.Millar
24	11	Alloa Athletic	1-0	4-1	682	B.Millar(2), McGivern, Cuthbertson
25	18	AIRDRIEONIANS	0-1	0-2	1711	
26	1 Feb	East Fife	1-2	2-2	940	Bryson(2)
27	8	MORTON	0-1	1-1	2252	Clarke
28	1 Mar	MONTROSE	3-0	3-0	1502	McNab, Bryson, McGuire
29	8	Hamilton	1-3	2-3	2345	McGivern(2)
30	15	ALLOA ATHLETIC	1-0	2-0	1260	McCafferty, McNab
31	22	Airdrieonians	0-1	0-1	1409	
32	25	Falkirk	1-0	1-1	2582	McNab
33	29	BRECHIN CITY	1-0	1-0	1511	Bryson
34	5 Apr	Clyde	1-0	3-1	820	McGivern(2), Bryson
35	9	EAST FIFE	1-0	2-0	1320	McGivern, McGuire
36	12	Forfar Athletic	0-0	0-1	874	
37	19	DUMBARTON	1-0	3-0	2821	Bryson, Clarke, McGuire
38	26	Partick Thistle	0-0	0-2	2835	
39	3 May	AYR UNITED	2-1	3-2	2369	McGuire(2), Bryson

Pos P. W. D. L. F. A. Pts.
3rd 39 18 8 13 62 49 44

Appearances / Substitutes / Goals

No.	Holland	Lowe	McLean	Robertson	Martin	P.Clarke	Cuthbertson	McCafferty	B.Millar	McGivern	Bryson	McCulloch	McNab	Cockburn	McKinna	Sarwar	McConville	G.Millar	Cook	McLeod	McGuire
1	1	2	3	4	5	6	7	8	9	10		11									
2		2	3	4	5	6	7	8	9	10		11	1								
3		2	3	4	5	6	7"	8	9	10		11	1	12							
4	2"	3	4	5	6	7	8	9	10*	11		1		14	12						
5		2	4	5	6	7"	8			10	11*	1		12	3		9	14			
6		2	4	5	6	7"		9		11	1			14	3	10*	8	12			
7		2	4	5	6		9	7		11	1			12	3	10"	8				
8		2	4	5	6	7"	9*		10	11	1			12	3	14	8				
9	7		4	5	6		9		10	11	1				3	8	2				
10		2	4	5	6	7"	9		10	11*	1			14	3	12	8				
11		2	4	5	6	7*	9		10	11"	1			12	3	14	8				
12		2	4	5	6	7	9		10		1				3	11	8				
13	3"		4	5	6	7	9*	10	12	1				14	11	8	2				
14			4	5	6	7	9		10	11	1				3	8	2				
15			4	5	6	7"	9		10	11	1			12	3	8	2				
16			4	5	6	7	9		10	11	1				3	8	2				
17			4	5	6	7	9		10	11	1				3	8	2				
18	12		4	5	6	7"	9*	10	11	1				3	14	8	2				
19			4	5	6	7"	14	9	10	11	1			3	12	8*	2"				
20			4	5	6	7*	12	10	11	1				14	3	9	8"	2"			
21			4	5	6	7	12	10	11	1					3	9	8"	2			
22	8*		4	5	6	7		10	11	1				12	3	14	2	9"			
23	3		4	5	6	7		10	11	1				12		14	8	2"			
24		2	4	5	6	12	7"	9	10	11	1				3		8				
25		2	4	5	6	7*	14	9	10	11*	1				3	12	8				
26		2	4	5	6		8			10	1				9		7		3		11
27		2	4	5	6		8			10	1				9		7		3		11
28		2	4	5	7	6	8		11	1		9		12				3		10
29		2	4	5	12	6	8		11	1	9						7"		3		10
30		2	4	5	14	6	8		11	1	9			12				7*	3		10
31		2		5	14	6	8		11	1	9		3*	12		7			4		10
32		2	4"	5	12	6	8		11	1	9			14			7		3		10
33		2		5	14	6*	8		11	1	9					7			4		10
34		2		5	6	8		11	1	9					7			3		10
35		2	5	4	6	8		11	1	9"		12			7			3		10
36		2	5	4	6	8		11	1	9"		12			7			3		10
37		2	5	4	14	6	8"	11	1	9					3	7*				10
38		2	5	4	6		11	1	9					3		8	7		12	10
39	8		5	4	7	6"				11	1			14	9	12			2*	3	10
Apps	1	4	31	32	31	38	22	22	21	36	37	38	11	23	11	19	10	15	1	12	14
Subs		1					7		4				1		12	5	13	3	1		1
Goals			3		1	6	6	1	7	11	14		3	1	2	2					5

League Cup

No.	Date	Opposition	H.T.	Res.	Att.	Goalscorers																	
2	20 Aug	St. Mirren	1-1	1-3	3435	B.Millar	2	3	4	5	6	7"	8	9	10	11	1	12						

Scottish Cup

No.	Date	Opposition	H.T.	Res.	Att.	Goalscorers																	
3	25 Jan	STIRLING ALBION	1-0	1-0	2199	McCafferty	2	4	5	6	7	10	11	1	9	8"	12	3			
4	15 Feb	Dundee United	0-0	1-1	6610	Bryson	2	4	5	6	7	10	11	1	9	8	3			
4R	19	DUNDEE UNITED	0-0	0-1	9054		2	4	5	6	12	7	10"	11	1	9	8	3		

Back row (l-r): Alan Robertson, Blair Millar, Ian Bryson, Barry Holland, Alan McCulloch, Paul Martin, Lawrie McKinna, Derek Cook. Middle row (l-r): Alex McAnespie (Youth Coach), Jim Shanks, Lenny Lowe, Bobby McConville, Stuart McLean, Mike Cormack, Gary Johnston, Rashid Sarwar, Tom McCafferty, Scott Cuthbertson, Hugh Allan (Trainer/Physio).
Front row (l-r): Hugh Houston, Rab Stewart (Reserve Team Coach), Jim Cockburn, Sam McGivern, Paul Clarke, Alistair McLeod, Graeme Miller, Eddie Morrison (Manager), Derek Mitchell.

SEASON 1986-87 — First Division

No.	Date	Opposition	H.T.	Res.	Att.	Goalscorers
1	9 Aug	East Fife	3-0	4-1	985	Bryson(2), Cook, McLeod
2	13	MORTON	2-1	2-2	2468	McGuire, Cook
3	10	Forfar Athletic	1-1	1-3	883	Bryson
4	23	MONTROSE	3-0	3-0	1447	Bryson, Martin, Cook
5	30	Queen of the South	0-1	1-2	2588	Cook
6	6 Sep	DUNFERMLINE	1-1	1-2	2862	Cook
7	13	Airdrieonians	1-0	2-3	1577	Bryson(2)
8	16	DUMBARTON	1-1	2-1	1664	Bryson, O.G.
9	20	Brechin City	1-1	2-2	572	Cook(2)
10	27	CLYDE	0-0	0-0	1761	
11	30	Partick Thistle	0-0	0-1	1828	
12	4 Oct	EAST FIFE	1-0	1-1	1306	Martin
13	8	Morton	0-1	0-2	1859	
14	11	Montrose	0-0	2-0	496	Harkness, McLean
15	18	FORFAR ATHLETIC	0-0	3-0	1440	Harkness, McGivern, Docherty
16	25	AIRDRIEONIANS	1-0	2-0	1996	Harkness, McLeod
17	29	Dumbarton	0-0	0-2	925	
18	1 Nov	Dunfermline	0-1	0-1	4179	
19	8	QUEEN OF THE SOUTH	1-1	3-2	2008	McGivern, McGuire, McLeod
20	15	BRECHIN CITY	0-0	0-1	1600	
21	22	Clyde	0-0	0-0	939	
22	29	PARTICK THISTLE	1-2	3-2	2502	Cuthbertson, R.Clark, McGuire
23	6 Dec	East Fife	1-0	1-2	1251	R.Clark
24	13	MORTON	1-0	2-0	1989	Harkness, McGuire
25	20	MONTROSE	1-0	1-0	1612	Harkness
26	27	Forfar Athletic	1-0	1-1	857	McGuire
27	1 Jan	Queen of the South	1-0	2-1	2009	Cook, McVeigh
28	3	DUNFERMLINE	0-1	2-2	4855	McGuire, Reid
29	24	AIRDRIEONIANS	0-0	0-0	1983	
30	27	DUMBARTON	1-2	1-2	2209	McVeigh
31	7 Feb	CLYDE	1-0	1-1	1769	McLean
32	17	Brechin City	0-1	0-1	513	
33	28	EAST FIFE	3-0	3-1	1434	Reid(2), Harkness
34	3 Mar	Partick Thistle	1-1	2-1	1383	Bryson, McGuire
35	11	Morton	0-2	1-2	1971	Cuthbertson
36	14	Montrose	0-1	1-1	417	Harkness
37	21	FORFAR ATHLETIC	0-0	2-0	1059	Reid, Bryson
38	28	QUEEN OF THE SOUTH	1-0	2-2	1675	Bryson, Reid
39	4 Apr	Dunfermline	1-0	1-0	3704	Harkness
40	11	Dumbarton	2-1	2-3	1030	Reid(2)
41	18	Airdrieonians	0-0	3-4	1028	Cuthbertson, Reid, McVeigh
42	25	BRECHIN CITY	0-1	0-1	875	
43	2 May	Clyde	0-0	1-0	638	Reid
44	9	PARTICK THISTLE	0-0	1-0	1453	McVeigh

Players (column headers, left to right): McCulloch, McLean, McLeod, Robertson, Martin, R.Clark, Cuthbertson, McCafferty, Cook, McGuire, Bryson, G.Millar, McGivern, Sarwar, J.Clark, Cockburn, McConville, B.Millar, McNab, Docherty, Lowe, Harkness, Holland, Houston, Marshall, McVeigh, Reid, Bell

Season summary

Pos	P.	W.	D.	L.	F.	A.	Pts.
6th	44	17	11	16	62	53	45

Appearance / Goal totals

	McCulloch	McLean	McLeod	Robertson	Martin	R.Clark	Cuthbertson	McCafferty	Cook	McGuire	Bryson	G.Millar	McGivern	Sarwar	J.Clark	Cockburn	McConville	B.Millar	McNab	Docherty	Lowe	Harkness	Holland	Houston	Marshall	McVeigh	Reid	Bell
Apps.	40	34	14	26	40	34	11	4	21	40	32	30	15		20	21	8	4	3	12	2	31	4	6	1	18	11	2
Subs	4	6				7	2	1	4				5	4	1	1		10	3	3	2			1			6	2
Goals	2	3		2	2	3		8	7	10		2						1		8						4	9	

League Cup

No.	Date	Opposition	H.T.	Res.	Att.	Goalscorers
2	20 Aug	AYR UNITED	0-0	1-2	3853	McCafferty

Scottish Cup

No.	Date	Opposition	H.T.	Res.	Att.	Goalscorers
3	31 Jan	Hearts	0-0	0-0	15227	
3R	4 Feb	HEARTS	1-0	1-1*	14932	Bryson
3R	9	HEARTS	0-1	1-3	14146	Martin

* After extra time

Action against Dunfermline

No.	Date	Opposition	H.T.	Res.	Att.	Goalscorers
1	8 Aug	HAMILTON	0-2	0-2	2178	
2	12	East Fife	1-0	1-2	711	Reid
3	15	Dumbarton	0-1	3-1	824	Cuthbertson, Harkness, McInnes
4	22	FORFAR ATHLETIC	1-2	2-2	1235	Harkness, Reid
5	29	QUEEN OF THE SOUTH	0-0	0-2	1720	
6	5 Sep	Meadowbank	1-1	1-2	698	Cook
7	12	RAITH ROVERS	2-2	3-4	1436	Cuthbertson, Harkness, McInnes
8	15	Clydebank	0-2	0-2	857	
9	19	Airdrieonians	1-1	2-3	1513	Bryson, O.G.
10	26	CLYDE	2-0	2-0	1732	Harkness, Bryson
11	29	PARTICK THISTLE	1-0	1-1	2030	Harkness
12	3 Oct	Hamilton	1-1	1-1	3236	Harkness
13	6	EAST FIFE	1-0	2-0	1425	Harkness(2)
14	10	Forfar Athletic	0-0	0-2	896	
15	17	Raith Rovers	1-0	2-0	2276	Gilmour, Harkness
16	20	CLYDEBANK	0-2	1-3	1733	McGuire
17	24	DUMBARTON	0-0	0-0	1571	Gilmour
18	31	MEADOWBANK	1-2	2-4	1442	Harkness(2)
19	3 Nov	Partick Thistle	0-1	0-1	1434	
20	7	Queen of the South	0-0	4-1	1487	Reid(2), Bryson, McInnes
21	14	AIRDRIEONIANS	1-0	1-0	1978	Reid
22	21	Clyde	0-2	0-2	1242	
23	28	HAMILTON	0-0	1-0	1922	Harkness
24	5 Dec	East Fife	1-0	1-2	605	Bryson
25	12	RAITH ROVERS	0-0	1-1	1654	Reid
26	19	Clydebank	0-0	0-1	981	
27	26	Meadowbank	1-1	3-1	751	Harkness(2), McFarlane
28	2 Jan	QUEEN OF THE SOUTH	0-0	0-0	3230	
29	9	Airdrieonians	1-1	3-3	1588	McFarlane(2), Gilmour
30	16	CLYDE	2-1	3-1	1754	Cuthbertson, Harkness, Bryson
31	23	Dumbarton	0-1	0-1	1048	
32	6 Feb	FORFAR ATHLETIC	0-1	0-2	1281	
33	13	PARTICK THISTLE	0-0	0-1	2432	
34	27	Hamilton	0-0	0-1	2048	
35	5 Mar	Raith Rovers	0-1	2-2	1536	Davidson, Cuthbertson
36	12	CLYDEBANK	1-1	2-2	1549	Martin, Bourke
37	19	MEADOWBANK	0-0	0-0	1662	
38	26	Queen of the South	0-0	0-0	1578	
39	2 Apr	Forfar Athletic	0-0	1-1	713	Gilmour
40	9	DUMBARTON	0-0	3-1	2205	Gilmour, McGuire, Bryson
41	16	Clyde	0-0	0-0	1120	
42	23	AIRDRIEONIANS	1-0	4-1	1953	McGuire(2), Bourke, Gilmour
43	30	EAST FIFE	0-3	1-3	2488	Gilmour
44	7 May	Partick Thistle	0-0	1-0	3103	Gilmour

Player columns (l-r): Holland, G.Millar, Cockburn, Robertson, McVeigh, R.Clark, McConville, McLean, Harkness, Reid, Bryson, McGuire, McInnes, Lowe, Bell, Cook, Davidson, Cuthbertson, Martin, Wylde, Gilmour, Houston, McCulloch, McFarlane, Kearney, Candlish, Marshall, Bourke.

Pos	P	W	D	L	F	A	Pts
10th	44	13	11	20	55	60	37

League Cup

No.	Date	Opposition	H.T.	Res.	Att.	Goalscorers
2	19 Aug	Hearts	1-2	1-6	9500	Bryson

Scottish Cup

No.	Date	Opposition	H.T.	Res.	Att.	Goalscorers
3	30 Jan	Motherwell	0-0	0-0	6499	
3R	3 Feb	MOTHERWELL	0-0	1-3	7591	Harkness

Back row (l-r): L. Lindsay, H. Houston, D. Cook, P. Martin, A. McCulloch, R. Clark, B. Holland, S. Marshall, A. Bell, F. Davidson. Centre row (l-r): S. Cuthbertson, R. McConville, C. Harkness, J. McVeigh, L. Lowe, G. Miller, I. McInnes, J. McGuire. Front row (l-r): R. Stewart (Coach), A. McAnespie (Coach), I. Bryson, J. Reid, A. Robertson, S. McLean, J. Cockburn, E. Morrison (Manager). H. Allan (Physio).

SEASON 1988-89   First Division

Player columns (left → right): McCulloch, Montgomerie, Robertson, Davidson, Martin, Marshall, McConville, Gilmour, Bourke, McDonald, McGuire, Cook, Harkness, McLean, Cuthbertson, Hughes, Wylde, McInnes, Brannigan, McFarlane, McQueen, Millar, McLaughlin, Reilly, Derek Walker, Flexney, Watters, David Walker, Lindsay, Spiers, Faulds, Stewart, Callaghan

No.	Date	Opposition	H.T.	Res.	Att.	Goalscorers
1	13 Aug	Queen of the South	0-0	2-2	1694	McGuire, Gilmour
2	20	PARTICK THISTLE	0-0	0-1	2442	
3	27	AYR UNITED	1-0	2-0	5387	McGuire, Marshall
4	3 Sep	Clydebank	1-1	2-2	1307	McGuire, Cuthbertson
5	10	Airdrieonians	0-2	1-5	2016	Cook
6	17	CLYDE	1-1	1-2	1745	McDonald
7	24	Dunfermline	0-1	0-3	5379	
8	1 Oct	MORTON	1-3	3-4	1865	Cook, Martin, McInnes
9	8	Forfar Athletic	1-1	2-2	685	McGuire, Gilmour
10	15	Meadowbank	0-0	2-0	1185	Cook, Montgomerie
11	22	RAITH ROVERS	1-1	1-1	1965	Wylde
12	29	St. Johnstone	0-0	0-2	2303	
13	5 Nov	FALKIRK	0-1	0-2	2561	
14	12	AIRDRIEONIANS	0-1	0-3	1958	
15	19	Clyde	2-0	2-0	1028	McFarlane(2)
16	26	DUNFERMLINE	0-2	2-2	2761	Gilmour, Brannigan
17	3 Dec	Partick Thistle	1-0	1-0	2498	McFarlane
18	10	ST. JOHNSTONE	0-1	0-3	2501	
19	17	Raith Rovers	0-0	0-0	1514	
20	24	MEADOWBANK	1-0	1-0	2405	Watters
21	31	CLYDEBANK	1-0	1-0	2760	McLaughlin
22	3 Jan	Ayr United	0-2	1-4	8585	Faulds
23	7	Falkirk	0-2	0-2	3972	
24	14	QUEEN OF THE SOUTH	1-1	2-1	2264	Derek Walker, Watters
25	21	FORFAR ATHLETIC	1-1	2-1	1813	Watters(2)
26	18 Feb	CLYDE	0-0	0-0	1953	
27	25	St. Johnstone	0-1	2-2	2393	Watters, Reilly
28	1 Mar	Morton	0-1	2-2	1807	Watters, Harkness
29	4	AIRDRIEONIANS	0-1	1-1	2376	McLaughlin
30	11	Ayr United	1-1	1-2	5476	Montgomerie
31	18	FORFAR ATHLETIC	2-2	2-2	1584	Harkness, Faulds
32	25	Dunfermline	0-0	0-0	5906	
33	1 Apr	FALKIRK	0-0	0-0	3780	
34	8	Meadowbank	1-0	2-1	866	Harkness, Watters
35	15	RAITH ROVERS	1-0	1-2	2218	Harkness
36	22	Morton	0-1	0-3	1623	
37	29	PARTICK THISTLE	0-0	0-0	2932	
38	6 May	Clydebank	2-1	2-3	1643	Harkness, Stewart
39	13	Queen of the South	1-0	6-0	1570	Watters(5), Reilly

Pos 13th   **P** 39   **W** 10   **D** 14   **L** 15   **F** 47   **A** 60   **Pts** 34

Summary (by player column):

- **Apps:** McCulloch 39, Montgomerie 31, Robertson 12, Davidson 26, Martin 11, Marshall 21, McConville 7, Gilmour 14, Bourke 2, McDonald 12, McGuire 11, Cook 8, Harkness 26, McLean 29, Cuthbertson 3, Hughes 11, Wylde 15, McInnes 19, Brannigan 4, McFarlane 12, McQueen 14, Millar 17, McLaughlin 9, Reilly 18, Derek Walker 20, Flexney 1, Watters 2, David Walker 4, Lindsay 13, Spiers 7, Faulds 11
- **Subs:** Gilmour 3, McDonald 3, Cook 2, McLean 2, Cuthbertson 4, Hughes 7, Wylde 3, McInnes 1, Millar 2, Reilly 4, Derek Walker 2, Watters 6, Lindsay 5, Spiers 8, Faulds 1, Stewart 1
- **Goals:** McCulloch 2, Davidson 1, Martin 1, Gilmour 3, McDonald 1, McGuire 4, Cook 3, Harkness 5, Hughes 1, Wylde 1, McInnes 1, Brannigan 1, McFarlane 3, McLaughlin 2, Derek Walker 1, Watters 12, Faulds 2, Stewart 1

League Cup

No.	Date	Opposition	H.T.	Res.	Att.	Goalscorers
2	17 Aug	FORFAR ATHLETIC	0-0	1-0	1523	Gilmour
3	23	Hibernian	0-1	0-1	8000	

Scottish Cup

No.	Date	Opposition	H.T.	Res.	Att.	Goalscorers
3	28 Jan	Queen of the South	1-1	2-2	2941	Watters, Spiers
3R	1 Feb	QUEEN OF THE SOUTH	0-1	0-1	5623	

Back row: H. Houston, D. Cook, P. Martin, A. McCulloch, B. Holland, F. Davidson, S. Marshall, J. McGuire.
Middle row: S. Cuthbertson, David Walker, M. Hughes, C. Harkness, A. Lindsay, S. Kearney.
Front row: R. Stewart, J. Clark, R. McConville, A. Robertson, S. McLean, E. Morrison (Manager), H. Allan.

No.	Date	Opposition	H.T.	Res.	Att.	Goalscorers
1	12 Aug	BRECHIN CITY	0-0	0-2	2402	
2	19	Arbroath	1-0	1-1	1070	Curran
3	26	Queens Park	0-0	0-1	1776	
4	2 Sep	EAST STIRLING	1-0	2-0	1767	Watters, Montgomerie
5	9	COWDENBEATH	0-0	0-0	1804	
6	16	Stenhousemuir	0-0	3-0	954	M.Thompson(2), D.Thompson
7	23	BERWICK RANGERS	1-0	1-0	1975	Curran, M.Thompson
8	30	Stirling Albion	1-0	1-0	1818	Curran
9	7 Oct	Montrose	0-0	1-0	810	Watters
10	14	EAST FIFE	0-0	1-0	2456	Reilly
11	21	Stranraer	0-0	0-1	2500	
12	28	DUMBARTON	0-0	3-0	2867	Watters(2), Tait
13	4 Nov	QUEEN OF THE SOUTH	1-0	2-0	2988	Reilly, D.Thompson
14	11	East Stirling	0-0	1-2	1333	McCabe
15	18	STIRLING ALBION	0-2	1-2	2473	Tait
16	25	Berwick Rangers *	0-3	2-3	784	Curran, Marshall
17	2 Dec	MONTROSE	0-0	1-1	2095	McFarlane
18	23	ARBROATH	0-0	3-0	3336	Watters(3)
19	26	Brechin City	1-1	1-3	1414	Burns
20	2 Jan	QUEENS PARK	1-0	2-0	4843	Watters, Callaghan
21	10	East Fife	1-1	2-4	1109	Watters, Burns
22	13	Cowdenbeath	0-1	1-2	961	Reilly
23	20	STENHOUSEMUIR	1-0	2-0	2777	Watters, Montgomerie
24	27	STRANRAER	0-1	0-1	3550	
25	17 Feb	Arbroath	1-1	4-2	891	Callaghan, Tait, Sludden, Watters
26	24	Berwick Rangers	1-0	4-1	992	Watters(3), Sludden
27	3 Mar	EAST STIRLING	1-0	2-0	2747	Burns, Reilly
28	6	STIRLING ALBION	1-0	1-0	3369	Watters
29	10	QUEENS PARK	2-0	3-0	3767	Watters(2), Montgomerie
30	13	Queen of the South	0-2	1-2	2058	Flexney
31	17	Stenhousemuir	0-0	1-2	1730	Sludden
32	24	Dumbarton	0-0	2-0	1609	Sludden, Tait
33	31	BRECHIN CITY	0-1	2-2	4767	Tait, Watters
34	3 Apr	Dumbarton	2-1	3-1	1475	Watters(2), Sludden
35	7	EAST FIFE	0-0	2-1	3266	Porteous, Tait
36	14	Stranraer	0-0	1-0	2410	Watters
37	21	QUEEN OF THE SOUTH	2-0	4-1	3362	Watters, Sludden, McArthur, McKinnon
38	28	Montrose	1-0	3-1	1597	Sludden, Watters, O.G.
39	5 May	COWDENBEATH	1-0	2-1	8526	Flexney, McKinnon

* Played at Tynecastle, owing to Berwick's ground being declared unfit

Pos P. W. D. L. F. A. Pts.
2nd 39 22 4 13 67 39 48

Appearance summary (players listed across top of grid):
McCulloch, Wilson, Davidson, Jenkins, Cody, Flexney, D.Thompson, Tait, M.Thompson, Reilly, Watters, Curran, Montgomerie, McLean, McFarlane, David Walker, McKinnon, McCabe, Geraghty, Callaghan, Marshall, Sludden, Burns, Spence, Wylde, McArthur, Quinn, Geddes, Porteous, McKellar

	McCulloch	Wilson	Davidson	Jenkins	Cody	Flexney	D.Thompson	Tait	M.Thompson	Reilly	Watters	Curran	Montgomerie	McLean	McFarlane	D.Walker	McKinnon	McCabe	Geraghty	Callaghan	Marshall	Sludden	Burns	Spence	Wylde	McArthur	Quinn	Geddes	Porteous	McKellar
Apps	24	6	3	7	12	34	8	37	4	30	35	12	32	19	5	13	33	4	2	20	1	22	22	17	5	2		10	5	5
Subs	1			6	8		7		1	3		1	3	4	3	2	2	1		9		1			6	1	3		2	
Goals					2	2	6	3	4	23	4	3		1	1		2	1		2	1	7	3			1			1	1

League Cup

No.	Date	Opposition	H.T.	Res.	Att.	Goalscorers
2	15 Aug	MOTHERWELL	0-2	1-4	3903	D.Thompson

Teams: McCulloch 1, Wilson 2, Davidson 3", Jenkins 4, Cody 5, Flexney 6, D.Thompson 7, Reilly 9*, Watters 10, Curran 11, Montgomerie 14, McLean 12, McFarlane 8

Scottish Cup

No.	Date	Opposition	H.T.	Res.	Att.	Goalscorers
1		Bye				
2	30 Dec	Stranraer	0-1	1-1	3700	Watters
2R	6 Jan	STRANRAER	0-0	0-0*	5033	

* After extra time, Stranraer won 4-3 on penalties. This was the first time ever that penalty kicks decided the outcome of a Scottish Cup tie.

Back row: R. Montgomerie, T. Spence, T. Tait, R. Geddes, P. Flexney, T. Burns, R. Reilly.
Front row: J. Sludden, G. Wylde, W. Watters, T. Callaghan, I. Porteous, D. McKinnon.

SEASON 1990-91   First Division

No.	Date	Opposition	H.T.	Res.	Att.	Goalscorers	Geddes	Montgomerie	Spence	McStay	Flexney	McKinnon	Stark	Tait	Watters	Callaghan	Shaw	Reilly	Sludden	Jenkins	Burns	Elliott	McKellar	Burgess	Curran	Wylde	Sloan	Williamson	McPherson	Smith	Agnew	Brayshaw	Campbell
1	25 Aug	Meadowbank	0-0	0-1	1787		1	2	3	4	5	6	6	7	8"	9	10	11*	12	14													
2	1 Sep	AIRDRIEONIANS	1-3	3-4	5287	Burns, Stark, Sludden	1	2	12		5	4	7		8*	9		14	11	10	3"	6											
3	8	Hamilton	1-1	1-3	2687	Tait	1	2	3	4"	5	6	7	8			12		9*	10	11	14											
4	15	FALKIRK	1-1	1-1	4629	Spence		2	3		5	4	7"	8		6			9	10	11	12	1										
5	18	Clydebank	3-1	3-1	2442	Burns, Reilly, Sludden	1	2	3		5	4	7	8	12	6		10"	9		11												
6	22	MORTON	1-0	3-1	4322	Stark, Watters, Sludden	1	2	3		5	4	7	8	12	6*		9"	10	14	11												
7	29	Dundee	0-0	1-1	4573	Callaghan	1	2	3*		5	4		8	12	6		9	10	7"	11				14								
8	6 Oct	Brechin City	1-0	2-0	1299	Callaghan, Sludden	1	2	3		5	4		8	9"	6		7	11*12		11				14								
9	9	RAITH ROVERS	1-0	1-0	3953	Watters	1	2	3		5	4		8	9"	6		7"	10		11	12			14								
10	13	AYR UNITED	0-1	3-1	9802	Elliott, Callaghan, Burns	1	2	3		5	4		8	12	6		9"	11*7		11				14								
11	20	Partick Thistle	0-0	0-2	4600		1	2	3		5	4	7	8		6			12	10"	11	9										
12	27	Forfar Athletic	2-0	2-2	1521	Sludden, Burns	1	2	3		5	4	7	8	9"	6			12	10	11											
13	3 Nov	CLYDE	0-0	2-1	3973	Sludden, Tait	1	2	3		5	4	7*	8		6			14	10	11	12			9"								
14	10	Airdrieonians	0-0	0-2	4400		1	2	3	7	5*	4	11	8		6			9	10						12							
15	17	MEADOWBANK	2-0	2-3	4198	Stark, Reilly	1	2*	3	5		4	11	8		12		6	10*		7						14	9					
16	24	Raith Rovers	1-1	1-1	2260	Burns	1	2	3	5		4	11	8		14		6*	10"		7						12	9					
17	1 Dec	BRECHIN CITY	1-1	2-1	3473	Williamson, Sloan	1	2	3		5	4	7"	8		6			12		11						10	9					
18	8	DUNDEE	2-0	2-1	4558	Williamson, Tait	1	2	3	14	5	4		8		6"			12		11	7					10*	9					
19	15	Morton	0-1	0-3	2724		1	2	3	14	5	4*	6	8					12		11	7"					10	9					
20	22	FORFAR ATHLETIC	0-0	1-0	3224	Williamson	1	2	3"		5			8		6			12	10	11	7			4			9					
21	2 Jan	Ayr United	2-0	2-1	9448	Burns, Sludden	1	2	3		5			8		6			12	10"	11	7			4			9					
22	5	PARTICK THISTLE	2-2	2-3	5508	Flexney, Callaghan	1	2	3		5			8		6				10	11	7			4			9					
23	12	HAMILTON	0-0	1-0	4767	Williamson	1	2	3*		5	14		8		6			12	10	11	7			4			9					
24	19	Falkirk	1-0	1-1	6749	Sludden	1		3		5	2		8		6				10	11	7			4			9					
25	2 Feb	CLYDEBANK	2-0	3-0	4169	Williamson(3)	1	2	3		5			8					12	10"	11	7*			4		14	9	6				
26	16	PARTICK THISTLE	1-0	1-0	6073	Williamson	1	2	3		5			8					12	10"	11	7			4			9	6"				
27	26	Clyde	1-0	1-1	1000	Silliamson	1	2		4	5			8		6					11	7						9	3"	10	12		
28	9 Mar	MORTON	1-0	1-1	4451	Williamson	1	2		4	5			8		6"		14			11	12						9	7	10*3			
29	12	Forfar Athletic	1-0	1-1	977	Williamson	1	2		4	5			8		6"		12			11							9	7	10	3		
30	16	Airdrieonians	0-1	0-2	5000		1		8	5		7	12			6		14			11				4			9	2	10	3*		
31	23	FALKIRK	1-1	1-1	6664	Stark	1	12	3	4	5		6*	8		7		9	10		11								2"	14		
32	30	HAMILTON	0-0	1-0	4449	Flexney	1	2	3	4	5			8					11	7						12	9		10"		6	
33	6 Apr	Raith Rovers	1-0	2-1	1761	Williamson, Campbell	1	2	3	4	5		6	8					11								9		12		7"		10
34	10	Meadowbank	6-0	8-1	1107	Williamson(2),Campbell(2),Burns(2),Smith,Stark	1	2	3	4	5"		6*						8	11				12			9		7		14		10
35	13	BRECHIN CITY	1-0	2-2	4543	Stark, Campbell	1	2	3	4	5		6"			12			8	11		14					9		7*				10
36	20	Clydebank	0-0	0-0	2005		1	2	3"	4			8						8	11					5		9		7	12			10
37	27	Clyde	1-1	1-2	1700	Jenkins	1	14	3	4			6*	12					8	11	7"				5				2	9			10
38	4 May	DUNDEE	0-0	0-0	5712		1	2		4				5		6"			8	11	12						9	3	7				10
39	11	Ayr United	0-1	0-1	6894		1	2		4		5			7	6"			8	11							9	3	12				10
		Apps.					38	35	32	18	34	20	21	34	5	26	1	13	23	8	37	14	1		10	1	3	23	11	9	3	2	7
		Subs					2	1	2		1		2	4	4	1		13	3	1		7		6		1	4			4	1	1	
		Goals						1		2			6	3	2	4		2	8	1	8	1				1	14		1			4

	Pos	P.	W.	D.	L.	F.	A.	Pts.
	5th	39	15	13	11	58	48	43

League Cup

No.	Date	Opposition	H.T.	Res.	Att.	Goalscorers	Geddes	Montgomerie	Spence	McStay	Flexney	McKinnon	Stark	Tait	Watters	Callaghan	Shaw	Reilly	Sludden	Jenkins	Burns	Elliott
2	21 Aug	CLYDEBANK	1-2	3-2*	4777	Spence, Stark, Callaghan	1	2	3	4"		6	7	8	9	14	11*12		5	10		
3	28	Rangers	0-0	0-1	32671		1	4	3"		5	6	7	8*	9	12	14	11		2	10	

* After extra time

Scottish Cup

No.	Date	Opposition	H.T.	Res.	Att.	Goalscorers	Geddes	Montgomerie	Spence	McStay	Flexney	McKinnon	Stark	Tait	Watters	Callaghan	Shaw	Reilly	Sludden	Jenkins	Burns	Elliott	McKellar	Burgess	Curran	Wylde	Sloan	Williamson	McPherson
3	26 Jan	ARBROATH	1-1	3-2	4991	Sludden(2), Burns	1		3		5	2		8		6"			12	10	11	7			4			9	
4	23 Feb	Dundee	0-2	0-2	7195		1	2	3		5			8					12	14	11	7			4"			9	6*

B&Q Centenary Cup

No.	Date	Opposition	H.T.	Res.	Att.	Goalscorers	Geddes	Montgomerie	Spence	McStay	Flexney	McKinnon	Stark	Tait	Watters	Callaghan	Shaw	Reilly	Sludden	Jenkins	Burns	Elliott
1	2 Oct	STIRLING ALBION	1-0	4-1	2612	Sludden(3), Burns	1	2	3		5	4		8		7	6"		9	10	11*12	14
2	16	ARBROATH	2-0	3-1	3437	Sludden, Elliott, Stark	1	2	3		5	4	12	8	14	6"		9*	10		11	7
QF	23	East Fife	1-0	2-1	2102	Sludden, Watters	1	2	3		5	4	7	8	9	12			10		11	6"
SF	30	DUNDEE	0-1	0-2	7933		1	2	3		5		7	8		6		9"	10		11	12

Back row (l-r): G. Wylde, S. McLean, R. Montgomerie, D. McKinnon, A. McCulloch, R. Geddes, J. Sludden, T. Burns, W. McStay, T. Spence. Centre row (l-r): A. Hollas (Stadium Manager), G. Shaw, F. Davidson, I. Brown, S. Quinn, D. McKellar, B. Stark, P. Flexney, E. Jenkins, T. Tait, J. Stewart (Goal Coach). Front row (l-r): M. Geraghty, H. Allan (Physio), D. Elliot, P. Curran, T. Callaghan, F. Coulston (Ass. Manager), J. Fleeting (Manager), J. McSherry (Ass. Manager), W. Watters, I. Porteous, R. Reilly, J. Clark (Coach), S. Cody.

SEASON 1991-92 First Division

No.	Date	Opposition	H.T.	Res.	Att.	Goalscorers	Geddes	McPherson	Reilly	Flexney	Burgess	Tait	Stark	Jack	Williamson	T.Burns	McSkimming	Porteous	Montgomerie	McStay	Mitchell	Campbell	McQuilter	Elliott	Callaghan	Brayshaw	Jenkins	H.Burns	Paterson	Black	Graham	Stephen	Clark	Reid	Roberts
1	10 Aug	STIRLING ALBION	0-0	0-0	4416		1	2	3	4	5	6	7"	8	9	10	11*	12	14																
2	13	HAMILTON	1-2	1-2	4347	McSkimming	1	2	3		5	6		8	9	10	11			4	7														
3	17	Partick Thistle	0-0	0-1	5537		1	12	3		5	6		8"	9	10	11		2	4	7														
4	24	Meadowbank	1-2	3-2	1222	Williamson(2), Mitchell	1	2	3		5	6"		12	9	10	11		14	4	7	8*													
5	31	AYR UNITED	0-0	1-1	8380	Montgomerie	1	2	3		5	6"			9	10	11	4"	12		7	8													
6	7 Sep	Clydebank	1-0	1-0	2576	Campbell	1	2	3		5	6"			14	9	10	11*	7	4		8	12												
7	14	MONTROSE	0-0	0-0	3478		1	2	3"		5				14	9	10	11	6	4		7*	8	12											
8	21	Dundee	1-1	1-2	3788	Williamson	1	2			5				8	9	10	3	12	6		7	11"		4*	14									
9	28	RAITH ROVERS	1-0	1-0	3385	Campbell	1	2			5				8	9	10	3"	14			7	11*		4	12									
10	5 Oct	Forfar Athletic	0-0	1-0	1019	Mitchell	1	2			5				10"	9	6		8	3		7	11		12			4							
11	8	MORTON	1-0	1-0	3677	Campbell	1	2	12	5					9	10	3		4			7	11		6"			8							
12	12	Stirling Albion	2-0	3-0	2065	Mitchell, McPherson, Williamson	1	2	12	5		4			9	10	3	14				7	11*		6"			8							
13	19	PARTICK THISTLE	2-1	2-3	4962	Williamson, Campbell	1	2		5		4			9	10	3					7	11		6			8							
14	26	CLYDEBANK	1-0	2-1	2231	T.Burns, Campbell	1	2	12	5		4			14	9	10	3				7	11*		6"			8							
15	29	Montrose	1-2	2-2	1074	Jack, Mitchell	1	2	12	4					10	9	6		3"			7	11					8	5						
16	2 Nov	Ayr United	3-0	3-0	6064	T.Burns, Mitchell, Williamson	1	2		4					10	9	6			3		7	11"					8	5						
17	9	MEADOWBANK	0-0	1-0	3828	McPherson	1	2		4					10	9	6	12				7	11"					8	5	3					
18	16	FORFAR ATHLETIC	3-0	4-2	3560	Jack(2), Mitchell(2)	1	2		4*		14			10	9"	6	12				7	11					8	5	3					
19	19	Morton	0-0	1-0	2637	Jack	1	2							10	9	6			4		7	11					8	5	3					
20	23	DUNDEE	1-1	1-2	7137	Mitchell	1	2							10"	9	6	12		4		7	11					8	5	3					
21	30	Hamilton	1-0	2-2	3893	H.Burns, Williamson		2		4					10"	9	6*	12	14			7	11					8	5	3	1				
22	3 Dec	Raith Rovers	0-1	1-1	2280	Williamson				4					9	14	6"	11	12	2		7	10					8	5	3	1				
23	7	STIRLING ALBION	0-0	2-0	3790	Williamson, H.Burns		2		4					10"	9		11	6			7	12					8	5	3	1				
24	14	Clydebank	2-0	3-0	2357	H.Burns, Mitchell, Campbell		2		4					9		11	6				7	10					8	5	3	1				
25	28	Meadowbank	0-0	0-1	1505			2							14	9	11"	12	6	4		7	10*					8	5	3	1				
26	1 Jan	AYR UNITED	0-0	1-1	8211	Campbell		2							9	6	11"		12			7	10					8	5	3	1				
27	4	Forfar Athletic	0-0	0-0	1185			2	11	4					12	9	6					7	10"					8	5	3	1				
28	7	MONTROSE	3-1	5-1	3183	Campbell(2), Jack, Black, O.G.	1	2	11	4					12	9"	6*		8			7	10					14	5	3					
29	11	MORTON	0-0	0-0	4988			2	11"	4					9		6		8			7	10					12	5	3	1				
30	18	HAMILTON	0-0	0-2	4662			2		4"		12			14	9		11	6			7	10					8*	5	3	1				
31	1 Feb	Partick Thistle	0-0	1-2	4483	Black		2							9	6	12		4	14		7	10					8	5*	3	1	11"			
32	8	Dundee	1-0	1-1	5988	Jack		2					10		9		6		4	14		7	11			12*		8	5*	3					
33	28	RAITH ROVERS	0-0	1-1	3657	McPherson	1	2	3		5				9	10"6		12	4			7	11					8							
34	29	FORFAR ATHLETIC	0-0	2-0	3076	H.Burns, Campbell	1	2			5				9		6		12	4		7	11					8		3			10"		
35	14 Mar	MEADOWBANK	0-1	2-1	2884	Tait, Jack	1	2			6		12		10		6				11	9						8	5	3		7"			
36	21	Ayr United	0-0	2-0	5530	Tait, T.Burns	1	2					10		11		6	12	8"	4	14	7	9*						5	3					
37	24	Morton	0-0	0-0	3015		1	2					10		11		6		8"	4		7						12	5	3					
38	28	Stirling Albion	0-1	0-1	2083		1	2					10		11"	12	6		8*	4		7	9					14	5	3					
39	4 Apr	PARTICK THISTLE	0-2	1-3	5640	Black		2					10		12	9	6			4		7	11"					8	5	3					
40	7	CLYDEBANK	0-0	1-0	2094	Mitchell	8						9"	10	6	11		4				7							2	5	3	1			12
41	11	Montrose	0-0	1-0	793	O.G.	1	8	3				9	10	6	11		4				7							2	5					
42	18	DUNDEE	1-0	2-0	4933	Tait, O.G.	1	10	3			12	9		6	11"8		4				7							2	5					
43	25	Hamilton	1-0	1-0	3449	Jack	1	8	3			14	9	6	11"7*		4	2	10	12								5							
44	2 May	Raith Rovers	0-1	1-1	1960	Porteous	1	8*	3			11	9	12	6		7	4	2	10"14															
		Apps.					33	42	15	27	1	18	1	27	33	41	23	16	26	5	42	35		6				28	28	23	11	1	1	1	1
		Subs						1	4			5			10	3		7	8	4		3		1	1	2	1	2	3						1
		Goals						3			3			8	9	3	1	1	1		10	10						4		3					

Pos P. W. D. L. F. A. Pts.
4th 44 21 12 11 59 37 54

League Cup

No.	Date	Opposition	H.T.	Res.	Att.	Goalscorers	Geddes	McPherson	Reilly	Flexney	Burgess	Tait	Stark	Jack	Williamson	T.Burns	McSkimming	Porteous	Montgomerie	McStay	Mitchell	Campbell	McQuilter
2	26 Aug	Cowdenbeath	0-0	1-0	1561	Williamson	1	2	3	5		6		12	9	10	11			4	7	8"	
3	28	HIBERNIAN	1-1	2-3	6507	Campbell, McSkimming	1	2	3	5		6		12	9		11	10		4"	7	8	

Scottish Cup

No.	Date	Opposition	H.T.	Res.	Att.	Goalscorers	McPherson	Burgess	Williamson	T.Burns	McSkimming	Porteous	Mitchell	Campbell	Elliott	H.Burns	Black	Graham	Stephen	Roberts
3	25 Jan	Meadowbank	0-0	1-1	2301	Mitchell	2	5	9	6	12	4	7	10	11"	8	3	1		
3R	4 Feb	MEADOWBANK	0-1	1-1*	4694	H.Burns	2	5	9"		4	14	7	10	11*	8	3	1		12

* After extra time, Meadowbank won 4-3 on penalties

B&Q Cup

No.	Date	Opposition	H.T.	Res.	Att.	Goalscorers	Geddes	McPherson	Reilly	Flexney	Burgess	Tait	Williamson	T.Burns	McSkimming	Porteous	Mitchell	Campbell	H.Burns
1		Bye																	
2	15 Oct	Morton	1-1	1-2*	2864	H.Burns	1	2	12	5		4	9	10	3	14	7	11	8

* After extra time

Standing (l-r): J. Stewart (Coach), E. Jenkins, A. Scott, C. Campbell, D. Elliot, W. Stark, I. Porteous, P. Flexney, R. Geddes, S. Burgess, R. Williamson, S. McSkimming, M. Reilly, T. Tait, A. Mitchell, T. Smith, G. Hollas (Stadium Manager).
Kneeling (l-r): A. Brayshaw, T. Callaghan, A. McPherson, J. McSherry (Ass. Manager), T. Burns, J. Fleeting (Ass. Manager), R. Montgomerie, W. McStay, R. Jack.

SEASON 1992-93 First Division

No	Date	Opposition	H.T.	Res.	Att.	Goalscorers	Geddes	H.Burns	Black	Montgomerie	Paterson	McPherson	Porteous	Skilling	Jack	Tait	Mitchell	Campbell	Reilly	T.Burns	Williamson	McCluskey	McStay	Furphy	Crainie	Wilson	Stark	McSkimming	Roberts	McCarrison
1	1 Aug	Morton	2-0	2-0	3274	Mitchell, Jack	1	2	3	4	5	6	7"	8	9	10	11	12												
2	4	Dumbarton	2-0	3-1	2109	Paterson, Jack, Tait	1	2	3	4	5	6	7*	8"	9	10	11	12	14											
3	8	RAITH ROVERS	0-1	1-1	4566	Mitchell	1	2	3	4	5		7"	8	9	10	11		6	12										
4	15	DUNFERMLINE	0-0	0-1	5511		1	2	3	4				8	9"	5	11		6	7	12					10				
5	22	Ayr United	0-0	0-2	5475		1	2	3	4				8	9	5	11	12	6	7"	14					10*				
6	29	MEADOWBANK	0-0	1-0	2821	Campbell	1		3	4	5	2"	12	8			7	9		6	10					11				
7	5 Sep	Clydebank	1-0	1-1	2216	Williamson	1		3	4	5	2"	8		14		7	9*		6	10		12			11				
8	12	Stirling Albion*	1-0	1-0	1441	Jack	1			4	5	2	8		9		7		3	6	10					11				
9	19	ST. MIRREN	0-1	1-2	5291	Williamson	1			2		8	10*	5	9"		7	12	3	6	14			4		11				
10	26	COWDENBEATH	1-0	3-0	2798	Williamson, Porteous, Jack	1			4		2	8	5	14		7	12	3	6	9	10*				11"				
11	3 Oct	Hamilton	0-0	1-1	2863	Skilling	1			4	5	2		8	12		7"		3	6	9	10				11				
12	10	MORTON	1-0	3-0	3991	T.Burns(2), McCluskey	1			4	5	2	12	8	14		7		3	6	9	10*				11"				
13	17	Raith Rovers	0-0	1-1	3718	Reilly	1			4	5	2	8				7	12	3	6	9	10				11"				
14	24	CLYDEBANK	1-0	3-3	3582	McCluskey(2), McSkimming	1			4	5	2	8				7		3	6	9	10				11				
15	31	Meadowbank	0-0	1-1	1104	McSkimming	1			4		2	8	5	12		7		3	6	9	10*				11				
16	7 Nov	Dunfermline	0-1	0-2	3924		1			4		2	8"	5	14		7		3	6	9	10			12	11*				
17	14	AYR UNITED	2-0	3-0	5709	McCluskey, Skilling, O.G.	1		3	4		8		5			7"	12		9					2	10		11	
18	21	St. Mirren	1-0	1-0	4686	Black	1		3	4		8		5			7		6	9					2	10		11	
19	28	STIRLING ALBION	1-0	1-0	3526	Skilling	1			4		2		5	14		12	7	3	6		9				10	8*	11"	
20	1 Dec	HAMILTON	1-0	1-0	3711	McPherson	1			4		8		5	11		7"		3	6		9			2	10		12	
21	5	Cowdenbeath	1-2	3-2	1176	Jack, Reilly, McPherson	1			4		8		5	11		7		3	6		9			2	10			
22	19	DUMBARTON	0-0	1-0	3591	Campbell	1			4		8		5	9		11"	7*	3	6	12				14	2	10		
23	26	DUNFERMLINE	1-1	2-3	5762	Stark, Reilly	1			4		8		5	9		14	7	3	6	12				2*	10		11"	
24	29	Morton	0-1	0-2	2822		1			4		8		5			12	7	3	6	9				2"	10	11		
25	2 Jan	Ayr United	0-0	1-0	8424	Porteous	1			4		8	7	5					6	11	9				2	10	3		
26	16	MEADOWBANK	4-0	5-0	3366	McCluskey(2),Porteous,Wlliamsn,McPhersn	1			4		8	7*	5			12		6	11	9"				14	2	10	3		
27	27	Hamilton	2-1	2-1	3106	Williamson, Porteous	1			4		8	7*	5					6	11	9				2	10	3		
28	30	RAITH ROVERS	0-0	3-0	7003	Porteous(2), Stark	1			4		8	7	5					6	11	9				2	10	3		
29	13 Feb	Dumbarton	0-0	0-1	2346		1			4		8	7"	5			9		6	11				12	2	10	3		
30	16	Clydebank	0-0	0-2	2107		1			4		2	7	5			12	8	6	11				9"		10	3		
31	20	COWDENBEATH	0-0	1-1	2928	Campbell	1	14	4			8	7	5			9"	12	6	11					2*	10	3		
32	27	ST. MIRREN	0-0	1-0	6555	McCluskey	1	2			4	8		5					6	11	9					10	3		7
33	6 Mar	Stirling Albion*	0-1	0-2	1386		1	2		4		8	14	5				12	6	11	9*					10	3"		7
34	9	MORTON	1-0	2-2	3407	Williamson, O.G.	1	2		4		8		5					6	11	9					10	3		7
35	13	Raith Rovers	0-1	0-2	4738		1	2		4	5	8	7				12		6	11	9"					10	3		
36	20	AYR UNITED	1-1	1-1	5660	Skilling	1		4	5		8					7		6	11	9				2	10	3"		12
37	27	Dunfermline	0-0	2-2	5224	Campbell, McSkimming	1		4	5		8					11"		6	12					2	10	3		
38	3 Apr	CLYDEBANK	4-0	6-0	3005	McClusky(2),Mtchll(2),McSkimmng,McPhrsn	1		4	5	7	8					14	11*	6	12	9"				2	10	3		
39	14	Meadowbank	1-1	1-1	1493	McSkimming	1		4	5	12	8					7		6	11"	9				7	10	3		14
40	17	STIRLING ALBION	1-0	3-0	3852	McCluskey, Mitchell, McCarrison	1		4	5	2	8					7		6"		9				12	10	3		11
41	24	St. Mirren	1-0	1-2	8432	Mitchell	1		4	5	2	8*					7		6	12	9				14	10	3		11"
42	1 May	DUMBARTON	1-0	1-0	3793	McCluskey	1		4	5	2	8					7		6		9				12	10	3		11"
43	8	Cowdenbeath	1-0	3-0	2754	Stark, Crainie, McPherson	1		4	5	8						7		6		9				11	2	10	3		
44	15	HAMILTON	0-0	0-0	12830		1		4	5	8						7		6		9				11		10	3		

* Played at Stenhousemuir's ground

Pos	P.	W.	D.	L.	F.	A.	Pts.
2nd	44	21	12	11	67	40	54

	Geddes	H.Burns	Black	Montgomerie	Paterson	McPherson	Porteous	Skilling	Jack	Tait	Mitchell	Campbell	Reilly	T.Burns	Williamson	McCluskey	McStay	Furphy	Crainie	Wilson	Stark	McSkimming	Roberts	McCarrison
Apps.	44	9	10	42	21	39	17	40	11	5	26	13	18	39	26	29	1	3	18	28	35	4	6	
Subs	1				1	3		7			6	11	1	7	2	1		6	1			1	2	
Goals		1		1	5	6	4	5	4	1	6	4	3	2	6	11			1		3	5		

League Cup

No	Date	Opposition	H.T.	Res.	Att.	Goalscorers	Geddes	H.Burns	Black	Montgomerie	Paterson	McPherson	Porteous	Skilling	Jack	Tait	Mitchell	Campbell	Reilly	T.Burns	Williamson	McCluskey	Stark	McSkimming
2	11 Aug	Morton	0-1	3-2*	3454	T.Burns(2), Jack	1	2	3	4	5*		7"	8	9	10	11	14	6	12				
3	18	HIBERNIAN	1-0	3-1*	7495	McSkimming, McCluskey, Jack	1	2	3	4			8	9	5	11	14	6	7"	12				10*
QF	25	ST. JOHNSTONE	0-0	1-3	8293	Campbell	1	2*	3	4	5		9	8	7	14	6	12	10"					11

* After extra time

Scottish Cup

No	Date	Opposition	H.T.	Res.	Att.	Goalscorers	Geddes	Montgomerie	McPherson	Porteous	Skilling	T.Burns	Williamson	McCluskey	Wilson	Stark	McSkimming
3	9 Jan	RAITH ROVERS	2-0	5-0	7309	Williamson(3), McCluskey, McPherson	1	4	8	7	5	14	0"	11*	0	12	2	10	3
4	6 Feb	ST. JOHNSTONE	0-0	0-0	9278		1	4	8	7*	5	12	14		9"	2	10	3
4R	10	St. Johnstone	0-0	0-1*	7144		1	4	8	7	5	12		6	11	9"	2	10	3

* After extra time

B&Q Cup

No	Date	Opposition	H.T.	Res.	Att.	Goalscorers	Geddes	Montgomerie	Paterson	McPherson	Porteous	Skilling	Mitchell	Reilly	T.Burns	Williamson	McCluskey	Wilson	Stark	McSkimming	McCarrison
1	29 Sep	CLYDE	2-0	2-1	2688	McCluskey, Mitchell	1	4	2	8	5		7	12	3	9	10"			11	6
2	20 Oct	AYR UNITED	1-0	1-0	7122	McCluskey	1	4	5	2	8		7	12	3	6	9	10"		11	
QF	28	MORTON	0-0	1-2	4956	T. Burns	1	4	2	8	12			3	6	9	10	5		11"	

Back row (l-r): T. Burns (Player/Manager), R. Williamson, H. Burns, T. Black, C. Paterson, R. Geddes, S. McSkimming, G. McCluskey, W. McStay, R. Jack, W. Stark (Player/Ass. Manager). Front row (l-r): R. Montgomerie, A. Mitchell, A. MacPherson, Cyril the Squirrel, M. Reilly, I. Porteous, M. Skilling.

SEASON 1993-94 Premier Division

No.	Date	Opposition	H.T.	Res.	Att.	Goalscorers
1	7 Aug	DUNDEE	0-0	1-0	8162	Brown
2	14	Aberdeen	0-0	0-1	13534	
3	21	MOTHERWELL	0-0	0-1	7555	
4	28	Rangers	0-0	2-1	43804	Roberts, Williamson
5	4 Sep	HIBERNIAN	0-1	1-1	7727	McCluskey
6	11	ST. JOHNSTONE	0-0	0-0	5670	
7	18	Hearts	1-0	1-0	8309	Skilling
8	25	PARTICK THISTLE	1-0	3-1	7411	Black, Williamson, McCluskey
9	2 Oct	Celtic	0-0	0-0	23396	
10	5	DUNDEE UNITED	0-0	1-1	7034	Roberts
11	9	Raith Rovers	0-2	2-2	4754	Mitchell, Williamson
12	16	ABERDEEN	0-0	1-1	9108	Mitchell
13	23	Dundee	0-1	0-1	4537	
14	30	Motherwell	1-0	2-2	7384	Mitchell, Roberts
15	6 Nov	RANGERS	0-0	0-2	19162	
16	9	Hibernian	1-0	1-2	6441	Brown
17	13	CELTIC	1-1	2-2	16649	Skilling, Williamson
18	20	Partick Thistle	0-0	1-0	6437	Crainie
19	27	St. Johnstone	1-0	1-0	4576	Williamson
20	30	HEARTS	0-0	0-0	6948	
21	4 Dec	Dundee United	0-0	0-0	7100	
22	11	RAITH ROVERS	1-0	1-0	6012	Brown
23	18	Aberdeen	0-1	1-3	10834	Skilling
24	1 Jan	MOTHERWELL	0-0	0-0	10511	
25	4	DUNDEE	0-0	1-0	7406	McSkimming
26	8	Rangers	0-0	0-3	44919	
27	15	HIBERNIAN	0-0	0-3	7358	
28	22	Hearts	1-1	1-1	9204	McPherson
29	5 Feb	ST. JOHNSTONE	0-0	0-0	6345	
30	12	PARTICK THISTLE	1-0	1-0	7511	Mitchell
31	1 Mar	Celtic	0-0	0-1	9887	
32	5	DUNDEE UNITED	0-1	1-1	7403	Brown
33	15	Raith Rovers	0-2	2-3	3585	Mitchell, McSkimming
34	19	ABERDEEN	0-1	2-3	8544	Black, McCloy
35	26	Dundee	0-3	0-3	3485	
36	30	St. Johnstone	1-0	1-0	5513	McPherson
37	2 Apr	HEARTS	0-1	0-1	8022	
38	16	CELTIC	0-0	2-0	11576	Black, Brown
39	19	Partick Thistle	0-0	0-1	7299	
40	23	RAITH ROVERS	0-0	0-0	7426	
41	26	Dundee United	1-0	3-1	8801	Williamson(2), McSkimming
42	30	Motherwell	0-0	0-1	8185	
43	7 May	RANGERS	0-0	1-0	18012	Black
44	14	Hibernian	0-0	0-0	9975	

Player columns (l-r): Geddes, McPherson, Black, Montgomerie, Skilling, Millen, Mitchell, Reilly, Brown, McCluskey, McSkimming, Crainie, Williamson, Roberts, Campbell, Porteous, Paterson, Stark, Burns, Lauchlan, McInally, Napier, McCloy

	Apps	Subs	Goals
Geddes	44		
McPherson	43		2
Black	44		4
Montgomerie	42		
Skilling	23		3
Millen	44		
Mitchell	34		5
Reilly	37		
Brown	26	1	5
McCluskey	16	5	2
McSkimming	40		3
Crainie	6	7	1
Williamson	36	8	7
Roberts	7	2	2
Campbell		6	
Porteous	7	1	
Paterson	4	6	1
Stark	6	2	
Burns	12		
Lauchlan		1	
McInally	2	6	
Napier	10	5	
McCloy	1	5	1

Pos P W D L F A Pts
8th 44 12 16 16 36 45 40

League Cup

No.	Date	Opposition	H.T.	Res.	Att.	Goalscorers
2	10 Aug	MORTON	1-1	1-2	5118	Mitchell

Scottish Cup

No.	Date	Opposition	H.T.	Res.	Att.	Goalscorers
3	29 Jan	AYR UNITED	1-1	2-1	12856	Black, McSkimming
4	19 Feb	Morton	1-0	1-0	7255	Williamson
QF	12 Mar	DUNDEE	1-0	1-0	10446	Brown
SF	10 Apr	Rangers	0-0	0-0	35134	
SFr	13	Rangers	1-0	1-2	29860	Black

Back row (l-r): A. Jack, R. Williamson, D. Cranie, M. Skilling, C. Meldrum, R. Geddes, C. Paterson, M. Roberts, D. McCarrison, J. Plunkett. Centre row (l-r): A. Hollas, T. Brown, A. Kerr, D. White, S. Hamilton, G. Mattews, P. Flexney, K. Doig, S. McCloy, I. Gallagher, D. Bagan, H. Allan. Front row (l-r): M. Reilly, S. McSkimming, G. McCluskey, T. Wilson, B. Stark (Ass. Manager), T. Burns (Manager), J. Stewart (Goal Coach), A. Mitchell, R. Montgomerie, T. Black, I. Porteous.

SEASON 1994-95 — Premier Division

No.	Date	Opposition	HT	Res	Att	Goalscorers	Geddes	MacPherson	Black	Montgomerie	Reilly	Millen	Mitchell	Napier	Williamson	Connor	Maskrey	McCluskey	Henry	McSkimming	Brown	Whitworth	McKee	Meldrum	Skilling	Anderson	Lekovic	Roberts	Lauchlan	McCarrison	Findlay	Wright
1	Aug 13	Partick Thistle	0-2	0-2	6606		1	2	3	4	5	6	7	8*	9	10	11	14														
2	20	Hibernian	0-0	0-0	9107		1	2	3	4	5	6	7			14	11	9	10*	8												
3	27	MOTHERWELL	0-1	0-1	7388		1	2	3	4	5*	6	7				12	10	9	8*	11	14										
4	Sep 10	FALKIRK	1-0	1-1	8021	Williamson	1	2	3		4"	6	7		9*	10				12	11	14	5		8							
5	17	Celtic	0-0	1-1	28457	Williamson	1	2		12	11	6	7*		9	10					4	3	5		8							
6	24	Hearts	0-2	0-3	9302		1		12	2	11	6	7*		9	10*					4	3	14	5	8*							
7	Oct 1	ABERDEEN	1-1	2-1	7445	OG, Brown	1		3	2	12	6			9	4	14				8	11	10	5	7*							
8	8	DUNDEE UNITED	0-1	0-2	7127		1	2	3	4	11*	6	12		9		14				8		10	5	7*							
9	15	Rangers	0-0	0-2	44099		1	2	3		4	6	7		9*						8	11	10	5	14							
10	22	PARTICK THISTLE	0-0	2-0	7023	McKee, Brown		2	3		4	6	7								8	11	10	5	9	1						
11	29	Motherwell	2-1	2-3	7436	Henry, McKee		2	3		4	6	7*			12		14			8	11	10	5	9	1						
12	Nov 5	HIBERNIAN	0-0	0-0	8319		1	2	3		11	6	7*			12		14			8		10	5	9					4"		
13	8	Falkirk	3-0	3-3	6134	Skilling, Black, OG	1	2	3		11	6	7			12		14			8		10*	5	9*					4		
14	19	CELTIC	0-0	0-0	13932			2	3		11		7					12			8		10	5	9*	1	4	6				
15	26	HEARTS	0-1	3-1	8069	Mitchell, McKee, Skilling		2	3		11		7				12	14			8*		10	5	9*		4	6	1			
16	Dec 3	Aberdeen	1-0	1-0	10345	Maskrey		2		4			7	3	12	10	11*						5	9*		8	6	1		14		
17	10	RANGERS	0-1	1-2	17219	McKee		2		4			7		14	10*	11	12					5	9		8*	6	1				
18	26	Dundee United	1-0	2-2	8468	OG, Mitchell		2	3		4		7*		14	10	11*						5	9		12	6	1				
19	31	Partick Thistle	1-2	2-2	5799	Maskrey, MacPherson		2	3		4					10	11*				8		14		9		5	6	1			
20	Jan 7	Hibernian	0-1	1-2	8918	McKee		2	3		4		7	12			10	11*			8*		14	5	9			6"	1			
21	14	Celtic	0-0	1-2	25342	Black		2	3		4		7			10	14				8		11*		9		5	6	1			
22	17	MOTHERWELL	2-0	2-0	7521	Black (2)		2	3		4		7			10					8		9	5	11			6	1			
23	21	FALKIRK	1-1	2-1	7648	Black, McKee		2	3	4	6		7			10	14				8		9*		11			1		5		
24	Feb 4	Aberdeen	2-1	3-1	9384	Maskrey, Brown, Roberts		2	3		4		7			10	11				9*		5				6	1		14		
25	11	Hearts	2-2	2-2	8374	Maskrey (2)		2	3		4		7			10	11				9*		5				6	1		14		
26	25	Rangers	0-0	0-3	44859			2	3	12	4		7			10	11*				8*		5	9			6	1		14		
27	Mar 4	DUNDEE UNITED	2-0	2-0	7630	Mitchell (2)		2	3		4		7			10	11*				8*		5	9		12	6	1		14		
28	21	CELTIC	0-0	0-1	10112			2	3		4		7*			10	11*				9		5	14		8	6	1			12	
29	25	Falkirk	0-1	0-2	5714			2	3		4"		7			10	11				9*		5	14			6	1			12	
30	Apr 1	Aberdeen	0-0	1-0	14041	Skilling		2	3		4"		7			10	14				10		5			8	6	1			12	9*
31	12	HEARTS	2-1	3-2	7239	Anderson, Henry, Whitworth		2	3	12			7			10	11				8		5			6*	1				4	9
32	15	Dundee United	1-1	2-1	8223	Whitworth, Henry		2	3				7			10	11				8		14	5		4"	6	1			12	9*
33	20	RANGERS	0-1	0-1	16532			2	3				7			10	11*						14	5		4	6	1			8	9
34	29	PARTICK THISTLE	0-0	0-0	9201			2	3				7			10	11				8		14	5		12	6*	1			4	9*
35	May 6	Motherwell	0-1	0-2	7760		1	2"		4	3		7				14				8		12	5	11*		10				6	9
36	13	HIBERNIAN	1-0	1-2	11676	Wright				4	3		7			10	11				6*		9	5		1	12			2	7*	8
		Apps.					12	33	9	31	13	33	2	7	27	19	2	28		8	18	30	22	4	13	20	20		2		5	7
		Subs						1	3	1		2	1	8	1	11	1	2		1	3		2			4		4		1	4	
		Goals						1	5			4			2		5			3	3	2	6		3	1	1					1

Pos	P	W	D	L	F	A	Pts
7th	36	11	10	15	40	48	43

League Cup

No.	Date	Opposition	HT	Res	Att	Goalscorers	Geddes	MacPherson	Black	Montgomerie	Reilly	Millen	Mitchell	Napier	Williamson	Connor	Maskrey	McCluskey	Henry	McSkimming	Brown	Whitworth
2	Aug 16	EAST FIFE	2-0	4-1	4243	Maskrey (2), Henry, McCluskey	1	2	3	4	5	6	7		12	11*	9	10*	8	14		
3	31	Raith Rovers	1-2	2-3	4181	Montgomerie, Williamson	1	2	3	4	5	6	7	8*	12	10	11			9		

Scottish Cup

No.	Date	Opposition	HT	Res	Att	Goalscorers																										
3	Jan 28	MORTON	0-0	0-0	8271			2	3	4		6		7"		14	10	12			8		9		11*			5	1			
3r	31	Morton	0-1	2-1*	6533	Maskrey (2)		2	3	4		10		7	14	11*		12			8		9	5				6*	1			
4	Feb 18	EAST FIFE	2-0	4-0	7003	Maskrey (2), Reilly, Black		2"	3		4		7			10	11				8		9	5	12			6	1			
QF	Mar 10	Celtic	0-1	0-1	30881			2	3		4		7			10*	11				8		5	9"		12	6	1		14		

*After extra time

Back row (l-r): M. Skilling, D. Anderson, R. Connor, T. Black, R. Geddes, C. Paterson, D. Lekovic, N. Whitworth, Findly, J. Henry, A. Kerr, A. McPherson, C. McKee. Front row: B. Williamson (Coach), D. McCarrison, P. Wright, M. Reilly, A. Mitchell, A. Totten (Manager), K. Thomson (Ass. Manager), R. Montgomerie, M. Roberts, S. Maskrey, S. McLoy, A. Hollas (Stadium Manager).

SEASON 1995-96   Premier Division

No.	Date		Opposition	HT	Res	Att	Goalscorers
1	Aug	26	Rangers	0-0	0-1	44686	
2	Sep	9	HIBERNIAN	0-3	0-3	7014	
3		16	Raith Rovers	0-0	0-2	4441	
4		23	ABERDEEN	0-2	1-2	7198	Brown
5		30	Motherwell	0-1	0-3	6356	
6	Oct	4	Partick Thistle	1-1	1-1	4000	OG
7		7	HEARTS	2-1	3-1	6721	McKee (2), Brown
8		14	Falkirk	2-0	2-0	4878	Mitchell, Wright
9		21	CELTIC	0-0	0-0	14011	
10		28	Hibernian	0-1	0-2	10400	
11	Nov	4	RAITH ROVERS	2-0	5-1	6440	Henry (2), Wright (2), Brown
12		8	RANGERS	0-0	0-2	14823	
13		11	Hearts	0-0	1-2	10442	McKee
14		18	MOTHERWELL	1-1	1-1	6608	Mitchell
15	Dec	2	Celtic	2-2	2-4	33812	Brown, Mitchell
16		9	FALKIRK	2-0	4-0	6017	Brown (2), MacPherson, Black
17		13	Aberdeen	1-2	1-4	14060	Wright
18		16	PARTICK THISTLE	1-1	2-1	6581	Wright (2)
19		26	Rangers	0-2	0-3	45173	
20	Jan	6	Raith Rovers	0-1	1-1	4781	Black
21		13	HIBERNIAN	0-2	3-2	6686	Henry, Wright, Maskrey
22		16	Motherwell	0-0	1-0	5781	Wright
23		20	CELTIC	0-0	0-0	16101	
24		23	ABERDEEN	0-1	1-1	6703	Wright
25	Feb	3	Falkirk	2-2	2-4	4143	Wright (2)
26		10	Partick Thistle	1-0	1-0	4800	Black
27		24	HEARTS	0-2	0-2	8022	
28	Mar	2	Aberdeen	0-1	0-3	7000	
29		16	MOTHERWELL	0-1	0-1	7035	
30		23	RAITH ROVERS	0-0	0-0	6143	McKee, Wright
31		30	Hibernian	0-1	1-1	8102	Wright
32	Apr	10	Celtic	1-0	1-1	36372	McIntyre
33		13	FALKIRK	0-0	1-0	6505	McIntyre
34		20	PARTICKTHISTLE	0-0	2-1	7276	Skilling, Black
35		27	Hearts	0-0	0-1	11329	
36	May	4	RANGERS	0-2	0-3	17056	

Pos	P	W	D	L	F	A	Pts
7th	36	11	8	17	39	54	41

Appearances grid (player columns):

No	Lekovic	Skilling	Black	Montgomerie	Whitworth	Connor	Mitchell	Henry	Wright	Brown	Reilly	Roberts	Geddes	MacPherson	McKee	Findlay	Anderson	Holt	Maskrey	Meldrum	Lauchlan	McIntyre
1	1	2	3	4	5	6	7	8	9*	10	11	12										
2		11	3	4	5	6*	7	8	9*	13	12	10	1	2								
3		8		4	5	6	7*	10	13				3"	9	1	2	11	12				
4	1	8			5	4	7	12	10*	11			3"	13	2	9			6			
5	1	8"	3		5	4	7*		10	11				2	9				6	12	13	
6	1	4	3		5		8	7	9	10*				2	11				6	12		
7	1	4	3		5		8*	7	9	10				2	11"				6	12	13	
8	1	4	3		5		8	7	9*	10*		13		2	11x				6	12	14	
9	1	4*	3		5		8	13	9	10x				2	11"	7			6	12	14	
10	1		3		5		8	12	9					2"	11"	7	6		4	13		
11	1		3		5		8	7	4	9	10*	12		2			6		13		11*	
12			3		5		8	7	4"	9	10*	12		2	11		6		13		1	
13	1		3		5		8	7	4	9			12	2	11		6		10*			
14	1		3		5		8	7	4	9	10*			2"			6		12	13		
15	1		3		5		8*	7	12	9*	10	4		2	13		6		11			
16	1		3		5		8*	7	4	9*	10	12		2			6		11	13		
17	1				5		8	7	4	9	10	3		2			6		11			
18	1				5		8	7	4	9	10	3		2					11		6	
19	1				5		8	7	4	9	10	3		2					11		6	
20	1		3		5		8*	7	12	9		13	4	2					11	10*	6	
21	1		3*		5			7	8	9			4	2	12		6		11	10		
22	1		3	12	5			7	8	9*			4	2	13		6		11	10*		
23	1		3		5			7	8	9			4	2	12		6		11	10*		
24	1		3		5			7	8	9	12		4	2	13		6		11*	10*		
25	1		3		5			8	9	10*	4	12		2	7		6		11			
26	1		3	5				8	9	10	4			2	7		6		11			
27	1		3*	5				8	9	10	4			2	11		6					
28	1		3	12	5	8	7	13	9*	10*	4			2	11		6					
29	1	12	3*		5		7	8	9		4*	13		2	14		6		11			10x
30	1	8		4	5*				9	13	12			2	7		3	6	11*			10
31	1			3	6				9	13	12			2	7		5		11*			
32	1	14	3	6					9	13	12			2	7"		5	11x	13			10*
33	1		3	4				12	8	9			6	2	7"		5	13	11*			10
34	1	8	3	4					9*	12	6			2	14		5	13	11*			10x
35	1	8	3	4			6	7*	9				13	2	12				11"	5		10
36	1	8x	3	4			14	7	9			6	13	2	12				11"	5		10*

	Lekovic	Skilling	Black	Montgomerie	Whitworth	Connor	Mitchell	Henry	Wright	Brown	Reilly	Roberts	Geddes	MacPherson	McKee	Findlay	Anderson	Holt	Maskrey	Meldrum	Lauchlan	McIntyre
Apps.	33	13	30	12	28	22	29	22	35	19	22	2	2	35	19	2	28	17	13	1	5	7
Subs		2		2		1	6	1	6	6	9				9	1	9		9			
Goals		1	4				3	3	13	6				1	4				1			2

League Cup

No	Date		Opposition	HT	Res	Att	Goalscorers	Lekovic	Skilling	Black	Montgomerie	Whitworth	Connor	Mitchell	Henry	Wright	Brown	Reilly	Roberts	Geddes	MacPherson	McKee	Findlay	Anderson
2	Aug	19	DUMBARTON*	0-0	1-0	5011	Roberts	1	6	3	4	5	10	7	8x	9	11*	13	14		2"		12	
3		30	Dundee	1-0	1-3	4130	Wright	1	2	3	4	5	6	7	8"	9	10	11"	13					12

* After extra time

Scottish Cup

No	Date		Opposition	HT	Res	Att	Goalscorers	Lekovic	Skilling	Black	Montgomerie	Whitworth	Connor	Mitchell	Henry	Wright	Brown	Reilly	Roberts	Geddes	MacPherson	McKee	Findlay	Anderson	Holt	Maskrey	Meldrum	Lauchlan
3	Jan	27	Hibernian	0-0	2-0	8350	Wright (2)	1		3*	14	5		7	8	9x	12	4			2	13		6		11	10*	
4	Feb	17	HEARTS	0-0	1-2	15173	Anderson	1		3	5			7	8	9	10	4			2	12		6		11*		

Kilmarnock v Celtic
BELL'S SCOTTISH LEAGUE, PREMIER DIVISION
Saturday 21st October 1995, Kick-off 3.00pm

A vital point for Killie from Celtic's first visit to the new Rugby Park.

SEASON 1996-97   Premier Division

No.	Date		Opposition	H I	Res	All	Goalscorers	Lekovic	MacPherson	Tallon	Reilly	Whitworth	Anderson	Mitchell	Henry	Wright	McIntyre	McKee	Lauchlan	Montgomerie	Roberts	Findlay	Brown	Holt	McGowne	D. Kerr	Meldrum	Bagan	A. Kerr	Burke	Hamilton	Prytz
1	Aug	10	Hibernian	2-1	2-1	8734	Mitchell, Henry	1	2	3	4	5*	6	7	8*	9	10	11x			13	14										
2		17	Hearts	1-2	2-3	10854	Wright, Lauchlan	1	2	3*	8	5	6	7		9	10		4		13	11*	12									
3		24	CELTIC	1-0	1-3	15970	Reilly	1	2	3	6	5		7		9		11*	4		13	12										
4	Sep	7	DUNFERMLINE	1-1	2-2	6623	Wright (2)	1	2		4*	5	3	7	8	9	10	12			13				11*	6						
5		14	Aberdeen	0-0	0-3	11826		1	2		4	5	3	7	8*	9	10	12							11	6						
6		21	RANGERS	1-0	1-4	14812	Reilly	1	2		4	5	3	7		9	10	11*							12	8	6					
7		28	Motherwell	0-1	0-1	5700		1	2		4*		3	7		9	10	11*		5			12	13	8	6						
8	Oct	12	Dundee United	0-0	0-0	7365		1	2					7	8	9*	10	12		5		4	13	11*	6	3						
9		19	RAITH ROVERS	1-1	2-1	5829	Brown, Wright	1	2					7	8	9	10*	11		5		4	12		6	3						
10		26	Dunfermline	1-1	1-2	5269	Findlay	1	2					7	8	9	10			5		4	11		6	3						
11	Nov	1	HIBERNIAN	2-2	4-2	10872	Henry, Wright, McIntyre, OG		2		12		6		8*	9	10	7		5		4	11			3	1					
12		16	MOTHERWELL	0-1	2-4	7087	Wright (2)		2		12			13	8	9	10	7		5		4*	11		6	3*	1					
13		30	Raith Rovers	0-0	0-1	3750			2					12	7x	9*	10	11*	4	5			13	14	6	3	1					
14	Dec	7	DUNDEE UNITED	0-1	0-2	5814			2		8			13		9		11	6	4*		14	12	10*	5	3	1	7x				
15		14	HEARTS	0-0	2-0	5832	McKee, Mitchell	1	2		8			7		9		11	4	5		6				3		10				
16		17	Rangers	1-1	2-4	39469	Montgomerie, Roberts	1	2		8			7		9*			4	5*	13	6			12	3		10x	11	14		
17		21	ABERDEEN	1-0	3-0	6114	Burke, Roberts	1	2		8			7			9*		4		12	6			5	3		10	13	11*		
18		26	Hibernian	1-0	1-0	8912	McIntyre	1			8			7			9*		4		12	6			5	3		10	13	11*	2	
19	Jan	4	Dundee United	0-0	0-2	8508		1			8		5	7		12	9	10*			13	6			4	3				11*	2	
20		8	Celtic	0-2	0-6	45535		1	2	4	8			7		9					13		12		5*	3		6		11*	10	
21		11	RAITH ROVERS	0-1	0-1	5505		1	6		8		4	7		9					13		12		5	3		10		11*	2*	
22		15	RANGERS	0-0	1-1	15662	McKee	1	2		8		4	7		9*	10	11*			6				5	3		12		13		
23		18	DUNFERMLINE	0-0	2-1	5813	Wright (2)	1	2		8		4	7	12	9	10	11*			6*				5	3				13		
24		21	Motherwell	0-2	0-2	5508		1	2		8		4	7*	12	9	10	11x	13		6				5	3				14	3*	
25	Feb	1	Aberdeen	0-2	1-2	8361	McIntyre	1	2		6		4	13	12	9					10		8*		5	3		7*		11		
26		8	Hearts	0-1	0-2	11020		1	2		6*		4	7	13	12	9				10*		8		5	3		11				
27		22	DUNDEE UNITED	1-1	2-3	6054	OG, Wright	1	2		6		13	7*	8	9	12	14		4					5	3*				11		
28	Mar	5	Raith Rovers	0-1	1-2	3306	McIntyre	1	2		6		3		8	9	12	13		4		7*	10*		5					11		
29		11	CELTIC	1-0	2-0	15087	Wright, Burke		2		6				8	9*	10	13		4			12		5	3	1	7*		11		
30		15	MOTHERWELL	0-0	1-0	7612	Wright		2		6			13	8x	9	10	12		4			14		5	3	1	7*		11*		
31		22	Rangers	1-0	2-1	50036	McIntyre, Wright	1	2		6			13	8	9	10	12		4					5	3		7*		11*		
32	Apr	5	HEARTS	1-0	1-0	7877	Wright	1			6				8x	9	10	12		4		13	14		5	3		7*		11*	2	
33		19	HIBERNIAN	1-1	1-1	10886	Wright	1	2		6				8*	9	10*	14		4			13	11	5	3		7x				12
34	May	3	Dunfermline	0-1	1-3	5904	McIntyre	1	2		6				8*	9*	10	13		4					5	3		7x				14
35		7	Celtic	0-0	0-0	42788		1	2		6		4	13		9*					14	12	10	5	3			7*		11		8x
36		10	ABERDEEN	0-1	1-1	10027	Holt	1	2		6			8		9*				4	13		12	10	5	3		7*		11		
			Apps.					30	33	3	31	6	16	23	18	29	29	14	7	20	2	15	7	10	30	27	6	16	2	14	6	1
			Subs						2		1		1	2				11		2	9	4	17	2	1		1	2	4			2
			Goals						2					2	2	15	6	2	1	1	2	1	1							3		

Pos	P	W	D	L	F	A	Pts
7th	36	11	6	19	41	61	39

League Cup

No.	Date		Opposition	H I	Res	All	Goalscorers	Lekovic	MacPherson	Tallon	Reilly	Whitworth	Anderson	Mitchell	Henry	Wright	McIntyre	McKee	Lauchlan	Montgomerie	Roberts	Findlay
2	Aug	13	AYR UNITED	0-1	0-1	8543		1	2	3	4	5	6	7	8"	9	10	11*			12	13

Scottish Cup

No.	Date		Opposition	H I	Res	All	Goalscorers	Lekovic	MacPherson	Reilly	Anderson	Mitchell	Wright	McIntyre	McKee	Lauchlan	Roberts	Findlay	Brown	Holt	McGowne	D. Kerr	Bagan	A. Kerr	Burke	Hamilton
3	Jan	23	EAST STIRLING	1-0	2-0	4783	McGowne, Brown	1	2	4	3	6	9*	11*		8		10		5	12	7			13	
4	Feb	15	Clyde	0-0	1-0	4483	Wright	1	2	6		7	9	11*		4		8		5	3	10			12	
QF	Mar	8	Morton	3-0	5-2	8826	Henry (3), Wright, McIntyre	1	2	6		8	9*	10	14	4	12	13			3	7*			11x	5
SF	Apr	14	Dundee United*	0-0	0-0	12391		1	2	6			8	9	10"	11	4		12		5	3			7*	
SFr		22	Dundee United*	0-0	1-0	9265	McIntyre	1	2	6		8	9*	10	12	4		13	11	5	3	7*				
F	May	24	Falkirk+	1-0	1-0	48953	Wright	1	2	6		12	13	9*	10x	4		14	11	5	3	7*			8	

* Easter Road
+ Ibrox

Back row: S. Walker, J. McIntyre, G. Holt, J. Henry, D. Anderson, D. Lekovic, N. Whitworth, M. Roberts, C. Meldrum, K. Doig, W. Findlay, J. Lauchlan, C. McKee. Middle row: Hugh Allan (Trainer/Physio), J. McClelland, S. Maskrey, R. Lennox, A. Burke, P. Finnigan, A. Hollas (Stadium Manager), S. Morrison, S. Davidson, D. Agostini, D. Bagan, G. Hay, S. Hamilton, R. Vincent, A. McLeod (Ass. Trainer/Physio). Front row: M. Graham, G. McCutcheon, M. Reilly, G. Tallon, A. Mitchell. A. MacPherson, K. Thomson (Ass. Manager), A. Totten (Manager), R. Williamson (Coach), R. Montgomerie, T. Brown, M. Skilling, A. Kerr, A. Ryan, J. Dillon.

SEASON 1997-98   Premier Division

No.	Date		Opposition	HT	Res	Att	Goalscorers
1	Aug	2	Aberdeen	0-0	0-0	13842	
2		23	Hibernian	0-2	0-4	9559	
3	Sep	13	Dundee United	1-0	2-1	6883	Wright (2)
4		21	Dunfermline	0-0	1-1	5374	Wright
5		24	RANGERS	0-0	0-3	15367	
6		27	HEARTS	0-3	0-3	7875	
7	Oct	4	Celtic	0-4	0-4	47955	
8		8	MOTHERWELL	2-1	2-1	6588	Vareille, Burke
9		18	ST JOHNSTONE	0-1	0-1	6572	
10		25	HIBERNIAN	0-0	2-1	7541	Roberts, Nevin
11	Nov	1	Rangers	1-1	1-4	49413	Mitchell
12		8	Motherwell	0-0	1-0	5346	Roberts
13		15	DUNDEE UNITED	1-0	1-3	7402	Roberts
14		23	Hearts	1-2	3-5	16015	Nevin, Holt, Roberts
15		29	DUNFERMLINE	2-1	2-1	6667	Nevin (2)
16	Dec	6	CELTIC	0-0	0-0	15676	
17		13	St Johnstone	0-0	1-1	4385	Mitchell
18		20	ABERDEEN	1-0	1-0	8452	Wright
19		27	Hibernian	1-0	1-0	10475	Wright
20	Jan	3	MOTHERWELL	3-1	4-1	8724	Wright (2), Mitchell, Roberts
21		10	Dundee United	0-1	1-1	7541	Reilly
22		17	HEARTS	1-2	2-2	11079	Wright, Reilly
23		31	Dunfermline	1-1	2-3	4903	Vareille, Roberts
24	Feb	7	ST JOHNSTONE	0-0	1-0	7408	Reilly
25		21	Celtic	0-2	0-4	48477	
26		24	RANGERS	1-1	1-1	15931	Wright
27		28	Aberdeen	0-0	0-0	10423	
28	Mar	14	Hearts	1-1	1-1	15338	Henry
29		21	DUNFERMLINE	0-0	3-0	8230	Wright, Nevin, McIntyre
30		28	St Johnstone	0-1	0-1	4982	
31	Apr	8	CELTIC	1-1	1-1	18076	Burke
32		11	Motherwell	1-0	1-1	6209	Holt
33		18	DUNDEE UNITED	1-0	1-0	7468	Burke
34		25	ABERDEEN	1-1	2-1	8212	Vareille
35	May	2	Rangers	0-0	0-0	50116	Mitchell
36		9	HIBERNIAN	1-0	1-1	12493	Roberts

Player appearances (Lekovic, MacPherson, Baker, Montgomerie, McGowne, Reilly, Mitchell, Findlay, Wright, McIntyre, Bagan, Vareille, Nevin, Hamilton, Meldrum, Whitworth, Vincent, Roberts, Burke, Henry, Kerr, McCutcheon, Holt, Anderson, Lauchlan, Doig, Marshall, O'Neill):

	Apps.	Subs	Goals
Lekovic	13		
MacPherson	25	1	
Baker	12		
Montgomerie	27	5	
McGowne	21		
Reilly	36		3
Mitchell	22	11	4
Findlay	2	3	
Wright	26	2	10
McIntyre	6	2	1
Bagan	4	3	
Vareille	24	10	4
Nevin	26	5	5
Hamilton	5	1	
Meldrum	11		
Whitworth	10	7	
Vincent			
Roberts	17	15	7
Burke	16	3	3
Henry	13	14	1
Kerr	20		
McCutcheon		1	
Holt	25	2	2
Anderson		1	
Lauchlan	22		
Doig	1		
Marshall	12		
O'Neill		2	

Pos	P	W	D	L	F	A	Pts
4th	36	13	11	12	40	52	50

League Cup

No.	Date		Opposition	HT	Res	Att	Goalscorers
2	Aug	9	East Fife	1-0	2-0	1169	Findlay, Vareille
3		20	Stirling Albion	0-2	2-6	2154	Vareille, Wright

Scottish Cup

No.	Date		Opposition	HT	Res	Att	Goalscorers
3	Jan	24	Stranraer	1-0	2-0	4304	Vareille, Roberts
4	Feb	14	Ayr United	0-0	0-2	9286	

European Cup-Winners' Cup

Rd	Date		Opposition	HT	Res	Att	Goalscorers
Q	Aug	14	SHELBOURNE	0-1	2-1	9041	Wright (2)
		28	Shelbourne (Agg 3-2)	1-1	1-1	8100	McIntyre
1	Sep	18	Nice	0-1	1-3	10812	Wright
	Oct	2	NICE (Agg 2-4)	1-0	1-1	8402	Reilly

Back row (l-r): R. Lennox, A. Kerr, M. Roberts, K. Doig, K. McGowne, C. Meldrum, D. Anderson, C. McKie, G. Tallon, G. Hay. Middle row: P. Finnigan, G. McCutcheon, D. Bagan, S. Hamilton, M. Baker, N. Whitworth, D. Lekovic, J. McIntyre, W. Findlay, A. Mitchell, A. Burke, R. Vincent, J. Dillon. Front row: H. Allan (Physio), M. Reilly, A. MacPherson, G. McCabe, R. Williamson (Manager), J. Clark, R. Montgomerie, P. Wright, G. Hollas.

No.	Date		Opposition	HT	Res	Att	Goalscorers	Marshall	MacPherson	Baker	Lauchlan	McGowne	Holt	Nevin	Mahood	Wright	Durrant	Mitchell	Roberts	Burke	Henry	Vareille	McCoist	Kerr	Montgomerie	Bagan	McCutcheon	Hamilton	Innes	Reilly
1	Aug	1	DUNDEE UNITED	1-0	2-0	8137	Wright, Nevin	1	2	3	4	5	6	7*	8	9"	10	11½	12	13	14									
2		15	St Johnstone	0-0	0-0	6210		1	2	3	4	5	6	11	8*	9*	10	7				12	13							
3		22	RANGERS	0-2	1-3	17608	Wright	1	2		4	5	6	14	13	9	10	7*		12		11"	8x	3						
4		30	HEARTS	1-0	3-0	10376	McCoist (3)	1	2			5	6"		8	9	10	12		13		7*	11½	3	4	14				
5	Sep	12	Celtic	0-1	1-1	58567	Vareille	1	2"	11		5	6		8	14	10x	7				9*	13	3	4	12				
6		19	Motherwell	0-0	0-0	9063		1	2	11½		5	6		13	9	10	7				8*	12	3	4					
7		23	DUNDEE	1-1	2-1	7069	McCoist, McGowne	1	2	11½		5	6			9*	10	7		12		13	8	3	4					
8		27	Aberdeen	1-0	1-0	13048	Wright	1	2			5	6			9x	10	7	13	12		11"	8*	3	4	14				
9	Oct	3	DUNFERMLINE	0-0	0-0	8346		1	2			5	6			9	10	8	12			7	11½	3	4					
10		17	Dundee United	1-0	2-0	8137	McGowne, Vareille	1	2	3		5	6		12	9	10*	8	11½	14		7x			4		13			
11		24	ST JOHNSTONE	0-1	2-2	9336	Roberts, OG	1		3			6		13	9*	10*	8	11	12		7x			4		14	2	5	
12		31	CELTIC	0-0	2-0	16695	Roberts, Mitchell	1		3		5	6		8	12	10*	7	9			11"			4		13	2		
13	Nov	7	Hearts	0-1	1-2	14363		1		3		5	6		8	13	10*	7*	9			11			4			2		12
14		14	Dundee	1-1	1-1	4249	Vareille	1	2	3		5	6			9	10	7	8			11			4					
15		21	MOTHERWELL	0-0	0-0	10176		1	2	3		5	6		14	11½	10	7	9"	12		8*			4	13				
16		28	Dunfermline	1-0	3-0	5608	Durrant (2), Holt	1	2	3		5	6		12	9	10*	7				8*	13		4					11
17	Dec	5	ABERDEEN	3-0	4-0	9785	Mitchell (2), Vareille, Wright	1	2	3		5	6		13	9x	10	7	14			11"	12		4					8
18		12	Rangers	0-1	0-1	49781		1	2	3		5	6		12	9*	10x	7	14			11"	13		4					8
19		20	DUNDEE UNITED	1-0	2-0	13538	Wright, Durrant	1	2	3		5	6		14	9*	10x	7	12			11			4		13			8
20		26	HEARTS	1-0	1-0	10668	Holt	1	2	3		5	6		13	9x	10*	7	12		14	11			4					8
21	Jan	1	Motherwell	1-1	2-1	8532	McCoist, McGowne	1	2	3		5	6			9	10	7				11			4					8
22		30	DUNDEE	0-0	0-0	7677		1	2	3		5	6		8"		10			12		9			4		11			7
23	Feb	6	Aberdeen	0-1	1-2	9299	Mahood	1	2	3		5	6		8	14	10		12	13		9 x		6*	11"					7
24		17	Celtic	0-0	0-1	59220		1	2	3		5	6		8x	12	10		14	11"	13	9"			4					7
25		28	RANGERS	0-1	0-5	16242		1		3		5	6			9	10	12	13	8		11"			4		2"			7
26	Mar	6	DUNFERMLINE	0-0	0-0	8032		1			4	5	6		8*	9"	10	12	14	13		11½	3				2			7
27		13	St Johnstone	1-0	1-0	5461	Holt	1	2		4	5	6*		14	9"	10x	8	12	13		11½	3							7
28		21	CELTIC	0-0	0-0	14472		1	2		4	5	6		14	9*	10x	8	12	13		11½	3							7
29	Apr	3	Hearts	0-2	2-2	14689	Henry, McCoist	1	2"		4	5	6		8	9x	10	11		14	12	13	3							7*
30		10	ABERDEEN	2-1	4-2	9048	McCutcheon (2), Mahood, MacPherson	1	2		4		6"		8	9*	10x	11		14	7				13		5			
31		17	Dunfermline	1-0	6-0	5585	Henry (2), Durrant, Mitchell, Vareille, McCoist	1	2		4				8	13	10	11½			7	9"	14	3			12		5	6
32		24	Dundee	0-1	1-2	4296	Innes	1	2		4				8	13	10	11			7	9x	12	3			14		5	6"
33	May	1	MOTHERWELL	0-0	0-1	15300		1	2	3	4	5	6			9x	10	12		14	7	8*	11				13			
34		8	Dundee United	0-0	0-0	7190		1	2	3	4	5	6			10	12	11"			7	9*					13			8
35		15	ST JOHNSTONE	1-0	1-1	15086	Roberts	1	2		4	5	6"		8	13	10	12	11		7x	9*		3			14			
36		23	Rangers	1-1	1-1	48835	McGowne	1	2		4	5	6		8		10x	9	11"	14	7*	12		3			13			
							Apps.	36	31	23	14	32	33	2	16	25	36	27	9	2	7	20	16	16	22	1	2	5	4	17
							Subs		1						12	8		6	13	16	4	3	10				4	11		1
							Goals		1			4	3	1	2	6	4	4	3		3	5	7				2		1	

Pos	P	W	D	L	F	A	Pts
4th	36	14	14	8	47	29	56

League Cup

No.	Date		Opposition	HT	Res	Att	Goalscorers	Marshall	MacPherson	Baker	Lauchlan	McGowne	Holt	Nevin	Mahood	Wright	Durrant	Mitchell	Roberts	Burke	Henry	Vareille	McCoist	Kerr	Montgomerie	Bagan	McCutcheon	Hamilton	Innes	Reilly
3	Aug	18	LIVINGSTON	1-1	3-1*	6565	Wright (2), McCoist	1	2		5	4	6	7*	9*	10	8	11½		14		13	12	3						
QF	Sep	8	AIRDRIEONIANS	0-0	0-1*	7897		1	2			5	6		10	7	8*	12	13			11	9*	3	4					

* After extra time

Scottish Cup

No.	Date		Opposition	HT	Res	Att	Goalscorers	Marshall	MacPherson	Baker	Lauchlan	McGowne	Holt	Nevin	Mahood	Wright	Durrant	Mitchell	Roberts	Burke	Henry	Vareille	McCoist	Kerr	Montgomerie	Bagan	McCutcheon	Hamilton	Innes	Reilly
3	Jan	23	Ayr United	0-1	0-3	10153		1	2	3		5	8"		12		10	11	6			9		4						7

UEFA Cup

No.	Date		Opposition	HT	Res	Att	Goalscorers	Marshall	MacPherson	Baker	Lauchlan	McGowne	Holt	Nevin	Mahood	Wright	Durrant	Mitchell	Roberts	Burke	Henry	Vareille	McCoist	Kerr	Montgomerie	Bagan	McCutcheon	Hamilton	Innes	Reilly
Q1	Jul	22	Zeljeznicar	0-0	1-1	22000	McGowne	1	2	3	6	5	8		11	9*	10	7	12					4						
		29	ZELJEZNICAR (Agg 1-0)	0-0	1-0	14512	Mahood	1	2	3	4	5	6	12	8*	9	10	7		11"	13									
Q2	Aug	11	Sigma Olomouc	0-1	0-2	3669		1	2	3	4	6	8		11	10	7			13		12		5						
		25	SIGMA OLOMOUC (Agg 0-4)	0-2	0-2	11140		1	2		4	5	6"	7*	12	9x	10		14	11		8		3			13			

Back row (l-r): S. Hamilton, A. McCoist, G. Holt, C. Innes, K. McGowne, G. Marshall, J. Lauchlan, D. Kerr, J. Vareille, M. Baker, A. Mahood. Middle row (l-r): G. Hollas (Stadium Manager), A. Mitchell, P. Wright, A. MacPherson. G. Hay, M. Roberts, C. Meldrum, J. Henry, S. Davidson, A. Kerr, M. O'Neill, R. Lennox, E. Young (Community Coach). Front row (l-r): A. Robertson (Youth Development), D. Bagan, A. Burke, R. Montgomerie, G. McCabe (Ass. Manager), R. Williamson (Manager), J. Clark (Ass. Manager), I. Durrant, M. Reilly, G. McCutcheon, H. Allan (Consultant Physio).

SEASON 1999-2000 SPL

No.	Date		Opposition	HT	Res	Att	Goalscorers
1	Jul	31	Rangers	0-1	1-2	48074	Mitchell
2	Aug	7	ABERDEEN	1-0	2-0	8378	Hay (2)
3		15	St Johnstone	0-0	0-2	4681	
4		21	MOTHERWELL	0-1	0-1	7732	
5		29	Dundee United	0-0	0-0	6621	
6	Sep	12	CELTIC	0-0	0-1	14318	
7		19	Hibernian	1-0	3-0	11219	Reilly, Jeffrey, McCoist
8		25	DUNDEE	0-1	0-2	7433	
9	Oct	16	RANGERS	0-1	1-1	15795	Jeffrey
10		23	Aberdeen	0-1	2-2	10352	Cocard, Mitchell
11		27	Hearts	0-0	2-2	12541	MacPherson, Cocard
12		30	Celtic	1-0	1-5	59791	Cocard
13	Nov	6	HIBERNIAN	0-0	0-2	8735	
14		20	DUNDEE UNITED	0-0	1-1	7012	Cocard
15		27	HEARTS	0-2	2-2	8326	Mahood, Reilly
16	Dec	11	Rangers	0-0	0-1	47169	
17		18	ST JOHNSTONE	0-2	1-2	6002	Wright
18		27	Hibernian	2-0	2-2	11900	Smith, Cocard
19	Jan	23	CELTIC	1-1	1-1	14126	Reilly
20		26	Dundee	0-0	0-0	4039	
21	Feb	12	MOTHERWELL	0-0	0-2	7057	
22		22	Motherwell	2-0	4-0	5813	Cocard (2), Vareille (2)
23		26	Hearts	0-0	0-0	14243	
24	Mar	4	DUNDEE	1-0	2-2	8460	Durrant, Dindeleux
25		15	Dundee United	1-0	2-2	6966	Durrant (2)
26		18	St Johnstone	0-0	0-0	4688	
27		25	HIBERNIAN	0-0	1-0	8068	Vareille
28	Apr	2	Celtic	0-2	2-4	55194	Wright, Lauchlan
29		8	DUNDEE UNITED	0-0	1-0	6037	OG
30		12	ABERDEEN	1-0	1-0	11525	Wright
31		16	Motherwell	0-1	0-2	5429	
32		22	Dundee	1-0	2-1	6208	Wright (2)
33		29	HEARTS	0-0	0-1	8057	
34	May	7	RANGERS	0-1	0-2	13284	
35		14	Aberdeen	1-3	1-5	9275	Lauchlan
36		21	ST JOHNSTONE	1-0	3-2	9192	Durrant, OG, Cocard

Pos	P	W	D	L	F	A	Pts
9th	36	8	13	15	38	52	27

League Cup

3	Oct	12	HIBERNIAN	2-1	3-2	6837	McCoist (2), Vareille
QF	Feb	2	HEARTS	0-0	1-0	6648	Jeffrey
SF	Feb	16	Celtic*	0-0	0-1	22926	

* Hampden

Scottish Cup

| 3 | Feb | 5 | ALLOA ATHLETIC | 0-0 | 0-0 | 5584 | |
| 3r | | 9 | Alloa Athletic | 0-1 | 0-1 | 1894 | |

UEFA Cup

Q	Aug	12	KR Reykjavik	0-0	0-1	2890	
		26	KR REYKJAVIK (Agg 2-1)	0-0	2-0*	11760	Wright, Bagan
1	Sep	16	Kaiserslautern	0-3	0-3	21000	
		30	KAISERSLAUTERN (Agg 0-5)	0-2	0-2	8074	

* After extra time

Back row: G. McCutcheon, S. Davidson, M. Baker, C. Innes, K. McGowne, J. Lauchlan, D. Kerr, J. Fowler, G. Hay. Middle row: E. Young (Community Coach), D. Bagan, P. Wright, M. Roberts, G. Holt, C. Meldrum, G. Marshall, C. Stewart, M. Jeffrey, J. Vareille, A. McCoist, A. Burke, A. Hollas (Stadium Manger). Front row: A. Macfie (Physio), A. Mitchell, A. Mahood, I. Durrant, J. Clark (Ass. Manager), R. Williamson (Manager), G. McCabe (Ass. Manager), A. MacPherson, M. Reilly, J. Henry, H. Allan (Consultant Physio).

SEASON 2000-01 SPL

No.	Date		Opposition	HT	Res	Att	Goalscorers
1	Jul	29	St Mirren	0-0	1-0	7388	Holt
2	Aug	5	RANGERS	2-1	2-4	14680	McLaren (2)
3		13	Celtic	1-0	1-2	57258	McLaren
4		16	HIBERNIAN	0-1	0-1	8672	
5		19	MOTHERWELL	1-1	3-2	6533	Dargo, Wright, Dindeleux
6		26	St Johnstone	1-1	1-1	3773	McLaren
7	Sep	9	DUNDEE UNITED	1-0	1-0	6380	Mitchell
8		16	ABERDEEN	1-0	1-0	6876	Mitchell
9		24	Hearts	1-0	2-0	10379	Wright, Dindeleux
10		30	Dundee	0-0	0-0	6170	
11	Oct	14	DUNFERMLINE	1-1	2-1	6454	Wright, Holt
12		21	ST MIRREN	0-1	2-1	7839	McLaren, Mahood
13		28	Rangers	2-0	3-0	49659	Cocard, Numan, OG
14	Nov	5	CELTIC	0-0	0-1	13412	
15		11	Hibernian	0-1	1-1	12588	Wright
16		18	Motherwell	1-1	2-1	6571	Wright, Cocard
17		25	ST JOHNSTONE	0-0	0-2	6330	
18		28	Dundee United	0-0	1-0	5497	Dargo
19	Dec	2	Aberdeen	2-1	2-1	11584	McLaren, Fowler
20		9	HEARTS	0-1	0-3	6828	
21		16	DUNDEE	1-0	2-3	6573	Cocard, Baker
22		23	Dunfermline	0-1	0-1	5337	
23		26	St Mirren	0-1	3-1	8142	Wright (3)
24	Jan	2	Celtic	0-1	0-6	59103	
25		30	HIBERNIAN	0-0	1-1	6385	Hay
26	Feb	3	MOTHERWELL	0-1	1-2	6018	Dargo
27		11	St Johnstone	0-0	2-1	6627	Dargo, Canero
28		24	DUNDEE UNITED	0-0	0-0	6289	
29	Mar	3	ABERDEEN	0-0	0-0	6577	
30		14	Hearts	0-0	0-3	9195	
31		31	Dundee	1-1	2-2	6719	Dargo, Mahood
32	Apr	7	DUNFERMLINE	1-0	2-1	6529	McCoist, MacPherson
33		11	RANGERS	0-2	1-2	14585	Hay
34		21	Hibernian	1-1	1-1	8113	Cocard
35		27	HEARTS	0-0	1-1	6867	McGowne
36	May	5	Dundee	0-1	1-2	6261	Dargo
37		12	Rangers	0-1	1-5	46577	Dargo
38		20	CELTIC	0-0	1-0	12578	Mahood

Player columns (left→right): Marshall, MacPherson, Baker, McGowne, Dindeleux, Mahood, Holt, Durrant, McLaren, Cocard, Vareille, Canero, Wright, Di Giacomo, Hay, McCoist, Hessey, Fowler, Mitchell, Dargo, Innes, Reilly, Davidson, Meldrum, Sanjuan, Calderon, Boyd

	Mar	MacP	Bak	McG	Din	Mah	Holt	Dur	McL	Coc	Var	Can	Wri	DiG	Hay	McC	Hes	Fow	Mit	Dar	Inn	Rei	Dav	Mel	San	Cal	Boyd
Apps.	31	32	14	20	35	33	19	12	30	16	2	16	15	2	27	11	6	3	25	16	23	11	2	7	3	7	
Subs		1						2		2	17	7		12	10	8	4	7		11	1	9	1	3		1	
Goals		1	1	1	2	3	2		6	4		1	8		2	1		1	2	7							

	Pos	P	W	D	L	F	A	Pts
	4th	38	15	9	14	44	53	54

League Cup

	Date		Opposition	HT	Res	Att	Goalscorers
2	Aug	22	Clyde	0-0	2-1*	2018	Dindeleux, McCoist
3	Sep	5	St Johnstone	0-0	1-0	3231	McCoist
QF	Oct	31	HIBERNIAN	0-1	2-1	7819	McLaren, Dargo
SFx	Feb	6	St Mirren	1-0	3-0	9213	McLaren, Dargo, Canero
Fx	Mar	18	Celtic	0-0	0-3	48830	

* After Extra Time
x Hampden

Scottish Cup

	Date		Opposition	HT	Res	Att	Goalscorers
3	Jan	27	PARTICK THISTLE	1-0	1-0	8836	Mitchell
4	Feb	17	Inverness Cal This	0-0	1-1	5294	Hay
4r	Mar	6	INVERNESS CAL THIS	0-0	2-1	6528	McGowne, Wright
QF	Mar	10	HIBERNIAN	0-0	0-1	8287	

Back row (l-r): A. Burke, S. Davidson, A. Mahood, C. Cocard, A. McLaren, M. Jeffrey, C. Meldrum, M. Baker, J. Vareille, T. McKinlay, P. Di Giacomo, P. Canero, J. Fowler. Middle row: A. Hollas (Stadium Manager), G. McCutcheon, S. Hessey, D. Beesley, N. McFarlane, K. McGowne, G. Marshall, C. Stewart, A. Smith, C. Innes, F. Dindeleux, G. Holt, G. Hay, E. Young (Community Coach). Front row: A. Robertson (Youth Coach), C. Dargo, A. Mitchell, I. Durrant, G. McCabe, R. Williamson (Manager), J. Clark (Ass. Manager), A. MacPherson, M. Reilly, P. Wright. A. Macfie (Physio).

Scottish League Champions 1965

Scottish Cup Winners 1997

Advanced Subscribers

Sir John Orr O.B.E, Chairman
Bill Costley, Joint Vice Chairman
Jamie Moffat, Joint Vice Chairman
Jim Clark, Director
Jim Murdoch, Director
Robert Wyper, Director
Brian Sage, Director

David Heath, Chief Executive
Kevin Collins, Secretary
Jim McSherry, Commercial Manager
Bobby Williamson, Manager
Jim Clark, Assistant Manager
Gerry McCabe, Assistant Manager
Alan Robertson, Youth Development

Hugh Irvine	A. McLelland & Son Ltd	James Flannigan	Kilwinning
Alastair Irvine	A. McLelland & Son Ltd	Dougal & Ian Rowan	Galston
Douglas Irvine	A. McLelland & Son Ltd	Sandy McCutcheon	Kilmarnock
Joe Cairns	A. McLelland & Son Ltd	Calum Lennon	Stewarton
Neil Ross	Middlesbrough	Paul Parker	Kilmarnock
David Ross	Dundonald	David Murray	Kilmarnock
Stuart Ross	Dunbar	Ewan J. McDowall	Kilmarnock
Richard Ross	Kilmarnock	Stephen Duff	Kilmarnock
Brian Caldwell	Beeston	Jackson Cree M.C.I.B.S	Kilmarnock
William Ross	Hurlford	William A Hair	Kilwinning
John Livingston	Kilmarnock	Andrew G Hair	Kilwinning
Daniel Andrew	Irvine	John Dixon	Darvel
Allan Morrison Jnr	Irvine	Christopher Adams	Galston
Ian G.M. Mackie	Troon	Craig Sharkey	Kilmarnock
Philip & Sarah Bentley	Lewisham	Christine Andrew	Irvine
David Steele	Carlisle	Campbell Andrew Mitchell	Stewarton
Vince Harvey	Giffnock	Frank Wragg	Kilmarnock
Eddie Dryden	Middlesbrough	Stewart Wragg	Kilmarnock
Frederick Pegg	Ballingry	Gordon Edgar	Dundonald
Adrian McCabe	Kilmarnock	Andrew & Edward Gorrie	Galston
John Hastings	Troon	Ross Strachan	Galston
Jim Hammill	Stoke Newington	Bob McWilliam	Kilmarnock
Gus Lauchlan	London	Ian Wallace	Kilmarnock
Charlie Walker	Rockcliffe	David Woodison	Cumnock
Stephen McCulloch	Irvine	David & Jean Cameron	Kilmarnock
Tony Galbraith	Kilmarnock	Bobby Gould	Galston
Drew Semple	Tarbolton	William A. Bradie	Saltcoats
Jim Irving	Aberdeen	Gordon Neilson	Dalry
Sandy Tyrie	Kilmarnock	Stuart J. Ferguson	Edinburgh
Eric Brown	Newmilns	Malcolm MacInnes	Darvel
Alan Brown	Newmilns	Malcolm Hunter	Troon
Lora Brown	Hurlford	James McFarland	Kilmarnock
Sam Stowe	Mauchline	Philip M. Harrison	Kilmacolm
Sam Young	Mauchline	John & Cathie Holmes	Troon
Alan Muir	Kilmarnock	Allan Collins	Kilmarnock
Bob Coburn	Ardrossan	Kerr Chalmers	Giffnock
Eddie Riley	Troon	J.Gary Torbett	Irvine
Thomas & Angela Clark	Lochwinnoch	David W Alexander	Troon
Harry Stewart	Ayr	Andy and Greg McSwiggan	Kilwinning
John L Woods	Kilmarnock	William Neasham	Mauchline
Robert Gilbert	Kilwinning	Angus Begg	Aberdeen

Vincent H. Godwin	Kilmarnock	John Robertson	Kilmarnock
Ian Moffat	Kilwinning	Douglas & Jean	Prestwick
Iain M MacInnes	Cheshire	Craig McAvoy	Ayr
Alasdair J Harvey	Torphins	Matthew A & Ailie Osborne	Ayr
Jack & Jill Parker	Prestwick	Craig Lamont	Catrine
Raymond Devlin	America	John Flynn	Troon
Gus McMillan	White Haven	Davy Murray	Troon
George C Mason	South Queens Ferry	James Hynds	Kilmarnock
Iain Bryson	East Kilbride	David & Kirsteen Adrain	Glasgow
Gavin Hill	Ayr	Malcolm Ewing	Surrey
George Brown	Dundonald	Robert Thompson Ward	Dalry
Billy Gibson	Sorn	Thomas & Margaret Adam	Irvine
Stan Babington	Irvine	Cameron Adam	Irvine
Andrew McRoberts	Kilmarnock	Douglas Adam	Irvine
Alastair Morton	Kilmarnock	Andrew John Notini Clark	Hurlford
Stuart Miller	Kilmarnock	Tom & Scott Kennedy	Glasgow
Gordon Sutherland	Kilmarnock	Iain Murray	Mauchline
Jane Orr	Dreghorn	Bob & Gary Martin	Tarbolton
Kenneth Paton	Darvel	Cameron Scott	Kilmarnock
Gordon Andrews	Fenwick	Alex. Taylor	Solihull
Alan Smillie	Newton Mearns	Jamie Hewitson	Kilmarnock
Robert J. Barnes	Bishopbriggs	Jemma Calderwood	Kilmarnock
Christopher J. Farmer	Edinburgh	Derek Stevenson	Kilmarnock
John G. Farmer	Edinburgh	Raymond Palmer	Derbyshire
Andrew Morton Hodge	Kilmarnock	Robert Morris	Irvine
Jim Craig	Kilmarnock	Ross McCulloch	Galston
Nicola Julie Sherry	Kilmarnock	Alec Harvey	Kilmarnock
Gordon C. Sherry	Kilmarnock	Robert Campbell	Mauchline
George & Hilary Whiteside	Troon	William Brown	Kilmarnock
Graeme Whiteside	Troon	Gregory McLelland	Kilmarnock
Jim & Neil Murray	Hurlford	Craig Hunter	Hurlford
R. Jefferson	Morayshire	Robert Neil	Galston
Andrew Miller	Kilmarnock	Andrew David Kerr	Kilmarnock
Cochrane Murray	Kilmarnock	Andy Waddell	Kilmarnock
Dr. David Brooks	Ayr	Joseph Neil	Kilmarnock
Mathew Train	Tarbolton	David Mawson	Kirkintilloch
David Hynds	Kilmarnock	James Ellis	Stewarton
Alan Graham	Perthshire	Alex Lamont	Cumnock
James Dick	Kilmarnock	Kevin Lamont	Dunfermline
Hugh Caldwell	Lugar	Scott Lamont	Mackalesfield
Colin C Stevenson	Troon	Dr William Murray	Inverness
Russell Blane	Mauchline	John Gibson	Kilmarnock
Allan T Scott	Kilmarnock	Don Martin	Kilmarnock
John D Kerr	Kilmarnock	Erik Schafer	Kaiserslautern
Stuart W Little	Kilmarnock	Bobby McDill	Irvine
James Hendry	Kilmarnock	Robert G McCluskie	Kilmarnock
David Hendry	Kilmacolm	Gordon Guthrie	Kilmarnock
Robert Burns	Ayr	Graeme Mackie	Kilmarnock
Jim Cockburn	Kilwinning	Angus Craig	Kilmarnock

Paul Martin Ross	Barrhead	Kevin Knapp	Kilmarnock
Gordon McCreath	Irvine	Scott Wilson	Darvel
Phil Morgan	Kilmarnock	Gordon Shields	Solihull
William Thomson	Kilmarnock	Jonathan Hamilton	Cambridge
Peter Cormack	Edinburgh	Mathew Hamilton	United States
William de Geus	The Netherlands	Alan Henry Taylor	Hamilton
John White Watters	Springside	Jim Wilson	Kilmarnock
Tom Barr	Dalkeith	Donald Maconochie	Girvan
Donald Stewart Cameron	Glasgow	Matthew Dodds	Galston
Gary Holt	Irvine	Ross Malcolmson	Kilwinning
Ralph Fallows	Australia	Alan Sime	Kilmarnock
Charles Watters	Cowes	Scott Brown Thomson	Kilmarnock
Neil & John Archibald	Northampton	Richard Cairns	Kilmarnock
Douglas B. Woodburn	Clitheroe	Stuart Hamilton	Kilmarnock
Michael Heald	East Kilbride	Kevin S. Dempster	Prestwick
Jim & Sharon Wilkinson	Irvine	Evelyn Cavens	Kilmarnock
William Boyd	Kilwinning	Gordon Smith	Irvine
Donald Faulds	Lewes	Andrew Gray	Kilmarnock
Allan Auld	United States	Taylor Gray	Kilmarnock
John Gilmour	Dundee	James Mitchell	Hurlford
Ally Hewitt	Livingston	Alan F.Reid	Newmilns
David & James Wallace	Scorton	Kevin Scoular	Kilmarnock
Jim Johnston	Kilmarnock	Kara Sim	Kilmarnock
Andrew Morran	Glasgow	Billy Kerr	Galston
Martin & Colin Goudie	Hedingham	Ian Mitchell	Glasgow
John & Ryan Burns	Bracknell	Howat Strachan	Kilmarnock
Jim, Grant & Andrew McKinlay	Newborough	Graham Steel	Galston
Eric, Ross & Mark MacKenzie	Kilwinning	Alan J. & Ian C. Rosamond	Ayr
Karen Steel	Kilmarnock	Francis Hunter	Darvel
Billy Steel	Kilmarnock	Rhuraidm Mathieson	Bishopbriggs
Fraser John Gall	Galston	Douglas & Mary J McAllister	Bishopbriggs
Gavin Smith	Kilmarnock	Gary Mason	Ayr
Robert Neil & Thomas Smith	Kilmarnock	Allan F. Presly	Kilmarnock
Hugh M.N Gordon	Hazlemere	Sam, Kirstie & Ken Haywood	York
John B Miller	Burnhouse	Daniel Cairney	Irvine
Graeme Stevenson	Paisley	Andrew William Taylor	Darvel
Jim,Neil & Craig McGuffie	Symington	Iain Inglis	Kilwinning
Paul Hume	Kilmarnock	Ross & Iain Clark	Kilmarnock
Lynne & Jacqueline Mossie	Kilmarnock	Bobby & Annie Fleeting	U.S.A
Jan M & James Richmond	Kilmarnock	Harry & Laurel Chadwick	U.S.A
Allan Campbell	Kilmarnock	Chris McMail	Seamill
Cllr.Daniel Coffey	Kilmarnock	David Blane from his Dad Allan	Kilmarnock
Kevin W. Wilson	Kilmarnock	Frank & Annette Alexander	Troon
Sam Elliott	Troon	Colin Mitchell	Montrose
Joe Robertson	Stewarton	Jimmy Hogg-Killie Til I Die	Stirling
Fraser Kilpatrick	Stewarton	Colin Hargreaves	Adrossan
Richard Caldwell	Stewarton	To Alistair from Allyson	Kilmarnock
Andrew & Heather Russell	Frankfurt am Main	Kevin Robertson	London
Katherine Simpson	Ashford	Denis Gibson	Kilmarnock